ST VINCENT DE PAUL
A BIOGRAPHY

St Vincent de Paul
Fondateur et premier Supérieur Général
de la Cong.^{on} de la Mission
et des Filles de la Charité

St Vincent de Paul
A Biography

Fr José María Román C.M.

translated by
Sr Joyce Howard D.C.

MELISENDE
LONDON

Translated from *San Vicente de Paúl I Biografía,* Madrid
© José María Román C.M., 1981

This edition in English
first published 1999 on behalf of
The Congregation of the Mission Trust
by Melisende,
an imprint of Fox Communications and Publications

Produced by
Fox Communications and Publications
39 Chelmsford Road
London E18 2 PW
England
Tel. 0181 498 9768
Fax 0181 504 2558
e-mail: 106040.2042@compuserve.com

General Editor: Leonard Harrow
Assistant editor: Alan Ball

ISBN 1 901764 08 7

Printed and bound in England by St Edmundsbury Press

CONTENTS

Contents

PART FIVE

HIS LUCID OLD AGE. (1653-1660)

FOREWORD

Forests and mists will always present a challenge to man's curiosity.

It has been said of St Vincent de Paul that his works encircle him like a forest and his humility envelops him like a mist.

Father José María Román valiantly guides us through that forest and mist. His work on St Vincent de Paul, the fruits of his reflection and study, is the most recent biography of St Vincent and it comes out very opportunely during the fourth centenary of St Vincent's birth.

As a professional historian, Fr Román is qualified to apply the methods of historical criticism to the information we have about the life and times of St Vincent. At the same time Fr Román is an experienced priest and he is a competent guide and excellent interpreter of the spirituality of this colossus of charity. This spirituality is expertly analysed in detail by Fr Antonio Orcajo in the second volume of this work.

St Vincent was a giant, not only of charity which was his special mission, but in other fields of activity, too. Like a giant, his thoughts range from the north of Scotland to Algeria and Madagascar, and from Paris to Poland. In his later years Vincent de Paul's active mind could organise a plan for the rescue of captives, and towards the end of his life he was wondering what would be the best method of ridding the world of pirates. From that thought he turned his mind to speaking to the first group of Daughters of Charity about the importance of mental prayer and the method they were to use for this. Later on that day he might be found in the royal palace in Paris for the Council of Conscience where he put forward his wise suggestions for the appointment of worthy bishops in France. At night he might be planning which missioners he could send to Madagascar to replace those who died there as victims of malaria.

What was the secret behind this colossal display of spiritual and charitable energy? Vincent would have replied simply ... 'The grace of Our Lord Jesus Christ'; that grace which is given to those who are simple and humble of heart. St Vincent said that simplicity was his gospel, and in his opinion, humility was the basic requirement for anyone who wants to love God and the poor.

The pages of this biography relate all these things and much more. We hope that people reading this book will be encouraged to read St Vincent's letters and conferences or his complete works. All these, fortunately, are published in Spanish. Or they might read the anthology by Fr Miguel Pérez Flores which completes the second volume of this present work.

I am sure that the readers of this biography and the writings of St Vincent published by the Library of Christian Authors to promote the spread of Catholic culture, will find, amid the forest and the mist, a shining light to guide them through life. After four hundred years, St Vincent remains a model for our times.

I pray for all who may read this book, using Vincent's favourite phrase for starting a letter, 'the grace of Our Lord Jesus Christ be with us for ever'.

RICHARD McCULLEN, C.M.
Superior General

ABBREVIATIONS

Anales   *Annals of the Congregation of the Mission and of the Daughters of Charity* (Spanish edition).

Annales   *Annals of the Congregation of the Mission and of the Daughters of Charity* (French edition).

Annali   *Annali della Missione* (Italian edition).

D.S.   *Dictionnaire de Spiritualité.*

D.T.C.   *Dictionnaire de Théologie Catholique.*

E.S.   Edition Sígueme (of St Vincent de Paul).

G.S.   *Gaudium et Spes* (Constitution of Vatican Council on the Church in the modern world).

L.G.   *Lumen Gentium* (Constitution *ibid*. on the Church).

M. et Ch.   *Mission et Charité.*

M.V.   P. COSTE. *Monsieur Vincent, Le grand saint du grand siècle.*

P.C.   *Perfectae Caritatis* (Constitution of Second Vatican Council on the renewal of religious life).

RAM   *Revue d'Ascétique et de Mystique.*

St Vincent de Paul

RHE	*Revue d'Histoire Ecclésiastique.*
RHEF	*Revue d'Histoire de L'Eglise en France.*
RSChI	*Rivista di Storia della Chiesa in Italia.*
Reg. com. CM	*Common Rules of the Congregation of the Mission.*
Reg. com. H.d.I.C	*Common Rules of the Daughters of Charity.*
S.V.P.	*St Vincent de Paul. Correspondence, entretiens, documents.* The volume quoted is given in Roman numerals and then the page reference is given.

INTRODUCTION

One of the saints whose life history has most frequently been written is Vincent de Paul. There have been as many as 1,500 biographies of Vincent, but the quality of writing has not always matched the quantity. Much of this literature was produced to celebrate special occasions and was directed at a reading public whose expectations differed widely. Strictly speaking, in the four hundred years since Vincent's birth, there have only been four major biographies of the saint, one for each century.

1. The seventeenth century biography was published in 1664, four years after Vincent's death. It was written by Louis Abelly, bishop of Rodez, and entitled: *La vie du vénérable serviteur de Dieu, Vincent de Paul, instituteur et premier supérieur général de la Congrégation de la Mission* (Paris, Florentin Lambert, 1664) three volumes (260, 480 and 372 pages).

Louis Abelly (1604-1691) was an old and a close friend of Vincent de Paul whom he had got to know about the year 1633 and with whom he had a close relationship until 1660. He was indebted to Vincent for various important steps in his ecclesiastical career: his nomination for the post of vicar general in the diocese of Bayonne as well as principal chaplain to the General Hospital in Paris. He was a prolific and widely-read author. His *Sacerdos Christianus* and his *Medulla Theologica* went through numerous editions in spite of Boileau who made a pun on the title of Abelly's best known work to satirise the author, describing him as *moelleux* or stodgy and viscous. When Vincent de Paul died, his priests wanted to publish a biography of their founder, and so they turned to this writer who was also a friend. They put at his disposal an impressive amount of documentation which ran to two or three large volumes and which had been compiled by Br Bertrand Ducournau who had been secretary to the dead man. This was supplemented by papers collected by other missioners including Fr Fournier and Br

Robineau. In addition there was the material gathered by Abelly himself who visited Vincent's birthplace; the papers sent by Canon Saint Martin, an old friend of Vincent who lived in the same locality, and finally, Vincent's original correspondence. There were far more of Vincent's letters than we have today. Abelly constructed his magnum opus from all this material which was classified by one of the priests of the Mission.

This is a very edifying biography with decidedly hagiographical overtones but it was radically and punctiliously accurate. Errors discovered later are due to lacunae or to mistakes in documentation; they were never deliberate. In spite of its sentimental style, the book continues to be one of the primary sources of information about Vincent, especially as many of the documents handled by Abelly have now been lost and we are left with just the transcriptions that he made. Perhaps the main defect of the work is that there is no sense of biographical development. Vincent de Paul is always the same, from the cradle to the grave.

In spite of everything, Abelly's work is still the first and the essential point of reference for all new biographies. Until proven otherwise, his information can be taken as reliable because it provides first-hand witness to most of the events related. His early readers who had known Vincent during his life, criticised the book for being long-winded, repetitive and cloying but never for being misleading. The only person bold enough to question its veracity was somebody who had no connection with the family, Martin de Barcos, and he took issue with only one point, viz Vincent de Paul's relationship with Saint-Cyran, the uncle of de Barcos, and with the Jansenist movement. Abelly refuted this accusation and proved that all his documentation was taken from the archives of the Congregation of the Mission and not from the Jesuits, as de Barcos claimed.

The work of Abelly has been recently translated into English: *The life of the Venerable Servant of God Vincent de Paul, Founder and First Superior General of the Congregation of the Mission* (New York, New City Press, 1993).

2. The eighteenth century saw the second great biography of Vincent. Pierre Collet wrote, *La vie de Saint Vincent de Paul, instituteur de la Congrégation de la Mission et des Filles de la Charité* (Nancy, A. Lescure, 1748), two volumes (XVIII + 588 and + 616 pages).

Pierre Collet was a distinguished theologian in the Congregation of the Mission. On the instructions of Cardinal Fleury he completed Tournely's work, *Institutiones Theologicae,* seventeen volumes which took him thirty-one years to finish. He also produced other works on moral and polemic theological issues. He was a fierce opponent of Jansenism.

Collet's biography of St Vincent was published shortly after the saint's canonisation. Because of Jansenist opposition, the book had to be published in Lorraine, and even then the author's name could not be revealed. In a methodical and systematic manner, Collet collected all Abelly's material and added to this the collection of documents that had been the basis for the beatification and the canonisation processes. He arranged all this in strictly chronological order for his book, and he added critical notes, something not found in Abelly's work.

It has been said of Collet that he was not very original. This criticism is only partly true. For the most part he followed Abelly fairly slavishly but he did introduce new material and he criticised many documents, argued against the Jansenist representation of Vincent de Paul, and high-lighted the political background to Vincent's work. This biography was an erudite work, written in the scientific style of the seventeenth century. It complements Abelly's work in more ways than one but it is less readable, because if Abelly's style errs on the side of being sugary, Collet's book is dry and rather heavy.

3. The major biography of the nineteenth century was the work of Ulysse Maynard, canon of Poitiers (1814-1893). He wrote *Saint Vincent de Paul. Sa vie, son temps, ses oeuvres, son influence* (Paris, Retaux-Bray, 1860) in four volumes.

Maynard's work was published to celebrate the bicentenary of Vincent's death and was commissioned by the Superior General of the Mission, Fr Jean Baptiste Étienne, who placed the archives of Saint Lazare at the author's disposal. Maynard made a thorough study of the documents with the intention of producing a work that was original. His aim was to present Vincent de Paul against the great historical background of that era. On the whole he succeeded in doing this although he did not always convey to the reader the relationship between the main character in the story and the world that Vincent lived in.

Maynard had skilfully managed to collect a vast amount of material and this meant he was able to include a lot of additional information in his biography of Vincent. It is a pity that his critical faculties are not always on the same plane as his painstaking research. At times he quite arbitrarily alters information or he accepts as authentic anecdotes which are more than a little dubious. The tone of the book very much reflects the nineteenth century taste for rhetoric with some lingering touches of romanticism. It continues to be an indispensable work of reference, especially with regard to certain

Vincentian enterprises such as the relief work he carried out in devastated regions and various other undertakings.

4. The twentieth century gave to Vincentian historiography the great work, *Le grand saint du grand siècle, Monsieur Vincent* (Paris, Desclée de Brouwer, 1932). This was written in three volumes and was the masterpiece of the Vincentian priest, Pierre Coste (1873-1935).

The author, who was archivist and secretary general of the Congregation of the Mission, had earlier edited the complete works of Vincent de Paul under the title, *Saint Vincent de Paul: Correspondence, Entretiens, Documents* (Paris, Lecoffre-Gabalda, 1920-1925), 14 volumes. This work brings together all the writings of Vincent de Paul that we know about to date—the letters he wrote and those he received, his spiritual conferences to the missioners and to the Daughters of Charity and a great number of miscellaneous documents (bulls, regulations, contracts and depositions, etc.). Strictly speaking, this is not a critical edition of Vincent's writing, as the editor dispensed with certain formalities, but this in no way detracts from its reliability, given the care Coste took to present the reader with Vincent's own words. The outstanding merit of this edition is the care taken by the author to bring together all the information which can throw light on the people, events, places and ideas referred to in the text of Vincent's writings. Since the publication of this work it is unthinkable that any biography or study of St Vincent de Paul could be undertaken without an in-depth study of Coste's writings. These are the primary source of all Vincentian research.

Coste himself was the first to systematically exploit his work, and the outcome of this was his biography of Vincent. The underlying concept of this book, and the way the work developed, are in accordance with the strictest demands of historical positivism. Facts are what interest him and, considered from this angle, Coste's biography leaves nothing to be desired. Apart from some discoveries that only came to light at a later date, we can say that this work draws together all the material facts connected with the history of Vincent de Paul.

Two objections might be raised with regard to this excellent work. For one thing, the author, following his convictions, is guilty of the excesses we connect with positive criticism. He set so much store on documentation that he refused to accept any evidence that was not in written form. Secondly, Coste may not have lacked talent but he certainly lacked the ability to interpret his material. His reading of the texts did not lead him to penetrate the deep, inner meaning behind words and events, something which is essential for any biography. Even so, Fr Coste's *Monsieur Vincent* is essential reading for any serious study of Vincent de Paul. There is an excellent English translation.

As for the minor biographies, the reader will find an outline of the more important in the bibliography. I will only mention here the four or five books which are the most original or of the greatest interest. In my opinion these would be the biographies written by A. Redier, P. Renaudin, J. Calvet, J. Mauduit and A. Dodin.

This last work (André Dodin, *Saint Vincent de Paul et la Charité* [Paris, Du Seuil, 1960], 188 pages), is a slender volume which is much more important than its small number of pages might suggest. It is an extraordinarily good synthesis which penetrates the interior world of Vincent de Paul and the inestimable work he did and it succeeds in rediscovering for us the living and smiling image of the saint of charity. At the same time, the author's skilful and thought-provoking questions move the reader to study the subject further by reading a longer and more detailed work.

The first book published in English on St Vincent de Paul was a small one written by an English emigré priest, Thomas Carre, with the title of *Pietas Parisiensis or a short description of the charities commonly exercised in Paris* (Paris: Moutier, 1666), which is mainly an abbreviated translation of the biography by Abelly. Nevertheles, it is interesting to note that English readers could have at their disposal an accurate account of the deeds of the saint founder of Charity only six years after his death.

There are numerous biographies written in Spanish but most of them are translations or adaptations of French works. The two outstanding ones are from the eighteenth and the twentieth century.

The first one, Father Juan del Santísimo Sacramento, *Vida del venerable siervo de Dios, Vicente de Paúl* (Naples, De Bonis, 1701, 12 + 572 pages) was published in 1701. It is the work of an Augustinian whose prestige was somewhat enhanced by the fact that he was the natural son of Philip IV. It is the Spanish translation of an Italian biography which came from the pen of the Oratorian priest, Domenico Acami (Rome, 1677), and this in turn was a translation of a French abridgement of the biography written by Abelly. But Fr Juan's translation is not a servile one. On the contrary, the author's easy flow of language and his well-turned phrases render his style superior to that of the original. It is a pity that subsequent editors felt free to modify the flowery sentences of the original text only to render dull and technical a prose style that has all the flavour of the Spanish classical writers of the Golden Age.

The last great Spanish biography was the work of Frs José Herrera and Veremundo Pardo, *San Vicente de Paúl. Biografía y selección de escritos.* (Madrid, BAC, 1950) X + 908 pages. This is a serious attempt to produce an original Spanish biographical work. The basis for its documentation is

Coste's biography and his edition of Vincentian writings. It is to be recommended for the soundness of its conclusions and for its easy style but it also reveals all the negative effects of the triumphalistic attitude prevailing at the time of publication and the authors take any Spanish link with Vincent and his work to extremes.

The book that the reader now has in his hands aims at continuing the on-going effort to discover and interpret the past from our present day standpoint, and this with regard to history in general, and to church history in particular. There is no difficulty in recognising the methodological principles that underpin the work. Nevertheless, I would like to make some of these explicit.

Ortega y Gasset wrote, 'All human life can be reduced to three major factors: vocation, circumstance and chance. When we write the biography of any human being we are expressing these values as an equation'.

The author's original intention, and his continued objective when writing this biography, was to remain faithful to this dictum of Ortega. From a Christian viewpoint, the three factors mentioned by Ortega are all related, not to a fourth factor, but to God, who is the guiding force behind every human story and who shapes all the events of history. It is God who reveals to every man his vocation to be the ideal self that each one of us is called to be.' It is God who places man in the circumstances that determine his life. What people call chance is in reality God; or, what amounts to the same thing, his providence.

In writing this book I have been concerned with two other factors that are deeply rooted in the Ortegan tradition. On the one hand, I wanted to view Vincent de Paul's life from the inside; that is to say, to look on it as a drama, or a story, whose plot would be the fulfilment or otherwise of a personal vocation all along its lifetime, with the help—or the obstacle—of circumstances. Secondly, I would try to refer each specific fragment of the historical reality that was Vincent de Paul to the authentic whole. There is no greater mistake than to isolate individual facts or else to consider them within a general setting where they are out of place. This, according to Ortega's diagnosis, constitutes an 'anatomical error'.

To organise the vast amount of different types of material on which the story of Vincent de Paul is based, and to make it into a coherent, intelligible and unified study in accordance with the three principles already indicated one has to bear in mind the five stages of human development which are biographically relevant: infancy, youth, early adulthood, later adult years and old age.

With this schema in mind, here is the outline synthesis of Vincent de Paul's biography:

1.   Chilhood and adolescence (1581-1600). No historical action.
2.   Youth (1601-1617). A period of instruction and apprenticeship, of searching for and discovering his vocation, or if you prefer the term, his fundamental option following on from a process of conversion.
3.   Early adult years (1618-1633). Period of gestation in which he is setting up the agencies which will put into action the programme he regards as his life's work, a time of conflict with the forces that had opposed him from the time he was admitted to influential circles.
4.   Later adult years (1634-1653). A period of dominance or management when he brought to fruition the great enterprises which are to mark his passage through the history of the Church and of the world.
5.   Old age (1653-1660). Vincent, now on the sidelines of life, and beyond the range of daily struggles, is eager to bequeath to future generations the fruits of his life's experience and his part in history.

It goes without saying that none of the above dates has been chosen at random. Anyone who has even a slight knowledge of Vincent de Paul knows that 1600 was the year of his ordination to the priesthood, 1617 was the year of Folleville and Châtillon when he knew for certain his vocation; the years 1632-1633 saw him established in Saint Lazare, the Congregation of the Mission unconditionally approved, the Daughters of Charity founded and the Tuesday conferences organised. The year 1652-53 corresponds with the time of his leaving the Council of Conscience, the approbation of the constitutions of the Congregation of the Mission by the archbishop of Paris, and the condemnation of Jansenism. 1660 is the year of his death.

In this introduction to the book we should also take on board the historical events at the time that Vincent de Paul lived. I hope these are dealt with explicitly enough in the text and, more importantly, that they are presented in a way that shows how they influenced Vincent's actions. For this reason, I must be true to my convictions, and refuse to paint a picture of events seen in isolation from the main character for whom they are meant to serve as a background.

JOSE MARIA ROMAN, C.M.

First Part

HIS CHILDHOOD—
HISTORY IS SILENT

(1581-1600)

Chapter I
A CHILDHOOD SPENT IN THE COUNTRY

It can be said of many famous people that the part of their life that we know least about is their childhood. This is very true of St Vincent de Paul. Who would be interested enough to note down for history the comings and goings of an insignificant country lad? Was this boy not destined to lead the same obscure existence as generation after generation of his forebears? Would he not turn out to be just another faceless peasant worn down by the exhausting labour of struggling to cultivate land that was barren? Yet the day would come when millions of people would look back, with interest, at the little French village that witnessed the first steps taken by a man whose fame has spread beyond all frontiers, and who, after four centuries, continues to challenge the passage of time.

A disputed date

The first problem we have with Vincent's childhood is the exact date of his birth. Up to about seventy five years ago there was absolutely no doubt that the saint was born on Easter Tuesday 24 April 1576. This was affirmed by his first biographer, Abelly.[1] Even before this work, Vincent's date of birth was reckoned to be 1576. Carved on his tombstone were the words, 'Died 27 September, 1660, aged 85 years'.[2] The same information is repeated in other contemporary documents—in the weekly *La Gazette de France* and in *Muze historique,* by the poet Jean Loret. Both these publications appeared

---

[1] L. ABELLY, *La vie du Vénérable serviteur de Dieu Vincent de Paul ...'* (Paris, F. Lambert, 1664), 1.1 c. 2, p. 6. We must remember that Abelly does not specifically state 24 April; he only mentions the year 1576 and the day celebrated in the liturgy, Easter Tuesday. We shall soon see that this is no idle observation.

[2] *'Obiit die vigesima septima septembris, anno millesimo sexcentesimo, aetatis vero suae octogesimo quinto'* (ABELLY, *op. cit.*, 1.1 c. 52, p. 259). The use of the ordinal number means that the years were not completed.

in October 1660.[3] From that time onward this same date was used in biographies and official documents.

In 1922, Fr Pierre Coste published a documented study with the strange title, 'The true date of Vincent de Paul's birth'.[4] He showed that contrary to traditional and universally held belief, Vincent de Paul was not born in 1576, but five years later, in 1581. Coste's argument was simple but solid and convincing, since it was based on the actual words of the man whose biography he was writing. His proposition can be summarised as follows: throughout the course of his long life, Vincent himself makes twelve statements about his age. All these references point to 1581 as being the year he was born. And who better than Vincent would know how old he was?[5]

---

[3] See the complete text of the news item from *La Gazette* and Loret's verses from *Annales* (1961) pp. 493-494 and (1929) p. 729.

[4] P. COSTE, 'La vraie date de la naissance de Saint Vincent de Paul', offprint from Bulletin de la Société de Borda (Dax 1922), 23 pages.

[5] Here we have, in chronological order the list of statements quoted by Coste:

1. 17-4-1628: This is a testimony about Francis de Sales' virtues: *'annos quadraginta octo aut circiter natus'* (*S.V.P.* XIII, p. 19).

2. 31-3-1639: The statement in the abbé de Saint-Cyran's trial: *'âgé de 59 ans ou environ'* (S.V.P. XIII, p. 86).

3. 12-10-1639: Letter to Louis Lebreton: *'J'entrerai au mois d'avril prochain en ma soixantième'*: 'Next April I will begin my sixtieth year'. (*S.V.P.* I, p. 593).

4. 25-7-1640: Letter to Pierre Escart: *'l'âge de soixante ans que j'ai'*: I am sixty years old (*S.V.P.* II, p. 70).

5. 21-11-1642: Letter to Bertrand Codoing: *'J'ai ... des expériences que soixante deux ans ... m'ont acquis'*: 'I have learnt from my 62 years experience and from my own mistakes' (*S.V.P.* II, p. 314).

6. 17-9-1649: Letter to Étienne Blatiron: *'le support que je le fais exercer depuis 69 ans qu'il me souffre sur la terre'*: 'He has had to be patient with me for the sixty nine years he has allowed me to be on this earth' (*S.V.P.* III, p. 488).

7. 27-4-1655 (= 5.° *kalendas maii*): Letter to Pope Alexander VII: *'Annum ago septuagesimum quintum'*: 'I am seventy five years old' (*S.V.P.* V, p. 368).

8. 3-11=1656: During repetition of prayer with the missioners: *'pour moi, me voilà à la 76 année de ma vie'*: 'I am seventy six years old' (*S.V.P.* XI, p. 364).

9. 6-1-1657: Conference to Daughters of Charity: *'Pour moi, cela se va sans dire, ayant soixante et seize ans ...'*: 'As regards myself, I am seventy six years old ...' (*S.V.P.* X, p. 252).

10. 17-6-1657: Conference to Daughters of Charity: *'Et moi qui, comme vous savez, suis âgé de soixante et dix et sept ans'*: 'As you know I am seventy seven years old' (*S.V.P.*, X, p. 283).

11. 15-7-1659: Letter to Cardinal de Retz: *'étant à présent dans la 79 de mon âge'*: 'Being now in my seventy-ninth year of age' (*S.V.P.* VIII, p. 26).

12. 24-8-1659: Letter to François Feydin: *'Ressouvenez vous, s'il vous plaît, en vos prières d'un veillard de 79 ans'*: 'Please, remember an old man of seventy nine in your prayers' (*S.V.P.* VIII, p. 91).

In spite of the difficulties implicit in Coste's theory, and particularly the question of how old the saint was when he was ordained to the priesthood (a subject that will be discussed in more detail later on), the theory seemed to be based on such solid reasoning that, once the work was published, his proposition was accepted in almost every detail by historians, biographers and ecclesiastical authorities alike. The only weak spot in Coste's interpretation is that the author understood Vincent to be speaking of incomplete, not completed years, whenever the saint referred to his age and this is a point that has not been fully substantiated. If we accept the latter part of this hypothesis, then the references quoted by Coste lead inevitably to the year 1580, and there are other powerful arguments for preferring this date.[6] In any event, the old date of 1576 has now been discarded once and for all. The mistake that all former historians made in favouring the earlier date is understandable, and there are no grounds for accusing the saint's followers and his immediate successors of inventing a pious lie or of being deliberately misleading. Some zealous biographers have made this charge and it is even implied by Coste himself.[7]

The only reliable document that the saint's companions had which could determine his age, and consequently his date of birth, was the official document concerning his ordination to the priesthood, and this stated that in the year 1600 the ordinand, Vincent de Paul, was of lawful age; that is to say, he was twenty four years old. So all they needed to do was a simple subtraction sum. The references that Vincent made to his age were not readily to hand and set down in chronological order. At best, people would remember the saint's words but they would have been vague as to the precise dates when these statements were made. This is how the mistake came to be made and the error persisted until Coste conscientiously checked his sources.

---

[6] Researchers such as A. POHAR, in his article 'Octogenarius ille' in *Vincentiana* (1959), p. 153-155, and F. DELCAMPO, in '1580-1980. IV centenario del nacimiento de San Vicente de Paúl', *Anales* (1977), p. 551-555, recently accepted the year 1580 as the date of St. Vincent's birth. Another reason for accepting that year is that Abelly only gives the specific date of Easter Tuesday which was on 5 April that year, the feast of St Vincent Ferrer. Perhaps, for this reason, the child was called Vincent in honour of the saint. St Vincent de Paul had a deep devotion to the Valencian Dominican who was like a second patron for him. *Cf.* ABELLY, *op. cit.*, 1.3 c. 9, p. 94.
J. DEFOS DU RAU accepts the years 1580 or 1579 as the time of St Vincent's birth. 'La date de naissance de Saint Vincent de Paul' (Auch, Frederic Cocharaux, 1958). Offprint of *Bulletin de la Société de Borda*.
J. M. ROMAN also prefers the year 1580. *Cf.* 'El nacimiento de San Vicente de Paúl. Preguntas en torno a una fecha' in *Semana Vicenciana de Salamanca* (10ª), p. 247-272.
[7] A. REDIER, *La vraie vie ...*, pp. 5-7 and 16-17. COSTE makes the same suggestion, but more cautiously in *M.V.* Vol.1, p. 18.

It could be that the new offshoot of the humble de Paul family was baptised on the day he was born. With the baptismal waters he received the name Vincent, a name he was to keep all his life and the only name he would be known by. His patron saint was the deacon from Saragossa who was martyred in Valencia. On one occasion Vincent de Paul asked somebody of influence who had friends and acquaintances in Spain if he would use his good offices to find out more information about the martyr than the scanty details given in the summary of his life.[8]

The years of Vincent's childhood and adolescence, then, would have been the period 1581-1600. What do we know about these first nineteen years? They were years which he spent exploring the world around him, key years for the development of his personality—vital years, whose influence on the saint's destiny has never been totally fathomed.

Apart from just a few quasi-legal details, the only source of information about this stage in Vincent's life is Abelly. In the early chapters of his book he brings together the limited source material which, after an interval of eighty years, might throw some light on Vincent's childhood. These documents are no longer available.

One such source of information was provided by the reports sent by Canon Jean de Saint Martin, an old friend of the saint. The canon took it on himself to go to the saint's birthplace and find out what friends and relatives remembered about Vincent. Canon Saint Martin's report is reliable,[9] in spite of some mistakes in dates which are easily verifiable, such as the date of Vincent's ordination to the subdiaconate and diaconate. The canon had belonged to the circle of Vincent's closest friends and over a number of years he had acted as intermediary between Vincent and his family on a variety of matters. So, for example, in 1630 we find two members of the St Martin family appointed executors for the goods that Vincent bequeathed to his brothers, sisters and nephews.[10] In 1656 the same Canon Saint Martin

---

[8] ABELLY, *op. cit.*, 1.3 c. 9, p. 94. Coste thinks that Vincent de Paul's patron is St Vincent de Xaintes, the first bishop of Dax, and the principal patron of that diocese, who was a martyr in Spain according to the Roman martyrology. This hypothesis not only contradicts Abelly's theories but, in accordance with local tradition, it contradicts the evidence that St Vincent of Xaintes was martyred in the place that bears his name, very close to Dax. If St Vincent of Xaintes were the patron of Vincent de Paul, Vincent would not have sought information from Spain about the saint's life. José Herrera has argued very convincingly in favour of St. Vincent of Saragossa. *Cf.* J. HERRERA, 'El santo Patrón de San Vicente', *Anales* (1961), pp. 220-223.

[9] Anyway, I judge Coste's categorical statement exaggerated: '... the memoirs of Canon Saint Martin are not reliable' (*M.V.* Vol. 1, p. 37 in the note). The statement has been often repeated without critical examination.

[10] *Annales* (1936), pp. 705-706.

will be responsible for distributing among the relatives the sum of one thousand *livres*, which Vincent had received as a gift to be used for this purpose from another friend of his, M. du Fresne.[11]

Moreover, one of the canon's nephews married into the Comet family, and this family would have had more information than anybody else on the subject of Vincent's early years since they had been the first patrons of the promising youngster. According to the second biographer, Canon Saint Martin's memoirs comprise various manuscripts which were written by different people.[12] So it is logical to suppose that some witnesses will be more reliable than others.

As well as the memoirs of Saint Martin, Abelly and Collet had at their disposal another manuscript about the family history of the founder of the Mission. This manuscript is now lost but it used to be kept in the archives of Saint Lazare.[13]

Finally, Abelly also had the information that he himself had collected. He tells us, in the prologue to his work, that he had visited the saint's birthplace and had got to know Vincent's closest relatives. He made this journey about the year 1639. He can therefore describe most of the things narrated in his book as, 'Seen with my own eyes or heard with my own ears'.[14] Let us now see what these sources have to tell us.

Rooted in the land

Vincent de Paul was French. He was a native of Pouy, a little village near Dax, in the Landes district of Gascony, not far from the Pyrenees.[15] Pouy,

---

[11] ABELLY, *op. cit.*, 1.3 c.19, pp. 292-293.
[12] P. COLLET, *La vie de Saint Vincent de Paul* (Nancy, A. Lescure, 1748), Vol. 1, p. 109.
[13] *Ibid.*
[14] ABELLY, *op. cit.*, *Avis au lecteur.*
[15] The fact that St Vincent de Paul was born in France, and more specifically in Pouy, is not only supported by historians, biographers and devotees of the saint, but it is authenticated by a long series of documents such as the leasing contract for the Abbey of Saint Léonard de Chaume which was signed on the 14 May, 1610. In this contract Vincent appears as *'natif de la paroisse de Poy (sic), diocèse d'Aqs, (sic) (Annales* [1941-1942], p. 261), notary's document concerning the saint's tranfer of the property he inherited from his father, in favour of his brothers and nephews. This deed of gift includes the words: *'natif de la paroisse de Poy, diocèse d'Aqs, en Gascogne'* (*S.V.P.* XIII, p. 62). The complete list of documents can be found in COSTE. *M.V.* Vol. 1, p. 19.
At the end of the nineteenth century some people thought that Vincent de Paul was born in Tamarite de Litera, in the province of Huesca, Spain. This theory was based on ancient local traditions, and also the fact that many families in Alto Aragón were called Paúl and Moras. The first person to publicly defend St Vincent's Spanish nationality

which since the nineteenth century has been renamed Saint Vincent de Paul, in honour of its most illustrious son, is today an elegant small town for retired people and summer visitors. The streets are asphalted, its neat country houses have well-kept gardens and the public buildings are modern and functional in design. Four centuries ago it was a miserable little hamlet made up of clusters of dwellings that were scattered about like islands in the marshlands of the Landes. At the close of the sixteenth century, the family of Jean de Paul and Bertrande de Moras lived in one of these farmsteads called Ranquine. The house which pilgrims know today as *le berceau de Saint Vincent* has very little in common with the house where Vincent de Paul was born. But it is near the original site, and in front of the dwelling is an ancient holm oak shored up with cement. This is a relic of a small number of trees (oaks, chestnuts and apple trees) which in earlier times would have been growing in the green space called the *airial* or *eriaou*. This opened out on to the collection of buildings comprising dwelling place, cowshed, pig sty, hen-run ...[16]

The landscape of the Landes district has changed a lot since the sixteenth century. At that time there would have been no dense pine forests or green plantations of maize. Alongside the river stretched a narrow band of common pasture land, and above this was the arable land that was difficult to cultivate because of the sandy soil. Lastly, there was a vast stretch of semi-desert land with a great number of stagnant ponds and treacherous clay pits covered by the vegetation so typical of that area. Here and there would spring up an oasis of greenery, bordering some tiny stream or buried in the depths of some hidden little valley. These were the outcome of a movement to colonise the Landes region which was begun in the Middle Ages and which received a new impetus during the sixteenth and seventeenth centuries.[17]

---

was Professor B. FELIU Y PEREZ, from Barcelona. This defence is in the appendix to the Spanish translation of the book *San Vicente de Paúl y su misión social* of A. LOTH (Barcelona, Jepus, 1887). Dr. Felíu, instructed Dr. A. HERNANDEZ Y FAJARNES, professor at the University of Saragossa, to write scientifically about St Vincent's Spanish nationality. The fruit of his work was the book entitled *San Vicente de Paúl. Su patria. Sus estudios en la Universidad de Zaragoza* (Saragossa, impr. La Derecha, 1888, 349 pages). In *San Vicente de Paúl, Biografía y selección de escritos,* by J. HERRERA and V. PARDO (Madrid, BAC, 1950), p. 35-40, can be found a summary of Fajarnés' theories. J. PEMARTIN vigorously refuted that hypothesis in a booklet entitled *Saint Vincent de Paul est né en France* (there is a Spanish translation). P. COSTE replies with ironic disdain (*M.V.* Vol. 1, p. 19). There is no foundation for the Spanish theory and this has not survived.

[16] COSTE, *M.V.* Vol.1, p. 20-21: S. SERPETTE, *Le berceau de Saint Vincent de Paul,* p. 12ff; COSTE, 'Histoire de la maison de Ranquine avant le XIX siècle', in the *Bulletin de la Société de Borda* (1906), p. 334ff.

[17] R. CUZAGO, *Géographie historique des Landes, le Pays landais* (Lacoste 1962); *Parc Naturel regional des Landes de Gascogne* (Paris, S.E.T.O).

By the year 1581 the de Paul family was established in Pouy but the date of their arrival there is not known. The husband's name was either Jean or Guillaume,[18] and the wife was called Bertrande. Fr Juan del Santísimo Sacramento, the first to write a biography of the saint in Spanish, made the observation in 1701 that the surnames were more Spanish than French, and he has a note to the effect that the family might possibly be of Spanish origin. 'This supposition is not unreasonable, given the fact that the village where the said couple lived is very near the border with Catalonia.'[19] Evidently Fr John's ideas about the exact location of Pouy were far from precise but this does not weaken the argument.

Coste is inclined to think that the family took its name from the Paul brook, which at midstream crosses the main road leading from the house where Vincent was born to the sanctuary of Buglose, or from a house of the same name that still exists in Buglose. However, there is a noticeable lack of documentary evidence to support this view.[20]

Leaving aside the question of birthplace, it is quite possible that the family was of Spanish origin. This is all the more probable[21] if we remember that, at the very time that the saint was born, a series of agreements called *lies et passeries* secured the free movement of people, flocks and merchandise from one part of Pyrenees to another. This guaranteed the right of French and Spanish people to trade with each other and allowed free access to territory even in times of war. The *passerie* decreed in 1513-1514 was of such importance that some scholars talk of a 'Pyrenees State' and this situation lasted until the end of the eighteenth century.[22] In such circumstances it is by no means improbable that Vincent de Paul had forbears who had emigrated from Aragon to France and settled there.

By 1581 the de Paul family had two sons, Jean and Bernard. After Vincent, who was their third son, came three more children—Dominic, known also as Gayon, and Manion, and then there were two daughters called Marie. One of these would later marry Gregoire Delartigue, and the second Marie

---

[18] 'Jean', according to Abelly (*op. cit.*, 1.1 c. 2 p. 7); 'Guillaume' according to the *Ristretto Cronologico*, p. 1 and Collet (*op. cit.*, Vol. 1, p. 5).

[19] JUAN DEL SANTISIMO SACRAMENTO, *Vida del Venerable Siervo de Dios Vicente de Paúl* (Nápoles 1701), p. 2.

[20] COSTE, *M.V.* Vol.1, p. 21.

[21] The corroboratory evidence collected by Hernández and Fajarnés was added to, around 1936, by the parish priest of Tamarite, José Merigó, and a lawyer from the same town, D. Joaquín de Carpi Zaidín, who wrote about the widespread usage of the surnames Paúl and Moras in the Aragon region generally and in La Litera in particular. This evidence is overwhelming. Cf. FAJARNES, *op. cit.*, pp. 99-141.

[22] J. F. SOULET, *La vie quotidienne dans les Pyrénées sous l'ancien régime du XVI au XVII siècles* (Paris, Hachette, 1974), p. 1.ª c. 3.

St Vincent de Paul

was married to Jean Daigrand who was also know as Paillole, which was the name of the house where he lived. Except for the eldest boy, all the brothers and sisters were alive in 1630.[23] In those days six children were not considered a big family. It was a stable and patriarchal rural family that needed plenty of hands for the agricultural unit it represented.

'Decent and fairly comfortable for their station in life'

In his saintly old age Vincent insisted on playing down anything about himself, and over and over again he would dwell on his humble beginnings[24] and lowly position in life,[25] on his poverty and misery.[26] If we were to take his words literally we would think that his family were almost beggars. This is certainly not true. Yes, they were peasants and as such belonged to the lowest echelons of a society which, in the Old Regime, was strictly hierarchical. But these peasants were their own masters. They were not simply hired hands or even tenants or tenant farmers. They owned small plots of land which might include woodland and arable fields, as well as a house and a farm with a variety of domestic animals such as sheep, oxen, cows and pigs.[27] They belonged to that social class which writers have said reflected the true history of France at that period, a France where the basic social unit was the rural village.[28] Collet states that even on their mother's side the family had the modest degree of social status which in villages and small towns was accorded to those who held certain minor offices. One member of the family had risen to the position of advocate in the parlement of Bordeaux.[29] On the father's side there were ecclesiastics of relatively high standing: a Stephen de Paul who was prior of the hospital of Poymartet,[30] and a Dominic Dusin, an uncle of Vincent, who was parish priest at Pouy when Vincent was a boy.[31]

---

[23] The saint's brothers and brothers-in-laws' names appeared, with some variations, in two notary deeds: the gift made inter vivos, 4 September 1626, published by Coste in *S.V.P.* (XIII, pp. 61-63) and the will, dated 7 September 1630, published in *Annales* (1936), p. 705-706. Coste was not aware of this.

[24] *S.V.P.* II, p. 3 and 51; IV, p. 215; VIII, p. 138; IX, p. 15; X, p. 681; XII, p. 21, 270, 279.

[25] ABELLY. *op. cit.*, 1.3 c.13, p. 204.

[26] *S.V.P.* XII, p. 220.

[27] ABELLY. *op. cit.*, 1.1 c. 2, p. 7; COLLET. *op. cit.*, Vol.1, p. 5; *S.V.P.* II, p. 3; IV, p. 215; XIII, pp. 61-63; *Annales* (1936), pp. 705-706.

[28] V.-L. TAPIE. *La France de Louis XIII et de Richelieu*, p. 34; R. MANDROU. *Francia en los siglos XVII y XVIII*, p. 10.

[29] COLLET. *op. cit.*, Vol.1, p. 110.

[30] S. SERPETTE. *op. cit.*, p. 9.

[31] *S.V.P.* IX, p. 81.

A humble family, yes, but in Vincent's own words they were able by their labours to 'live decently and fairly comfortably according to their station in life' and they could fulfil the divine precept to 'earn their bread by the sweat of their brow'.[32] As always in the country, this demanded the hard-working collaboration of every member of the family just as soon as they were old enough to do useful work. In his old age Vincent will recall, with veiled tenderness, the diligent and self-sacrificing activity of his mother and sisters. He will urge the Daughters of Charity to take as their model the virtues of good village girls which, he says, 'I know about from experience and from what happened in my own family since I am the son of a poor farmer and I lived in the country until I was fifteen,'[33] and he describes a scene which his young eyes must have witnessed countless times:

The girls come home from work exhausted, to take a brief rest. They are tired and worn out, wet through and covered in mud, but no sooner have they arrived than they have to set to and work again if there is anything to be done, and if their father or mother tells them to go out again they do so straight away, without thinking about their tiredness or the mud, and without stopping to think what they look like.[34]

With a stroke of his pen, Vincent evokes the frugality of the family table, in a way reminiscent of the pictures of peasant life painted by the Le Nain brothers or by Georges Latour:

In the country districts where I come from, their diet consists of a grain called millet which is cooked in an earthenware pot. At meal time it is poured out on to plates, and all the household gather round to take their portion before they go off to work. Most people are often satisfied with soup and bread even though their work is constant and exhausting.[35]

When Vincent paints an idyllic picture of the virtues of these country people he is no doubt idealising the situation and this is on two levels. Maybe he exaggerates the scarcity of food, but his sober descriptions are in singular agreement with the studies of modern social historians. His words are also

---

[32] ABELLY. *op. cit.*, 1.1 c. 2, p. 8 and 1.3 c. 19, p. 291.
[33] *S.V.P.* IX, p. 81.
[34] *S.V.P.* IX, p. 91.
[35] *S.V.P.* IX, p. 84.

immensely valuable for putting before us the circumstances of his family background when he was a child.

'I have kept flocks'

Vincent had to learn very early in life to bring his own contribution to this modest and hard-working family. One particular work seems, by its very nature, to have been set aside for farmers' children to do even from their earliest years: tending the flock, whether this was large or small. Vincent became a shepherd at a very early age. He looked after sheep, cows and pigs, though later on when speaking about himself he would try to sell himself short by emphasising the pigs.[36] His contribution to the family's resources was no small one. The shepherd is a key figure in the organisational structure of the Landes region where the main occupations were farming and cattle rearing.

We can imagine the young son of the Paul family, perched high on his tall stilts that enabled him to go safely about the swampy, muddy land. He would be dressed in a heavy sheepskin coat, and would be leaning on a long stick whose forked end would provide a precarious seat during the interminable stops he was obliged to make while the sheep grazed at their leisure, or the greedy pigs rooted under the oak trees. Slung over his shoulder would be the leather pouch containing his meagre lunch, and the horn which he would blow when it was time to gather in the flock for the journey home, or to sound the alarm if he spotted a wolf.

He would have in his hand the country bagpipes that he played to while away the hours of solitude, or perhaps he would be carrying a spinning wheel which was another means of augmenting the family income. At least this is what social historians and folklorists have discovered, and it helps us, in our day, to reconstruct what the shepherd of the Landes district must have been like at the close of the sixteenth century.[37] The shepherd might not always return at night. His search for good pastures could sometimes take him as far as Montgaillard, about fifty kilometres distant from Pouy. We know this because one day Vincent mentioned it to Persin de Montgaillard, the bishop of Saint Pons, thinking that the castle which gave its name to the prelate's family was the Montgaillard in his part of the country: 'I know it well; when I was a child I used to look after the flocks and I would take them to that place.'[38] This mistake is a valuable one because it enables us to follow

---

[36] *S.V.P.* II, p. 3; IV, p. 2 15.

[37] *Parc Naturel regional des Landes,* p. 22.

[38] COLLET, *op. cit.*, Vol. 2, p. 195.

on the map one of the journeys made by our young shepherd and it helps us to realise the relative importance of the flock committed to his charge, for nobody would go that distance with just a few animals.

Was the Paul family a devout one? The conventional hagiography of those who first wrote Vincent's biography would almost make us despair: 'Their seeming lack of prosperity was made up for in piety, candour and innocence before God', writes one of them.[39] Another says, 'Poor in this world's goods but rich in heaven's blessings'.[40] Vincent will be more clear-sighted and have less regard for convention when he paints the canvas of rural piety based on his childhood memories:

> Have you ever seen anyone with more confidence in God than good country people have? They sow their seed and wait for God to bless the harvest. It God allows the harvest to fail they still trust that he will provide them with food for the year. At times they have losses but, in their love of poverty and their submission to God's will they say: 'God has given, God has taken away, blessed be his holy name'. Provided they have enough to exist on, and that is something they never lack, then they are not concerned for the future.[41]

This was the strong, elemental faith of Europe's early churches that gave solidity to Western Christianity and which, at different times, has almost miraculously caused certain ancient rural family trees to bear the tender flowers of sanctity that the world will come to know by the name of Joan of Arc, John of the Cross, Jean Marie Vianney or Vincent de Paul.

The flowers of childhood

Since Vincent was brought up in such circumstances it is not surprising that early on he showed signs of a piety that was both solidly-based and intelligent. The witnesses interviewed by Abelly remembered that when young Vincent was bringing flour from the mill he would open the sack and give away handfuls of the flour to poor people he met on the way, and they recalled that his father, 'who was a good man, did not take it amiss.'

At other times he would give away part of the bread in his shepherd's pouch and on one occasion, having managed to save up as much as thirty

---

[39] COLLET, *op. cit.*, Vol. 1, p. 5.
[40] FRAY JUAN DEL SANTISIMO SACRAMENTO, *op. cit.*, p. 2.
[41] *S.V.P.* IX, pp. 88-89.

sous (a fortune for somebody his age and in a region where money was scarce) he gave the whole lot to a beggar who seemed in particular need.[42]

Both early and later hagiographers, who were traditional in outlook (and Coste is no exception), have seen in these accounts the unmistakable signs of a precocious generosity that foreshadowed the lofty destiny of the future apostle of charity. The other extreme is shown by biographers who have set out to demythologise Vincent and have claimed that there is no historical proof for such stories, which they dismiss as figments of the imagination on the part of worthy peasants wanting to boost 'their' saint.[43] There is nothing in these humble narratives to make us doubt their authenticity. Basically, the charitable acts attributed to the boy Vincent are nothing more than the docile response of a young and generous heart to his good upbringing in a Christian family. That same environment would explain other pious traits often attributed to the young shepherd Vincent, his frequent visits to the old, ruined sanctuary of Our Lady of Buglose (the new one did not exist at that time), or the placing of a picture of Our Lady in the hollow of an oak tree in his father's *airial* to offer her the homage of his prayers in this improvised oratory.[44] These pious acts are far more questionable than Abelly's descriptions of the boy's generosity, and perhaps we should attribute them to the popular taste for embellishment that people weave around those they cherish.

What we do know for certain is that young Vincent stood out among his brothers and companions for his keen, lively mind and for the quickness and inventiveness of his intelligence. His calculating peasant father saw this as an asset to be exploited. He decided to send him to study. In the closed, hierarchical society of that time, study was the only avenue to promotion open to members of the third estate, and this was especially true if study helped somebody to enter the ranks of the clergy.

In the neighbouring town of Dax, the Franciscans were in charge of a boarding school which was alongside a college which would be classified today as a secondary school. The boarding school fees were not excessive (seventy *livres* a year) but this represented a heavy financial burden for the hard-pressed farmer from the Landes. Nevertheless, he thought it worthwhile making the effort. Jean de Paul had in mind the example of a prior who had

---

[42] ABELLY, *op. cit.*, 1.1 c. 2, p. 9; COLLET. *op. cit.*, Vol.1, pp. 6-7.

[43] A. REDIER, *La vraie vie de Saint Vincent de Paul* (Paris, Grasset, 1947), p. 13.

[44] U. MAYNARD, *Saint Vincent de Paul* (Paris 1886), Vol. 1, pp. 5-7. With regard to problems about the sanctuary of Buglose, it was not known for certain that this sanctuary existed until 1620. *cf.* COSTE, *M.V.* Vol.1, pp. 25-28.

come from a similar social background and whose income from the benefice had vastly improved the financial position of his relatives.[45] It was the year 1594, and Vincent was nearly fifteen years old. It was high time to take a decision.

---

[45] ABELLY, *op. cit.*, 1.1 c. 2, pp. 6-10; COSTE, *M.V.* Vol. 1, pp. 29-30.

Chapter II
A PROMISING ADOLESCENCE

'Paris is well worth a Mass'

The years 1593, 1594 and 1595 were important ones for France and it was at this very time that the peasant from Pouy decided to send his son, Vincent, to study. These were key years, not only for this bright young shepherd boy, but for the whole of France as well. In some mysterious way the development of France's history synchronises with the dynamic progress of Vincent de Paul's life. Both begin their climb at the same moment and man and nation reach their peak at the same time.

In 1594, the former Huguenot, Henry of Bourbon, became recognised almost everywhere as king of France. One year earlier, on 25 July 1593 (perhaps at the very time that Vincent was giving the beggar the only thirty *sous* he had), Henry had solemnly abjured heresy in the church of Saint Denis and returned once more to the bosom of the Catholic Church. Was this a calculated move, a step taken from conviction, or a patriotic gesture? Thanks to his conversion, whether this was sincere or motivated by self-interest, and thanks to a shrewd policy of concessions and awards, Henry gradually managed to get himself accepted by his Catholic subjects.

After a quarter of a century of bloody religious strife, domestic peace began to be a reality for France. In February 1594 Henry was consecrated at Chartres with the oil used at the coronation ceremony of all previous Christian monarchs and within a month he had made his triumphal entry into Paris ('Paris is well worth a Mass') while the Spanish garrison that had occupied the capital withdrew without any military engagement. The following year, after long hesitation, consultation and prayer, Pope Clement VIII absolved the former heretic. The war with Spain was to drag on for a further three years. Then, with the exception of a brief period of hostilities, the Edict of Nantes and the Peace of Vervins in 1598 put the official seal on peace at home and abroad. France had started on the path to greatness. The powerful nation recovered its strength and, under the direction of an able monarch who was energetic, astute, clear-sighted and cynical, the country prepared to unite all its forces for the great plan, *le grand dessein*, for the supremacy of Europe. It would take three reigns and eighty years (the eighty years of Vincent's life) to achieve this but the great task was set in motion. The monarch's reign had begun and even though it was perhaps less brilliant than the two that followed, it was nevertheless of fundamental importance as it signalled the dawn of a new era.[1]

How much of all this religious, political and military confusion reached that obscure village at the other end of the kingdom? Echoes of the exhausting negotiations (the Estates General and Suresnes discussions) would reach them via the slow mail of that period or by the occasional arrival of some visitor. They would learn, too, about defeats and victories in far away, unknown cities—Doullens, Cambrai, Calais, Fontaine-Française, Amiens, Paris—and there would also be decrees from the bishop and from the pope. During the long wintry evenings the de Paul family would sit round the hearth discussing any news or rumours.

Many years later Vincent would perhaps recall the impression made on him by his father's account of these happenings:

> You know about the riots that took place in France during the reign of Henry IV. That prince had previously been a heretic and apostate, and if he had declared himself an enemy of the Catholic religion for a second time, then his subjects would no longer be bound to obey him. This king followed his conscience and renounced the error of his ways. He knew that the townspeople might refuse to obey him and he immediately indicated to Rome that he wished to be reconciled ...[2]

The famous phrase, 'Paris is well worth a Mass' had not yet been heard in the humble home of Pouy. The king's conversion came when 'he followed his conscience.' Can we see in these lines a revelation of the first political stance taken by Vincent de Paul when he was a young man? By the time he reached old age, any wounds to Vincent's conscience were now only scars; and former hatreds, if any such ever existed, were now forgotten. Buried in history were the excesses of Jeanne d'Albret's troops, the atrocities committed during the campaigns of Montluc and Montgomery, the sacrilegious destruction of the sanctuary of Buglose and attempts by the

---

[1] For specific information about the history of France, see E. LAVISSE, *Histoire de France*, Vol. 6 and 7. R. MOUSNIER's book, *L'assassinat d'Henri IV* (Paris 1964), gives an original interpretation of Henry IV and his reign.

[2] *S.V.P.* XII, p. 347.

heretics to attack Dax. By now Protestants had ceased to be a growing force in France. It was not a question of fighting them but of winning them over. Here we can see, perhaps, the roots of Vincent's gentleness in dealing with dissidents; a gentleness that was to prove contagious.[3]

'How disobedient I used to be'

With the coming of peace, life returned to normal and so it was back to school again. One day at the beginning of autumn in 1594 or 1595,[4] father and son arrived at the door of the Franciscan friary in Dax. It was from behind that door that Vincent would begin the long journey that would eventually take him far away from his native region, but which would never be able to break the bonds that linked him to the land and to country places. But for the moment he had to cope with the rudiments of Latin, because in those days this was the compulsory basis of humanistic studies. Surrounded by a swarm of school companions who perhaps belonged to families of somewhat higher social status than his own (sons of attorneys or provincial lawyers, of traders or merchants who were trying to better themselves, sons of some nobleman or other), Vincent began to feel further and further distanced from the obscure family tree that was his origin. We know this from a couple of colourful anecdotes which he himself would later relate, to his public embarrassment:

---

[3] P. DEFRENNES, 'La conversion de Saint Vincent de Paul', *RAM* (1932), p. 391.

[4] Abelly states that Vincent began his studies 'about 1588' (*op. cit.*, 1.1 c. 3, p. 10), that is to say when he was twelve years old, according to his way of reckoning. Collet agrees with this way of calculating. 'Vincent de Paul was twelve years old when his father decided that his son should begin to study' (*op. cit.*, Vol. 1, p. 8). But Vincent himself stated that he remained in the country 'till he was fifteen' (*S.V.P.* IX, p. 81). With this in mind, and taking 1580 or 1581, as the date of Vincent's birth, we are led to understand that Vincent began his studies in the year indicated in the text. Herrera is more inclined to agree with Abelly (*Vicente de Paúl, biografía y selección de escritos*, p. 48). None of these theories has the backing of a definite date and there are four different possibilities:

a) Abelly's theory: Vincent was born in 1576. He began his studies in 1588, when he was twelve years old. The drawback with this theory is that it prolongs Vincent's humanities studies for nine years.

b) Herrera's theory: Vincent was born in 1576. He began his studies in 1591, when he was fifteen years old. This theory reduces the time of study to six years.

c) Coste's theory: Vincent was born in 1581. He began his studies in 1595 when he was fourteen. This would seem too short a period of study.

d) Vincent was born in 1580 or 1581, and began his studies when he was between twelve and fifteen years old (1592 to 1595). We have to accept that it is almost impossible to determine these dates more accurately.

I remember that when I was a lad my father used to take me to town with him. He was badly dressed and a bit lame and so I was ashamed to go with him and acknowledge him as my father. Wretched me! How disobedient I was.[5]

Or again:

In the school where I was studying, they told me that my father, who was a poor peasant, had called to see me. I refused to go out and talk to him and so I committed a grave sin.[6]

Perhaps it was in reaction to these peccadilloes of childish vanity that Vincent, in later years, was to insist on his humble family background. These stories are useful because they give us a more complete picture of Vincent at the outset of his career. A generous heart and a child's openness are set alongside an adolescent's conceit and the seeds of rebellion. It is the human face of a youth whose character is still being formed and who has not yet experienced the powerful promptings of grace.

Vincent's studies with the Franciscans in Dax were short-lived; they lasted barely two years. So according to the French educational system, he would have followed fifth and fourth grade classes. Vincent himself used to say that he was only a poor fourth grade student, and what we have always taken to be a sign of his humility should perhaps be interpreted literally.[7]

The father guardian of the Franciscans noted the lad's lively intelligence and recommended Vincent to an unexpected patron who may have been known to the family. This benefactor was M. de Comet, a lawyer from Dax and judge at Pouy. M. de Comet's patronage brought a twofold benefit to Vincent: it allowed him to continue his studies without too much of a financial burden being put on his family, and it also pointed him in the clear direction of an ecclesiastical career.[8] M. de Comet had him removed from the Franciscans and brought to his own house as tutor, or perhaps we should say as monitor and older companion for his children. From now on it would not be necessary to scrape together the seventy *livres* for his board. At the same time he began to see that his real calling was to the priesthood.

At the suggestion of M. de Comet, Vincent received the tonsure

---

[5]   *S.V.P.* XII, p. 432.
[6]   COSTE, *M.V.* Vol. 1, p. 30.
[7]   *S.V.P.* XII, p. 135 and 293.
[8]   ABELLY, *op. cit.*, 1.1 c. 3, p. 10.

and minor orders on 20 December, 1596, when he was just over fifteen years of age.[9] With the permission of the chapter of Dax, this ceremony was performed at Bidache because the episcopal see was vacant at the time. Vincent began his university studies the following year. His father had complete confidence in the boy's ability and, trusting in the bright future that lay ahead for his son, made one more sacrifice so that the ambition could be realised: he sold a pair of oxen.[10] The good peasant continued to take an interest in this, the most gifted of his children, and this continued even after his death, which occurred during Vincent's first year at university. In his will, dated 7 February 1598, he arranged that no effort should be spared so that his son could continue his studies, and to this effect he disposed of his property in terms as favourable to Vincent as the law allowed.[11]

Spanish 'intermezzo'

There were two different scenarios for Vincent de Paul's academic career. These were Toulouse and Saragossa, although most of his student days were spent in the French city. A certificate signed by the academic authorities of Toulouse in 1604, and later found in the saint's room after his death, confirms his seven years of theological studies.[12] His stay in Saragossa seems to have been a brief one. The information we have on this point is not very precise but the dates given lead us to believe that he spent several months there, or possibly a complete academic year. We do not know, either, if Vincent studied here before going to Toulouse, or whether this course was followed at some time during a break from his main studies. There is no doubt, however, that he did study at Saragossa. We have categorical statements about this from his two biographers, Abelly and Collet (both of them Frenchmen), who had access to the earliest documents.

Abelly writes:

> It is true that during this period (the seven years of theological studies) he went to Spain and that he lived and studied in Zaragoza for a time.[13]

---

[9] *S.V.P.* XIII, p. 1-2.
[10] ABELLY, *op. cit.*, 1.1 c. 3, p. 10.
[11] COLLET, *op. cit.*, Vol. 1, p. 13; ABELLY, *op. cit.*, 1.1 c. 3, p. 12.
[12] ABELLY, *op. cit.*, 1.1 c. 3, p. 12; COLLET, *op. cit.*, Vol. 1, p. 10.
[13] ABELLY, *op. cit.*, 1.1 c. 3, p. 10.

Collet says:

> We cannot be sure whether he went to Aragón before beginning
> his studies in Toulouse. What we do know for certain is that
> he did study in Zaragoza for a time, but he did not stay there
> long.[14]

No consideration, such as an increase in personal prestige, or a covert attempt to make the saint's life history more interesting, could have induced these biographer-witnesses to invent such an isolated piece of information. It stands out like some solid landmark that keeps alive the memory of a path, which will later be obliterated.

At various times Vincent made indirect, but unmistakable references, to the fact that he had lived for a time in Spain. He referred specifically to the teaching methods that were in vogue in Spanish universities. The saint does not give the impression that he is speaking from hearsay; his words reflect lived experience. He was always opposed to the very widespread practice of dictating notes and to support this view he would put forward, with boring insistence, the example of universities in Spain.

> Pupils in Spanish schools are not allowed to write in class.[15]
> What can be said of the universities where this business of
> taking notes in class is absolutely unheard of? The lecturers
> are content to explain their subject verbally and yet everyone
> agrees that they produce the most profound theologians.[16] I
> believe it has never been the custom to dictate notes in Spain
> or Italy. That is why Spaniards are very scholarly and they
> study the sciences in greater depth than students do anywhere
> else.[17]

Pedro de Cerbuna, the founder of Saragossa University, and his collaborator, Diego Frailla, laid down the university statutes in 1583. These required lecturers to expound subjects and to make sure that their students understood and memorised what they heard. They were not to wait for the students to take notes since 'the practice of dictating notes conveys little

---

[14] COLLET, *op. cit.*, Vol. 1, p. 9.

[15] *S.V.P.* II, p. 212.

[16] *S.V.P.* II, p. 235 and 240.

[17] *S.V.P.* IV, pp. 322-323. More references to this subject can be found in *S.V.P.* VII, p. 291;
VIII, p. 107 and 381.

information to the listener, and does not help him to understand what he hears because the subject has not been adequately explained.'[18]

More precise is Vincent's reference to some of the customs followed by Carmelite nuns in Spain.

> The Carmelites are very austere and they aim at practising great mortification. Unlike their sisters in France who wear sandals, these nuns go barefoot. I do not know very much about Carmelites in this country, but I do know that in Spain they wear neither stockings nor sandals. They have only a bit of hay or straw to sleep on even during the harsh winter.[19]

The fact that Vincent de Paul is more conversant with the customs of Spanish Carmelites than he is with those followed by the nuns in his own country can only be explained by his having been in Spain at some time. Vincent also speaks of the Carmelites' meals, and again we see that he had first-hand knowledge of their way of life:

> They eat very simply and have large plates of soup and rotten eggs. This is their diet even though they come from wealthy families and have been delicately nurtured. I am quite certain about what I am telling you. The eggs served to them are putrid and they have to eat them.[20]

If, in the earlier quotation, he admitted that he did not know much about the Carmelites in France, in the second quotation he is so certain of his facts that he could only be speaking about the Spanish nuns whom he knew well. The Carmelite foundation in Saragossa dates from 1588, some ten years before this university freshman arrived in Aragón.

The final piece of evidence is of a more general nature and it has political connotations. Perhaps this is why Vincent does not name the country in question.

> I was once in a country—he told the Daughters of Charity on 6 January 1658—where there was a certain religious who went to see the king and he asked for news of what was happening at court. The person he was addressing answered, 'But why would a religious want to meddle in the affairs of royalty?' In

---

[18] J. HERRERA refers to them, *op. cit.*, p. 52.
[19] *S.V.P.* X, p. 124.
[20] *S.V.P.* X, p. 60.

this country people never discuss the king. He is sacred and they have such respect for everything concerning him that such matters are never spoken about. So in this country everyone is loyally united to the king and nobody is allowed to say a word about his commands.[21]

This Catholic kingdom that Vincent said he had been in can only refer to Spain. No other European state at that time could fully match the description given; either the countries were not kingdoms, or they weren't Catholic or they were not characterised by blind obedience to the monarch. On the other hand, Spain in the last years of Philip II's reign fits the description perfectly. Furthermore, apart from his visits to Rome, we have not the slightest indication that Vincent de Paul ever stayed in any other country.

We know absolutely nothing about Vincent's reasons for coming to Saragossa or for his speedy return to France. It may be, as Spanish tradition has always held, that he had family connections with influential clergy in Aragón.[22] Collet's theory about Vincent's return to France was favourably received by biographers until it was discredited by Coste. Collet suggested that Vincent, who was peace-loving and charitable by nature, left Saragossa in disgust because he could not stand the bitter disputes among theologians over the controversial questions of *scientia media* and the decrees on predestination.[23] This romantic interpretation of the situation is flawed because it conflicts with the sad reality of what was happening, during these same years, at the university of Toulouse.

There would be frequent and violent quarrels among students from different regions—Burgundy, Languedoc, Lorraine, France and Champagne etc.—and these quarrels would often degenerate into armed combat. Every year the parlement of Toulouse was obliged to prohibit the use of arms by students, and this on pain of death. There were house searches, fines, arrests and other harsher penalties. No way could be found to teach these riotous students a lesson or to put an end to such behaviour. They demanded a 'welcome' from all foreigners whether these were students or not and, on at least one occasion, two of them were found guilty of murder, after they had caused the death of one of the officials of the municipality. They were condemned to death for this crime but later reprieved by the parlement because

---

[21] *S.V.P.* X, p. 446.

[22] A. HERNANDEZ Y FAJARNES, *op. cit.*, p. 247-349.

[23] COLLET, *op. cit.*, Vol. 1, p. 9; U. MAYNARD, *op. cit.*, Vol. 1, p. 22. In Lavedan's work this theory is regarded as a certainty and we see here the influence of Merimée's *Carmen*. H. LAVEDAN, *San Vicente de Paúl* (Buenos Aires, Difusión, 1944), pp. 40-41.

of their youth.[24] If Vincent was looking for peace he would not have gained much by leaving Saragossa for Toulouse. A more reasonable explanation, based on the information we have available, is that Vincent began his studies at Saragossa in 1597, and was obliged to return home half way through his course when his father died in February 1598. Then, as he had not the money to return to Saragossa (he could not sell another pair of oxen) he transferred his course to Toulouse and it was here that he completed his first year in theology. Toulouse consequently awarded him a certificate in 1604 stating that he had studied there for seven years.[25]

Unfortunately, researchers have been so preoccupied with these particular problems that their attention has been diverted from more interesting questions such as the quality of education that Vincent received in Toulouse and Saragossa, the doctrinal persuasions of his teachers, and the influence that this *alma mater* of Western Christian culture had on his thinking. And yet these are the things that we would be more interested in knowing about.

When Vincent was at Saragossa and Toulouse he was at an age when he could be both formed and informed. From the world around him he selects his own particular ideological baggage; he forms his own personal view of the world and adopts convictions and points of view that he will adhere to all his life. As there are no monographs written on this subject we

---

[24] R. GADAVE, *Les documents sur l'histoire de l'Université de Toulouse et spécialement de sa faculté de droit civil et canonique (1229-1798)* (Toulouse 1910). Referred to by COSTE, *M.V.* Vol. 1, pp. 33-36.

[25] Nearly all the earlier and later biographers are agreed on Vincent de Paul's stay in Saragossa. Only Coste has some reservations, but we think these are not justified: 'It is hard to believe that young Vincent, being so short of money, left the University of Toulouse, would go to Saragossa University and, shortly after his arrival there, would come back to Toulouse. Before we can accept the authenticity of this journey, which is mentioned in reports sent from Dax to Vincent's first biographer, we would like to know what grounds there are making this statement. Collet assumes that Vincent found the University of Saragossa deeply embroiled in the old scholastic disputes about *scientia media* and the question of predestination, and that this would have made him return quickly to France. Such a theory is not very plausible and the question itself is even less plausible (*M.V.* Vol. 1, pp. 36-37). The esteemed editor of the Vincentian *Opera omnia* has obviously made several errors because he discards sources of information and took it for granted that Vincent began his studies in Toulouse. He ignores definitive phrases by Abelly and Collet like 'it is true', and 'it is certain' and, as though to forestall possible objections, he changes 'a short stay' as given in the original version. He makes an objective and irrefutable obstacle out of what was a subjective judgement about the improbability of such an event; he rejects a priori the indisputable, formal, and disinterested testimony of witnesses who were most directly involved in the affair, and he comes to the conclusion that the explanation is flawed because the events themselves were only imaginary. Sound historical criticism rejects the idea that we solve a problem by denying that it exists.

can only come to very general conclusions, viz: the solid scholastic training he received, the mental gymnastics of academic dissertation and the habit of painstakingly thinking a question through that Vincent would have acquired from his contact with the great masters. This is only a small fraction of what we would like to know about how Vincent developed a way of thinking which, even if it was never speculative or brilliant, always reflected the soundness and coherence of a solid corpus of doctrine that was deeply rooted in the very fibres of his being.[26]

'Private tuition'

The young student's financial position became much worse when his father died. Vincent was reluctant to take advantage of the small bequests left to him in his father's will because this would have meant his mother and family receiving less.[27] If he was to continue his studies and pay his expenses, then he would have to provide the resources himself. His experience of working in the de Comet household and perhaps, too, his memories of early experiences in the Franciscan boarding school, suggested the course of action he should take. Like so many students in every age, he would teach and study at the same time. The boarding school that Vincent directed was opened at Buzet-sur-Tarn, about thirty kilometres from Toulouse. The school proved to be a success and it began to have a good reputation in that small country place. Pupils came from as far away as Toulouse as Vincent explained to his mother in the first letter we have that tells us anything about himself, the first of thousands and thousands of letters he would write in the course of his long life. Unfortunately, that letter is now lost. We know nothing about it except the brief reference that Abelly salvaged. But it is good to think that the first letter written by a man, whose pen was to prove the most powerful means of governing and of influencing people, was a letter to his mother, such as any schoolboy studying away from home might have written.

Some of his pupils came from families that were influential in that

---

[26] In line with Hernández and Fajarnés, Herrera is happy to speculate about Vincent's contact with Jesuit teachers from San Carlos school where Vincent was supposed to have lived during the months he stayed in Saragossa, and with the professors from the Faculty of Theology. But the whole argument shows that no serious effort was made to collate dates and events. It also lacks a systematic analysis of the hypothetical Saragossan masters' way of thinking. The same could be said about Toulouse. Paul Dudon's well-known study of the subject just repeats what is already known about Vincent passing through the lecture halls of Toulouse, without any critical examination of what was taught there. *Cf.* P. DUDON, 'Le VII centénnaire de l'Université de Toulouse', *Etudes* Vol. 199 (1929), p. 724-738.

[27] ABELLY, *op. cit.*, 1.1 c. 3, p. 12.

region because parents wanted their sons to be educated in an environment where discipline was upheld. Collet assures us that they even included two great-nephews of Jean de la Valette, famous master of the Order of St John of Jerusalem which forty years earlier, in 1565, had defended Malta with 15,000 men from an attack by the Turkish army which boasted a force of 150,000. When Vincent had to return to Toulouse to continue his studies, he took his pupils with him and the parents readily consented to this. The life of teacher-student was a hard one. Vincent could not have had much time left to prepare his university work. Imagination cannot be far removed from the reality of the situation, when Collet pictures him going to bed late, getting up at the crack of dawn, and having no time to spare for leisure activities or for legitimate relaxation.[28] He had to find a way out of that situation and discover a less arduous way of life. In the society of those days, the answer would be to acquire an ecclesiastical benefice early in life. Vincent decided to be ordained to the priesthood as soon as possible.

'If I had only know what the priesthood involved ...'

There is no uncertainty about the date of Vincent's ordination to each stage of the priesthood. Copies still exist, both of dimissorial letters and correspondence that confirms each stage of ordination. According to these documents, Vincent was ordained subdeacon and deacon on 19 September and 19 December 1598, respectively, by Sauveur Diharse, bishop of Tarbes. Authorisation for his subdiaconate was signed by the vicar general of Dax, Guillaume Massiot, because by 10 September the episcopal see had become vacant. Guillaume Massiot also signed the authorisation for his admittance to the diaconate but this time he did so in the name of Jean Jacques Dussault, the new bishop, who would have been appointed by then but not officially confirmed in office, and the documents were drawn up on 11 December. In both cases there was scarcely a week's interval between authorisation for, and conferring of, the appropriate stage of Vincent's advance to the priesthood. On 13 September 1599, the same vicar general and bishop of Dax granted permission for priestly ordination but Vincent delayed using this permission for over a year. He did not present himself to the bishop of nearby Tarbes but was ordained priest on 23 September 1660, in the diocese of Périgueux, quite a distance from Dax and Pouy as well as from Toulouse. He was ordained by the elderly bishop of that diocese, François de Bourdeille,

---

[28] Information about Vincent's stay in the boarding school at Buzet-sur-Tarn in ABELLY, *op. cit.*, 1.1 c. 3, p. 12, and COLLET, *op. cit.*, Vol. 1, pp. 9-11.

in the church of St Julien at Château l'Évêque, the bishop's country residence. On each occasion Vincent made use of the university vacation period to be ordained.[29]

This tiny handful of indisputable dates conceals a few problems for historical and biographical interpretation.[30]

We have to grapple, particularly, with the problem of Vincent's age at this time. If he was born in 1581 or 1580, by September 1660 he would have been nineteen or, at most, twenty. According to the prescriptions of the Council of Trent which insisted on candidates being twenty-four years old, he was not canonically eligible for ordination. But it was only later on that the prescriptions of the Council of Trent were applied in France, and its decrees were not promulgated until the General Assembly of Clergy in 1615. In the mean time and for a considerable period afterwards, there were many abuses.

We have written evidence that many ordinations to the priesthood were irregular because candidates were under age. This led to numerous appeals to Rome for a dispensation.[31] The vicar general of Dax who authorised Vincent's ordination stated that the candidate was of lawful age but this was not true.

Was he acting behind the back of Mgr Dussault, the new bishop? As Diebold has shown, the bishop, who was a reforming prelate, set up a programme of religious and ecclesiastical reform during the diocesan synod of 18 April 1600[32]—between the dates for authorisation and the actual ceremony of Vincent's ordination. In any case, the fact remains that it was an irregular ordination because the candidate was below the age required by canon law.

The new bishop's determination to introduce reforms could explain another riddle that has puzzled scholars:[33] the reason why Vincent would have gone to no less a place than Périgueux to be ordained by an eighty-four years-old bishop, Mgr Bourdeille, who was to die on 24 October 1600, barely

---

[29] *S.V.P.* XIII, documents 2, 3, 4, 5, 6, 7 and 8, pp. 2-7.

[30] This question is studied in detail in the article by E. DIEBOLD, 'Saint Vincent de Paul. Sa nomination à la cure de Tilh (diocèse de Dax) en 1600', *Annales* (1959), pp. 389-397.

[31] COSTE, *M.V.* Vol. 1, p. 39. On 21 July 1609, the Cardinal-Secretary of State expressed to the Nuncio in Paris his astonishment at the great number of French priests having recourse to Rome for absolution because they were under age canonically when they were ordained. When Sebastian Zamet took possession of his diocese of Langres in 1615, he found as many as 200 priests who were ordained before reaching the age prescribed by canon law. More information is given in COSTE, 'La vraie date de la naissance de Saint Vincent de Paul'. Offprint from *Bulletin de la Société de Borda* (Dax 1922), pp. 15-17.

[32] E. DIEBOLD, *art. cit.*, p. 392.

[33] F. CONTASSOT, 'Saint Vincent de Paul et le Périgord,' *Annales* (1949-1950), pp. 161-203.

a month after the ceremony.[34] The idea that Vincent searched out a distant diocese and an unknown bishop in order to dodge the disciplinary rules of his new prelate does not seem as fanciful now as when Rédier suggested it, in one of those apt and intuitive inspirations which he had from time to time.[35]

The history of Vincent's ordination to the priesthood is most important if we are fully to understand his personality. At the age of twenty Vincent de Paul was not the saintly priest, full of apostolic fervour, that traditional hagiography would have us believe. If this had been the case he would never have dared, in conscience, to contravene the prescriptions of Trent. But neither was he a corrupt young man, insensitive to the 'gravity' of the sin he committed in being irregularly ordained before he was of canonical age, a sin which at a more mature age he would keep silent about, so as not to besmirch the memory of the prelates who were accomplices in his fraud.[36] This particular abuse was so frequent, and so firmly established, that neither the ordinand nor the prelate, if in fact the latter knew about the canonical irregularity, would have felt any shame in complying with so prevalent a custom.[37] He was just a poor youngster who saw the priesthood as a quick means of securing a respectable position in society (the quicker the better). He was not too concerned that in order to do this he would have to contravene a certain number of juridical formalities which had recently been introduced, and find a shrewd way of evading the excessive zeal of a new pastor who was not familiar with old, and generally accepted, customs.

The fact that the ordination was irregular could not have had any adverse effect on the bishop of Dax's opinion of his subject—nor, for the moment, did it worry the young man himself. Eight years later, Vincent had no hesitation in asking the bishop of Dax for a reference since, and these are Vincent's own words, 'You have always known me to be an honest man.'[38]

It was by just such an expeditious route that Vincent, when he was barely twenty years old, achieved the goal that by common consent his father, the farmer from Pouy, and his benefactor, M. de Comet, had pushed him towards. From what we know of his later history, it was also the path that God was pointing out to him. But was it for Vincent a vocation that sprang from deep conviction? We cannot be sure of this. Years later, one of his nephews thought he had a vocation and this brought to the saint's mind the time leading up to his own ordination.

---

[34] *Ibid.*, p. 162 in the note.
[35] A. REDIER, *La vraie vie ...*, p. 16.
[36] A. REDIER, *ibid.*, p. 17.
[37] F. CONTASSOT, *art.cit.*, p. 164.
[38] *S.V.P.* I, p. 15.

As for me, if I had known what the priesthood entailed when I was rash enough to enter this state, as I found out about it later on, I would rather have gone on tilling the fields than commit myself to such an exalted calling.[39]

He is even more explicit when talking to a lawyer whom he tried to dissuade from becoming a priest:

... experience obliges me to warn those who ask my advice about the priesthood, that they should not commit themselves to this unless they have a real vocation from God, a pure intention of pleasing the Lord by practising the same virtues that he did and other unmistakable signs that the divine will is calling them to it. And I feel so strongly about this that if I were not already a priest, I would never become one.[40]

On another occasion, in the presence of his missioners, Vincent paints a picture of the priesthood which puts before us the contemporary scene and, at the same time, is a self portrait (a painful one because by this time he was a saint).

After studying philosophy and theology for a few years, and having only a smattering of Latin, a young man would go off to a parish and administer the sacraments after his own fashion.[41]

'A real vocation from God', 'a pure intention of honouring God' and an adequate pastoral preparation—these are the three things which, after nearly seventy years of priestly life, Vincent thought he lacked when he took the decisive step.

What were his dispositions at that time? What motives did he have for becoming a priest? On the one hand there is the element of rashness referred to in the first of his letters just quoted. Another factor would be self-will; he made his own decision without trying to discover if it was God's will; and then there was his worldly outlook. He had too materialistic a view of the priestly state, and all we can say to excuse this fault, is that Vincent was the product of his age.

---

[39] *S.V.P.* V, p. 568.
[40] *S.V.P.* VII, p. 463.
[41] *S.V.P.* XII, p. 389.

How wretched are those who enter the priestly state through the window of their own choice and not by the door of a genuine vocation. However, there are many people who view the ecclesiastical state as a peaceful way of life, where they seek, not to labour, but to find their ease.[42]

'The twenty year old is a fearsome animal'

No, at the age of twenty (Mateo Alemán, a Spanish contemporary of Vincent, wrote 'the twenty year old is a fearsome animal'), Vincent de Paul had not come to grips psychologically or effectively with his vocation. And yet this was his God-given calling. There is no paradox here. Do we need to invoke the hackneyed phrase that God writes straight with crooked lines? For Vincent de Paul at the age of twenty the priesthood is not a special way of life; it is just a way of life. When he embraced this state he expected to find his ease, not toil. He was soon to be disillusioned.

It is with great respect and a deep fear of being misunderstood, that the author writes these lines. Vincent de Paul is not a heartless individual; he never was that, even at the age of twenty. Looked at simply from the historical perspective of his times and background, he is just one of many poor but ambitious young men who have been made to regard the ecclesiastical state as a means of bettering themselves. This utilitarian view of the ecclesiastical state as opposed to an appreciation of the real meaning of the priesthood does not preclude a certain natural goodness, sense of duty, and willingness to meet the obligations of the calling. These might also have been young men of piety and if their piety was perhaps superficial, it was none the less sincere.

Vincent disciplined himself to wait some time before celebrating his first Mass and this showed he had the dispositions which leading bishops of the reform movement required.[43] This first Mass was celebrated in a locality that had witnessed Vincent's labours and his ambitions. According to tradition, this place was a little chapel dedicated to Our Lady, high up in the mountains, surrounded by woods and bordering on Buzet-sur-Tarn where Vincent had had his school. There was nobody else present except the altar boy and the assisting priest.[44] All the evidence suggests that he said this Mass with great

---

[42] *S.V.P.* VII, p. 463.

[43] E. DIEBOLD, 'La première messe de Saint Vincent de Paul', *Annales* (1957), pp. 490-492.

[44] ABELLY, *op. cit.*, 1.1 c. 3, p. 11; COLLET, *op. cit.*, Vol. 1, p. 14.

fervour, and this view is supported by tradition and by the most rigorous contemporary research.[45]

When he became a priest, Vincent bade a decisive farewell to his childhood and adolescence. He was now on the threshold of early adulthood— at an age when he wanted to know about things, an age of searching and of making plans. Vincent felt no qualms as he moved into this stage. He had made his own decision. He had plans that he had thought out for himself without bothering to make sure that they were in accordance with God's will. All through this next stage in life he would insist on carrying out these plans, in spite of repeated failures. Gradually, and, it must be said, very gradually, he will discover another plan. This plan will not be of his making but of God's. And when Vincent discovers God he will also discover himself. In other words, he will find his vocation.

---

[45] E. DIEBOLD, *art. cit.*, p. 492; COSTE, *M.V.* Vol. 1, p. 40.

Part Two

THE YEARS OF PILGRIMAGE AND APPRENTICESHIP

(1600-1617)

Chapter III
PLANS AND SETBACKS

The first project

No sooner is Vincent ordained than it seems he achieved the objective he had so much set his heart on: an ecclesiastical benefice. He was to devise many schemes between the years 1600 and 1617 but this was his first specific project. Vincent was a young man and he had his life to plan. It still had not dawned on him that he should be relying on God and trying to discover the vocation to which he was being called.

Very soon after Vincent's ordination (it might have been that same year, 1600) the vicar general of Dax appointed him parish priest of Tilh, a good parish in that diocese. It is strange that this nomination should have come from the vicar general and not the bishop, because contrary to what Abelly believed, the see was not vacant at that time. And yet it was in similar circumstances that the vicar general had authorised Vincent to proceed to the subdiaconate and diaconate.[1]

A powerful influence was at work in Vincent's favour, that of Monsieur de Comet. Thanks to Monsieur de Comet's introduction, the parish was granted to Vincent. In the background to all this, could there have been a secret struggle going on between the old authority and the new, between the vicar general and the bishop?

One thing was certain, this appointment would turn out to be his first failure. Two obstacles cropped up to prevent Vincent's induction at Tilh. Firstly, this brand-new parish priest continued to study at Toulouse and

---

[1] Abelly says, in fact, that it was the 'vicars general of Dax *sede vacante*' who appointed Vincent to the parish of Tilh because at that time the see of Dax was vacant (*op. cit.*, 1.1 c. 3, p. 11). Coste realised that Abelly was mistaken about the see being vacant and so felt justified in saying that Vincent's appointment came from the bishop (*M.V.* Vol. 1, p. 40). The situation is by no means clear. It was the vicars general who issued the dimissorial letters even though the see was occupied (*S.V.P.* XIII, p. 5 and 6). This was what caused Abelly's mistake and there was confusion, too, about the dimissorial letters for the subdiaconate.

so could not reside in the parish. During a diocesan synod the new bishop had recommended all parish priests to be resident in their parishes. Secondly, a rival appeared on the scene in the person of a certain M. Saint-Soubé who had been appointed to the parish by the curia in Rome.

If Vincent wanted to keep the parish he would have had to file a lawsuit so he gave up his claim. Early biographers have attributed this act of renunciation to Vincent's repugnance for all forms of litigation, a repugnance based on the precepts of the gospel. But that would be to project on to the young man the attitudes and maxims of a much more mature Vincent. There is probably a much more down-to-earth explanation. Vincent's age was against him, as was the full weight of the Roman Curia, and there may have been opposition, too, from his own bishop who had been party to neither his ordination nor his appointment to the parish. Maybe it was at this period that the thought first entered his mind—a thought he was to put in writing years later:

> How wretched are those who enter the ecclesiastical state by
> the window of personal choice and not by the door of a genuine
> vocation.[2]

Vincent was now experiencing for himself something of the turmoil that was unsettling France as the Tridentine reforms came to be implemented. It was an experience he would never forget.[3]

In Rome 'I was moved, even to tears'

It might just be, though, that Vincent decided to go somewhere else to pursue his claim to the parish. The place in question was Rome and Vincent moved there some time in 1601.

Early biographers knew nothing about Vincent's first stay in the Eternal City (we will deal with his second stay there in due course). We are aware of this first visit because Vincent says on several occasions, 'I had the honour of seeing Pope Clement VIII.'[4] Well, Clement VIII died in 1605. Another reference made by Vincent helps us to pinpoint more precisely the date of his visit. Writing on 20 July 1631 to one of his early companions who had influence in Rome at that time, Vincent says that he himself had been

---

[2]   *S.V.P.* VII, p. 463.
[3]   *Cf.* E. DIEBOLD, 'Saint Vincent de Paul. Sa nomination à la cure de Tilh (Diocèse de Dax) en 1600', *Annales* (1959), pp. 389-397.
[4]   *S.V.P.* IX, pp. 316-317, 468; X, pp. 365 593; XII, p. 347.

there 'thirty years ago'.[5] So that must have been in 1601. We have no information at all regarding his motives for making this journey. Was it, perhaps, to obtain a dispensation for his irregular ordination? The most likely conjecture, as we have suggested, is that he undertook this journey in the hope of obtaining the disputed parish of Tilh. He soon realised that he had no chance at all against his rival.

On the other hand, we have quite a good idea of Vincent's religious dispositions during his first stay in Christendom's main city. We need this knowledge if we are to reconstruct his spiritual itinerary. The letter we have just referred to lifts, for a few brief moments, the veil of secrecy with which Vincent always jealously guarded his spiritual life.

> At last you've arrived in Rome where you will find the visible head of the Church on earth, where you will find the bodies of St Peter and St Paul, and those of many other martyrs who in ages past shed their blood and spent their lives in the service of Jesus Christ. What a happiness it is to be able to tread the same ground that so many great and holy people walked! This thought affected me so much when I was in Rome thirty years ago that, although I was weighed down by sin, I think the experience never ceased to move me, even to the point of tears.[6]

So it was the Rome of 1601 that awakened his devotion to the Roman pontiff, then Clement VIII, whom Vincent always regarded as a saint. We know that this pope used to weep as he went up the *Scala Sancta*. Could it be that Vincent was performing this same act of devotion when he, too, burst into tears? Vincent loved to quote the sayings of this pope whose handling of the thorny question of Henry IV's absolution was presented to his priests as a model of how to act in times of temptation.[7] All the indications are that this journey to Rome introduced Vincent to the mysterious world of holiness. Perhaps it was a first call. A good many years would have to pass before Vincent responded to it with his whole heart and soul. In the meantime he had his way to make; he had to complete his studies and find another benefice which would make up for losing the parish of Tilh and he had to enjoy all the benefits he could rightfully expect from his newly acquired

---

[5] *S.V.P.* I, p. 114. We think, however, that there is no foundation for the theory that Vincent went to Rome to gain the jubilee indulgence for the year 1600. It is more likely that this journey took place in 1601.

[6] *Ibid.*

[7] See texts quoted in note 4 to this chapter.

priesthood. Even though he was pious, even though he could be moved to tears, Vincent was not yet a saint. He was a young man with a career ahead of him. Nobody could reproach him for this. Such aspirations were lawful and reasonable in his day ... as they are in ours. It is just that they were not the aspirations of a saint.

'A project so rash that I dare not speak about it'

Once he is back in Toulouse Vincent resumed the life he was leading before his journey to Rome and his ordination to the priesthood—a life of teaching and of study. For the moment, the boarding school would provide an income sufficient to meet his needs; in the future, his studies will open doors which at present remain closed to him. Vincent never felt drawn to a purely academic career. He regarded study as a means, not an end. In 1604, when he was twenty-four years old, he decided to finish his university studies for good. Three certificates crowned his academic career: one of these credited him with seven years study, the second was his degree in theology, and the third was a certificate authorising him to explain the second book of *The Sentences* of Peter Lombard.[8]

Now, at last, he could seriously consider more lofty ambitions. He now had patrons who were even more influential than de Comet. He could count on the patronage of no less a person than the Duke of Epernon who, from his magnificent castle in Cadillac near Bordeaux, exercised unofficial but none the less effective power in the region of Gascony. Vincent returned to his dreams and these become more and more ambitious. No longer is it a question of some country parish, however important a one; Vincent had his sights set on a bishopric. This must have been the business 'the rashness of which I dare not speak about' that Vincent referred to in a letter which we will study in more detail later on.[9] This second project of his crashed to the ground even more quickly than the first, because of a whirlwind of unforeseen events. It could be said that some invisible hand was taking delight in showing him the inadequacy of plans that are purely human.

---

[8] ABELLY, *op. cit.*, 1.1 c. 3, p. 12; COLLET, Vol. 1, p. 11.

[9] *S.V.P.* I, p. 3. *Cf.* ABELLY, *op. cit.*, 1.1 c. 4, p. 14; Collet thinks that the question of a bishopric is mere conjecture (*op. cit.*, Vol. 1, p. 15); Coste casts doubt on the Duke of Epernon's patronage (*M.V.* Vol. 1, p. 37 and 43).

'That wretched letter'

We need to pause here. All the information that we have about Vincent's life during the next three years, 1605, 1606 and 1607, comes from two of his letters. One of these was dated 24 July 1607, and the other 28 February 1608. The first letter was written in Avignon and the second in Rome. It is obvious that these texts are autobiographical and their discovery should mean, that after so many calculations and conjectures, we must be on firm ground as we try to reconstruct the early stages of Vincent's life. In actual fact we have the exact opposite happening. There is no way of evading the fact that a fierce controversy was to rage round these letters for nearly half a century.

The authenticity of the letters has never been questioned. The originals, written in Vincent's own hand, have been preserved, and scholars have patiently reconstructed the history of their preservation. Both letters are addressed to M. de Comet, who was the brother of Vincent's former benefactor and the one who became the young priest's new patron. The letters passed from the de Comet family's archives into the possession of his son-in-law, Louis de Saint Martin, the lord of Agès and a lawyer at the presidial court of Dax. He was married to Catherine de Comet and was the brother of Canon Jean de Saint Martin who has been mentioned earlier.

The letters were then bequeathed to César de Saint Martin d'Agès, who was the son of Louis and Catherine.[10] One day this man decided, out of curiosity, to look through his grandfather de Comet's old papers and he discovered the letters. This happened in 1658 and by this time Vincent was a person of high standing, with a reputation for sanctity. Young Saint Martin trembled with excitement. Here was the great man's own account of his early life. How delighted he would be to read about the most exciting adventure of his long life! He lost no time in telling his uncle, the canon. The good canon, in his turn, wrote in haste to M. Vincent, telling him of their unexpected find. But Vincent's reaction was very different from the one they expected. He wrote back immediately, begging them to send him the originals and he obviously intended to destroy them.

At this point other people become involved. The saint's secretary brought the matter to the knowledge of the priests who were the assistants to the superior general of the Mission. There was a council of war. At all costs these letters had to be rescued from the imminent threat of destruction, and to prevent this happening they had to make sure that the letters did not fall

---

[10] Coste is mistaken when he gives the name Jean to both the Saint Martin brothers, one of whom was a canon and the other a layman (XIII, p. 539 and 540). In St Vincent's will, 1630, he calls the latter Louis, and his son, whom Abelly refers to as simply as Saint Martin d'Agès, is called César *(Annales* [1936], 706).

into the hands of the man who wrote them. They instructed the secretary to explain the situation to Canon Saint Martin and asked him to send the letters, not to M. Vincent, but to somebody they could trust, Fr Watebled who was then superior of the foundation house of the congregation and out of Vincent's reach. The canon did as he was asked.

Meanwhile the poor old man was weary waiting for a reply. He saw death approaching and those letters were still in the hands of strangers and open to God knows what interpretation. On 18 March 1660, he wrote again to Canon Saint Martin:

> In the name of all the graces that God has bestowed on you, I adjure you to send me that wretched letter about Turkey. I mean the one that Monsieur d'Agès found among his father's papers. I earnestly beg you, in the name of Jesus Christ, Our Lord, to do me the favour I ask, as quickly as possible.[11]

These are moving words but by then Canon Saint Martin could not be touched by them. The letters that Vincent so desperately wanted back had been kept safe for two years in the hands of M. Alméras, the saint's first assistant, and later his successor. Six months later, Saint Vincent would die without being able to lay his hands on what he had written as a young man. Thanks to the pious machinations of his secretary, the assistants, and the canon, these papers had been preserved for posterity.[12]

---

[11] *S.V.P.* VIII, p. 271. Coste emphasises the fact that Collet was mistaken in thinking that it was after receiving this letter that Saint Martin sent the letters about the captivity to Fr Watebled at the Bons Enfants. He did indeed make a mistake, but this was only about the date the letter was sent, and not about the person to whom it was dispatched.

[12] The story of the letters about Vincent's captivity has been told many times. Note particularly the account given by Abelly (*op. cit.*, 1.1 c. 4, pp. 17-18) and by Collet (*op. cit.*, Vol. 1, pp. 22-23). The documents on which these are based are to be found in *S.V.P* I, pp. 1-2; VIII, pp. 271, 513-515.

Chapter IV
THE STORY OF HIS CAPTIVITY

An unexpected legacy

Let us now read the letters that Vincent de Paul, in his old age, had tried so hard to destroy.[1]

In the early months of 1605, Vincent's affairs seemed to be progressing very favourably. This is the first piece of information we can glean from the first letter. He had just come back from a short trip to Bordeaux when he discovered that a good old lady from Castres had left him in her will some land and furniture which were worth about 400 *écus*.[2] These were owed to her by an individual of very dubious character. It was just what Vincent needed. The money would pay off his debts and meet the expenses of the rash enterprise referred to earlier, his designs on a bishopric.

Not one to let the grass grow under his feet, Vincent hired a horse and set off for Castres. This is the first time we hear of Vincent riding a horse; it will not be the last. During his life he travelled many leagues on horseback and he became so familiar with equestrian terms that he used many of them in the talks and conferences he gave.[3]

---

[1] The complete text of the letters is in volume two of *S.V.P.* I, pp. 1-17. We recommend you to read the whole text. References in the following text are taken from it.

[2] In the seventeenth century, French coinage kept to the medieval monetary system which dates back to the time of Charlemagne and which continued to operate in England until the second half of the twentieth century. The monetary unit was the *livre* which was subdivided into coins of lesser value. The *livre* was divided into 20 *sous* which, in turn, were divided into 12 *denarii*. Before decimalisation the English pound was worth 20 shillings and the shilling was worth 12 pence. In the seventeenth century the French *écu* was a silver coin worth 3 *livres*. It is more difficult to estimate the present day value of these coins because prices and wages have changed so much over the years. It might be helpful to know that in 1629 the income of a French parish priest was fixed at 300 *livres* (100 *écus*) a year while a casual labourer's pay could vary between 7 and 11 *sous* (approximately half a *livre*) a day.

[3] A. DODIN, *Lecciones sobre vicencianismo*, p. 235.

An unpleasant surprise was waiting for him at Castres. The villain had disappeared in the direction of Marseilles where he was said to be living in grand style off the fortune he had dishonestly acquired. Vincent decided to pursue him. The only difficulty was that he had no money to pay for the journey but he very soon found the answer to the problem. Without giving the matter a second thought, he sold the horse he had hired (he would pay for it on his return) and set off again on his journey. Luck, or rather providence, was on his side. When he arrived in Marseilles, he had the fugitive thrown into prison and then came to an agreement with him. The rogue paid him 300 *écus* in ready cash and Vincent was satisfied. He immediately got ready to return to Toulouse. Then came the setbacks.

The ship is boarded

Vincent took the advice of a gentleman who was following the same route and decided to go by sea to Narbonne, which was the first stage of his return journey. The sea was calm, the wind favourable, and everything bespoke a pleasant and speedy voyage. He would arrive more quickly and it would be cheaper. As things turned out 'he would never arrive and he would lose everything he had.'

A few miles off Marseilles, three Turkish brigantines were lying in wait near the coast of Provence (it was now July) for boats coming from the fair at Beaucaire, 'the finest fair in Christendom'. On board were Berber corsairs from the regency of Tunis, who specialised in the capture and sale of Christian slaves. They rammed Vincent's boat. There was a brief struggle and the French ship had to surrender to the enemy who were superior in numbers, but not before losses were inflicted on both sides. One of the Turkish squadron commanders died and four or five rowers died too. The French suffered two or three losses and many wounded. Vincent was wounded by an arrow, and this injury was to serve him as a 'clock'* for the rest of his life. In reprisal for their losses, the Turks cut the French pilot to pieces. They ill-treated the rest of the crew and passengers and took them captive. With these prisoners on board, they continued on their course for about a week, attacking and looting any ships they encountered. Perhaps it was because

---

* Translator's note: the author uses the word 'clock' because in St Vincent's time the barometer was not yet invented. Vincent's wound would be affected by the weather and it would keep him awake (hence, 'clock').

their boats were overloaded that the pirates set free any people who had surrendered without resistance. Finally, they headed for Barbary and arrived at Tunis.

The slave market

As soon as they disembarked, the slaves were led to the market place. Here their clothing was removed and they were each given a pair of breeches, a linen jacket and a cap. In this guise, and with a chain round their necks, they were marched round the city. Those who were selling the captives took good care to make it known that this cargo had been captured from a Spanish ship. This was a necessary cover-up so as not to provoke the intervention of the French consul. France had made a series of treaties with the Turks which guaranteed freedom of trade and of navigation for her ships. Everything was carried out in an orderly fashion, according to the good and time-honoured customs of the slave markets. Merchants could probe wounds to judge how serious they were, could check the appetite of their merchandise, calculate their strength, see how well they could walk, examine their teeth ...

The fisherman and the doctor: his first two masters

Once the inspection was over and the sale agreed upon, there began for Vincent two years of captivity that were relatively peaceful. He was first bought by a fisherman but the new slave proved to be such a bad sailor that his owner had to get rid of him. Vincent then fell into the hands of a colourful character who was a doctor of metallurgy, an alchemist and something of a wizard, who boasted of his powers to turn base metals into gold. He had not yet discovered the philosopher's stone (but he was very close to it). He distilled the five essences, he had remedies for all manner of sicknesses and he could even make a skull talk. For this latter achievement, he had invented a contraption which deceived the gullible people into believing that it was Mohammed speaking through the mouth of the skull.

Vincent did not have a bad time at all. His main duty was to keep the dozen or so ovens lit, day and night, because these were needed for the old alchemist's concoctions. This man was both humane and approachable. He took a liking to the young slave and tried to interest him in the Islamic religion, promising to bequeath him his wealth and his discoveries. Vincent contented himself with learning the treatment for stone, an illness that had afflicted his friend and benefactor, M. de Comet.

He was certain (prisoners always are certain) that one day he would

63

be free, and that this remedy would alleviate the pains of the aged gentleman who was suffering, even if he had not been able to save Monsieur de Comet, senior, who had died of the same disease. If only he had known sooner about this effective remedy! Now that he was deprived of human resources, Vincent sought help from heaven and commended his cause to the intercession of the Blessed Virgin. She would surely obtain for him the freedom he so earnestly desired.

From one owner to another: the renegade

Vincent's peaceful existence in the doctor's house came to an abrupt end when the Grand Turk summoned the doctor to Constantinople. Vincent now became the property of one of the doctor's nephews. This was in August 1606. The doctor died during the voyage and his nephew immediately got rid of Vincent because he found out that a French ambassador was coming to Tunis with authorisation from the sultan to free any French slaves. Monsieur Savary de Brèves did arrive in Tunis on 17 June 1606. This gentleman was a skilful negotiator but his talents brought only minimal results. He left for France on 24 August with a band of 72 slaves from among the thousands who were left either to languish in the slave prisons of the bey of Tunis or to stay in the clutches of private owners.[4] Vincent was not one of the lucky few. The next person to buy him was a renegade from Nice or from Annecy.[5] He took Vincent inland with him (well out of the reach of the investigating French envoy) and brought him to his farm, a *temat* or *to'met* which he apparently cultivated for the great lord who was theoretically the owner of all that land.

A change of scenery meant a change of occupation for the slave. He now had to dig the soil in the heat of North Africa's burning sun. The work was difficult but the slave enjoyed more freedom. The renegade had three wives. Two of them showed an affectionate interest in the captive. One was a Christian belonging to the Greek schismatic Church and the other wife was a Mohammedan. This latter used to like going to the fields where Vincent was working, and she would ask him to sing. Vincent, who remembered so well the breviary he used to recite every evening in his humble student's lodging, and the Old Testament passages he had studied in the lecture halls of Toulouse, would intone with great emotion and a feeling of nostalgia the

---

[4] BAUDIER, *Inventaire de l'Histoire des Turcs* (Paris 1631), 1.17, p. 235; refered by COLLET, *op. cit.*, Vol. 1, p. 19; JACQUES DU CASTEL, *Relation des voyages de Monsieur de Brèves* ... (Paris 1628); referred by COSTE, *M.V.* Vol. 1, p. 50.

[5] It is not easy to read this word. It has been traditionally interpreted as Nice, but modern editors think it should read Nissy or Niçy, that is to say Annecy.

psalm of the Israelites in captivity, *Super flumina Babylonis,* and followed this with the *Salve Regina* and other hymns. The pure notes of the Gregorian chants soared into the silence of the sun-filled fields. The Turkish woman was moved and filled with wonder. What a sublime religion that must be if it inspired such beautiful and evocative hymns! Her husband had been very wrong to abandon it; she told him so that very night. The renegade agreed. He was more than repentant. The words of his wife, (likened by Vincent to 'another Caiaphas or Balaam's ass') meant that the man's secret feelings of repentance could be contained no longer. The next day he told Vincent of his plan to flee to France at the first opportunity.

Set free

The opportunity did not arise, however, until ten months later. It was then that master and slave embarked one day in a small skiff and made for the sea. They were in luck and they made the Mediterranean crossing without mishap. On 28 June 1607, two years after Vincent's capture, they disembarked at Aigues Mortes and made their way to Avignon.

In that pontifical city, Vincent's restless compass was to find another North Star which would point him towards the third of his youthful projects and also, though here we are anticipating future events, to the third of his failures. The papal vice legate in Avignon (we must remember that at this time the city and its surrounding territory constituted an enclave of papal sovereignty on French soil) received back the penitent renegade and promised to help him enter the monastery of the Fate bene fratelli in Rome. He also took a fancy to the intrepid priest from Pouy. Vincent won the hearts of de Comet, the generous old lady from Castres, the alchemist, the renegade's wife and this, his fifth benefactor, by no other means than his kindness which seems to have been contagious, and perhaps by his air of vulnerability which belied his apparent self-assurance. These were weapons he was to employ in pursuit of nobler aims for the rest of his life.

Pietro de Montorio, as the vice legate was called, was preparing to return to Rome after completing his three-year appointment.[6] He would return

---

[6] Vincent states that the vice legate completed his three year term of office on the feast of St John. Other documents would suggest that the date was 14 June, but this may be due to a misreading of the text. Anyway, Vincent's statements tally perfectly with what we have learnt from other sources. In fact, on 27 July 1607, Monsignor Montorio wrote to Cardinal Borghese, informing him that he would remain in Avignon until the arrival of his successor, Giuseppe Ferreri, archbishop of Urbino. The phrase that Vincent used is almost word for

as soon as his successor arrived. He told Vincent that he had a good relationship with this man. He undertook to procure a good benefice for him, the benefice that Vincent had been seeking in vain for five years. That rash project which had taken Vincent from Toulouse, first of all to Bordeaux, and then to Castres and Marseilles, and finally to the coasts of Tunisia, had been a complete failure. Vincent's two years in captivity saw the plan collapse like a pack of cards—if indeed there was ever any substance to it. Vincent accepted the vice legate's proposals with enthusiasm. Here was a new avenue opening up to him. For the plan to be successful he would need, as he told his benefactor, documentary proof of his ordination to the priesthood and his degree in theology. On the face of it, this was Vincent's reason for writing the first letter to Monsieur de Comet. He also wanted to reassure his relatives and close friends about his sudden disappearance, and finally, he wanted to satisfy his creditors, even if, for the moment, he could only offer promises. He did have some money as the renegade convert had made him a present of about 120 *écus*. But for the moment he needed these to pay for the journey and his stay in Rome, even though he could count on the vice legate for support and for lodgings. He would pay later on ... At the age of twenty-seven, Vincent did not have too many scruples about taking other people's money without permission and using it for his own purposes.

Back in Rome again

Vincent found himself in Rome for the second time in less than eight years. He lived in the monsignor's house and enjoyed his confidence. His board and lodgings were assured. He used his free time to study at one of the universities in Rome. In return, he acted as servant to the Roman prelate and entertained him as a jester. In renaissance and baroque Rome this was a common enough practice and Vincent turned to his advantage the tricks he had learnt from the old Turkish doctor—the little secrets of alchemy,

---

word the same as Montorio's. He arrived in Rome on 30 October 1607. We have no information about Montorio's departure from Avignon but it must have been sometime after 31 August that year. For these matters and general biographical information about Montorio, *cf*. JEAN PARRANG, 'Un mécène de Saint Vincent de Paul: Pierre François Montoro (dit Montorio) (+ 1643)', *Annales* (1937), pp. 245-259; *ibid*. (1938), pp. 615-623; *ibid*. (1943-1944), pp. 224-28. The latter part of this article was written by P. Raymond Chalumeau from notes by Parrang who died before he could finish the work.

Archimedes' mirror and the talking skull. It was Ginés de Pasamonte at the court of Rome!*

Pietro de Montorio used to brag about the skills his servant had learnt and even mentioned them to the sovereign pontiff, then Paul V, the Borghese pope who had just entrusted to Maderno the work of completing Michelangelo's basilica. The vice legate continued to promise favours to this talented and likeable servant. This led to a further request for a copy of his university certificates and letters of ordination. The previous ones were invalid because they did not bear the signature or seal of the bishop of Dax. Vincent hoped that Monsieur de Comet would intervene again on his behalf in this matter. He signed his second letter to him, as he had done the first, with his surname written in one word, Depaul. He never wrote it any other way, although his contemporaries and consequently all Vincentian biographers were accustomed to write it in two words—de Paul. This detail is of no great significance. The registers of the Landes district, and certain legal documents relating to Vincent, use both forms indiscriminately. Neither form is indicative of nobility. The particle *de* just indicates the place of origin. Thousands of lowly peasant families on both sides of the Pyrenees used it in their surname.

---

* Translator's note: Ginés de Pasamonte was a character in *Don Quixote* by Cervantes, and may have been inspired by the historical figure 'Jerónimo de Pasamonte' who, like Vincent, was a captive in Algeria. The fictional character, Ginés de Pasamonte, was involved in various escapades and at one time had a puppet show.

Chapter V
FICTION OR HISTORICAL FACT?
A SERIOUS PROBLEM FOR THE CRITICS

A long-standing controversy

We could continue happily with our story if we did not have to contend with the serious historical problem that we referred to before our study of the letters. For three centuries Vincent's account of his captivity was accepted without question. Then contemporary researchers cast doubts on it just as they had questioned the accepted date of Vincent's birth. They did not doubt that Vincent had written the two letters but they considered the contents to be a complete fabrication. A possible explanation might be that Vincent had embarked on some adventure or other, and for two years had completely lost touch with his acquaintances and familiar surroundings. When he surfaced again, and the episode of his voluntary or enforced disappearance was closed, he might have invented the story of his captivity to explain away that long absence to his family and friends.

It seems that the first person to suggest that Vincent's story might be untrue was Fr Pierre Coste,[1] though he only spoke about it in private and did not put his opinions in writing. The first public allegation that appeared in print was made by Antoine Rédier, in 1927. Rédier's initial stance was relatively moderate but in later editions of his work it became more radical.

---

[1] A. REDIER, *La vraie vie de Saint Vincent de Paul* (Paris 1947), preface, p. X-XII. Coste's opinion on this point is ambiguous. In public he agreed that the captivity was historically authentic (*M.V.* Vol. 1, pp. 58-59). When speaking in private (*cf.* A. REDIER, *op. cit.*, XII and XV), or writing off the record, as in the unsigned letter included in P. GRANDCHAMP *(La prétendue captivité ... II. Observations nouvelles)* or in some of his unpublished writings (*cf.* J. GUICHARD, *Saint Vincent de Paul esclave à Tunis*, p. 187), he is among those who most strongly reject the captivity as historical. Being a priest he may have had good reasons for acting like this, and for prudently avoiding scandal. It might be, too, that he didn't want to compromise the views expressed in his books. He may have had other good reasons. R. Laurentin refers to these when he describes Coste's attitude to St Catherine Labouré's sanctity. 'Father Coste', wrote Laurentin, 'has a cleric's mistrust of anything extraordinary, either in

He states here, 'It is impossible to say for certain whether the events related in those two letters did actually happen.' 'The most we can say is that they are obviously a mixture of truth and invention.'[2]

In the following year, 1928, a scholarly French official at the general residency in Tunis, Pierre Grandchamp, author of a monumental work on the French presence in Tunisia, was stimulated by Rédier's claims to make a detailed study of the letters that Vincent wrote in captivity. This was published as a preface to volume VI of his work. In this book he came to the conclusion that it is 'almost certain that the journey to Barbary and the captivity did not take place.'[3] In the volume that followed he returned to this theme with *Nouvelles Observations*. These were meant to reinforce his argument and answer some critics. Grandchamp's thesis was countered by other works, notably the writings of the French Vincentian, J. Guichard, whose style was most erudite and fairly bristled with the techniques of literary criticism. But it also received enthusiastic support, even if this had little critical value, from such writers as the Church historian, Fr Debongnie. Ever since then there has been no end to the controversy. The most recent findings of any weight are those of André Dodin, who takes a negative view of the letters' authenticity, and the work of Guy Turbet-Delof who strongly supports the account given by Vincent.[4]

---

the religious or the scientific meaning of that term, because extraordinary happenings are not in accordance with either scientific strictures or the precision of faith' (R. LAURENTIN, *Catherine Labouré et la Médaille miraculeuse*, Vol. 1, p. 35). In a Church and a society that had a very strict code of conduct and narrow conventions and where everyone had to be extremely careful about what he said and did, Fr Coste, like many others of his time, had a great sense of duty and he respected the rules and conventions of his position. But he cultivated, in a secret garden, liberal views that went to extremes at times because they were a way of compensating for official policy and they acted as a sort of safety valve ...' (*ibid.*, p. 36).

[2] A. REDIER, *op. cit.*, p. 34 and 24.

[3] P. GRANDCHAMP, 'La prétendue captivité de Saint Vincent de Paul à Tunis (1605-1607)'. Extract from *La France en Tunisie au XVII siècle*, vol. 6 (1928), 20 pages.

[4] P. GRANDCHAMP, 'La prétendue captivité ... II Observations nouvelles', in *La France en Tunisie ...*, vol. 7, p. XXII-XXXIII; *idem.*, 'De nouveau sur la captivité de Saint Vincent de Paul à Tunis', *Revue Tunisienne* (1931), pp. 155-157. Grandchamp's three articles have been reproduced in *Les cahiers de Tunisie* (1965), pp. 51-84; J. GUICHARD, *Saint Vincent de Paul esclave à Tunis. Étude historique et critique* (Paris 1937); P. DEBONGNIE, 'La conversion de Saint Vincent de Paul', *RHE* (1936), pp. 313-339; A. DODIN, *Saint Vincent de Paul et la Charité* (Paris 1960), pp. 144-168; G. TURBET-DELOF, 'Saint Vincent de Paul et la Barbarie en 1657-1658', *Revue de l'Occident mususlman et de la Méditerranée* 3 (1967), pp. 153-165; *idem.*, 'Saint Vincent de Paul a-t-il été esclave à Tunis?', *RHEF* 58 (1972), pp. 331-340. For a very exhaustive list of writings on this subject, S. POOLE, *Saint Vincent's captivity in Tunis. A survey of the controversy*. Caramillo (mimeographed). And other titles in our bibliography: A. BELLESORT, J. CALVET (pp. 23-40), P. COSTE, P. DEBONGNIE, J. DEFOS DU RAU, R. GLEIZES (pp. 1-67), P. GRANDCHAMP, H. LAVEDAN (pp.

Putting the problem into focus

Before going on to a detailed analysis of the question, we need to make an observation about methodology. It is this: the debate over whether Vincent gave a true account of his captivity in the letters or not was originally based on a false premise. Everything was made to depend totally on a vision of Vincent's sanctity. If Vincent had lied in those letters it would have meant that his progress towards sanctity was uneven. Vincent would have been a sinful young man who only became the saint we now venerate after a process of conversion. If, on the other hand, the contents of the letters were authentic, then his development would have shown continuity. From adolescence, and early manhood, Vincent would have moved imperceptibly through trials and sufferings, in a gradual progression towards sanctity. As late as 1960 A. Dodin inclines to this view. But it is a false dilemma. The hypothetical arguments for and against the letters' integrity should not substantially alter our judgment of Vincent at the time he wrote them. Quite apart from whether he was lying or not, Vincent had not become a saint by 1605 and had not begun to be one by 1607. In any case, Vincent could never penetrate the mysterious world of holiness without undergoing a conversion experience. At a time when hagiographers were making extraordinary claims about Vincent's childhood and adolescence, it may have been thought necessary to depict him as a fraud in order to put an end to all those myths about him. In our day such an argument would not hold water. The riddle of Vincent's captivity, whatever the answer to it might be, should be approached from a perfectly neutral standpoint.

The arguments against his captivity

We will now summarise the arguments against Vincent's captivity. The first bombshell was the argument that throughout his long life Vincent de Paul maintained complete silence about his captivity in Barbary. Until the fortuitous discovery of the letters in 1658, nobody had ever heard him say that he had been a prisoner in Tunis. Priests of his community who had been living with him for nearly fifty years knew nothing about it. He had never referred to his extraordinary adventure, either when sending his missioners to North Africa, when he welcomed captives back to freedom, or when he reflected in his conferences on the sad plight of prisoners.[5] On the contrary, we have seen how much effort he put into recovering the letters from M. de St Martin as

---

56-66), J. MAUDUTI (pp. 67-96), A. PRAVIEL, A. REDIER, P. RENAUDIN, J. M. ROMAN, G. F. ROSSI.
[5]   COSTE, *M.V.* Vol. 1, p. 58.

soon as he learnt they were still in existence and that he pleaded for their return 'by all the graces God has been pleased to bestow on you' and 'through the tender mercy of Jesus Christ', describing what he had written in his youth as that 'wretched letter'.[6] 'His silence is truly amazing and has no plausible explanation. Therein lies a mystery,' wrote Coste[7] for whom the traditional explanation, based on the saint's humility, had no validity whatsoever. Would he not be more likely to remain silent if the letters were a fabrication and this fact had been kept hidden for years?

Critical analysis of all the data contained in the letter has only served to confirm Grandchamp's original suspicions. Step by step he gathered together all the inaccuracies and improbable facts in the letter, and then set these against other sources of information, including historical and geographical data, that tell us about the customs of those times, and the events and people alluded to by Vincent.

Here is a summary of his arguments:[8]

1. The archives of the Languedoc coastal region contain no reference to the battle in which Vincent was taken prisoner.

2. Vincent says nothing about what happened to his fellow passengers or to the captured ship. Such silence is unusual in accounts of this kind.

3. It was not the custom for pirates to set free people who had surrendered peacefully. These could have alerted the coastal authorities and the pirates would have run the risk of being pursued by French galleys.

4. The brigantines could not have managed the seven or eight days crossing plus the time needed to come from Tunis, because they would not have had enough victuals and fresh water on board.

5. It is surprising that after his arrival in Tunis Vincent did not try to approach the French consul in a bid to regain his freedom.

6. Vincent does not seem to know the exact location of Tunis, which is not a seaport but a lakeside city. In fact he says that after he and

---

[6] *S.V.P.* VIII, p. 271.

[7] GRANDCHAMP, 'Observations nouvelles', *Les cahiers de Tunisie* (1965), p. 71.

[8] A summary of the arguments against the captivity is readily available in the works we have mentioned by P. GRANDCHAMP and P. DEBONGNIE.

his companions had been paraded through the streets of Tunis, they were brought back to the ship. Well, it was impossible for ships to navigate the lake. Only very small craft called 'sandals' could do this.

7.   Vincent was sold to a fisherman who got rid of the new slave because he was seasick. Well, in the first place, no fisherman would have been rich enough to buy a Christian slave. Secondly, Tunisians did not go fishing in the sea but only on the lake so there could be no question of seasickness.

8.   In the space of a year Vincent could not have learned enough Arabic to converse with his second master about medicine, religion and alchemy.

9.   It is incredible that in 1607 an anonymous Turkish alchemist should have discovered the transmutation of metals and invented the phonograph three centuries before Edison.

10.   The doctor who had been summoned to Constantinople 'died on the road'. One would not use this expression to describe a sea voyage. In his later writings Vincent always used the expression to signify journeys by land.

11.   The doctor's nephew, and Vincent himself, would not have had enough time to hear that the doctor had died 'on the road' before the third sale went ahead.

12.   Vincent says that the doctor's nephew who had left for Constantinople in August, came back immediately, because 'he had heard that the French ambassador was coming.' Savery de Brèves had arrived in Tunis on 17 June and he left on 24 August. So how could he 'have been coming'? The difficulty is compounded when one thinks of the time it would take for news of the doctor's death to reach Tunis. The nephew could not possibly have sold Vincent before September.

13.   According to Vincent, the apostate owned a *temat*. This was a farm that belonged to the state but was leased out. Neither the word *temat* nor the system existed in Tunis.

14.   The *temat* was in mountainous desert country. There are not any

mountains near Tunis and of course you cannot farm desert land.

15.   It is strange that the Turkish, rather than the Greek woman, should have befriended Vincent.

16.   It is contrary to Islamic custom for women to be able to speak so freely to a Christian slave.

17.   Nothing further is said about the women's attitude during the ten months that elapsed before the escape.

18.   The whole account is riddled with improbabilities:

a) To choose the route Tunis-Aigues Mortes would be sheer fantasy.

b) To sail 625 miles in a small skiff is quite a feat.

c) How they managed to escape the vigilance of the Turkish authorities along the coast, and collect enough provisions for the journey without rousing suspicion, does not bear scrutiny at all.

19.   An escape would have provoked serious reprisals from the Turkish authorities. There is no record of Vincent's escape with his master in the archives of Tunis.

20.   If Vincent really had been in Tunis, and if he had been familiar with the Moslem mentality, it would never have occurred to him to send his missionaries there nor to buy the consulates of Algiers and Tunis.

21.   M. de Comet attached not the slightest importance to Vincent's letter and did not bother to answer it. He accepted it for what it was, a cock and bull story invented by an over-imaginative southerner.

22.   If Vincent disembarked at Aigues Mortes on 28 June, he could not have arrived in Avignon the next day, which was when the apostate, whose name appears in the archives as Guillaume Gautier, was reconciled.

23.   Vincent's companions in captivity did not try to get in touch with him when he became well-known.

24.   In his letter to St Martin on 18 March 1660 Vincent wrongly calls Tunisia, Turkey. This is sure proof that he did not know for certain where either place was.

The vast amount of evidence accumulated by Grandchamp, and those who came after him, contradicting the humble writings of young Vincent de Paul is impressive. So it is not surprising that most experts were convinced by it. This long list of allegations reduces the letter to a web of statements that are untrue, inaccurate or improbable. We must patiently reconstruct the work, step by step, in order to restore its credibility.

The Defence

From the outset, two general criticisms were levelled against those who opposed the slavery theory.

First, the frequent and repeated use of arguments that are purely negative. These point to the absence of supporting proof from other sources and to Vincent's own silence on some points—a silence which may be deliberate or it may show ignorance of the facts. Turbet-Delof has described this methodology very precisely in the phrase, 'It is a form of professional distortion to reduce historical reality to the written word alone.'[9] This objection can be applied to arguments 1, 2, 17, 19 and 23.

Secondly, the gratuitousness and lack of proof for many of the assertions that challenge the letter, 'It is not the custom among pirates', 'This is not the case in other similar accounts', etc.

Anyhow, the accusations called for a detailed study, both of Vincent's letters and of contemporary parallel sources that have some connection with points in the story which are being called into question. This was the principal merit of Guichard's work even though his critical methods had their faults. Perhaps the work was too much for one man and later researchers have uncovered an ever-increasing amount of documentation. I now present a synthesis of this counter-research. The synthesis must, of necessity, be condensed and I have presented the arguments in the same order as the points raised against them.

---

[9] Arguments in favour of the captivity theory are quoted in the writings of J. GUICHARD, G. TURBET-DELOF, R. GLEIZES, J. M. ROMAN, J. MAUDUIT. I will only give detailed references when quoting the actual text. The corresponding passage for note 9 is to be found on p. 333 of the second article by G. TURBET-DELOF.

1. The argument *a silentio* is purely negative. Barbary pirates captured ships so frequently that we can be certain that only a small number of these incidents were recorded in the archives.

2. Another negative argument. Fr Jerónimo Gracián, who also was captured by Turkish pirates eight years before Vincent de Paul had the same misfortune, does not mention either his companions or the ship. So in at least one story of this genre, things work out just as they did in Vincent's account. We know that ships were often sunk after they had been pillaged. It may be that Vincent was separated from his companions and never heard any more about them. This would account for his silence on the subject.

3. We know from writers who were Vincent's contemporaries that in quite a number of cases the ships were allowed to go free and this was particularly true if they were French. The pirates were content to 'stroke them', that is to plunder their cargo and provisions. The Turkish brigantines could be manoeuvred so rapidly that it would be impossible for the cumbersome Christian galleys to overtake them and in skirmishes like these the Turks made mockery of the enemy's vessels.

4. The pirates' expeditions often lasted quite a bit longer than a week. Very reliable witnesses speak of expeditions lasting as long as a month or a month and a half. The problem of drinking water could be solved in various ways. To begin with, the Turkish brigantines were not as small as Grandchamp thought. Also, the Turks used to take on fresh water at unguarded spots along the coast. They requisitioned the water supplies of ships they attacked and, finally, to make sure that there would be enough water for the crew, they ignored the needs of the galley slaves and of their prisoners. We learn from reliable sources that these wretched men were often reduced to drinking salt water or else they died of thirst.

5. It would not be possible for a slave with a chain round his neck to leave the ranks and go off and visit the consul. The pirates resorted to various tricks to elude the vigilance of the French consul and we are told they sometimes circumcised French captives to make them look like Moslems.

6. Vincent's vague manner of writing was nothing unusual; other witnesses who were very familiar with the geography of Tunisia wrote in a similar vein. Vincent does not state that he was taken back to the 'brigantine' or the 'ship'—terms which he used earlier—but to the *bateau*. In seventeenth century French, this word was used to describe a small craft whose precise function was to navigate rivers and lakes.

7. It frequently happened that a group of fishermen owned Christian slaves in common. Vincent makes no mention of the social status of his first owner and it is possible that this man was a wealthy fisherman. Neither does he expressly state that he was seasick. He uses the more general expression that the sea did not agree with him. There is nothing to indicate that the fisherman lived in Tunis; he might have lived in another locality along the coast. Finally, we know from other documents that people fished on the lake and in the sea, but fish from the lake were of poor quality.

8. *The lingua franca*, the international language of Mediterranean ports, would be a mixture of Arabic, Turkish, Spanish, Italian, Portuguese and French and it was quite widespread in Algiers and Tunis. Among those who vouched for this were the Spanish writers Haedo and Cervantes. There would be no problem of communication between Christian slaves and their Moslem owners.

9. This is an incredibly naive suggestion even though it comes from Coste. Vincent is obviously referring here to the tricks and contrivances of a magician or ventriloquist. Such ruses are mentioned in other stories about slaves in Vincent's time.

10. There is nothing in Vincent's letters to indicate that the doctor had just embarked. He could have died during the overland journey from Tunis to Bizerta. People commonly made the journey from Tunis to Constantinople by travelling overland as far as Sfax or even Tripoli. In such a case the expression 'on the road' would be most appropiate. The same expression is used by Spanish writers of that time when speaking of sea voyages. When Vincent uses this expression in later writings he is, in fact, referring to land journeys, but there are no parallel passages where he uses different expressions when speaking of sea voyages.

11. If the doctor had died during the journey from Tunis to Bizerta or from Tunis to Sfax, the news could have reached Tunis immediately. Even if he had died at sea, we should not forget that a very effective Moslem postal service had been in operation since the eighth century. News could have been transmitted in a relatively short space of time from any of the stopping-off points on the journey.

12. We can see from the two previous arguments that it was a mistake to suppose that the third sale could not have taken place before September 1606. It could quite well have coincided with Savery de Brèves' stay in Tunis. The phrase 'was coming' did not strictly mean 'he was going

to come'. The phrase indicated, rather, 'the reason for his visit was ...' (he was coming in order to ...). The presence of M. de Brèves in Tunis from 17 June to 24 August allows an elastic use of temporal expressions.

13. In 1936 Grandchamp recognised that the word *temat* could be the Arabic transcription of the Turkish *timar* and that the proper translation was 'owner'. We can be more certain that Vincent's *temat* is the equivalent of the Arabic word *to 'met*—a non-hereditary fief, which is exactly the sense in which Vincent used the term. Other sources have attested that there was such a custom in Tunis.

14. The mountains that Vincent refers to could well be the hills that surround the city from a radius of between twelve and thirty kilometres. There is nothing in the letter to indicate that they may not have been even further away, in the direction of Goleta or the Cape Bon.

In the language of the seventeenth century the word 'desert' does not necessarily imply the land was barren or infertile; it simply means that there were few inhabitants. Le Vacher, a missioner sent by St Vincent to North Africa, visited 'tenant holdings' and rural dwellings or farms in 'the mountains, in places more inhabited by lions than by men', and these were, six, eight, ten or twelve leagues away from Tunis.

15. Human behaviour does not have to comply with the dictates of literary critics. It just happened that the Greek woman was the first to show affection for the captive and it was the Turkish woman who intervened on his behalf. There is nothing implausible in that. We have no indication that there was any romance between the slave and his owner's wives. A recurring feature in Vincent's biography is the attraction that a certain type of woman felt for him. In every case (Madame de Gondi, Louise de Marillac, the Duchess d'Aiguillon, etc.) he used his influence for good. From a psychological point of view this is the trait of Vincent's character that we can be most certain about.

16. All writers of this 'genre', whether their work be history or fiction, have testified to the easy relationship between Moslem women and Christian slaves which at times led to immoral situations. Such writers range from Haedo and Gracián to Gómez de Losada and from Fr Dan to Aranda or Rocqueville.

17. Yet another negative argument. If Vincent had had to relate everything the critics want to know, he would have had to write a treatise, not a letter.

18.   a) Passengers who did not regularly travel by sea did not 'choose' their route—this would surely depend on circumstances—winds, tidal currents, the vigilance of Turkish galleys, etc.

b) The 'small skiff' must have been carefully chosen (ten months would have been more than ample time for that) and great care would he needed to make sure that it was safe and could travel fast. There are many accounts of escapes that were as spectacular as Vincent's or even more so, and which were more perilous. We note particularly, that of Fr Dan, whose escape from La Calle to Marseilles took less than seven days and that of an unnamed French slave who, in 1650, used a leather raft that had neither sail nor rudder. It was possible to cross from Tunis to Marseilles in three days.

c) This was why the apostate took so many precautions and waited ten months to make the crossing as comfortably and as safely as possible.

19. Reprisals and punishments were carried out when the Turks managed to capture the fugitives or when the owner reported an escape. As master and slave had escaped together there would be nobody to report the fact and for this reason it is not mentioned in the archives.

20. Turbet-Delof describes this argument as contradictory, philistine and a masterly example of *a priorism*. It was precisely because he knew the dangers that Christian slaves were exposed to in North Africa, that Vincent was moved to send his missioners there and to buy the two consulates. He was unlikely to have done this had he not himself been a captive. He did know the Moslem mentality, and this made him warn the missioners to be very careful to avoid proselytising Moslems and apostates.

21. It is not true that de Comet did not answer the first letter. In his second letter, Vincent acknowledges receipt of his ordination papers but these did not have the bishop's seal and so he was obliged to ask for a second set. If de Comet set no store by the letter, how is it that he preserved it so carefully and bequeathed it to his heirs?

22. This argument is no longer put forward by the anti-captivity faction. It was based on the mistaken identification of the apostate as Guillaume Gautier. Investigations carried out at a later date than Grandchamp's writings prove beyond all doubt that Vincent's renegade was someone else. The reconciliation, therefore, did not take place on 29 June, but at the beginning of July (cf. *Annales* [1936], pp. 182-188).

23. Another negative argument. All the time that he was a slave Vincent never mentioned that he was a priest. If any of his companions at this time remembered his name, they would not have identified him as the famous M. Vincent. Or it could be that none of them was still alive and at liberty by 1630, the date when Vincent began to be well known.

24. Tunis was, in fact, under Turkish sovereignty. In the seventeenth century French people thought that the Turkish empire extended as far as Salé in Morocco.

M. Vincent is silent

Vincent de Paul's life-long silence about this extraordinary adventure, and his anxiety in the last days of his life to recover and destroy the 'wretched letter,' are perhaps the most compelling arguments and merit a more detailed examination.

First of all, we should note that there is a strange reversal of dialectical position with regard to the date of Vincent's birth and the controversy over his captivity. In the first case, the saint's own words are used to support the argument in favour of the traditionally held date. In the second case, Vincent's words (his letters) are called into question and the argument based not on what he said, but on what he left unsaid. Does not this suggest that sources and documents are being quoted on two different levels and used for contradictory purposes?

We cannot analyse Vincent's silence without reference to the total personality of the man, and at this stage in the biography we have not enough information to make a judgement. But even if it means jumping ahead and using information about the saint that was available later, we have to put on record that Vincent, in his mature years, and even more so in his old age, was complete master of himself and we never hear of any uncontrolled outbursts in unguarded moments. He always says what he wants to say and nothing more. He never talked much about other events in his life that are perfectly well documented in other sources. He never told anyone that he had studied at Toulouse University, nor that he had been chaplain to Marguerite de Valois; he never referred to the fact that he had been abbot of St Laurent de Chaumes, canon of Ecouis and prior of Grosse-Sauve. If we have to erase from the life of Vincent de Paul everything that he deliberately kept silent about, we would have to cross out with one stroke of the pen whole chapters of his life.

At this point in the debate we can already glimpse some of the reasons for his prolonged silence and for his fears that the letters might be published. Leaving aside the question of his humility, though his contemporaries who recognised the extent of his virtue were convinced by this, and disregarding, too, Vincent's leanings towards the secrets of alchemy which were nothing more than innocent tricks of 'white magic', there is one aspect of the problem that Turbet-Delof has emphasised, namely, the remorse that Vincent must have felt after his conversion for having, throughout his captivity, concealed the fact that he was a priest. Conscious of this incident in his earlier life, what moral authority would he have for exhorting his missioners in Tunis and Algiers to be faithful witnesses to Christ, even unto death? Does it not also conceal something more serious (something painfully odious to the saint's heart) his conviction that captive priests were 'irregular' and the sacraments they administered might have been invalid?[10]

Moreover, in 1658 Vincent was committed to touching the hearts of people in France over the terrible plight of slaves in North Africa and appealing for funds to pay the ransom of the consul Barreau, a brother of the Mission, who had been detained by the Turkish authorities. In these circumstances, would not the discovery of the letter he had written as a young man, painting a somewhat rosy picture of life in captivity, give a different message from the one he was urging in his appeal? 'Wretched letter ...'!

And does not the whole letter breathe such self-confidence, and a certainty that God was guiding his steps, that contrasts sharply with Vincent's later spirituality when he would be at such pains to discover the mysterious signs of providence? Would he not consider this letter to be contrary to the teachings he was then trying to instil into his missioners? Defrennes was certainly right when he wrote, 'For a man who was as self-controlled and master of himself as M. Vincent was, there can be a thousand good reasons for his silence.'[11]

Final observations

Another contradiction can be seen in the writings of those who denied the historical authenticity of Vincent's captivity, and this is particularly true of Rédier's work. The letter is factually correct up to the point where Vincent de Paul arrives in Marseilles. At this point the fiction begins. The Bordeaux affair is authentic and so is the inheritance from the old lady of Castres. It is true that Vincent was in debt and that he sold the horse. He would agree that Vincent was covetous, even to the point of having a man put in prison for failing to pay his debts. The only part that is not true is Vincent's captivity.

---

[10] *S.V.P.* V, p. 85; VII, p. 117.
[11] P. DEFRENNES, *art. cit.*, p. 395.

Such a reasoning can only come from manipulation of the historical documents; it would be to accept whatever is in accord with a preconceived theory and to reject whatever contradicts it. The letter must be accepted or rejected in its entirety.

Those who come out against the captivity would deprive us of the true picture of Vincent before his conversion—the reckless young fellow who was not too scrupulous in money matters, who trusted too much in himself and was inclined to regard his own intuitions as divine interventions ... Those who do not believe in Vincent's captivity would give us back the precocious little saint they wanted to demythologise.

On the other hand, is not the fact that Vincent begged Canon St Martin to send the letter back an indirect proof of their authenticity? If Vincent wanted all traces of his youthful fantasy to disappear, why was he not simple and straightforward enough to tell his good friend that this was a story he had invented about a wild episode in his youth? From the moment anyone got to know about it there would have been no point in destroying the letters. Also, those who knew would have talked about them. It was not enough to destroy the letters, it was absolutely essential to deny that the contents were true. In 1659 Vincent did not lack the humility to accuse himself of that sin. He did not fail to describe that letter as 'wretched' but he never said that what he had written was untrue.

Let us add one final methodological consideration. In any rational historical criticism one cannot reject an argument (in our case, Vincent's letters) because a difficulty remains unsolved: his later silence. As René Laurentin wrote about Coste's difficulties in accepting that Catherine Labouré was a saint: 'Coste emphasised difficulties that other people were trying to diminish. It is a good way of finding a solution. But this method was carried to extremes, and the exaggerated claims of so much German scientific literature in the nineteenth century are reflected in Coste's writings.'[12] Neither is his allegation against Vincent de Paul 'free from the excesses of mistrustful criticism and a strong bias towards polemics. His conclusions often go beyond the original premise. His negative assessments are disproportionate to the information on which they are based.'[13]

Conclusions?

After listening to the arguments for and against Vincent's captivity, what, finally, are we to make of it? We believe that the reader now has at hand all

---

[12] R. LAURENTIN, *op. cit.*, Vol. 1, p. 35.

[13] *Ibid.*, p. 37.

the necessary information to make his own judgement. The author feels that the following conclusions cannot be argued against.

1. The difficulties put forward by those who reject Vincent's account of his captivity are groundless if compared with many parallel and contemporary testimonies.

2. Much of the information given by Vincent receives overwhelming confirmation when it is subjected to similar comparisons, and it is also borne out by what we know of Vincent's character in his later years.

3. Recent findings have seriously weakened the argument based on Vincent's silence, which remains as a difficulty which has yet to be solved, not as a definitive proof.

To sum up then; we should add Turbet-Delof's conclusions: 'I do not say that everything happened in the way Vincent de Paul describes it. I just say that everything could have happened like that. There is nothing in Vincent's writing, or in other sources, that would lead us to reject this testimony. In conclusion, we must accept one of two alternatives: either Vincent de Paul was a prisoner in Tunis from 1605 to 1607, or we must regard his letter of 24 July 1607, and the postscript dated 28 February 1608, as a brilliant fraud without any possible parallel in any literary or other sources.'[14]

As long as we have no proof that Vincent was in some other part of France, or in some other foreign place, between 1605 and 1607, we have to accept his statement that he was a captive in Tunis at that time.

---

[14] G. TURBET-DELOF, second article quoted, p. 339. From a literary point of view, Vincent's letters about the captivity bear some resemblance to the French *turquerie*, or to the picaresque and moorish genres in Spanish literature. Turbet-Delof, who was an authority on French *turqueries* says that Vincent's journeys might be a historical or travel *turquerie* but not a fictional one. There might be a connection between Vincent's story of his captivity and similar stories in *Quixote* or certain episodes in *Guzmán de Alfarache* by Mateo Alemán, since both these Spanish works were published before 1607. But nobody has been able to prove such a link. In fact, the opposite would seem to be true; the Cervantes and Guzmán accounts of captives and *pícaros* show that Vincent's story rings true. The reality of such situations is part of Mateo Alemán and Cervantes' literary creations but it is part of the life history of Vincent de Paul. See our article 'Las cartas vicencianas de la cautividad, ¿novela picaresca?', *Anales* (1980), pp. 137-147, and further references in the works of J. GRACIAN, D. HAEDO, E. ARANDA, P. DAN, G. GOMEZ DE LOSADA, in the Bibliography and in our article, 'Corsarios berberiscos y cautivos cristianos. Nuevos datos para el tema de la cautividad tunecina de Vicente de Paúl', *Anales* (1979), pp. 445-465.

Chapter VI
FROM ROME TO PARIS,
A CHANGE OF SCENE

Third project, third failure

Once again we are back in Rome with our Vincent de Paul in the palace of Mgr Montorio. Vincent has embarked on his third project to find a secure position in life. This time it is the generous prelate who thought up the idea, not Vincent. And once again it is a purely human undertaking. Over and over again Montorio had promised him a benefice, a good benefice, an excellent benefice. Vincent waits hopefully. Meanwhile, he tries to put his time to good use. He does some study and gets in touch with some pastoral initiatives in the Eternal City. For instance, he gets to know the Confraternity of Charity in the Hospital of the Holy Spirit and this organisation will later serve as a model for the first charitable association that he founds.[1]

He probably comes into contact, also, with the parish charity of San Lorenzo in Damaso, a church near the Montorio palace. Their rules show a surprising similarity to those that Vincent will set down for his own associations.[2] Vincent is an excellent pupil in the school of life. He is living out his years of pilgrimage and apprenticeship. None of the lessons learnt during these years will be wasted.

During the two or three months he stayed in Avignon, Vincent had had the occasion to come in contact with the missions organised by the vice legate for the conversion of the Huguenots.[3] Charity and mission—almost without realising it, he is accumulating experiences which will one day help him to fulfil his own mission in the Church. For the moment he has not the faintest idea what this might be. He is still firmly wedded to his own project, that desirable benefice promised by monsignor. But this project, too,

---

[1] *S.V.P.* XIII, p. 423.
[2] A. ARMANDI, 'Une étrange coïncidence: Saint Vincent de Paul à Rome et les conférences dites de Saint Vincent de Paul', *M. et Ch.*, n. 10 (1963), pp. 224-226.
[3] R. CHALUMEAU, *Annales* (1943-1944), p. 225ss.

comes to nothing; we do not know for certain when or how this happened. One thing we do know is that two years later, on 17 February 1610, he writes to his mother from Paris. This is the only letter he wrote to her that has been preserved. It contains a humble admission of failure, which is a far cry from the arrogant confidence of his letters to de Comet. Vincent is learning a lot about life.

> I would like one of my brothers to send his son to study. My misfortunes, and the little help that I have been to the family so far, might discourage him from doing this.[4]

What misfortunes is he referring to here? To those now distant troubles of his capture and slavery at the hands of Barbary pirates? To more recent mishaps which caused him to lose favour with Mgr Montorio? It is significant that for the rest of his life Vincent will have no further dealings with the former vice legate of Avignon whose death did not occur, however, until 1643. It is clear, too, that the monsignor fell out of favour when the pro-French pope, Urban VIII, ascended the pontifical throne in 1623, and that before that date very few of Vincent's letters were preserved.[5] So Vincent left Rome without any tangible outcome to all Montorio's promises.

Paris: 'The time I have left in this city'

Contrary to what we might have expected, Vincent did not return to Toulouse, or to his native region, Dax, after he left Rome. Towards the end of 1608 he left the Eternal City for Paris. Abelly attributes Vincent's journey here to motives which are as honourable as they are improbable! The French ambassador to the Holy See, Cardinal d'Ossat, must have entrusted the young priest with a secret mission to the king, Henry IV; this mission being so confidential and of such a delicate nature that it was too dangerous to commit it to writing. It could only be transmitted verbally.[6] Such a theory is highly improbable and that for a very simple reason. Cardinal d'Ossat had died in 1604 so he could hardly have confided a mission to somebody four years later! Later biographers than Abelly who knew more about secular history than he did, repeat the story of this mission, but they say Vincent was sent, not by d'Ossat, but by no less a commission than the three ministers who were accredited to Rome by the French monarchy in 1608. These were

---

[4] *S.V.P.* I, p. 19.

[5] R. CHALUMEAU, *Annales* (1943), p. 228.

[6] ABELLY, *op. cit.*, 1.1 c. 5, p. 20.

the Marquis de Savary de Brèves, (the same man who two years earlier had been sent to Turkey and to Tunis to procure the release of French captives), Denis de Marquemont, the auditor of the Rota, and the Duke of Nevers, Charles Gonzaga.[7] It is a pity that this information about Vincent's mission should have such little foundation. Vincent only made his entrance on to the historical scene during the reign of the next monarch. So writers who are fond of making historical comparisons have been deprived of the opportunity to describe for us an interview between the jovial, exuberant Béarnese monarch and the up and coming young priest from Gascony.

Vincent's reason for going to Paris was not simply that he felt attracted to the capital. After his recent failure in Rome, Paris was the only place where he could try once more to win the benefice he so desperately wanted, and which was so necessary for the stabilisation of his finances. Besides, he only expected to stay in the capital for a short time. He indicates this in the letter to his mother:

> The time I have left in this city to try and better myself (advancement that has been thwarted by my misfortunes) makes me unhappy because I cannot leave here to render you the services I owe you.[8]

Vincent's affairs had become complicated and this was to continue; so much so that his brief stay lasted till the end of his life.

'God knows the truth'

Then came the biggest complication of all but Vincent was in no way responsible for it. When he arrived in Paris he took up residence in the Faubourg St Germain, an unpretentious district on the left bank of the Seine. He chose this place, not because it was the university and student area, as it still is today, but for the more practical reason that it was the Gascon quarter. Vincent was too poor to own his own house. He hired a room and shared it with a man from his own part of the country, a minor judge from Sore, in the region of Bordeaux. Shared accommodation has its drawbacks as Vincent was soon to find out.

One day Vincent felt unwell and he had to stay in bed. His companion, the judge, left early to attend to some business in the city. Vincent

---

[7] *Ristretto cronologico ...*, p. 14; COLLET, *op. cit.*, Vol. 1, p. 25.

[8] *S.V.P.* I, p. 18.

sent to a nearby apothecary for the medicines he needed. The apothecary's assistant was looking in the cupboard for a glass when he discovered the judge's purse containing 400 *écus*. The temptation proved too strong for the lad. As he rummaged about for the glass, he stealthily pocketed the money, and as soon as he had attended to the sick man he left the house and was never seen again.

Who should come back soon afterwards but the judge, and almost immediately he discovered his money was missing. Who could have stolen it? It must surely have been this fellow who had pretended to be ill and stayed in bed as though nothing had happened. He swore he had not taken it and that he had not seen anybody else take it. The judge was a hasty and a violent man. Shouting at the top of his voice, he accused Vincent of the theft, threw him out of the house, and denounced him to his friends and acquaintances. He even caused the ecclesiastical authorities to issue a *monition*.[9] Poor Vincent, who was just beginning to lift his head up again after those earlier disasters, felt that adversity was dogging his steps yet again.

At that time Vincent had got to know some very influential people in Paris. He had just made the acquaintance of Pierre de Bérulle, the future cardinal, who was to have such a decisive influence on his life. The exasperated judge could not contain his anger even in the presence of the cardinal and he accused Vincent of being a thief. Vincent's reaction was exemplary, and here we come across one of his characteristics that presaged the mettle of his sanctity. It did not even occur to him to throw suspicion of the crime on to the apothecary's assistant. He contented himself with the meek reply, 'God knows the truth.' Six years were to pass before the truth was discovered because this incident unfolded in a manner worthy of some Byzantine fiction where all is made clear at the end.

If the story had not been told by Vincent himself Coste would have dismissed it as fiction. But it so happened that six years later the guilty party was arrested in Bordeaux for some other crime. Overcome by remorse, he asked the judge from Sore to come to the prison and he confessed his misdeed. The judge was no less ardent in his apologies than he had been in his accusations. He wrote to Vincent and begged his pardon, assuring him that

---

9 A *monition* was an order from the ecclesiastical authorities, granted at the request of a secular judge. It required people to declare everything they knew about a given offence, and this under pain of excommunication. The monitories were read out by the parish priest during Mass on 3 consecutive Sundays. The ease with which monitions were granted constituted a serious abuse which was deplored by the clergy. *Cf.* M. MARION, *Dictionnaire des Institutions de la France aux XVII et XVIII siècles* (Paris, J. Picard, 1969); R. MOUSNIER, *Les institutions de la France sous la monarchie absolue*, Vol. 2, p. 391.

if he did not receive this in writing, he would go to Paris and publicly ask pardon on his knees and with a halter round his neck. This was not necessary. Vincent generously granted him the pardon he asked.[10]

All this happened in 1609. When Vincent wrote to his mother early in the following year the letter we have already mentioned, he could rightly complain about his disasters and misfortunes. Pierre Debongnie has seen the false accusation of theft to be the key event in Vincent's conversion.[11] This is too simplistic a view. Vincent's conversion is much more complex and the process takes far longer. Over the years he will be touched by a whole series of events and influences; this accusation of theft is only the first step.

However, there can be no doubt that Vincent's reaction on that occasion marks a significant turning point in his standards and in his conduct. 'Are you going to justify yourself?' They are accusing you of something that they cannot prove. 'No', he said to himself, raising his mind to God, 'you must suffer it patiently'and that is what he did.[12] He tells the story in the third person and adds, 'Let us leave it to God to reveal the secrets of men's consciences.'[13]

In spite of this, in February 1610, Vincent still seems entrenched in attitudes we have noticed earlier; he wants to direct his own life and he trusts in fortune and in human resources. He is still waiting for 'an opportunity for promotion', his horizons and hopes are still limited to the prospect of a comfortable 'retirement' and his mind is still set on devoting the rest his days (he is now thirty!) to looking after his mother and helping his brothers and nephews. He still clings to the philosophy expressed in the letters of his captivity, that 'present misfortune heralds future success.'

But this disillusionment aside, we can already read between the lines and see a subtle change in outlook. 'I trust in God that he will bless my work and quickly grant me the means of securing a decent retirement.'[14] 'Raise your heart to God'—'hope in God'—this is the lesson he has learnt from his captivity, from the calumny, and from other misfortunes that he doesn't name. He will soon have occasion to put this very much into practice. The life he thought was over, was just about to begin. Ten years of planning and of sounding out human resources were to be followed by seven or eight years when he would slowly and gradually discover the real plan, the divine plan which would shape his conversion process and at the same time would clearly spell out his vocation.

---

[10] ABELLY, *op. cit.*, 1.1 c. 5, pp. 21-23; COLLET, *op. cit.*, Vol. 1, pp. 27-28.

[11] P. DEBONGNIE, 'La conversion de Saint Vincent de Paul', *RHE* 32 (1936), pp. 313-339.

[12] *S.V.P.* XI, p. 337.

[13] ABELLY, *op. cit.*, 1.1 c. 5, p. 23.

[14] *S.V.P.* I, pp. 18-20.

Chapter VII
THE PATHS OF CONVERSION

A decisive year

It is generally accepted by the saint's biographers that at this period Vincent de Paul was going through a process of conversion.[1] By 'conversion' we understand, first of all, the fundamental discovery of a religious dimension to life. 'Life is permeated with a new power and it is perceived in a totally different way. It is radically altered and renewed.'[2] The person experiences conversion as the masterful presence of God bursting into the innermost depths of his personality. Conversion and vocation are complementary realities, the two sides of a coin. This divine outpouring into the soul causes the person to break with his former way of life and to view the world, and his own existence, in a way that is completely different. Conversion carries with it a call; there is born a new dynamism and a clearly defined programme of action.

Conversion is not always a sudden phenomenon. In most cases it is the result of a long progression towards maturity, though the final stage of conversion is often crystallised in some rather extraordinary event which gives the impression that conversion is something sudden and immediate. The fall on the way to Damascus and Augustine's *tolle, lege,* are typical examples of how these things happen.

---

[1] The first writers to make a serious study of the question of Vincent de Paul's conversion were: P. DEBONGNIE, 'La conversion de Saint Vincent de Paul', *RHE* 31 (1936), pp. 313-339, and P. DEFRENNES, 'La vocation de Saint Vincent de Paul'. Étude de Psychologie surnaturelle', *RAM* (1932), pp. 60-86, 164-183, 294-321, 389-411; The subject is taken up again, and interpreted in an original way by A. DODIN in *Saint Vincent de Paul et la Charité*, pp. 148-150. Recently there has been a systematic analysis of the question and the different approaches to it, presented by L. Mezzadri in 'La conversione di San Vicenzo di Paoli', *Annali* 84.3 (1977), pp. 176-182, translated in *Anales* (1978), pp. 9-15.

[2] G. VAN DER LEEUW, *La religion dans son essence et ses manifestations* (Paris 1955), p. 520.

The discovery of God's sovereign presence and his radical demands in the conversion experience does not mean that up to this point the person had no knowledge of God, and neither does it imply that the earlier way of life was sinful. In many cases conversion takes place when a person simply turns away from a life that was not really God-orientated.

From the information we now have at hand, we must suppose that this happened in Vincent's case. However excessively humble Vincent might be in his later years, he never believed himself to be a wicked man and neither did other people make this judgement about him. In 1608 we can be quite sure that his bishop had no difficulty in testifying that he had always been of good character.[3] His conversion to a life of complete and utter surrender to the divine will follows on from a way of life characterised by mediocrity and by aspirations that were purely materialistic. Spiritually, it was rather superficial with scant attention paid to the supernatural.

We see this reflected in his youthful peccadilloes—he was ashamed of his shabbily dressed and crippled father, he was careless about money (his debts and the sale of the hired horse) and his continual search for wealthy ecclesiastical benefices.[4]

Let us now consider the events leading up to his conversion. It was in 1610 that Vincent confided his disappointment and disillusionment to his mother. This was to be a decisive year in the life of the priest who was still a young man. It would prove to be no less important a year in the history of France. Once again we come across the relentless parallels between the course followed by this young man and the direction in which the country was heading. This convergence in their development becomes now more marked and its implications more significant for both of them.

14 May of that year was marked by two events that took place almost simultaneously and in localities that were very close to each other. The two events were very different but they symbolised the beginning of a new and important stage in the life of Vincent de Paul and the destiny of France.

That evening, in a house on the rue de Coutellerie in the parish of Saint Médéric, Vincent signed a contract whereby he received from the archbishop of Aix, Monsignor Paul Hurault de l'Hôpital, the abbey of Saint Léonard de Chaumes in the diocese of Saintes together with all its titles, revenues and responsibilities. Vincent thought he had now achieved the goal

---

[3] *S.V.P.* I, p. 15.
[4] A. DODIN, *op. cit.*, pp. 149-150.

that he had striven so long and so hard to attain; at long last an important ecclesiastical benefice was his.[5]

At almost that identical hour, between four and five o'clock in the evening, and just a few blocks away in the rue de la Ferronerie, the king, Henry IV, was driving in his carriage from the Louvre to the house of his chief minister, Sully, when he was stabbed twice by a half crazed fanatic called François Ravaillac and thus ended his life and his reign. The death of this gallant king brought to a close a chapter in French history; the military campaign he had inevitably started up against Spain and the empire was left in abeyance, and there followed a period of instability and power struggles because the new king, Louis XIII, was a minor and his mother, Marie de Medici, was queen regent.[6]

Vincent was deeply affected by the king's murder and not just because he was so close to where this happened. The abbey of Saint Léonard was not the first appointment he managed to secure. For a few weeks now his life had been revolving round that magnetic nucleus of power that was the royal household, even though he was only on the periphery. At some date between 28 February and 14 May he had also managed to secure the position of chaplain to the ex-queen, Marguerite de Valois. This title is ascribed to him in the lease contract for the abbey.[7]

Queen Marguerite

We don't know for certain just what Vincent's duties were as chaplain to Marguerite. She was Henry IV's first wife and the last direct descendant of the house of Valois. Her marriage to the king was annulled (and rightly so!)[8] in 1599. She lived in a sumptuous palace on the left bank of the Seine.

> Around the former queen there swarmed, as though at court,
> a motley crowd of poets, playwrights, theologians, nobles,
> religious and charlatans. While Marguerite did not altogether

[5] F. COMBALUZIER, 'L'Abbaye de Saint Léonard de Chaumes et Saint Vincent de Paul (14 mai 1610-29 octobre 1616)', *Annales* (1914-1942), pp. 249-265. This is an introductory study of the history of the abbey and it also gives four legal documents concerning the acquisition of the abbey by Saint Vincent. The remaining documentation can be found in *S.V.P.* XIII, pp. 8-13.

[6] V.-L. TAPIÉ, *La France de Louis XIII et de Richelieu*, pp. 11-12.

[7] *S.V.P.* XIII, p. 8; ABELLY, *op. cit.*, 1.1 c., p. 21 and 25; COLLET, *op. cit.*, Vol. 1., p. 30.

[8] It is said that during the wedding the king, Charles IX, had to tap her on the head when it was time to say 'Yes'. Cardinal de Bourbon, who officiated at the ceremony, had not been able to obtain a dispensation from disparity of cult.

refrain from courtly flirtations, she combined an interest in the arts and sciences with a taste for religion. At her own expense she maintained a community of Augustinians who chanted morning and evening office in her chapel and she was in the habit of hearing three Masses every day. These were celebrated by her chaplains who were at least six in number. One of these was Vincent de Paul who owed his nomination for the post to the good offices of M. Le Clerc de la Forêt.[9]

So that he could live near the palace Vincent set up house in the rue de la Seine. His dwelling had a certain air of distinction because its facade bore the insignia of Saint Nicholas.[10] As chaplain-almoner (the word *aumonier* would have retained its original meaning in seventeenth century French) Vincent's duties would be to celebrate Mass when it was his turn to do so and to distribute the generous supply of alms that the extravagant lady provided. Many of these donations were destined for the nearby Hospital of Charity which was under the direction of the St John of God Brothers, the Fate bene fratelli, whose monastery in Rome had admitted the ex-apostate from Tunis. We will soon see him in action there.[11] Vincent continued to gain experience and his apprenticeship gave him a more specific training for the great works he would undertake during his lifetime. As the years passed, he would become, in a very real sense, the grand almoner of France, though this title was never his. He would also become spiritual director to the lawful queen of France. A very profound change came over Vincent de Paul in 1610, the year when he crossed the dividing line between youth and maturity as he reached the age of thirty.

The abbey of Saint Laurent de Chaumes turned out to be a less promising acquisition than Vincent had imagined. According to the deeds of purchase the church was in ruins, there were no monks living there and the lands that had been neglected would need to be developed. As if that was not enough, there followed a whole series of lawsuits. Vincent was unable to produce the 3,500 *livres* he was expected to pay annually to Hurault de

---

[9] Abelly and Collet think that it was Charles du Fresne, Queen Marguerite's secretary, who introduced Vincent into the queen's household. Dodin, basing his ideas on the unpublished biography of Antoine le Clerc, suggested it was he who arranged it.

[10] *S.V.P.* XIII, p. 8.

[11] The Hospital of the Brothers of Charity or, to give it its more abbreviated name, the Charity Hospital, was founded by Henry IV's second wife, Marie de Medici, and she had four St John of God brothers sent from their monastery in Florence for this purpose. Marguerite de Valois had this hospital moved to another building which was near her palace and she endowed it generously. C. F. GUILLET, *L'Hôpital de la Charité* (Montévrain 1900); referred to by COSTE, *M.V.*, Vol. 1, p. 68.

l'Hôpital who had given him the benefice. After six years he got rid of such a costly acquisition by handing it over, irrevocably and in perpetuity, to François de Lanson, the prior of Saint Etienne d'Ars.[12]

A truly priestly life

Let us return to the year 1610. As well as trying to put his financial affairs on a more solid footing, Vincent had a variety of worries and problems to contend with during those months. There are several pointers to the changes that were beginning to take effect in Vincent's soul. In spite of what he had written to his mother early in the year, neither the chaplaincy to Queen Marguerite nor the abbey of Saint Laurent (to some extent the 'decent retirement' he had been seeking for so long) led him to return home and devote himself to the interests of his family as he had planned. As we know, he had moved house. The unfortunate experience he had while lodging with the judge from Sore, had opened his eyes to the dangers of life in the world.

Before he was falsely accused of theft, Vincent had become acquainted with Pierre de Bérulle (1575-1629), one of the most significant figures in the Church in France at that time. This was the man that Vincent de Paul chose as his spiritual director. It was just a small gesture but it showed a profound change of attitude. Vincent was beginning to set himself higher goals than just improving his social position; he started to seek a more spiritual orientation to his life and his objectives became less materialistic. 'God had inspired him', comments Abelly, 'with the desire to lead a truly priestly life.'[13]

De Bérulle brought Vincent into contact with the most active and the most fervent religious movements in the Church in France. For almost half a century these had been trying to introduce into the country the reforms promulgated by the Council of Trent. At this particular time the campaign to have the Tridentine decrees accepted in France was at its most successful.

Although these measures were defeated by the Estates General of 1614, the reforms were eventually introduced during the General Assembly of Clergy of 1615, notwithstanding Gallican resistance.[14]

---

[12] *S.V.P.* XIII, pp. 40-41.
[13] ABELLY, *op. cit.*, 1.1 c. 6, p. 24.
[14] L. WILLAERT, *La restauración católica,* vol. 20 from *Historia de la Iglesia* of FLICHE-MARTIN, Spanish translation, pp. 409-422.

'Cardinal de Bérulle, one of the holiest men I have ever known'

Pierre de Bérulle was born into the lower aristocracy. He was educated by the Jesuits and received a sound ecclesiastical and classical education. As a young man he was outstanding for his fervour and innocence of life. Family connections and his own preoccupation with religious matters placed him at the centre of the reform movements. Even before his ordination to the priesthood in the final decade of the sixteenth century, he had been part of a group centred around Mme Acarie (1566-1618) and directed by a French Carthusian, Dom Richard Beaucousin, and an English Capuchin, Benet of Canfield (1562-1610) who was an Anglican convert. It was through them that groups of devout people in France were being introduced to the spirituality of Rhenish-Flemish mysticism and the Spanish Carmelites.

Among its members, too, were men like Michel de Marillac, the future Keeper of the Seals in France, André Duval (1564-1638) a doctor of the Sorbonne, and François Leclerc de Temblay (1577-1638) Baron de Maffliers, who would later become the famous Père Joseph, the *éminence gris* of Cardinal Richelieu.[15] Vincent would get to know all these people at some time or other during his life. This group, and especially de Bérulle and Duval, would implement the initiative of Jean de Quintadueñas to bring Carmelite nuns into France. Jean de Quintadueñas was the Franco-Spanish lord of Brétigny who devoted his life and his fortune to establishing more foundations of St Teresa's spiritual daughters, letting other people and particularly de Bérulle occupy centre stage in all matters connected with the work of introducing the Carmelites into France.[16] It was, in fact, de Bérulle who went to Spain in 1604 and brought the first group of Spanish Carmelite nuns to Paris. De Bérulle, Duval and Gallemant would jointly be their first superiors.

Many other religious and political enterprises lay ahead for de Bérulle. His numerous publications would initiate what has come to be called 'the French school of spirituality'. His political action was backed by the Marillac family who would continue his work, and as we shall soon see,

---

[15] For information on de Bérulle and his rôle in reforming the Church in France *cf.* P. COCHOIS, *Bérulle et l'École française* (Paris, De Seuil, 1965) and the indispensable work by H. BRÉMOND, *Histoire littéraire du sentiment religieux en France* ... (Paris, Blond, 1916-1932), Vol. 3. Benet of Canfield's influence on the movement in general is dealt with by OPTAT DE VEGHEL, *Benoît de Canfield (1562-1610). Sa vie, sa doctrine et son influence* (Rome, Institutum Historicum O. Fr. Min. Cap., 1949), XXIII, 516 pages, and ETTA GULLICK, 'The life of Father Benet of Canfield', *Collectanea Franciscana* 42 (1972), pp. 39-67 and *DTC* II, col. 718-719; *DS* I, 1446-1452.

[16] P. SEROUET, Jean de Brétigny (1556-1634). 'Aux origines du Carmel de France, de Belgique et du Congo' (Lovaina, *RHE,* 1974), XXII.

would constitute the only valid alternative to Richelieu's political policies. But above all, those who worked to reform the French clergy from within were to find in him their spiritual guide and mentor. Inspired by the writings of St Philip Neri, he was to found the Oratory, an association of secular priests whose particular charism was a vision of the clerical state as the ideal of Christian holiness. This was very different from the outlook of many people whose ideals were superficial and even materialistic and who looked on the priesthood merely as a way of procuring sinecures and benefices.[17] The new approach was just what Vincent de Paul needed.

In 1610 Vincent came into contact with this man and years later he was to say, 'He was one of the holiest men I have ever known.'[18] It was through him that Vincent was able to join the small but influential circle of reformers. He read the *Rule of Perfection* by Benet of Canfield which had been published the previous year, he became friendly with Duval and got to know the Marillac family. Obviously, if he was going to take part in the reformation of the Church then reformation would have to start with himself. It was this new circle of friends and the intervention of divine providence that would bring about this change.

Pierre de Bérulle is the first of the great spiritual directors of Vincent de Paul. He was the one to rouse Vincent from the golden dreams of his mediocre way of living and to help him through the crucial crisis of his life. But de Bérulle's influence over Vincent was not absolute, neither was it permanent.

At the time when Vincent put himself under de Bérulle's direction, the eminent ecclesiastic was putting the finishing touches to the basic outlines of the Oratory, and a year later, 11 November 1611, the first community came into being. Vincent lived for a time with the first small group of future Oratorians but Abelly makes a subtle distinction when he adds, 'not with a view to joining that holy congregation since he himself would later declare that this was never his intention. He just wanted to find a refuge from his secular commitments to discover God's designs for him and to prepare himself to carry these out.'[19] Whatever admiration Vincent might have felt for the founder of the Oratorians, it was not strong enough to attract him to the new congregation.

---

[17] H. TÜCHLE, *Reforma y Contrarreforma,* Vol. 3 from *Nueva historia de la Iglesia* (Madrid, Cristiandad, 1966), p. 250.

[18] *S.V.P.* XI, p. 139.

[19] ABELLY, *op. cit.*, 1.1 c. 6, p. 24. Abelly assures us that Vincent lived in de Bérulle's house for two years. Coste thinks that such a long stay would not have been possible. He bases this opinion on documents which give details of places where Vincent lived, and also on the fact that the Oratory was founded on 11 November 1611, and Vincent de Paul took up his appointment at Clichy on 2 May 1612.

As far as we know de Bérulle's direct influence on Vincent lasted for seven or eight years. Vincent would retain from this contact quite a number of spiritual guidelines and would always have a great veneration for his first master. But when the right moment came Vincent would discover his own path and his own spirituality, something beyond the teachings of de Bérulle. This is evident in spite of Brémond's efforts to demonstrate the contrary.[20]

It is curious to note that in the fourteen volumes of Vincent's writings we find no more than a dozen direct quotations from de Bérulle. Several of these relate to fairly topical matters and de Bérulle's reflections seem rather banal, as for example the dangers inherent in holding the office of superior.[21] There was an abrupt end to the harmonious relationship between master and disciple. We are not very sure about the details because of Vincent's extreme discretion in such matters. The break probably happened in 1618. A serious crisis had arisen in de Bérulle's circle just before that date. The future cardinal had insisted on imposing a fourth vow on the Carmelite nuns by which they would undertake to become the slaves of Jesus. This proposal met with fierce resistance from many of the nuns and was vigorously opposed by one of the other superiors, M. Duval, who did not hesitate to denounce the matter to Cardinal Bellarmine. In January 1618 de Bérulle had a violent disagreement with Mme Acarie, now Mother Mary of the Incarnation, and this led to a decisive break in their relationship. Mme Acarie died in April of that same year without making her peace with de Bérulle. Several of the Carmelites took the grave decision to leave their convent in Paris and seek refuge in the Spanish Netherlands. Vincent does not appear to have been very much involved in this unhappy affair but we can be sure he was on M. Duval's side. Had there not been a serious conflict between de Bérulle and Vincent it would be impossible to explain the former's bitter opposition to the Holy See's approval of the Congregation founded by his former disciple.

'Good M. Duval'

Vincent moved from de Bérulle's spiritual direction to that of Dr André Duval. It is very likely that he was influenced by both men for a short period. He looked to de Bérulle for guidance on the professional level, in matters concerning his works and occupations, but he followed Duval's advice more in matters of conscience. Duval was not as brilliant as de Bérulle but he was just as wise and he was certainly more impartial in his judgements and more

---

[20] J. CALVET, *op. cit.*, p. 240.
[21] *S.V.P.* XI, p. 62 and 139.

saintly. Vincent said of him, 'He was a great doctor of the Sorbonne but even greater for the holiness of his life.'[22] 'Good Dr Duval'—another of Vincent's favourite ways of describing him[23]—was outstanding for his devoted loyalty to the Holy See. He was, in the French sense of the word, an 'ultramontane'. At the insistence of Cardinal Barberini, later to become Urban VIII, whose friend he had been since Barberini's days as nuncio in Paris, he wrote a treatise on the authority of the Roman Pontiff.[24] This was to refute the anti-Roman propaganda of Richer. On a practical level, he laboured, though without too much success, to make the Sorbonne a focal centre of spirituality. He translated the *Flos sanctorum* of Père Rivadeneira and wrote the lives of French saints and the biography of Venerable Mother Mary of the Incarnation, the famous Mme Acarie. Until his death in 1638 he would be Vincent's unfailing counsellor. Vincent found Duval's teaching more to his liking—the idea that the unlearned will compete with the wise for entrance into heaven[25] and that they will be admitted appealed to him more than de Bérulle's notion that the shepherds of Bethlehem were unworthy to pay homage to the Word Incarnate because of their lowly condition. 'The honour he received from them could have been of little consequence. We might say that they came to gaze on the Son of God rather than pay him homage.'[26] Can we see here the root of some deep divison which will eventually cause the future apostle of poor country peasants to distance himself from de Bérulle?

'Since he was living in idleness he experienced great temptations against the faith'

But we have jumped too far ahead of events. In 1610 the friendship between de Bérulle and Vincent has just begun[27] and they have a very good relationship; so much so that we might perhaps say that de Bérulle is much more to Vincent than patron and counsellor; he is his novice master.[28] The

---

[22] *S.V.P.* XI, p. 154.

[23] *S.V.P.* XI, p. 100, 376.

[24] A. DUVAL, *De suprema Romani Pontificis in Ecclesiam potestate* (Paris 1614).

[25]. *S.V.P.* XI, p. 154.

[26] Referred to by J. ORCIBAL, in *Le cardinal de Bérulle ...*, p. 122. About Duval, *DTC*, IV, col. 1967.

[27] It is very difficult to fix the exact date of this meeting between Vincent and de Bérulle. According to Abelly (1.1 c. 5, p. 22) and Collet (*op. cit.*, Vol. 1, p. 26), it happened shortly after Vincent's arrival in Paris. It may not have been as early as that. The first time that we know for certain that de Bérulle came into Vincent's life was on the occasion when the judge from Sore lodged a complaint about the alleged theft. So we have to put the date of the meeting back to 1609 or 1610.

[28] P. DEFRENNES, *art. cit.*, p. 397.

first significant event to have a spiritual impact on Vincent was when he was accused of theft; the second major event that would decisively put him on the road to sanctity was his meeting with de Bérulle. The third and most important event was soon to follow. Sometime between 1611 and 1616, we cannot pinpoint the date more exactly, Vincent went through a very severe spiritual crisis. This was his desert journey or what the Carmelites would call 'his dark night of the soul'.

This is Abelly's account of what happened. One of Queen Marguerite's palace coterie was a famous doctor who had formerly held the office of canon theologian in his diocese and who was well-known for his eloquence and his zeal during the controversy with the Protestants. The idle life of the sinecure he held left him prey to grave temptations against the faith. These temptations became so violent that the poor man felt violent urges to blaspheme, he lost all hope of salvation and even felt driven to commit suicide by throwing himself out of the window. Just reciting the Our Father brought dreadful images to his mind. He had to be dispensed from saying the office and celebrating Mass. This man confided his troubles to Vincent de Paul whose advice was that when the temptation was at its worst, he should just point in the direction of Rome or the nearest church to indicate he believed all the teachings of the Roman Church.

The man was still in this state of mind when he fell seriously ill. Vincent was afraid he would yield to these temptations in the end and he asked God, if it were his will, to transfer the doctor's trials to his own soul. The doctor felt his darkness of spirit disappear immediately, he began to see the truths of faith with radiant clarity and he died with great spiritual peace and consolation.[29]

Then the trial began for Vincent. His soul was plunged into darkness. He found it impossible to make an act of faith. He felt all his childhood beliefs and certainties crumble around him. The only thing that helped him in this time of darkness was the conviction that this trial came from God and that eventually God would have pity of him. He redoubled his prayers and penances and took the most practical measures he could devise. The first of these was to write down the act of faith on a piece of paper and wear this over his heart. He made a pact with God that every time he put his hand to

---

[29] The account of the doctor's temptation is given by Vincent himself (*S.V.P.* XI, pp. 32-34), although he does not specifically say that he was the person involved. The detail of Vincent asking God to let him suffer the trial comes from Abelly who says that he has it on very good authority from somebody who did not know about Vincent's account. If this is the only available testimony then we have reason to doubt whether this happened. The actual temptation, however, as we go on to describe it, is not open to question (ABELLY, *op. cit.*, 1.1 Vol. 3, c. 11, pp. 116-119).

his heart he was resisting temptation even though he did not say a single word of the Creed. 'In this way', says Abelly with penetrating psychological intuition, 'he vanquished the devil without having to speak to him or to look at him.' The second remedy was to live out in practice what his confused state of mind prevented him from thinking about. He devoted himself to works of charity, visiting and consoling the sick in the St John of God hospital. The temptation lasted three or four years. He was finally delivered from it when, inspired by grace, he took the firm and irrevocable decision to devote his whole life to the service of the poor out of love for Our Lord Jesus Christ. 'Scarcely had he made up his mind to do this when the suggestions of the evil one vanished. His heart which had been oppressed for so long was now filled with sweet liberty and his soul inundated with a wonderful light that let him see all the truths of faith with perfect clarity.'

We would love to know more details about Vincent's spiritual journey during those three or four years. It is useless to speculate. Unlike other saints who have described their mystical experience in great detail, Vincent has left us no record of what took place. But everything points to the fact that this was the most crucial turning point in his life. His spirit was being slowly fashioned by this painful trial and he emerged from it purified and transformed. There would be other experiences and other graces during his life but the fundamental change had already taken place. He had found God, and found himself, even though his vocation had not as yet found expression in any particular way of life or in any specific activity. So he will go on groping blindly for a few years yet.

It would take many years for Vincent's radical conversion to come to maturity and blossom into a tree bearing much fruit, but one incident in 1611 would lead us to think that Vincent was already a changed man. On 20 October of that year Vincent entered into a legal contract by which he freely and voluntarily donated to the Hospital of Charity the sum of 15,000 *livres* which he had received the previous day from M. Jean de la Thane.[30] Was this a pure and disinterested act of charity or was he merely directing the alms to their intended destination? In either case Vincent was chosen to carry out this charitable act and this clearly shows that we are now dealing with someone very different from the insouciant debtor of Toulouse. The fact that he was still not completely cleared of the robbery charge had in no way undermined the confidence that his Parisian friends had in him. If they did not reckon him to be a saint at this time, they at least recognised him as a man of honour.

---

[30] *S.V.P.* XIII, pp. 14-16. Strangely enough, this M. de La Thane, director of the Royal Mint in Paris, was at this very time in conflict with de Bérulle because he (La Thane) refused to hand over to him (de Bérulle) the buildings of the Royal Mint conferred on de Bérulle by royal decree for the establishment of the Oratory (quoted from an article by DEFRENNES, p. 396).

Parish priest in a country district for the first time

Vincent's director, Fr de Bérulle, showed yet another mark of confidence in him. François Burgoing (1585-1662), who was about to become one of de Bérulle's first companions in the Oratorian Congregation, was at this time parish priest of the small country place called Clichy-La-Garonne, near Paris. In order to join the new community he had to give up his parish. De Bérulle thought that Vincent was the man to replace him. Burgoing finally withdrew from the parish on 13 October 1611,[31] and his resignation was accepted by the Holy See on 12 November. Vincent was no longer the inexperienced aspirant to the parish of Tilh; he knew it was important to leave no loose ends untied. On 2 May 1612, all the legal formalities had been complied with and he took up his appointment with all due ceremony. He went through the door of the church and the presbytery, sprinkled the church with holy water, knelt down and prayed in front of the crucifix and the high altar, kissed the missal, laid his hands on the tabernacle and the baptismal font, rang the church bells and took his seat in the parish priest's stall.[32] After twelve years he was, for the first time in his priestly life, taking responsibility for souls. He would continue this work for more than fourteen years but only for the first two years would this be his main concern. After that would come other tasks, and other demands would be made on him so that he would have to give up the direct service of people in this country parish, and leave the day to day running of the parish to a curate. Until such time as Vincent discovered the true direction of his life, Clichy would always be for him a safe and continual means of support and he kept this appointment in reserve for a very long time, as he was entitled to do by the customs and religious ordinances of these times.[33]

In 1612, Clichy was a fairly large parish. Parts of it are now incorporated into the VIII, IX, XVII and XVIII *arrondissements* of Paris. Few people lived there at that time—about six hundred souls, out of which number only three hundred would have been old enough to have made their first communion. In spite of its closeness to the capital, the inhabitants were humble peasants and simple folk like those Vincent had known in his native Pouy. The new parish priest devoted himself to the task with all the ardent zeal of a neophyte. He was still suffering the trial mentioned earlier but this only served to redouble his fervour. He was convinced that the root cause of the initial temptation was idleness and it was only by living a completely

---

[31] COLLET, *op. cit.*, Vol. 1, p. 36.

[32] *S.V.P.* XIII, pp. 17-18.

[33] COSTE, *M.V.* Vol., 1 pp. 77.

different way of life that he would eventually conquer the insidious temptation.

His activities were many and varied. The church was in bad condition and Vincent undertook to have it repaired. He furnished it and provided vestments as well as a new pulpit and a new baptismal font. He got the necessary funds from his friends in Paris. Vincent already had the gift of being able to inspire the rich to practise generosity towards the poor and this gift was to play an important part in his life. He himself did not hesitate to get into debt for the same noble motives. After six months in Clichy he had to attest before a notary a debt of 320 *livres*.[34]

'Happier than the pope'

He devoted himself with even greater zeal to the spiritual needs of his flock. His preaching was enthusiastic but, more importantly, it was persuasive. He visited the sick, consoled the afflicted, helped the poor, reproved wrong doers and encouraged the weak. It was a happy time for him and in old age he would look back on it with nostalgia.

> I was once parish priest in a certain village (a poor parish priest!). My people were so good and so obedient in doing everything I asked of them that when I told them to go to confession on the first Sunday of the month they did not fail to do so. They came to confession and every day I could see the spiritual progress they were making. This gave me such consolation and I felt so happy that I used to say to myself, 'My God, how happy I am to have these people in my care!' And I would add: 'I do not think even the pope can be as happy as a parish priest with such good-hearted people.' And one day Cardinal de Retz asked me, 'How are things going? How are you?' I told him, 'Monseigneur, I cannot explain how happy I am'. 'Why?' 'Because I have parishioners who are so good and so obedient in doing everything I ask them, that it seems to me that neither the Holy Father, nor you, Your Eminence, could be as happy as I am.[35]

Not only were they good people but they were musical.

---

[34] *S.V.P.* XIII, p. 19.
[35] *S.V.P.* IX, p. 646.

I must confess, to my shame, that when I was in a parish I did not know what to do. I used to listen to these country people intoning the psalms without a single wrong note. And I would say to myself, 'You are their spiritual father and you do not know anything about this.' It made me very sad.[36]

Vincent's activities in Clichy spread to neighbouring parishes whose priests were moved by his example. Once, when he had to go away for a short time, there was a letter from his curate begging him to return as soon as possible because all the priests and the citizens of the surrounding parishes wanted him back. A religious who was also a doctor of the Sorbonne was frequently invited by Vincent to preach and hear confessions in the parish, and this man said that the parishioners of the future founder of the Congregation of the Mission were like angels. Trying to instruct them, he fancied, was as vain a task as bringing light to the sun.[37]

Vincent started another initiative during his stay in Clichy. He gathered round him a small group of ten or eleven young men who wanted to become priests.[38] One of these was called Antoine Portail and he was twenty years old at this time. He is the first of Vincent's followers that we know by name. He was destined to be his constant collaborator; he would spend his whole life with Vincent and both were to die in the same year, within seven months of each other. Portail was the unwitting occasion for Vincent to practise another virtue, that of pardoning injuries. One day, for some unknown reason, good M. Portail was attacked by a group of men from the neighbouring town of Clignancourt. They set on him, struck him, and threw stones at him. The people of Clichy came out to defend the unfortunate young man and managed to lay hold on one of the attackers who was put into prison. Vincent intervened on his behalf with the local magistrate, and had the prisoner released.[39]

In a certain sense Clichy is the rough draft of Vincent's completed work. Even at this juncture his work in the parish includes, on a small scale, all the main features that will characterise the way his future missionary work will develop—his concern for the evangelisation of poor peasants, his motivating the powerful to help the needy, his charity, his work of instructing the clergy. As yet this is just a glimpse of the vague, sketchy outlines of his work but future events are already casting their shadow. To discover what his future work would be, and to accomplish this mission, Vincent had need

---

[36] *S.V.P.* XII, p. 339.
[37] ABELLY, *op. cit.*, 1.1 c. 6, p. 26.
[38] ABELLY, *ibid.*, p. 28.
[39] Brother Robineau's manuscript, p. 157.

of different horizons, a wider framework to work in, and a more specific call. Once again de Bérulle was to be the unwitting instrument of Providence. Towards the end of 1613 he invited Vincent to leave Clichy and become tutor to the de Gondis, one of the most illustrious families in France.

We can understand how sad the people of Clichy felt when he left their village. He did not leave them for good because he retained the incumbency of the parish till 1626, and from time to time he would go back there for a christening[40] or to be with his parishioners when the bishop made his pastoral visitation, as happened in 1624. Mgr Jean François de Gondi found everything in order; the liturgy was celebrated with dignity, catechism classes were held, the parish records were up to date, there was a good relationship between the parish priest and his curate, and the priests and people got on well together.[41]

Monsieur Vincent

The good people of Clichy always had happy memories of their best parish priest, Vincent de Paul, or as they familiarly called him, 'Monsieur Vincent'. He himself preferred to be called this, just as one might speak of Monsieur Pierre or Monsieur Antoine, explains Abelly.[42] This was his way of covering up the rather ostentatious 'de Paul' of his surname. And for the rest of his life he remained simply Monsieur Vincent. He was called this by the queen, Cardinal Mazarin, the priests of the Mission, the Daughters of Charity, the poor people of Châtillon, and by cardinals and bishops. Through over-use the name may now lack some of its original freshness and spontaneity but he is still known to us today as Monsieur Vincent.

---

[40] COSTE, *M.V.* Vol. 1, p. 77.
[41] *Annales* (1929), p. 729.
[42] ABELLY, *op. cit.*, 1.3 c. 13, p. 199.

Chapter VIII
THE DISCOVERY OF A VOCATION

A breed of captains

On de Bérulle's instructions, M. Vincent left his parish in Clichy towards the end of 1613 and settled with his few belongings in the Paris house of the de Gondi family, in the rue des Petits Champs in the parish of St. Eustache. This was the second time he was to live in a palace. This one was rather less luxurious than that of Queen Marguerite but it was still very grand. After all, the de Gondis were one of the leading families in the country and had inherited, along with their Florentine blood, a renaissance taste for luxury and refinement.

The first de Gondi to settle in France was Antonio. He was a banker by profession and his financial interests had brought him to Lyons at the beginning of the sixteenth century. In the city of Rodano he had married a noble lady of Piedmontese origin, Marie Cathérine de Pierre Vive. His business affairs did not flourish but the couple found other ways of making a fortune. When Cathérine de Medici had occasion to visit Lyons they managed to gain the sympathy of their royal compatriot. Antoine was appointed steward to the dauphin, Henry III, and Marie Catherine became governess to the royal children. It was rapid promotion.

Later on we will discuss their two sons' success. The elder son, Albert, became Marquis of Belle Isle and the Golden Islands, a peer and marshal of France, general-in-chief of the royal armed forces, General of the Galleys, governor of Provence, Metz, and Nantes and, through his marriage to Catherine de Clermont, Duke of Retz.

With his Florentine genius for intrigue, he was one of the chief instigators of the Massacre of St Bartholomew's Day and this massacre, in his opinion, should also have included the king of Navarre who later became Henry IV. This did not prevent him from becoming an ardent supporter of the Huguenot pretender and retaining all his titles and privileges when Henry became king.

In a different area, the Church, his brother Pierre had a career that was no less meteoric. At thirty-two years of age he was bishop of Langres, and at thirty five, bishop of Paris. Charles IX named him as his confessor and appointed him head of his council. Henry IV entrusted to his care the thorny problem of negotiating with Pope Clement VIII his pardon for heresy and, later on, the annulment of his marriage with Marguerite de Valois. In reward for his services he was made cardinal.

Albert de Gondi and Catherine de Clermont had four sons. Two of them, Henri and Jean François, succeeded in turn to their uncle Pierre's episcopal see in Paris. Henri, coadjutor bishop with right of succession from 1596, governed the diocese during the last eight years of his uncle's life and he succeeded him in 1616. This was the man to whom Vincent had said he was happier in his parish than the pope. He died of 'army fever' while he was accompanying King Louis XIII at Béziers. He, too, was a cardinal, the first Cardinal de Retz. Jean François had earlier joined the Capuchins. Then he became dean of Notre Dame and coadjutor to his brother, and was consecrated bishop in 1623. He did not become a cardinal but he did have the satisfaction of seeing his episcopal see raised from being suffragan diocese to Sens, to the status of archbishopric. So he was the first archbishop of Paris and he held this office for more than thirty years. We will refer to this man many times as our story unfolds.

Two of Albert de Gondi's daughters were religious in the abbey of Poissy. In this family noted for its intrigues and wranglings, another daughter was outstanding for her holiness. This was Charlotte de Gondi, better known as the Marquise de Maignelay through her marriage to Florimund d'Halwin. Left a widow at the age of twenty, she dedicated her life and her fortune to every kind of religious and charitable work.

The other two male children, who were the third generation of the French de Gondi family, were called Charles and Philippe Emmanuel. They both followed a military career. Charles succeeded his father as Duke of Retz and inherited other titles. He married Antoinette d'Orleans of the French royal house and lived a fairly peaceful existence. Philippe Emmanuel inherited the titles of General of the Galleys, Marquis of the Golden Isles, Count de Joigny and Baron de Montmirail, Dampierre and Villepreux. He was a gallant and distinguished gentleman, pleasant-mannered and resourceful. He was brave to the point of recklessness but basically he was an upright and sincerely pious man. In 1600 he married a lady from Folleville, Marguerite de Silly, who emulated her sister-in-law, Charlotte, in her piety and penances.

As well as owning the family castle of Montmirail and other country residences, the de Gondis had a house in Paris, first of all in the rue des Petits Champs, and later on in the rue Pavée. It was this house that Vincent de Paul came to in 1613 when he was at the height of his fortune. The de Gondis had asked Father de Bérulle for a priest because they needed a tutor for their children. De Bérulle could not release any of his companions from the small, infant community of Oratorians but he thought of Vincent. He knew that Vincent had been tutor to de Comet's sons when he was a young man and that he had earlier directed a boarding school in Toulouse. These facts weighed in Vincent's favour. It should not be difficult for the parish priest of Clichy to resume his former occupation. Vincent obeyed.

The General of the Galleys had two sons, Pierre who was twelve, and Henri who was then three. The elder boy, who inherited the family titles, succeeded his father as General of the Galleys. He liked meddling in politics and was always on the side of the opposition, first against Richelieu whose murder he plotted and then against Mazarín. The second son was destined for the Church but at the age of twelve he died after being thrown from his horse. A third offspring, destined to be the most illustrious son of the family, was born that same year, 1613, and was baptised on 20 September, just a few days before or after Vincent entered that household. He was given the names Jean François Paul, but history was to know him as Cardinal de Retz, the terrible Cardinal de Retz of the turbulent years of the Fronde, and the man whose scandalous memoirs are the most cynical testimony to the greatness and to the misery of a whole epoch.[1]

A flood of benefices

Vincent silently prepared to discharge his duties. Silently, because he still had to live with the spiritual trial that was tormenting him. Besides this, in 1615 a serious illness affected his legs and this made him withdraw from company even more. It was an illness that would trouble him all through his life.[2] This may be the reason that he lived in this house which was frequented by all manner of people, 'like a Carthusian, and his room was like a monastic cell.'[3] Grace continued its mysterious work of purification. The de Gondis were quick to recognise the worth of their discreet guest and they made great efforts on his behalf, heaping benefices upon him.

In 1614 they procured for him the parish of Gamaches in the diocese of Rouen. The right to nominate priests for this benefice was vested in the Count de Joigny.[4] In 1615 Vincent was made canon in charge of relics and

---

[1] Cf. J. CORBINELLI, *Histoire généalogique de la maison des Gondi* (Paris, J.-B. Coignard, 1705), 2 vols; RÉGIS DE CHANTELAUZE, *Saint Vincent de Paul et les Gondi* (Paris 1882), pp. 83-89.

[2] RISTRETTO, pp. 20-21; COLLET, *op. cit.*, Vol. 1, p. 46.

[3] ABELLY, *op. cit.*, 1.1 c. 7, p. 28.

[4] *M. et Ch.* 8 (1961), p. 495.

treasures in the collegiate church of Ecouis which was also under the patronage of Emmanuel de Gondi. It was probably for reasons of ill health that Vincent only took possession of this by proxy on 27 May. Four months later, on 18 September, he made his appearance at the collegiate church to swear his oath of allegiance and to receive the *osculum pacis* from his companions. The next day, in accordance with the customs of the collegiate chapter, he invited them to dine *pro suo iucundo adventu.*[5]

The benefices he had worked so hard to obtain over the past years were now being showered on him. By early 1616 the tutor to the de Gondi family was simultaneously parish priest of Clichy, abbot of Saint Laurent de Chaumes, parish priest of Gamaches and treasurer-canon of Ecouis. He had now achieved the career goals he had dreamed of all those years ago in Dax and Toulouse. If Vincent de Paul had been satisfied with these aims then that would have been an end to him as far as history was concerned. Fortunately, the decisive turning point he had reached some months earlier, was about to be ratified. Vincent may not have known St Teresa's witty dictum but he was soon to give the lie to her words 'They begin by wanting to be saints and they end up as canons.'

As regards the parish of Gamaches, we do not even know if he ever took possession of it. The only relevant document to be preserved is concerned with his appointment to the benefice. We know that he got rid of the abbey of Saint Laurent during the year 1616.[6] Still preserved are the canonical documents relating to Ecouis and these state he had to answer the charge of not residing in the parish, something 'which threatens to completely wreck the foundation.'[7] A letter from the General of the Galleys and another from the Duke de Retz, the general's brother and co-patron of the church, persuaded the canons to extend to a fortnight the time granted to M. 'de Paoul' (this is the first time we see this spelling of his surname) to justify his absence.[8] Lack of documentation prevents us from learning the outcome of the conflict. The fact that there is no further mention of the canonship of Ecouis leads us to suppose that Vincent eventually disposed of the honour.

Vincent's silent and self-imposed withdrawal did not prevent him from scrupulously carrying out his duties as chaplain and tutor. Obviously he would not be required to do anything for the new baby, Jean-Paul. He initiated the two elder boys into the mysteries of Latin and tried to inculcate in them high standards of Christian living. But this did not satisfy him. Like all their Italian and French ancestors, these passionate and high-born boys were less

---

5   *S.V.P.* XIII, pp. 19-22.
6   *S.V.P.* XIII, pp. 37-39.
7   *S.V.P.* XIII, pp. 22-24.
8   *S.V.P.* XIII, p. 25.

biddable than the humble provincial lads of Toulouse. Vincent came to experience a painful sense of failure. Basically, he felt that he was being idle, like the famous doctor in the household of Marguerite de Valois.

Vincent began to do things on his own initiative. His duties as chaplain obliged him to accompany the family as they moved around Joigny, Montmirail, Villepreux and other places that were part of their considerable estates. More and more Vincent devoted himself to looking after the spiritual needs of his master's servants and dependents. Within the household he would instruct the servants, visit them when they were ill, console them in their troubles and on the eve of solemn feasts would prepare them to receive the sacraments. When they went to country places he would instruct the peasants, preach to them, and exhort them to go to confession.[9]

We still have one of his letters, dated 1616, in which he asks the vicar general of Sens for permission to give absolution for 'reserved sins' because, 'sometimes you meet good people who would like to make a general confession and it makes you sad to see them go away' because of their reserved sins.[10] Little by little he was sounding the depths of the spiritual abandonment suffered by these poor country people. His loving heart was touched by so much misery. No other reason could explain the pity he felt for those who could not receive absolution. Unknown to himself, he was being prepared for the revelation of his mission. It is a pity that Abelly's vague estimate of 'three or four years' as the time that Vincent's temptations against faith lasted, does not allow us to pinpoint the exact moment when Vincent took the resolution to devote his life to the service of the poor and found himself delivered from the nightmare. This evidently coincides with the time he spent wandering about the de Gondi estates. It is not by chance that the first of his sermons to be preserved was that of 1616, and its theme was the importance of knowing the catechism well.[11]

From chaplain to director of conscience

Almost without realising it Vincent began to have an influence on his patrons, too. When he entered their service he had made up his mind to view this situation in a spirit of faith. He explains this on several occasions.

> When it pleased God to call me to the house of the General of
> the Galleys I looked on the general as somebody in the place

---

9   ABELLY, *op. cit.*, 1.1 c. 7, p. 28.
10 *S.V.P.* I, p. 20.
11 *S.V.P.* XIII, pp. 25-30.

of God, and his wife as being in the place of Our Lady. I do not remember ever receiving an order from the General of the Galleys without thinking that it came from God, or that it came from the Blessed Virgin if his wife requested it. By the grace of God, I do not know that I ever acted in any other way. I make bold to say that if God has been pleased to grant his blessing to the company of the Mission, I think this must be on account of the obedience I always showed to the general and his lady, and for the spirit of submission with which I entered his household. To God be the glory for all this, and to me confusion![12]

For once M. Vincent was not talking about his sins, but about his virtues, and this allows us to recognise the profound changes at work in his soul. It was not long before the situation was reversed. M. and Mme de Gondi began to look on their chaplain as a man sent by Providence, someone truly sent by God for the salvation of their family. It was the wife who first realised this. Marguerite de Silly was a troubled, complex soul. She was beautiful and she was delicate. Her fragile beauty was like that of the lady of Ghirlandaio and she was so pious that she told Father de Bérulle she would rather her sons be saints in heaven than great lords on earth.[13]

God, to her, was more of a judge than a father. She tormented herself, and her confessors too, with her unfounded scruples. Before Vincent had been two years in the house she thought of taking him as her spiritual director. When the chaplain resisted this suggestion she had recourse to de Bérulle and once more Vincent obeyed. He began to direct this soul with an energy that combined gentleness and respect. She wanted to keep him at her side always and was fearful that some accident or illness might carry him off. Vincent made her go to other confessors, especially a certain Recollect father who was a master in spiritual direction. He was gently trying to detach her from himself and teach her to be dependent only on God.[14] Using the remedy he had tried out on himself, he firmly pointed her in the direction of charitable works. He encouraged her natural generosity and almsgiving, trained her to visit the poor in person and to serve them with her own hands, and got her to ensure that her stewards administered justice fairly and without delay.[15] Even so, there would come a time when Vincent would feel obliged to go away so that he could be free of her, and also to help her overcome the

---

[12] *S.V.P.* IX, p. 9; X, p. 387.
[13] R. CHANTELAUZE, *op. cit.*, p. 85.
[14] ABELLY, *op. cit.*, 1.1 c. 9, pp. 36-37.
[15] ABELLY, *op. cit.*, 1.1 c. 8, p. 31.

excessive attachment she had for her director. But before this happened they would have made together the most important discovery of Vincent's life.

M. de Gondi was equally appreciative of his children's tutor but he was more reserved. Vincent won him over one day when, with an unusual display of independence, he dared to intervene in his affairs. M. de Gondi was about to fight a duel, something that was customary at that time. One of his relations had been killed and de Gondi felt himself responsible for avenging the family honour, so he challenged the killer who was a nobleman at Court. Before he left for the duel he wanted to fulfil his duty as a Christian gentleman and hear Mass. A strange piety that would try to make God act in accordance with human passions! Vincent was on hand to set things right. When Mass was over and the servants and the family had left, Vincent bent low before the master of the house who remained kneeling in the chapel for a few minutes.

'My lord', he said, 'allow me in all humility to tell you from God whom I have just held up before you and whom you have just adored, that if you do not turn away from this evil design he will pass judgement on you and on all your posterity.' Having said this, the chaplain withdrew.[16]

This courageous admonition had its effect. M. de Gondi gave up the duel. To calm his anger he set off for a tour of his estates. The aggressor was sentenced to exile.[17] Vincent had gained his lord's confidence.

In the eight years that had gone by since he first arrived in Paris, Vincent was a transformed character. He was now a man of distinction, in full possession of the rich resources of nature and of grace given him by God. He was eloquent and persuasive in speech, and was able to speak convincingly to men's minds and to move their hearts. These were *par excellence* the gifts of an apostle. With these qualities he had stifled the evil seed of vengeful hatred and murder in the heart of the general. He used these gifts to enlighten and console the poor country people who were prey to the same ills as their masters. With these gifts he channelled Mme de Gondi's morbid sensibilities towards charitable goals. He was now rid of the burden of his unworthy ambition for honours and comfortable benefices. He had widened his horizons to embrace the infinite. He was now ripe for the discovery of his vocation. God would soon reveal this to him.

Folleville: 'It was here that the first sermon of the Mission was preached'

The revelation came through one of those unforeseen events by which Vincent was to develop spiritually and discover the will of God. Providence worked

---

[16] *S.V.P.* XI, p. 28.
[17] COSTE, *M.V.* Vol. 1, p. 84.

in the guise of fate.

One day in January 1617, we find Vincent accompanying Mme de Gondi to her castle in Folleville, in Picardy. From nearby Gannes, two leagues away, came the news that a dying peasant wished to see M. Vincent. Immediately he hurried to the sick man's bedside. In that humble dwelling he sat down by the sick man's bed to hear his confession. He urged the man to make a general confession of all the sins of his life. The peasant began to recite the sad rosary of his sins. It was worse than Vincent expected.

The man had a reputation for being honourable and virtuous but buried in his conscience were burdens that he had never revealed. Year after year, and confession after confession, he had kept silent—through ignorance, shame or hypocrisy—about the most serious sins he had committed. Vincent had the feeling that in a final moment of grace he was dragging a soul from the clutches of the devil. The peasant felt the same. Remorse for a whole lifetime of sin lifted the guilt from his soul. He felt liberated. If it had not been for that general confession he would have been damned for eternity. He was filled with unrestrainable joy. He had his family brought to his home, together with the neighbours and Mme de Gondi herself. He told them his story. In the three days left before he died, he publicly confessed the sins which previously he had not dared to reveal even in secret. He gave thanks to God who had saved him through that general confession. Mme de Gondi trembled in terror:

> M. Vincent, what is this we have just heard? The same thing
> must be happening with most of these people. If this man who
> was supposed to be good was near to damnation, what will
> happen to the rest of them who lead such bad lives? Oh, M.
> Vincent, how many souls are going to be lost! What can we do
> about it?[18]

By common consent Vincent and the lady found a solution. The following week Vincent would preach in the church at Folleville on the subject of how to make a good general confession. He chose to do this on Wednesday 25 January, the feast of the conversion of St Paul. Vincent went up into the pulpit. In front of him were humble country folk as found in every corner of France. He saw men similar to those he had known in his distant country home of Pouy—men whose crushing labours had made them brutish. He saw a similar type of women who were both ignorant and pious. Similar young men and similar children whose faces were still innocent but whose eyes already reflected the secret bite of the serpent. Vincent had nothing but

---

[18] *S.V.P.* XI, p. 4.

his words; his words and a burning compassion for these abandoned brothers of his.

This sermon was powerful and easily understood. He instructed them, he moved their hearts and encouraged them. 'God was pleased to bless my words,' he says simply, and attributes their success to madame's faith and trust, saying that his own sins would have rendered the sermon fruitless.

> The people, that poor good people, came to confession in droves. Vincent and his assistant priest could not cope. They would have to ask the Jesuits of Amiens to help. Mme de Gondi undertook to arrange this. The rector himself came and was later replaced by one of his companions, Fr Fourché. Even so, they were swamped by the number of penitents. They repeated the sermon and exhortations in the neighbouring villages and always had the same resounding success.[19]

It was a revelation. Vincent decided this must be his mission; this was what God was calling him to, he was to take the gospel to these poor country people. He did not found any congregation that day. Perhaps the idea of forming one never entered his head. He just preached a sermon, 'the first sermon of the Mission'.[20] Eight years were to pass before he set up the Congregation of the Mission and yet throughout his life he would have his missioners celebrate 25 January as the birthday of the company.

Vincent used to tell the story of that mission over and over again, with some variations in the telling. In the second version dated 25 January 1655, and still preserved, Vincent discloses another fact that he had not dared to mention earlier because some of the people concerned were still alive. We will leave him to tell the story.

> One day, while she was still a young girl, the wife of the General of the Galleys went to confession to her parish priest. She realised that he was not giving her absolution but was murmuring something between his teeth and that he did this on other occasions when she went to confession. This worried her somewhat, so one day she asked a religious who was visiting her if he would write down for her the formula for absolution. He did this and that good lady, when she went to

---

[19] *S.V.P.* XI, pp. 2-5; ABELLY, *op. cit.*, 1.1 c. 8, p. 31-35; COLLET, *op. cit.*, Vol. 1, pp. 46-48.
[20] *S.V.P.* XI, p. 5.

confession the next time, asked the aforementioned parish priest to pronounce over her the words that were written on the paper. He read them aloud. She continued to do this every time she went to confession to him, handing him that piece of paper because he was so ignorant he did not know the words he should have been saying. When she told me this I took note of it and I paid more attention to the priests who heard my confession. I discovered that all this was true and that some of them did not know the words of absolution.[21]

We now see Vincent in possession of two basic elements of his profound religious experience—the spiritual misery of a Christian people without the gospel, and the frightening lack of training for the clergy who were ignorant of even the most elementary rules for the exercise of their ministry. These were two evils vigorously denounced by the Council of Trent which suggested catechetical work should be undertaken and centres set up for the training of priests. As we have seen, France had only come to accept the Tridentine decrees in 1615. From the year 1609, or the following year, Vincent had had close ties with those groups of people most committed to reforming the Church along conciliar lines. He had generously worked at his own personal renewal. Providence was pointing out to him the great collective task that was coming along. He was happy to take it on. The events that followed would complete the revelation just made to him, and clarify the third, and perhaps the most important aspect of that revelation, his own vocation.

---

[21] *S.V.P.* XI, p. 170.

Chapter IX
THE INITIAL RESPONSE, CHATILLON-LES-DOMBES

The gilded cage

The day after that marvellous experience at Folleville, Vincent began to reflect on his own personal response to God's call, a call he had so unmistakably heard in the faltering voice of the dying man at Gannes and in the hundreds of whispers from anonymous voices behind the grille of the confessional. He still felt ill at ease in his work as tutor to the children of the General of the Galleys, and had come to the conclusion that he was not cut out to be a teacher. Everything he tried to do was frustrated by the example given to the boys by their shallow and often insensitive compatriots and kinsfolk.[1]

The general's wife was harassing him with her continual scruples, her tormented religiosity and her cloying, self-centred devotion. Perhaps he could see in this something even more dangerous, though it was hidden under a sincere preoccupation with spiritual matters. Does not Abelly imply something of the kind when he explains the reasons why Vincent left the de Gondi household? Let us listen to his words:

> The general's wife had such an exaggerated regard for M. Vincent and put so much trust in him that she began to fear she might lose him. How could anyone replace this man so filled with grace and enlightenment that he could give her peace of conscience, soothe her spiritual pains and direct her in the path of true and solid virtue? Her fears increased to the point where she could hardly bear him to be absent, and when Vincent's affairs made it necessary for him to go on some journey she was always anxious and afraid lest the heat or some other accident might make him ill or cause him discomfort.[2]

---

[1] *S.V.P.* I, p. 21.
[2] ABELLY, *op. cit.*, 1.1 c. 9, p. 36.

The de Gondi family's deep involvement in public affairs made the general picture even more sombre. Coinciding once again with the main stages in Vincent's life, the year 1617 signalled a new era in the history of France. It marked the time when Louis XIII effectively took over the government of the kingdom, having been declared of age three years earlier. The year is marked by a bloody coup d'état; the assassination of the queen mother's favourite, Concino Concini, who had been the real usurper of royal power.

The plot was hatched in the young monarch's cabinet by his favourite, Albert Luynes, and the assassination carried out on 24 April 1617, on the drawbridge of the Louvre by Baron de Vitry, Commander of the Bodyguard. Immediately after the murder, the king made it clear that he wanted to direct the nation's affairs himself. The queen mother lost control of the kingdom and was banished to Blois, and Concini's wife, Leonora Galigai, was tried for witchcraft, condemned to death and executed on 8 July. The ex-regent's ministers were dismissed and among these was the then little-known bishop of Luçon, Armand du Plessis, who was later to become the all-powerful Cardinal Richelieu. Surprisingly, he was allowed to accompany Marie de Medici into exile at Blois as head of her council. Ministers who had held office under Henry IV were reinstated.[3]

Paris then witnessed the sort of violence that usually accompanies political change. The mob sacked the homes of Marshal d'Ancre, his friends and accomplices, but in spite of their Italian origin the de Gondi family was not attacked. The de Gondis do not appear to have taken any part in these tragic events. The general retained his important post with the royal fleet and on more than one occasion the bishop of Paris acted as impartial mediator between the queen mother and her son. We can be certain, however, that very disturbing rumours found their way into the household. Collet leads us to believe that Vincent felt deeply upset by these violent events[4] and his anxiety on this score was yet another reason for leaving the capital.

Testing out a response

What Vincent had been contemplating ever since 25 January was not, in fact, an escape, but rather a response to a call. He had discovered his vocation and he realised he was not called to stay with the de Gondis, looking after their unruly young sons and directing a rather neurotic lady who would

---

[3] P. CHEVALLIER, *Louis XIII,* pp. 133-208; V. L. TAPIÉ, *La France de Louis XIII et de Richelieu,* pp. 11-12.

[4] COLLET, *op. cit.*, Vol. 1, p. 52.

have liked to monopolise him. The people were calling, the poor, simple country folk. Clichy was not the answer because it was too near Paris and it might be argued that he could attend to those people and still live with the de Gondis. He put his ideas and plans before Father de Bérulle, who according to Abelly 'did not oppose them.'[5] We should note the nuance here. The young priest was beginning to distance himself from his former spiritual guide and was about to go his own way. De Bérulle found out from the Oratorian Fathers at Lyons that Châtillon-les-Dombes, a parish in that diocese, was vacant and that they were looking for an able and zealous pastor. He offered the post to Vincent who set off immediately for his new destination. He made the excuse that he needed to go away for a little while on urgent business and did not let the de Gondis know his real intentions. It was Lent 1617.[6]

Châtillon-les-Dombes, which today is called Châtillon-sur-Chalaronne, had been incorporated into France only seventeen years before Vincent arrived there. By the Treaty of Lyons, 1601, the two kingdoms of France and Savoy had exchanged the territories of Saluzzo and Bresse. Being a frontier town, Châtillon had been pillaged by both armies on far too many occasions. Its proximity to Geneva meant it was tainted with Calvinism and some of the leading families followed the new religion. The church was in a fairly good state of repair, as were the vestments and sacred vessels, according to the bishop of Lyons[7] after his canonical visitation in 1614, but the spiritual situation was deplorable.

The small hospital and the presbytery were practically in ruins. The town had six chaplains whose lives were far from exemplary. They frequented taverns and gaming places, took money for hearing confessions, obliged children to make a public confession in front of their friends, and some of these chaplains had women of doubtful repute in their houses. The rest of the

---

[5] ABELLY, *op. cit.*, 1.1 c. 9, p. 37.

[6] Enquiries made among the people of Châtillon in 1665 confirm this. Coste agrees with this date because Vincent took possession of the parish on 1 August. Vincent's many activities in Châtillon make it hard for us to believe that all this work was accomplished in less than five months, since, as we shall see later on, Vincent left Châtillon in the middle of December. It was common practice for a parish priest to take up his duties even before he was officially installed. This happened with Vincent's successor in Châtillon. After careful consideration we would be inclined to agree with the date suggested by the enquiry, namely, March or April 1617.

It is the second report on Vincent's activities in that parish and is signed by Charles Demia, the parish priest, and by leading parishioners. It was published in *S.V.P.* XIII, p. 45-54. The results of the first enquiry, dated 1664, are not available to us today but Abelly and Collet consulted these.

[7] COSTE, *M.V.* Vol. 1, p. 94.

inhabitants followed the clergy's example. The Huguenots lived licentiously and this was approved and encouraged by their own ministers. The lax morals of Catholics gave the lie to the faith they professed. Vincent had a daunting task ahead. He looked round for help and found a good priest from Bresse who was a doctor in theology. Louis Girard agreed to be Vincent's assistant. So Vincent set to work.

Reforming the clergy

First of all he set an example. When he arrived in the town he was advised by Fr Bence, superior of the Oratory in Lyon, to take lodgings with one of the leading Protestant families, so he stayed with a wealthy young man called Jean Beynier. Vincent would not allow any women, even his host's sister-in-law, to enter his room under any pretext whatsoever but tidied it, himself, every day. He would rise at five o'clock and, together with his companion, would make half an hour's meditation. Then he would say Mass and visit his parishioners. Vincent wore a hair shirt and was always dressed in a long cassock. His example and his words were contagious. Won over by Vincent, the six chaplains renounced their sinful ways and came to live together as a community. Vincent was more than ever convinced that the clergy had to be reformed before the people could be converted.

Converting heretics

Of course he did not wait for the clergy to be reformed before he started to change people. His zeal was directed at Catholics and Protestants alike, and he was soon successful in dealing with both. His host, M. Beynier, changed first of all his life-style and then his religion. Vincent left to others the honour of accepting his formal disavowal of heresy. Seven of Beynier's nephews and nieces, surnamed Garron, were converted in their turn and became reconciled with the Church. The head of the family could not be persuaded, however. Jacques Garron, an old man who had once been an officer in the Duke of Montpensier's Guards, remained unmoved. Not only did he refuse to become a Catholic but he denounced Vincent before the joint tribunal of Grenoble. These joint tribunals had been set up after the Edict of Nantes to hear cases brought by litigants of different religions. Half their members were Catholics and half were Huguenots. It was a similar tribunal that adjudicated in the case of the old lady of Castres who left her fortune to Vincent. The old man's case was dismissed. The young Garrons persevered in their new faith. One of them became a Capuchin and one of the girls entered a convent. They all rivalled each other in using their wealth to serve the needy. The old father died of grief and neither his sons nor Vincent had the consolation of witnessing a change of heart.

Combating lax morals

The new parish priest was equally successful in his work with Catholics. As at Clichy and Folleville, the liturgy was celebrated with dignity and the office recited with due attention. To this was added Vincent's eloquent and passionate preaching. His style was direct and almost commonplace, but his words were full of love and conviction and his hearers found this disarming. Vincent learned the local dialect, Bressain, so as to have closer links with the people and he was soon able to teach the children their catechism in this language. One of these children would later recall how the zealous parish priest would never let a day go by without reminding them of their duty to give alms.

He was a tireless preacher. For the most important feasts he invited the Jesuits from Lyons and religious from other orders to speak. He spent long hours in the confessional and visited his parishioners in their homes every morning and evening. The people were astonished at such tireless activity and his pure, ardent zeal for souls. They began to look on him as a saint and Châtillon may have been the first place where people thought he would one day be canonised. Even lapsed Catholics felt drawn to him.

Two young ladies who were members of high society (the 'high society' of that remote provincial place) had gained quite a reputation for their frivolity and flirtations. Françoise Baschet de Mayseriat, mistress of Chaissagne and Charlotte de Brie, mistress of Brunand, filled their days with dancing, parties and amusements. As they listened to the first public sermon given by their new parish priest their hearts were moved by his impassioned words. They visited him in private and Vincent spoke to them so vehemently but so graciously that they were won over. They gave up the diversions of their dissipated, pleasure-seeking way of life and became, instead, the parish priest's collaborators.

More remarkable still was the conversion of a nobleman, the Count of Rougemont. This gentleman from Savoy had been serving under Henry IV when his estates in Bresse were annexed to the French crown. He was known for his quarrelsome nature and was famed for his swordsmanship. He liked nothing better than fighting a duel. A tall man, he was strong and agile, and this was a great advantage when he used his sword. His opponents could certainly expect to be speedily dispatched. Nobody could count the number of people he had wounded, mutilated or killed.

He was intrigued by Vincent's reputation and went to see him. The parish priest's words (once again it was his words) were like a two-edged sword that pierced his very soul. His conversion was as swift as any of his rapier thrusts and no less spectacular. He sold his estates in Rougemont for 30,000 *écus* (90,000 *livres!*) and gave the money to found monasteries and to help the poor. He also wanted to dispose of his castle in Chandée but Vincent would not allow this. He got his own back by turning the castle into a religious guest house and a hospice-refuge for the sick and for beggars. These he served with his own hands. He also paid the clergy to see to their spiritual needs. He was distressed when his spiritual director would not allow him to dispose of all his possessions.

'I do not understand', he would say, 'how a Christian can possess anything of his own when the Son of Man was so poor when he was on earth.' He obtained permission from the archbishop of Lyons to have the Blessed Sacrament reserved in the chapel of his castle. He would spend long hours there, meditating on Christ's passion. He wanted to know how many strokes of the lash Our Lord had received at his scourging so that he could give the equivalent amount of alms to the Oratorians. One day he asked himself if he still felt any inordinate attachment to anything. He mentioned this to M. Vincent who spoke about it, years later, to the priests of the Mission. Let him tell the story.

> He called to mind his business affairs, his wealth, his friends, his reputation, his rank, his innocent pleasures. He ponders, reflects and meditates and finally the answer comes to him— his sword! 'Why do you wear that sword?' he asked himself. 'Could you manage without it? What! Give up this sword which has served me so well on numerous occasions and which, after God, has delivered me from so many dangers! I would be lost without it if somebody were to attack me. But it is also possible that somebody could insult you, and if you had your sword you would not be strong-minded enough to refrain from using it and then you would offend God. Oh my God, what am I to do? Can I let my heart be ensnared by this instrument of my shame and of my sin? There is nothing more precious to me than this sword; it would be cowardly of me not to be detached from it.' Just then he saw a boulder. He got off his horse and whiz, bang, wham! He ended up breaking the sword into bits and went on his way. He told me that this act of detachment was like breaking an iron chain that held him prisoner, and it left him with such a feeling of freedom that in spite of the heartache, for he really loved that sword, never

afterwards did he have any affection for earthly things. He desired God alone.[8]

Imaginative Charity

Something else was needed before Vincent could understand the special requirements of the Mission that providence had destined for him. He was to discover what this was at Châtillon. One Sunday, while he was vesting for Mass, the mistress of Chaissagne came to the sacristy to tell him that on the outskirts of the town there was a family in desperate need. The whole family was ill and there was nobody to help them. They had neither food nor medicine.

The good priest's heart ached at the news. He gave a very moving homily to the parishioners about this distressed family. His compassion proved contagious or, as he would say, 'God touched the hearts of his listeners.'

After vespers that evening, Vincent set off to visit the unfortunate family, accompanied by a good man of the town. To his great surprise, he met on the way a crowd of people on that same charitable errand. It was a hot day (probably 20 August) so many of these people sat down by the roadside to have a rest and something to drink. It was just like a pilgrimage. When Vincent arrived he saw for himself the family's extreme poverty and he administered the sacraments to those were most seriously ill. Vincent also saw the great pile of provisions that the parishioners had left and this made him think. Yet another event and another sign from providence had just pointed out the path he was to follow. 'These poor people', he mused to himself, 'have suddenly got more food than they need. Some of it will go bad and then tomorrow they will be just as badly off. This charitable work is very haphazard.'[9] What was needed was organisation.

Three days later, on Wednesday 23 August, Vincent put his plan into action. He called a meeting of the pious ladies in the town and these included, of course, Françoise Baschet and Charlotte de Brie. He urged them to start up an association to help the poor sick people of the area.[10] They undertook to begin this good work the next day. It would be carried out on a rota basis, according to the date that members joined, and it would be headed by the chatelaine of the district.

> No good work of importance can fail to succeed if the Mother of God is invoked, so these ladies (states the record of this meeting) took her as patron and protectress of the enterprise.[11]

---

[8] *S.V.P.* XII, pp. 231-232.

[9] ABELLY, *op. cit.*, 1.1 c. 11, p. 46.

[10] *S.V.P.* XIV, p. 125.

[11] *Ibid.*

The first charity association was born. Later on, the association would have to function and develop according to canonical statutes. They did not have long to wait before this happened because Vincent acted promptly. It was three months later, on 24 November, that the vicar general of Lyons gave formal approval to the rules of the association which now became a confraternity.[12] The constitutions of this confraternity were issued on 8 December, Feast of the Immaculate Conception, during a solemn ceremony in the hospital chapel and many people witnessed this public act.[13] The new confraternity had twelve members and Françoise Baschet, mistress of Chaissagne, and Charlotte de Brie, mistress of Brunand, were elected prioress and treasurer, respectively. After this, Vincent had no hesitation in launching into charitable works all the people who came under his spiritual leadership.

The first rules

The rules of the Châtillon charity reveal something of Vincent's greatheartedness when, at the age of thirty-seven, he reaches full maturity. In this nascent apostle of charity, moulded by his experiences at Folleville and Châtillon, we see something of the man's heart and also his talent for organising, because with Vincent, the impulse to act was always moderated by careful planning.

Everything was worked out in detail, from the spirit and aims of the association to the procedures for electing officers; from the spirituality that animated its members to the manner in which they were to serve the poor. Vincent admits to taking his inspiration from the Hospital of Charity in Rome. It was his life-long policy to profit from all his experiences and to build on these, but the substance and the form of the charity's rules are written in a sort of lyrical prose that is special to Vincent.

His main concern was that the sick should be cared for and so all the ladies were to be servants of the poor. They were to work on a daily rota so that there would be no gaps in the service, neither would there be too many helpers. They were to be careful to attend to the spiritual and material needs of these poor people, to distribute food, clothes and medicine, but they were also to invite the sick to go to confession and holy communion. When they visited anyone for the first time they were to take them a white shift and, if necessary, some sheets. They would also take a crucifix and

[12] *S.V.P.* XIII, pp. 423-437.
[13] *S.V.P.* XIII, pp. 437-438.

place it where it could be seen by the sick person and they would provide any basic furniture.

Vincent's sensitivity and far-sightedness shine through the whole text but they are especially evident in his rules for the corporal service of the sick.

> The one whose turn it is will prepare the food and take it to the sick. When she gets there she will greet the sick person cheerfully and in a charitable manner; she will put a little table near the bed and on it place a serviette, a bowl and a spoon; she will wash the sick person's hands and say grace. Then she will pour the soup into the bowl, arrange everything carefully on the bedside table, and charitably invite the person to eat for the love of Jesus and his holy Mother. She will do everything with love, as though she were serving her own son, or rather serving God who takes as done to himself the good that is done to the poor. If necessary she will cut up their meat and pour their drink into a glass. [While doing this] she will say a few words to them about Our Lord, trying to console those who are most distressed.[14]

This page of the text is an admirable description of Christian courtesy and charity. The rules also deal with the menu for these sick people as we see in the following recommendations. These might appear somewhat strange to our eyes but they were in keeping with the customs of those days.

> Each sick person will have all the bread they need, together with a quarter of a pound of cooked veal for the mid-day meal and the same quantity roasted for supper, except on Sundays and feast days when they can have chicken. Two or three times a week they will have mince for supper. If they do not have a temperature they can have a quart of wine each day, half to be given in the morning and half in the evening. For their mid-day meal on Fridays and other days of abstinence they can have soup, a couple of eggs and some butter. They will have the same for their supper and can have their eggs cooked any way they want. If fish can be bought at a reasonable price they may have it, but only for supper.[15]

---

[14] *S.V.P.* XIII, pp. 427-428.
[15] *S.V.P.* XIII, p. 428.

The rule ends by reminding the members of the association. 'They will perform all their actions purely out of love for the poor and not from any motive of human respect.'

The Mission and the Charity Confraternities: their objectives

Saint Vincent was to repeat many times during his life, 'The poor country people are dying of hunger, and they risk damnation.' These words sum up Vincent's frequent meditation on his experience at Folleville and Châtillon, the two major events in his life which opened his eyes to the spiritual and material poverty of the peasants. The response to these needs will be his two great works, the Mission and the Charity. These are really one single work because the Mission includes Charity and Charity includes the Mission. Both organisations sprang from the same basic experience, the needs of a people who were abandoned, humiliated, and exploited, a people who were slaves to the greed of wealthy men and beasts of burden in a society based on privilege. They reflected the sombre reverse picture of that century's glory, luxury and brilliance.

These people knew hunger and poverty but they also suffered from spiritual abandonment because their pastors were so ignorant. Moreover, they had become enslaved to their passions, and this meagre compensation for so many privations put at risk their eternal salvation. In 1617 Vincent can at last view the situation clearly. He now knows what the Lord is asking of him as a priest, and this in spite of all the twists and turns of his past misguided calculations. When he hid himself away in Châtillon he thought that he was giving the appropriate answer. This time, he was wrong again. Buried in the far-off plains of Bresse, he might also have been a saint there, a saint like the Curé d'Ars or one in those traditional medieval saints renowned for their almsgiving. But his vocation was meant to span wider horizons, and the unwitting instrument of providence to arrange this was Mme de Gondi. We have her to thank for it.

A desperate struggle

The surreptitious departure of their chaplain brought consternation to the de Gondi household. His short journey was lasting too long. Where could M. Vincent have put himself? Could he have abandoned them altogether? In the middle of September, a letter from Vincent to the General of the Galleys who was in Provence at the time because of some duties, confirmed their worst fears. In the letter Vincent begged the general to accept his resignation since he had neither the grace nor the aptitude for teaching his sons. He had said nothing of this to Mme de Gondi or to anyone in the house but he had no intention of returning.[16] The general wrote to his wife:

> I am desperate after reading M. Vincent's letter which I am sending on to you to see if there is any way we could still prevent the misfortune of losing him. I am greatly astonished that he said nothing to us about what he intended to do ... I beg you to do everything in your power to prevent him from leaving. Even if he is right in saying that he is not qualified to teach the youngsters [the original letter refers to teaching methods—this is the era of Descartes] he could always have an assistant to do that. Anyway, I am most anxious for him to return to my house. He can live his own life but with him at my side I trust that one day I may become a virtuous man.[17]

If that was the general's reaction, one can easily imagine how his wife felt. Her desolation knew no bounds. She wept continually and could neither eat nor sleep.

> 'I never thought M. Vincent could do such a thing', she exclaimed, 'he had too much charity for my soul to abandon me like this. Blessed be God! I am not blaming him for anything. I am sure he has acted out of pure love of God and in accordance with God's special designs for him.'[18]

In her own way, the general's wife was too practical a woman to do no more than lament her misfortune. She began by consulting Father de Bérulle who assured her he would do everything he could to make Vincent return, though he recognised that Vincent had acted from the highest motives. The sorrowful lady did not need to be told twice. She wasted no time in starting her campaign. She moved heaven and earth. She enlisted the help of anyone who might be able to influence Vincent, though she recognised that her chaplain was not a man to do things by halves, and that before he left he would have anticipated anything she might say or do. She bombarded him with a shower of letters—letters from herself, her sons, Cardinal de Retz, all her relatives, the chief officials in her household, de Bérulle, doctors, religious

---

[16] ABELLY, *op. cit.*, 1.1 c. 9, p. 38.
[17] *Ibid.*, p. 39.
[18] *Ibid.*

and other important and pious people. Only one letter, written by Mme de Gondi, has been preserved and we have to admit that it is a model of religious sentiment, diplomacy and female perspicacity.

> I had every reason to fear that I would lose your help. I have said this so many times and now it has happened. I would not be able to bear the anxiety of it were it not for a special grace from God which I do not deserve.

She refers to what has happened and then appeals to his charity, believing this to be the most persuasive argument for his return.

> I beg God and the Blessed Virgin to send you back to our house for the salvation of our family and that of many others who would benefit from your charity. I beg you to show that charity to us.

She does not stop at blackmail either, even though it is spiritual blackmail:

> 'If, in spite of everything, you refuse me this request, I will hold you responsible before God for anything that happens to me and will charge you with all the good works I neglect to do without your help'. 'I know that my life is not important since it serves only to offend God, but when I am dying my soul will need your assistance.'[19]

Father de Bérulle was more discreet. He contented himself with telling Vincent about Mme. de Gondi's despair and how anxious the general was to have him back in his household. He left it to Vincent's prudence to decide what course of action he should take.[20] De Bérulle realises, perhaps, that he is no longer directing Vincent who has begun to follow his own path and act on his own initiative.

In a final attempt to overcome Vincent's resistance, Mme de Gondi sent a personal representative to Châtillon. For this mission she chose an intimate friend of Vincent, M. du Fresne, who had previously been his companion in the household of Marguerite de Valois and had taken service with the de Gondis on Vincent's recommendation. Vincent's determination began to waver. He agreed to go to Lyons and consult Fr Bence, the superior

---

[19] *S.V.P.* I, pp. 21-22.
[20] ABELLY, *op. cit.*, 1.1 c. 10, pp. 43-44.

of the Oratory. At this priest's suggestion, he then decided to go to Paris and seek the advice of people who knew him well and would be best able to help him discern the will of God. Vincent confided his plans to the general and to du Fresne who was overjoyed at the news.[21] Nobody doubted that if Vincent left Châtillon it would be forever. Leave he certainly would, but who was he leaving for?

Defeat or victory?

Vincent said goodbye to the faithful in Châtillon about the middle of December. He assured them that when he first came to the town he had intended to spend the rest of his life there, but this was not God's will and he had to obey. It was a moving farewell. Vincent shared his clothing and even his linen among the poor. The people burst into tears and loudly expressed their sorrow.[22] A poor man named Julien Caron had to fight tooth and nail to protect a hat given him by Vincent and which other people wanted to carry off as a relic. For a good part of the journey the whole town followed the carriage that was taking Vincent away from Châtillon. From the carriage window Vincent commended them to God and gave them his final blessing.[23] The carriage went tottering on its way through the bleak, wintry countryside. The people of Châtillon raised their hands in a last gesture of farewell. They had lost the man who, in less than six months, had transformed their town. They would never forget him.

The seed that Vincent had sown flourished in his absence and bore much fruit. Shortly after his return to Paris, the spectre of famine afflicted Châtillon and the surrounding districts, as it was to do on so many occasions. M. Beynier, and the ladies of Charity headed by the once coquettish Mme de Chaissagne and Mme de Brunand, put into practice the teachings of the founder of the confraternity and devoted themselves, with exemplary selflessness, to the service of those poor, starving people. They hired a barn and put into it a part of their own harvest. Then they launched a charity appeal among the comfortably-off neighbours at Châtillon and the surrounding districts. They distributed food to the needy with their own hands. Shortly after this came the plague, the second apocalyptic horseman of that violent century. They repeated their wonderful work. The two generous ladies, with the support of their fellow members, took up residence in some rustic cabins

---

[21] *Ibid.*

[22] *S.V.P.* XIII, p. 53.

[23] COLLET, *op. cit.*, Vol. 1, p. 84.

they had had specially made for them on the outskirts of the town. Here they set up the general headquarters of the Charity, prepared food for the starving, and medicines for the sick. Faithful and brave hands carried these to houses where people were struck down with plague.[24] The Confraternity proved to be very efficient and the solid principles on which it was founded were clearly evident. So it is not surprising that thirty years later it was still flourishing, and people would remember with affection the parish priest who was with them such a short time. In 1646, M. Vincent received this striking letter which must have filled him with nostalgia.

> I am one of your sons in Jesus Christ and I have recourse to your fatherly kindness which I have experienced several times already. I was reborn into the Church after you publicly absolved me from heresy in the church of Chatillon-les-Dombes in 1617, and I learnt from you the principles and beautiful maxims of the Catholic, apostolic and Roman faith. By the grace of God I have persevered in this, and hope to do so for the rest of my life. I am that little Jean Garron, the nephew of M. Beynier at Chatillon, in whose house you stayed while you were there.
>
> I beg you to give me the help I need so as not to do anything contrary to the designs of God. My only son has decided to become a Jesuit when he has completed his studies. He is the most gifted young man in this province. What do you think I should do? I am hesitating for two reasons ... I am afraid of doing the wrong thing and also I thought you might do me the favour of giving me your advice which I beg most humbly. I think you will be pleased to know that the charitable association of servants of the poor is still flourishing.[25]

Of course M. Vincent was delighted to learn this. Was not the confraternity at Châtillon the first blossoming shoot from that tree of charity which by this time had put down solid roots everywhere on French soil? Châtillon with its haughty nobility, its 'precious' and frivolous ladies, its ignorant and lazy clergy, its selfish merchants, its hungry and ignorant peasants, was a microcosm of French society and of the whole Church in France which sorely needed the leaven of apostolic charity. So we can say that Vincent's

---

[24] COLLET, *op. cit.*, Vol. 1, pp. 65-66.
[25] *S.V.P.* III, p. 29.

escape from Châtillon was something more than mere flight. Châtillon had been the first rehearsal, a full dress rehearsal, for all Vincent's work. The show was ready to start immediately.

Vincent arrived in Paris on 23 December 1617. The following day, Christmas Eve, he went back to the de Gondis for the second time and was welcomed. 'like an angel from heaven.'[26] Vincent promised Mme de Gondi that he would stay with her and help her until the day she died. He, in turn, was given the assurance that he could spend his time and energy doing the work to which he had been called. He had not come back by choice but had been forced to return. His withdrawal to the Aventine had turned him into a conqueror. He could impose conditions.

All that remained to be done was formally to give up his title of parish priest at Châtillon. It was in a spirit of submission that Vincent did this, on 31 January 1618. On 18 July of that same year, Louis Girard, who had been such an able assistant to Vincent, took his place at Châtillon. In the story of Vincent's life we have now turned over the pages of the chapters that relate to his youth.

---

[26] ABELLY, *op. cit.*, 1.1 c. 9, p. 45.

Part Three

CREATIVE MATURITY

(1618-1633)

Chapter X
A PERSONAL COMMITMENT

'Who decided we should work for the Mission?'

For Vincent, the fifteen years between 1618 and 1633 are a period of growth. They are creative years when Vincent is groping his way, following any indication given by providence, and taking his own personal decisions. In doing this he becomes aware of the ways in which he will fulfil his special vocation; he creates specific organisations and he sees them fully operational. These are also years when Vincent abandons himself more and more to the influence of grace and reaches a level of human maturity that is very close to sanctity.

When he returned from Châtillon in December 1617, Vincent was determined to devote himself completely to working for the salvation of poor country people and to relieving their physical sufferings. He would do this through the Mission and by founding the Charities. He had permission from the de Gondis to do this work and, as they were anxious to keep him in their household, they gave him, as promised, an assistant who would be tutor to their sons. This man was Antoine Portail.[1] So Vincent now has the time and the freedom to move about and follow what he now knows to be his vocation. His immediate horizons are the de Gondi[2] estates and he very quickly puts into action a plan to evangelise the people there. His missionary activity is restricted geographically and also by lack of personnel. Vincent himself is the Mission. Has he already glimpsed the possibility of founding a new community and been given a hint of the vast horizons, both national and international, of his vocation? According to Vincent no such thought had ever entered his head.

---

[1] *Annales* (1933), pp. 72-80.
[2] ABELLY, *op. cit.*, 1.1 c. 13, p. 53.

Who was it that founded the company? Who sent us to work on the missions and with the ordinands, etc.? Was it I? Most certainly not. Was it Fr Portail whom God sent to join me right at the start? Definitely not. We never thought of such a thing or had any plans like that. Who, then, was the creator of all this? It was God, in his providence and utter goodness.[3]

Here we come to a problem which has long been debated: the question of Vincent de Paul's lack of imagination and spiritual initiative, as well as his natural timidity. Some people think Vincent is rather limited, he does not rise to great heights of contemplation and he cannot see the long term consequences of the task he is undertaking. His imagination worked from the particular to the general, and he created nothing more than a chain of minor projects that answered limited needs; the final outcome was far beyond what he had planned. All Vincent's works were a response to specific but quite minor events that showed up some moral or social evil. His projects were based on experience, not on natural creativity.[4]

On the other hand there are people who detect in Vincent a certain boldness. He liked things to be on a big scale and was happy to take risks. Any apparent lack of decisiveness or initiative was simply because Vincent was making a very determined effort to carry out to the letter de Bérulle's teaching on total submission to God's will. In his striving after sanctity Vincent deemed it absolutely essential to abase himself completely before the divine majesty. This means, in effect, that he was ready to give up his own plans and rely totally on God for guidance.[5] We recognise here a principle that is so characteristic of Vincent de Paul and one which he will repeat over and over again, that of never anticipating providence but always following its guidance.[6] We will see how he lives this out during the year in question. Vincent makes strenuous efforts to subdue nature by practising strict, ascetic discipline and he tries to correspond as fully as possible with the demands of his recent conversion. So we should not be surprised by Vincent's voluntary renunciation of his natural inclination towards ambitious projects such as those we noted in the early and eventful years of his priesthood.

It is clearly evident, however, that during his second stay with the de Gondis, between 1618 and 1625, Vincent devoted himself to the work of the Mission and the Charities. He did this single-handed except for occasional

---

[3] *S.V.P.* XI, pp. 38 and 3.
[4] P. RENAUDIN, *op. cit.*, pp. 59-62.
[5] A. REDIER, *op. cit.*, pp. 145-147.
[6] *S.V.P.* I, pp. 68, 241; II, pp. 137, 208 418-419, 453, 456, 466, 473; III, pp. 188, 197; IV, p. 34; V, pp. 164, 396; VI, p. 8; VII, p. 10, 543; VIII, pp. 152, 255, 402.

help from companions who only joined him for certain specific and limited projects. In the year 1618 he preached three missions that we know about; those of Villepreux, Joigny and Montmirail which were all part of the de Gondi estates. During these missions he received help from good priests some of whom we know by name: Jean Coqueret, a doctor in theology at the college of Navarre, together with Berger and Gontière who were ecclesiastical councillors to the parlement of Paris.[7] These three accompanied him on the first mission he preached at Villepreux. But we should not let this statement pass lightly over us as though we fully realised its significance. What precisely was the Mission? More than three centuries of familiarity with the term has trivialised its meaning. Let us try to rediscover this meaning in the pure, clear light of the Mission's origin.

On the de Gondi estates: the Mission and the Charities

In Gannes, in Folleville, and in Châtillon Vincent had discovered the profound spiritual dereliction of these poor country people, their ignorance of the fundamental truths of faith, their routine practice of a mildewed, musty Christianity and their lack of even basic preparation for the sacraments. The results of all this were only too evident and Vincent's heart was seared at finding 'a people who risked being damned because they were ignorant of the truths necessary for salvation and because they did not confess their sins.'[8] A radical solution had to be found and the missions aimed at providing just this.

Each mission was like planting the seeds of Christianity afresh. Shortly after they arrived at the village, the small team of two, three or four missioners would unload their scanty belongings and begin days of intensive preaching. Depending on the size of the place, the work could go on for five or six weeks or even for two months. The missions always lasted a fortnight at least, even in the smallest villages. The programme was adapted to suit the work routine of the peasants. Early in the morning there would be a sermon on the basic truths of the faith, the virtues, and common sins. At one o'clock in the afternoon there would be catechism class for the children and these youngsters hurried eagerly to it because for so long nobody had bothered about them. And now one of these gentlemen who had come all the way from Paris was going to put on a show especially for them and the performance would not be without its stratagems and ploys to capture a child's imagination.

---

[7] ABELLY, *op. cit.*, 1.1 c. 10, p. 47.
[8] *S.V.P.* I, p. 115.

Late in the evening, when the farm work was finished, there would be the *grand catéchisme*, during which the adults would be instructed on the articles of the Creed, the commandments of God and of the Church, the sacraments, the Lord's prayer and the Angelus. The mission ended with a joyful celebration. In the morning those children who had not already done so made their first communion and, that evening after Vespers, there was a splendid procession of the blessed sacrament. The children carried lighted candles and behind them walked the clergy and the congregation. The people remembered the mission for a long time. It was an intensive course in Christianity for all who took part in it.

But the course was not just theoretical. Explanations of the truths of faith went hand in hand with strong exhortations for a change in life style, and a call to conversion which would be sealed by a good general confession and receiving holy communion.[9] The people who had been neglected for so long discovered afresh the ancient treasures of their dormant faith. They felt they were living a new and marvellous spiritual adventure; it was a re-encounter or, for many of them, their first serious encounter with Christianity. To crown this, the mission put before them the fundamental goal of the Christian vocation, the practice of charity. The missions invariably ended with the founding of a charity confraternity like the original one that Vincent started at Châtillon.

We know that between the years 1618 and 1625 Vincent preached missions throughout the entire estates of M. and Mme de Gondi and that these comprised a nucleus of thirty or forty key towns. He founded a Confraternity of Charity in each one.[10] We still have the constitutions for the confraternities of Joigny, Montmirail, Folleville, Courbon and Montreuil[11] as well as the general constitutions which, with some local variations, were to provide the broad outlines for the particular constitutions.[12] All of these clearly show the workings of the same practical mind, the same attention to detail, the same concern for efficiency, the same combination of spiritual and material assistance and the same compassion for the needy that we saw in the constitutions drawn up for the Charity at Châtillon.

Everything was worked out in great detail: the acts of piety to be practised by the associates, the sick people's diet, the duties of officers, possible sources of funding for the Charity, the manner of persuading people to receive the sacraments and arrangements for the burial and funeral of those who died. So as not to duplicate resources, the new confraternity would combine

[9] ABELLY, *op. cit.*, 1.2 c. 1, pp. 12-14 and 21-22.
[10] ABELLY, *op. cit.*, 1.1 c. 10, p. 47.
[11] *S.V.P.* XIII, pp. 439-521.
[12] *S.V.P.* XIII, pp. 417-422.

with one or other of the pious associations already in existence and, according to the locality, this would be the Confraternity of the Blessed Sacrament or that of the Holy Name of Jesus or that of the Holy Rosary.[13]

The Confraternities of Charity were originally set up to channel the religious fervour of pious ladies. Vincent soon realised that this promising mobilisation of charity could also include men. So men's confraternities were set up and the first of these seems to have been in Folleville, which was founded on 23 October 1620.[14] The main difference between the two types of confraternity was that the ladies' work was specifically to care for poor sick people while the men worked with the able-bodied. Consequently their activities were not the same. One of the principal commitments of the men's confraternities was the setting up of workshops. Here, children and young people between the ages of eight and twenty, lived together under ecclesiastical direction, and learned a trade which they, in their turn, undertook to teach other apprentices gratis. Without expressing it in so many words Vincent had discovered the maxim, 'Give a man a fish and you feed him for a day; teach him how to fish and you feed him for life.'

There were also some Charities which had mixed membership. Those of Joigny, Montmirail, Courbon and Montreuil had both men and women members.[15] But these were only moderately successful and had to be disbanded. In the light of experience Vincent concluded that it was not the women's fault that these Charities failed.

> When you have men and women working together they cannot agree on matters of administration; the men want to be in charge of everything and the ladies do not like this. In the beginning the Charities of Joigny and Montmirail had mixed membership; the men took charge of the able-bodied poor while the ladies cared for the sick, but as their funds were held in common we found it necessary to withdraw the men. As for the ladies, I can only speak highly of them; nobody could fault their administration for they were very careful and most trustworthy.[16]

One woman in particular played a decisive role in the development of that floodtide of charity that Vincent unleashed. This woman was Mme de Gondi, whom we know about already. Prompted by her chaplain's contagious

---

[13] *S.V.P.* XIII, pp. 521, 527.
[14] *S.V.P.* XIII, p. 484.
[15] *S.V.P.* XIII, pp. 446, 511, 521.
[16] *S.V.P.* IV, p. 71.

fervour, she took an active part in Vincent's missions, not just by giving alms but by going in person to visit and console the sick. She also saw that disputes and lawsuits were settled and her involvement lent authority to all the initiatives undertaken by Vincent and his companions.[17] Her influence was crucial for the founding of the Charities. When illness prevented Vincent from being present, it was she who presented to the local parish priest the official approbation of the confraternity that the archbishop of Sens had granted them. The new confraternity elected Mme de Gondi its prioress and received its first funding from the money she set aside from the taxes that mariners paid for sailing their boats and barges under the town's bridges on Sundays and festivals.[18] At the request of the countess, the bishop of Soissons approved the constitutions of the Charity confraternity at Montmirail and in other parts of the de Gondi estates that belonged to his diocese. The countess refused to be elected to any office in the confraternity but in the end she had to agree to being nominated assistant to fill this post that was left vacant.[19]

Like concentric circles of waves in the sea, Vincent's work was spreading, through force of circumstances, to ever more far-flung territories. Vincent's name began to be known in all parts of the de Gondi's domains because these estates belonged to different dioceses and the fruits of his charitable work were appreciated in Paris, Beauvais, Soissons, Sens ...[20] Unforeseen, or perhaps we should say providential happenings, were soon to expand these enterprises nationwide.

'I have seen these poor people treated like animals'

The office of General of the Galleys that Philippe Emmanuel de Gondi held was one of the most prestigious posts in France's armed forces. It provided Count de Joigny with opportunities for deeds of valour commensurate with his reputation for bravery. Among many other armed conflicts that he engaged in, we should remember his intervention in the siege of La Rochelle in October 1622. The French fleet was under the personal command of the general who decided the outcome of the engagement in a very practical way. On the day after the attack on the fleet of La Rochelle, the rebel city conceded defeat and sued for peace.[21] But, as was customary at that time in history, this glorious

---

[17] ABELLY, *op. cit.*, 1.1 c. 13, p. 54; COLLET, *op. cit.*, Vol. 1, pp. 87-88.
[18] COSTE, *M.V.* Vol. 1, pp. 123-124.
[19] *S.V.P.* XIII, p. 466.
[20] COLLET, *op. cit.*, Vol. 1, p. 88.
[21] R. CHANTELAUZE, *op. cit.*, pp. 142-144.

navy sailed on an ocean of misery, pain and blood—the labours of the galley slaves. It was these men, the scum of society, whose arms toiled at rowing and whose backs were lacerated by the overseer's implacable whip, who sailed the ships that proudly flew the fleur de lys ensign.

There were few situations more heartrending in the sixteenth and seventeenth centuries than the plight of men sentenced to the galleys. The only comparison we might make would be to compare them with prisoners in the concentration camps of the twentieth century. The horror began the moment they were imprisoned in the Conciergerie in Paris, waiting for the time when they would be part of 'the chain' that took them to the ports. It was there that they languished in infectious and nauseous prisons, chained together in pairs, famished with hunger and worn out by fever or by worms. The situation was no better when they were put aboard ship. Awaiting them were endless days of painful rowing when they were scorched by the fierce Mediterranean sun or lashed by rain and storms, as they were whipped by heartless and cruel slave-drivers. The worst thing was that they had no legal redress. If they were condemned to two or three years in the galleys they might find their sentence arbitrarily extended for an indefinite period. This might be due to bureaucratic chaos or to the navy's demand for manpower.[22]

Vincent de Paul began to visit the galley slaves in Paris in 1618.[23] That same heart which had been touched by the spiritual abandonment and the physical hunger of the peasants of Châtillon and on the de Gondi estates now shuddered at the sight of this untold misery. Talking to his spiritual daughters forty years later, he could still remember how he felt at that time.

> What happiness, my Daughters, to serve these poor prisoners left abandoned in the hands of men who show them no pity. I have seen these poor people treated like animals and their sufferings moved God to show compassion for them.[24]

Vincent's compassion was never passive or sterile. He immediately set about looking for ways of making the prisoners' painful situation a little easier even if he could not remedy the problem entirely. His first step was to persuade the general to have the prisoners in Paris moved to a more habitable building in the Faubourg St Honoré near the church of St Roch and here the prisoners were allowed a more substantial and healthy diet. On Vincent's initiative, the bishop of Paris issued an injunction ordering parish priests,

---

[22] ABELLY, *op. cit.*, 1.1 c. 14, pp. 58-59.
[23] COLLET, *op. cit.*, Vol. 1, pp. 94-95.
[24] *S.V.P.* X, p. 125.

assistant clergy, and preachers, to urge the faithful to participate in the work of helping the condemned men.[25] Vincent was just as concerned with the spiritual welfare of the galley slaves as he was with their material welfare. He visited the gaols and showed great zeal in preaching missionary style to these people who were as distanced from God as they were abandoned by men. His success was beyond all expectations. There were remarkable conversions and these were all the more sincere as they were in no way dependent on any expectation of material reward such as liberty or a reduction in sentence. The preacher was very careful not to promise this.[26] In this same year, 1618, he made a first journey to Marseilles to take the same consolation to the unfortunate wretches still sentenced to the galleys.

At this juncture it would be well to put into context a rather dubious anecdote which tells how Vincent took the place of a galley slave for a short time so that the man could go free and help his family. Although different witnesses testified to the historical accuracy of the story during the beatification process, it has always raised doubts in the minds of biographers. Even Abelly, who was the first to tell the story, showed a certain scepticism.[27] This led Collet to argue strongly against it.[28] The controversy has continued ever since.[29] Taken in its most radical version as Vincent having actually replaced a galley slave, and this would mean accepting, too, the complicity of those in charge in allowing the man to go free, the story seems highly improbable. Taken as a sudden impulse on Vincent's part to take the seat of an exhausted galley slave and spare him a couple of lashes the story might be more plausible. This is how modern biographers tend to explain the incident. They are fascinated by such a noble gesture, which is very much in keeping with Vincent's burning charity.[30]

Another of Vincent's initiatives to help the galley slaves at Marseilles was destined to have a more lasting effect. Under the auspices of the General of the Galleys, they started to build a hospital. Unfortunately the project was soon halted through lack of funds and was not taken up again till twenty-five years later.[31]

Vincent's selfless labours in Paris and Marseilles induced M. de Gondi to look for some way of legalising and perpetuating the work. It came into his mind to create the post of chaplain royal to the galleys in France and

---

[25] COLLET, *op. cit.*, Vol. 1, p. 95.

[26] ABELLY, *op. cit.*, 1.1 c. 14, pp. 58-60; R. CHANTELAUZE, *op. cit.*, p. 117.

[27] ABELLY, *op. cit.*, 1.3 c. 11, pp. 114-115.

[28] COLLET, *op. cit.*, Vol. 1, pp. 100-102.

[29] COSTE, *M.V.* Vol. 1, pp. 149-155.

[30] J. CALVET, *op. cit.*, p. 71.

[31] COSTE, *M.V.* Vol. 1, p. 141.

this work was entrusted to Vincent. The king, 'moved with pity for the prisoners and wishing them to derive spiritual profit from their bodily affliction,' approved the plan. On 8 February 1619, a brief was issued to set up the new post 'with authority over all other chaplains' and it was conferred on Vincent de Paul. It carried with it an annual salary of 600 *livres* and the rank of officer in the Levant navy. Four days later, on the twelfth day of that month, Vincent took the oath of office in the presence of the general and assumed responsibility for the work.[32] It was the first of Vincent's charitable works to be carried out on a national scale. Vincent was to retain the title all through his life. Shortly before his death he succeeded in having the title linked to the office of superior general of the Mission in perpetuity. It was no sinecure.

From the outset, Vincent's personal dedication to the work was matched by the commitment shown by his two close collaborators, Fr Belin and Fr Portail.[33] Later on he would appoint a number of missioners to help in this work and would enlist the help of the Daughters of Charity to look after the corporal needs of the galley slaves. The Daughters would go down into the prisons like veritable angels of consolation. In the brief intervals that Vincent had free after giving missions to the peasants on the de Gondi estates, he would go to either the Hospital for Galley Slaves in Paris or to the galleys themselves to bring to the prisoners, too, the benefits of a mission. He did this in Marseilles in 1622 and in Bordeaux the following year. We will see this a little later on.

'When I founded the Charity at Mâcon ...'

On one of his journeys in September 1621, Vincent passed through the town of Mâcon. It was there that providence was waiting to launch him into a new enterprise, which would establish beyond any doubt, his organising ability and the effectiveness of the confraternity he had set up in Châtillon.

Mâcon was swarming with beggars who were a real scourge for the city because of their demands, their wranglings and the inconvenience they caused. Straightaway Vincent tackled the problem and he was particularly concerned about the dreadful condition of these poor people who, in addition to all their bodily miseries were a long way from the practice of their religion. Why should not he apply to the city's problem those same remedies that he had used in the small villages? The plan that he conceived was on a grand

---

[32] *S.V.P.* XIII, pp. 55-56.
[33] ABELLY, *op. cit.*, 1.1 c. 14, p. 60; COLLET, *op. cit.*, Vol. 1, p. 96.

scale, so much so that when he was bold enough to present it, some people thought that the man who conceived this plan was interfering or crazy. Those who were more pious recognised the good intentions behind the idea but were sceptical about its chances of success. His plan was to organise a charity on a city-wide scale and thus put an end to begging and to the corporal and spiritual abandonment of these poor wretches. The idea began to gain support. Vincent managed to interest the magistrates of the town, the bishop, the two canonical chapters, the municipal councillors, the burghers and the leading merchants of the town. He presented his plan at a meeting held in the Hôtel de Ville on Thursday 16 September.

The basis of Vincent's plan was that they should set up two associations of charity, one for men and the other for women. The general outline of his plan provided, first of all, for the compiling of a list of all poor people living in the town and these numbered three hundred. Then they would set up a relief fund which would draw on voluntary donations covenanted annually by the clergy and well-to-do citizens, as well as agreed revenues specially assigned to this good work from entrance dues exacted from all the professions in the city and from collections taken up by the ladies of Charity every Sunday. On Sundays the poor people would go to the church of St Nizier to hear Mass and eventually to go to confession and communion. After Mass they would all be given bread and money, according to their family circumstances, except for those who were caught begging during the week. Poor people who were passing through the town would be given a night's lodging and the next day they would be sent on their way with an alms of two *sous*. The bashful poor would be discreetly helped by the ladies who gave them food and medicine when they were sick. Men who were able to work were only given enough money to supplement their miserable wages because the association did not believe in encouraging idleness. Members of the confraternity were to meet once a week to update the list of poor people, to delete the names of those who no longer needed help and to impose the appropriate sanctions on those who did not deserve to be helped or who had broken the rules.

The plan worked. The sum of two hundred *écus* was raised to cover initial expenses. In less than three weeks the scheme was fully operational. Each Sunday 1,200 pounds of bread and 18 or 20 *livres* of money were distributed. The ladies received 12 or 15 *livres* for the bashful poor, the apothecaries were paid 100 or 120 *livres* for their medicines, the surgeon drew 20 *livres*, and the women who attended to the sick were given 4 *livres* a month. The officials whose duty it was to ensure that no beggars from outside the area stayed in the town, were each given 20 *livres*. This total did not include the cost of clothing, firewood and coal, which would have come to a considerable sum.[34] One might perhaps be surprised at this mixture of organised charity and preoccupation with good behaviour. Vincent de Paul was no dreamer, but a prudent and realistic organiser. His heart was always moved at the sight of suffering but that did not prevent him from recognising measures that were necessary for the preservation of good public order and he was well aware of roguery's thousand disguises. In a century when social assistance was unheard of, the charity association at Mâcon represents a massive attempt to meet the needs of the poor. He was preparing, or perhaps we should say that providence was preparing him, for the even more far-reaching tasks he would have to undertake.

Once again he had shown that he could rouse people's goodwill, mobilise forces and channel relief aid. Strangely enough it is Vincent himself who has left us the most convincing proof of his success at Mâcon even though this is in a private letter to Louise de Marillac, his principal collaborator and closest confidante. We have already quoted some of the words he wrote to her on 21 July 1635.

> When I started the charity at Mâcon everybody laughed at me and pointed at me in the street, but when the work was finally accomplished they all shed tears of joy. The local magistrates paid me such honour when I was leaving that I could not bear it, and I had to creep away to avoid their praise. And now Mâcon is one of the most solidly established charities.

And, in order to justify this unwonted avowal of personal success, he adds:

> I hope that the confusion you experienced as your work began will be turned into consolation and the enterprise will thus have a more solid foundation.[35]

His duties as chaplain royal to the galleys and his success in organising the charity at Mâcon meant that Vincent's work was beginning to spread beyond the confines of the de Gondi estates. Both these works would

---

[34] ABELLY, *op. cit.*, c. 15, pp. 61-63; COLLET, *op. cit.*, Vol. 1, p. 104-108. In *S.V.P.* XIII, pp. 490-504, we have a collection of documents about the charity at Mâcon which include Abbé Laplatte's history of Mâcon, the testimony of Father Desmoulin, superior of the Oratory, who was an eye-witness, the minutes of the meeting that took place in the Hôtel de Ville, on 16 April 1621, and those of the assembly which was held on the following day in the capitular church of Mâcon.

[35] *S.V.P.* XIII, p. 833.

soon reveal the true stature of this humble priest who was still in the early stages of his marvellous and providential vocation.

'I begged Our Lord to change my nature'

However, the development of Vincent's works should not distract our attention from his on-going spiritual progress during these early years of his apostolate. Guided by de Bérulle and Duval—and he was soon to encounter the third person to have an important influence on his life—and corresponding more and more to the promptings of grace, Vincent was making progress along the difficult path of personal sanctification. Still preserved are a few but significant watersheds in his life that help us trace the secret path of his spiritual progress. It is almost by chance that we have first-hand testimony of his personal asceticism. No matter how much he wanted to conceal his departure from Mâcon he had, of course, to tell the Oratorian fathers who had been his hosts in that city. On the day he was leaving some of them went into his room very early in the morning to say goodbye to him. It was then that they noticed that this energetic organiser of charity was in the habit of removing the mattress from his bed and sleeping on the bare straw. When this regular act of penance came to light all Vincent could do was to murmur a confused and not very convincing explanation. Vincent was faithful to this penitential practice all his life.[36]

In that same year, 1621, Vincent had made his retreat at Soissons. Among other graces he received there, and we will discuss these later on, one particular grace contributed to his personal maturity which is the subject now under discussion. Vincent was not by nature a gentle and affable person. Perhaps he exaggerates to some degree but he often accused himself of 'black moods' and of having a 'harsh and aggressive manner'.[37] This surliness found expression, not so much in angry outbursts as in a brooding silence when he would be closed in on himself, and in periods of deep melancholy. Mme de Gondi suffered from her chaplain's fluctuating moods. She was worried that he was fretting and that one day he might leave them again. One day she summoned up courage and very courteously brought this fault to the priest's notice. Vincent thought about it. Feeling himself called to live in community— significantly this is the first time we find him thinking along these particular lines—he realised that he would have to live with all types of people and so he resolved to mend his ways. During the retreat at Soissons he reveals, 'I

---

[36] ABELLY, *op. cit.*, 1.1 c. 15, p. 63; COLLET, *op. cit.*, Vol. 1, p. 107.
[37] *S.V.P.* XI, p. 64.

turned to Our Lord and begged him to change my brusque and forbidding character and I asked him to help me to become gentle and kind.' Vincent was no doubt influenced by Marguerite de Silly when he made this petition, and he was even more strongly influenced by the example of St Francis de Sales whom he had just come to know. Vincent not only prayed but he also made firm resolutions. He began to make strenuous efforts to acquire the virtues he prayed for and eventually became one of the most amiable men of his time.[38]

In 1621 we have one final indication that Vincent was acquiring a reputation for sanctity and indirectly it points to other things that Vincent did though we have no details of these. On 26 February of that year, Fr François de Maida, superior general of the Minims, presented Vincent with a certificate of affiliation in recognition of his outstanding piety and the services he had rendered to these religious. Being granted associate membership meant he would share in the prayers, sacrifices, almsgiving, indulgences and other good works of the order.[39] One might consider this a routine act of gratitude towards a benefactor. Unfortunately we do not know the precise reasons that prompted the superior of the Minims to take this action but we do know that a letter of aggregation was not granted lightly and neither was it a reward for just any ordinary service. Perhaps it was not just by chance that the bishop of Mâcon belonged to that same religious order of Minims, and that Mâcon was the city where eight months later Vincent's charity was to reap such a rich harvest. The certificate of affiliation accorded to the de Gondi chaplain was something more than a mere document.

---

[38] ABELLY, *op. cit.*, 1.1 c. 12, p. 179; COLLET, *op. cit.*, Vol. 1, p. 99.
[39] COLLET, *op. cit.*, Vol. 1, p. 100.

Chapter XI
FURTHER SIGNS FROM PROVIDENCE

The third man, Francis de Sales

In these early days of commitment to his recently discovered vocation, Vincent came into contact with the third man whose influence was to play a decisive part in his life: Francis de Sales (1567-1622).

The bishop of Geneva arrived in Paris in November 1618. His reasons for making the journey were partly religious and partly political. He was accompanying the cardinal of Savoy who was responsible for arranging the marriage between the prince of Piedmont and Princess Christine of France, the sister of Louis XIII. It is a well-known fact that in the time of the *Ancien Régime* there were many implications for royal marriages, so negotiations could be very complicated. The negotiations entrusted to Francis de Sales went on for nearly a year. He could not return to Savoy until September 1619, but he made good use of his time. His main objective was to finalise these negotiations but Francis had his own reasons, too, for making the journey. The private business he had to attend to was the founding of the first convent of his Visitation nuns in Paris. With this in mind, the saintly bishop's inseparable companion, Mère Jeanne Françoise Frémiot de Chantal (1572-1641) also moved to Paris and brought with her the first group of Visitandine nuns for the new convent.[1]

'I was honoured with his confidences'

We do not know how it happened but Vincent de Paul came into contact with these two holy people. It would not be over-presumptuous to guess

---

[1] Concerning St Francis de Sales *cf.* H. DE MAUPAS DU TOUR, *La vie du vénerable serviteur de Dieu François de Sales* (Paris 1657); H. BRÉMOND, *Histoire littéraire du sentiment religieux ...*, I, pp. 62-128; P. LAJEUNIE, 'Saint François de Sales, maître spirituel' (Paris 1967), *DTC* VI, col. 736-762.

that the de Gondis engineered this meeting since their family belonged to the exclusive circle of high society that the saintly bishop frequented. The bishop visited the General of the Galleys at his residence in Paris.[2] Vincent and Francis de Sales soon became friends but the relationship had a supernatural basis. We have a most valuable witness to this, the testimony of Vincent de Paul himself. When the bishop of Geneva arrived in Paris Vincent was not in the capital. He had left for Montmirail with Mme de Gondi and he stayed in their country house for the best part of December.[3] However, he could recall in detail what happened when the saintly bishop preached his first sermon in the capital on 11 November 1618. Francis de Sales himself described what happened in a conversation he had with Vincent and Saint Frances de Chantal. Let us listen to Vincent:

> The first time he preached in Paris during his last visit there, they came from every corner of the city to hear his sermon. Members of the court were present and it was a congregation worthy of such a celebrated preacher. They were all expecting to hear one of his marvellous sermons that showed how well the great man could captivate his listeners, but what did this great man of God do? He simply told them the story of St Martin and he did this deliberately in order to humble himself before these high-ranking people whose presence would have excited any other preacher. Through this heroic act of humility he himself was the first to profit from the sermon.
>
> Shortly afterwards Francis related this incident to Mme de Chantal and myself saying, 'How I must have humiliated our sisters who were expecting to hear marvellous things in such exalted company! One of them—he was referring to a postulant who later became a religious—remarked during the sermon, 'This is the preaching of a clown and a country bumpkin. He need not have come all this way to preach like that and try the patience of so many people.'[4]

Obviously, such details about the event, the preacher's motivation, and his reflections on the incident, could only be disclosed in the context of mutual trust between friends. And yet at first sight there would seem to be little in common between the illustrious prelate, Francis de Sales, and the little-known priest, Vincent de Paul. The former belonged by birth and

[2] *S.V.P.* I, pp. 353-354; XI, p. 26.
[3] COSTE, *M.V.* Vol. 1, p. 158.
[4] *S.V.P.* V, pp. 472-473.

education to the highest and most refined social class while the latter was a peasant who had only shed his family's rusticity by frequenting the homes of the aristocracy and he did this as chaplain, a position not far removed from that of servant. St Francis de Sales moved in the highest ecclesiastical circles, not only on account of his rank, but also because of his publicly acclaimed sanctity. Vincent, who had just resolved the crisis of his vocation, was a novice in the paths of holiness and he held no office that gave him any status in the eyes of those who knew him. What secret affinity existed then between these two men who were so very different? We know what it was that attracted Vincent. He discovered in St Francis de Sales what he had sought in vain from de Bérulle, a saint. And this contact with holiness made him commit himself, heart and soul, to following the same path. On Francis's part there must have been a divine intuition which helped him discern that he and the chaplain to the de Gondis were kindred spirits in striving for union with God, and he recognised the saint in the making.

One thing we can be certain about is that in the space of just one year, which was the time Francis de Sales spent in Paris, the two men became very close friends. In the declaration Vincent made ten years later during the process for the beatification of his illustrious friend, he repeats with rather tiresome insistence, 'M. Francis de Sales often honoured me with his confidences ...'; 'from his own lips I heard him say in familiar conversation ...'; 'I can add that honouring me with the intimacy I have already mentioned, he opened his heart and said to me ...'[5]

'Our Blessed Father'

The admiration that Vincent felt for the saint and their close friendship based on personal contact was not diminished either by the bishop of Geneva's departure from Paris or by his death in 1622. Living and dead, Francis de Sales continued to be Vincent's spiritual mentor. The saintly bishop's writings, and in particular his *Treatise on the Love of God* and the *Introduction to the Devout Life* were always part of Vincent's spiritual reading and he never tired of recommending them to his spiritual sons and daughters.[6] He wrote this outstanding eulogy on the *Treatise on the Love of God*:

> This is a very noble and immortal work, a worthy testimony of his most ardent love of God. It is certainly a book to be admired

---

[5] *S.V.P.* XIII, pp. 67-69.

[6] A. DODIN, 'Lectures de Saint Vincent: Introduction à la vie devote. Étude de spiritualité vincentienne', *Annales* (1941-1942), pp. 239-248 and 'Le traité de l'amour de Dieu de Saint François de Sales', *Annales* (1945-1946), pp. 447-464; *ibid.* (1947-1948), pp. 479-497.

and it will preach the goodness of its author as many times as it is read. I have therefore earnestly made sure that it is read in our community, as a universal remedy for tepid souls, as a mirror for the sluggish, and as an incentive to make progress in love for those who are aiming at perfection. I greatly desire everyone to make fitting use of it. Its warm appeal is for everybody.[7]

As for the *Introduction to the Devout Life,* he recommends it as spiritual reading and as a guide to the spiritual exercises,[8] as a meditation book for the Daughters of Charity,[9] as spiritual reading for members of the Confraternity of Charity,[10] and as an essential piece of luggage for the missionaries to Madagascar.[11]

Vincent's letters and conferences contain a great many quotations from the writings of Francis de Sales. Even more numerous are the implicit references to the bishop's ideas which are undoubtedly one of the sources of Vincentian spirituality. But most striking of all is the personal veneration that Vincent kept all through life for the man who had opened up to him the vast horizons of sanctity and had shown him the way to achieve it. He had the bishop's portrait hung in the conference room at St Lazare, the mother house of the Congregation of the Mission,[12] and whenever he spoke to the missioners or to the Daughters of Charity he referred to Francis as 'our blessed father'.[13] Forty years after his first and only encounter with him, Vincent wrote to the pope, Alexander VII, earnestly petitioning him to grant the speedy beatification of this venerable servant of God and he recalled once more their friendship and the numerous intimate conversations they had had.[14]

'How good you must be, O my God, since your creature is so loveable!'

What did Vincent owe to Francis de Sales that would explain this lasting gratitude and the unswerving veneration he had for him? As we have already said, the most important thing was Vincent's living contact with holiness. There was, too, all the help that Vincent received both in his personal life,

[7] *S.V.P.* XIII, p. 71.
[8] *S.V.P.* I, pp. 155-156.
[9] *S.V.P.* IX, p. 13 and 50.
[10] *S.V.P.* XIII, pp. 435, 822.
[11] *S.V.P.* III, p. 283.
[12] *S.V.P.* XI, p. 393.
[13] *S.V.P.* II, pp. 70, 212.
[14] *S.V.P.* VII, pp. 584-586.

and towards a wider vision and more organised effort with regard to his spiritual life and the apostolate. For Vincent, who was preoccupied with his faults and striving to acquire a friendly and outgoing disposition, the gentleness of Francis de Sales was a revelation. So much so that one day when he was in bed ill, Vincent remembered Francis de Sales and exclaimed aloud, 'My God, how good you must be since Francis de Sales, your creature, is so good and kind.'[15]

The example of Francis de Sales was crucial for prayer and the resolutions that Vincent made during the retreat at Soissons. He attributed the grace of being freed from his surliness and melancholy to the saint's intercession.[16] Moreover, Francis de Sales was a herald of the doctrine that sanctity is for everyone, irrespective of their condition or state in life; it is for seculars and religious, married and single people, men and women, rich and poor. This is the message of the *Introduction to the Devout Life*. Vincent was an ordinary secular priest committed to the task of setting up small teams of lay people dedicated to charitable activities and at this point he was probably just touching the surface of the project he had scarcely formulated. His plan to establish a new type of apostolic community found theological backing in this doctrine which endorsed his creative activities. He also discovered in it a simple path to sanctity. To reach perfection he did not have to master the complex, intellectual structures of his first master, de Bérulle. It was enough to follow the humble and gentle way preached by Francis de Sales.

He was indebted to the bishop for this doctrine and for a great many practical favours. The first of these was that Vincent was introduced to another saint, Mother Chantal. As we have already seen, Vincent was allowed to share in the private conversations of the founders of the Visitation order. When Francis died Mother Chantal took Vincent as her spiritual guide. We still have a small number of exquisite letters which reveal his individual style of spiritual direction. They are different from any other letters written by Vincent. Their tone is affectionate and full of Salesian gentleness but at the same time they are more solemn and respectful. It could be said that Vincent is both master and pupil. Not without reason does he think of her as 'Mother' and address her by this name.[17]

---

[15] *S.V.P.* XIII, p. 78.

[16] CALVET, *op. cit.*, p. 63.

[17] *S.V.P.* I, pp. 561, 574; II, pp. 45, 85, 97, 185. On Saint Chantal *cf.* H. DE MAUPAS DU TOUR, *La vie de la Vénérable Mère Jeanne Françoise Frémiot* (Paris); L. E. BOUGAUD, *Histoire de Sainte Chantal et des origines de la Visitation* (Paris 1874); H. BRÉMOND, *op. cit.*, I, pp. 68-127; II, pp. 537-584.

Mother Chantal's daughters, the Visitation nuns, also came under Vincent's direction. When he left Paris, Francis de Sales needed to confide to some priest the direction of the nuns in the convent he had established in the capital, as well as the four future foundations. The saintly bishop would have had no difficulty at all in finding important people who would be only too willing to take on the spiritual direction of his daughters, but he chose for the task the practically unknown chaplain to the de Gondis. With St Chantal's consent, he put Vincent's nomination before the bishop of Paris. In 1622 the appointment was extended[18] and Vincent kept this office all through life, though he several times tried to relinquish it, and on one occasion seemed to go on strike.[19] But if Vincent was zealous in his duties for the nuns, and his work was very successful, he did not intervene in the education of the aristocratic young ladies that the nuns received into their convents as pupils. It would be wrong, then, to attribute to the saint (as one enthusiastic writer has done)[20] an influence he did not exert on the education of young girls at that time.[21]

There was an even more important legacy that Vincent inherited from St Francis de Sales. In spite of fairly recent efforts to contradict this,[22] we can be certain that St Francis's original intention in founding the Visitation order was to create a new type of community for women who would not be cloistered but, as their name suggests, would devote themselves to visiting abandoned sick people and performing other works of mercy. Under pressure both from the archbishop of Lyons and the Holy See, he had to abandon his original plan and content himself with founding yet another cloistered order which followed the rule of St Augustine but was endowed with a new and original form of spirituality.[23] Vincent was careful to preserve the confidences that St Francis de Sales shared with him on this matter and, when it came to his turn, he skilfully got round the obstacles that the bishop of Geneva had not been able to sidestep. The result of all this was the company of the Daughters of Charity.

---

[18] ABELLY, *op. cit.*, 1.2 c. 7, p. 314.

[19] ABELLY, *op. cit.*, 1.3 c. 14, p. 231; COLLET, *op. cit.* Vol. 2, p. 76.

[20] A. MENABREA, *St. Vincent de Paul. Le Maître des hommes d'État* (Paris, La Colombe, 1944), pp. 85-86.

[21] J. CALVET, *op. cit.*, p. 61.

[22] FRANÇOIS VINCENT, 'Autour de Saint François de Sales', *Revue d'Apologétique* (1925), p. 677ff.

[23] *L'esprit de Saint François de Sales recueilli de divers écrits de Jean Pierre Camus, évêque de Belley, par Pierre Collot* (Paris 1727), pp. 188-189.

'A globe of fire'

The favours that Vincent de Paul received did not end with the saint's death. It was to St Francis de Sales and to St Jeanne Françoise de Chantal that Vincent owed the one extraordinary mystical experience that we know about in his lifetime. This took place in 1641 on the very day that St Chantal died. As soon as Vincent received the letter telling him that the venerable Mother was gravely ill, he made an act of contrition. Immediately he had a vision of the two holy founders going to heaven. He had the same vision again as he celebrated Mass after receiving the news that the Mother had died.[24] Speaking in the third person, Vincent himself has described the vision.

> When he received news that our dear departed lady was seriously ill, this person (we know from the letter quoted earlier that this was Vincent himself) knelt down to commend her soul to God. His first impulse was to say an act of contrition for her past sins and day to day failings. He immediately perceived a small globe of fire that rose from the ground and joined another bigger and more shining globe higher in the air. Then both globes melted into one, rose higher in the air, and then entered and were lost in another globe which was infinitely greater and more luminous than the previous ones. He heard an interior voice telling him that the first globe was the soul of our worthy mother, the second was that of our blessed father, and that they were both in God, their sovereign beginning. He also said that he was celebrating Mass for our most honoured mother as soon as he heard news of her holy death, and when he came to the second memento and prayers for the dead, he thought he really ought to pray for her as she might be in purgatory for some things she had said some time previously and which might have constituted a venial sin. But scarcely had this thought come to his mind when he had the same vision again; the same globes united and this gave him the inner conviction that her soul was in heaven and had no need of prayers. This idea was so firmly fixed in this person's mind that whenever he thought of her it was always in this state.

Vincent, who is always prudent and realistic, ends his testimony with the following words of caution:

---

[24] *S.V.P.* II, pp. 212-213: (letter to Father Codoing).

Something that might lead us to question this vision is the fact that this person had such a high regard for the sanctity of that blessed soul that he always regarded her letters as being inspired by God so that he could never read them without weeping. Consequently he might have imagined the vision, but what leads us to believe that it was authentic is that the person concerned is not given to seeing visions and this is the only one he has ever experienced.[25]

Led on by the strong and gentle hand of his friend in heaven, and his heart filled with the wholesome joy of the Salesians, Vincent prepares to meet the final signs that will prepare him for his mission in the Church.

The ultimate sign

At this juncture, 1620-1621, did Vincent really need yet another sign that his destiny was unquestionably to evangelise poor peasants? To judge from his passionate commitment to missionary work on the de Gondi estates one would say no. However, divine providence was again to provide unexpected confirmation of his mission.

Once again this confirmation came (the repetition is significant) through Mme de Gondi. It was she, who during a mission that Vincent preached in Montmirail, 1620, invited him to instruct three heretics in that locality who seemed ready to be converted. For a whole week the three men came every day to the de Gondi palace where Vincent would set aside two hours to instruct them and answer their difficulties. Shortly afterwards two of them said they were convinced, abjured their errors, and were readmitted to the bosom of the Church. The third proved more unwilling. This man was a self-sufficient character, careless in morals and given to dogmatising. One day he put forward an objection which wounded Vincent deeply since it touched on something he was deeply concerned about.

'According to you,' he said, 'the Church of Rome is guided by the Holy Spirit but I cannot believe that since there are Catholics in country places who are abandoned to the care of wicked and ignorant pastors who do not know their obligations and do not even know the Christian religion while the big cities are full of priests and friars doing absolutely nothing. In Paris alone there could be as many as 10,000 while these poor country

---

[25] *S.V.P.* XIII, pp. 126-127.

folk are left in frightening ignorance which could bring about their damnation. And you are trying to convince me that all this is under the guidance of the Holy Spirit? That I cannot believe!'

It was the most brazen statement that Vincent had heard on the subject of a scandal that had been gnawing at his own heart for three years. Naturally he tried to justify the situation. Things were not quite as the objector suggested. A fair number of priests from the cities often went to the country districts to preach and to catechise; others used their time profitably in writing learned treatises or singing the divine office, and finally, the Church could not be held responsible for the failings and negligence of some of her ministers.

The heretic was not convinced and maybe in his heart of hearts, Vincent was not convinced either. He could see only too plainly that the people's ignorance and the lack of zeal among the clergy were the great scourge in the Church that had to be remedied at all cost.

With redoubled zeal he travelled about the small towns and villages, continuing his work of evangelisation. The following year, 1621, it was his turn to preach at Marchais and other small villages on the outskirts of Montmirail. As usual he was accompanied by a handful of priests and religious who were friends of his. Among these were Blaise Féron and Jérome Duchesne who were both at the Sorbonne. Later they would gain their doctorates there and go on to become archdeacons of Chartres and Beauvais respectively. Nobody remembered the man from Montmirail who had refused to be converted. But he had not forgotten Vincent. He came to the mission services out of curiosity. He saw the zeal with which these ignorant people were instructed and the efforts made to come down to the level of the least intelligent among them, and he witnessed wonderful conversions on the part of hardened sinners. One day he came back to Vincent and amazed him by saying:

> Now I can see that the Holy Spirit is guiding the Roman Church since it is concerned for the instruction and salvation of those poor peasants. I am ready to come back to the Church as soon as you will receive me.

Vincent's joy was twofold. He rejoiced first of all that this straying sheep had returned to the fold, and secondly, that this conversion was a striking vindication of the direction in which he himself was to lead his life and follow out his apostolate. However, the new convert had a last-minute problem. This time it concerned statues.

> How can the Church of Rome think there is any supernatural virtue in pieces of stone that are as badly fashioned as the

statue of Our Lady that people venerate in the church at Marchais?

It was a question dealt with in first year catechism classes. A child could have answered it. Vincent called over one of the many lads in the country church and put the question to him. Without a moment's hesitation the boy repeated the catechism answer:

It is right to venerate images, not because of the material they are made of, but because they represent Our Lord Jesus Christ, his glorious Mother and the saints in heaven who, having overcome the world, exhort us by means of these images, to follow their example of faith and good works.

Vincent repeated the child's answer, developing it in some depth, but he judged it prudent to defer the Huguenot's abjuration for some days. This finally took place in the presence of the whole parish, to the edification and consolation of everybody.

This incident was etched on Vincent's memory for ever, and later on he would speak of it to his missioners. The double task of evangelising the poor and reforming the clergy now took on a new light; they were an answer to Christians separated from the Church. For this reason he ended his story with the moving exclamation,

How blessed are we missioners to be able to show that the Holy Spirit is guiding the Church when we work for the instruction and sanctification of the poor.[26]

The final temptation

Before he could be completely satisfied with the path that providence was pointing out to him, Vincent still needed to overcome one final temptation. This temptation was all the more insidious as it suggested to his mind specious motives for his apostolate and at the same time appealed to his natural feelings of affection which in themselves were admirable.

In 1623, after the mission to the galleys anchored at Bordeaux following their brilliant intervention at the siege of La Rochelle, Vincent

---

[26] The episode is related at length by ABELLY, *op. cit.*, 1.1 c. 13, pp. 54-57 and COLLET, *op. cit.*, Vol. 1, p. 88-93. Coste took St Vincent's words from Abelly's account and he published it in *S.V.P.* XI, pp. 34-37.

thought he would escape, for the first time in twenty-six years, to his native village which was so close at hand. He hesitated before doing so. He had seen so many fervent and self-sacrificing priests lose their fervour after long and fruitful years in the apostolate because of their desire to give financial help to their relations. He was afraid that the same thing might happen to him. But he put his fears to two of his best friends and they both advised him to go; the visit would be such a consolation for his relatives!

Vincent went to Pouy and stayed there for about a week or ten days. He lodged with the parish priest, Dominic Dusin, who was a relative. There was a local and family celebration in the little village. In the parish church he renewed his baptismal vows at the font where he had received the sacrament of regeneration. On the final day he went on pilgrimage with his brothers and sisters, his friends and nearly all the village, to the newly erected shrine of Our Lady of Buglose. He travelled barefoot the league and a half distance from Pouy. Was it not a blessing from heaven to return to that forgotten landscape of his childhood and to tread once more those paths he had followed with his father's flocks in the majestic solitude of the countryside? Now he seemed to be leading a different flock, his good peasants. Many of them were his kinsfolk who crowded round him, happy to have him back, happy to touch the soutane of their famous compatriot who had risen to such important positions in their country's far-off capital. He celebrated High Mass at the shrine. In the homily he showered on his family and neighbours advice which was tender, simple and full of apostolic zeal. He repeated what he had said to them in private, intimate conversation; that they should rid their hearts of any desire to become rich and that they were not to expect any financial help from him, for even if he had coffers full of gold and silver he would not give them anything because everything a priest has belongs to God and to the poor.

He was still feeling the aftermath of these emotions when he set off on his journey the next day. It was then that the temptation made itself felt. First of all came the tears. The further he travelled the more he felt the anguish of separation. He turned away and wept uncontrollably. All through the journey he wept ceaselessly. After the tears came the reasoning. He felt a great desire to help his relations towards an easier way of life. With a sudden rush of tenderness he planned to give this to one and that to another. In his imagination he was sharing out what he had and what he did not have.

So here we have Vincent de Paul at this crucial crossroads in life, in the throes of a temptation frequently experienced by people just reaching maturity. To what unforeseen point of destiny might he not be led if he followed the hazardous road he had started on six years earlier at Folleville and Châtillon? Would not the right thing be to follow the plan he had toyed with when he was in Toulouse, Avignon, Marseilles and Rome? That plan was that he should become a good priest respected by his family and the people of his neighbourhood and he would lead his kinsfolk and the people who belonged to the same social background as himself along the road to heaven just as he had led them to Buglose the previous day; he would lift his family out of their poverty and help them towards a more comfortable way of life, relieving them of their uncertainty and their anxious toil to earn their daily bread ... Like the Israelites after they had crossed the Red Sea and like Jesus in the desert, Vincent heard the insidious invitation, 'Go back to Egypt', 'Command these stones to turn into bread.' The temptation was all the more serious as it came cloaked in the guise of virtue. At that moment the whole significance of his life could have been altered. According to the answer he gave would depend whether Vincent was to become St Vincent de Paul or just one of so many venerable ecclesiatics worthy of mention in biographical dictionaries ...

The struggle, and it was a fierce one, lasted for three whole months. When the enemy's attacks had abated somewhat, Vincent begged God to deliver him from the temptation. He kept on till his prayer was granted. Once the struggle was over he was freed from the temptation for ever and now, after breaking the ties of flesh and blood, he could follow more closely the path that God was pointing out to him. A few days after returning to Paris he started a new mission in the diocese of Chartres.[27]

---

[27] The main source of information about the incident of St Vincent's visit to his home town, in 1623, can be found in COLLET, *op. cit.*, Vol. 1, pp. 109-111. This is based on an old manuscript, which is now lost, and it was entitled *Généalogie de M. Vincent de Paul*. This manuscript collected the testimonies of Pouy's inhabitants. The temptation account was given by St Vincent in a conference to the missioners and it was related by ABELLY, *op. cit.*, 1.3 c. 19, pp. 289-290. This account is identical with the one preserved in the manuscript of the conferences published by COSTE in *S.V.P.* XII, pp. 218-220.

Chapter XII
FOUNDATION PROJECTS

The new France: Richelieu on the horizon

While Vincent de Paul was successfully overcoming the last great crisis of his life, a new France was emerging from the first confused years after Louis XIII began to govern the country himself, 1617-1624. This new France would witness the end of Spanish domination and would eventually claim supremacy in Europe. One name is irrevocably linked with the task of forging France's greatness and that name is Richelieu.

On 29 April 1624, the bishop of Luçon who two years earlier had been raised to the purple and made a cardinal, rejoined the royal council and assumed the function, if not the name, of prime minister. He had been dismissed seven years previously and it took all the astuteness and tenacity of this second son of an aristocratic family to overcome the king's resistance. The king mistrusted Richelieu's ambition for power and feared his intelligence which was widely recognised. Marie de Medici, the queen mother whom the bishop as a follower at court had served and attended, not without self-interest, for the seven years she was in conflict with her son, pleaded his cause with all the womanly passion she could muster. Little did she then suspect the irreparable damage her intervention would cause to her.

Richelieu, who was always a cautious man, took one step at a time to achieve the objective he had set his heart on, to gain the confidence of the king and, ultimately, to wield absolute power. In the six years from 1624-1630 he had to temporise, because there were still powerful forces opposed to his taking power. These forces were headed by de Bérulle, the leader of the queen's council. From the outset Richelieu's actions followed a clearly defined policy. This policy may have been formulated at a later date but it has often been summarised in some lines from his *Political Testament* which was probably drawn up in 1638; 'I swear to Your Majesty that I will spare no effort and I will use all the powers you have been pleased to bestow on me to put an end to the Huguenot faction, to humble the pride of the nobility and bring all your subjects to fulfil their obligations to you and to raise your name to its rightfully exalted position among foreign nations.' Whether this policy document was drawn up beforehand or not, these four propositions encapsulate the work of one of France's greatest politicians of all time.

The country immediately sensed that a new style of government and a different political programme were beginning to emerge. The new policy would affirm the king's power over dissident factions, Huguenots or nobles, within the realm. It was a policy that defended national interests and resolutely pursued the goal of French supremacy abroad, especially with regard to Spain and the Austrian empire. It must be said that it was also a policy that would bring in its train a long period of misery and suffering for a large part of the nation, for the poor who were ground down by taxes, forgotten by the government, crushed by every army and victims of every campaign. It was precisely to these poor people that Vincent de Paul had dedicated his life, and on more than one occasion we will see his path cross that of the all-powerful minister. At the very time that Richelieu was taking the reins of power into his own hands, Vincent was thinking of formally establishing his work and seeing what had been 'The Mission' become 'The Congregation of the Mission.'[1]

'Our first foundress'

Who was the first person to think of changing Vincent's individual apostolate into a project for establishing a new community? Vincent liked to repeat, with boring insistence, that it was Mme de Gondi. It was she who urged Vincent to preach at Folleville the first sermon of the Mission on the day after the peasant from Gannes had made his confession. She recognised the terrible inadequacy of spiritual care brought to light by that first sermon as well as by her experience as a young woman when her confessor did not know the words of absolution, and she decided to extend the benefits of the mission to all the estates that she and her husband owned. To put the work on a solid and permanent footing she got Vincent to ask different communities to be responsible for it. These requests were unsuccessful. After consultation with their major superiors, the Jesuits made it known through their provincial,

---

[1] P. CHEVALLIER, *Louis XIII* (Paris 1979), p. 269-317; V. L. TAPIÉ, *La France de Louis XIII et de Richelieu* (Paris 1967), pp. 129-167. There is a very extensive bibliography on Richelieu. For works on this subject see *Lettres, instructions diplomatiques et papiers d'État du cardinal de Richelieu,* ed. D'AVENEL (Paris 1853-1857); *Testament politique du cardinal de Richelieu,* critical edition by L. ANDRÉ (Paris 1947); L.BATIFFOL, *Richelieu et le roi Louis XIII* (Paris 1934); M. HOUSSAYF, *Le cardinal Bérulle et le cardinal Richelieu. 1625-1629* (Paris 1875); P. ERLANGER, Richelieu (Paris 1972); C. J. BURCKHARDT, *Richelieu* (Paris 1970-1975), 3 vols.

Fr Charlet, that they could not take on the foundation as it was contrary to the aims of their institute. The Oratorians also refused and so did other communities. In her will, which she renewed every year, Mme de Gondi began to assign the sum of 16,000 *livres* to any community that would be responsible for preaching missions throughout her domains.

Meanwhile, Vincent continued his work as travelling preacher in the towns and villages, and was always accompanied by temporary helpers who were often drawn from the most illustrious and zealous clergy of Paris. It was Mme de Gondi, too, who had the idea, 'Why should not M. Vincent turn that fluctuating group of missioners into a new community dedicated to preaching missions and why should not he direct it himself?'[2] After much reflection Vincent agreed. The plan evolved slowly. In a few years time, as we shall see later, its definitive form would be settled in a formal contract between M. and Mme de Gondi on the one hand, and Vincent de Paul on the other. So Vincent was right to call the general's wife 'our first foundress'.[3] The company was indebted to her for both financial backing and for being the inspiration behind its foundation. But we should not be completely taken in by appearances.

Vincent, with his profound and perceptive humility, was past master at attributing to others the ideas that he had quietly slipped into their minds. Be that as it may, the year 1624 is the year when Richelieu effectively assumed power, and the year when Vincent began to shape the congregation he had in mind.

'God delivered me from hastiness'

To Vincent's way of thinking, not all the obstacles had been surmounted. His delicacy of conscience after his conversion experience raised two different types of doubt in his mind. Firstly, when he heard confessions, and this was an indispensable part of preaching missions, he was frequently subjected to temptations against chastity. Would it not be better to give up this work rather than lose his peace of soul or even risk damnation? Secondly, the idea of founding the Congregation filled him with such joy, and such a sense of

---

[2] Saint Vincent described the origins of the Congregation of the Mission on at least three different occasions: *S.V.P.* XI, pp. 2-5, 169-172 and XII, pp. 7-9. For additional information see ABELLY, *op. cit.*, 1.1 c. 7, p. 35 and c. 17, p. 66 and especially COLLET, *op. cit.*, Vol. 1, pp. 111-113. The information about Mme de Gondi's legacy that was renewed annually comes from Abelly and Collet. However, there is no mention of this annual bequest in the only known copy of her will. *(cf. Annales* [1933], pp. 67-80).

[3] *S.V.P.* III, pp. 399.

urgency, that he began to wonder if it really came from God or if it was merely a natural impulse or even, perhaps, a suggestion from the devil.

Divine objectives need divine assistance. Vincent made two retreats, one at the Carthusian monastery of Valprofonde and the other at Soissons. During the first retreat, a Carthusian dispelled his fears by reminding him of the story of a bishop in the early Church who experienced temptations whenever he baptised women.

> He begged God many times to deliver him from this temptation but as God did not grant his prayer he finally lost patience and retired to the desert. God showed him three crowns, one of which was more precious than the others. This was the one that God had prepared for him if he had persevered, and God told him he would only win the smallest crown since he had not trusted in him to keep him from falling into temptation. 'This example,' concluded St Vincent, who was telling the story to one of his companions who was constantly tormented by scruples, 'dispelled a very similar temptation that I experienced at that time as I fulfilled the duties of my vocation.'[4]

The second difficulty was more subtle. The account we have of it reveals Vincent's attitude towards the project of founding the Congregation of the Mission, something he attributed to Mme de Gondi. It also shows, indirectly, his preoccupation with the question which was so central to the asceticism of his day: the discernment of spirits.

> When I began to plan the establishment of the Mission my constant concern was about the spirit that inspired me to do this. I was in a state of doubt and did not know whether the idea was just a natural impulse or some suggestion of the evil one. I made a retreat at Soissons for the particular intention that God might take from me the pleasure I felt in this project and my urgent desire to see it accomplished. God was pleased to hear me and he rid me both of this desire and my over-hastiness, leaving me in quite the opposite dispositions.[5]

Confidence in God and holy indifference: Vincent is painfully acquiring those dispositions of soul that will transform him into a docile

---

[4] *S.V.P.* II, p. 107.
[5] *S.V.P.* II, pp. 246-247.

instrument of God's will. Let us take a quick glance at the ground he has covered from the time he was an impatient man, as we know from his letter in captivity, to the mature person who works things out; from being someone who light-heartedly plans his own life, to becoming a man who will scrupulously seek out signs from providence. This change has left its mark on his life. From now on he will desire to remain

> 'faithful to the practice of not finalising or embarking on any enterprise while I am so buoyed up with hope at the thought of all the good that might be achieved.'[6]

It was precisely when he put aside every natural impulse that God's work was most tangibly evident. The last obstacles had been overcome. The final impetus was to come from the man who, together with Pierre de Bérulle and Francis de Sales, was most influential in bringing about Vincent's spiritual transformation.

The impetus given by Duval

In his efforts to be completely submissive to God's will, Vincent was guided by Benet of Canfield's *Rule of Perfection* and had learnt that if God's will is made known by interior promptings of grace, it is even more clearly revealed through the will of superiors. At Soissons he had reached the state of complete spiritual indifference. He thought this was a sign that his plans for founding the company were of divine origin. He wanted something more; he needed to know that the work was positively willed by God. So he went off to discuss the matter with his spiritual director, André Duval.

In the Sorbonne doctor's austere and almost monastic room, Vincent gave a minute account of his works, his experiences and his hopes. He spoke about the peasants' spiritual poverty; their ignorance of their religion, their hunger for the bread of God's word, the frightening lack of good pastors in country parishes, the success of the missions and the blessings these had received from God. It was a long monologue during which he poured out his soul to this man, as he would have done to God himself. At last he fell silent and he trembled as he waited for his director's response. Duval gave it in a single sentence from Scripture; *Servus sciens voluntatem Domini et non faciens, vapulabit multis.* 'The servant who knows his master's will and neglects to do it, will receive many strokes of the lash.'

---

[6]   *S.V.P., ibid.*

165

As soon as he heard these words Vincent felt in his heart a powerful upsurge of grace. It was the divine mandate he had been seeking. He hesitated no longer. God was calling him, and those who wished to follow him, to dedicate themselves completely to the mission of bringing the word of God to country areas, to preach, catechise, hear confessions, settle disputes; in a word, to offer every kind of spiritual help to the people in the villages. After God, and after Mme de Gondi, the good M. Duval was the founder of the new company. It was he who had cut the last cable that moored the little barque, and had provided the decisive impetus which would launch it into the deep waters of the Church.[7]

Preparations for take-off

Vincent's progress was not confined to the spiritual life. Experience had taught him to prepare carefully every step of his career, to anticipate any difficulties that might arise, and to provide himself in advance with the necessary resources for achieving his objective. The founding of a new congregation called for serious preparation. Above all, he had to make sure that there would be support for his ideas and he would have to be very careful about administration.

This realistic approach to life was one of Vincent's chief characteristics, and three particular things he did in 1624 are clear evidence of this.

First of all he acquired a new benefice, the priory of St Nicolas de Grosse-Sauve, in the diocese of Langres, which was granted to him by the Holy Father. We have this information from a legal document dated 7 February 1624. It is a deed authorising a proxy to take possession of the priory in Vincent's name. The proxy was not named, as was common practice with this type of document, so that the name could be filled in later. It would seem that this was never done, so we can take it that Vincent did not take possession of the priory. This is hardly surprising as St Nicolas de Grosse-Sauve was not, in fact, vacant. A year earlier, on 22 June 1623, it had been given to the Oratorians by Sebastian Comet, bishop of Langres. So there was a clash of interest between the bishop's nomination in favour of de Bérulle's community, and Vincent's nomination by Rome. This is not an isolated case in that era's tangled legislative jungle. As it happened, the bishop's decision prevailed, and was confirmed by letters patent from the king and recorded by the

---

[7] *La vie de Mr. André Duval, Prêtre, Docteur de la Sorbonne ... par Robert Duval, son neveu ...*, pp. 43-45; manuscript quoted by J. M. IBAÑEZ in *Vicente de Paúl y los pobres de su tiempo*, pp. 339-340.

parlement of Paris. In 1627, three years after Vincent's unsuccessful nomination, further letters patent gave new responsibilities and granted new favours to the Oratorians in charge of the priory.[8]

Should we read into Vincent's tardy nomination for a new and quite considerable benefice yet another attempt on his part to secure a 'decent retirement' and add to the positions he had accumulated during the second decade of the century? Neither Vincent's state of mind in 1624 nor the advanced stage his plans had reached would support this theory. We should rather think of it as his first attempt to provide living quarters for the congregation he had in mind and secure for it some financial backing. When this attempt failed because of the obstacles mentioned earlier, Vincent and the de Gondis looked for other solutions to the problem.

In fact, just one month later, on 2 March 1624, there was another similar document authorising two priests, Blaise Féron and Antoine Portail, to take possession of the Collège de Bons Enfants of the University of Paris in the name of Vincent de Paul who, the previous day, had been named director and chaplain of the said college by Jean François de Gondi, the general's brother. This time the formalities were observed and there was no delay in taking over the property. On the 16 March Antoine de Portail, in virtue of the authority delegated to him, repeated Vincent's ritual at Clichy; he opened and closed the college church, knelt down to pray before the crucifix and the statue of Our Lady, kissed the altar, took his seat in the rector's stall, rang the bells, went through the outbuildings, entered and then left the principal's room and opened and closed the doors of the main building ...[9]

In this second document there is a minor, but for us an important variation, because it gives us interesting information about Vincent's preparations for his new life. The two procurators of the Bons Enfants are named, and we have the first reference to Vincent's degree in canon law. Apparently he had only recently obtained this degree. In the document relating to his nomination for Grosse Sauve he is referred to simply as 'parish priest of Clichy-la-Garonne'. So he must have acquired his new academic title after that. It would seem that in the free time left to him after his apostolic journeys, his duties in the de Gondi household, his work as chaplain to the galleys and director of the Visitation nuns, he found time to study for his law degree. This information should be considered too, in the context of his plans for

---

[8] The notarial deed referred to here and published by Coste in *S.V.P.* XIII, pp. 56-57, was a defective copy. F. Combaluzier published it again in *Annales* (1941-1942), pp. 265-271, and he appended to the original document a short study, and it is from this that we have taken the information in question.

[9] *Annales* (1940), pp. 458-460; ABELLY, *op. cit.*, 1.1 c. 17, p. 67; COLLET, *op. cit.*, Vol. 1, p. 113.

founding the company. If the cradle of the new company was going to be a university college then its director should have more qualifications than the mere bachelor's degree in theology Vincent had obtained after those now long distant years of study in Toulouse.

The 'Bons Enfants' was something more than we would understand by the term 'college' today. It is better translated as college 'for children of the aristocracy' rather than the traditional rendering of college 'for good sons' or 'for good children' and it took in students who had scholarships from the Sorbonne. Founded in the thirteenth century by the king, St Louis, and restored in the fifteenth century by Jean Pluyette, ex-rector of the Sorbonne, in Vincent's time the college was on the point of closing down. Louis de Guyart, the former director or 'principal', to use the academic term, made it available to the archbishop in return for an annual income of 200 *livres*. It covered approximately 1,600 sq. metres but most of the buildings were in ruins and completely uninhabitable. Anyway, it would do to house the small group of missioners that constituted the first nucleus of the infant community.[10]

Vincent did not move to his new residence straight away. His duties as chaplain and spiritual director kept him at the de Gondi's house, close to his illustrious penitent. He was detained, too, by other duties he had taken on previously. He was still titular parish priest of Clichy. The last things he did here as parish priest are recorded in the report of a pastoral visitation made by the archbishop of Paris on 9 October 1624. The archbishop found everything in good order; the parish priest had no complaints about his people and the faithful were happy with their priests. Altars, sacristy, vestments and sacred vessels were all clean and in good condition; the divine office was celebrated according to the rubrics, catechism was taught, the registers were up to date, there were 300 communicants and 100 parishioners had been confirmed. Through the good work done by his assistant, Grégoire le Coust, Vincent was able to watch over the spiritual welfare of his parishioners.[11] It might have been Vincent himself who suggested this episcopal visitation just before his departure to take up his new duties as founder. He liked to leave everything in good order.

'I never called M. de Saint-Cyran master'

Meanwhile, Vincent's circle of friends was widening. The various positions he held, and the new acquaintances these brought, opened increasingly

---

[10] *S.V.P.* XIII, pp. 24-26; *cf.* COSTE, *M.V.* Vol. 1, pp. 172-175.
[11] *Annales* (1929), pp. 729-730.

important doors to him. Through de Bérulle he came into contact with one of the most restless and influential minds of that epoch, someone who was to unleash on the Church in France, the most serious crisis it suffered that century. This was the famous and controversial Jean Duvergier de Hauranne, abbot of Saint-Cyran (1581-1643). The two men were almost compatriots.[12] Saint Cyran, as he was commonly called, was born in Bayonne right next to the Landes region of Gascony which was Vincent's birthplace.

There was a very practical reason why the two men should meet. A nephew of Saint-Cyran had been arrested in Spain for his part in a forgery crime. De Bérulle thought that Vincent might use his influence with Mme de Gondi who was the sister-in-law of the French ambassador in Madrid, to have the prisoner set free. It was with this in mind that he arranged a meeting in his own house.[13] According to Vincent, this took place sometime around 1624.[14] One way or another, they would have met anyway. They were both very concerned about Church reforms; both had a great desire for spiritual perfection and both men moved in the same circles. Although their reasons for doing so were different, both venerated de Bérulle as master. At this period, Saint-Cyran used to come and talk to the founder of the Oratorians every evening between six and seven o'clock. He soon became de Bérulle's apologist and confidant so the cardinal entrusted to him his administrative and literary concerns.[15]

Vincent and the abbé de Saint-Cyran were kindred spirits. What had started as a casual acquaintance motivated by self-interest ripened into friendship. They often dined together.[16] Mgr Pallu, founder of the Paris Foreign Missions Society, would have us believe that they even shared a common purse,[17] but from what we know about their separate living quarters and also the fact that Vincent gave away money shortly afterwards, this expression should not be taken literally. At most it would have meant that they shared the cost of some things.

There were also very considerable differences between Vincent and Saint-Cyran. Vincent, who now had close links with Dr Duval, was

---

[12] Martin de Barcos, the nephew of Saint-Cyran, objects to the term 'compatriots' that Abelly uses when speaking of Saint Vincent and the Abbé de Saint-Cyran (*op. cit.*,1.2 c. 12, p. 409), He claims that Bayonne and Dax were in different provinces and under different regional authorities. *cf.* M. DE BARCOS, *Défense de feu M. Vincent de Paul ...,* p. 10. For Saint-Cyran's bibliography *cf. infra* c. 36.

[13] *Journaux de M. des Lions,* unpublished; referred to by COSTE, *M.V.* Vol. 3, p. 137; J. ORCIBAL, *Les origines du jansénisme,* II, p. 399.

[14] *S.V.P.* XIII, p. 87.

[15] J. ORCIBAL, *Saint-Cyran et le jansénisme,* pp. 11-14.

[16] *S.V.P.* XIII, p. 94.

[17] *Restrictus probationum circa zelum servi Dei contra errores Sancyranii et Jansenii* (Rome 1727), p. 10.

distancing himself more and more from de Bérulle, whereas Saint-Cyran was becoming more deeply involved with him. Vincent's two directors took opposing sides in the controversy over the Carmelites' vow of slavery. In other matters the position taken by each party was not so clearly defined.

In spite of his close friendship with de Bérulle, Saint-Cyran continued for a time to be the friend of Richelieu and undertook to publish his *Instructio Christiana*. There was a time when the abbé de Saint-Cyran had the not very honourable role of confidant and informer[18] to the prime minister, and in return Richelieu offered Saint-Cyran an abbey. In spiritual matters Saint-Cyran was moving more and more towards a rigorously pessimistic doctrine, taking to extremes de Bérulle's teaching about the intrinsic worthlessness of the creature while Vincent trusted more and more to the merciful love of Christ who came to save all men and whose messianic sign par excellence was the evangelisation of the poor. In the future there would be more serious differences to alienate the two men who met in de Bérulle's room one evening in 1624. But that was a secret that the future kept to itself. For the moment, if we are to believe one Jansenist witness, Vincent was 'inspired, inflamed and enraptured' by what Saint-Cyran said. Yet he never was fully convinced intellectually by Saint-Cyran, and in 1639 he would say categorically, 'I have never acknowledged M. de Saint-Cyran as master.'[19]

'Wait patiently for his holy will to be made manifest'

Vincent was to find more lasting support from another friendship that started at this time, his friendship with Louise de Marillac (1591-1660).[20] It seems quite extraordinary that Vincent de Paul was forty-four years old before he

---

[18] J. ORCIBAL, *op. cit.*, pp. 27-28.

[19] DES LIONS, p. 70, referred to by COSTE, *M.V.*, p. 137; *S.V.P.* XIII, p. 89.

[20] The foundation biography of Saint Louise de Marillac was published in 1676: *La vie de Mademoiselle Le Gras, fondatrice et première supérieure de la Compagnie des Filles de la Charité, servantes des pauvres malades, par Monsieur Gobillon, Prêtre et Docteur de la Maison et Société de Sorbonne, curé de Saint Laurent* (Paris 1676). Among more recent biographies we should give special mention to L. BAUNARD, *La Vénérable Louise de Marillac, Mademoiselle Le Gras, Fondatrice des Filles de la Charité de Saint Vincent de Paul* (Paris 1898); J. CALVET, *Louise de Marillac par elle même* (Paris 1958); M. D. POINSENET, *De la angustia a la santidad, Luisa de Marillac, fundadora de las Hijas de la Caridad* (Madrid 1963). A great deal of research has followed the publication of P. Coste's Monsieur Vincent which accentuated the numerous problems for historical criticism posed by St Louise de Marillac's life and also provided a catalogue of unpublished documents about Louise which are preserved in various archives (*M.V.* Vol 1, pp. 209-263). We must highlight, too, the works of Fr Benito Martínez, mentioned earlier in the bibliography. The reader can find in the works we have referred to, all the documentation on which the following biographical summary is based.

met this woman who was destined to bring into being at least one half of his charitable works. It is also striking that Louise de Marillac should appear at the very moment when support and stimulus from Marguerite de Silly was on the wane. So unless we call it fate, we must see this as the designs of providence.

Vincent must have seen Louise de Marillac before 1624. Louise, who was born in 1591, belonged to a family of high social rank and it was this type of company that Vincent frequented. The Marillac family, who came from Haute Auvergne, could trace its family tree back to the thirteenth century. The most important members of the family at the beginning of the seventeenth century were three brothers, two of whom were called Louis and the other was named Michel. A surprising mixture of politician and saint, Michel was a close friend of de Bérulle and his collaborator in the task of bringing St Teresa's Carmelites into France. He rose to the highest positions in the government: Superintendant of Finances, Keeper of the Seals in 1626, and presumed prime minister in 1630. The second brother named Louis was a marshal in the army. The first Louis was not as gifted as his two brothers; he was a less stable character and less successful. This man was Louise's father. She was an embarrassment to him because she was illegitimate. However, Louise received an excellent education. Her childhood was spent at the famous Dominican convent at Poissy, and the prioress there belonged to the de Gondi family. One of the nuns at Poissy was a cousin of Louise. She was well versed in the classics, knew Latin and Greek, and had written or translated various pious works into pure, classical French.

Louise found her cousin was a great teacher. She learnt Latin, studied philosophy, and took up painting, though this did not last for long. In 1604, on the death of her father, she was removed from the convent and placed in a boarding school run by 'a poor lady' which turned out to be a sort of sewing workshop and family boarding house, so that she might learn 'the skills proper to a woman.' Her father's family distanced themselves somewhat from Louis's offspring. He had left his property to Innocente, a daughter of his second marriage, and Louise had only a modest allowance.

When she was young, Louise tried to enter the Poor Clares but was not accepted for health reasons. Her family then arranged a marriage for her and while it was not a very brilliant match it was respectable and likely to provide security. On 5 February 1613, she was married in the church of Saint Gervais to a gentleman named Antoine le Gras who was one of Queen Marie de Medici's secretaries. After that she would be known by her husband's surname with the prefix 'Mademoiselle'. This was the recognised form of address at this time, since she was not entitled to be called 'Madame' on account of her husband's low status in society. They had a son and called him Michel.

Louise conscientiously carried out her duties as wife and mother. Perhaps she was too conscientious. Deprived of genuine affection during her childhood, and haunted by the dark shadow of her unknown parentage, she tended towards introspection, scruples and anxiety. From time to time she felt racked by terrible spiritual crises which her directors (and she had very good ones) were not able to relieve. She was directed by Francis de Sales while he was in Paris, and then by Mgr Camus, who was a friend of the bishop of Geneva, and had inherited his spirituality. She was also able to count on the rather distant affection of her intelligent and spiritual uncle Michel, whose letters to her were full of practical wisdom. Louise suffered. Her sufferings were indescribable. When her husband's long and painful illness began, an illness which was to last four or five years and cause him to become irritable and uncongenial, she thought this was a punishment for not being faithful to the vow she made in her youth to join the Poor Clares. She began to think it was her duty to leave her husband and son. This notion became a veritable obsession which resulted in a very painful crisis.

On the Feast of the Ascension 1623, some days after making a vow of widowhood if her husband were to die, Louise suffered the dark night of the soul. Everything was darkness for her. She had doubts about herself, about the immortality of the soul and about the existence of God. They were ten days of terror. Finally, on Pentecost Sunday, in the church of Saint Nicolas des Champs, she was enlightened. Her doubts suddenly vanished. She understood that it was her duty to stay with her husband until God should take him. She would then be free to make vows and dedicate her life to the service of her neighbour. In another revelation she saw her future director, and at that time she felt a certain repugnance towards him. But more than anything else, she felt God was speaking to her. Never again could she doubt his existence for she had so deeply experienced his mysterious, consoling presence. [21]

Shortly after this purifying experience, she came within Vincent de Paul's sphere of influence. He was the priest she had seen in her vision at Saint Nicolas des Champs. It seems that Mgr Camus, whose pastoral duties in his diocese of Belley were keeping him very far from Paris, had recommended him.

---

[21] The account of her severe trial and unexpected deliverance from it is given by Louise, herself: LOUISE DE MARILLAC, *Écrits spirituels*. (Paris 1983), pp. 3-4. Another edition of Louise's writings is *Louise de Marillac, veuve de M. Le Gras. Sa vie, ses vertus, son esprit* (Bruges 1886) 4 volumes (the first one contains Saint Louise's life by Gobillon; the second one is about her spiritual writings, the third and fourth contain her letters). In English there is the translation published in 1991: *Spiritual Writings of Louise de Marillac. Correspondence and thoughts* (New York: New City Press).

At first Vincent considered the spiritual direction of this tormented soul to be a burden and a possible hindrance to the commitment he had already made to founding the Congregation of the Mission. Here was another Marguerite de Silly, but an even greater nuisance. It was only gradually that he came to realise what a wonderful collaborator in the apostolate this woman could become if he showed patience in guiding her. From Vincent Louise would receive peace of soul and discover the true meaning of her life but Vincent was going to find in Louise the most vitally important woman among all his female co-workers. God's ways are mysterious. Just as Vincent is about to begin his great work he has at hand everything he needs. 'Wait patiently for God's holy and adorable will to be made manifest', he wrote to Louise in the first letter we still have that was addressed to Mlle le Gras.[22] He knew from experience that God's will would always reveal itself eventually.

---

[22] *S.V.P.* I, p. 26.

Chapter XIII
THE CONGREGATION OF THE MISSION IS BORN

'They will give themselves to the service of poor country people'

In the afternoon of 17 April 1625 the de Gondi palace in the rue Pavée in the parish of Saint Sauveur witnessed some unusual activity. Shortly after midday two notaries from Châtelet, M. Dupuyis and M. Le Boucher, arrived there. They were immediately received by the master and mistress of this household together with their chaplain, M. Vincent. There then followed a simple ceremony during which a contract was read and duly signed. However routine an event that may have been for the notaries, who must have concluded dozens of these formalities every year; in the eyes of one person present, M. Vincent, the signing of that contract was of overwhelming importance. It was at this moment, and by means of this contract, that a new ecclesiastical community was born, the Congregation of the Mission.

It was still not very clear what sort of a child this would turn out to be—a pious association, 'company, congregation, or confraternity'. It could have been known by any of these names. And at this stage nobody knew who would be in this community. In fact, only one member was present and this was the founder, who committed himself to recruit within the space of a year six ecclesiastics or at least the number of these who could be supported financially by the foundation.

However, the motives and the aims of this pious work were crystal clear. Whereas the townspeople had their spiritual needs attended to by a good number of priests, doctors and religious, the poor people in country areas were left abandoned. The distinguished and influential M. Philippe Emmanuel de Gondi and his wife, Marguerite de Silly, thought that they could remedy this evil by setting up a pious association of priests who would decline all offers of work in the big cities and would 'dedicate themselves completely and exclusively to the salvation of poor country people; going from village to village at the community's expense to preach, instruct, exhort and catechise these people, and encourage them all to make a good general confession of their past life.'

The juridical structure of the new association was no more than rudimentary. It only named M. Vincent superior and director for life, leaving it to his discretion to choose his collaborators. These would have to renounce any other office, benefice or dignity for at least eight to ten years, and at the end of this period the superior could authorise them to accept any parish that the bishop might wish to give them. The association was meant to be a permanent one. In the event of Vincent's death provision was made for the remaining members to elect a new superior by a majority vote.

Certain distinctive characteristics were already apparent; the commitment not to preach in towns where there was an archbishop, bishop or presidial; the members 'will dedicate themselves entirely to the care of poor country people' and their services will always be given free of charge since it was the intention that the missioners should be supported from community funds so that they could freely give what they had freely been given by the liberal hand of God.

The contract provided for the compilation of community rules and it traced their basic outlines: life in common in obedience to M. Vincent, giving missions from October to June, a spiritual retreat lasting three or four days to be made in the house at the end of each month's work, helping parish priests and curates on Sundays and feastdays during the summer when requested.

Their field of action was to be the estates of M. and Mme de Gondi and they were obliged to preach missions, covering the whole area, every five years. If there was any time over they were free to devote it to apostolic work elsewhere, and in particular to giving spiritual help to the galley slaves.

In return for all this the de Gondis donated to the association the capital sum of 45,000 *livres*, 37,000 *livres* of which was counted out in cash and handed over in the notaries' presence. The balance would be paid within a year, and in the meantime the donors' possessions were mortgaged to this amount. This capital was to be invested in property or established revenues. M. and Mme de Gondi, their heirs, and successors, were named founders of the work in perpetuity with the rights and prerogatives set down by canon law. But they renounced all claims to office and made no demands regarding funeral or anniversary Masses.

Once the document had been read, the contracting parties and the notaries put their signature to the document. Vincent signed his name in a bold, firm hand in the centre of the page just below the signature of Marguerite de Silly.[1]

---

[1]   The complete text of the contract is given in *S.V.P.* XIII, pp. 197-202. The phrases in quotation marks are taken word for word from the original text.

That contract gave shape and form to the timid little light that had been lit eight years earlier by the bedside of the dying peasant in Gannes. For Vincent, it was not the end of anything, but rather a starting off point for a task whose magnitude could never have been foreseen. At the age of forty-five, and at the height of his maturity and creative powers, Vincent, now sure of God's will, convinced about his mission and confident in his strength, felt ready to take on the work and the struggles that lay ahead. There was one minor clause in the document that he must have been very reluctant to accept. This stipulated that 'the said M. de Paul should continue to reside with the de Gondis and to give them and their family the spiritual assistance he had provided for so many years up to now.' Events were soon to release him from that burdensome obligation.

A perfume that fades away

It was just as though Marguerite de Silly's only reason to go on living was the foundation of the Mission, because she survived the signing of the contract by barely two months. On 23 June 1625, she died a holy death in her Paris home at the age of forty-two.[2] Once her work was over she disappeared quietly and discreetly, like a flower which has given all its perfume. At the time of her death, her husband was a long way from Paris, on duty as General of the Galleys, in the southern ports of France. Mme de Gondi, however, had the consolation of being attended and comforted by Vincent de Paul, as she had always wished.[3] She left him and his assistant, M. Portail, a grateful remembrance in her will. She bequeathed two legacies to Vincent, one worth 1,500 *livres* and the other 900 *livres*, while M. Portail received 300 *livres*.[4] She begged Vincent never to leave her husband's house and to stay with her children when M. de Gondi died.[5] It was a request that Vincent regretfully could not comply with. The countess, whose entreaties had caused him to return to Châtillon, was now dead, and his mission in the de Gondi household was at an end.

---

[2] There is a discrepancy of detail regarding the exact date of Mme de Gondi's death. According to Abelly (*op. cit.*, 1.1 c. 18, p. 71), it occurred on 24 June. Collet gives the date as 23 (*op. cit.*, Vol. 1, p. 117), Chantelauze (*op. cit.*, p. 181) as 22 June. Collet's version is the best documented so Coste adopted this in *Monsieur Vincent* Vol. 1, p. 176, and it is his text that we follow.

[3] ABELLY and COLLET, *ibid.*

[4] *Annales* (1933), pp. 72-80.

[5] ABELLY, c. 1.1 c. 18, p. 72.

From nobleman to priest

However, he still had one painful duty to perform; he had to break the sad news to the General of the Galleys. As soon as Mme de Gondi was buried in the Carmelite convent at rue Chapon, Vincent made his way to Provence. The general was not in the best frame of mind to accept calmly the sad news, A few days earlier there had occurred a very unpleasant incident which had put him out of temper.

On 16 June his return to the port was not marked by the customary gun salute because the governor had kept the ammunition and gunpowder locked away. A few days later the governor paid a visit to de Gondi, and he was accompanied by an armed escort. This was an insult, not only to the supreme commander of the fleet, but also to the royal standard on the flagship as no arms were allowed past that. M. de Gondi reminded the governor of this, but the latter defied him again, expressing his anger with the port authorities and went on to say it was very hot there. De Gondi retorted that they would get even hotter if he dared to repeat the offence. Action followed words when he ordered his men to disarm one of the governor's guards they found walking along the quay, and throw him into the sea. The governor's response was to order the city officials to arm the surrounding areas. For his part de Gondi drew up his galleys with their prows pointing towards the port and ready to fire. The terrified town hall officials hastened to say that they did not want to jeopardise the peace of their town by getting involved in a quarrel between two individuals. De Gondi gave the order for the galleys to change course.

That was not the end of the conflict. The governor retired to his property in Soliers and he let de Gondi know that he thought it very strange that the latter should stay in the city while he himself was away in the country. De Gondi took this as a challenge. He went to Soliers and sent word to his adversary that he was going hunting and that if the governor wanted to join in, he would find it very entertaining. Some captains of the galleys went in search of their leader and persuaded him to return to the town. But when he reached the gates of the city the soldiers on guard did not salute him and, worse still, they had their weapons drawn. The irascible general charged at them and wounded two soldiers with his sword. There then followed a skirmish which lasted for some hours. The city magistrates were alerted and they hurried to the scene. They calmed down the two antagonists and placed the general under the protection of the city guard. Meanwhile the governor had been informed of the turn of events and he then set off for Toulon with a force of 120 men. His uncle, the bishop, went out to meet him and made him return to Soliers. The two adversaries were separated, and the mediation of influential people, together with a peremptory order from Richelieu, brought the matter to a bloodless if not very amicable conclusion.[6]

Notwithstanding his pious initiatives, Philippe Emmanuel de Gondi was still the haughty descendant of a breed of captains. In these difficult circumstances the news of his wife's death came like a thunderbolt from heaven. Vincent used all his eloquence to try and console him. He also asked the general to dispense him from the obligation of complying with Mme de Gondi's dying wish that Vincent remain in their household. The general agreed to this all the more readily since he himself had decided to leave the house and enter holy orders. The troubled events he had just lived through were, for him, a call to conversion that he could not ignore. But doubtless he was also influenced by the political turn of events following the rise of Richelieu. The general was far-sighted enough to realise that the de Gondi star was in eclipse. So in less than a year after his wife's death he entered the Oratorian Order and began to prepare for the priesthood. That was 6 April 1626. Thereafter he would be known as Fr de Gondi.[7]

'We would leave the key with a neighbour'

Once the bonds that tied him to the de Gondi palace were broken, Vincent found himself free to devote all his time to the missions and to developing the infant congregation. In October or November of that year he moved into the Collège des Bons Enfants.[8] His sole companion at that time was the ever-faithful Antoine Portail. To comply with the obligations laid down for the foundation, they had to find a third priest and they paid him 50 crowns a year.[9] These were heroic times for the foundation. Vincent would recall them later with evident nostalgia:

> The three of us would go from village to village giving missions. When we left we would leave the key with one of our neighbours and ask him to go and sleep in the house. However, at that time I had just one sermon which I preached with a thousand variations, its subject was the fear of God.[10]

---

[6] R. CHANTELAUZE, *op. cit.*, pp. 172-176.

[7] COLLET, *op. cit.*, Vol. 1, p. 119.

[8] *S.V.P.* XIII, pp. 60-61.

[9] It is unlikely that this third priest was Fr Belin, as Coste suggests. (*M.V.* Vol. 1, p. 178). St Vincent would not refer to him just as 'a good priest' and not give his name. Even in 1634 St Vincent considered him a perfect missioner who would have been in the Congregation if unavoidable duties had not prevented this; *cf. S.V.P.* I, p. 288.

[10] *S.V.P.* XII, p. 8.

His main concern was to bring together the small group of missioners he was committed to recruiting. He had a year in which to do this but recruitment was proving more difficult than he had expected. It was one thing to preach missions occasionally but it was a very different matter to commit oneself to it permanently and to give up the security one had acquired. And so there began for Vincent a period in his life when he would struggle to consolidate his project in the face of resistance and lack of understanding. Two candidates he had counted on for the Mission let him down at the last minute. Father Belin, who had been his companion for years in the service of the de Gondi family and in ministering to the galley slaves, withdrew because it was clearly God's will that he remain at Villepreux where he was chaplain to a noble family,[11] and Louis Callon, a priest from Aumale, was obliged to return to his parish because of ill health.[12]

Vincent thought that things would be easier once the community had ecclesiastical approval. He had no difficulty in obtaining this. It was granted by the archbishop of Paris, Jean François de Gondi, on 24 April 1626.[13] A curious case of a community being approved before it existed! In fact, just four months later, on 4 September, the first three companions signed, in the presence of a notary, the act of affiliation to the infant congregation, company or confraternity. These were Fr Portail and two priests from the diocese of Amiens: François du Coudray and Jean de la Salle who had been living with Vincent since March and April respectively.[14] The first thing they did together was to go on pilgrimage to Montmartre but Vincent was not able to accompany them because of illness. Their reason for going was to ask the holy martyrs to obtain for them the grace of poverty. Was this a deliberate wish to repeat the gesture made by the first Jesuits who joined St Ignatius in going to Montmartre for the same intention?[15]

Shortly afterwards another four members joined the community; Jean Becu, Antoine Lucas who was not yet ordained, Joseph Brunet and Jean d'Horgny. The 'little company', as Vincent was to call it all through his life, was at last a reality and not just a project written down on paper.

---

[11] *S.V.P.* I, p. 288; COLLET, *op. cit.*, Vol. 1, p. 96.

[12] *Vie du Vénérable M. Jacques Gallemant* (Paris 1653), pp. 319-328, quoted by COSTE in *M.V.* Vol. 1, p. 181.

[13] *S.V.P.* XIII, pp. 202-203.

[14] *S.V.P.* XIII, pp. 203-205.

[15] *S.V.P.* XII, p. 411. *Cf.* PEDRO DE RIBADENEIRA, *Vida del Padre Maestro Ignacio de Loyola ...* (Madrid, Madrigal, 1595), p. 33.

Burning the boats

Vincent realised that the time had come for him to burn his boats. He had reached the point of no return. He decided, first of all, to dispose of his personal property. On the same day, and in the same notary's office as the three companions had signed their act of entrance into the institute, he freely and irrevocably renounced all his paternal inheritance in favour of his brothers and sisters and their children. This is an interesting document because it gives us some idea of Vincent's property and the financial situation of his family.

The most important item was the sum of 900 *livres* (had he inherited this from Mme de Gondi?) that Vincent had already advanced to his brothers to pay off their debts, and a farmstead comprising farmhouse, woods and arable lands which he left to one of his sisters. Problems must have arisen at the time the deed was to be executed and this explains why four years later, in 1630, Vincent had a new will drawn up, leaving the same goods to the same beneficiaries. The properties donated by Vincent now came into the hands of his executors, M. Louis de Saint Martin d'Agès and his son César. There are some interesting differences between the first and second documents. The most significant difference is that in the deed of gift of 1626 there is only mention of goods inherited from his father; in the will dated 1630 reference is made to inheritances from father and mother.[16] So the death of Vincent's mother must have occurred in the interval between the two wills being made and not, as Coste thought, when he calculated she must have died before 1626.[17] If this was the case then providence had asked of the new founder an even more painful act of detachment than his voluntary renunciation of his property.

Another death during these years was to sadden Vincent's heart. Cardinal de Bérulle died suddenly while saying Mass on 2 October 1629. A contemporary poet captured the impression made by this event in a beautiful couplet: *Coepta sub extremis nequeo dum Sacra Sacerdos perficere, at saltem victima perficiam,* 'If I cannot complete the holy Sacrifice as priest then I will at least do so as victim.'

The departure of de Bérulle, as we shall see, was to have important political consequences. In spite of the fact that Vincent had been distancing himself from his former spiritual guide, and that in latter years they were practically enemies, de Bérulle's death saddened Vincent who continued to

---

[16] The text of the donation is found in *S.V.P.* XIII, pp. 61-63; that of the will is in *Annales* (1936), pp. 705-706.

[17] *Annales* (1936), p. 299. Coste did not know about St Vincent's will because it was discovered after Coste's death.

speak of him with affection.[18] In was as if some invisible hand were knocking down, one after another, the pillars which had been his support at the beginning of his mission. Marguerite de Silly in 1625, his mother in 1627 or 1628, de Bérulle in 1629. He was losing past friends but future friends were gathering round him.

The foundation contract stipulated that would-be members of the congregation had to renounce every ecclesiastical office or benefice. Vincent had to be the first to comply. Of all the benefices he had acquired in the years of his worldly aspirations, only one remained. This was the one he loved best, the parish of Clichy, whose titular appointment he had retained through all the trials of the previous 15 years. Now the time had come to give up Clichy. He did this in that same year, 1626. We know this because according to yet another legal document, 1630, we learn that he had received from his successor, Jean Souillard, the last 100 *livres* of the 400 *livres* stipulated for the transfer. Vincent's realism and strong financial acumen would not allow him to hand over the parish 'purely and simply as a gift, with no pension' as Abelly believed.[19] Such were the customs of his time. Had not his predecessor as principal of the Bons Enfants exacted an annual pension of 200 *livres* for the rest of his life?[20] Perhaps it is in this sense of not asking for a life pension that we should understand Abelly's phrase 'purely and simply'. After all, the flourishing parish of Clichy was worth a good deal more than the pile of ruined buildings known as the Collège de Bons Enfants.[21]

Vincent gave up the Bons Enfants, too. The college had been made over to him personally but the archbishop of Paris had intended it to house the congregation. So as soon as the institute received official approval from the same archbishop, Vincent had the property put in the name of the congregation. The archbishop issued the decree of collective ownership on 20 July 1626. But there must have been a legal problem, perhaps because the congregation had not, as yet, received royal approval. Once this was obtained a second episcopal decree was published.[22]

'The most distinguished member of my family'

Vincent's detachment from temporal goods was matched by a degree of spiritual detachment that is hard to assess because there is no direct testimony

---

[18] COLLET, *op. cit.*, Vol. 1, pp. 161-162.
[19] *S.V.P.* XIII, pp. 85-86; ABELLY, *op. cit.*, 1.1 c. 6, p. 27.
[20] *Annales* (1940), p. 461.
[21] *S.V.P.* I, pp. 24-25.
[22] *Annales* (1940), pp. 460-462; *S.V.P.* XIII, pp. 208-213.

to it. One single incident at this time can shed some light on this hidden process. One day, it must have been in 1629 or 1630, one of Vincent's nephews turned up at Bons Enfants. You could tell a mile off that the good man was a peasant. His appearance, and especially his clothes, marked him out as a typical peasant. Vincent felt ashamed to acknowledge that desperately poor and down-at-heel relation. He arranged for the man to be brought in unobtrusively. This was the old demon of his youth coming back to tempt him: the embarrassment he felt at having to go through the streets of Dax with a father who was badly dressed and lame. The bad impulse only lasted a moment and he quickly overcame it. He ran out of the house and embraced and kissed his relative openly in the street. Then he took him by the arm and led him into the college courtyard. He sent for all the members of the company and introduced his nephew to each one saying, 'This is the most distinguished member of my family.' It was visiting time. Vincent repeated the introduction for every visitor. Canon Saint Martin personally witnessed the event and it is he who tells the story.

It seems that the main reason for the nephew's visit was that he had come to consult his uncle about a promise of marriage. Might he not have come also to present some claim to the property allocated by Vincent in 1626? In actual fact, by the terms of the will drawn up in 1630, one of the nephews, Thomas Daigrand, who was the son of Vincent's older sister, was better provided for. Vincent had to drain the chalice to the dregs. His nephew had no money for the return journey. He was reluctant to use community money so he begged an alms from the Marquise de Maignelay, the pious sister of M. de Gondi. With the 10 crowns she donated, the young man set off on the 180 leagues (700 kilometres) return journey which he made on foot of course. Furthermore, at the next community exercise Vincent accused himself in front of everyone of having been ashamed of his rough and badly dressed nephew and of wanting him to be brought secretly to his room.[23] At last the earlier Vincent, who dreamed of worldly success and looked on the priesthood as a means of advancing his family's fortunes, was buried once and for all.

Vincent had crossed all the bridges and had now reached the other bank of his life in the company of that handful of young priests. Only one of them, du Coudray, had turned forty; the friend he had known longest, Portail, was not yet thirty-six—and they all looked to Vincent as their father and spiritual guide, the motivating force behind their apostolate, the one who

---

[23] ABELLY, *op. cit.*, 1.3, p. 208 and 292; COLLET, *op. cit.*, Vol. 1, pp. 108-109; *S.V.P.* XIII, pp. 61-63; *Annales* (1936), pp. 705-706.

would orientate them in doctrine and organise the little group. It was a community that had to be built up from the foundations even while the stones that comprised it were still being fashioned. Vincent, without daring to say so (he would say it later on when old age and the passage of time would help him overcome any inhibitions of false modesty) was thinking of St Benedict, St Bruno and St Ignatius as they started their life's work. The task ahead was enormous and there would be no shortage of problems.

Chapter XIV
THE STRUGGLE TO CONSOLIDATE HIS APOSTOLIC WORKS

'Just as Our Lord won over and directed the apostles'

The de Gondi lands were waiting. As soon as the new community came into being it was launched into the work for which it had been founded. No fewer than 140 missions were preached during the first six years of its history when the missioners had their first home at the Bons Enfants.[1] This figure is all the more remarkable since there were no more than seven priests until 1631. In that year the number rose to fourteen[2] thanks to the ordination of some clerics who had been admitted to the company some years previously and these were joined by two more priests. This meant that two mission teams could be set up and they would work a total of 290 days in the year. Vincent worked just like the others. The office of superior did not demand much in the way of supervisory duties. Vincent was more than superior; he was their leader. He was gradually laying the foundations of a congregation that was destined to last.

Life at the Bons Enfants was well-ordered. There were rules for all the community exercises which regulated the time to be given to prayer, to study and to 'controversy', a term which signified debates with the Huguenots. These regulations were taken from a manual written by the Belgian Jesuit, Martin Becan, which was much in vogue at that time. Vincent made sure that the order of day was observed even when he was absent.[3]

There were some picturesque aspects to the mission journeys. To honour the terms of the foundation and not place any burden at all on the places where missions were being given, the missioners used to take with them the basic items of furniture they would need and these even included portable beds[4] which would be put in a little horse-drawn cart. They made

---

[1] ABELLY, *op. cit.*, 1.2 c. 1, p. 21.
[2] *Notices sur les prêtres, clercs et frères défunts de la Congrégation de la Mission*, Vol.1 (Paris 188), pp. 453-455.
[3] *S.V.P.* I, p. 66.
[4] *S.V.P.* II, pp. 77-78.

the journey from one place to another on foot but when they grew weary they would take it in turn to ride the one horse[5] they had at their disposal. As superior, Vincent was attentive to the smallest details. Life on the missions was to follow the Paris regime as much as possible. They kept to a fixed time for rising and for going to bed, for meditation, for reciting the divine office, for going to the church, for mission services and for returning. Vincent attached great importance to things being done at the same time and on a regular basis, not according to people's whims and passing moods. He wanted to inculcate habits of regularity and exactness.[6] He was even more anxious to teach his collaborators those virtues he deemed most necessary for living in community. He insisted on prudence, thinking ahead and on meekness. He urged them to struggle against sensuality, selfishness and any form of vanity in their preaching.[7]

But Vincent was no dreamer. He knew that communities are made up of men who all have their little faults, their different temperaments and moods which could sometimes cause friction. For that reason he had to smooth away rough edges and settle minor differences. On one occasion he exhorted Portail to forego his seniority and in charity give complete support ('I repeat, complete support') to the young and inexperienced Fr Lucas. 'This was the way Our Lord won over and taught his apostles' and the way Portail was to act since he was older in years and the second eldest in vocation. It was just like a father gently, very gently, correcting his son, 'As you are the eldest ...'[8]

At other times he had to offer encouragement and congratulation. Vincent did this discreetly and when he gave praise he mentioned at the same time the qualities that person still lacked. This same M. Portail was a shy man who even in 1630, after 20 years at Vincent's side, had not the courage to preach from a pulpit. Vincent praised him for his perseverance and begged for him the grace of being an example to the community when conversation showed any lack of modesty, meekness or mutual respect.[9]

He was not only concerned for their spiritual welfare. Health and happiness are equally important if a community is to function well. 'Are you all well? Are you all happy?' he would ask when he was away from them. His letters would frequently end with this practical recommendation, 'I beg you, take care of your health.'[10]

---

[5]   *S.V.P.* I, p. 175.
[6]   *S.V.P.* I, p. 177.
[7]   *Ibid.*
[8]   *S.V.P.* I, p. 112.
[9]   *S.V.P.* I, p. 88.
[10] *S.V.P.* I, p. 67.

'I thought the gates of Paris were going to fall on top of me'

But his greatest concern was to share his zeal; that burning spiritual desire for souls who were at risk, his indefatigable spirit of work, his hunger and thirst for God's glory. All these things were an obsession he wanted to pass on to others.

> The poor people run the risk of losing their souls because they are ignorant of the truths necessary for salvation and they do not know how to go to confession. If His Holiness knew of their needs he would not rest until he had put the matter to rights. It was our awareness of this problem that caused us to found the company.[11]

Vincent himself was so consumed with this zeal that he believed he had no right to take any rest. The following disclosure on his part is absolutely invaluable for revealing to us the spiritual dispositions of the founder during those early years, that same M. Vincent who just ten years before had limited his aspirations to the procuring of a good benefice and leading the quiet, peaceful life of a worthy canon or respected abbot.

> Whenever I came back from a mission and drew near to Paris I had the feeling that the gates of the city were about to fall on me and crush me to pieces. That thought was in my mind nearly every time I returned from giving a mission. I used to think to myself. 'Here are you coming back to Paris while there are many other villages expecting you to do for them what you have just done elsewhere. If you had not gone to that particular village then such and such a one would probably have been damned if they had died in the state you found them in. Having experienced this, and knowing that such sins are being committed in that parish, do you not think that the same sins and similar faults are being committed in the other parishes too? They are waiting for you to go and do for them what you have just done for their neighbours. They are expecting a mission and you go off and leave them there! If people die in the meantime, and they die without repenting of their sins, you will be responsible in a way for their damnation and you should tremble lest God call you to account for it.' Fathers

---

[11] *S.V.P.* I, p. 115.

and Brothers, these were the thoughts that went through my mind.[12]

Anxious to put the company on a solid foundation, Vincent proposed a practice which was widespread in most communities, that of making vows. Most of his followers took the advice given by their father and master.

> From the very beginning God granted the company the desire to live in the most perfect way possible outside of the religious state. These are the reasons why we made vows: to unite ourselves more closely to Our Lord and to his Church, for the superior of the company to be more united to its members and for the members to be in closer union with its head. This custom has been followed since the second or third year of the company's existence. These vows of poverty etc. were simple vows and we renewed them after two or three years.[13]

Without rushing things, but avoiding procrastination too, he was tracing the main outlines of his institute. Vincent considered it most important to have the foundations solidly laid. At the same time he was creating a style or ‚as he would say, a spirit (this was a popular word in that century). He was fashioning apostles and seeing in his mind's eye the benchmark of the institute. The Congregation of the Mission is the first of his works and in a certain sense it will give support to all the rest. Without realising it Vincent was becoming a patriarch, a role he assumed without any trace of arrogance. He felt conscious of his unworthiness and this was a burden he would carry all through life. He was very far from considering himself a saint but paradoxically that is precisely what other people were beginning to think that he was.

'Depravity among the clergy is the ruin of the Church'

As the new congregation developed, a new apostolate was opening up, that of retreats for ordinands. Given Vincent's habit of denying that any work he undertook was done on his own initiative, and his attributing all of them to the unforeseen and mysterious designs of providence,[14] it is hard to judge how far this new work sprang from Vincent's concern and preoccupation

---

[12] *S.V.P.* XI, p. 445.
[13] *S.V.P.* V, pp. 457-458.
[14] *S.V.P.* IX, pp. 57, 113-114, 208-210, 242-243, 313, 455-457, 682-683; X, p. 90; XII, pp. 7-9, 390, 437-438.

about the question, or how much it was the result of fortuitous circumstances which obliged him to take on the work and thus comply with providence.

The need to correct abuses among the clergy was a cause of deep concern to those members of the reform movement whose company Vincent had been frequenting since the early days of his conversion.[15] This rehabilitation was the underlying principle of the Tridentine reform project. So there were swarms of people trying to get the Tridentine directives and initiatives for the reform of the clergy introduced into France. This was a crying need as is proved by statements from contemporary witnesses attesting the relaxation of morals among the clergy. There were three main reasons for this: firstly, the system of allocating benefices which was largely in the hands of lay people (the crown, parlement or feudal lords); secondly, the practice of allowing lay people and even children to assume the title of abbot, prior or even bishop; and finally, the lack of centres for training priests.

As well as the three conditions just mentioned there was widespread abuse of every kind. There were irregular ordinations (we remember Vincent's own ordination) and the appointment as bishops, abbots and canons, of individuals who had no vocation for the task, or rather, whose only vocation was a hereditary right to certain ecclesiastical benefices. A great number of dioceses were either without a bishop or the prelate did not comply with the obligation to reside in that place. In addition there was the scandal given by numerous clergy through their gambling, concubinage and addiction to drink. There was widespread ignorance of liturgical rites and ceremonies and ignorance, too, of even the basic truths of the faith.[16]

As a remedy for such a sad state of affairs the Council of Trent proposed the setting up in every diocese of seminaries where aspirants to the priesthood would be educated from an early age and instructed in those subjects necessary for the exercise of the sacred ministry.[17] But as we know, the Tridentine decrees were not accepted in France until 1615. Before that date the assemblies of clergy and provincial councils issued numerous

---

[15] P. BROUTIN, *La réforme pastorale en France pendant la première moitié du XVII siècle* (Tournai 1956), 2 vols.

[16] There is abundant evidence concerning the decadence of the French clergy in the seventeenth century. It is very easy to draw from all this a very pessimistic picture of the situation. A typical example of this would be the book by E. MOTT, *Saint Vincent de Paul et le sacerdoce* (Lille 1903) and the work of Coste, himself, in *M.V.* Vol. 1, p. 283-290. Modern researchers are cautious about generalisations made from particular examples or cases. However, the general view is far from optimistic. See J. ORCIBAL, *Les origines ...* II, p. 1-13, which has an extensive bibliography; E. PRECLIN, *Luchas políticas,* pp. 226-227.

[17] Dec. *Cum adulescentium aetas* ses. 23 c. 18. *Cf.* L. CRISTIANI, *Trento* (Vol. 19 *Historia de la Iglesia,* by FLICHE-MARTIN), pp. 235-243.

decrees in the last quarter of that century, urging the establishment of seminaries and general measures to reform the clergy. But none of these seminaries flourished and sooner or later they all closed. In 1624 the situation had improved only marginally. The conciliar documents continued to be a dead letter.[18]

At the beginning of the seventeenth century a solution began to emerge. It came from the nucleus of reformers grouped around Dom Beaucousin, Canfield, Duval, Mme Acarie, de Bérulle and Marillac. Vincent had become acquainted with this group. The basic thrust of de Bérulle's action, and something that Saint-Cyran continued and reinforced, was to make people realise the dignity of the priestly calling. De Bérulle's Oratorians put their best men and their biggest effort into the training of priests.[19]

The same objectives were pursued, although by different methods, by another friend of de Bérulle and Vincent de Paul, Adrien Bourdoise (1583-1655) who, in the parish of St Nicolas du Chardonnet in Paris, had set up a community of priests where a small number of aspirants to the priesthood received some training in spirituality and ministry. Michel le Gras, the son of Louise de Marillac, was one of these aspirants. So, too, was Claude Lancelot[20] who was to become the famous Jansenist leader.

From the very outset Vincent was well aware of the deplorable state of the clergy. The people were deprived of pastoral care because their priests were unworthy of their calling and lacked training. This situation was the crucial factor in the three decisive experiences that determined Vincent's vocation. When he was with the de Gondis there had been the confessor who did not know the words of absolution. In Châtillon there were the six chaplains who scandalised the faithful by their irregular conduct. At Marchais there was the heretic's accusation that the Church had thousands of idle priests in the big cities while the poor people were served by unworthy clergy who were ignorant of even the basic truths of their religion.

During his apostolic journeys Vincent came across many proofs of this alarming state of affairs. The following diagnosis of the situation which

---

[18] A. DEGERT, *Historie des séminaires français jusqu'à la Révolution* (Paris 1903); E. PRECLIN, *Lucha políticas*, pp. 224-226.

[19] J. ORCIBAL, *Les origines*, Vol. 2, pp. 24-25; H. BRÉMOND, *op. cit.*, III, pp. 154-157; L. COGNET, *La reforma del clero,* in H. JEDIN, *op. cit.*, pp. 57-68; H. KAMEN, *El siglo de hierro pp,* 282-284; *DTC* XI, 1104-1120.

[20] For information on Bourdoise, *cf.* Ph. DESCOURVEAUX, *La vie de Monsieur Bourdoise* (Paris 1714); J. F. DARCHE, *Le saint abbé Bourdoise*, 2 vols. (Paris 1883-1884); P. SCHOENHER, *Histoire du Séminaire de Saint Nicolas du Chardonnet* (Paris 1909-1911); J. HARANG, *Bourdoise* (Paris 1949); E. PRECLIN, *Luchas políticas*, p. 224. The information on Lancelot is taken from the preface to his work: C. LANCELOT, *Mémoires touchant la vie de Monsieur de Saint-Cyran* (Colonia 1738), Vol. 1, p. I-XXXVIII.

we read in his writings could hardly be more pessimistic. He presents us with the sombre picture of many unlettered priests.[21] Their most common failings, and here their conduct was worse than that of lay folk,[22] were avarice, hard-heartedness towards the poor, excessive drinking,[23] immoral behaviour[24] and negligence in ensuring that church property was kept in good order. 'I was full of confusion at hearing what was being said about the dirt and the bad condition of churches in France.'[25] What he has to say about liturgical abuses is particularly hard, and at the same time revealing, because he speaks from lived experience:

> If you had seen, I do not say the wrong actions, but the different ways they interpreted the rubrics for saying Mass forty years ago (writes Vincent in 1659), you would have been ashamed. I think there is nothing more unbecoming than to see so many variations in the way Mass is celebrated. Some priests begin Mass with the *Pater Noster;* others have their chasuble over their arm while they say the *Introibo* and put it on afterwards. I was once in St Germain-en-Laye and I noticed seven or eight priests who each said Mass his own way. Each one had his own ceremonies. Such diversity was really pitiful.[26]

Vincent, however, had no wish to generalise and he was happy to recognise that there were also priests who were very holy. In Paris itself there were many very good priests.[27] But, all in all, his deep conviction was that:

> In many places the Church is falling into disrepute because of the bad lives of priests. It is these who are ruining and bringing down the Church, it is only too true that the depraved state of the clergy is the main reason for the downfall of God's Church.[28]

Reading this account of those deeply felt experiences, it is hard to believe Vincent altogether when he says he never thought of devoting himself

---

[21] *S.V.P.* XII, p. 289.
[22] *S.V.P.* XII, p. 374.
[23] *S.V.P.* XI, p. 9, 25. *S.V.P.* IV, p. 326.
[24] ABELLY, *op. cit.*, 1.2 c. 2, p. 214.
[25] *S.V.P.* IV, p. 326.
[26] *S.V.P.* XII, p. 258.
[27] *S.V.P.* XI, p. 9.
[28] *S.V.P.* XI, pp. 308-310.

to the reform of the clergy. Such statements should be understood to mean that he would never, on his own account, have dared to take on a work so bristling with difficulties. As always he awaited the manifestation of God's holy and adorable will without anticipating Providence.' In the end God spoke to him one day through the words of a certain prelate and this gave him more reassurance 'than if an angel had revealed it to him.'[29]

'The ordinands are our richest and most precious asset'

It turned out like this. Among the bishops that Vincent had dealings with through giving missions in their dioceses, parts of which included the de Gondi estates, was one of the most austere and zealous prelates in France, Augustin Potier, bishop of Beauvais (+ 1650). On more than one occasion both men lamented the deplorable state of the diocesan clergy. Vincent had put forward very clearly his view of the problem: it was useless to try and reform the elderly priests who had lived irregular lives for many long years and had become used to that situation. A more radical remedy was needed. They would have to impart a truly priestly spirit to ordinands and not admit to holy orders those who lacked this spirit or who were incapable of fulfilling their priestly duties. Notice it was Vincent who put forward the *status quaestionis*. The idea took root in the prelate's mind.

In the middle of July 1628, Vincent and Monseigneur Potier were travelling together in the prelate's carriage. The bishop seemed to be dozing. His companions kept a respectful silence. But Potier was not dozing. After a while he half opened his eyes and murmured:

> I think I have found a quick and effective way of preparing candidates for the priesthood. Gather them together in my house for a few days, and see that they practise works of piety and receive instruction about their duties and their ministry.

Vincent took up the suggestion immediately. 'That thought has come from God, my Lord. I, too, think that is the best way of setting the clergy of this diocese on the right path.'

'Well, let us set to work', said the prelate. 'Draw up a programme, prepare the list of subjects to be dealt with, and come back to Beauvais two or three weeks before the September ordinations to organise the retreat.'

---

[29] ABELLY, *op. cit.*, 1.1 c. 25, p. 118.

This was the divine signal Vincent had been waiting for. He arrived at Beauvais on 12 September. The three days from 14 to 16 September were devoted to examinations of the candidates. On Sunday 17 September the retreat began and the bishop himself gave the opening address. Then Vincent, helped by three members of the Bourdoise community, directed the retreat. He kept for himself the task of explaining the commandments. Duchesne and Messier, who were doctors of the Sorbonne, explained the sacraments and the Creed. It was Duchesne who had accompanied Vincent on the mission at Marchais, and had helped with the conversion of the heretic. One of his brothers, assisted by a graduate, gave instructions on the liturgy. The retreat was a resounding success. All the ordinands made a general confession to Vincent. Duchesne was very moved and did likewise.[30]

So began the new work of the Congregation of the Mission which was still in its infancy: retreats for ordinands, 'the richest and most precious deposit the Church could place in our hands', as Vincent used to say to his missioners.[31]

Looked at from today's perspective, Vincent's ways of tackling the terrible problem might seem to us inadequate. And some harsh critics of that period, like the Jansenists, were of the same opinion.[32] The retreats for ordinands were, in fact, a sort of professional sandwich course. In the space of ten or fifteen days, the aspirants to holy orders made the retreat proper, and also received basic instruction in morality and doctrine as well as practical experience in the rites of celebrating Mass and administering the sacraments. So it was a case of applying an urgent remedy to a state of affairs that called for immediate action. A complete programme for training priests would require the setting up and organising of seminaries. Vincent would come to that but the work would take many years and the Church, in the meantime, could not afford to wait. As long as the system of recruiting clergy remained unchanged, and each candidate was able to study as he chose, the bishop could only see to it that ordinands received the short, sharp, shock of a retreat to make them reflect seriously on their vocation and to provide them with the basic theory and practice of the way they should perform their pastoral duties. In time to come, the retreats for ordinands would put the finishing touches to a long period of training in the seminary.

The new institution was an immediate and outstanding success. Within three years the practice was adopted in the diocese of Paris. The

---

[30] ABELLY, *op. cit.*, 1.1 c. 25, pp. 116-119; *S.V.P.* I, p. 65.

[31] *S.V.P.* XII, p. 9.

[32] M. DE BARCOS, *op. cit.*, pp. 74-80.

archbishop confided the work to Vincent de Paul. Many other dioceses followed suit, as we shall see later on, and even in Rome itself the retreats became obligatory and were always directed by priests of the Mission.

'A special confraternity called a charity'

The 'charities', or confraternities of charity, which were the first works established by Vincent, continued to occupy a good deal of his time during these creative years. Everything points to the fact that Vincent had hit on just the right formula from the very moment they were first founded at Châtillon-les-Dombes. The initial foundation proved very successful but there was still need for modification and development.

Following established guidelines, every mission closed with the founding of a confraternity. Vincent and his companions were always faithful to this practice. Very soon there were charities on all the de Gondi estates and from there they spread to neighbouring districts. Paris, itself, began to see charities set up in 1629. The first ones were established at St Sauveur and St Nicolas du Chardonnet. By 1631 they numbered six; the two just mentioned plus those of St Eustache, St Benoît, St Sulpice and St Méderic. Soon afterwards there followed those of St Paul, St Germain l'Auxerrois and St André. They increased gradually until there was not a single parish in the capital which did not have its confraternity.[33]

The second episcopal city to have the charities was Beauvais. Monseigneur Potier, that same bishop who had inspired Vincent to give retreats to ordinands, summoned him to establish charities in the main city of his diocese.[34] At Beauvais Vincent repeated, though perhaps more cautiously, his experiment at Mâcon to turn a whole city into a confraternity of charity. His precautions proved to be well-founded. The royal lieutenant became alarmed at Vincent's activity and sent a strong note of protest to the authorities in Paris. He also asked them to investigate what was going on and present the facts to the Procurator General.

According to the note:

> for the past fortnight there has been in this city a priest called Vincent who, disregarding the king's authority, and without informing either the court officials or any other appropriate authority, is holding meetings for a great number of women

---

[33] ABELLY, *op. cit.*, 1.1 c. 23, pp. 108-109; *S.V.P.* I, pp. 100, 112, 117; II, p. 156; IV, p. 425; XIII, p. 599.

[34] ABELLY, *op. cit.*, 1.1 c. 23, p. 108.

whom he has persuaded to join a confraternity which goes by
the particular name of a Charity. By means of this society, he
proposes to help the sick people of the said city of Beauvais,
by giving them food and other necessities. Money is collected
every week for this purpose. It has been organised by the said
Vincent who, having founded the said confraternity, has
admitted to it some 300 women who meet frequently to
undertake the above named functions—a matter which cannot
be tolerated.[35]

We have no documents to tell us what effect the royal deputy's
bureaucratic prose had. It must have been nil because the charities continued
to function in the town's eighteen parishes.

A woman's hand is needed

As the charities began to spread, Vincent had to consider the problem of
finding some central organisation which would co-ordinate the charities and
see that a good spirit was maintained in each. Some abuses had crept in;
some charities were finding it hard to function; here and there the first fervour
had waned, and many charities felt the need for instructions on how to proceed
in face of unforeseen difficulties. Vincent thought there should be periodic
visitations to reanimate the members' enthusiasm and correct any little failings.
The best person for this would be a woman. A small group of ladies who had
caught something of Vincent's charitable zeal, had gathered round him.
Vincent had recourse to this group and addressed himself in a special way to
the most fervent and devoted woman among them, Louise de Marillac. But
first of all he had to train her. Vincent set about the task.

Louise had been a widow since 21 December 1625. Her husband,
Antoine le Gras, had died after a long and painful illness. He suffered a lot
and the night before he died he vomited blood seven times. Nevertheless he
had great peace of soul. Some days earlier he had taken the resolution to
devote the rest of his life to God. His last words were, 'Pray for me since I
cannot pray any more.' When morning came, Louise, who had been
completely on her own that terrible night, hurried to church to go to confession
and communion and then consecrate herself to Our Lord as the only spouse
of her soul.[36]

---

[35] A. FEILLET, *La misère au temps de la Fronde et Saint Vincent de Paul* (Paris, Didier, 1868),
pp. 212-213.

[36] GOBILLON, *op. cit.*, pp. 21-24.

Shortly after her husband's death, Louise's young son Michel, who was thirteen years old, entered the parish seminary of St Nicolas du Chardonnet. This was not to be the final solution because the poor lad was idle and unstable. He was to prove a constant source of worry for Louise but for the moment he seemed to want to be a priest. His entrance into St Nicolas du Chardonnet set him on this path and relieved his mother of not a few worries.

During the three years that followed, Vincent kept Louise in a state of something like holy idleness. She devoted this time to innumerable acts of piety. We still have the rule of life she imposed on herself at this time. Not even the most austere conventual rule could have been more demanding. Every day she had two hours of mental prayer, recitation of the Little Office of the Blessed Virgin, Mass, visit to the Blessed Sacrament, spiritual reading, rosary, examination of conscience and all these at the appointed time. Every hour she would make at least four acts of the presence of God accompanied by ejaculatory prayer. Every week she would re-read what she had written in 1623, the account of her great temptation, in order to remind herself of her obligation to serve God all her life. On the first Saturday of every month she would renew the vows and review the other resolutions she had taken. She received holy communion four days a week, and on these days she would practise special penance. As well as observing the fasts of Advent and Lent, she fasted every Friday of the year. She took the discipline three times a week and wore a hair shirt all day Friday and on the mornings she went to communion. Every year she made two eight-day retreats, one during the octave of the Ascension and the other in Advent.[37]

'I will think for both of us'

In the beginning Vincent let her continue like this. Then, little by little, he took over the reins to direct this ascetic novice. The correspondence between them, which is still preserved, introduces us to another of Vincent's talents, the art of spiritual direction. His letters are full of affectionate concern and are written in affectionate and even tender terms; something we would not have expected from one who so harshly criticised the failings of the clergy. But it was just the tone that the afflicted widow le Gras needed.

Vincent's spiritual direction led her to overcome her fears and place herself in the state of perfect indifference, and of confidence in the merciful love of God.

---

[37] LOUISE DE MARILLAC, *Ses écrits*, pp. 887-890.

'Continue to be happy and remain in the dispositions of
wanting whatever it is God wants of you.[38] Try to find
contentment in circumstances that bring you unhappiness
and always honour the inactivity and the hidden life of the
Son of God. This is the basic reason why God created you and
it is what he asks of you at present, in the future and for ever.
If his divine Majesty does not let you know, beyond any
shadow of doubt, that he is asking something else of you, do
not think about that matter, keep your mind off it. Leave me to
be responsible for it. I will do the thinking for both of us.'[39]
'Read the book on the love of God, (*Treatise on the Love of
God* by St Francis de Sales) especially that part where he
writes about the love of God and the virtue of indifference.'[40]
'Why should your soul not be full of confidence since, through
his mercy, you are the beloved daughter of Our Lord.'[41]

Young Michel did not find the seminary at St Nicolas to his liking
and Louise was very anxious about him. There is scarcely a letter written by
Vincent at this time in which he does not refer to the problem. He holds to
the same principle, motherly love must also give way to confidence in God's
love.

How blessed it is to be a child of God, since He loves those
who have the happiness of being his sons even more than you
love your son; though you show more tenderness than any
other mother shows her children. Have complete confidence
that since Our Lord has given you such charity towards other
people's children, you can expect Him to take special care of
your son. Rest in this hope, and live with the joyful heart of
one who is conformed to Our Lord's will in everything.[42]

Louise also needed to detach herself from her devotion to certain
pious practices which, to someone of her meticulous and scrupulous
temperament, were more of a hindrance than a help on the road to perfection.
She had to learn to distinguish between the essential thing which was to

---

[38] *S.V.P.* I, p. 39.
[39] *S.V.P.* I, p. 62.
[40] *S.V.P.* I, p. 86.
[41] *S.V.P.* I, p. 90.
[42] *S.V.P.* I, p. 77.

love God, and her devotions which were of lesser importance. Vincent's counsels led her gently on towards this goal.

> As for the thirty three acts of devotion in honour of Our Lord's sacred humanity and those other devotions, do not be worried when you omit them. God is love and he wants us to go to Him through love. So do not feel that you are obliged to perform all these good practices. I am very pleased that you should practise devotion to Our Lady provided you go gently.[43]

'Go in God's name'

The main problem was whether God wanted her in the cloister, as she had thought when she was young. Neither she, nor Vincent, had a clear answer to this question. So there was a delay of three years while they waited for some unequivocal sign from providence. In the meantime, Vincent used the same tactics as he had done with Mme de Gondi: he got Louise interested in works of charity. In the early stages he did this indirectly and kept her in the background, more in the role of administrator. Together with the other ladies from Vincent's circle, Louise would send material, chemises, money and food from Paris to help the charities in country districts.[44] Finally, he judged her sufficiently mature to undertake visitations. The journeys began. To prepare her for the first one, Vincent sent her a letter which is both an itinerary and a spiritual guide.

> I am sending you letters and the report you will need for your journey. Go then, Madamoiselle, in the name of Our Lord.[45]

It meant a lot of work right from the outset. In 1629 Louise visited, as far as we know, the charities at Montmirail and Asnières. In 1630 she went to Saint Cloud, Villepreux, Villiers-le-Bal and back again to Montmirail and Beauvais. The following year she visited the charities of Montrueil-sous-Bois, Montmirail for the third time, Le Mesnil, Bergères, Loisy, Soulières, Sannois, Franconville and Herblay. In 1633 she went to Verneuil, Pont-Sainte-Maxence, Gournay, Neufville-le Roy, Bulles ...

---

[43] *S.V.P.* I, p.86.
[44] *S.V.P.* I, pp. 31, 32, 33, 39, 40.
[45] *S.V.P.* I, pp.73-74.

Their journeys by ramshackle coach were most uncomfortable and they had to find lodgings wherever they could. They stopped at abandoned, wretched villages, where the accommodation was often not very respectable. The serious faces of Louise and her companions soon took on some of St Teresa's joyfulness. Louise always travelled with an attendant, and often this would be one of the ladies she was friendly with, especially her cousin Isabelle du Fay.

The visitations were not easy either. In some places they met opposition from the priest or even from the bishop of the diocese.[46] Vincent tried to smooth out difficulties beforehand by sending letters of introduction to the priest or providing her with a reference from Fr Gondi if the charities were on his estates.[47] Each charity had its own particular problems. In Villepreux they had given up visiting the sick. In Sannois they did not keep the accounts. In Franconville the procurator had taken charge of the funds and used them as he liked. The treasurer at Verneuil was tight-fisted: she refused to take in any more sick people and sent home too soon those sick people already admitted. There was such division among the members at Bulles that one group refused to visit the poor with ladies from the other group.[48]

During these visitations Louise would remedy any faults, check abuses, remind them about points of rule, praise good actions, encourage, exhort and renew fervour. Moreover, she did not go to these charities purely as an administrator. Louise took an active part in the charitable works; she visited the poor, looked after the sick and distributed alms. Her special care was to teach young girls their catechism. Louise would gather them together and explain the doctrines of faith and a Christian's duties and obligations. She used a catechism which she herself had drawn up and which is still preserved. Like all the catechisms of that time, it was based on question and answer, and contained a clear and simple summary of the articles of faith together with instructions on the sacraments and the Christian's rule of life. Before leaving the town Louise would show the schoolmistress, if there was one, how to continue the work she had started. If there was no schoolmistress, she tried to train one of the youngsters to do the work.[49]

---

[46] *S.V.P.* I, p. 82.

[47] *S.V.P.* I, pp. 119-120.

[48] LOUISE DE MARILLAC, *Pensées* , ed. a., p. 125ff.

[49] GOBILLON, *op. cit.*, p. 38; R. CASTAÑARES, *op. cit.*,Vol. 3, pp. 349-362; A. LOPEZ, 'La obra catequética de Santa Luisa', *Anales* (1980), pp. 220-230.

Humility in triumph

The most remarkable visitation was the one she made at Beauvais in 1630. Vincent sent her there to put the finishing touches to the eighteen charities which, as we have seen, he founded in that town. Her visit won applause from the outset, so much so that Vincent had to give her this warning:

> When you find yourself honoured and esteemed be united in spirit with the mockery, scorn and ill-treatment that the Son of God suffered. It is quite true, Mademoiselle, that a truly humble soul can find humiliation as much in acclaim as in abuse and, like the bee, can make honey from the dew that falls on wormwood equally well as from that which falls on the rose.[50]

Louise solved a lot of practical problems but not without first consulting Vincent by letter. Vincent answered in the same way. Thanks to details in this interchange of correspondence we learn to what extent Vincent was prepared to use his talents as organiser. The treasurer could delegate to another person the provision of wine and so devote herself to her special duties of admitting and discharging the sick, but they were not to pay wages to this assistant or she would, says Vincent, with a deliberate play on words, prove 'the costliest thing the community had.' It is all right for members of the confraternity at Basse-Oeuvre to attend the funeral of poor people from their own charity as well as that of Saint Gil, but this should not become a regular practice since each parish had enough to do to look after its own poor. A collection should be taken up on as many days as was necessary; nobody should sell medicines if they did not know what they cost; it would be as well to inform the bishop about their principal works etc.[51]

During the visitation Louise would summon the ladies to a general meeting. No men were allowed to attend but the interest roused by that kindly and intelligent lady from Paris was so great that some men hid in the building where the meetings were being held, to listen to what she said. We are not told whether the king's suspicious deputy was among the listeners!

At last the day came for them to leave. It was a noisy farewell. The whole town gathered round the coach that Louise was to travel in, and they followed it to the outskirts of the town, shouting blessings and thanks. A dangerous accident might have spoilt their jubilation but in fact it added to their happiness. A little boy was jostled by the crowd and he fell to the

---

[50] *S.V.P.* I, p. 98.
[51] *S.V.P.* I, pp. 96-98.

ground in front of the coach. One of the wheels went right over his body. Louise saw the accident and immediately started to pray. As she looked back she could see the boy get up, completely unscathed, and go happily on his way. Whether it was a miracle or not, the golden legend began to weave its web round Louise, too.[52]

'What a beautiful tree'

Vincent's tactics had the outcome he had been hoping for. One day, while she was at prayer, Louise was divinely inspired to devote her whole life to the service of the poor.[53] Vincent was overjoyed at the news.

> Yes, at long last, my dear Mademoiselle, I think it is a good idea. How could it not be, since it was Our Lord who put this good thought into your mind? So go to communion tomorrow and prepare that useful general confession you planned to make. After that you can begin the retreat you had in mind. I cannot tell you how earnestly I want to see you, to find out how all this has come about, but I will mortify myself in this for the love of God which is the one preoccupation I desire you to have.
>
> I can imagine you must have been deeply moved by the words of today's gospel. How powerfully they must speak to a heart that loves with a perfect love. Oh what a tree you must have seemed in God's eyes, today, since you brought forth such fruits. May you always remain a beautiful tree of life producing fruits of love.[54]

Early in 1633, Vincent's co-operation with God's work succeeded in fashioning Louise, after seven years probation, into a fitting instrument for charitable works. With her support he was about to embark on the last, and in some ways the most important, of all his initiatives. This subject needs to be studied in depth. We shall come to it later on.

---

[52] GOBILLON, *op. cit.*, pp. 40-43.

[53] ABELLY, *op. cit.*, 1.1 c. 23, p. 105.

[54] *S.V.P.* I, pp. 51-52. Coste is inclined to date this letter as 30 July 1628. We cannot be sure about it. It seems that even in 1630 Louise was thinking of joining a contemplative order (*cf. S.V.P.* I, pp. 86-87). Louise's resolution to devote herself completely to the service of the poor did not necessarily precede her visit to the charities as Coste supposed. It is more likely that the charities inspired her resolution.

Chapter XV
THE STRUGGLE TO PUT THE
CONGREGATION
ON A MORE SOLID FOUNDATION

Behind the scenes politics

Like it or not, we have to turn our minds back to politics. The year 1630 saw yet another key event in Louis XIII's reign. It affected both Vincent and Louise though to different degrees. Cardinal Richelieu had been putting his political policies into action between 1624 and 1630. The first of his objectives to be achieved was the dismantling of Protestant power within the kingdom. To secure this he engaged in a war that lasted four years (1625-1629) and the most outstanding event of this war was the siege, and ultimately the surrender, of La Rochelle. While the war was going on Richelieu had to conceal his hostility towards Spain and he signed the Treaty of Monzón (5 March 1626) which was negotiated by two of Vincent's friends, Pierre de Bérulle and Charles d'Angennes, Lord of Fargis, who was married to Madeleine de Silly, the frivolous sister of Mme de Gondi. That treaty which ended the war of La Valtelina, could almost be considered a victory for Spain. The queen mother and the most fervent Catholics in France had always favoured a policy of maintaining good relations with Spain. They were delighted with this turn of events in French foreign policy and gave enthusiastic support to Richelieu in his struggles against the Huguenots. Their joy was to be short-lived. The peace of Alès (28 June 1629) saw an end to the Protestant problem but the question was settled by the granting of an Act of Pardon and while this rescinded the political and military privileges enjoyed by Protestants it reaffirmed religious concessions made to them.

A political party of some importance gathered round Marie de Medici who was still jealous of Richelieu's rise to power. This group soon became known as the 'Devout Party' and it took offence at the terms offered at Alès. Their recognised leader was de Bérulle who had been a cardinal since 30 August 1627. With him were the two Marillacs, Louis the Marshal and Michel, Keeper of the Seals, Fargis and his wife and others of lesser importance. In opposition to the 'Devout Party' Richelieu's followers called themselves

'The Good Frenchmen'. Tension mounted between the two, especially over the War of Mantua which broke out between France and Spain over the question of who was to succeed to the duchy. This was a further indication that Richelieu's anti-Spanish policy had not changed. It was in these circumstances that the sudden death of de Bérulle (2 October 1629) mentioned earlier, deprived the Devout Party of their strongest support. Up to now they had had a cardinal to oppose another cardinal and de Bérulle enjoyed the advantage of his formidable intelligence, his influence at Rome and his reputation for sanctity.

The king's serious illness in 1630 and a fresh outbreak of the Italian campaign with the taking of Pignerol, made them realise that their time for action was running short. The queen mother was already in open conflict with Richelieu whom she reproached for taking over from her in the management of public affairs and for alienating her from the king's affection. So the events of one of the most famous days in French history were being hatched.

'The day of the Dupes'

On 10 November 1630 the king held a council at which the queen mother was present together with Richelieu and the Keeper of the Seals, Michel de Marillac. It was the final attempt at a reconciliation. Richelieu made concessions and even accepted the nomination of Louis de Marillac as commander-in-chief of the army in Italy. It was to no avail. When the council was over the queen mother informed the cardinal that she no longer had any confidence in him and that from now on he was relieved of all his duties in her household: controller, head of her council and principal chaplain. Also dismissed were Richelieu's trusted companions who held office in the queen's household and, in particular, his niece, Marie de Wignerod, the future Duchess d'Aiguillon who had been lady of the bedchamber. When these dismissals were made public the whole court believed that anyone losing the queen's favour would then be in disgrace with the king.

The following day, 11 November, the queen prepared to deal the final blow. About eleven o'clock in the morning she had an interview with her son during which she tried to get Richelieu dismissed. This meeting took place at the queen's residence, the Palais du Luxembourg. The queen took the precaution of locking all the doors leading to her apartments as she wanted the interview between herself and the king to be strictly private. But Richelieu went to the palace, too, on the pretext of taking his leave of the queen. As soon as he arrived he realised the gravity of the situation. He came to a desperate decision. He went to the chapel. At the back of the sacristy was a half-concealed staircase which led directly to the queen's apartments. It was hardly ever used and in all probability nobody had bothered to lock it. The doors were, in fact, unlocked. He pushed his way through the last of the gates and burst into the room where Marie de Medici and Louis XIII were in conference.

'I wager your Majesties are discussing me', were his first words. After a moment's attempt to pretend this was not so, the queen admitted it.

'Yes, we were saying you were the most ungrateful and wicked man alive.'

Then followed a long tirade during which the queen lost all self-control. She shouted, insulted the cardinal, and reproached her son for preferring a servant to his own mother.

Faced with this torrent of accusations Richelieu considered himself lost. He began to weep and then knelt down and kissed the hem of the queen's robe. Apparently the king was the only one not to lose his nerve. He gave a sign for Richelieu to withdraw, and then, bowing to the queen, he also left. He went down to the courtyard to prepare for the journey to Versailles. Richelieu was already in the courtyard and bowed low to the king who did not even look at him. Richelieu then retired to his residence.

The news spread like wildfire all through Paris: Richelieu had fallen from power. Michel de Marillac rushed to the Luxembourg Palace pretending he knew nothing about it. The queen received him in her boudoir and, in the presence of Madame de Fargis, brought him up to date with what had happened and told him he was to be the new prime minister. This was a resounding victory for the Devout Party. Marillac began to prepare his new government which would embrace all the different elements that surfaced after these important political changes: sincere party members, opportunist climbers, ambitions flatterers and yesterday's enemies who were now life-long friends.

However, the battle was not won. During the afternoon the king summoned Richelieu to Versailles and the two were reconciled. The cardinal offered to resign but the king assured him that he looked on him as his most loyal and devoted servant and that he would continue to protect him and keep him in power in spite of all intrigues against him. He knew that Richelieu had not acted against the queen but against a scheming cabal whose members were enemies of the realm.

Immediately following this there was an emergency meeting of Richelieu's party ministers and it was then that de Marillac's fate was decided. Evening saw a complete reversal of the way events had earlier promised to turn out. Everyone was proved wrong, the queen mother, Marillac and even

Richelieu himself who thought he was in disgrace. One of the courtiers coined the phrase which has gone down in history, *La journée des Dupes,* 'the Day of the Dupes'.

Michel de Marillac was ordered to Glatigny near Versailles. This time the Keeper of the Seals was under no illusion; he knew he was defeated. He hurriedly burned any incriminating documents and hastened to the rendezvous. It was one o'clock in the morning. Early in the day, a royal comissary arrived while Marillac was hearing Mass. He asked to be allowed to stay till the end and his request was granted. When he left the chapel he was ordered, in the king's name, to hand over the royal seals. He did so. Then a captain of the guard ordered Marillac to follow him; he was a prisoner. The ex-minister was taken first to Caen, then to Lisieux, and finally to Châteaudun where two years imprisonment awaited him. This proved too much for him and he died in the castle in 1632.

An even worse fate befell his brother Louis. On that same night, 11 November, a secret messenger left for Italy with orders to relieve the marshal of his office and to arrest him. This order was immediately carried out by two of his colleagues, Marshals Schomberg and Laforce, and Marillac was dispatched to France. Louis was a greater threat than Michel because he had married a cousin of the queen and also because he had close links with the army. It was not difficult to find some pretext for bringing him to trial; he was accused of misappropriating funds. There were few officials at that time who could have thrown the first stone from their glass houses. After a mock trial on 8 May 1632 he was condemned to death. The execution was carried out two days later in the Place de la Grève, Paris.[1]

Others who had participated in the 'Day of the Dupes' suffered reprisals, too. The queen mother never recovered political influence over her son. After a lengthy banishment at Compiègne she fled to the Spanish Netherlands where she remained until her death in 1642. Madame de Fargis, Madeleine de Silly, was condemned to be beheaded but she escaped death by fleeing to the Low Countries where she, too, died in 1639. Her husband, the former ambassador to Spain, was imprisoned in the Bastille. He was to end his days in the Congregation of the Mission, on 20 December 1648. People who played a minor role in the drama were given lighter sentences. It spelled complete defeat for the Devout Party. For Richelieu and his 'Good Frenchmen

---

[1] Many works have been written about 'The day of the Dupes'. The most important of these are: L. BATIFFOL, *La journée des dupes* (Paris 1925); G. MONGRÉDIEN, *10 novembre 1630. La journée des dupes* (Paris 1961); V. L. TAPIÉ, *op. cit.*, pp. 221-230. In recent times P. Chevallier has done research into new sources of information which correct many traditionally held ideas. *Cf.* P. CHEVALLIER, *Louis XIII*, pp. 373-401 We have used his findings.

Party' it was an overwhelming victory. The astute cardinal's power was consolidated once and for all.

Two policies

A superficial reading of the events of the Day of the Dupes would lead one to think that it was just a struggle between the personal ambition of Marie de Medici and Michel de Marillac on the one hand, and Richelieu on the other. Really it was the final quarrel between the two policies. It was Richelieu's policy to wage war against Spanish supremacy even though this meant indirect support for the Protestant cause and led to increased taxes which crushed the people. De Bérulle's policy, which was backed up and continued by Marillac, was a policy of peace or at least of *détente*, and it was based on two principles. The first of these was a religious principle, and attempts were made to come to an agreement with Spain about Catholic interests in the field of international politics. The second principle was social in character, and its object was to relieve the enormous economic burden weighing down the people and provoking serious disturbances throughout the country. Marillac was a mystic whose deeply spiritual life was in no way incompatible with political activity and personal ambition, and his convictions were all the more deeply-rooted as he considered them to be matters of religion and of conscience.

These were two diametrically opposed policies yet both were possible options for France in the first third of the seventeenth century. Richelieu's policy put the emphasis on military and political power; Marillac's stressed the welfare of the people and the triumph of Catholic interests. The time had come to choose which policy to follow. Against the background of the Thirty Years War's which began in 1618 and in which France had not as yet played a direct part, Louis XIII sided with Richelieu. Five years later this policy would lead to war being declared against Spain and the empire.[2]

Did Vincent de Paul play any part in this duel between Richelieu and Marillac? Whatever his sympathies might have been, and in spite of his friendship with nearly all the members of the Devout Party, everything suggests that he kept aloof from the political skirmish. De Bérulle had died before this great political storm blew up, but Vincent's friendship for him had already begun to cool off. Over the next few years we are to see Vincent drawing closer to Richelieu. This does not seem compatible with Vincent's taking up a political stance, given the spiteful character of the cardinal minister. However,

---

[2] GUY PAGES, 'Autour du "Grand Orage". Richelieu et Marillac: deux politiques', *Revue Historique* 179 (1937), pp. 63- 97.

Vincent had friends in Richelieu's party, too. By this time he had come into contact with the wives of ministers and members of the legal nobility and in particular with Marie de Wignerod, the cardinal's niece and the only person for whom Richelieu was known to show any affection.

Louise de Marillac was more directly affected by events. She was grief-stricken by the disgrace of her two uncles and especially by the execution of Louis. Vincent wrote her a letter and we do not know which to admire more, the sober asceticism and the sublime challenges of the counsels he showers on her, or the total political neutrality with which it is expressed. This is what he wrote:

> What you tell me about M. le Maréchal de Marillac is very tragic and I am most upset about it. But let us honour God's will in this and reflect on the happiness of those who, through their own pains, honour the sufferings of the Son of God. It matters not how our relations go to God provided they are with him. Putting this manner of dying to good use is one of the surest means of attaining eternal life. So let us not grieve but rather let us find peace in God's adorable will.[3]

'In the beginning every congregation has worthy motives'

Although he was a contemporary of Richelieu and shared his preoccupations with the problems of their day, Vincent's concerns followed a different direction altogether. He was preoccupied with obtaining official approval for his congregation and having it put on a sound juridical basis. The speed with which Vincent accomplished this is remarkable but so, too, is his calculation of every move. Each step was only taken after careful preparation.

The early stages proved relatively easy. We have already noted how the archbishop of Paris—he was a de Gondi, remember—had given his approbation even before the first companions had officially joined the company on 24 April 1626.[4] It was not difficult, either, to get the consent of the king, who granted them letters patent in May 1627.[5]

The problems began when they tried to get the royal assent ratified by the parlement of Paris. For some unknown reason Vincent had left this formality so late that he had to obtain a second royal letter in case the first one expired and became invalid.[6]

---

3   *S.V.P.* I, pp. 153-154.
4   *S.V.P.* XIII, pp. 202-203.
5   *S.V.P.* XIII, pp. 206-208.
6   *S.V.P.* XIII, pp. 225-227.

The parish priests in Paris heard about the moves that were being made and they expressed their opposition to the ratification. Their syndic, Etienne le Tonnelier, wrote to the parlement saying that while it was not his intention to impede the work of the new congregation, he wanted to avoid the trouble and dissension this might arouse though put forward in the guise of piety. In view of this the parish priests demanded a guarantee that the new institution would agree to three conditions: firstly that 'the missioners should completely renounce employment in the churches and parishes of all towns in the kingdom'; secondly, that they would refrain from entering any church without the authorisation of the bishop and the permission of the parish priest, and not conduct any services at the same time as ordinary parish services; and thirdly, that they would renounce 'all hope of claiming or ever asking for any payment or salary from the benefice in which they preached or from the local people.' The syndic added to the petition a long series of arguments liberally spiced with clerical mistrust. Here is an example:

> 'Every congregation is born of deep piety and starts off with the purest of intentions but over the years these motives are completely debased by avarice and ambition.' It was for this reason that he considered the foundation clause requiring them to renounce all work in the city inadequate and he demanded that 'the court oblige, constrain and order that no person should enter the congregation unless he had specifically agreed to this condition.' It was not out of self-interest, of course, that the curés refused to allow priests of the Mission to work in their parishes; they were merely doing what was their duty in charity, 'defending all rural parishes in every diocese throughout France from the damage that could ensue from granting approbation to this new institute.'[7]

Vincent and his missioners made a formal declaration that they would comply with the guarantees demanded.[8] They found no difficulty at all in doing this, since the conditions laid down by the curés in Paris were in complete accord with the special characteristics of their Congregation as defined in the foundation contract. Vincent was careful to safeguard the distinctive marks of his community: withdrawal from the cities, non-payment for missions, and submission to parish priests and the bishop. He was doubtless influenced in this by the vigorous opposition shown by the curés of Paris. It was the

---

[7] *S.V.P.* XIII, pp. 227-232.
[8] *S.V.P.* XIII, p. 233.

first opposition to his plan that he encountered. We should not be surprised by it, since this was the price he had to pay for his novel approach.

The parlement took no heed of the priests' opposition and on 4 April 1631 they recorded and ratified the letters giving royal approval to the Congregation of the Mission. This recognition of its civil identity was achieved in just under five years.[9]

Victory in Rome

Vincent was not satisfied with just having diocesan and royal approval. He also cherished the hope that his congregation would be recognised by the Holy See and this would give it an ecclesial dimension. The most surprising part of all this is the speed with which Vincent acted. For someone who, as we have seen, declared that it was never his idea to found the congregation, it is hard to explain the haste with which he threw himself into the task of gaining papal approval. We can be sure that even from the beginning Vincent's project was more ambitions than the terms of the contract would suggest.

In 1627, two years after the foundation of the Mission and a few months or days after it had received royal approval, Vincent set about winning the approbation of the Holy See. This shows how certain he was that the work he was undertaking was in conformity with God's designs and that it fulfilled a need in the Church as a whole as well as the Church in France.

It is quite true that the step he took in 1627 was only a very small one. All he was asking from the recently established Sacred Congregation for the Propagation of the Faith was a special blessing from the Holy Father and the usual faculties to be granted to the missioners. For the moment it was not a question of founding a society of pontifical right, whose members lived in community. So for this reason the text of the petition makes no mention of community, but only of 'mission', a technical term then applied to different groups of people devoted to apostolic work even in Catholic countries. These groups were often comprised of religious communities whose apostolic work had to be approved by the Sacred Congregation for the Propagation of the Faith.

The petition was presented by Blaise Féron, the doctor of the Sorbonne who accompanied Vincent and Duchesne on the mission to Marchais. Although he did not belong to the main body of the congregation he considered himself one of its missioners and he, too, was following the same sign that the Lord had given to Vincent.

Considering how things usually worked in Rome, the sacred Congregation acted with unusual promptness. On 5 June the matter was

---

[9] *S.V.P.* XIII, pp. 232-233.

studied for the first time in plenary session, and it was decided to ask the nuncio in France to send a report. They wrote to him on the eleventh of that month and he sent back a letter on 26 September which was full of praise for Vincent.

> The opinion of people who are absolutely trustworthy confirms my own judgement regarding the worthiness of the said M. Vincent and the eight companions who live in community with him; they will be warmly welcomed in many dioceses in France and this country can expect a rich harvest from their labours.

It was with this important recommendation before them that the Sacred Congregation met again, this time in the presence of the pope and they confirmed and approved Vincent de Paul's Mission on 5 November.

As we can see, the sacred congregation also confined itself to speaking of 'mission' and did not use the term 'congregation', 'company' or 'confraternity'. For the moment this was sufficient. No longer was Vincent's work to be merely diocesan based; it was to be an ecclesial mission. There were some limits put on the approval that was granted: submission to the ordinaries in the use of faculties that were granted, restriction of these faculties to a seven year period and, something which the Sovereign Pontiff himself suggested, that the archbishop of Paris be nominated protector of the new mission. The first step had been taken, Vincent's name had become known to the curia in Rome. The pope and the cardinals had given great praise to the mission's founder.[10]

'It is something more than a mission'

After the success of his first venture in Rome Vincent was encouraged to take the second step. This time he wanted more. So with this in mind, in June 1628, Vincent addressed to Pope Urban VIII a long and carefully reasoned petition. He signed this himself, and so did his first eight companions including Louis Callon who, as we know, did not sign the document for admission into the company and left shortly afterwards.[11]

The gist of the petition was a request that the institute be confirmed

---

[10] No Vincentian biographer or historian knew about the first approval granted by Rome to St Vincent de Paul's mission. The relevant documents were discovered, and published for the first time, with an excellent commentary, by A. COPPO, 'La prima approvazione pontificia della Missione nel 1627', *Annali della Missione* (1972), pp. 222-255. We have used dates and quotations from this article in our text.

[11] The history of negotiations carried out in 1628 for the approval of the Congregation of the Mission, was written by Coste (*M. V.* Vol. 1, pp. 184-185), and was based on documents that were available at the time and which he published in *S. V.P.* I, pp. 42-51 and 52-62 and XIII,

and approved, with a new foundation if necessary; that Vincent be nominated president or superior general; that permission be given for them to accept new members, be these priests or laymen; and to establish norms and rules, subject to the approval of the Holy See, as was the case with other orders and congregations; permission to open new houses even outside the diocese of Paris with the consent of the bishop of the locality; to receive donations and to use these without having recourse to diocesan authorities; in short the permissions usually granted to missionaries *ad gentes*. The most important matter was his petition to the Holy See for the new congregation to be canonically exempt from the authority of the ordinary and to be directly dependent on the Apostolic See.[12]

Vincent had this petition presented by the papal nuncio in Paris, Giovanni Franceres Guidi dei Conti di Bagno, or Mgr Guidi for short. This was the man who had given such a favourable report in the 1627 negotiations. Once again he gave his strong support and in a letter, dated June 21, which accompanied Vincent's petition, he recommended it be granted 'with some privileges'. This was a kindly strategy which was meant to minimise the important concessions that were being requested.[13] Not content with this, in a further communication of 23 July, he sent the sacred congregation two letters from the king of France. One of these letters was addressed to the pope and the other to the ambassador in Rome. In his letters the king strongly recommended that approval be given to the institute. The nuncio took advantage of the occasion to inform the congregation that he himself was confident that the new congregation would do great work for souls.[14] Vincent had certainly tied up the loose ends. He had come a long way since those naive days when he petitioned for the parish of Tilh or for the abbey of Saint Léonard de Chaumes.

But Rome was not to prove so easily influenced by kindly nuncios or devout monarchs. The sacred congregation studied Vincent's petition in minute detail. Mgr Ingoli, their secretary, who had given a favourable report when the Mission was approved in 1627, was under no illusions about these far-reaching new petitions. They seemed to him 'exorbitant'.[15] If the request were to be granted the foundation would no longer be a simple mission but

---

pp. 218-225. A. Coppo rewrote the whole sequence of the negotiation in a work which presented ten as yet unpublished documents, some of which shed new light on the subject by providing information that Coste did not know about: 'Le due supliche del 1628 per l'erezione dell'Istituto in Congregazione di diritto pontificio, non accolte dalla Sacra Congregazione', *Annali della Missione* (1973), pp. 37- 73.

12 *S.V.P.* I, pp. 47-50.
13 *S.V.P.* XIII, p. 218.
14 *S.V.P.* XIII, pp. 219-221.
15 A. COPPO, *cit. art.*, p. 51.

would turn into something resembling a religious order with its own spirituality and its own special works.[16] He communicated this to the congregation of cardinals. His advice was that they should only authorise the mission to be founded in France with a maximum number of 20 or 25 priests and that it should not be accorded the title of order, confraternity or congregation of the Mission. A 'mission' was, by its very nature, something temporary and it should be disbanded once the need that had created it had been met.[17]

Vincent had been unlucky in coming up against Mgr Ingoli. Later on this man would be a great help to Vincent de Paul but by and large he was not very favourably inclined towards the religious communities that were already in existence. He was even less happy about new ones being established.[18] What is more, Vincent's projects were rejected by some very important assessors. Among these was no less a personage than his former guide and protector, Cardinal de Bérulle. In 1628, this man who was so influential in political and church circles, wrote to Fr Bertin, his representative in Rome.

> You write to me that these people are planning to present the mission question in various and, to my mind, devious ways. This is highly suspect and it could oblige us to forsake the moderation and straightforwardness that I consider the right way of acting in matters that pertain to God, providing others do likewise.[19]

So here we have the great cardinal prepared to use all his influence against his former disciple, even to the point of 'being forced' to act in a not very 'straightforward', that is to say, a not very honourable way. Vincent was not Richelieu, so he was unsuccessful of course. On 22 August, the Sacred Congregation settled the 'mission affair' as de Bérulle called it. Vincent's petition was rejected out of hand because it 'went further than the term "mission" implied, and was veering towards the foundation of a new religious order.' The rejection did not take up (and this was the only concession given) the secretary's suggestion that they limit the number of missioners. To sweeten the pill a bit he advised the nuncio to persuade 'M. Vincent' and his companions to forget the idea of a new congregation and to keep within the limits of a simple 'mission'. The illustrious cardinals promised to have

---

[16] *Ibid.*, p. 41.
[17] *S.V.P.* XIII, pp. 222-224.
[18] A. COPPO, *art. cit.*, p. 46.
[19] Referred to by COSTE, *M.V.* Vol. 1, p. 185.

this confirmed by the Holy Father with all the faculties normally accorded to missions in France.[20]

But Rome did not know Vincent de Paul. When it was a question of giving glory to God he, too, could be obstinate. As Richelieu was to have two years later, Vincent had suffered his 'Day of the Dupes'. No matter how long it took to win the battle, he refused to concede defeat. Before the first petition was looked at in Rome he had already dispatched a second one, dated 1 August, and the wording of this was only slightly different from the previous one.[21] Again he looked for people to give him references. Once again he was recommended by the nuncio. Then came a new factor: he also sent a recommendation from the reigning queen, Anne of Austria, and not the queen mother, Marie de Medici.[22] We need to emphasise this point; it is a detail that Coste did not know about. It may perhaps help us to assess Vincent's stance in the political crisis which was then brewing at the French court. It is the first time we see Vincent dealing with Anne of Austria, the queen who was to play an important part in the way his future works of charity developed. The second petition and new references were late in arriving. By then the matter was already settled. At a meeting on 25 September the sacred congregation limited itself to acknowledging receipt of the communication and it referred back to the decisions taken on 22 August.[23]

Vincent did not give up hope. He continued negotiations bearing well in mind the reasons for previous failures. When we speak of Vincent not wanting his congregation to be considered a religious order one must keep in mind the secular nature of the work he was undertaking but we must not forget either, and Vincent himself would never forget, that his first attempt to have the congregation approved by the Holy See had been rejected because it was a new form of 'religious life'. Vincent was a man of experience who was always ready to learn from events and looked on these as signs sent by providence.

'If Your Holiness only knew the need there is ...'

Vincent had a new objective and a different way of working for the second assault on Rome's fortress. Instead of going to the Congregation of Propaganda he addressed himself to the Congregation of Bishops and

---

[20] *S.V.P.* XIII, p. 225 and A. COPPO, *cit. art.,* pp. 51-52.

[21] *S.V.P.* Vol. 1, pp. 52-57; A. COPPO, *cit. art.,* pp. 53-54.

[22] A. COPPO, *cit. art.,* pp. 57-58.

[23] A. COPPO, *cit. art.,* p. 62.

Religious, and instead of working from a distance with all the hazards of correspondence, he detailed Fr François du Coudray to go to Rome as his personal representative. This priest was one of the original three companions and after Vincent he was the oldest. He was certainly the most learned and brilliant of them all. He had such a good knowledge of Hebrew that Vincent was wont to say, 'he could argue the Son of God's case in Christ's own language'. The same could be said for his knowledge of Syrian, so much so that it was suggested that while in Rome he should translate the Syriac Bible into Latin.[24]

Du Coudray arrived in Rome in the middle of 1631.[25] Through their frequent correspondence Vincent was able to follow closely every step in the negotiations. Unfortunately there are very considerable gaps in the letters that are still preserved, but we can still follow the main stages of the negotiation.

A letter dated 1631 reveals the base line beyond which Vincent refused to make any concessions. His approach is based on a personal and fundamental religious experience that gave rise to his congregation:

'They must be made to understand that poor people are losing their souls because they are ignorant of the truths necessary for salvation and because they do not know how to go to confession.'

This is Vincent's overriding conviction, the goad that will allow him no rest nor let him abandon his plans; the guiding force that impels him to fight on for the congregation to be approved. It is his message for the Church, the *raison d'être* of all his work, and indeed, for his whole life.

'It was knowing this state of affairs that made us establish the company.'

He had no doubt that the person with supreme responsibility for governing the Church would share this conviction. If told about it he would share Vincent's sorrow and his anxiety for the salvation of souls:

---

[24] *S.V.P.* I, pp. 251-252.

[25] *S.V.P.* I, p. 114. According to Barcos, Saint-Cyran did two things for Vincent at this time: he offered first of all to translate the rules of the company into Latin and, secondly, to send his nephew, Bernard d'Arguibel, to negotiate the approbation. We have no proof that Vincent accepted either offer. His only procurator with the Holy See was du Coudray. *Cf.* M. DE BARCOS, *op. cit.*, pp. 13-14; J. ORCIBAL, *Les origines ...,* II, p. 400.

'If His Holiness knew about this need he would not rest until he had done all in his power to right the matter.'

With the exception of some passages from conferences given towards the end of his life, never has Vincent's voice been more prophetic.

He then comes down to a more practical level and states the five maxims he considers basic for the congregation. They are in fact the five conditions already stated in the foundation contract and reaffirmed after the controversy with the parish priests: submission to the bishops and parish priests in matters concerning missions, the total gratuity of their work, the missioners of the congregation were to keep away from the towns, and the superior was to be autonomous with regard to the internal affairs of the company. His insistence that these conditions were not negotiable was based on the teaching of someone who, for him, embodied the highest moral authority, M. Duval.[26]

'Act in the most Christian way possible'

Vincent's efforts were to meet with opposition just as they had done in 1628. We know from the correspondence that has been preserved, some of the objections put forward and we have a general idea from which quarter the opposition came.

They said apparently, that the fact that the missioners were based in Paris proved that they were not as exclusively dedicated to the poor people in country areas as they would have had people believe:

'In Paris', replied Vincent,' we live as solitary a life as that of Carthusians. As we do not preach, give instructions or hear confessions in the city, hardly anybody has any dealings with us and we have nothing to do with them; this solitude makes us long to work in country places and that work makes us long for solitude.'[27]

'Carthusians at home and apostles abroad' is the phrase which traditionally has encapsulated this thought of Vincent's. This interpretation is a far too sweeping generalisation of an idea which is not meant to be a rule of life for the community but a description of the reality of the situation

---

[26] *S.V.P.* I, p. 115-116. The paragraphs in inverted commas are the actual words of this letter.
[27] *S.V.P.* I, p. 122.

where they had to contend with ill-informed opponents.

Who were these opponents? We do not know any names but we certainly do know the group they belonged to; it was a section of the Oratorians who wanted to continue acting in the same way as their founder. Some of them tried to cause complications at the various stages of the negotiations. There was one particular person who was actively engaged in this and he was 'someone from whom, after God, we would have expected most help.'[28]

Vincent was certain that this attitude was not shared by Fr Condren, superior general of the Oratorians, and de Bérulle's successor. This man disapproved of such manoeuvres and gave Vincent every help he could. More interesting than anecdotes about the tricks they played and the snares they put in the founder's path was Vincent's reaction to all these. It demonstrates the high level of human and supernatural development that Vincent had reached by the time he was fifty-one, nearing the highest point of his creative powers and within reach of his most cherished ambitions.

'I beg you to act', he writes to du Coudray, 'in the most Christian way possible to those who are trying to make difficulties for us. I often meet these people and by God's grace I am able to show them the same cordiality as before. It seems to me that by the grace of God I not only have no aversion for them but that I show them more honour and affection. And I will tell you something else—I have never complained to Fr de Gondi for fear of unsettling him in his vocation. I beg you, Father, do not stop seeing these priests; practise in their regard what Our Lord counsels us to do to those who vex and baulk us, and please ask all those whom God inspired with charity towards us not to do them any harm either by word or by action.'[29]

One would not want to write a panegyric but these lines leave us in no doubt about the deep transformation grace had worked in the soul of the humble Gascon priest; the man who years earlier was falsely accused of theft and had merely replied, 'God knows the truth.' That reply now answered the most sublime demand of the Gospel, that we love our enemies.

'Salvatoris nostri'

In spite of the opposition, negotiations followed their normal course. Du Coudray presented the petition to the sacred congregation for approval. It was a long document in Latin and Italian and it kept strictly to the instructions

---

[28] *S.V.P.* I, p. 162. Efforts to identify that person have so far proved unsuccessful. It is obvious, from what follows in the letter, that it cannot be Philippe de Gondi.

[29] *S.V.P.* I, pp. 163-165.

received from Vincent.[30] The sacred congregation studied it for the first time on 13 February 1632 and designated Cardinal Bentivoglio assessor for the final scrutiny. He had played the same role when previous petitions had been presented to the Congregation of Propaganda in 1628 and had been rejected. The four years that had elapsed since then and Vincent's new tactics had made the cardinal change his mind. At the session held on 30 April 1632 he gave a favourable report, merely pointing out that they would have to get the necessary reports from the nuncio and the archbishop of Paris.[31] Vincent lost no time in requesting these.[32]

In the end, the outcome of all the negotiations was an undreamed of success. The Congregation of the Mission received approval under just those conditions that the founder wanted; not by a simple rescript of the Sacred Congregation for Bishops and Religious, but by the most solemn of all Pontifical documents, a bull issued by the Holy Father himself. On 12 January 1633 Urban VIII signed the bull *Salvatori nostri* which officially approved and established the Congregation of the Mission.[33]

The bull began with a brief history of the foundation of the Congregation by Philippe Emmanuel de Gondi and his wife, Marguerite de Silly. Then followed a statement giving the reasons which had led the pious founders and Vincent himself to start the congregation. Using thoughts and phrases taken from the petition, it described the terrible spiritual condition of poor country people and those in neighbouring towns, villages and territories. The state of people in these areas was very different from that of people living in the big cities. People in rural areas were ignorant of the truths of faith and did not know how to go to confession; they were ignorant of all the things necessary for salvation, and thus many souls redeemed by the blood

---

[30] This important document was discovered by Giovanni Mazzini and it was published in *Annali* (1925), pp. 174-186: 'Per l'appovazione della Congregazione della Missione. Un documento dell'anno 1632'. It was reprinted in *Annales* 1926 (pp. 140-144, Latin text) and in 1941 (pp. 27-30, Italian text).

[31] For all these negotiations, see G. MAZZINI, article, pp. 177-178.

[32] This is confirmed by a letter on 12 July, 1632; cf. *S.V.P.* I, p. 162.

[33] The bull is dated 12 January 1632, *anni incarnationis Domini*. Coste took this date literally when he included it in *S.V.P.* XIII pp. 257-267. But such a date is inconsistent with what we know about the Sacred Congregation's meetings in February and April, 1632, and with St Vincent's letter quoted in the previous note. Mazzini solved the problem by pointing out that the year of the Incarnation began on 25 March, not on 1 January. So 12 January of the year of the incarnation, 1632, would correspond to 12 January 1633, in the normal way of reckoning. Mazzini suggested to Coste that he correct this date and put it in its right chronological sequence in any new edition of the work that might be published (*art. cit.*, pp. 177-180). Coste altered the date in *Annales* (1925), p. 139; *ibid.* (1926), p. 140, and later on in *M.V.* Vol. 1, p. 187.

of Christ were being lost. The pope had taken up Vincent's challenge, 'If His Holiness knew the need.'[34]

Vincent, who was so accustomed to seeing the decisions of the Church as so many manifestations of God's will, must have been particularly consoled that the Supreme Pontiff had accepted that the inspiration for the foundation had come from God:

> And having begun this worthy project, the said Vincent whom
> God, the author of all good had inspired with his thought,
> took upon himself the task of starting this congregation.

The pope said this idea had come from God and for Vincent there could not have been a more authoritative or decisive endorsement of his project. It was just as M. Duval had said. Vincent would use these words of the Holy Father to affirm that the works of the congregation, and the congregation itself, were not his doing, but God's.

The main part of the bull traces the basic outlines of the institute. It gives a more detailed definition of its objectives: the members would devote themselves to their personal sanctification and to that of poor people in country towns and villages; they would not preach in the cities except to give retreats to ordinands. Then follows a description of their ministry: teaching the truths of religion, giving instruction on how to make a good general confession, administering the sacraments, preaching, catechising, setting up confraternities of charity, settling disputes, giving retreats to parish priests and promoting meetings of the clergy to study matters of conscience. The juridical structure is set out. This is to be a congregation of secular priests and laymen under the authority of the superior general for life, Vincent de Paul, who had authority to change the rules and statutes with the approval of the archbishop of Paris. Also defined is the method of electing Vincent's successor and permission is given for the congregation to own property, to open houses and to acquire and transfer goods. Their ministry is to be gratuitous and they are exempt from the jurisdiction of the ordinary except in matters pertaining to their ministry. The bull also maps out the framework of the new congregation's rules: daily Mass, communion for lay members, one hour's mental prayer each day and examination of conscience. It emphasises the key points of this approved congregation's spirituality: devotion to the Blessed Trinity, to the Incarnation and to the Blessed Virgin.[35]

---

[34] *S.V.P.* I, p. 115.

[35] The Latin text of the bull that we have summarised is given in *S.V.P.* XIII, pp. 257-267. However, it would seem that this is based on a copy, not on the original text. F. Combaluzier has painstakingly noted the slight differences between this and the Latin text. *Cf. Annales* (1941), pp. 31-32.

The bull *Salvatori Nostri* marked the decisive establishment of the Congregation of the Mission. No longer was it to be a simple 'mission' with the limitations of time and space imposed by its definition in 1625 and ratified by the Sacred Congregation of Propaganda in 1627. It had now become a religious institute of pontifical right, freely available for service within the wider horizons of the universal Church. A canonical entity of extraordinary originality had come into being since the new institute was exempt from the ordinary while at the same time retaining its secular character. For Vincent the most important thing was that its basic message, 'the poor people are being lost', had been accepted by the Church and such a grave need was being met. Religious reforms would now reach the mass of poor people who needed them most. So it represented a triumph for Vincent but no way was it the end of his career; in fact it was the starting point for great enterprises.

Chapter XVI
THE STRUGGLE TO PUT THE COMPANY ON A MORE SOLID FINANCIAL BASIS

'We have no right to refuse what people give us out of love for God'

Vincent knew that establishing his congregation's juridical structure was not enough to safeguard its status within the Church. It was also essential to see that the company's finances were secure, in order to provide for the needs of its members and also to ensure freedom of action in the apostolate. This was all the more necessary since all its members, and particularly those engaged in the work of preaching missions, had to give their services free.

The basic financial assets held by the congregation between 1625 and 1632 came from income from the capital given at the foundation, the 45,000 *livres* donated by the de Gondis and invested as the contract stipulated in land investment.[1] This capital sum was meant to provide for the needs of six or seven missioners. Well, the congregation was beginning to expand. In addition to the coadjutor brothers, whose vocation consisted in helping the priests' apostolic work by striving after personal sanctification and carrying out domestic tasks, there were 11 members of the congregation in 1627, 18 in 1629, 23 in 1630 and 26 in 1631. This brief résumé of statistics gives us some idea of the little company's satisfactory progress with regard to personnel. But it also reminds us of the corresponding increase in expense. Of course the Collège des Bons Enfants which, as we mentioned earlier, Vincent donated to the congregation, must have provided another modest source of income from the contributions paid by the priests who lived there and, as it was still a university college in the strict sense of the term, it drew income from some independent properties. But we have no records to help us evaluate these sources of income, which in any case would have been of no great value. On the other hand we do know that major repairs had to be carried out.[2] So it is not surprising that Vincent had to take out loans which were sometimes

---

[1] *S.V.P.* XIII, p. 199.
[2] *S.V.P.* I, pp. 24-25.

endorsed with money belonging to Louise de Marillac,[3] and that when the time came to buy an organ he went to a second class tradesman and not to one of the exclusive firms that made musical instruments. It is moving to note that in the contract for constructing this organ, Vincent expressly stipulated three or four times that it had to be solidly made—this shows the mentality of someone who had to practise economy and wanted to make sure that his money would be well spent. The price of the said organ was 150 *livres*.[4]

The congregation also received gifts occasionally and Vincent tried not to refuse these. One day Fr de la Salle, keeping strictly to the rule that mission work should be gratuitous, refused to accept a gift from Fr de Gondi. Vincent wrote to him to rectify this;

> You have no need to worry about accepting charity from Rev. Father de Gondi. If you have been refusing it up to now, make your apologies to M. Ferrat. He is our founder. We have no right to refuse anything that is given to us for the love of God, or that is donated by someone not living in the place where we are giving a mission. This was the way St Paul used to act. He would never accept anything from the people among whom he was working but he would take offerings from other churches so as to be able to continue his labours in other places ... *Spolians Ecclesias Macedoniae, ut non essem vobis oneri* he writes to the Corinthians, though he adds that he glories in preaching the gospel without payment.[5]

Here we have a picture of the real Vincent de Paul as portrayed in his own words. He was no utopian dreaming about some unattainable Arcady, but the practical realist who was willing to bleed the rich to help the poor. It could be true, too, that the inaccurate quotation from St Paul revealed the subconscious workings of his mind. To take from the rich in order to aid the poor, this was the secret of very many of his enterprises.

If certain sources are to be believed, there came a time, round 1628, when the company's finances were reaching a critical stage. An eighteenth century Oratorian, Fr Joseph Bicaïs, spread a rumour—'You can read in a certain work', he said—that at one time Fr de Gondi was thinking of taking back the gift he had made to Vincent de Paul for the establishment of his congregation. He went to consult the abbé de Saint-Cyran about this but the abbé dissuaded him and pointed out the benefits the foundation could bring

[3] *Annales* (1937), pp. 239-244.
[4] *Annales* (1936), pp.702-704.
[5] *S.V.P.* I, pp. 136-137.

to the Church.'[6]

Most probably, the work from which Bicaïs alleged that he had taken this information, would be a small book by Martin de Barcos, a nephew of Saint-Cyran, who wrote it to counteract Abelly's Biography of Vincent. The learned Oratorian must have read the pages from de Barcos's work in a great hurry because the text could be interpreted in different ways. He says of Fr de Gondi:

> He honoured with his friendship the now deceased abbé de Saint-Cyran, whose piety and learning he held in high esteem. He told him that he had been advised to change his mind and transfer to others the foundation gift of the Collège de Bons Enfants that he had made to the priests of the Mission. He had made this endowment during the lifetime of Madame General of the Galleys, and his wife had been in complete agreement. He asked the abbé what he should do. Saint-Cyran dissuaded him from making the change and encouraged him to keep to his original plan. Fr de Gondi did this, and gave no more thought to the alternative which others had proposed. One could therefore say that the late M. de Saint-Cyran saved the company of the priests of the Mission from being smothered at birth.[7]

De Barcos is not speaking here of any decision made by Fr de Gondi, rather of 'advice he was given', and this advice left the former General of the Galleys with only one doubt in his mind, and this was immediately dispelled by his consultation with Saint-Cyran. There is no doubt at all that the existence of the Congregation of the Mission would have been seriously threatened if Fr de Gondi had taken any notice of those who gave him such bad advice. De Barcos does not say who these people were, and maybe he did not know, but it would not be hard to guess. Think back to the way de Bérulle and other Oratorians fiercely opposed the approbation of Vincent's congregation. It would be easy to understand Fr de Gondi's dilemma, too, if the advice had come directly from the founder and superior general of the Oratory.

Understood in these terms, the information given by de Barcos, and repeated by Bicaïs, is reasonable. This would not be so, however, if the

---

[6] The biographical note about Philippe-Emmanuel de Gondi is taken from *Notice de l'Oratoire de France,* by Father Joseph Bicaïs and published by F. Combaluzier in *Annales* (1940), pp. 272-287. This quotation referred to is on page 287.

[7] M. DE BARCOS, *op. cit.,* p. 11.

statement were taken to imply that de Gondi had made a definite decision. There are facts that prove the contrary was true. Throughout all the long drawn-out formalities for obtaining Rome's approval, Vincent never hesitated for a moment to say that his work was founded by de Gondi and he was always supported on this point by another de Gondi, the Archbishop of Paris. In 1631 as we have already noted, Fr de Gondi spontaneously made a gift to Vincent's missioners[8] and this is hardly in keeping with his alleged plan to withdraw the foundation. We shall see later on that, in 1632, de Gondi stands guarantor for a large debt contracted by Vincent, and there is also the fact that Vincent did not want to mention the opposition he was experiencing from leading members of the Oratory for fear of undermining his vocation.[9] This is yet another proof that Vincent was convinced of de Gondi's firm support for the foundation. Even if de Barcos has used this incident to enhance his uncle's reputation, and this indeed was his object in writing the book, that is no reason why we should reject the information once it is understood in its right context.

Furthermore, there are statements in later reports given by Bicaïs, which, in the light of documentation available to us today, cannot be substantiated. He claims that when the de Gondis made their gift, it had not been their intention 'to found a new congregation but to establish a house of the Oratory.' It was the abandonment of this original plan that caused Fr de Gondi's temporary displeasure.[10] All the information given in the preceding chapter will prove to the reader how mistaken were these ideas of Bicaïs.

However, quite apart from this threat to the company's initial capital, the finances of the Congregation of the Mission in 1630 must have been quite precarious. Then, completely out of the blue, came the answer to their problems.

A rich priory

In Vincent de Paul's time , on the outskirts of Paris in the direction of St Denis, was to be found the fine priory of St Lazare. It was an ancient foundation dating back at least to the twelfth century and it had originally been built as a *leprosarium*. Over the years kings and popes had endowed it with riches and privileges, and at the beginning of the seventeenth century it served as an ecclesiastical court which dealt out justice at all levels. We have evidence of this in the pillories and stone columns, both within the priory and at the

---

[8]   *S.V.P.* I, pp. 136-137.
[9]   *S.V.P.* I, p. 163.
[10] J. BICAIS, *op. cit.*, in *Annales* (1940), p. 287.

adjacent crossroads. But there were hardly any lepers left. One of the favours granted by the monarchs was the privilege of welcoming the king on his solemn entrance into Paris at the beginning of his reign to receive the capital's oath of fidelity. Similarly, when the monarch died, the funeral cortege halted at the Church of St Lazare on its way to St Denis. It was at St Lazare that the body was handed over to the monks of St Denis, the final absolution was pronounced, and all the bishops of the realm went in turn to sprinkle the catafalque with holy water.

The priory comprised a small thirteenth century gothic church which had been extensively restored in the seventeenth century, and the community dwellings that were built on to the north side of the church, with a cloister round a spacious interior courtyard. In addition to these were several buildings that were more or less separated from the others by courtyards or gardens; these were the leper-houses, the prison, a mental asylum, the dovecote, the farm, the windmill, the cowsheds and stables and the abattoir. The surrounding 32 hectares or so of property today covers two districts of Paris. This land was used for sowing wheat, rye and alfalfa. Outside of the main precinct, the abbey held lands in many of the neighbouring towns— Argenteuil, Belleville, La Chapelle, Le Bourget, Cormeilles, Drancy, Gonesse, Lagny, Marly, Rougemont, Sevian and Paris itself. Also dependent on the abbey was the cattle fair of St Laurent, whose lands were on the other side of the St Denis road, next to the parish from which it took its name.

For a long time the administration of the priory had been confided to the Knights of St Lazare, a sort of confraternity of priests and laymen who lived together in community. They followed the rule of St Augustine but did not take vows. They lived under the authority of a prior who was designated by the bishop of Paris from among the clergy of his diocese. At the beginning of the sixteenth century, Bishop Etienne de Poncher suppressed the confraternity, and handed over the priory to the canons of St Victor, while retaining the right to change the administrators whenever he judged it necessary.[11]

In 1630, the community of canons at St Lazare was going through a

---

[11] The history of St Lazare is in COSTE, *M.V.*, p. 189-193. and the information given in this book is taken from there *cf.* ABELLY, *op. cit.*, 1.1 c. 22, p. 94 and 1.3 c. 16, p. 256 and c. 17, p. 263; COLLET, *op. cit.*, Vol. 1, pp. 163-165; A. COPPO, *De antiqua Domus S. Lazari forma nuperrime inventa: Vincentiana* (1960), p. 266 and *De antiqua S. Lazari forma iuxta casalense ms. nuper repertum: ibid.* (1961), pp. 361-366. The secular nature of the priory of Saint Lazare is significant in the history of St Vincent. During the beatification process, one of the objections raised by the Promoter of the Faith, was precisely the fact that St Vincent had accepted the priory of St Lazare contrary to the juridical maxim *regularia regularibus*. This objection was overruled because the priory was proved to be a secular establishment. (COLLET,

bad time. There were clashes of temperament, and maybe clashes of interest, too, between the prior and his religious. The prior, Adrien Le Bon, began to sound out the possibilities of exchanging the priory for some other benefice. There was no lack of tempting offers, including an abbacy. Mutual friends intervened in the conflict, and suggested they hold a meeting at which each party would state its grounds for complaint. They had the meeting and came to an agreement which satisfied everybody. This soon became a dead letter. The disagreements continued and the prior thought of a more radical solution, he would withdraw from the priory.[12] But who was going to succeed him?

'What sort of a man are you?'

Some friends put forward to Adrien Le Bon the name of Vincent de Paul, who was someone the prior did not know. He asked for reports on Vincent and these reports were all excellent; that new congregation had done so much good for souls; it well deserved to have its future assured by the gift of a priory. Adrien Le Bon thought the matter over carefully and one day came to a decision. He summoned the parish priest of St Laurent, Nicolas de Lestocq, and set off for the Collège des Bons Enfants.

When the introductions were over, the prior revealed the reason for his visit. Vincent's reaction was most unexpected. He was stunned; it was as though he had just heard a cannon shot. He could not speak; he was stupefied.[13]

'What! Are you trembling?' exclaimed the prior. When Vincent at last found his voice, he explained,

> Yes, indeed my lord. Your offer frightens me. We are not on
> that plane at all so I dare not even think about it. We are poor
> priests and our only desire is to serve the poor country people.

---

ibid., p. 165). In the lawsuit that Vincent had to bring before he could take possession of St Lazare, the fact that the archbishop of Paris had the right to confer this property, was definite proof that the priory was secular, and this put the judgement heavily in Vincent's favour.

[12] We know the history of the negotiations for the donation of St Lazare from an account given by the parish priest of St Laurent which Abelly included in his biography (*op. cit.*, 1.1 c. 22, pp. 95-99). Coste took that report from Abelly's work and published it in *S.V.P.* XIII, pp. 244-248.

[13] The effect on Vincent that is likened to a cannon shot, is a quotation from Vincent himself (*S.V.P.* V, p. 533). Nicolas Lestocq has the same idea because he compares the prior's offer to a thunderbolt.

Your kindness is much appreciated, and we are very grateful,
but we cannot accept.

Adrien Le Bon insisted, but he met with the same determined refusal. It seemed as though the roles were being reversed so that the donor was pleading and the recipient was refusing the gift. After a useless tussle Le Bon withdrew but he did not accept defeat. He took leave of Vincent, after giving him six months in which to reflect.

When the six months were up, he came back to the Bons Enfants, accompanied once again by Lestocq. He repeated his offer and this was warmly seconded by the parish priest of St Laurent. Vincent could not be moved; he urged that they were few in number; they had only just been established; he did not want people to be talking about him; that all this would be noised abroad; that he hated the limelight; in short, that he was unworthy of such a great favour.

At this point the bell rang for the community meal. Le Bon begged to be admitted to Vincent's table. Vincent gladly agreed. The circumspection shown by this small group of missioners, the orderliness of their refectory, the silence in which they listened attentively to the reading, all reinforced his esteem for these men. He was now absolutely determined; whether they wanted it or not, he would give them his priory.

He kept up his efforts for a further six months but Vincent still refused. Then one day the prior had a bright idea.

'What sort of a man are you?' he said to Vincent. 'If you, yourself, do not want to hear about this matter, at least tell me this: who is your director, the man whose judgement you can trust? Tell me who it is so that I can go to him. My religious have already agreed, all I need is your consent. Nobody who has your good at heart could ever advise you to refuse my offer.'

Vincent gave him the name of his faithful friend and mentor, André Duval, and added, 'We will do whatever he says.' Duval believed he should take up the offer and since it was the voice of God speaking through his spiritual director Vincent accepted.

All Vincent's biographers have been intrigued by his refusal to accept St Lazare. Always, or nearly always, they have suggested that the reason for this was the saint's humility. It is true that humility is an important factor in this question, but this is not the only factor, because humility has its own reasons. As with all true humility, that of Vincent was based on reality. When Adrien Le Bon made his first offer at the end of 1630, the total number of missioners was no more than 23—nine priests, nine clerics and five brothers. Were they not really too few to live on the biggest estate in Paris? St Lazare seemed to be too big a suit for the tiny little body. Again, the future of the congregation was not too clear in 1630. It was too soon after Propaganda had rejected their petition for approval, and negotiations with the Sacred Congregation for Religious had not yet begun. In these circumstances how could they possibly embark on the adventure of moving to St Lazare? If his dream of winning juridical support for the new congregation were suddenly to come to nothing, there would be all the scandal and talk that Vincent dreaded so much, and would not all this be far worse if they were settled in St Lazare? Finally, was the priory really the most suitable place for a group of secular priests totally committed to apostolic work? Would it not mean complications for their life-style? The negotiations with the prior and the canons to settle the terms of the contract, only served to increase Vincent's fears. The offer of St Lazare was a crucial dilemma for Vincent. 'Expand or perish' could well have been his motto. Accepting St Lazare meant that the tiny barque of the congregation was irrevocably launched on the high seas. It was natural that Vincent should hesitate; he always did hesitate at any important crossroads.

That, then, is the handful of objective details which, to my mind, explain Vincent's thinking at this juncture. Obviously, underpinning all of them must be the saint's humility.

'I would rather we stayed in our poverty'

Working out the terms of the contract proved to be a difficult task. Adrien Le Bon had a very different mentality from that of Vincent so they both regarded the proposed merger from a very different standpoint. Adrien Le Bon had in mind that missioners would continue the work previously undertaken by his religious. Although Vincent was prepared to take on the responsibility of looking after the lepers, which was the principal work of the foundation, his congregation's move to St Lazare signalled the beginning of a new era in the history of the priory, and he would not want it to entail any changes for the missioners or for the company's life-style. So there were times when it seemed the negotiations would break down. Vincent could not agree to his missioners chanting the divine office in choir, dressed in *mozetta* and hooded robe, or that they should live together with the former religious. Acceptance of the first proposal would give the impression that the missioners were canons, and that they had renounced their fundamental option for serving the poor people in country areas. To accept the second proposal would pose a threat for the new community's habits of regular observance and of silence, and tempt the missioners to follow the more liberal life-style of the canons. The best thing would be for the canons to have private rooms and the missioners to keep to their community quarters. Unless these conditions were changed, Vincent was prepared to refuse the foundation.

> Since this is fundamentally a question of God's glory and the salvation of souls, and having in mind, also, the inconveniences that could arise if matters turned out the way he (Prior Le Bon) plans, I have the utmost confidence that he will graciously accept this humble representation I am making to him, that I would rather we stayed in our poverty for ever than that we deviate from the designs God has in our regard.[14]

There were differences of opinion, too, about money matters, and in particular about the contribution to be paid by those canons who decided to go on living at the priory. This problem was easily solved. Vincent was satisfied with the annual sum of 200 *livres* offered by the prior, who was well aware that a canon's keep cost considerably more. An ordinary student at the Bons Enfants paid 90 crowns or 270 *livres*.[15] At last, the difficulties were all resolved, and on 7 January 1632, the contract was signed.

Contract and decree of union

The three following considerations helped to settle the agreement. Firstly, by this time there were hardly any lepers to be looked after. When Adrien Le Bon said this, he was only stating an obvious historical fact. Leprosy, one of the spectres that terrified Europe in the Middle Ages and had occasioned the establishment of a network of *leprosaria* or pest-houses, was now eradicated. These *leprosaria* had been under-used since the sixteenth century as patients became fewer. In France first of all, and then throughout Europe, there was a widespread movement in favour of returning these *leprosaria* to public ownership, a sort of early disentailment. St Lazare in Paris was only one of many such cases. So this gesture of Adrien Le Bon shows his awareness of the needs of his time.[16] His second motive for relinquishing the priory was that the Congregation of St Victor, who used to own the priory, had now been disbanded, following a decision taken by the chapter of that same community on 25 December 1625. The third reason was that the income from the priory was meant to benefit lepers and, in default of this, the most natural thing to do, and something which was most in keeping with the

---

[14] *S.V.P.* I, p. 141.
[15] *S.V.P.* I, p. 139.
[16] P. CHAUNU, *I La civilizacion de la Europa classica*, pp. 231-233.

intentions of the founders, was to use these funds to help those working for the salvation of poor peasants 'infected with the leprosy of sin' by donating this money to the priests of the Mission, thus co-operating in the work of consolidating and expanding this congregation.

The clauses dealing with rights and obligations were very precisely worded. The prior was to enjoy an annual pension of 2,000 *livres* and would retain his title; he was to have free use of the places where he chose to reside, and the abbey lands in Rougemont, and the Benedictine benefice of Ste Marie Madeleine de Limouron, in the diocese of Chartres. Each canon would receive an annual pension of 500 *livres* whether he stayed at St Lazare or moved elsewhere. If he had his meals with the new community, then his pension would be 200 *livres*. In addition to this, the canons retained the right to live in their own rooms and apartments so they were very comfortably housed. The prior and religious also enjoyed various spiritual privileges such as funeral rites, burials, and anniversary Masses.

The man who stood guarantor for the financial commitments taken on by the Congregation of the Mission, was Fr de Gondi. In doing so he was rendering a worthy and a new form of service to his former chaplain. It was as though this action was giving the lie, in advance, to the rumour that some historians would spread in their own self-interest: the rumour that de Gondi had changed his mind.

In the name of his congregation, Vincent accepted all responsibilities connected with the priory and, in particular, the hospitalisation and care of lepers, as well as the orderly celebration of the Divine Office, which was to be said aloud but not chanted.

Once the union had been approved by the archbishop of Paris, the Holy See, and the appropriate civil authorities, the Congregation of the Mission would, in return, take full and lasting possession of the priory with all its goods, movable and immovable, and all its assets, incomes, and emoluments. Since negotiations for this could be protracted, the missioners were authorised to take up residence immediately.[17]

The expenses Vincent incurred must have been fairly heavy. He had to pay out 7,000 *livres* a year in pensions for the religious alone. Added to this, the archbishop of Paris, in his letter confirming the union which he signed the day after the contract, imposed two burdens which were no less onerous, but at the same time most pleasing to Vincent's apostolic heart— the priory income was to cover the expenses of at least eight of the twelve priests who would devote themselves to giving missions, all through the year, in all the villages of his diocese, and the same priory funds would provide free board and lodging for as many Paris clergy as the archbishop

---

[17] The whole text of the contract is in *S.V.P.* XIII, pp. 234-244.

wished to send there for a fortnight's retreat prior to their ordination.[18] The episcopal decree of union was followed by letters patent from the king, in that same month, January 1632. The municipal authorities of Paris gave their approval on 24 March. As was customary the royal letters needed to be ratified by the parlement. It was then that the problems started.[19]

'The religious of St Victor are in dispute with us over St Lazare'

The ownership of St Lazare was such an important issue that there were rival claimants for it. During the years just mentioned, Fr Charles Faure, a canon regular from Ste Geneviève, Paris, was trying to reform the Augustinian canons and bring them together in a congregation called 'The Congregation of France'. He received support and encouragement for this undertaking from the titular abbot of Ste Geneviève, Cardinal de la Rochefoucauld. Both men felt that St Lazare was slipping through their fingers. Before the contract was signed they approached Charles de Beaumannoir de Lavardin, bishop of Le Mans, who was a great friend of Adrien Le Bon, to persuade him that it would be much better to give the priory to his brothers in religion. Le Bon and his canons had no wish to submit to Fr Faure's reforms and said as much to the officious mediator. For his part, Vincent made a personal visit to the cardinal, and to the religious, begging them not to put any obstacle in the way of the prior's plans. The opposition from the canons of Ste Geneviève was overcome without too much difficulty, and the cardinal, too, seemed convinced by Vincent's words. But Fr Faure would not give up the fight, and wrote a report to the archbishop of Paris who replied, somewhat curtly, that the nomination of St Lazare's prior had always been the prerogative of the bishop of Paris and he had no intention of relinquishing this.[20]

Other forms of opposition were less easy to overcome. The canons of Ste Geneviève were followed by the canons of St Victor, who also pressed their claim to the priory. St Lazare had, in fact, belonged to their community. But the Congregation of St Victor had been disbanded in 1625. This was one of the factors that had led Vincent de Paul to sign the contract with the religious of St Lazare.

In spite of this, the religious of St Victor thought they were in the right. On two occasions—once, on 17 December 1631, before the contract was signed, and again on 13 May 1632, after the agreement was concluded,

---

[18] *S.V.P.* XIII, p. 252.
[19] *S.V.P.* XIII, pp. 254-257.
[20] *Histoire des chanoines réguliers de la Congregation de France* Vol. 3 c. 13; quoted by Coste in *M.V.*, Vol. 1, pp. 196- 199.

they went to the parlement to try and have the royal letters disallowed. This led to a lawsuit which was heard by the highest court in the land. Vincent felt tempted to give up the project. The ever-devoted Duval and some other friends, including the abbé de Saint-Cyran, dissuaded him, and assured him that he was in the right. Saint-Cyran won for him the support of the two leading figures in the court hearing: the president, Le Jay, and Bignon, the advocate general. These had both been inclined, earlier, to favour the St Victor claim.[21] Vincent could also count on the unqualified support of the abbot of Quincy and the parish priests of Paris. So Vincent went to court.

Will we ever really be able to fathom Vincent? Hagiographers and biographers who have interpreted some of the words spoken or written by Vincent, without giving due consideration to the far-off times and influences that occasioned them, and judging the facts *a priori* rather than in context, have often presented us with a picture of Vincent who was always meek and kind, the sworn enemy of all lawsuits and unable to defend himself against anyone who wanted to rob him. This was not so. Vincent was very keenly aware of his duties as head of a congregation. He knew that in defending his rights, he was also defending thousands of poor people who would receive from his companions and himself the spiritual and material assistance they would get from no other quarter. The St Lazare question threatened the whole future of his congregation and he was convinced that it also posed a threat to the salvation of poor peasants. Vincent has reached the point where he believed it was God's will that he should accept St Lazare. For this reason he was as tenacious in fighting for it as he had previously been in refusing it. It was at this period of strenuous effort to secure St Lazare that Vincent was fighting, too, to have his congregation approved by Rome.

'More disinterested than ever'

But he fought, and went to litigation, in the spirit of the gospel, completely without self-interest or worldly concerns, and totally indifferent to the outcome.

'You are well aware', he wrote at that time, 'that the religious of St Victor are disputing our claim to St Lazare. You cannot imagine how submissive I have been to them, in accordance with the maxims of the gospel, though these religious are, in fact, in the wrong. M. Duval assures me that everyone who knows anything about the case, agrees that this is so. Let what Our Lord wills be done, because he truly knows that on this occasion his goodness

---

[21] *S.V.P.* XIII, p. 105; BARCOS, *op. cit.*, pp. 11-13.

has rendered me more indifferent about this matter than any other business which I have had to deal with.'[22]

According to Abelly, however, Vincent sought refuge in La Sainte Chapelle on the day the parlement debated the case, and remained in prayer throughout the hearing, praying not that his claim would be successful, but that whatever the outcome his heart would always be submissive to the designs of providence.[23]

Apparently there was just one exception to that deliberate indifference. Vincent spoke about it years later, without realising, perhaps, that his words might shed some light on his conduct and his character:

> When we came to this house the prior had two or three poor insane people here and, when we replaced him, we had to take responsibility for looking after them. At that time we were involved in a lawsuit to decide whether we would remain at St Lazare or have to leave, and it was then that I remembered asking myself this question, 'If you had to leave this house right now, what would you find hardest about leaving? And it seemed to me, then, that the worst thing would be to have to abandon these poor people and not be able to look after them and serve them.[24]

Vincent won the lawsuit. The parlement gave its verdict on 7 September 1632, confirming an earlier decision of 21 August of the previous year,[25] but because of some irregularities in the wording it ordered that the archbishop of Paris be requested to issue another decree of union between the priory and the Congregation of the Mission.[26]

Everything had to be done all over again. Vincent, and this is no cliché, had the patience of a saint. Moreover, it gave him the opportunity to reword certain clauses that were not to his liking. He got the prior to concede, in the contract, that it was not necessary to have the transfer confirmed by the Holy See since this was entirely within the province of the archbishop of Paris.[27] In the new decree of approval he wanted the archbishop to waive his

---

[22] *S.V.P.* I, p. 151. It is interesting to note that in this letter, which was written about the same time as the lawsuit was in progress, St Vincent makes no direct mention of the help given by Saint-Cyran which the abbé, and his nephew Barcos thought so important. This is the assistance referred to in an earlier note.

[23] ABELLY, *op. cit.*, 1.1 c. 22, p. 101; COLLET, *op. cit.*, Vol. 1, p. 174.

[24] *S.V.P.* XI, pp. 21-22.

[25] *S.V.P.* XIII, pp. 268 and 271.

[26] *S.V.P.* XIII, p. 396.

[27] *S.V.P.* XIII, p. 270. Adrien Le Bon's declaration is dated 29 December, 1632.

right to demand an examination of the priory's accounts. The archbishop was not prepared to do this. Vincent threatened to withdraw completely from the deal if this was not granted. 'And I would have had no hesitation in doing so if he had persisted in his demands', added Vincent.[28] The archbishop had to agree. Had he already received the news from Rome that the Holy See had approved the Congregation of the Mission as an institute of pontifical right, exempt from the authority of the ordinary and that the bull *Salvatori Nostri* was on the point of being issued? The king granted further letters patent[29] and these were again ratified by the parlement[30] as well as by the *Chambre des Comptes* and the *Cour des Aides*.[31]

When all these formalities were finally ended, Vincent and his companions took possession of the priory in peace. As a matter of fact, they had been living there since early in 1632, after the contract was signed because, as we have already noted, this was expressly stipulated in the contract.[32]

In order to put the property beyond the reach of any future litigants, or the unforeseen whims of bishops, Vincent started the long, drawn-out negotiations to have St Lazare annexed, once and for all, to the Congregation of the Mission. It could be said that this new negotiation would last till the end of the founder's life time.[33] As late as 18 April 1655, the papal bull to this effect had not yet been obtained,[34] and it was only six months before he died that Vincent could have in his possession the letters of Louis XIV which gave full and legal effect to the papal bull.[35]

'They have put bread into our hands'

It had been a long battle. Was it really worth such a struggle? There is no doubt that Vincent thought it worthwhile. Why was this? Firstly, we have to bear in mind (as Vincent certainly did), something we have not given much attention to up to now: the move to St Lazare was in the nature of a new foundation, and this time it was Adrien Le Bon and his canons, who with the

---

[28] *S.V.P.* IV, pp. 70-71. The new decree issued by the archbishop is dated 31 December 1632, and can be found in pages 271-277 of volume 13.

[29] *S.V.P.* XIII, p. 277; January 1633.

[30] *S.V.P.* XIII, p. 397, dated 21 March 1633.

[31] *S.V.P., ibid.* The approval of the *Chambre de Comptes* and the *Cour des Aides* are dated 18 October 1633 and 9 January 1634, respectively.

[32] *S.V.P.* XIII, p. 243.

[33] *S.V.P.* I, pp. 255-272.

[34] *S.V.P.,* XIII, pp. 372-380.

[35] *Ibid.*, pp. 412-415.

archbishop's consent, provided the capital. It was very much more important than the foundation at the Bons Enfants. The obligations laid down by the archbishop were more far-reaching than those of the first foundation, but they followed the same guidelines. Preaching missions to poor peasants was now complemented by the second aspect of the Vincentian vocation, the reform of the clergy through retreats for ordinands. This work had not got under way at the time the contract was signed in 1625. It represented the ultimate expression of the Vincentian mission, as confirmed later by the bull *Salvatori Nostri.*

The second reason has to do with living quarters. The Bons Enfants was too small. St Lazare, on the other hand, would allow for unlimited expansion of the Congregation. In actual fact, it was to remain the mother house of the community for nearly two centuries, until the outbreak of the French Revolution. At some periods, even in Vincent's lifetime, it would shelter hundreds of people within its walls.

Finally, there were financial considerations. We have not the information to help us calculate with certainty the expenses of St Lazare in 1633. But taking into account the level of commitments taken on,[36] perhaps it would not be too bold to suggest that expenses would be at least 40 or 50,000 *livres* a year.

The vicissitudes of the times, and the increasing burdens that Vincent's charity made them undertake, meant that St Lazare passed through some difficult times financially. But taken as a whole, it could be said that thanks to Adrien Le Bon, the congregation had emerged from its poverty. Vincent wanted them to look on Adrien Le Bon as a father.

'Many of us suffered want and it was he who provided the means to feed and maintain us.'[37]

'He put bread into our hands.'[38]

At times Vincent was afraid that St Lazare

'Might prove too attractive on account of the good bread and

---

[36] We have to remember that these financial obligations included more than 7,000 *livres* in pensions for the former religious occupants, the expense of maintaining 8 priests whose exclusive work was to preach missions in the diocese of Paris, the free board and lodging for a fortnight that was given to the ordinands at all the retreats before ordination in Paris. There would be at least 5 of these ordinations a year and there would be numerous candidates at each.

[37] *S.V.P.* XI, pp. 155-156.

[38] *S.V.P.* XIII, p. 639.

meat one could eat there, the good air one could breathe, the open spaces for walking and all the amenities it provides.'[39]

'We have splendid courtyards and a walled garden. As for food, where would you find better bread and better wine? Where would you find better meat? better fruit? What do we lack? How many people in the world can enjoy all this?'[40]

Even if we disregard the large dose of rhetorical exaggeration in the words used by the founder to urge his missioners to preserve their spirit of poverty in the midst of what was relatively material comfort, there is no doubt that St Lazare assured the expansion of the infant community's assets. We will soon see the use that Vincent, the apostle-businessman, was to make of these resources from St Lazare. For the moment, suffice it to say that when Vincent simultaneously took on the struggle to institutionalise his community, confirm its work objectives, and put it on a sound financial basis, he was laying up for it very many years of security and fruitfulness in all kinds of apostolic endeavour. St Lazare would be the new stepping-off point, so it is quite fitting that Vincentians in France should be known as Lazaristes.

---

[39] *S.V.P.* VI, p. 516.
[40] *S.V.P.* XI, pp. 247-248.

Chapter XVII
FOUNDATION WORKS
THE TABLEAU IS NOW COMPLETE

The 'Tuesday conferences'

The year 1633 is Vincent de Paul's year of successes. With the publication of the bull, *Salvatori Nostri,* his congregation was accorded papal approval and the juridical status it was never to lose. Their move to St Lazare had the king's unqualified support and so they now had a permanent operational base. However, some parts of his works' mechanism still needed to be pieced together.

Retreats for ordinands were just the beginning of Vincent's efforts to reform the clergy. This was the aspect of his missionary work that had been delayed the longest. The year 1633 was to put into his hands yet another tool for the development of this work, the 'Tuesday Conferences'. As usual, Vincent assures us that this was not his idea, but that the suggestion came from one of the more fervent priests who had made his retreat for ordinands. We know that very early on Vincent and his companions had taken advantage of the missions they preached to bring together the local priests and give some talks to them, too. They instructed them in their pastoral duties,[1] and later welcomed them, first to the Bons Enfants, and later to St Lazare, for a retreat. The bull, *Salvatori Nostri,* mentions this and other works that the missioners undertook for the clergy: the monthly meetings for curés and rectors to study together cases of conscience and ways of administering the sacraments.[2] All this proves that Vincent had, for years, been thinking about and trying out new ways of working for the clergy, in addition to the retreats for ordinands.

At the beginning of the seventeenth century, a devout prelate, Cardinal François Escoubleau de Sourdis, had introduced into his diocese the practice of assembling the rectors and other priests to discuss questions

---

[1] ABELLY, *op. cit.*, 1.2 c.1, p. 15.
[2] *S.V.P.* XIII, p. 261.

of moral theology.[3] A similar programme had been started by Fr Bourdoise, founder of the community of St Nicolas du Chardonnet, both in his seminary in Paris and in various dioceses in the north of France.[4] But meetings of the clergy to discuss the virtues proper to their state and to give mutual support in practising these and so advance in virtue were something completely new. At least Vincent de Paul had never come across anything like them.[5]

The young clerics who had made a pre-ordination retreat in Vincent's house were beginning to be conspicuous among the priests in Paris. They lived a more orderly life, occupied their time in exercises of piety, visited hospitals and prisons and genuinely desired to live a truly priestly life.[6] Sadly, this first fervour was, of its nature, something ephemeral and easily dissipated when it came into contact with others who were tepid or more relaxed in life-style. Vincent was aware of this and he wondered how he could make the fruits of the retreat more lasting.[7]

One day Vincent received a visit from one of these priests who shared his concern.

> M. Vincent, why do you not start an association to help us
> keep alive to our first fervour?

Once again, Vincent believed it was the voice of God speaking. His own special way of listening to God was not through visions or apparitions, but through concrete situations brought to his notice either by the entreaties of somebody in need, or somebody speaking on their behalf. This is what happened at Châtillon, at Folleville and in the carriage of the bishop of Beauvais. Even when Vincent was aware of a need, he would always wait for providence to reveal its plans to him. So sometimes the accusation has been made, even by contemporaries, that he was slow to make a decision.[8] Anyone who thinks that does not know Vincent. Vincent was slow, desperately slow, when he could not see clearly what was God's will. This was the case with St Lazare, when he took over a year to make up his mind. But once the divine will was manifest through some event, an order from someone in authority, or through the advice of some spiritual person, Vincent made up his mind with astonishing speed. The idea of forming an association of priests is a case in point. Only a few days after receiving the confidences of this good

---

[3] *S.V.P.* XI, p. 13.
[4] J. F. DARCHE, vol. 1, pp. 213, 273, 372, 488.
[5] *S.V.P.* XI, p. 13.
[6] *S.V.P.* I, p. 204.
[7] ABELLY, *op. cit.*, 1.2 c. 3, p. 246.
[8] ABELLY, *op. cit.*, 1.1 c. 19, pp. 75-76; COLLET, *op. cit.*, Vol. 1, p. 123.

priest Vincent had drawn up his plan and put it into action. He was inspired by the memory of the Early Fathers who used to meet in the desert from time to time for spiritual discussions.[9]

'We have every reason to expect that much good will come from this company!'

At that time, Vincent had on hand the priests who had just been ordained. Under his instructions, they were preaching a mission to the stonemasons and carpenters who were working on the Visitation nuns' convent chapel in the Faubourg St Antoine, a chapel paid for by Brûlart de Sillery,[10] whom Vincent had once directed. After explaining his idea to the archbishop, and getting his approval, Vincent went to see them. It was the feast of St Barnabas, 11 June 1633.[11] He interviewed each one of them and told them his plan. They all agreed enthusiastically. This was Saturday and he arranged for them to meet at two o'clock the following Monday, in his house at St Lazare.[12]

This was just an introductory meeting where Vincent explained in more detail the aims and nature of the association he had in mind. Unfortunately, we do not have the text of his address, but the résumé given by Abelly lets us hear an echo of Vincent's eloquence and his style, as he addressed an audience which included some priests he would greatly esteem all his life: the then very young Jean Jacques Olier, future founder of St Sulpice, Nicolas Pavillon, later bishop of Alet, Antoine Godeau who would become bishop of Grasse, François Perrochel, who was destined to become bishop of Boulogne, and Michel Alix, abbot of Colenge.[13]

Vincent talked to them about the dignity of the priesthood, a truly holy state for those who consecrated themselves entirely to the Lord. Then he pondered on the unfortunate condition of priests who lose their first fervour and become contaminated with the spirit of the world. He exhorted them to seek the means of remaining faithful to the spirit of their vocation as they went about their daily duties or mixed with their families. He backed up each statement with quotations from scripture—the ploughman who looks back, the lustreless gold mentioned by Isaiah, the temple stones scattered in

---

[9] ABELLY, *op. cit.*, 1.2 c. 3, p. 246; *S.V.P.* XI, p. 13.
[10] *S.V.P.* I, pp. 41-42.
[11] ABELLY, *op. cit.*, 1.2 c. 3, p. 247.
[12] *S.V.P.* I, p. 201.
[13] COLLET, *op. cit.*, Vol. 1, p. 189.

the streets, Baruch's stars where each shines from its appointed space and joyfully answers the call of its maker.[14]

Vincent's preaching had a great impact, too, on the learned members of the audience. By this time he was already a saint, and every phrase he uttered was the fruit of long meditation and personal experience. He was very concerned for these inexperienced young men. He wanted this select group, which only admitted priests who were known for their piety and innocence of life, to be the leaven among the clergy of France, and to form a brotherhood where they would be closely united in and with Christ, for their mutual help towards progress in virtue. He wanted them to try and mirror Christ in everything. More than anything he wanted them—and here we have Vincent's own personal vocation persuasively winning over disciples— to imitate the Saviour's love for the poor. He wanted each to follow his own particular inspiration, labouring for God's glory, not just among the poor people in the cities, but with those in country areas, too.

He suggested they make it a definite rule to keep at least to this basic daily programme: always to rise at a fixed time, to have mental prayer, Mass, meditative reading of the New Testament, particular and general self-examen, and spiritual reading. There would also be their annual retreat and the weekly conferences on spiritual matters and on the duties, virtues, and pastoral work of a good priest.[15]

He gave them a month to think it over. They would meet again on Saturday 9 July to set up the association. There was nobody missing from this meeting; in fact a few more came after seeing the zeal of the first members. The only one to be absent was the priest who had first thought of the project for he was out of Paris, giving a mission. Vincent wrote to tell him about it:

> The idea you recently paid me the honour of sharing with me has been so well received by the priests. They all came together a fortnight ago and decided to implement your proposals. There was such unanimity in this that it seems the plan must come from God. There are having another meeting today. O Lord, what reasons we have for expecting much good to come from this company. You are its inspiration, and will see that everything works well for God's glory.[16]

---

[14] ABELLY, *op. cit.*, 1.2 c. 3, pp. 247-248.

[15] *Cf. Règlement des ecclésiastiques membres de la Conférence des mardis; S.V.P.* XIII, p. 128-132; COLLET, *op. cit.*, Vol. 1, pp. 186-187.

[16] *S.V.P.* I, pp. 202-203. Up till now, all attempts at identifying the priest who first suggested to St. Vincent the idea of the Tuesday conferences, have been unsuccessful. Quite a few indications lead us to think it could have been Abelly, who deliberately omitted his name from the account, but we cannot be certain of this.

At the second meeting they drew up a provisional rule based on Vincent's guidelines, elected the organising committee and decided that Tuesday was the most convenient day to meet. This is how the association came to be known as the 'Tuesday conference'. However, the first conference, properly so-called, took place on the following Saturday 16 July.[17]

'Vincent was the soul of that pious assembly'

The only thing we know about that first conference is its theme. The subject under discussion was the priestly state, motives for attaining it, its nature, and the means of achieving, preserving and making progress in it. But the conference would have developed along the same lines as others that we know about. Vincent had a horror of the empty oratory in vogue at that time. So there were to be no discourses, just the simple and clear presentation by one of the priests of the thoughts he had at prayer and meditation. Then the others would join in and there would be a common sharing of reflections and sentiments. Vincent spoke little. Usually he was content just to listen. Only at the end would he speak, to emphasise some of the ideas expressed, to add his own feelings on the matter, put forward his own reflections, amplify, exhort and correct.

They would drink in whatever he had to say. As the years passed, Vincent was becoming more and more and more the prophetic voice of the church in France. The most distinguished member of the conferences, the incomparable Bossuet, would recall with emotion:

> I, too, belonged to that association which he founded and directed. Its aim was to bring together some priests every week to talk about spiritual matters. Vincent was the soul of the pious assembly. We listened eagerly to what he had to say. We felt that as he spoke he was fulfilling the apostle's maxim, 'If anyone speaks, let his speech be as coming from God.'[18]

Right from the outset, Vincent had high hopes for this new work. Shortly after the association started, he wrote to his faithful friend and

---

[17] This is the date given by Abelly. (*op. cit.*, 1.2 c. 3, p. 249). Coste's reason for changing the date, and for thinking that it took place on Tuesday 19, are not convincing. (*cf. M.V.* Vol. 1, p. 309).

[18] In COLLET, *op. cit.*, Vol. 2, p. 600 and 606. Bossuet's letter to Pope Clement XI petitioning the beatification of Vincent de Paul.

companion in his works, François du Coudray, who was still in Rome working on the congregation's business:

> 'The object of these meetings is for the members to commit themselves to aiming at perfection. They will strive to discover ways of avoiding offending God and, on the contrary, of making him known and served by all communities. Through the association both priests and the poor will give glory to God. Somebody from here will be the director, and they will meet here every week. Since God has blessed the retreats that so many parish priests from this diocese have made here, these gentlemen would like to make a similar retreat and, in fact, they have already started. If Our Lord is pleased to bless the work we have reason to hope that great good will come of it, so I recommend it specially to your prayers.'[19]

In keeping with his method of directing souls, Vincent was not content to give just a theoretical lead to the members of the association. He immediately did with them what he had done with Marguerite de Silly and Louise de Marillac: he set them to work. During that same year, 1633, they preached in the Hospital of the Three Hundred, a refuge for blind people, which had been founded in the capital by Louis XIII. This mission was not confined to the blind and their families, but was open to anyone living near the hospital who wished to attend. That mission was followed by others: to soldiers of the royal guard, to labourers in Paris workshops, to stonemasons and hired hands, to the poor people of the Hôpital de la Miséricorde, to the women in the house of correction,[20] and many other missions which we will study later on. Vincent's energetic charity, which relied on the Congregation of the Mission to evangelise the poor peasants, could now, through the Tuesday conferences, reach out to the poor people of the cities, a work that the congregation could not undertake.

'Every good priest wanted to belong to it'

It became fashionable to attend the conferences. A very reliable witness, the Jansenist, Lancelot, was to say, 'There was not any good priest in Paris who did not want to belong to it'.[21] Even the young son of the de Gondi family, a

---

[19] *S.V.P.* I, pp. 204-205.
[20] ABELLY, *op. cit.*, 1.2 c. 3, pp. 256-257.
[21] *Mémoires touchant la vie de Monsieur de S. Cyran,* Vol. 1, p. 287.

tearaway, who at that time was only abbot of Buzais but who would later become the famous Cardinal de Retz, was admitted to the conference even though his conduct was far from edifying. No doubt this inclusion was due to Vincent's influence, and his affection for the young man whom he regarded as an erring son that he always hoped to bring back to the right path. 'He is not very pious, but all the same, he is not far from the kingdom of heaven', is what de Retz claimed that Vincent had said about him.[22] This was the weakness of a father, perhaps the only perceptible weakness in Vincent de Paul, and an understandable one, as it concerned the son of his benefactor, a boy he had known almost from the cradle and someone who, as archbishop of Paris, would become Vincent's bishop.

The conference's reputation spread rapidly. Richelieu, who had his finger on every tiny movement within the kingdom, wanted to have first-hand information. He arranged a meeting with Vincent that was not without some political purpose. As far as we know, this was the first meeting between the humble priest and the mighty prime minister who was also a churchman and, in his own way, a reformer. Richelieu wanted to know the reasons for these meetings, the matters discussed there, who went to them, and the works they took on. Perhaps he was just a little suspicious of the activities of someone who had earlier been the friend of de Bérulle, the de Gondis, the Fargis and the Marillacs. He was completely reassured. This was no political cabal but a genuine religious association. He ended up by asking Vincent which of those priests would make a good bishop, and he wrote the list in his own hand. Vincent maintained strict secrecy about the interview. He had no wish to see the conferences turn into a springboard for climbers and plotters.[23] Rather, it was to become a seedbed of zealous reformers, and from its ranks would come twenty-three bishops and archbishops, as well as numerous vicars-general, archdeacons, canons, parish priests, directors of seminaries, religious superiors and provincials, and confessors for religious.[24] Vincent de Paul's reform movement was penetrating the highest echelons of the Church. But we are anticipating events. In 1633, the Tuesday conferences were just one more tool forged by Vincent for his work of reforming the clergy and serving the poor.

The Charities finally take shape

If Vincent had collaborators on hand to give spiritual help to the poor, and to

---

[22] COSTE, *M.V.* c.2, p. 307; *Mémoires,* I,pp. 177-178.
[23] ABELLY, *op. cit.*, 1.1 c. 27, p. 125.
[24] COLLET, *op. cit.*, Vol. 1, p. 191.

assist the clergy, the same could not be said about the material help he wanted to give. This was the other side of his vocation as he discerned it at Châtillon-les-Dombes or in dungeons for galley slaves. Vincent had conceived the idea of confraternities of charity at Châtillon, but when these moved to Paris a certain insensitivity crept in among the members. We have already seen that periodic visitations were necessary to put right any failings in these small, isolated associations. In Paris the situation got worse. The ladies of the capital had been enthusiastic at first, but then they found going in person to serve the poor a burden.[25] So they sent their servants instead. Vincent could not tolerate this mercenary way of practising charity. For one thing, it clashed with his conviction that charity, for a Christian, is a matter of personal commitment. Secondly, it meant that the poor were being left unattended because what they needed was continuous help from people who would be utterly dedicated to the work. Without dispensing with the charities altogether, he began to plan a new association whose members would make up for any deficiencies in the charity confraternities, and would dedicate all their time to the service of the poor. The search for such an association lasted for some years. We know that when Vincent was unsure of God's will, he was slow to make up his mind. He was no utopian political thinker, anxious to find a solution to specific evils in society. He was a man of God who strove to distinguish the voice of God, amid the clamours of the world.

'The first Daughter of Charity'

One day, early in 1630,[26] Vincent was giving a mission when he met a young village girl whose soul was obviously touched by the invisible finger of grace. Her name was Marguerite Naseau and she came from Suresnes, a small town not far from Paris. It was she who would prove to be the answer to what Vincent was looking for. But let Vincent himself tell us about it:

> She was just a poor, unlettered girl, who minded cows. A powerful inspiration from heaven gave her the idea of instructing young people. She bought an alphabet, and since she could not go to school to learn to read, she used to ask the parish priest or the curate to tell her the first four letters; later on she would ask about the next four, and so on with the

---

[25] *S.V.P.* IX, pp. 209, 244, 455, 601.
[26] *S.V.P.* I, p. 76.

others. She studied her lessons as she minded the cows. If she saw somebody passing by who looked as if he could read, she would ask, 'How do you pronounce this word, sir?' And so, little by little, she learnt how to read, and then she taught other girls in her village. Then she made up her mind to go from village to village, with two or three girls she had trained, so that they could teach others. What a marvellous work! She undertook all this, even though she had no money, and no other support but divine providence. Often she would fast for days on end, and she lived in dwellings that only had the walls standing. However, she devoted herself, sometimes by night as well as by day, to teaching not just girls, but older people as well, and she did this without any vanity or self-interest, but purely for the love of God who saw to her needs without her thinking about them. She herself told Mlle Le Gras, that on one occasion when she had been several days without bread, and had not told anybody about the poverty she was living in, she came back from Mass to find enough provisions to feed her for quite a long time. The more she laboured at teaching young people, the more she was calumniated and jeered at by the peasants. She was so detached from things, that she gave away everything she had even though that meant going without necessities. She helped some poor students to pursue their studies, provided them with food for a time, and encouraged them in the service of God. These young men are now good priests.

Finally, when she learnt that there was a confraternity of charity in Paris for poor sick people, she went there. She had a great desire to do this work and, although she still wanted very much to continue instructing young people, she nevertheless abandoned this charitable work, to take on the other service which she judged to be more perfect and more necessary. And God wanted her to act in this way so that she would be the first Daughter of Charity, servant of the sick poor, in the city of Paris. Her example attracted other young girls, whom she had helped to give up all sorts of frivolities in order to embrace the devout life.[27]

To Vincent's way of thinking, the story of Marguerite Naseau, together with the charity confraternity at Châtillon-les-Dombes, was, for the

---

[27] *S.V.P.* IX, p. 77 ss.

Daughters of Charity, what the peasant's confession at Gannes and the sermon at Folleville had been for the missioners. So he told the story over and over again, each time adding new and interesting details. He nearly always attributes to Marguerite herself the initiative in going to Paris to work in the charities. But just on one occasion, he slips into the first person, and says, 'I suggested to her that she should serve the sick. She agreed to the suggestion at once and with great pleasure, and I sent her to St Sauveur.'[28] This is for us a precious slip of the tongue which helps us realise, once again, Vincent's understanding of the gentle ways of providence.

'They began to join, almost without realising it'

Other young girls followed Marguerite Naseau, some of them recruited by her. Mlle le Gras took charge of them in Paris. Soon a large number of girls joined them and the group seemed to go on increasing. Vincent was to say,[29] 'They began to meet and almost without realising it they would join.' After a few weeks' elementary instruction, which often had to begin with teaching them the alphabet, and a religious formation which consisted basically of some spiritual exercises, the practice of Buseo's method of mental prayer, and spiritual reading from Fr Granada's *Guide for Sinners,* they were launched into the works.[30] They were nothing more than some extended version of the charity confraternities in each parish. For this reason they received their orders from the ladies of the confraternity, and at this time were not united by any bonds of community. From now on they came to be known as *les filles de la Charité,* i.e., the charity girls or lasses.[31]

Soon the project surpassed all expectations. The number of girls increased rapidly, and gradually the idea took shape of forming them into a separate body which would be organised on a more permanent basis. This plan would entail many difficulties. No matter what their title might be, they would always be regarded as some new religious congregation. This was a big risk, because the term 'religious' meant cloistered; they would be enclosed behind grilles and that would mean goodbye to caring for the sick, and

---

[28] *S.V.P.* IX, p. 209. All St Vincent's allusions to the story of Marguerite Naseau are to be found in: *S.V.P.* I, pp. 76, 131, 185, 187; IX, pp. 77, 209, 244, 455, 601; X, p. 10.

[29] *S.V.P.* IX, p. 209.

[30] *S.V.P.* I, pp. 197-198.

[31] No serious study has been made of the original meaning of the phrase 'Daughters of Charity'. The text indicates that the name followed on from what they did. Later on St Vincent interpreted it in the spiritual sense of 'Daughters of God', because God is Charity. *Cf.* CALVET, *Luisa de Marillac. Retrato* (Salamanca, Ceme, 1977), p. 80.

goodbye to the service of the poor. Vincent remembered the frustrations experienced by St Francis de Sales when he started the Visitation nuns. He would have to tread very carefully, and make it absolutely clear that these were not nuns, but a group of secular women, living in community but keeping the same freedom to come and go through the streets of the city, the wards of hospitals or the cells of a prison. Modesty was to serve them as religious garb, and they would wear the grey serge robe and white coiffe of the village girls in country areas near Paris. They were not to live in convents, but in houses. They would not have a 'novitiate', but their months of formation would be known as the 'seminary'.

A capable, intelligent, and pious lady would have to be found to train and direct these girls, and she would need to give wholehearted commitment to the work. Louise de Marillac appeared to be the obvious choice. For years now she had been training these girls to work in the parish charities, but Mlle le Gras was still a long way from solving her own personal problems. We must pause here and trace in some detail her spiritual journey between 1630 and 1633, though precise dates are unavailable. There are many gaps in the correspondence between Vincent and herself, so it is difficult to be sure about dates. She continued to be very anxious about her son who, at the age of eighteen or nineteen, had still not decided what to do in life. He was often ill, he changed schools, and he decided not to be ordained, a decision that Vincent supported.[32] From time to time, Louise herself still thought of entering a contemplative order. In 1630, Vincent praised 'your generous resolution to honour the hidden life our adorable saviour practised from his early years.'[33]

'Your angel has spoken to mine'

The following year, if Coste's dating of the letters is correct, it is Vincent who is hesitant. This would seem to be the obvious sense of one of the letters that Abelly interprets, and I think rightly so, as the director putting the brakes on the impatient woman he was guiding.

> As for the other matter, unless Our Lord lets you see with absolute certainty that he desires something different of you, I beg you once and for all, not to give it any more thought, since at the moment he is letting you feel quite the opposite

---

[32] *S.V.P.* I, pp. 102, 106-107, 109, 123, 128, 129, 131-132, 135, 142.
[33] *S.V.P.* I, p. 87.

sentiments. We often desire good things, and this desire seems to come from God, but it is not always so; God allows it so that the soul may be prepared to be as he wills. Saul went in search of an ass, and found a kingdom, St Louis went to conquer the Holy Land, and he conquered himself, thus winning a heavenly crown. You are trying to become the servant of these poor girls, and God wants you to be his servant, and perhaps the servant of many others, whom you could not help if you continued like this. And if you were to be just the servant of God, would not God be satisfied that your heart is honouring the tranquillity of Our Lord?[34]

Vincent seems to want Louise to have the same experience that he had during his retreat at Soissons, to put aside all haste and wait patiently for God's will to be made known. Even as late as Pentecost 1633, he was still undecided, but Vincent was so sparing with words that we do not know the reason for this hesitation:

With regard to the matter you have in hand, I still have not had sufficient enlightenment from God, and I find it difficult to see whether this is his divine Majesty's will. I beg you, Mademoiselle, to pray to him for this intention during these days when he bestows the graces of the Holy Spirit more abundantly and gives the Holy Spirit himself. Let us keep up our prayers, then, and I beg you to remain joyful.[35]

The retreat he made in August, or September 1633, proved decisive. As at Soissons, ten years earlier, Vincent's hesitation and Louise's doubts vanished and the way was now open for a new community to be established. At the end of this retreat Vincent writes a letter to Louise which is tantamount to giving her the green light:

In the name of Our Lord I beg you, Mademoiselle, to look after yourself as much as possible, not now as a private individual, but as someone whose health concerns many other people.

This is the eighth day of the retreat and with the help of God I hope to continue till the tenth.

I think your good angel must have done what you wrote to me about. Four or five days ago, your angel spoke to mine

---

[34] *S.V.P.* I, pp. 113-114; ABELLY, *op. cit.*, 1.1 c. 24, p. 113.
[35] *S.V.P.* I, p. 200.

about the charity of your daughters. He has often brought this to my mind, and I have given serious thought to this good work. God willing, we shall talk about it on Friday or Saturday, unless you advise me to the contrary before then.'[36]

29 November 1633

The following months were spent looking for, and selecting, the young girls who were to form the first nucleus of the new community. They all had experience of working for the poor in the parish charities.[37] On 29 November 1633, on the eve of the feast of St Andrew, a small group of girls, whose names are unfortunately not known to us, moved into the house of Mlle le Gras to begin their training in 'solid virtue'. Thus was born the company of the Daughters of Charity.[38] Marguerite Naseau was not to be one of them. A few months earlier she had died, the victim of heroic charity, after sharing her bed with a woman who had the plague.[39]

The Charity Association of the Hôtel-Dieu

Yet another institution was to be added to the list of those destined by Vincent to bring about the reforms he felt called to make, reforms in, and for, charity. This happened early in 1634, though it had begun to develop much earlier. The final piece of Vincent's charity apparatus was the association of ladies of the Hôtel-Dieu, or Central Hospital in Paris, and although at first sight it seemed less important than his other works, in fact it was to prove indispensable for their functioning.

 Once again, the inspiration for this work came from an outside source and once again it was the initiative of a generous lady. The Madame Presidente, Goussault, whose maiden name was Geneviève Fayet, was one of those pious ladies who gathered round Vincent during the years 1625-1633, attracted by the powerful appeal of his ardent charity. Her husband, Antoine Goussault, Lord of Souvigny, member of the royal council and president of the Chamber of Finance, had died in 1631, and his widow retained the name and title of her deceased husband. As Vincent had previously

---

[36] *S.V.P.* I, pp. 217-218.

[37] *S.V.P.* I, p. 219.

[38] GOBILLON, *op. cit.*, pp. 51-52.

[39] *S.V.P.* IX, p. 79; X p. 101. There is some doubt about the date of Marguerite Naseau's death. Early biographers give the date as 1631. Coste puts it back to the year 1633, but the dating of the letters on which he bases this supposition is questionable. *Cf. S.V.P.* I, pp. 185-189.

done with Louise de Marillac, he got Mme Goussault to visit the charities. It is from her that we have the liveliest, and most colourful accounts of their journeys, real gems that reveal the language, and the good taste, of the aristocracy of those days. She, too, had worked hard to recruit and train the first aspirants to the Daughters of Charity. It has sometimes been suggested that Vincent's final hesitation in authorising Louise to take charge of the work might have come from his indecision about which of these two ladies should be superioress of the institute. Madame Presidente was just as spiritual and fervent as Louise, and she was, moreover, a more lively and enterprising woman. Perhaps, though, she lacked that final touch of mysticism which was ultimately to make Louise de Marillac a saint. [40]

Mme Goussault's innate generosity had moved her to start visiting the hospital of her own accord. What she found there filled her with dismay. The physical and spiritual needs of the sick people were neglected. The hospital was directed by the cathedral chapter, but all these canons did was to designate two of their members to visit the hospital, and these, in their turn, delegated their responsibilities to a group of chaplains presided over by a 'spiritual master'. None of these people was particularly zealous. The hospital was run by a community of Augustinian nuns whose observance of rule and regularity of life style also left much to be desired. It was the sick who suffered from this state of affairs. If we discount conditions that could be attributed to lack of medical knowledge at that time, conditions such as several people being crowded into the same bed, or practically non-existent standards of hygiene, there were still other deficiencies that could easily have been put right. The food was poor and unappetising, and there was no such thing as personal hygiene. The sick were obliged to go to confession as soon as they were admitted, and they were not helped with this. Nobody bothered about confession again until the person was dying.[41]

Many pious people were concerned about conditions at the hospital. This was particularly true of the Company of the Blessed Sacrament, a semi-secret association of clergy and laity, which had been established to attend to various needs within the Church, and which had tried to alleviate the worst evils.[42] Mme Goussault, who may have been inspired by some member of that company, thought it could, and should, be doing more. The idea came to her of setting up a confraternity of charity devoted exclusively to serving

---

[40] *S.V.P.* I, pp. 158, 191-196.
[41] A. CHEVALIER, *L'Hôtel-Dieu de Paris et les Soeurs Augustines* (Paris, H. Champios, 1901): M. FOSEYEUX, *L'Hôtel-Dieu de Paris au XVII siècle et au XVIII siècle* (Paris, Berger-Levrault et Cie, 1912).
[42] R. VOYER D'ARGENSON, *Annales de la Compagnie du Saint Sacrement* (Marseille, Beauchet-Filleau, 1900).

the hospital. She went to Vincent de Paul to ask him to start the work and be its director.

'On someone else's pitch?'

As always, and perhaps this time even more so than on previous occasions, Vincent asked himself if this really was God's will for him. There were so many people connected with that hospital: canons, chaplains, nuns, knights of the Blessed Sacrament. If he sent a new association of ladies there, would it not be trespassing on someone else's pitch? Gently, but firmly, he refused. She may have been expecting this, but she was not a lady to take no for an answer. She was only too well aware of the weak spot in Vincent's defences, and went off to see the archbishop. He gave his blessing to the project and told Mme Goussault to inform Vincent that he wished him to undertake this work. Vincent had no option but to comply with the order from his bishop, even though this had been contrived by the manoeuvres of an enterprising lady.

The introductory meeting of the association took place in Mme Goussault's house, early in 1634. Present at this meeting were a good number of ladies who all came from distinguished families: the elegant and precise Isabelle Blandeau, chatelaine of Villesavin, and widow of Marie de Medici's secretary; Isabelle Marie Mallier, the wife of Nicolas Bailleul, Lord of Wattetot-sur-Mer and of Soisy-sur-Seine; the celebrated and accomplished Marie Dalibray, widow of the former treasurer of France, an intimate friend of Pascal and member of his circle, and the young and beautiful Marie Lumague, chatelaine of Pollalion, who was also a widow and had for years devoted her time to visiting the charities.[43]

They decided to hold a second meeting in a few days time, and in the meantime they would look around for new recruits. This second meeting, which was now legally constituted, had even more ladies present. Among others, were Isabelle d'Aligre, the chancellor's wife, Anne Petau, the widow of Traversay, and the famous Mme Fouquet, Marie de Maupeon, who was the mother of two future bishops and of the famous and ill-starred

---

[43] ABELLY, *op. cit.*, 1.1 c. 29, p. 132; *S.V.P.* I, pp. 229-230 and I, p. 158. We cannot be certain about the date of this first meeting. Collet (*op. cit.*, Vol. 1, p. 232) says it took place after 25 July. This cannot be right because St Vincent's letter of 25 July speaks of the association as being already a constitutive body. (*S.V.P.* I, pp. 253-254). Coste thinks it took place sometime before April. This, too, is doubtful. The dating of the letters n. 159 and 162 is very much open to question, especially, as we suspect from the date of St Vincent's visit to the Magdalen convent, letter 162 should be dated 1635 (*cf. Annales* [1934], p. 650).

superintendent of finances under Louis XIV, as well as five daughters who entered the Visitation Order.[44] Of course Louise de Marillac was there, too. When the officers were elected, Mme Goussault was voted president, or 'superior', the title laid down in the rules. Vincent was appointed director for life.

'How long is it since you have been to confession?'

The rule was drawn up with the greatest care not to wound anyone's feelings. The first thing the ladies had to do when they went to the hospital was to introduce themselves to the nuns in charge and offer their services. The association had for its principal aim, not the corporal care of the sick, but spiritual help, and the ladies were to instruct them and prepare them to make a good general confession of their past life. With this in view, Vincent drew up for the ladies' use a manual of instructions which they were to have in their hands as they talked to the sick people, so that it would not look as though they were preaching to them. Those high-ranking ladies were not unlike those that Molière satirised in *Les Précieuses Ridicules* and Vincent de Paul, the peasant from the Landes, teaches them how to use direct and simple language which is both concise and clear.

> My dear sister, is it a long time since you have been to confession? Would you like to make a general confession if I told you how to do it? I have been told that it is very important for my salvation that I make one before I die, so that I can put right any ordinary confessions that I might have made badly, and also so that I will have greater sorrow for my sins.

He obliged them—and this is another thing that Molière ridiculed because he did not understand it—to dress as simply as possible when they visited the poor, with no trappings of luxury, lest their obvious wealth distress those who lacked the barest necessities. This shows the depth of Vincent's psychological insight, and his acute awareness of the resentment and frustration which, as he knew so well, the poor can feel.

Above all, he recommends them to treat the sick with humility, sweetness and gentleness.

---

[44] *S.V.P.* XIV, p. 218-220; ABELLY, *op. cit.*, 1.1 c. 29, p. 133; COLLET, *op. cit.*, Vol. 1, p. 234. Coste omits the name of Isabelle d'Aligre, and replaces it with that of Mme Séguier. (*M.V.* Vol. 1, p. 179). This is incorrect. In 1634, Etienne d'Aligre was chancellor and Seguier was the Keeper of the Seals. Séguier was appointed chancellor in 1635.

Vincent was putting at the disposal of these high and mighty ladies, his long experience in dealing with the needy; his loving and patient service of the poor.[45]

To ensure that this spiritual help would be more favourably received, the ladies were to add to their pious words some small material comforts which would supplement the dull and unappetising meals provided by the hospital. Helped by the Daughters of Charity, they would distribute each morning good big mugs of milk, and in the evening they would give out 'white bread, biscuits, sweets, ice-cream, grapes or cherries in season, and in winter, lemons or pears cooked in sugar'.[46]

The association proved very successful. Within a few months the membership had risen to nearly 100, and all these ladies belonged to the aristocracy.[47] Results were encouraging. Apart from the number of Catholics who went to confession in the first year alone, there were more than 700 conversions from among Lutherans, Calvinists and Turks.[48]

The association of ladies of the Hôtel-Dieu differed from the other charity confraternities in that it was not linked to any particular parish; it was an independent organisation whose members were drawn from every district in Paris.

Another distinctive and more important characteristic was that, although it was founded primarily for the pious motives we have already mentioned, it became, in the end, a society for giving charitable relief, and Vincent would appeal to it on behalf of those most in need. The 'Ladies of Charity of Paris', as they came to be called, provided the most solid financial support for the charitable enterprises that Vincent was to undertake in later years. Their foundation in 1634, was like establishing a chancellor of the exchequer for Vincentian charity. The inauguration of their association meant that the picture was now complete and all the necessary institutions were in place for the new stage that was just beginning.

---

[45] In ABELLY, *op. cit.*, 1.1 c. 29, pp. 136-138, the reader can find the complete text of the exhortation to make a general confession and also a summary of the rules.

[46] ABELLY, *ibid.*, p. 136.

[47] *S.V.P.* I, p. 253.

[48] ABELLY, *ibid.*, p. 140.

Part Four

TWENTY YEARS OF ACHIEVEMENT

(1634-1653)

Chapter XVIII
PANORAMIC VIEW FROM
SAINT LAZARE

Vincent lived in St Lazare from 1632-1660, that is, from the time he was fifty till he reached the age of eighty. All his great projects would be directed from the command post he set up in the old priory. It was there that two generations of Frenchmen would come to know him. His role in society and in the Church was firmly established and never seemed to alter. This was probably why a famous bishop was heard to exclaim, after paying him a visit, 'Monsieur Vincent is always Monsieur Vincent.'[1] This was not true. All those long thirty years Vincent's human development had kept pace with the expansion of his works and the deepening of his spiritual life.

Portraits of M. Vincent

Something we unfortunately cannot know about, is the change in Vincent's appearance over the years. Unlike the great majority of his contemporaries, Richelieu, de Bérulle, Mazarin, Descartes and Saint-Cyran, Vincent would never agree to sit for a portrait. The only portraits we have of him (and these were done secretly), were painted when Vincent was an old man. The missioners thought up a strategy to get round the humble priest's opposition to having his portrait painted: they commissioned an artist for the work, and he lived at St Lazare for a few months. This artist was given a place in the refectory, facing Vincent, so every day he could observe him at his leisure, and perhaps make some sketches on the sly. Then he painted the model's features on canvas, working from memory.[2] This was not a famous artist (which great master would ever have agreed to work under these conditions?); his name was Simon François, and he was a native of Tours. He may have

---

[1]   ABELLY, *op. cit.*, 1.3 c. 21, p. 310.
[2]   [L. ROBINEAU], *'Remarques ...'*, p. 30.

been given this assignment because he had a nephew studying with the missionaries in the seminary of Le Mans.[3]

Simon François may have painted two portraits. In the first one, Vincent is dressed in the soutane, and the second one pictures him in a surplice. We have two portraits that claim to be original works by François, or copies of them. One is kept in the sacristy of the present day church of St Lazare, and according to reliable tradition, it used to belong to Anne of Austria. The other portrait is in the house of the Daughters of Charity at Moutiers-Saint-Jean.

In the first portrait Vincent is wearing his normal clerical garb, and in the second he is in choir rochet. During the seventeenth century copies of one or other of the two originals were made by four different engravers, Nicolas Pitau, Peter van Schupper, René Lochon and Gerard Edelinck. As well as these portraits we have two other paintings which might be originals: an unsigned miniature which is also preserved at St Lazare, and a pencil sketch by Angélique Labory which is dated 1654. This sketch belonged to the de Comet family and it is now kept at Le Berceau de St Vincent de Paul.[4]

Thanks to these eight pictures, we can have a fairly accurate idea of what Vincent looked like when he was an old man.

As far as we can tell, Vincent de Paul's face was neither too fleshy nor too emaciated, and it was attractive if not handsome. His compelling gaze was gentle but penetrating. He had a rather large mouth, with thin lips arching gently into a faint smile, and etched round them were whitish traces of his goatee beard. He had a prominent and broad nose, a wide forehead, and big ears. The black skull cap concealed a large head which lent character to the face, and suggested a hidden dynamism in the portrait. It is no ordinary face that looks out on us from the quiet tranquillity the artist wanted to capture. Vincent has a gentler expression in the portrait that now hangs in the sacristy of St Lazare, while the one in Moutiers-Saint-Jean gives a greater impression of vitality. So, taken together, the two portraits reveal a personality that combines strength and tenderness. This is how Vincent's contemporaries would have seen him.

Abelly describes Vincent as being, 'of medium height and stockily built.'[5] His remains were examined in 1830, on the occasion of the solemn translation of the relics. These were found to measure five feet five inches (1.63 m.).[6] so we would consider him rather on the small side, even allowing

---

[3] *S.V.P.* VIII, p. 349.

[4] P. COSTE, *M.V.* Vol. 3, pp. 431-440.

[5] ABELLY, *op. cit.*, 1.1 c. 19, p. 73.

[6] *Annales* (1949), p. 286.

for the extra two or three centimetres of height he would have had when alive.

To discover the Vincent who was still a young man when he took over St Lazare in 1632, we would need to paint out from the picture the imprint of heavy burdens left by passing years. But if we did this we would not have two authentic portraits. One thing we know for certain: in spite of the good prelate's remark quoted by Abelly, the years had not left Vincent unchanged.

We must put events in chronological order

Before we begin the story of the fourth period of Vincent's life we need to give a rapid outline of events in chronological order.

The period 1634-1653 marked the most productive years of Vincent's life. This was a time for organising the management of his works, and it may be subdivided into two periods centring on the years 1642 and 1643. The first period is prior to these dates and relates to the years 1634-42, a time of expansion. With all his institutions now in good working order, Vincent is becoming increasingly well-known. The Congregation of the Mission is spreading throughout every province in France and the Charities are answering new and pressing needs such as the foundlings (1638), or the sending of aid to war-torn Lorraine, (1639). After 1635, his concern for the clergy takes on new dimensions with the establishment of seminaries. The sending of chaplains to the army (1636), the first mission preached at Court (1638), and the trial of Saint-Cyran (1639), would all bring Vincent into contact with the most powerful forces in the land. The internal organisation of his two congregations is being constitutionally recognised and the first stage of this will be completed as the procedure for taking vows in settled. (1642).

Between 1642 and 1643 several things happened that are of importance for Vincent's biography. The Congregation of the Mission held its first assembly in October 1642; in December of that year there was the death of Richelieu; May 1643, saw the death of Louis XIII and Vincent's appointment to the Council of Conscience. These events belong to that part of Vincent's life when his influence was most marked, and after this period he enters the final stages of his career.

As a member of the Council of Conscience, Vincent is, in a certain sense, at the forefront of the Church in France. The Congregation of the Mission continues to expand and becomes an international force when it is established in Italy, (1642) Poland, (1651) North Africa, (1645) and Madagascar (1648). There is a similar, but less spectacular development, among the Daughters of Charity. The rules and constitutions of both congregations are finalised. The Congregation of the Mission drew up what was to be almost the definitive form of their rules and constitutions during the 1651 assembly, which also settled the question of taking vows. The Daughters of Charity are granted recognition for the first time by the archbishop of Paris in 1646. From 1649 onwards, this decade witnesses another sphere of action, the tremendous outpouring of charitable aid by all the Vincentian institutions working together for the relief of the devastated regions of Picardy, Champagne and Ile de France. Vincent becomes famous throughout the land for his intervention in the serious crisis of the Fronde (1649-1652), and famous throughout the whole church for his stand against the threat of Jansenism.

A certain respite comes in 1653, after years of feverish activity. Mazarin's return (1653) brought an end to the Fronde, the calamities abated somewhat, and Jansenism was formally condemned in the bull *Cum occasione*. All this came as a tremendous relief for Vincent and considerably lessened his responsibilities. His departure from the Council of Conscience (October 1652), marks an end to his work for the government. Vincent's influence will take on a different form but it will be no less important. He is the great moral authority within the French church, and bishops, cardinals and the pope himself consult him on serious matters. And he will devote himself, with increasing determination, to putting the final touches to the works he has started. But this last endeavour belongs to the final stage of his life, to his clear-sighted and hard-working old age.

The century of the poor

The single and ever-constant pivot of Vincent's marvellous human career was the poor. Ever since 1617, when he realised the double misery of physical and spiritual deprivation that the poor suffered, he had devoted all his energies to finding ways of alleviating their plight. Every foundation he accepts, every work he undertakes, and every responsibility he assumes, are all centred on the service of the poor. The poor are his whole *raison d'être* and his obsession, or, as he would say on more than one occasion, 'his burden and his sorrow.'[7]

There has been much research into the causes of poverty in the seventeenth century, the century that Henry Kamen has echoed Cervantes in describing as 'the iron century'. These causes may be briefly classified as structural and politico-economic. In the first case, we have to reckon with the nature of society itself under the *Ancien Régime*, as well as the state's

---

[7] ABELLY, *op. cit.*, 1.3 c. 11, p. 120; COLLET, *op. cit.*, Vol. 1, p. 479; Vol. 2, p. 168.

absurd system of taxation which weighed most heavily on the poorer classes and became a real mechanism for creating poverty. The economic situation of this century had been following a downward trend from 1620 onwards, and a series of short or mid-term crises put the heaviest burdens on those who were less wealthy, and this led to their gradual impoverishment. Another contributory factor to this poverty was the war that caused uninterrupted devastation to vast areas of the country. It is very difficult to give statistics for the number of poor people, but it has been estimated that the poor, or those impoverished by taxation, accounted for half the population. The concept of poverty itself is difficult to define. In the seventeenth century everything turned on the concept of ownership. According to Furetière's dictionary, a poor man is defined as 'someone who possesses nothing, who lacks the necessities of life, or is unable to maintain his social position.' Today socio-economists think of poverty in terms of consumer power. Economists and historians both agree that this century was characterised by indisputable and crushing poverty.[8]

Vincent de Paul never attempts to define the poor. It is obvious that he gives different meanings to the word 'poor', and he often uses this adjective to describe a situation, which for any number of reasons might evoke pity or the need to help.[9] This is particularly the case when he speaks about peasants, and he invariably refers to them as 'the poor peasants'. We should remember that for people in seventeenth century, the term peasant, farmer, or villager, was synonymous with poverty. It is with some optimism that Furetière explains in his dictionary that, 'in France the towns are rich and the country areas are very poor.' Vincent de Paul had somewhat the same idea, though he would have made more distinctions. In any case, when Vincent uses the phrase 'poor man', he is referring to someone who would be an only too obvious and frightening reality for the people of his country and his times, and they would immediately grasp the significance of the term.

'Turn the medal over'

Vincent's main preoccupation was the suffering that these poor people had to endure. 'The poor do not know what to do or where to go. They suffer

---

[8] R. MANDROU, 'Francia en los siglos XVII y XVIII' pp. 40-54; R. MOUSNIER, 'Los siglos XVI y XVII' pp. 171-178; P.CHAUNU, 'La civilización de la Europa clásica', pp. 67-108; P.GUTTON, 'La société et les pauvres en Europe (XVI -XVIIIsiècles'), (Paris 1974).

[9] CARVEN, 'The poor. An attempt to fathom the mind of St Vincent', *Vincentiana* (1979), pp. 42-56.

greatly, and every day their numbers increase.[10] When their meagre harvest is exhausted, there is only one thing left for them to do, and that is to dig their own graves and bury themselves alive.'[11] These people are the object of all his concern. As a result of the war, the suffering of the poor gets worse.[12] These people are the focal point of his compassion and of his charitable works. More than anything else, Vincent was a man who felt himself overwhelmed by the sufferings of the poor. He was, moreover, someone who felt intuitively the tremendous injustice of that century's hierarchical structure of society, though he denounced this injustice in religious rather than in political terms. Vincent used to say to his missioners, 'The rich are living off the sweat of the poor; it is the poor who are feeding them by their labours and their fatigue'[13]. So they deserve the work and the help of those who live at their expense, and all the more so, since true religion is to be found among the poor, whose patient acceptance of suffering brings them close to complete confidence in God[14] and to the simple, living, faith of the saints.[15]

Indeed, in the eyes of Vincent, who was religious to the very core of his being, the poor were transformed by suffering, into an image of the patient and poor Christ. This idea is firmly rooted in the gospel and it is not original to Vincent. Obviously, this idea was in circulation in earlier times, but Vincent enriched the ancient symbolism with images and convictions of his own.

'I should not judge a poor peasant or a poor woman by their appearance or by what I take to be their level of intelligence, because very often they appear so gross and earthy that they seem to lack the features and the mind of rational beings. But turn the medal round and with the eyes of faith you will recognise that these poor people represent, for us, the Son of God, who chose the poor. During his passion, he was scarcely recognisable as a man; the Gentiles considered him a fool, and he was a stumbling block for the Jews, so he describes himself as the 'evangeliser of the poor.' *Evangelizare pauperibus misit me.* O my God how beautiful it is to go to the poor when you see them in God, and reflect on the esteem Christ had for them. But if we judge them according to human standards, and the spirit of the world, they will seem contemptible.[16]

The obvious conclusion was that serving the poor meant serving

---

[10] COLLET, *op. cit.*, Vol. 1, p. 479.

[11] ABELLY, *op. cit.*, 1.3 c. 11, p. 120.

[12] *S.V.P.* XI, p. 200.

[13] *S.V.P.* XI, pp. 201-202.

[14] *S.V.P.* XI, p. 200; XII, p. 170.

[15] *S.V.P.* IX, p. 89.

[16] ABELLY, *op. cit.*, 1.3 c. 2, p. 9; *S.V.P.*

Christ himself.[17] No honour could be compared to that of being chosen to perform this service, and Vincent considered himself blessed because the two companies he founded were destined by God for the spiritual and corporal service of the poor.[18] In Vincent's eyes, the service of the poor was a sort of sacrament and, when the need arose, this service could, and should, supersede not just the observance of rules or community exercises, but even the obligation to hear Mass on Sundays, because leaving prayer or any other devotion in order to serve the poor was, in a very real sense, 'to leave God for God.'[19]

Those who practise charity towards the poor, become the servants of the poor who are their 'lords and masters'. The phrase 'The poor are your lords and masters' was no mere figure of speech for Vincent[20] and his followers; it was a daily reality.

Again, this idea was not exclusive to Vincent. Others had said it before him but few had lived it with the same intensity.

Vincent knew from experience the right way of serving these masters who could be so demanding at times. This service should be joyful, enthusiastic and consistent; it should be given with the same humility, patience and respect that would be paid to real masters.[21] In short, in Vincent's eyes, service of the poor was just another name for love; effective and authentic love translated into action.

A life given to serving the poor merits the highest reward, because if God has promised to repay a cup of water given to the needy, what will he not give to those who have spent their whole life serving the poor? The poor will intercede for them with God,[22] and since it is the poor who open the gates of heaven, it is they who will lead them into the eternal dwelling places.[23]

But Vincent did not dwell on the promise made to those who are merciful; the mere fact of serving the poor was pure delight for him. 'I confess', he used to say, 'that I have never felt so much consolation as when I was serving the poor.'[24] He thought the same must be true for the Congregation of the Mission:

---

[17] *S.V.P.* IX, pp. 59, 252.
[18] *S.V.P.* V, p. 60; IX, pp. 119, 324; X, p. 681; XI, p. 364; XII, pp. 79-87.
[19] *S.V.P.* IX, pp. 5, 34, 42, 126, 215, 216, 218, 319, 326, 432, 692; X, pp. 3, 95, 203, 226, 541, 554, 595, 685.
[20] *S.V.P.* X, p. 332.
[21] *S.V.P.* IX, p. 593; X, pp. 679-680.
[22] *S.V.P.* IX, pp. 252-253.
[23] *S.V.P.* X, p. 332.
[24] *S.V.P.* X, p. 681.

God loves the poor, so he also loves those who love the poor, because when you love a person very much, you also show affection to their friends and to their servants. Well, this little company of the Mission tries to devote itself to serving the poor, with affection, because these people are God's chosen ones, and so we have every reason to hope that God will love us, because of them. So then, my brothers, let us serve the poor with renewed affection, and let us search out the very poorest and the most abandoned; let us recognise before God that they are our lords and masters, and that we are unworthy to render them our paltry services.[25]

'... In the sweat of our brow'

Vincent's reflections on the Gospel, and his understanding of the nature and mission of the Church, are the key to his thinking which we have briefly summarised here, and these were intensified and developed during his lifetime. Vincent had been introduced to the devout life when he joined the most fervent members of a group that was working to reform the Catholic religion in France, at the beginning of the seventeenth century. He discovered his own personal vocation when he realised that this renewal movement had to return to the basic Gospel message of preaching love. If this proclamation was to be something more than empty words, the work would entail effort and great labour. This is how Vincent explained, in a deep and warmly-worded conference, his vision of the role of those who work in the apostolate:

Let us love God, my brothers, let us love God, but let it be in the strength of our arms and in the sweat of our brow.

This was just the renewal that the Church needed, since the big failing among many of the clergy, and some very learned religious and nuns, was that their apostolic and charitable works lacked precise and effective direction.

There are many people who are very concerned about looking recollected and having wonderful feelings about God in their hearts, but they stop at this, and whenever an opportunity for action arises, they fall short. They are very pleased with the

---

[25] *S.V.P.* XI, pp. 392-393.

images conjured up by their lively imagination, and well content with the pleasant conversations they have with God during prayer; they speak almost as though they were angels, but when it is a question of labouring for God, practising mortification, instructing the poor, going out in search of the lost sheep, being willing to be deprived of something, accepting illness or any other unpleasant thing—ah—everything crumbles and they lose heart. Let us not deceive ourselves, *Totum opus nostrum in operatione consistit* ('All we have to do is to work').

Vincent was too prudent a man to single out anybody in particular, and he applied all these observations to his own life, and to the members of his two congregations. But reading between the lines, we can see his sharp criticism of the clergy of his day, and it is easy to understand why he always refused to have his communities identified as religious orders:

These days there are many people who seem to be virtuous, and indeed they are so, but they are inclined to lead a quiet, easy life rather than one of solid and active commitment. The Church is like an immense harvest that needs labourers, but labourers who are willing to work. There is nothing more true to the spirit of the Gospel than gathering light and strength in prayer, and then going out to share this spiritual food with others. This is what Our Lord did, and the apostles followed his example. To do this, we must combine the role of Martha and of Mary; we have to imitate the dove which takes only half its food and feeds the rest into the beaks of its young. This is how we should act, and prove our love for God through our labours. *Totum opus nostrum in operatione consistit.*[26]

'A priest should have more work than he can manage'

Vincent de Paul took the active service of the poor as his rule of life, and based it on one of the maxims of his master, M. Duval: 'A priest should have more work than he can manage.'[27] The amount of work that Vincent did is truly astounding. In 1634, he was superior of the Congregation of the Mission

---

[26] *S.V.P.* XI, pp. 40-41, the three previous quotations belong to this passage.
[27] *S.V.P.* XI, p. 202.

and of its mother house St Lazare; superior of the Daughters of Charity, chaplain royal to the galleys, superior of the Visitation nuns in Paris, director of the ladies of Charity, president of the Tuesday conferences, and he also organised and directed the confraternities of charity. In later years he would take on more responsibilities; especially after 1643, when he became a member of the Council of Conscience. None of these posts was a sinecure. On the contrary, each one added to his burden of responsibilities. It was his duty to give a mission, or see that one was preached, in all the de Gondi territories and every parish in the diocese of Paris; to welcome and organise the groups who came to the retreats for ordinands; to work for the expansion of his two communities, administer their goods and see to the formation of their members; preside at the weekly conferences for the clergy, look after the spiritual and physical needs of the galley slaves, attend the community chapters of the Visitation nuns and make visitations of their convents, watch over the functioning and good order of the charities, and encourage the ladies of the Hôtel Dieu to take on ever more ambitious projects.

Each one of these activities had its own organisational structure, with Vincent as leader, but they were all dependent on his spiritual driving force and very often needed his personal intervention in specific matters. Not only was he personally responsible for the spiritual formation of the missioners and the Daughters of Charity, or for presiding over the assemblies of ladies and conferences for the clergy, but, in addition, he continued to preach missions into his old age. And, of course, one duty that he could not delegate to anyone else, was his attendance at meetings of the Council of Conscience. Added to this, there could be extra and unforeseen demands made on him, by ecclesiastical authorities and other important personages.

It was only because he used every available minute to its full advantage that he was able to take on so many tasks. But Vincent was the embodiment of work. To realise this, one has only to cast a glance at the habitual timetable he kept to for nearly 30 years while living at St Lazare. This timetable is provided by Vincent himself in a letter to St Jane Frances de Chantal, dated July 1639.[28]

It reads as follows:

a.m.	p.m.
4.00 ... Rise, wash, dress.	12.30 ... Private work
4.30 ... Meditation	14.00 ... Vespers. Work.

---

[28] *S.V.P.* I, p. 563.

5.30 ... Recite Small Hours	17.30 ... Matins. Particular.
5.45 ... Mass. Thanksgiving.	17.45 ... Evening meal
Examen.	18.15 ... Recreation
6.30 ... Private work	19.15 ... General examen.
10.30 ... Particular examen.	Angelus, recreation.
Lunch.	Work.
11.30 ... Visit to Blessed	21.00 ... Bed.
Sacrament	

Altogether, he devoted 3 hours to prayer, 9° hours to work, 4° to meals, recreation and miscellaneous activities, and 7 hours to sleep. But it was not always possible to keep to this timetable, and extra work was taken on at the expense of recreation or sleep. He was often prevented from taking part in the community recreation owing to unforeseen commitments, and he was often an hour or two late going to bed because he had to keep his correspondence up to date. In addition, there were weekly engagements that interrupted his routine. After the evening meal on Friday, he would give a spiritual conference to the community of missioners. He did the same for the Daughters of Charity each Sunday. Twice a week he would have repetition of prayer before Mass, and on Fridays there would be the chapter of faults. All these required serious preparation on Vincent's part.

The written word—his correspondence

One activity that took up a lot of Vincent's time was his correspondence. As the works and the personnel became scattered over ever-widening distances, he had to take on an overwhelming amount of letter writing. It has been calculated that during the final thirty years of his life, Vincent penned some thirty thousand letters and that would mean an average of three or four a day. After 1645, he had a secretary amanuensis, brother Bertrand Ducournau, and soon he had to take on a second one, brother Louis Robineau. Even so, many of the letters are entirely in Vincent's own handwriting. These letters were addressed to all sorts of people—from popes, kings, bishops and ministers, to humble brothers of the Mission or simple Daughters of Charity, consoling them in some spiritual trial or giving them instructions on how to carry out their office. For a long time he was in the habit of writing a weekly letter to the superiors of the principal houses of the Mission. His most assiduous correspondent was Louise de Marillac. Some four hundred of his letters to her are still in existence. The subjects dealt with are just as varied as his correspondents and range from serious matters of state to the smallest problem of conscience, from questions of government and administration to notes of a purely personal nature. Vincent's heart was open to every need. His orders, advice, admonitions, supplications as well as his observations on current events, his praise, and his reservations, are so many reflections of the author's rich, varied and dynamic personality. And all these letters were written in simple, direct, language. There was no seeking after effect in this clear, precise, style. There is no better way of getting to know Vincent de Paul than by reading and studying his letters.

The spoken word: his conferences

A good part of Vincent's life was taken up by his correspondence and also by the talks he gave. He was required to speak in public on an average of six times a week. As we have already mentioned, he would speak to the missioners three or four times a week, once or twice a week to the Daughters of Charity, and he would give a weekly talk to the Tuesday conferences, not to mention the times he was called on to address the ladies' assemblies, the occasional talks he gave to the Visitation nuns, and to meetings and councils of other associations.

His method never altered—the conference, or to give it the French name he used, the *entretien* or 'conversation', was on a theme that had been the subject of meditation. Vincent would begin by asking some of his listeners among the missioners or Daughters of Charity to speak on the subject they had been notified about earlier. After an informal exchange of views Vincent would make his comments, and this was very much the case with the Daughters of Charity, when he would stress the positive aspects of what had been said, and lend his authority to this for the encouragement of everyone present. Sometimes those called upon to speak made the excuse that they had not prepared what they were going to say, through laziness, vanity, or false modesty. Vincent would then reproach them. At other times people gave their thoughts spontaneously, and Vincent would have to call a halt to the avalanche of speakers. He would end up by summarising what had been said, and then making his own contribution, which was the basic core of the conference. Towards the end of his life, Vincent's conferences got longer, and other people's contributions were minimal. It was as though Vincent wanted to take full advantage of these last opportunities to talk to his sons and daughters, and bequeath to them the treasure of his teaching on the fundamental spirituality of the two congregations. He explained the rules and the virtues proper to priests of the Mission and to Daughters of

Charity; the love and service of the poor, the vocation of members of both congregations, submission to God's will, poverty, obedience, fraternal charity, mutual correction, the virtues and example of deceased missioners and sisters ...

Vincent took the opportunity, during conferences, and especially during repetition of prayer, to share any community news, to commend to God the difficulties his foundations and subjects were experiencing, to correct outstanding misdemeanours and to impose some penance on incorrigible or recalcitrant subjects. His talks thus became a living expression of community experience and everyone felt part of it.

Vincent's language is colourful, and his remarks could be trenchant, and somewhat caustic. When he spoke to the sisters he would give many comparisons and a good sprinkling of anecdotes. He had the gift of story-telling and was a master of dialogue. Telling the life story of a saint, or describing some incident he had experienced personally, he would spontaneously change into direct speech to let the people in the story tell the event.

He would accompany his words with gestures and mimicry. When he referred to lazy people he would fold his arms or leave them dangling by his side. He would huddle himself together to describe those who wanted to avoid the tiring labours of the apostolate, or who did not want the company to take on any risky and dangerous enterprises.

But whenever he gave an admonition, he always followed it with an act of humility, acknowledging that he, too, was guilty of the fault he was condemning. He blamed himself for any failings within the community. One day, when speaking about poverty, he exclaimed:

Oh Saviour! Who am I to be talking about this; I who am wretched enough to have had a horse and carriage, and even now my room has a bed with good curtains; I have a brother to look after me so that I want for nothing. What scandal I must give to the company by my failings in the vow of poverty, in these and in other matters. I ask pardon of God, and of the company, and I beg you to put up with me in my old age. May God grant me the grace of making amends at this stage of my life, and help me to get rid of all these things as soon as possible. Stand up brothers. (The community had all knelt down while he made this act of humility.)[29]

---

[29] *S.V.P.* XII, p. 384.

A superior's room

Poor M. Vincent! Anyone listening to him would think that he lived in luxury. The very opposite was true. All his life he had a simple room with a bare floor and bare walls; there was no rug or carpet, and it had only four pieces of furniture—a wooden table without a cloth, two cane chairs and a bed that had only a mattress, blanket and pillow. Once, when he was ill, they put a canopy over his bed, but as soon as he was better he ordered it to be removed. He did the same with some holy pictures that his secretary had hung on the walls. When he noticed these he said that one picture was sufficient, so the brother had to take down the others. He had a small office on the ground floor where he could receive visitors. It was so bare that the cold winds of Paris used to blow through chinks in the door. Somebody, probably one of the brothers, made a curtain out of a piece of carpet, and hung it behind the door. M. Vincent ordered it to be removed at once. It was only in the last four or five years of his life, when he was worn out by constant illness, that he consented to have a fire in his room and a canopy over his bed. Even so, he tried to use as little firewood as possible, so as not to waste the property of the poor.[30]

He practised the same austerity with regard to food. He never took breakfast; it was not customary in those days. However, a few years before his death, they persuaded him to take something. He agreed and asked for an infusion of wild chicory and clear barley, which people said was more like a medicine than a beverage. He fasted, not only in Lent, but twice a week throughout the year. His duties often caused him to arrive at the refectory after the community had dined, so he would sit at the 'second' table with the servants, and have exactly the same food as they did. On one occasion, the cook managed to deceive him and served him fresh fish instead of the dried fish that the rest of the community had been given. But this trick soon came to light, and Vincent made it known that in future he would have the same food as everybody else. Only once did he make an exception to this rule. One day, he was served raw eggs by mistake. Without a word he ate these as though they had been done to a turn. For many years his evening meal consisted of a piece of bread, an apple, and a glass of water with a few drops of wine in it. But he considered himself too well done to. He would often come back from the city after working late, and would go to his room without having anything to eat. And very often when he did go to the refectory, he would say to himself, 'Miserable wretch. You have not earned the bread you are eating.'[31]

---

[30] ABELLY, 1.3 c. 18, pp. 273-274.
[31] COLLET, *op. cit.*, Vol. 2, pp. 259-261.

A community with complications

This was certainly not a boss's life-style. And yet his humble room in St Lazare was the general headquarters of an extensive apparatus whose invisible wires would influence every corner of the world. Even within the precincts of the old priory, Vincent's administrative duties were many and varied. It was not just a question of directing the quite considerable numbers of priests, brothers, students and seminarists, who made up this community. There were five or six groups of ordinands every year, private retreats every week, the beggars who came to the door looking for food and alms, the consecration of bishops that took place from time to time in the church there; after 1642 there were the junior seminarists of little St Lazare; there were the deranged people who lived in a small asylum in one of the buildings, the unruly youngsters who were kept locked up in another part which was something like a reformatory, and finally, there were visitors of every rank and condition who flocked to Vincent for recommendations, advice, or help. He also had over-all responsibility for the harvests from the priory lands, for maintaining the wine presses, the ovens and the mill, as well as the hiring of stalls for the St Laurent fair and appointing bailiffs who would see justice administered at all levels throughout the priory domain.

The former prior

Permanent guests at St Lazare included the canons of the former community who would continue living there till the end of their days. Sharing accommodation with them was not easy. The former prior, Adrien Le Bon, who had shown such detachment and generosity, was not an easy man to live with. As stipulated in the foundation contract, he kept his title and certain prerogatives that went with it.[32] His extreme touchiness bordered on the neurotic. This was particularly so during the first five or six years, when every tiny incident made him regret his decision to relinquish the benefice. It only needed the door keeper to be a few minutes late letting him in, or for some visitor to say he had not been able to see him, for the prior to fly off the handle and begin his lamentations. The same thing would happen if any lay person criticised his decision to leave his property to another community. Vincent had to go on his knees, and ask pardon for the real or imagined insults offered him by the community or one of its members. The prior would then be mollified and his affection for the community would be restored ...

---

[32] *S.V.P.* XIII, p. 326.

until the next time. Vincent recalled more than fifty occasions when he had to go on his knees to him.[33]

However, it was Vincent, himself, who provided the most serious cause for complaint. On the queen's orders, and with Vincent's approval, an abbess from an illustrious family had been shut up in a convent on account of her scandalous behaviour. The prior had received important favours from this nun. At her insistence, he went to Vincent and asked him to use his influence to have the nun released. Vincent told him frankly that he could not in conscience do this. The prior's reaction was predictable. At the height of his wrath over this refusal, he exclaimed, 'What! Is this the way you treat me after I have put my house in your hands? Is this the way you repay me for the benefice I gave you to help your company?', 'I realise', answered Vincent, 'that you have showered honours and benefits on us, and we are as grateful to you as sons would be to their father. My lord, I beg you to take it all back again, since you judge us so unworthy.'

The old man was not disarmed by this calm and firm reply and retired to his room, obviously offended. It was only some days later, when he received more detailed reports of the abbess's scandalous behaviour, that he realised his mistake and rushed back to Vincent to apologise and take back what he had said.[34]

Vincent behaved towards Adrien Le Bon as though the prior was really in charge of the house. When Vincent came back from a journey, the first thing he would do after paying a visit to the Blessed Sacrament, was to greet Adrien Le Bon. Every Sunday they would take their evening meal together. Vincent always regarded him as father of the community, and wanted all its members to consider themselves his sons.[35]

On Easter Sunday 9 April 1651, Adrien Le Bon gave up his soul to God. Vincent took particular care to repay his generous benefactor. He made the whole community come to the prior's room to receive his last blessing, and he personally led the prayers for the dying. As soon as the dying man had breathed his last, Vincent gave a very moving funeral oration from beside the death bed, praising the dead prior's virtues and exhorting all present to pray for the repose of his soul. The funeral ceremonies were carried out with the utmost solemnity. Vincent also wrote a circular to all the houses of the community enjoining suffrages for the dead man's soul, and he gave orders that the former prior's remains should be laid to rest in the church of St Lazare, in the centre of the chancel. His tomb was decorated with a long and eloquent epitaph, written in Latin, and praising the deceased's virtues. The

---

[33] *S.V.P.* XIII, pp. 638-639.
[34] ABELLY, *op. cit.*, 1.3 c. 22, pp. 318-319.
[35] ABELLY, *op. cit.*, 1.3 c. 17, p. 270.

fine phrases that introduced and concluded this epitaph were the work of the community's greatest classicist, the learned and resourceful, Jacques Corborand de la Fosse. (1621-1674).[36]

Havens of joy

Life at St Lazare had a humorous side, too. One of the most amusing incidents that would often been related in the community concerned Jacques de la Fosse. Shortly after ordination in 1648, he was sent by Vincent to teach humanities in the seminary of St Charles or Little St Lazare.[37] From time to time he would write religious plays and his young students would perform these to great applause. [38] This was the era of Corneille and Racine. Neither St Lazare nor Vincent could remain completely untouched by the fashions of the day. De la Fosse made a name for himself by writing a prodigious number of Latin verses in elegant renaissance style.

One day he was invited to a famous university college to see a play, which happened to be a tragedy written in Latin. De la Fosse went into the auditorium and sat down in one of the seats reserved for distinguished guests. The principal of the college did not know who he was, and he sent one of his servants to ask him to move. But de la Fosse answered in Latin that he was very comfortable where he was, and had no wish to move. When the messenger reported to the principal that the stranger only spoke Latin, he took him to be an Irishman and sent a junior professor to repeat, in Cicero's tongue, the invitation to find another seat. De la Fosse then spoke in Greek and very courteously repeated that he wanted to stay where he was. The junior professor decided that the man must have come from Lebanon, and said this to his superior. The superior was getting tired of all this coming and going and he sent the professor of rhetoric to deliver his message but de la Fosse answered this man in Hebrew. Things went on like this till eventually one of the university staff recognised the learned missioner and conducted him, with all due ceremony, to a place in keeping with his rank.

De la Fosse enjoyed the joke more than anybody and when he got back to St Lazare he wasted no time in telling his friends about it. The story passed from mouth to mouth until it eventually reached Vincent's ears. He immediately sent for the joker, and made him see that no humble man would be looking for a place of honour. As a penance, he told him to go and ask

---

[36] ABELLY, *op. cit.*, 1.1 c. 31, pp. 190-191; *S.V.P.* IV, pp. 168-170; XI, p. 155.
[37] *S.V.P.* IV, p. 438.
[38] COLLET, *op. cit.*, Vol. 1, p. 326.

pardon of the college principal and the professors for his unedifying conduct. De la Fosse was not only a man of learning, he was also a good missioner, and without trying to excuse himself set off for the college and humbly complied with his superior's instructions. The college principal was a liberal and understanding man, and he replied that if he had previously appreciated him for his learning, in future he would appreciate him just as much for his virtue. Another incident in the life of Jacques de la Fosse will be related later on, and it will show that the principal was not mistaken in his judgement. [39]

The mentally deranged and the people in custody

As we have already indicated, two other sorts of inmates were housed in buildings that were separated from the community quarters: a small group of mentally deranged people, and another small group of recalcitrant young people who were locked up there on the orders of their families. Vincent was quite content to take on both these works and tried to discharge his responsibilities in the spirit of his community. [40]

As regards the mentally deranged, Vincent declared that the thought of having to abandon these unfortunates was the only argument that influenced him when there was question of St Lazare being handed over to the canons of St Victor.[41] Vincent put his best effort into seeing that both groups of inmates were well looked after and he made sure that they were served exactly the same food as the community had. Any occasional negligence in complying with this order brought the gravest reprimand for the brothers.[42]

Vincent's zeal in this quarter is all the more to be admired as both the mentally deranged, and the young people in custody, gave him more trouble than satisfaction and at times threatened to compromise the good relations he had with other people. There was, for example, the incident where no less a personage than Jean de Montholon escaped from custody. This young man was the younger brother of Duke Guy François de Montholon, (1601-1679), one of the wealthiest men in the land. The duke had had his brother and ward locked up for secretly marrying, at the age of twenty-one, a young woman of very much lower station in life. Vincent had to make all sorts of excuses to the nobleman, especially as the young man had made his

---

[39] COLLET, *op. cit.*, Vol. 1, pp. 277-279.
[40] *S.V.P.* XI, pp. 20-24; XII p. 88.
[41] *S.V.P.* XI, p. 21.
[42] *S.V.P.* XI, p. 331.

escape almost under his nose, and almost certainly abetted by one of the former religious of St Lazare.[43]

A systematic analysis is needed here

Governing the mother house of his congregation was just a small part of Vincent's activities in the twenty year period from 1634 to 1653. During these twenty years of management, Vincent's activities expanded over an ever-widening radius. His concerns become more broadly-based and diversified, his network of contacts is strengthened; his influence in national decisions of major importance is limitless, and his spiritual life is purified and refined to the point of sanctity.

At this point it is impossible to keep strictly to the chronological order of events. To do so would make us lose the thread of the story of how the different works developed and it would entail boring repetition. For this reason we shall have to consider Vincent de Paul's achievements, section by section, in parallel blocks that cut across the vibrant reality of a life-story that shows remarkable continuity. The disadvantage of this procedure is that it artificially isolates parts of Vincent's life that were essentially connected. This is the price demanded by all methods of systematic study.

---

[43] *S.V.P.* I, pp. 291-293. *Cf.* J.MELOT (R. CHALUMEAU), 'Les pensionnaires de Saint Lazare aux XVIIe et XVIIIe siècles', *M. et Ch.* 13-14 (1964), pp. 49-55.

Chapter XIX
EXPANSION OF THE CONGREGATION

The Congregation of the Mission mirrored the many facets of Vincent himself; it shared his charisma and was destined to inherit and continue it. The full flowering of Vincent's vocation would depend on the degree to which it was shared by the small group of men gathered around him. This group was the focal point of all Vincent's activities and whenever he delegated authority to others, the impetus and inspiration for doing so came from this central work. It is only to be expected, therefore, that Vincent's best efforts and most of his energy would be put into developing his most important work, the one that would prove a continuation and expansion of the man himself.

'Let us honour the small number of Christ's disciples'

At the present time we have no monographs on the men who belonged to the Congregation of the Mission during the founder's lifetime. Although the data I am about to offer is reliable in broad outline, it cannot be as precise and definite as one would wish.[1]

In the first ten or twelve years of the congregation's history there was a fairly slow increase in numbers. Vocations were few and averaged three or four a year. Up to 1636 the numbers would be about fifty; of these thirty were priests, ten or so were clerics waiting to be ordained, and another ten were lay brothers. Was such slow growth due to prevailing circumstances or was it Vincent's deliberate intention not to recruit candidates too quickly,

---

[1] There is no lack of documentary evidence for these findings. The figures and the facts quoted are based on a personal study of the original registers of the Congregation of the Mission, and in particular, on *Notices sur les prêtres, clercs et frères coadjuteurs défunts de la Congrégation de la Mission* Vol. 1, p. 453-509 and *Catalogue du personnel de la Congrégation de la Mission, depuis l'origine (1625) jusqu'à la fin du XVIII siècle* (Paris, rue de Sèvres, 1911), 640 pages.

so that new members could assimilate and be imbued with his spirit? What we know of Vincent's attitude to the vocation of the company makes us incline to the latter view. It was during this particular period we are studying that Vincent made these revealing observations:

> 'Since you left', he wrote to Antoine Portail, on 16 September 1635, 'the number of men entering our congregation has risen to six. How fearful I am, Monsieur, of big numbers and expansion. And how many reasons do we not have to bless God who allows us to be few in number, like the disciples of his Son.!'[2]

'It is for God alone to choose those he wishes to call'

As a matter of principle he did not go looking for vocations but was content with those that the Lord deigned to send him. He kept to this practice all through his life so that as late as May 1660 he kept back a letter, which one of his missioners had written to a priest to try to persuade him to join the company. This gave him the opportunity to express his thoughts on the question of recruiting vocations. The religious principle underlying his words was the simple but profound conviction that a vocation comes from God.

> We have the principle ... of never urging anyone to join us. It is for God alone to choose those he wishes to call, and we are convinced that one missioner given by his fatherly hand will do more good than many others who do not have a true vocation. We must beg him to send labourers for his harvest, and to live such good lives that our example will attract them and not deter them from working with us.[3]

He was even slow to accept the idea of praying for vocations:

> For more than twenty years I have not dared to ask this grace from God, believing that, as the congregation was his work, I should leave concern for its preservation and growth to providence alone; but after reflecting on the gospel's counsel that we should pray to him to send labourers for his harvest, I

---

am now convinced of the importance and efficacy of such
acts of devotion.[4]

When assessing the qualities of aspirants, he was very demanding,
not so much as regards their intellectual or physical endowment, but
concerning their spiritual outlook and the purity of their intentions.[5]

The most striking feature of Vincent's attitude to vocations is his
complete lack of self-interest. This prevented him from capitalising on the
contacts he made with good people seeking guidance about their vocation,
contacts made in the course of retreats for ordinands, and similar works. The
directives he gives on this point might seem uncompromising, and even
inhuman, if we did not know that they were based on his personal
understanding of the Gospel. Here are a few examples:

> Fathers, and especially those among you who direct retreats,
> be very careful not to urge anybody to join the company, but
> be satisfied with encouraging them in their good resolutions
> and trying to help them decide for themselves the place they
> believe God is calling them to be. I go further: even if they
> manifest this desire, and tell you that they feel a certain
> attraction for our way of life, be very much on your guard
> about saying they should be missioners; do not advise or
> exhort them to do this. Simply say to them that it is all the more
> important that they put this plan in God's hands, and that they
> should consider it very carefully, as it is a matter of supreme
> importance. Point out, too, the difficulties that human nature
> would have to contend with and how necessary it is, if they
> do decide to embrace this state, to expect to endure much
> labour and suffering for God's sake. If after all this, they make
> up their minds to join—well that is all right—you can arrange
> for them to speak to the superior and discuss their vocation
> with him in greater depth. Let us allow God to act, Fathers, and
> let us humbly await and depend on his providence. By his
> mercy the company has acted in this way up to now, and we
> can say that there is nothing in the company which has not
> come from God, and that for our part we have never gone
> looking for men, possessions or foundations. In God's name,
> Fathers, please keep to this practice, let God act and let us be

---

[4] *S.V.P.* V, p. 462.
[5] *S.V.P.* VI, pp. 155, 186; VII, pp. 237, 523.

content to co-operate with him. Believe me, Fathers, if the
company continues to act in this way God will bless it. So we
must be satisfied with the candidates God sends us.[6]

Somebody comes to make a retreat to decide on his future state in
life—you see one going to the Jesuits, another to the Carthusians. What! Is
not the Mission a holy congregation, too, and you can save your soul there
just as well as in other places? Human prudence! I remember a certain occasion
when one of the most intelligent men on earth, somebody who had held the
office of councillor advocate, consulted me about his vocation. He was
hesitating between becoming a Carthusian or a missioner. I felt honoured
but God gave me the grace never to speak to him about becoming a missioner.
He went to the Carthusians. I told him, 'God is calling you to the Carthusians,
go wherever God is calling you.[7]

He even wanted men with a vocation to the company to rise to the
heights of heroism.

My very dear Fathers and Brothers, would to God that all
those who enter the company could come with the desire for
martyrdom, wishing to suffer martyrdom in the company and
to consecrate their whole lives to God's service, either in far-
off lands, here, or in any place he may wish to use this poor
little company.[8]

'Not many of us come from noble families'

In spite of his precautions, or maybe indeed because of them, the congregation
increased in number more rapidly after 1637. The cause, and also the effect,
could have been the establishment that year of a sort of novitiate for aspirants.
Vincent used the term 'internal seminary' so that this congregation would
not be confused with a religious order. After this year the average number of
new entrants was twenty-three and of these, again we are talking of averages,
sixteen would be priests or clerics, and seven would be lay brothers. The
year 1645 saw the highest number of entrants, a total of thirty-eight. Between

---

[6] *S.V.P.* XI, pp. 426-427; ABELLY, *op. cit.*, 1.1 c. 34, p. 139.

[7] *S.V.P.* XII, pp. 315-316. *Cf.* XII, pp. 441-443.

[8] *S.V.P.* XI, p. 371. *Cf.* A. ORCAJO, 'La promoción de vocaciones a la C.M. según San
Vicente', *Annales* (1978), pp. 17-32.

1648 and 1652 there was a notable drop in the number of vocations and these were at their lowest level in 1652 with only three new entrants. Such a large decrease in numbers was no doubt due to the upheaval caused by the Fronde, which interrupted the usual flow of aspirants to St Lazare. Once these adverse circumstances were reversed things returned to normal and in 1653 there were twenty-five new entrants.

Altogether, there were 614 aspirants received into the congregation during the founder's lifetime, and of these, 425 were priests and 189 were lay brothers. Some did not complete their probationary period and quite a number of others left the congregation after a few years' study or work. If we add to this the number of those who died—life expectancy in the seventeenth century was short and the missioners' work, especially in aiding victims of the plague, was very dangerous—we find that the total number of active members of the congregation which rose to 200 in 1645 was never to be more than 250. This was a very small number compared with those of the large and well-established communities and it was small in proportion to the enormous task it carried out, but all the same it was a fairly acceptable figure for the young congregation which was growing up during a period in history when there was a superabundance of religious communities, both old and new. Vincent always called his community, 'the little company'. He meant this title to reflect the lowliness of its members and the modest works they performed but the name was also appropriate in a numerical sense.

As we might expect, vocations to the company came from those regions where there was the strongest community presence. Most of the missioners came from northern France, from Champagne, Artois, Picardy, Ile de France, Normandy and Brittany. The four dioceses of Amiens, Paris, Rouen and Arras alone, provided a contingent of more than 140 missioners. On the other hand, places south west of a line Loire-Rhône provided fewer than thirty. It is a strange fact that during Vincent's lifetime there was not a single missioner from Dax, the diocese the founder came from. When the congregation began to spread outside of France there was an immediate influx of foreign vocations. About twenty came from Ireland and as many again from Italy, together with a few from Poland and from Switzerland. There were a considerable number, too, from Lorraine and from Savoy but the political development of these regions was such that we cannot call them non-French in the strict sense of the term.

Vincent always insisted that his company was made up of ordinary people with no rank, wealth, or learning. In this he recognised the hand of God who is pleased to choose the weak and the foolish of this world to confound the strong.[9] Perhaps he was exaggerating slightly for some

---

[9] *S.V.P.* XI, pp. 38, 132; XII, p. 105

important people did put on the missioner's habit. One such was M. de Fargis, Charles d'Angennes, the former ambassador to Spain and brother-in-law of the de Gondis. He joined the congregation towards the end of his life and died in it twelve months later, on 20 December 1648, before completing his period of probation.[10] A similar case was that of M. René Alméras who was admitted into the company his son already belonged to, after serving as secretary royal, treasurer of France, secretary to Marie de Medici, master of the accounts and controller general of the mail, he joined the company at the age of eighty-one and lived in the internal seminary from 1657-1658. It seemed to Vincent that this man accepted death with as much trust and resignation as any saint.[11] Apart from these truly exceptional cases, there were other missioners who came from families noted for their rank or their intellectual endowments. Among these were René Alméras Junior, the two Fathers Watebled who were related by marriage to the famous Vatable,[12] and there were the Fathers Le Vacher who were nephews of Dr Duval.[13]

Vincent's early companions included many graduates from the Sorbonne and gifted people like François de Coudray or Jean Dehorgny. But on the whole we have to agree with Vincent that most of his missioners were good French countrymen who belonged to the same social class as the people they were called to evangelise. And that was a good thing. Vincent abhorred nothing so much as a company made up of learned men or noble gentlemen who could not adapt themselves to working among the poor and lowly people of the country districts.

In the early years nearly all those who entered the congregation were ordained priests, and these joined Vincent straightaway in his work of preaching missions or giving retreats to ordinands. As the institute became more stable and began to develop along the lines of traditional communities, so the number of young entrants who were not ordained increased. These men were called 'clerics' in community parlance, though at this stage they had not yet received the tonsure. Of the 425 mentioned earlier, only 125 were ordained before they entered the company. So more than two-thirds were aspirants to the priesthood who saw in the congregation the answer to their apostolic calling.

It is even more difficult to calculate the ages of these new members. One thing we do know for certain, is that the two-thirds of those entering the community before ordination were below the age of twenty-six. The bull, *Salvatoris nostri*, fixed the minimum age for admission at seventeen or

---

[10] *S.V.P.* III, p. 398. *Cf.* COLLET, *op. cit.*, Vol. 2, p. 28; *Notices* ..., II, pp. 425-430.

[11] COLLET, *op. cit.*, Vol. 2, p. 29 *Notices* ..., II, pp. 453-461; *S.V.P.* III, p. 26 and VII, p. 41.

[12] *S.V.P.* III, p. 249.

[13] COLLET, *op. cit.*, Vol. 2, p. 23.

eighteen.[14] Even so, about a dozen lads were admitted before their seventeenth birthday. So it was not just the novelty of its works, but also the ages of its members, that made the Congregation of the Mission burst out like a youthful tidal wave over the weary scene of life in France during the second third of the seventeenth century.

'You will be tried like gold in the crucible'

For the first ten or twelve years Vincent himself took responsibility for training aspirants. The congregation had no educational structure, properly so-called. The new entrants received their training from living in direct contact with the older members of the congregation and especially with the founder. The fact that they were few in number made for a direct spiritual osmosis and Vincent intensified this, as much as possible, by means of his talks and conferences, his repetitions of prayer and his letters. Rather than use the term 'congregation' in the strict sense of the word, we should perhaps speak of a team whose leader was at once superior, spiritual director, master of novices and spiritual guide. We have already noted Vincent's skill and sureness of touch in the exercise of these offices and he continued this work until he died. But as numbers increased it became necessary to devise a specific system for welcoming new recruits and imbuing them with the spirit of the community. To prepare for this, he sent Jean de la Salle, the youngest of his first three companions, to spend some months in the Jesuit novitiate, following their practices and seeing how these could be adapted for an institute of secular priests such as the Congregation of the Mission.[15] De la Salle was a great missioner; he was extremely devout and an excellent debater. When he was in charge of the seminary he managed, in barely a year, to create such a pleasant and welcoming atmosphere that the older missioners regretted that they and their contemporaries had not been able to enjoy such benefits. He died in 1639, at the age of forty-one. In his dying moments he felt the urge to strip himself completely naked in imitation of St Francis of Assisi whose life he had listened to with great devotion, a saint who stripped himself so as to be like Our Lord in all things.[16] He was succeeded as director by Frs Dehorgny, Alméras, Dufour, Jolly and Delespinay.

The period spent in the internal seminary lasted for two years. At the end of the first year the seminarists declared their intentions, i.e., they stated publicly that they intended to live and die in the congregation. Until

---

[14] *S.V.P.* XIII, p. 261.
[15] COLLET, *op. cit.*, Vol. 1, p. 272.
[16] *S.V.P.* I, p. 35, 591; II, p. 334; XII, p.293.

1642, this bond which had already been prescribed in the bull of foundation[17] was the only official record of membership.

Before Vincent accepted postulants he would subject them to a rigorous scrutiny of their natural and spiritual dispositions. The two years probation period was not only meant to test the candidates' suitability, but to strengthen them in their vocation and build on to this foundation the virtues that constitute a good missioner.[18] Vincent's aim was to inculcate solid virtue. What he understood by this expression is summarised in one of the finest passages that ever came from his pen.

> Anyone who wishes to live in this community must be prepared and determined to live like an exile on this earth and live only for Christ; to change his ways and mortify his passions, to seek God alone, to be submissive to everybody and to be convinced that he has come here to serve, and not to govern, to suffer, and not to have an easy life, to labour, and not to live in ease and idleness. He must realise that he will be tried like gold in the crucible, and that it is impossible for him to persevere unless he humbles himself before God, and finally, that the true way of being happy is to nourish himself with the thought of martyrdom and the desire to attain it.[19]

There were no esoteric forms of initiation and no extraordinary ascetic practices in the Vincentian novitiate. The order of the day was more or less that prescribed for everyone, with time for a few personal acts of devotion. Importance was given to reading the New Testament, to knowing the works of spiritual writers, to maintaining a pure conscience through frequent confession, and to the assimilation of the doctrines and disciplines of Trent.[20] Vincent kept a close eye on the workings of the seminary and he interested other missioners in it by often giving them news about the increase, or the lack, of new vocations, the number of seminarists, and the type of formation they were receiving.[21]

Later on, as the congregation began to grow in number, other seminaries besides that of St Lazare were needed, so seminaries were opened at Richelieu, Genoa and Rome.[22] It often happened that if seminarists were

---

[17] *S.V.P.* XIII, p. 261.
[18] *S.V.P.* VI, p. 155.
[19] ABELLY, *op. cit.*, 1.1 c. 34, p. 162; COLLET, *op. cit.*, Vol. 1, p. 275.
[20] *S.V.P.* XIII, p. 261.
[21] *S.V.P.* I, p. 539; II, pp. 127, 323, 489; III, p. 97; V pp. 68, 239, 349, 573; VI, pp. 143, 238, 247, 610; VII, p. 17.
[22] *S.V.P.* IV, pp. 156, 541; VI, pp. 431, 592.

already ordained priests, they would be sent out to give missions during the second year of their probationary period.[23] On the other hand, Vincent was not so happy about seminarists pursuing a course of studies during their formation period, seeing that this might prove an obstacle to the validity of the vows.[24]

'Learned and humble missioners are the treasure of the company'

As more and more young men joined the company before completing their ecclesiastical studies, the establishment of internal seminaries was followed by that of the scholasticate. We have nothing resembling a *ratio studiorum* preserved from those early days but we do know that included in the programme was the study of philosophy and theology, and that these courses were followed either at the Bons Enfants or at St Lazare. We have the names of quite a few of the professors and among these were Damiens, Dufour, Gilles, Watebled, just to mention a few of the names that will crop up in other contexts.

Vincent kept careful watch on the training that these men gave, and he too joined in the work. He was firmly opposed to the dictating of notes in class in these seminaries or in seminaries for externs. The method he favoured was for teachers to give an explanation of the manuals they used; he recommended 'disputations' and trained students in the art of preaching through the talks and sermons they were required to give in the refectory. He chose the textbooks to be studied, especially those written by the Jesuits, Becan and Binsfeld,[25] and he was involved in the day-to-day events of life in the scholasticate.

As so easily happens among young people, a row broke out one day. This occurrence became grist to Vincent's pedagogical mill as he pondered aloud and somewhat rhetorically the gravity of the fault. He even went so far as to compare it with an incident that took place about that time in an Augustinian monastery in Paris when parlement troops had to intervene to restore order and two religious were killed.

> Shall I tell you something else; something that happened here at St Lazare? What I am about to tell you took place among the students. They went out for a walk in the courtyard, and two of them who were walking ahead of the others found a game of

---

[23] *S.V.P.* II, p. 360.
[24] *S.V.P.* VII, p. 479; VIII, p. 382.
[25] *S.V.P.* XIV, p. 534.

skittles so they started to play. Then the others arrive and say that they want to join in. One of them knocks over the skittles and, when one of the students who started the game sees this, he picks up one of the skittles and hits the one who knocked them over in the stomach with it. Not content with this, he strikes him again, this time on the back, and with such force that the student still feels the pain. Just think, please, of the extremes he went to when he let himself be carried away by anger; just reflect whether this company has not reason to lament over this. Oh, if such things can happen when men are just starting out in the company, what could happen after a few years when their first fervour and observance of the rules has become more lax? There was nothing for it but to have this student locked up.[26]

The founder's directives were not always welcomed by the students, and Vincent's moral authority was not so strong as to suppress a certain degree of opposition. One of the professors of theology, Father Damiens, had a certain sympathy for Jansenist teachings and he expressed his opinions in his lectures. After several warnings, which were all to no avail, Vincent had to take him out of teaching. But the students had taken a liking to him. They came in a body to Vincent's room to ask him to revoke the decision. Vincent refused to listen to them and sent them away with a stern reprimand.[27]

At the beginning of every year the students, led by their director, would come to Vincent's room to ask for his blessing. The founder would take advantage of such occasions to inculcate in them the right dispositions they should have with regard to study. People have spoken, sometimes too lightly, about Vincent's mistrust of learning. Some of his words taken out of context might give the impression that this was so. All that can safely be said on this subject is that Vincent was too practical a man to take empty satisfaction in knowledge that did not lead to action. Was not one of the first things to stimulate his vocation, the fact that thousands of men with doctorates were living idly in Paris, while the poor people were in danger of damnation because of their ignorance? Vincent was not an intellectual, but an apostle whose concern was for the salvation of souls. Whatever the cost might be, he had to make sure that his congregation did not fall into the very vices he claimed to be remedying.

Then there were the usual pitfalls for students that he knew about

---

[26] *S.V.P.* XII, pp. 59-60.
[27] ABELLY, *op. cit.*, 1.3 c. 2, p. 6; COLLET, *op. cit.*, Vol. 1, p. 214; *S.V.P.* IV, p. 356.

from experience and from observation. The greatest risk was that they might come to value knowledge more than piety.

> The transition from seminary to study is a very dangerous step and causes the downfall of many ... It is very dangerous to go from one extreme to the other; just as glass that is taken from the heat of the oven and put in a cold place is in danger of breaking.

For this reason he recommended that study should always go hand in hand with piety.

> If every time we grasp the meaning of something, we could also make the effort to strengthen our will, then we can be sure that study is a way of serving God.[28]

A second danger could be vanity—studying just to excel, to be esteemed, to have the reputation of being a learned intellectual.

> To prevent this evil falling upon us, my brothers, do not be anxious for success, for carrying off prizes, or for earning a reputation as a debater whichever side you may be representing; you should rather wish, yearn for, and often beseech Our Lord for the grace to practise humility in everything and for everything ...[29]

Finally, there was the danger of curiosity. People could seek knowledge for its own sake, knowledge of abstract things that is far removed from real life; they could have no understanding of the real aim of knowledge and they might make it an end in itself, divorcing it from its true function in the Church. So they had a duty 'to study in moderation, desiring to know only those things that are in keeping with our state in life.'[30]

None of these reservations can be taken to mean that Vincent was against the acquisition of knowledge; on the contrary they show his strenuous efforts, after meditating on the subject, to put knowledge and study in the context of his vocation and that of his followers; that is to say, to use them for the apostolic aims of the company.

---

[28] *S.V.P.* XI, pp. 28-29.
[29] *S.V.P.* XII, pp. 63-64.
[30] *S.V.P.* XI, pp. 126-128.

Although all priests need to be well instructed, we have a special obligation in this matter, because of the retreats and other works confided to us by divine providence, such as the ordinands, our direction of ecclesiastical seminaries and missions. We need knowledge. And he added that those men who combined learning with humility were the treasures of the company, just as good and pious doctors are the greatest treasure of the Church.[31]

Vincent himself has left us the best summary of his thinking on the usefulness and the dangers of study at the end of a repetition of prayer given at the relatively early date of October 1643. In it we can admire the vigour and the coherence of his ideas, as well as the fine irony of its closing words:

We have to have knowledge, my brothers, and woe to those who neglect to use study time well. But let us be afraid, my brothers, let us fear and tremble, and tremble a thousand times more than I can say. Those with talent have every reason to be afraid, for *scientia inflat*, and it is even worse for those who lack talent unless they humble themselves.[32]

'Am I dying? What do I need to do?'

Vincent's labours, and his concern to set up a fine training ground for young and holy seminarists, were crowned with success. There emerged from the internal seminary and the scholasticate that small but hardy phalanx which would sow the missionary seed in every corner of France. One of Vincent's achievements, and possibly his most creative one, was the formation he gave to men like Thomas Berthe, Jean and Philippe Le Vacher, René Alméras, Edmund Jolly, Lambert aux Couteaux, Charles Nacquart, Claude Dufour, Jean Martin, Etienne Blatiron and many others whose work we will describe in later chapters. Others were destined not to reach the stage of working in the apostolate; they had matured so early that they were ripe for heaven's harvest. Such was the case with Martin Jamain who entered St Lazare on 8 October 1640, at the age of twenty-one, and died four years later before he could finish his studies. Vincent gives an account of his death, in a fine letter that

---

[31] *Ibid.*
[32] *Ibid.*

reads something like a legend, or rather, it reflects the sense of awe which a person feels when he has come into contact with sanctity.

> These few lines are just to let you know that recently the number of missioners who have been called home to heaven has increased after the blessed death of one of our students, good Brother Jamain, who came from Verdun. God allowed him to miss out on scholastic theology here, so that he could understand heavenly theology straightaway. His exemplary life, and his holy death, lead us to the pious belief that he is already enjoying the immortality of the saints ... His final illness only lasted a week but he suffered more for Christ during that week than he had done in the whole of his life till then. He suffered intense pain and practised great virtue, so much so that we were all astonished that his mind could be completely on God. On the fourth Sunday of Lent he was suddenly struck down with this illness. It started off as very violent colic and after a few days this turned into inflammation of the lungs which quickly rotted away. You cannot imagine the intense pain and distress he suffered, yet he showed extraordinary patience and wonderful peace of mind. When they told him that death was near, he showed he was quite prepared for this, and without any trace of anxiety he said, 'Very well, Father. What do I need to do?' He received the sacraments with unusual devotion and peace, and had the happiness of gaining the jubilee indulgence. Right to his last breath he continued to practise the virtues that merit heaven, sometimes praying in his heart, and sometimes aloud, especially when anyone spoke to him. His agony lasted only a very short time. Perhaps this was God's way of rewarding him for having struggled so hard during life to practise the virtue of mortification.[33]

The pace of establishing foundations

As numbers swelled there was a corresponding increase in the number of houses of the congregation. The dioceses of France seemed to have caught the contagion and bishops wished to take advantage of one or other of the pastoral movements initiated by the missioners. As we follow the history of successive foundations it is just like following Vincent himself, as his sphere

---

[33] *S.V.P.* II, pp. 513-516.

of influence progressively widens. Each new establishment is a replica of the original foundation, but with different people and a different setting. Vincent returns again and again to the origins of the company; he recalls its basic objectives, he lays down conditions, and he adapts to circumstances. Unlike St Theresa, he does not travel to all the towns where he is going to send his companions, but controls and directs everything from his room in St Lazare. He discusses matters with benefactors in his letters, he strikes bargains, makes concessions, signs contracts. The result of all this is a network of missionary posts scattered over different regions, each one with its own individual characteristics, and these spread ever more widely the work of renewal. At the same time, each house he establishes gives added touches to the traditional works. So Vincent's achievement is enriched and diversified. The time will come when it will cross frontiers to reach Italy, Poland, the British Isles—all the vast world of missionary territories.

Until the year 1635, the congregation only had the two houses in Paris. We know that the congregation did not have many members at this time and further expansion was not possible. Most of the missioners lived in St Lazare. Four or five had stayed at the Bons Enfants to continue the work laid down in the founding contract, giving missions on the de Gondi estates and providing lodgings for the students whose numbers were gradually decreasing. Vincent changed the work of the house. About the year 1636 he set up the first seminary there. This was modelled on the directives of Trent and catered for young boys and adolescents. In 1645 this seminary was moved to a building inside the precinct of St Lazare. It was then renamed St Charles. So now there were three houses in Paris. The Bons Enfants, which was not very roomy, became an ecclesiastical seminary for ordinands. At the same time its buildings were used as a retreat house, a theological scholasticate for clerics in the company, and also, at times, it was used to house foreign students who were spending a short time in the capital.[34]

The first foundation outside Paris was made at Toul, in Lorraine, in 1635. Then followed the foundation at Aiguillon (1637) which was soon to be moved to the sanctuary of Notre Dame de la Rose; then came Richelieu, Luçon and Troyes in 1638; Alet, which only lasted three years. Annecy in Savoy followed in 1639 and then Crécy was founded in 1641.

---

[34] The following references are presented in the context of the different works.
Conferences: *S.V.P.* I, p. 33; II, p. 564; VII, p. 390.
Ordinands: *S.V.P.* I, pp. 92, 106, 107, 308, 525-526; VII, p. 390.
Retreats for other people: *S.V.P.* I, p. 308.
Junior Seminary of St Charles: II, pp. 226, 535.
Seminary for clerics at the Bons Enfants: *S.V.P.* II, p. 225, 535; VII, pp. 483, 610.
Theological studies: *S.V.P.* I, p. 539; IV p. 518.
Guests: *S.V.P.* V, pp. 28, 597.

The year 1642 is a watershed in the history of the company. With the official opening of the house in Rome, the Mission crossed frontiers, and at the same time continued its programme of expansion throughout France, as houses were set up in Cahors, Marseilles and Sedan (1643), Montmirail and Saintes (1644), Le Mans and Saint Méen (1645), Tréguier (1648), Agen (1650), Périgueux which only lasted a few months, and Montauban (1652), so that the missionary influence was making itself felt in ever more distant regions. The foundation at Genoa followed in 1645, the same year that the missioners went to Tunis, and then to the British Isles (1646), Algeria (1646), Madagascar (1648), and Poland (1651).

Towards the end of Vincent's life the pace of expansion is slower and more hesitant. Several of the foundations he had in mind were only finalised after his death. This happened at Metz, Amiens and Noyon. Other houses, like those of Agde (1654), Meaux (1657), and Montpellier (1659), only lasted a short time. The only solidly established foundations were those of Turin (1654), and Narbonne (1659).

The rate at which houses were established each year from 1632 to 1660 is a good indication of the young congregation's healthy growth, and it shows that the works they undertook responded to very real needs in the Church in France.[35]

'We have never requested a foundation'

The setting up of new foundations always followed the same basic pattern. As Vincent was often to repeat, the initiative did not come from him:

> Some years ago we made a commitment that we would never ask for a foundation, since we have always experienced God's special providence in our regard. It is this same providence that has established us in all the foundations we now have, and this without any initiative on our part, so that we can truly say that we own nothing that has not been offered and given to us by Our Lord God.[36]

---

[35] Abelly compiled a list of all the foundations of the Mission made during St Vincent's lifetime and gave a short description of each (*op. cit.*, 1.1 c. 46, pp. 219-227). Further details are given in *Notices* ... Vol. I, pp. 510-535, in the foundation contracts, and in the registers of personnel. Coste (*M.V.* Vol. 2, pp. 75-162) made an exhaustive study of each foundation and collated all the original foundation contracts that had been preserved. Only a few of these were published in Vol. XIII, *S.V.P.* Since our study is a synthesis, and in order, also, to avoid frequent repetition of the same sources, we think it better to refer the reader to the works mentioned above.

[36] *S.V.P.* III, p. 194; IV, p. 138.

The usual procedure for setting up a new house was as follows: some pious person (secular or ecclesiastic) would see the need to have missioners in a particular locality and take his request to M. Vincent, who would consider the proposal and satisfy himself that the work was in keeping with the aims and spirit of his congregation. Then he would study the conditions, and if the initiative had come from some outside source, he would seek approval from the bishop. Only then would he accept the foundation and sign the contract.

Foundations made before 1642 were devoted exclusively to the work of preaching missions and giving retreats to ordinands. They were new versions of the Bons Enfants and St Lazare. After this date many of the houses took on the additional work of directing seminaries. This was the way that Vincent's efforts to reform the clergy had developed, and later on we will examine the scope and the characteristics of this work.

In many cases, and this was particularly true during the second period of expansion, the initiative for making a foundation came from the bishops who wanted their dioceses to benefit from missions, or wanted to open a seminary in order to guarantee the supply of new priests. This happened at Toul, Saintes, Alet, Cahors, Saint Méen and some other places. In Sedan the impetus came from the royal government seeking to halt the spread of Protestantism in territories recently annexed by the crown. In many other places it was private individuals who took the initiative in setting up foundations. Troyes and Annecy, for example, were the work of Commander Noël Brulart de Sillery (1577-1640), a distinguished layman who was converted by the joint efforts of Francis de Sales and Vincent de Paul, and followed Vincent's spiritual direction until he died.[37] Montmirail was established by Pierre de Gondi, the eldest son of the family Vincent had once worked for, and who had been tutored by him as a boy. The foundation at Crécy owed its origin to M. de Lorthon, a councillor and royal secretary, who also secured royal patronage for the house. Cardinal Richelieu was responsible for establishing the missioners in the town that bears his name, as well as at Luçon, the episcopal see of his former diocese. However, the tangled state of the cardinal-minister's personal finances and his sudden death posed not a few financial problems which were finally settled through the intervention of his niece, the Duchess d'Aiguillon. This lady was the generous benefactress

---

[37] For information on Brulart de Sillery, *cf. Vie de l'illustre Serviteur de Dieu Noël Brulart de Sillery* (Paris 1843). Noël, knight commander of the Order of Malta, was the brother of Nicolas, the famous chancellor, who served under three monarchs (1607-1624). After his conversion, and his ordination to the priesthood in 1634, (*cf. S.V.P.* I, p. 235) he donated his considerable properties to charity and to helping various religious communities: the Visitation nuns, Jesuits, Carmelites etc.

of the foundation at Aiguillon (transferred and annexed to the sanctuary of Notre Dame de la Rose by the bishop of Agen), and the houses at Marseilles and Rome. It was through her efforts, too, that the missioners were established in Tunis and Algeria. The pious Duchess d'Aiguillon was the most outstanding of all the Mission's benefactors. She was able to do so much for them because she had an immense fortune, but this in itself would have been of no use if she had not been endowed with intelligent and fervent piety. Marie de Wignerod was the great cardinal's good angel. Her life, however, was suffused with sadness. At the age of 16 she entered into a politically arranged marriage with the Marquis de Combalet, nephew of Luynes, the favourite of Louis XIII. The political alliance between Luynes and Richelieu at this time was therefore strengthened by the bonds of kinship. Neither of these two unions was destined to last. Luynes died suddenly, leaving the field wide open for Richelieu's ambition. The marriage lasted an even shorter time. Two years after the marriage Combalet died in military action outside the walls of Montpellier. His young widow of eighteen renounced the world and entered Carmel. She was brought out from the cloister by her influential uncle who had procured a papal brief forbidding Mme de Wignerod to embrace the religious life. She then held several important positions at court. After the Day of the Dupes that we have already referred to, she devoted her time and her fortune to pious and charitable works. It was not long before she came into contact with Vincent de Paul, who was to find in this lady an inexhaustible provider of funds for his charitable works. Later on we will see the results of this alliance, between the noble lady and the humble shepherd of Pouy.[38]

'The missioners should have what they need for their livelihood and their work'

Special mention should be made of the financial aspect of these foundations. The missioners gave their services free so this meant they had to find other sources of guaranteed income. Vincent de Paul is adamant on this point:

> I do not pay the slightest heed to all these people who come with plans for a foundation but have not the resources to put the plan into practice, people who are full of good intentions but who do not want to spend any money ... It is not sufficient to provide lodgings for the missionaries, for these should have what they need for their livelihood and for their work. This

---

[38] *S.V.P.* I, pp. 329-330.

must be provided because they are not allowed to take up collections and it is not fitting that they should do this.[39]

The commitments of each house, and the number of missioners who could live there, depended on the amount of capital put into the foundation. The endowment capital, however, could come in very different forms and it could be said that every means of producing income known to pre-industrialised society was represented in contracts for Vincent's foundations.

When bishops were involved in the business transaction the usual procedure was to link the missioners' house to some ecclesiastical benefice. In Toul they were given the Hôpital du Saint Esprit; in Cahors the priories of Vairette and Saint Martin de Balaguier; in Saintes the parish of St Preuil; at St Méen the abbey of that name; at Agen a chapel and the priory of La Sainte Foi; at Montauban the parish of St Aignan and the chapel of Notre Dame de l'Orme etc.

Another source of income was derived from the transfer of rights to claim tax duties. Noël Brulart de Sillery handed over to the house at Troyes the money he received in taxes on merchandise, food and wines in the two parishes at Ponts-de-Cé, and to the house at Annecy he ceded his rights to the *aides*[40] at Melun which provided the capital sum of 40,000 *livres*. The foundation at Crécy was established on the basis of a house left to them in perpetuity by the king, together with an income of 8,000 *livres*, derived partly from the revenue of five estates and partly from dues collected from the salt vendors at Largny-sur-Marne.

Some foundations were better provided for and one such was Sedan. In his will, Louis XIII had bequeathed the sum of 64,000 *livres* for the preaching of missions, and 24,000 *livres* from this was specifically allocated to the work of giving two missions a year in the city of Sedan. His widow, the queen, provided all the capital for the foundation of a permanent mission and the abbot of Mouzon gave them the parish of Sedan. Vincent invested the capital in the construction of thirteen small houses near St Lazare and he let these to the Ladies of Charity as a refuge for the foundlings.[41] Good provision was also made for the house at Le Mans. This foundation enjoyed the amenities of the estates belonging to the collegiate church of Notre Dame de Coëffort which included farms, farm houses, dwellings, lands,

---

[39] *S.V.P.* VII, p. 208.

[40] The 'aides' were a tax levied on drinks and other consumer goods. These could be leased out by the state to private individuals. *Cf.* MARION, *Dictionnaire ...*, pp. 9-20; MOUSNIER, *Les institution ...*, II, pp. 420-425.

[41] *S.V.P.* XIII, pp. 303-306.

woods, meadows, orchards, kitchen gardens, and the right to present candidates for the parishes of Montbézat and the Maison-Dieu. The poorest house was Montmirail which only had the priory of La Chausée, and the state of this building left much to be desired.

The initial capital for the house at Marseilles was reckoned to be 14,000 *livres* and this was given by the Duchess d'Aiguillon to invest in any way Vincent thought proper.[42] The house in Rome, and that of Notre Dame de la Rose, were also founded through the generosity of the duchess, while the main source of income for the missions in Algeria and Tunis were the coach-routes businesses of Chartres, Rouen, Orleans, Soissons and Bordeaux. Vincent was the concessionary for these businesses and he contracted out this prerogative in return for an annual income.[43] We have to remember, too, that the early foundations often received further gifts of money from other benefactors.

'In the diocese of the saints'

Each foundation had its own individual history with a mixture of incidents that could be mundane, edifying, surprising, curious or mysterious. All these help to give us a more detailed picture of Vincent's style of governing the community.

The bonds between Vincent and St Jane de Chantal were strengthened when missioners were sent to Annecy. Vincent wrote her a precious letter to explain the spirit, the aims, and the life-style of the missioners who were to be her neighbours, and after expressing his joy at being able to send companions to work in 'the diocese of the saints', he gives a summary of the congregation's rule as it was lived in 1639.[44] If Vincent was a father to the Visitation nuns in Paris, the missioners at Annecy were to find a mother in St Chantal. This is how the indefatigable collaborator of St Francis de Sales described her first impressions of the newly arrived missioners.

> The bishop of Geneva and myself were consoled beyond words. They seem just like brothers to us, as we have so much in common, and there is great simplicity, openness and mutual trust. We talked together and for me it was like speaking to Visitations nuns. They are all very kind and very open. The

---

[42] *S.V.P.* XIII, pp. 298-301.
[43] *S.V.P.* II, pp. 275, 284, 367, 390, 396, 406, 413, 501; VI, pp. 49, 434.
[44] *S.V.P.* I, pp. 561-567.

third and the fifth missionaries (Jacques Tholard and Etienne Bourdet) need a little encouragement to draw them out of themselves, and I will say as much to the superior (Bernard Codoing) who is just the right man to do this. Fr Escart is a saint. I gave each one a practice ... Well, they are all very pleasant and since they have the same spirit as my dear Father, they have given a very good example to this town in the three days they have been here.[45]

'We have no wish to bring a lawsuit against our benefactor'

After the missionaries had been working in Crécy for a fair number of years the founder had second thoughts about his good intentions, and decided to divert to the hospital the income which had been destined for the missionaries. This left them without resources, so much so that Vincent recalled them, leaving only one priest and one brother. He was quite prepared to give up the foundation but the bishop of Meaux, Dominique Séguier (+ 1659), the brother of the chancellor, intervened.

'This good prelate', relates Vincent, 'took our cause in hand. Since God has granted the company the grace to be ready to leave everything rather than vex the man who made that foundation, we wanted to satisfy him by leaving. We did this purely out of love for God and for no other reason. During the proceedings, the bishop told me that we should make another attempt to go back. I asked him to excuse us as we had no wish to go to court against our benefactor. 'It was he who established us there, and now he wants to use the foundation for some other purpose. We do not mind, we want him to do as he thinks best.'

'Well, you can do that but I will act differently and try to thwart this man's plans.'

In fact, the bishop paid the cost of that lawsuit and continued to give us support until justice was done. We stayed there and they allocated to us the funds that would have gone to the main hospital. Providence moved the person who started the foundation to come and apologise for his

---

conduct, when he learnt that out of respect for him we would have preferred to leave rather than defend our case.'[46]

'... some joker is making these noises'

The house at Saintes had other problems and these show us Vincent's natural common sense and his realistic outlook on life. For several nights on the run, mysterious bangs had been heard in the house and the missioners decided this must be the work of the devil. The superiors consulted Vincent about it and his reply was both reassuring and faintly ironic.

> The first thing that occurs to me about all this is that some joker is making these noises so as to have a laugh at you and enjoy your discomfiture, or maybe someone wants to stop you having any peace or rest so that in the end you will leave the house. I spoke to the penintentiary about your letter and he agrees with me. I am even more convinced about this when I think back to something very similar that happened here in St Lazare. Some people amused themselves by making strange, wailing, noises to frighten everyone else. Well, if this particular noise is, as you say, like that of a rafter crashing down from the roof, it could also be similar to the noise made by a rattle that is used on Good Friday. This can be heard a good distance away, and is used to summon people to the church services. This noise can be heard all over the house and, if it is set off in the cellar, then it sounds even louder. So, Father, what you are hearing might be something like that, and somebody could be banging hard against the woodwork from somewhere underground or even inside the house, or in the house next door. If they are doing it for a joke they will keep it up and enjoy your panic, but if there is something more sinister about this or if someone is using an illegal workshop, perhaps to make counterfeit coins, as people have suggested, then they will stop this activity as soon as they find out that people have noticed these thudding noises at night, and they will be so afraid they will be discovered that they will move to another district. So make sure this is not some human trickery. If you judge this is not the case, and you think it possible that some

---

[46] *S.V.P.* XII, pp. 243-244.

evil or demonic spirit is causing this noise to disturb you, then
the penitentiary says you should have recourse to the
blessings that the Church permits in such cases; you should
sprinkle holy water and recite some appropriate psalms from
the ritual ...[47]

There is a gap in Vincent's correspondence so unfortunately we do
not know how this story ended.

'... how you settled the house's debts'

Some of the houses had a more complicated history and this was true of the
foundation at Marseilles. It was originally established for the purpose of
bringing spiritual help to the galley slaves in the hospital there, and to ensure
that a mission was preached every five years on board each galley.[48] To do
this more effectively, Vincent managed to secure permission for his personal
title of chaplain to the galleys to be linked to his position as superior general
of the Mission, with the right to pass on this title to his successors and
delegate it to other missioners.[49]

The original work soon expanded to include other forms of service.
In 1648 a seminary was opened[50] and most of its students came from the
abbey of St Victor. The project fell through because most of those aspiring
to the religious life were young men who had no genuine vocation, but
whose parents had forced them to enter the monastery so that they could be
sure of a benefice.[51]

But their biggest problems were financial. The superior was Fr Firmin
Get who was an enterprising man but somewhat too reckless. He did not
hesitate to take on debts for the building of the seminary, but he concealed
the extent of these debts from Vincent. When at last Vincent got to know the
exact state of their finances, he sent the superior a stern reprimand, reproaching
him particularly for the lack of trust between father and friend that this
indicated.

May I ask you, Father, what reasons you had for concealing
the matter you wrote to me about in your last letter, the fact

---

[47] *S.V.P.* VI, pp. 83-85.
[48] *S.V.P.* XIII, pp. 298-301.
[49] *S.V.P.* XIII, pp. 302-303.
[50] *S.V.P.* III, pp. 258, 271, 403, 417.
[51] *S.V.P.* XIII, pp. 370-371.

that you borrowed 1,300 *livres* from the hospital administrators. How did you manage to pay 1,500 *livres* to settle part of the house's debts and how much will you need to pay off these debts in full? I must say, Father, that I was astonished because nothing like this has happened for a long time. If you came from Gascony, or Normandy, I would not be quite so surprised, but for an honest fellow from Picardy, whom I know to be one of the most upright members of the company, to have concealed this from me is something I could never have imagined, any more than I can imagine how we are going to pay for all this. Mon Dieu! Why did you not you tell me? We would have seen to it that the works continued as far as our resources or, maybe I should say, our lack of resources, allowed.[52]

Once the culprit had admitted his fault Vincent stopped reproaching him, and promised to set the situation right as soon as he could.[53] He was more concerned about settling the debt than about the actual amount involved. Except for a short interval when he was negotiating the foundation of Montpellier, Firmin Get continued as superior until after the founder's death. His management of affairs in Barbary, where he acted as Vincent's delegate, reveals his skill and sureness of touch. The financial situation of the house improved considerably in 1659, when he received a legacy of 18,000 *livres* from the Marquise de Vins. This was for the purpose of preaching missions to peasants and for organising retreats for priests on her estates. To comply with this, Vincent sent two extra priests to the house at Marseilles.[54]

'We will be sent to prison'

The most colourful episode in the history of any of Vincent's foundations happened in Brittany, at the abbey of St Méen. The bishop of St Malo had ruled that this property should be given to the priests of the Mission so that they could open a seminary there. However, the Reformed Benedictines of the Congregation of St Maur thought that the bishop was exceeding his powers, as the abbey was only held *in commendam*. They took their case to the Breton parlement and obtained an injunction stating that the missioners had to leave the abbey.

---

[52] *S.V.P.* V, pp. 198-199.
[53] *S.V.P.* V, p. 211.
[54] *Annales* (1944), pp. 239-244 and 264-269.

This order was put into effect during the early hours of 23 July 1646. The commissary of the parlement, accompanied by several officials and nine Benedictines, forced the doors of the building, which had been barricaded by the seminarists who were led by the vicar general. The missioners and their companions took refuge in the abbot's house while the monks occupied the community premises. This uncomfortable situation lasted for a fortnight. The seminarists and servants did everything they could to make life difficult for the monks. One night they filled the wells with rubbish. Finally, they were obliged to leave the building on 7 August, after a new order was issued by the parlement. Before they did so, the vicar general promulgated an excommunication of the monks and an interdict on their church. The bishop was not content with spiritual warfare, and took even stronger action than his vicar general. Armed with letters patent from the king authorising him to occupy the abbey, he went to the lieutenant of Brittany, Marshal de La Meilleraye.

The marshal sent a squadron of horsemen with an officer at its head, and this detachment entered the church, still on horseback, and with drawn swords. This happened in the early hours of August 20 and, to the shouts of 'Out with the monks', the military took possession of the abbey. The missioners and their seminarists were reinstated. Then the parlement was petitioned once again by the Benedictines and launched a counter-attack. On 28 August they issued a warrant for the arrest of the superior of the Missioners, Fr Bourdet, his assistant, Fr Beaumont, the vicar general, the captain of the guard, and some other individuals, and all these were ordered to leave the seminary forthwith.

The man responsible for seeing that this order was carried out was the advocate general who was accompanied by the provost general at the head of all his armed men. An armed struggle seemed inevitable, but when the small army arrived at the abbey they found it deserted. That night Marshal de La Meilleraye had given his soldiers the order to retreat. The missioners had no option but to follow suit. Fr Bourdet, the superior, fled on horseback and galloped for a whole night and a day without stopping. He was exhausted by the time he reached a hostelry which was a good distance away from where these events had taken place. However, when he went into the stables he saw two horses there, and was told that these belonged to two of the parlement's ushers who had just arrived. Without waiting to hear any more he got on his horse again and continued his frenzied ride till the poor beast dropped dead under him.

Fr Beaumont had more valour. When the others left he agreed to stay behind and guard the house. He was arrested by the deputies and sent to prison where his feet were put in fetters. He was only there for four days because the president of the parlement judged these measures to be too harsh and the missioner was set free. Meanwhile, the bishop's efforts did not slacken. He obtained a royal edict which ordered the monks to leave the abbey immediately, and vehemently denounced two councillors and the parlement's procurator general, and had them dismissed. On 22 September a nephew of the bishop enforced this order from the king, and this time there was no opposition. The parlement presented the king with a humble and reasoned petition but this fell on deaf ears. In an attempt to have the matter settled once and for all, they appealed to the Holy See, which imposed a cooling-off period of 12 years, and then issued a bull annexing the abbey of Saint Méen to the diocesan seminary of Saint Malo which was to be directed by the priests of the Mission to whom they gave fulsome praise.[55]

At Vincent de Paul's beatification process the devil's advocate exploited this episode to the full, but his efforts were counter-productive. The postulator of the cause had Vincent's letters in hand and showed that the founder's conduct was irreproachable. The conflict and all its ensuing vicissitudes had been engineered by the bishop, not by Vincent. Just a few months earlier, the founder who had written to his missioners that 'it was better to withdraw than go to court',[56] remained faithful to that maxim even during the most critical moments in the dispute. He ordered his missioners to stay at their posts only out of deference to the bishop whom he considered to be absolutely in the right. Indeed, on 1 September 1646, he wrote to the superior of the abbey-seminary, unaware, at this time, of the missioner's flight on horseback:

> If the company had any say in the matter we would have recalled you as soon as the trouble broke out, but we were working with a bishop who had some problems and was negotiating to help other people. If we had thought that by not going to court we were following the evangelical counsel, then we would have been guilty of gross ingratitude, which is the greatest crime of all. It is true that the company holds to the principle of preferring to lose everything rather than initiate a lawsuit, and I beg God to grant us the grace of always being faithful to this. But this principle is for matters that we can control. In this instance, it is not we who are bringing the lawsuit, but a prelate. He has called us to serve God in his diocese but other people are trying to have you moved out.

---

[55] *S.V.P.* XIII, pp. 387-395. Saint Méen Abbey's events were related in detail by Coste (*op. cit.*, Vol. 1, pp. 414-418). The main details are also in St Vincent's letters which are mentioned in the following quotations.
[56] *S.V.P.* II, p. 569.

In virtue of this and some other important considerations, Vincent exhorted Fr Bourdet to show courage in facing up to the sufferings that might ensue:

> What dangers will the company have to face in all this? 'We will be sent to prison', you say. That is the worst that can happen. Mon Dieu! What will we ever be able to put up with if we cannot suffer this for God? Can we see regiments of 500 soldiers, from the most meanly-born men to royal princes, all fighting for their country, and risking not just prison, but death itself, while Our Lord cannot find five or six brave and faithful souls to serve him?[57]

If this strong clarion call had arrived earlier we do not know whether the good Fr Bourdet would have found the courage to stand firm when the parlement's troops arrived, instead of escaping at the gallop. Fr Beaumont's conduct earned great praise from Vincent,[58] who had petitioned the president of the Breton parlement for his release. In his letter, he pleaded the innocence of the arrested missioner, 'one of the best men in the world, whose work for the peasants has brought many blessings from God'. Then he presented a calm and respectful account of the affair saying that, if it had depended on the missioners, they would have left everything as soon as the disagreement started. He further states that the conflict has no way lessened his affection for the Benedictines:

> There is nobody in the world who loves and esteems them as much, thank God, as I try to do, and they themselves can testify to this.[59]

Vincent's spirit of detachment, and his charity, were vindicated by the setback. Whether the bishop had any right or not to secularise the property of religious was not for him to say. His duty was to show obedience to the bishop and to the king. Faced with Vincent's humility and his common sense, the devil's advocate had to concede defeat.

---

[57] *S.V.P.* III, pp. 36-40.
[58] *Annales* (1926), pp. 233-235: *S.V.P.* III, pp. 45-48.
[59] *S.V.P.* III, pp. 46-49.

'Is the Catholic any less guilty just because he is a Catholic?'

Sedan had problems of a different kind. The town had a great number of Protestants and this made for continual tension between them and the Catholics. In a climate of religious strife fuelled by doctrinal theories and by self-interest, the missioners allowed themselves to be carried away by polemic attitudes which bordered on the unjust. This was particularly true of the superior, Fr Gallais, who was a fiery, argumentative man. Nothing could have been more contrary to Vincent's convictions. In a century where violence in the name of religion was the general rule—let us not forget the Thirty Years' War was escalating at this time—Vincent made the gentleness he had learnt from St Francis de Sales his invariable rule of conduct when dealing with dissidents. For this reason he wrote to the superior at Sedan in 1643:

> When the king asked for you to be sent to Sedan it was on condition that you would never enter into dispute with the heretics, either from the pulpit or in private. Little good comes of this for often it is more of an outward show than something that bears fruit. A good life, and the good odour of the Christian virtues you practise, attract the lapsed back to the right path and strengthen Catholics in their faith. This is how the company can profit from its work in Sedan; by adding good example to our practice of virtue, by instructing the people just as we usually do, by preaching against vice and evil habits, by persuading people to lead a good life and speaking to them of the beauty and the necessity of practising different virtues as well as the means they have to acquire these. This is your main task. If you want to discuss some controversial topic you should only do so if it follows on naturally from the Gospel of the day. In that case you could state and prove truths that heretics are attacking. You could reply to their objections but on no account must you mention heretics by name or speak of them.[60]

In spite of Vincent's advice, Fr Gallais's stout heart and his partisan feelings, that are understandable in this situation, carried the day and he leapt to the defence of Catholics who were in litigation against the Protestants. Happy fault which meant we now have one of the most eloquent proofs of Vincent de Paul's equanimity and sense of justice which could rise so far above party or factional bitterness.

---

[60] *S.V.P.* VIII, p. 526.

O Fr Gallais, my dear brother! What good missioners you and I would make if we could inspire people with the spirit of the Gospel which would lead them to live as Christ did! I assure you that this is the most powerful means we have of sanctifying Catholics and converting heretics. There is nothing more likely to confirm heretics in their wrong ways than for us to act in any other way. Remember, Father, Our Lord's words to the man who complained about his brother, *Quis me constituit iudicem inter te et fratrem tuum?* So you should say to those who want you to take up their case, *Quis me constituit advocatum vel negotiatorem vestrum?*'

'But', you will say to me. 'am I to see a Catholic persecuted by someone of the other faith and not do anything to help him?' I would answer that there must be some reason for the persecution; it might be on account of some debt that the Catholic owes the Huguenot, or some injury or damage that he has done. Well, in that case, is it not only right that the Huguenot should seek satisfaction through the court. Is the Catholic any less guilty just because he is a Catholic?[61]

The good superior's breviary

Towards the end of his life Vincent put together the experiences of more than thirty years in office when, in the course of a private conversation, he drew up for the young and inexperienced Fr Durand what might be called, 'the good superior's breviary' before sending him out to take up office in the house at Agde. It shows us the way of life that Vincent wanted his congregation to follow and it reveals the secret of the congregation's success, in spite of the fact that there were still not enough missioners to staff so many foundation, as Vincent, himself, realised.[62] Vincent's thinking may be summarised as follows:

Above all, the superior should let himself be ruled entirely by God, and be filled with his spirit. The means par excellence of governing well is to have recourse to prayer. The superior must pray so that he himself will persevere in virtue, and also

---

[61] *S.V.P.* II, pp. 449-450.
[62] *S.V.P.* III, pp. 153.

to beg God to grant graces to the companions entrusted to his care. He must exercise his office as superior in the same spirit of humility and service which characterised the Son of God, and not rule in any spirit of domination or pride. If he wants to find the right words and make the right decisions he must let the conduct of Jesus be his constant guide. On the other hand, the authority given to the local superior is subject to that of the superior general, and all important matters must be referred to him. Vincent's vision of how authority should be exercised tends towards centralisation. The successful superior will shun all singularity. It is vital that the superior exercise a good influence on his brothers in community. Finally, the good superior must be concerned for the temporal interests and material needs of those in his care, as well as for their spiritual welfare. Vincent's realism causes him to read the Gospel through the wary eyes of the peasant he would always remain. The more attention that was paid to the physical needs of the missioners the better would be their spiritual dispositions.[63]

'We are having a visitation here'

Instructions sent by letter were soon reinforced by another instrument of government which has a long tradition in religious communities viz, the canonical visitation. Vincent carried out many of these himself, but he often delegated to others this task which he considered to be of the utmost importance. He saw it as a means of spiritual renewal for the company and something essential for the preservation of its spirit. He wrote about the visitation to St Lazare in 1640 as follows:

> We are having a visitation here just now. I have never before seen so clearly our need to use this occasion, given to us by providence, for our greater spiritual progress. In God's name, say as much to the company, and tell them how important it is to give all the time we can to carrying it out properly. We should therefore stop doing any other sort of work, even preaching or visiting places where we intend to give missions,

---

[63] *S.V.P.* XI, p. 342-351.

and leave this for another time. We must strive to let God reign fully in our lives and then in the lives of others.[64]

Those authorised to make visitations were Frs Alméras, Berthe, Dehorgny, Lambert, Le Gros, Portail and a few others. A detailed study of their journeys would provide material for a much longer book. Suffice it to say that all the houses had several visitations and Vincent was always satisfied with the results.

He himself was pleased to submit to this obligation imposed by rule on the congregation in 1642, and gave an account of how the visitor's recommendations were carried out. In 1641, he wrote to Fr Lambert who had made a visitation at St Lazare:

I think we have been quite faithful in following out the directives given at your visitation and we have read these every two months since you left. I myself have tried to recall what you said in the language of your beloved region (this is a reference to Lambert's habit of speaking the Picardy dialect) although I have failed once or twice, and I have also neglected to visit two of the sick in the infirmary. You cannot imagine how frequently and how earnestly I speak of our duty to observe these directives faithfully.[65]

The congregation was beginning to express its way of life in concrete terms and norms conceived independently of its founder and superior.

---

[64] *S.V.P.* II, p. 96.
[65] *S.V.P.* II, pp. 208-209.

Chapter XX
THE MODEL AND SPIRIT
OF THE RULES

Development is slow

The bull *Salvatori Nostri* accorded only a minimal juridical structure to the Congregation of the Mission. It simply named Vincent as superior general for life with the authority to draw up, promulgate, revoke, and modify all manner of statutes and ordinances which would otherwise have needed the approval of the archbishop of Paris who was the apostolic authority's delegate. It also provided for the election of Vincent's successor by the members of the congregation. That was all. So it could be said that Vincent was the congregation. However, he was not prepared to let this situation continue. He thought that community structures should be made more objective and it would take him the rest of his life to see this accomplished. We can distinguish three phases in the process.

During the first period, from 1633-1642, it might be said that everything was dependent on Vincent's personal wishes. Whether we regard these as rules or not, he is imposing a set of practices which will later be codified to form the basis of the rules and constitutions. Collegiality plays no part in government. All authority is vested in Vincent alone and he does not even rely on a group of councillors. As we have seen, it was his decision alone to set up the internal seminary in 1637 and we shall see later that it was Vincent himself who decided to promulgate an order which obliged all future members of the Mission to take vows.

Vincent convoked the first assembly of the congregation in 1642 to study questions of government. This was the first step towards broadening the concept of authority. We will study this in more detail later. For the moment it is enough for us to know that the basic work of this meeting was to review a project dealing with rules and constitutions.

The second period, (1642-1653), saw a preoccupation with the definitive form of the rules and constitutions and a study of the role and nature of community vows. In 1651 Vincent called a second assembly and its sole objective was to study these two points. The rules were finalised, submitted to the archbishop of Paris, and approved by him in 1653.

The third period (1653-1660), does not fit into the chronological sequence of this part of the story. However, so as not to lose the thread of this institutionalising process, let us just say that during these final years there is a further revision of the rules and constitutions entailing some changes in detail and that this was the period when the company particularly strove to obtain the Holy See's approval for the vows. This approval was granted by Pope Alexander VII in 1655.

'The little regulations'

Let us now examine each of these stages in detail. In the prologue to the *Common Rules* of the congregation distributed in 1658, Vincent de Paul declared that 33 years had elapsed between the founding of the company and the printing of its rules. This is absolutely correct. A few lines later he adds the words:

> You will not find anything in these (rules) that you have not been practising for a long time, to our great consolation and your mutual edification.[1]

It was true. We have already noted that Vincent's writings referred to the rule or the rules.[2] We are not sure whether these were referring to written rules though Vincent's words would lead us to think this was the case. As for the content of the rules, there were prescriptions laid down for the order of the day,[3] pious exercises,[4] silence,[5] and the virtues proper to missioners.[6]

The most complete document we have regarding this first rule is a letter written by Vincent to Mother Chantal. It is dated 14 July 1639, and as we have no other texts that refer more directly to the subject, we must consider this as an authoritative summary of the primitive rules of the Mission.[7]

---

[1] *Reglas comunes,* prefatory letter.
[2] *S.V.P.* I, pp. 66, 176, 311.
[3] *S.V.P.* I, p. 176.
[4] *S.V.P.* I, p. 204.
[5] *S.V.P.* I, p. 139.
[6] *S.V.P.* I, p. 88; ES p. 151.
[7] *S.V.P.* I, pp. 561-567.

'We have still not settled the question of our rules'

The validity of this outline of the rules was purely private since it had never been officially approved. This meant that Vincent lived in constant fear that his sudden demise would leave the congregation without any written rules. Sometime around 1635, we cannot be more definite about the date, he wrote these lines:

> Two or three days ago I was gravely ill and this led me to think about my death. By the grace of God I can adore his will and cleave wholeheartedly to him. When I ask myself if I have any cause for regret, I cannot find anything to worry about except that we still have not formulated our rules.[8]

We should note, in passing, the great progress made by Vincent during these years in his favourite virtue of submission to the divine will, and also his extraordinarily pure conscience since he had nothing else to reproach himself about except that he had not given rules to his congregation. It was Vincent's wish that the compilation of these rules should be a collective task and not something he worked out on his own.[9] This is indicated by the sudden change from singular to plural in the subject of the last sentence. In fact, in 1640, when they were actively working on the drawing up of the rules, Vincent had the most widely representative body of missioners engaged in the task.[10] And when in 1642 there at last appeared a rough draft which was more or less complete, he convoked the first general assembly of the congregation to revise and finalise it. The superior of each house was summoned to attend; exceptions were made for those prevented from coming because of distance or for other reason and in these cases Vincent chose substitute delegates. Altogether there were eleven representatives at the assembly.

'My first act of obedience to the company'

The 1642 assembly marks the coming of age of the Congregation of the Mission. During the proceedings Vincent, who was the only legislator recognised in the bull *Salvatori Nostri,* handed over his powers to that

---

8 *S.V.P.* I, p. 291; ABELLY, *op. cit.*, 1.1 c. 2, p. 252.
9 *S.V.P.* II, p. 137.
10 *Ibid.*

representative body and did it in such a way that he gave full recognition to the corporate identity of the community. As the session held on 22 October came to a close, he fell on his knees and resigned his position as superior general, saying that he was not competent to continue, and he urged them to choose somebody else. Having said this he retired to one of the tribunes in the church which looked on to the high altar. The assembly delegates were astonished beyond measure but they did not hesitate at all. They would not even consider the proposal. A delegation was immediately sent to look for Vincent and to tell him how they felt about the matter. The delegates searched the whole house without finding Vincent until it occurred to them to look in the chapel and they found him kneeling there before the tabernacle, absorbed in prayer. He repeated that he had resigned and that he already considered himself out of office; they were to proceed immediately to the election of his successor. The delegates went back and reported to the rest of the community. Then they all went in a body to the church.

'We cannot choose another superior', they told him, 'as long as the one whom God, in his goodness, appointed for us, is still living.'

Vincent remained adamant but then the assembly delegates took a line of argument which could not be refuted.

Very well, then we choose you, and we will have no other superior for as long as God preserves your life.

They had turned the tables on Vincent and he had to agree.

'It is my first act of obedience to the company'[11] he said.

The first biographer, Abelly, relates this incident in the chapter where he is treating of Vincent's humility. It certainly was a splendid act of humility but there was more to it than that. After Vincent's act of renunciation the company became master of its own destiny. There it was, in front of his very eyes, deliberately taking responsibility for its actions. At that moment it ceased to be just something that the founder had established and became a corporate body with sovereign, independent, rights. Conscious of its new powers, it elected by secret ballot the superior general's two assistants. These were Frs Portail and Dehorgny and from now on they would form his council. It had already been decided to divide the houses of the congregation into provinces and so they established four groups of houses; one with Paris and Crécy, a second with Toul and Troyes, a third comprising Richelieu,

---

[11] ABELLY, *op. cit.*, 1.3 c. 13, p. 212; *S.V.P.* XIII, p. 296.

Luçon, Saintes and Notre Dame de la Rose, and the fourth one that took in Annecy and Rome. These areas would be governed by a provincial superior known as the visitor.

The main aim of the assembly was to study the rules, and they devoted eighteen sessions to this work. They discussed not only the rules as such, but also the constitutions dealing with the election and powers of the superior general, and those concerning general assemblies, visitors and provinces. Unfortunately we do not have available the text that the assembly delegates were given to study, and neither do we have any record of their observations on this. All we know about the assembly is a few details relating only to constitutional matters. It was a complicated business, perhaps more complicated than they had realised.

Observations were made and amendments introduced. For this reason, and also so as not to prolong the assembly unduly, it was decided to appoint a committee of four members who, together with the superior general, would finalise the definitive edition in the light of observations made. Frs Portail, du Coudray, Dehorgny and Lambert were chosen and Fr Alméras was nominated as substitute for any of these who might be absent.[12] We have already mentioned the first two men who were the two most senior members of the company; Dehorgny entered in 1627, and Lambert in 1628. Alméras was the last of these to enter, since he joined in 1637. By 1642 these five were the best trained and the most competent men in the company.

'To delay the rules as long as possible'

The compilation of the rules and constitutions evolved at what we would consider a fairly slow pace between the years 1642 and 1651. Vincent consulted other missioners in addition to those who were members of the commission.[13] The founder himself gives the reason for the delay in a letter in 1648 to Fr Portail, when writing about much the same thing, the regulations for the hospital for galley slaves in Marseilles.

> It often happens with people whom God uses to start new and holy works that they take as long a time as possible to draw up rules for these. Experience teaches us that what may be appropriate at the beginning can sometimes be harmful later on, or have unfortunate consequences, and for this reason,

---

[12] The detailed minutes of the Assembly are in *S.V.P.* XIII, pp. 287-298; *cf. S.V.P.* II, p. 307.

[13] *S.V.P.* II, pp. 307, 362.

some communities, like the Carthusians, only drew up their constitutions after a hundred years. St Ignatius only left a brief outline of his rules so his company formulated them in their present form in accordance with the inspiration they received as time went on. The bishop of Geneva was too hasty in drawing up the rules for the Daughters of St Mary, so that very soon he had to add a directory.[14]

At this time there was some hesitation over which tactics they should pursue. In 1644 Pope Urban VIII died, and Vincent sounded out the possibilities of seeking approval for the rules directly from the Holy See and also of revoking the powers delegated to the archbishop of Paris in the bull *Salvatori Nostri*.[15] However, they could not have done much in that line, since a few months later they again tried to have them approved in Paris[16] and in 1648 the superior of the house in Rome, Fr Alméras, was asked 'to begin to get them approved.'[17] In 1646 it would seem they were on the point of being presented to the coadjutor of the archbishop of Paris, his nephew, Jean Francois de Retz, who was temporarily in charge of the diocese during his uncle's absence.[18] The text must still not have been finalised, since in 1647, and again in the following year, Vincent ordered Portail, Alméras and Dehorgny, who occasionally met in Rome, to devote six days to revising the rules.[19]

'The final touch'

The text was finally completed in 1651. Vincent convoked a second general assembly which was held at Saint Lazare from 1 July to 11 August. There were fourteen delegates including Vincent. We have two different records of this assembly: the official minutes and the private diary of Fr Antoine Lucas,[20] one of the delegates. The main purpose of the assembly was to 'put the final touch' to the rules.[21] At the same time they discussed other practical matters, particularly the question of the community's vows. We will return to this subject later. Most of the time was spent studying the rules. In the end, the

---

[14] *S.V.P.* III, p. 272.
[15] *S.V.P.* II, p. 475.
[16] *S.V.P.* II, p. 488.
[17] *S.V.P.* III, p. 381.
[18] *S.V.P.* III, p. 8, 73.
[19] *S.V.P.* III, p. 236.
[20] *S.V.P.* XIII, pp. 326-332, 333-356, 357-359.
[21] *S.V.P.* XIII, pp. 326, 358.

delegates decided that they had worded them 'the best way they could'[22] and that there was no point in discussing them further, since revising the rules is like washing your hands; the more you wash them, the more you need to wash them or like hens pecking the ground they have been over a hundred times already.'[23] Added to this was the possibility that the superior general might die before the rules were approved, and a successor could only be elected if he swore,' to observe, enforce and approve the rules in their present form.'[24] It was Vincent's wish that the compilation of the rules should be a collective task on the part of the company, but he was evidently weary of this revision process that was going on for too long and leaving the basic norms of the community in a continual state of flux. So on the day the assembly ended, he drew up a solemn document, signed by all those present, in which he affirmed that the rules and constitutions were in conformity with the life-style, aims and nature of the congregation as well as the terms of the foundation bull, and that they had been practised for nearly 25 years. In view of this he petitioned the archbishop of Paris to give then his approval in virtue of the authority delegated to the prelate by the apostolic see.[25] This time they did not have to wait long for the archbishop's decision. He had the rules studied by a panel of doctors of theology and then gave his approval which was confirmed by a decree issued on 23 August 1653.[26]

We know from a study of the assembly minutes, and from Vincent's letters on the subject, that the text approved in 1651 comprised at least the *Common Rules*, the ordinance and formula for the vows, the rules concerning the superior general and the visitor, as well as matters relating to assemblies of the congregation at general, provincial and local levels. We are talking here of a complex ascetic-juridical collection of rules which was the depository of the teachings and the spiritual standards that were to direct the life of the whole community, and the constitutional rules for its various branches of government. But we have neither the original nor any copy of the approved text. It is thanks to Fr Angelo Coppo's discovery that we know about the documents which the archbishop of Paris approved in 1653.[27]

---

[22] *S.V.P.* XIII, p. 329.

[23] *S.V.P.* XIII, p. 356.

[24] *Ibid.*

[25] *S.V.P.* XIII, pp. 357-359.

[26] *S.V.P.* XIII, p. 366.

[27] In 1957, Fr Angelo Coppo discovered a manuscript codex in the archives of the Congregation of the Mission's house in Sarzana (Italy). This codex has a copy of all the documents submitted for Mgr Jean François de Gondi's approval in 1651. Fr Coppo accounted for his discovery in a meticulously critical work entitled 'La prima stesura delle Regole e Costituzioni della Congregazione della Missione in un inedito

'Here at last are the *Common Rules* and the Constitutions'

This approval of the rules brought to an end the second stage in the constitutional development of the company. In the third and final stage (1653-1660) the rules would still need some rewording. The rules first went into print in 1655, but there were so many errata that the edition had to be withdrawn before distribution.[28] Vincent took advantage of this mishap, as well as some other unforeseen circumstances, to revise some details[29] and once again he sought the help of his collaborators.[30] These changes meant they had to seek the archbishop's approval yet again. Approval was given by the new archbishop, Cardinal de Retz, but we do not have the date for this.[31]

A second edition was printed in 1658 and Vincent distributed copies to the missioners at an emotional ceremony on 17 May.[32] It seems that even this was not thought to be the final text. Two letters, dated 1659, speak of further alterations, and approval for these was sought from the archbishop of Paris. He was authorised by the Holy See to approve the amendments since the text was substantially unaltered except for some minor details.[33] There is some doubt, however, as to whether these referred to changes made after the rules were printed, apart from correcting a simple printer's error that slipped into article three of chapter two of the *Common Rules*. It is more likely that Vincent made some slight changes to the 1658 edition and sought approval from the bishop *a posteriori*.[34] At long last, when he

---

manoscritto del 1655-1658', *Annali* (1957), pp. 206-254; This codex is at present kept in the general curia of the Congregation of the Mission where we were able to photocopy it. The index contains the following documents: 1) *Common rules;* 2) ordinance of 1641 about the vows, with the formula for them and the explanation of the vow of poverty; 3) the archbishop's approval of the previous ordinance; 4) the rules for the superior general, visitor and local superior; 5) the regulations concerning general, provincial, and local assemblies; 6) the text of the approval given to the collection of previous documents granted by the archbishop of Paris on 23 August 1653; 7) a statement by notaries that one of the documents is an exact copy of the original.

[28] *S.V.P.* V, p. 337.

[29] *S.V.P.* V, p. 600. The French text reads as follows: *Pour les règles ne sont pas en état d'être montrées; nous y travaillons à cause de quelque occasion qui est arrivée, qui nous oblige d'y toucher.*

[30] *S.V.P.* VI, pp. 344, 366, 507.

[31] *S.V.P.* VIII, p. 26.

[32] *S.V.P.* XII, pp. 1-14.

[33] *S.V.P.* VII, p. 480.

[34] This would seem to contradict Vincent's solemn assurance to Cardinal de Retz that only slight changes were introduced, 'And I give Your Eminence my solemn word on this, before God to whom I will one day have to account for the actions of my wretched life' (*S.V.P.* VIII, p. 2).

was almost at death's door, Vincent had finally settled the juridical structures of his company.[35]

'You are to look on them as something given by God'

The *Common Rules*, which had been a matter of so much concern for over thirty years, are the basic core of all Vincentian legislation. They are the code of spiritual perfection that Vincent de Paul proposed to his missioners. From what we know of the slow and painstaking development of these rules, we can say they are the embodiment of everything that Vincent hoped for and wanted from his followers. In the prefatory letter that introduces their printed form, Vincent himself says they should be thought of as 'not as something produced by the human mind but as inspired by God, the giver of all good gifts.'[36]

The rules are quite concise and are contained in a small book measuring 12cms. x 6cms. which has just over 100 pages divided into twelve chapters entitled, 'The purpose and nature of the congregation'; 'Gospel teaching'; 'Poverty'; 'Chastity'; 'Obedience'; 'Matters concerning the sick'; 'Decorum'; 'Getting along with each other'; 'Getting along with non-confreres'; 'Spiritual practices used in the congregation'; 'Missions and other ministries of the congregation on behalf of the people' and' Some useful means needed for properly and effectively carrying out the ministries just mentioned.'

With just a very few exceptions the rules do not give detailed prescriptions for the order of the day or particular community practices. They are more geared to presenting the spirit in which a missioner is to face the demands of his vocation to perfection and to the apostolate. An essential feature of the work is that each chapter opens with a call to imitate Christ by practising the virtue proposed in the chapter. Vincent's gaze was increasingly fixed on the Saviour as pattern and model of Christian holiness, and this is his unique way of interpreting de Bérulle's teaching that we should adore the different characteristics of the Word made flesh.

Vincent is a child of his times when he elevates the role of superior in the rules. He gives superiors almost total control over their subjects'

---

[35] The history of the rules of the Congregation of the Mission was given by Coste in *M.V.* Vol. 2, pp. 1-38. A new study giving interesting details was made by Coppo in the article to which we have referred (*cf.* nt. 27: *La prima stesura ...*). Although we have both studies on hand we have used the original documents so we have been obliged to interpret some details of the texts differently.

[36] *Common Rule*. Prefatory letter.

activities and even of their spiritual life. Furthermore, the rules are not entirely original. Many of the more specific precepts are taken, and sometimes taken word for word, from legislation which is common to earlier or to contemporary religious orders, especially to the Society of Jesus.[37]

The authentic Vincent is seen particularly in the choice of Gospel teachings he puts at the beginning of the book. The passages selected show us how Vincent had throughout his life read Christ's message; 'Seek first the kingdom of God', 'I always do what is pleasing to my Father', 'Be wise as serpents and simple as doves', 'Learn of me for I am meek and humble of heart', 'Whoever would come after me, let him deny himself and take up his cross daily', 'He who does not hate father and mother cannot be my disciple ...'

When Vincent de Paul read the gospel it was no mere speculative exercise but a dynamic act of commitment. The *Common Rules* are the fruit of this experience and so we can find in them the spiritual portrait of their author. For the moment we will content ourselves with this observation, as our story unfolds we will see how true it is.

---

[37] COSTE, *M.V.* Vol. 2, p. 13. Cf. J. M. ROMAN, 'San Vicente de Paúl y la Compañía de Jesús', *Razón y Fe* 162 (1960), pp. 303-318; 163 (1961), pp. 399-416.

Chapter XXI
THE VOWS, AN IDEAL AND A SAFEGUARD

'We have been taking vows ever since the second or third year after our foundation'

The practice of taking vows was not yet incorporated into the constitutions of the Congregation of the Mission. Vincent thought it would be inappropriate to include it in the *Common Rules* since no other community did so.[1] We have already noted that private vows had been taken in the community, on a voluntary basis, from the second, third or fourth year after the foundation of the congregation, i.e. from 1627 or 1628[2] onwards. These were the traditional vows of poverty, chastity and obedience common to all religious communities, together with a fourth vow of stability, so that missioners would devote their whole lives to working for the salvation of poor country people. Vincent has explained the reasons why these first missioners made this decision. Firstly, it was 'the desire to embrace the most perfect state possible without becoming a religious', a desire no doubt inspired by Vincent himself. Secondly, 'to become more closely united to Our Lord and to his Church, the superior of the company to its members and the members to its head.[3] The practice of taking vows only came about after a long process similar to that followed by the development of the rules. In some ways it was more difficult and more controversial to legislate for the vows. As happened with the rules, the process developed over three stages: 1633-1642, 1642-1653 and 1653-1660.

Vincent spoke about the way the vows had developed when he told the company about the pontifical brief approving them. The summary he wrote in a letter to Fr Edmund Jolly gives us further guidance on this point.

---

[1] *S.V.P.* XII, p. 367.
[2] *S.V.P.* V, pp. 319-320, 458; XII, p. 379. The register of personnel states that vows were taken for the first time on 8 September 1629 *(Notices ...,* I, p. 493). According to a reference quoted by Coste, the date was 9 September of the same year. (*S.V.P.* V, p. 458).
[3] *S.V.P.* V, p. 458.

We have presented the Holy Father's brief to the family here and it is directed to the priests as well as to the lay brothers, giving them to understand how from the very beginning of the company God granted it the desire of being in the most perfect state possible short of becoming a religious order and it was for this reason that we took vows: to unite ourselves more closely to Our Lord and to the Church, the superior of the company to its members, and the members to its head. This was already being done in the second or third year after the community was founded. These vows of poverty etc. were simple vows and we renewed them after two or three years. We finally made a rule which was approved by the archbishop of Paris and after that time we all took our vows together, but no sooner had we started to do this than some of the community began to complain and these complaints were noised abroad.

We were obliged to summon the leading doctors of theology in Paris to ask them if we had acted rightly. They agreed that we had. So we called an assembly here of the main superiors and some former superiors in the company and among other matters we dealt with this question. They agreed with the theologians that we should continue the practice, in spite of difficulties both within and outside the company. But the evil spirit tries to thwart the works of God and only gives up after battling to the bitter end so these difficulties continued and even increased. This meant we had to consult these doctors again to see if they were of the same opinion in spite of the difficulties that had arisen. They kept to their original decision and put this in writing for us in a statement signed by three of the most distinguished Jesuits. Yet all this did not satisfy people. We called a second assembly of the principal superiors of the company and they agreed, as they had done on the first occasion, that we should continue in this way. But ever since then there has been disagreement. We finally had recourse to the oracle of God's will, who eventually gave us the brief which confirms our manner of taking vows.[4]

During the period 1633-1642 there was no constitutional ruling on the taking of vows. Each individual was free to take vows or not after he had

---

[4] *S.V.P.* V, pp. 458-459. As the reader will observe, the subheadings for this chapter are taken from the paragraph we have copied.

prayed about it and sought advice.[5] The bull *Salvatori nostri* makes no mention of any vows at all when giving approbation to the congregation. In spite of this, the practice continued. In 1639 most of the missioners had taken the four vows and they even considered introducing an extra vow of obedience to the bishops in the exercise of works proper to the congregation.[6] But Vincent was determined to incorporate the taking of vows into the constitutional framework of the company. It was one of those areas where Vincent was most adamant even though he met with all kinds of opposition from within and outside the community. The battle continued right to the end of his life but never for a moment would he yield to pressure, even though this came from people who were very dear to him. There can be no doubt that this attitude was rooted in his unshakeable conviction that this was God's will in the matter. As we know, in such cases Vincent was never prepared to compromise.

'I am perplexed and full of doubts'

Vincent was not happy with the idea of vows being optional as was the custom up to 1639, so he began to seek approval for the vows from the Holy See.[7] It is worth mentioning that this was the year that the first missioners who had entered the congregation under the new system would complete their internal seminary. This must have been the catalyst that moved Vincent to start making arrangements. Early that year he sent to Rome a missioner who was new to the congregation, though he was not too young in age. This man was Fr Louis Lebreton and he was given the task of bringing before the curia the question of approval for the vows and other matters that were of interest to the community.[8] He expected to achieve his first objective without much delay but it was not as simple as that.

There were numerous objections from Rome but the greatest obstacle was that it was considered inappropriate for a congregation of secular priests to take vows. Vincent confessed himself bewildered in face of these never-ending objections and so tried various solutions which mark several changes in his thinking. His first plan was to abandon the idea of solemn vows and petition, instead, for four simple ones (November 1639). Then he began to think in terms of one single vow of stability with excommunication

---

[5]   *S.V.P.* V, p. 458.
[6]   *S.V.P.* I, p. 563.
[7]   *Ibid.*
[8]   *S.V.P.* I, pp. 547-553.

for those who did not observe poverty and obedience (February 1640). Then he suggested three simple vows on completion of the internal seminary, followed by a solemn vow of stability some years later (August 1640). This was changed to a proposal to have a single vow of stability (October 1640) then a simple vow of stability after two years novitiate to be followed by a solemn vow eight or ten years later, and then a sworn oath binding under pain of excommunication instead of the other three vows (November1640). At one point it seemed the congregation was prepared to declare itself a religious order if that was the only way they could have vows and they even petitioned to take religious vows.[9]

'We made a rule'

The impossible task of overcoming all the difficulties put forward by Rome made Vincent try another track. As we know, the bull, *Salvatori nostri,* authorised the archbishop of Paris to approve all kinds of statutes and ordinances (*ordinationes*) relative to the life style and government of the congregation. Applying this pontifical concession to the letter, Vincent drew up an ordinance (*ordinatio*) by which all future members of the congregation would, at the end of their second year in the seminary, pronounce simple vows of poverty, chastity, obedience and stability in working for the salvation of poor country people. These vows were to be pronounced during Mass, in the presence of the superior but not addressed to him, and dispensation from these vows could only be granted by the sovereign pontiff or the superior general. In this way the congregation would not constitute a religious order and its members would still belong to the secular clergy. This ordinance was not compulsory for those who were already members of the company but the superior could allow these to take vows, too, if they wished. Vincent respected the liberty and the rights of the individual.[10] The ordinance was followed by the formula for the vows and an explanation of the vow of poverty.[11]

The ordinance had to be approved by the archbishop of Paris in order to be valid and Vincent petitioned for this. The archbishop found not a

---

[9] The texts referring to the negotiations can be found in *S.V.P.* I, p. 600; II, pp. 28, 90, 100, 124, 137-138; XIII, p. 338. *Cf.* H. DE GRAAF, *De votis quae emittuntur in Congregatione Missionis* (Rome 1955).

[10] References in several documents led people to believe that the *Regula sive Ordinatio de votis simplicibus in Congregatione Missionis* existed but the actual text only came to light with the discovery of the *Codex Sarzana* which includes it in p. 39-41, *Cf.* A. COPPO, *La prima stesura ...*, pp. 219-220.

[11] Codex Sarzana, pp. 41-42.

few difficulties in this original idea put forward by Vincent, and before giving his approval he consulted the doctors of his council. After considering the proposal for three years he finally gave his approval which dated from 19 October 1641.[12] A few months later, on 24 February 1642, the feast of St Matthias, Vincent and the vast majority of his companions either took their vows or renewed them.[13]

The matter was still not completely settled. From within and from outside the community came protests from those who questioned the validity of the ordinance and its approbation. To pacify these dissenters Vincent held a consultation with the leading doctors of theology in Paris, and their opinion was favourable. Not content with this, he had the ordinance ratified by the 1642 assembly.[14] He had won this first battle but he was still a long way from winning the war.

'They immediately started to complain'

Indeed, during the second period we mentioned, (1642-1653) the debate about the vows became so acrimonious that it provoked the most serious crisis the young community had ever known.

The nub of the matter was the question of whether vows would make the congregation into a religious order something contrary to its original secular character. Those who opposed the vows declared it did and Vincent assured them this was not so. He had foreseen the danger and thought he had averted it by repeating, almost word for word, in the ordinance's final clause, the archbishop's decree of approval, 'notwithstanding the taking of these said vows, the congregation will not be deemed a religious order and therefore it will not cease to be part of the secular clergy.' For many canon lawyers at that time it seemed like squaring the circle but Vincent was convinced of the validity of his formula:

'God's providence has finally inspired the company to embrace a state of life where we have the happiness of being religious in the sense that we take simple vows but we remain part of the secular clergy. We are as much under obedience to the bishop as are the humblest priests in their diocese in all matters

---

[12] *S.V.P.* XIII, pp. 355 and 366. Similarly, the text of the approbation of the rules is given in Codex Sarzana, pp. 42-46. Coste published it in *S.V.P.* XIII, pp. 283-286, and made some errors of transcription, as Coppo pointed out in (*La prima stesura ...*, pp. 212-213, 219).
[13] *S.V.P.* V, p. 319: *Notices ...*, I, pp. 453, 454, 457.
[14] *S.V.P.* V, p. 458.

concerning our works ...' 'We are not a religious order and we maintain that although we take simple vows we do not claim to be religious but remain part of the clergy.[15]

After the archbishop's approval of the ordinance and its ratification by the assembly of 1642, the official position was favourable to the vows. In spite of this there continued to be criticism and in fact this increased. In no other matter did Vincent de Paul experience so much opposition from within the congregation. Neither his authority as superior general nor his prestigious position as founder was sufficient to disarm his critics. Vincent faced this situation with unrelenting tenacity and we see the level of his patience, firmness and his negotiating skills. In 1647 the conflict was brought out into the open. When it was time to renew the vows, and it was customary to do this during a retreat, a small group of missioners led by a priest and a cleric, refused to renew their vows, stating that these had no validity. Vincent launched a counter-attack during a brief and fervent address.

> I gave them a short talk on two points; the first was on the reasons we have for renewing them [the vows] since God wishes to give us the grace attached to taking vows, and the second point was on the means we have of doing this. On this second point I mentioned two things: first, I begged those who did not feel able to persevere to leave and, secondly, I said that a sign that someone has this grace is that he is determined never to speak against this holy action but to defend it on every occasion against those who attack it, since it must happen that these vows will be contested by people in the community and outside of it.[16]

Vincent's eloquence won them over. Even the ringleader of the small rebellion came and humbly begged permission to renew his vows. He brought along 'a pile of things he had laid by in private' and Vincent, with his usual combination of severity and gentleness, allowed him to keep his bits and pieces.[17]

However, Vincent had no illusions that the problem was solved. Opposition to the vows intensified and he had to find a radical solution. Once again he had recourse to his friends, the doctors of theology in Paris. The penitentiary Jacques Charton, Duval the younger, Pereyret, Cornet and

---

[15] *S.V.P.* III, pp. 246-247.
[16] *S.V.P.* III, p. 245.
[17] *Ibid.*

Coqueret again pronounced in his favour. He took further steps to have the vows approved by the Holy See through the efforts of Frs Portail, Dehorgny and Alméras, but it was not an easy task. The francophile pope, Urban VIII, was succeeded in 1644 by Innocent X whose portrait was painted by Velázquez. This pontiff was more inclined to favour the Spanish and he had little regard for the religious state of life. Vincent waited patiently for better times. He was so convinced of the rightness of his cause that he refused to back down and this conviction inspired him with optimism and confidence.[18]

'We held a second assembly'

Approval from Rome seemed to be a long time coming. While Vincent never gave up hope that approval would eventually be given, he decided on a quicker course of action; he would bring the matter before another assembly of the congregation and, as we have previously mentioned, this was convoked for July 1651. As in the 1642 Assembly the main business concerned the rules, this time the main topic of debate were the vows. We need to follow the proceedings in some detail so as to understand Vincent's system of government.

Four possible options

Scarcely had the assembly begun, on the morning of 1 July, when the problem was raised with great frankness and four possible solutions were suggested: 1) that they continue to take vows in the manner agreed on at the previous assembly; 2) that they scrap them; 3) that they omit the more difficult points like dispensations being reserved to the pope and the superior general, and 4) that they find another way of retaining the vows.

It is not easy to follow the course of the debate in detail because all four solutions are often combined in the propositions put forward by the assembly delegates and because Fr Lucas' diary, which is our source of information, contains phrases which are not very clear because his notes were brief and fragmentary. For this reason there have been different interpretations of what happened. The explanation we are about to offer comes after long and thoughtful analysis of the texts.[19]

One thing that is absolutely clear is that the delegates enjoyed complete freedom of speech throughout the assembly. As he had done in

---

[18] *S.V.P.* III, pp. 246-248, 378-383, 453-454.

[19] The diary of Fr Lucas is in *S.V.P.* XIII, pp. 333-336. The following pages are based on this, so I do not need to give detailed references for all the statements.

1642, Vincent came before his sons as an equal, without trying to impose his opinion which was well known right from the start. During the evening session of the first day he outlined the arguments in favour of each of the solutions mentioned in the opening address.

He gave the following reasons for retaining the vows:

> Fr Condren disagrees with St Thomas and it is his opinion that Our Lord took vows; taking vows is a very ancient and holy practice in the Church and even in the synagogue; vows are a very pleasing holocaust to God who is offered both the tree and its fruits; actions performed in virtue of the vow are more meritorious and individuals who, left to themselves are as unstable as water, are strengthened in their good intentions; the company will be more perfect and its subjects will be more available for distant or difficult missions.

Then he gave the reasons for discontinuing the vows:

> Quite a few congregations such as the Oratory in Rome, St Nicolas and St Sulpice in France, flourish and do good works even though their members do not take vows. Many members of the company are strongly opposed to taking vows. There is more freedom without vows, and more merit. Without vows we are more like the clergy to whose ranks we belong. Ecclesiastics will have more confidence in us and feel more at ease. The bishops will have no reason to be suspicious. All our difficulties will vanish.
>
> As for the proposal to omit those aspects of the vows which cause most difficulty, such as dispensation being reserved to the pope and the superior general, the only reason advanced for this is that the bishops would retain their authority over the missionaries.
>
> The fourth solution—that we find some other way of retaining the vows—really means that we should ask the Holy See to approve them. This course of action is based on the following reasoning: there is some doubt about the validity of our present vows even though the archbishop of Paris believes he had the authority to approve them and he is supported in this by his council and some of the theologians, although other theologians disagree. If we were to send to Rome a missioner who could devote all his time exclusively to this project then we would be successful, because everything can be settled in

Rome given time and patience. Our present difficulties will eventually disappear because our decision was only taken after lengthy consideration and much prayer.

On the following day, Sunday 2 July, there was a brief summary of what had been said the previous day, Vincent taking the opportunity to complete some ideas, and then the debate reopened.

The second and third days were devoted to studying the first two options: the preservation or the discontinuance of the vows. Straightaway three different viewpoints emerged. Frs Grimal, Thibault, Gilles, Becu and Le Gros declared themselves in favour of keeping the vows as they were; Frs Dehorgny, Alméras, Lambert and Cuissot were against the principle of taking vows, and a compromise solution with some minor changes was proposed by Blatiron, Portail and du Chesne.

The strongest argument for retaining the vows was put forward by Fr Gilles. Among other things, he said,

> The company cannot exist without vows. So everyone should be obliged to take vows at the end of the two years of seminary. However, we should not pressurise older members into taking vows as this might lead them to criticise the practice. Neither should there be any recriminations against those who choose not to take vows.

The strongest case against taking vows was put forward, strangely enough, by one of Vincent's most faithful friends, Fr Alméras. His juridical training led him to reject them. As they stand the vows are invalid, he argued, and they were not acceptable to Popes Urban VIII and Innocent X. At this point, Vincent interrupted him to say he had instructed Fr Lebreton to ask for religious vows, not vows as they were then practised by the company. Fr Alméras continued his speech. The vows are invalid because the powers delegated to the archbishop of Paris in the bull *Salvatori nostri* were of a very general nature and did not cover such specific areas as the vows, which required special authorisation. Moreover, he doubted very much whether they should be taking vows, since the practice caused so many difficulties within the community and outside of it; they were an obstacle for new members of the community and, finally, if they took vows they would be religious.

He then gave the counter-arguments. It would be said that theirs was an arduous ministry which required the strength given by the vows. He would answer that people did not work any less hard if they did not take vows or that those who did take vows did not necessarily work harder; the Capuchins, for example, cannot find anybody willing to go to Picardy. The superior's decision would be accepted with regard to mission as much as in other matters, and his firmness would serve just as well as compliance with a vow. Anything else would show a want of confidence in God. It might also be argued that discontinuing the vows would involve change. But change is sometimes a good thing as M. Vincent has shown by reforming the liturgy. Finally, it has been said that taking vows is the more perfect course of action. It is also more perfect to embrace the religious state and yet Rome puts so many obstacles in the way of those who wish to do this.

The third position was defended by Blatiron and du Chesne. The main point that they made was that vows should be optional. Blatiron favoured the Jesuit system where some members took vows and other did not. His reason for wanting vows to be optional was that he had been superior at Genoa and knew from experience that there was great opposition in Italy, both to the custom of taking vows and to the religious state itself. Du Chesne was in favour of complete freedom in this matter for then there would be no need to petition Rome.

The third day closed with a brief address given by Vincent who gave a spiritual dimension to all the points discussed.

> We must pray earnestly to know what is God's will for the company and how we can put an end to whatever causes divisions in it. Let us continue to study this question until we get a greater consensus of opinion.

'Most of us are in favour of taking vows'

On the fourth day the debate entered a new phase. Once again Vincent opened the proceedings to clarify some points concerning the real nature of the problem, which turned on the question as to whether or not the company would become a religious order if its members took vows. Basing his remarks on the bull *Ascendente Domino* he argued as follows;

> For a community to be constituted a religious order because its members take vows, these vows would have to be made within an approved religious order. Well since the Council of Lyons and the Lateran Council in Pope Innocent III's time, it has been forbidden under pain of nullity to found new religious orders unless these followed one of the four approved monastic rules. The popes and the council of Trent have made an exception only in the case of the Jesuits. The Congregation of the Mission does not come into this category. Therefore it is not a religious order.

Having clarified this point, he went on to dismiss some of the objections brought forward on previous days:

> Nobody is obliged to take vows if he does not enter the community, just as no woman is obliged to marry and no widow is obliged to enter a community founded for widows. But if they do marry or join a community they must fulfil the duties of their state. To discontinue the vows is a backward step. It is not easy to revoke a law once it is established practice. As for it being a good idea to adapt ourselves to what people around us think, you have to remember that one cannot please everybody. It is like the tale of the father and his son who go off on a journey with their donkey. No matter what they did they always found somebody ready to criticise.

Then he opened the debate on the third point which was whether or not it would be right to restrict to the pope and the superior general, the right to dispense from the vows.

Once again there were differences of opinion although the positions taken were somewhat different from those of the previous debate.

Becu and Thibault were in favour of retaining the vows but against the reservation clause. Blatiron, as might be expected from his ideas on freedom of choice, was also against the reservation:

> If we were to take vows it would make people think we were religious and this is particularly so in Italy so we would not be well received there. We would find it hard to get any priests to join us. We are the bishop's coadjutors. If the bishops had to select from religious orders they would choose more learned men like the Jesuits. If the vows are going to be reserved then it is better not to take them at all. We could restore unity in the community by authorising those who wish to take vows to do so and by not allowing dispensations. This would make it easier for us to have the vows approved.

The trio who supported the vows, Grimal, Gilles and Le Gros, were also in favour of the reservation, Grimal because 'some bond is essential', and Le Gros because he saw the company as an edifice whose foundations were the rules and the vows: 'If we cannot do without the first, then we cannot do without the second either.'

As on the previous occasion it was Fr Gilles who delivered the *tour de force*.

'I have a horror,' he said, 'of altering any resolution taken at a general assembly. Does not the Holy Spirit guide these assemblies? Then where is this guidance? All these changes are very disturbing. As for myself, it was the vows that kept me in the community when I had a young fellow of 25 as my superior. If we change things now we will be shillyshallying again at the next assembly and this is very bad for the company. *Omnis mutatio morbus* (all change is weakness) says Aristotle. You cannot change from hot to cold. A statesman once remarked to me one day, "It is easy to change one's state in life but I would rather die five deaths than change." And an Oratorian admitted to me, "The Oratory is just a respectable lodging house."'

> We are very different from the Jesuits. Their vows are made within a recognised religious community as we know from the bull *Ascendente Domino*. Not even the lay brothers retain their right of inheritance. Their fourth vow is a solemn one. The houses of professed religious are not allowed to own goods. They are exempt from the ordinary. Those who leave are excommunicated and regarded as apostates, the only future open to them is to join the Carthusians. They make various vows and promises. Their ministries and habits are very different from ours.

> Most of us are in favour of having vows. There is nobody in the company who is not prepared to take them. So what, if the Italians do not like them? The daughter should follow the mother, not the mother follow her daughter! It is not morally sound to follow the opinion of one single theologian ... I have read that there is not a single opinion, no matter how stupid it might be, that has not been defended by some learned man. I would rather leave the company than see the vows discontinued. I do not think there is anything to discuss on this question.

'Our Lord wishes us to take them'

With Gilles' speech, matters seemed to be at an impasse and yet this opened the way to a compromise solution. This was the fourth suggestion, put forward by Vincent, that they should have recourse to Rome.

This was acceptable to those in favour of the vows and to those who opposed them. In the previous debate this had been suggested as the only solution by Dehorgny, Portail and Lambert. Alméras, who was so much against the current practice of taking vows, agreed with them. Really, the question under discussion was not so much whether they should take vows or not, but rather the question of whether the community should continue in that state of uncertainty in which it found itself because of the doubtful validity of episcopal approval for their vows. Fr Lambert put the position very clearly 'It is good to take vows but we need to consult Rome.'

Vincent, who had kept silent throughout this long discussion, closed the proceedings with a speech in which he defended the vows.

Our Lord wishes us to take vows. As soon as I can I will send somebody to Rome for the sole purpose of negotiating this.

They had come to a unanimous decision, something which had seemed impossible at first. Vincent was satisfied. He had saved the vows and the juridical structure would afford them more importance than previously.

There now remained just one practical matter that caused anxiety to the assembly delegates—how were they to reply to anyone who asked them about their vows? On 20 July when the assembly had been debating other matters for a fortnight, this question was put in writing and they asked for an answer. Vincent gave his reply in a long and vigorous speech which showed very clearly his thinking on the subject.

'Let us make a distinction', he said, 'between two sets of people, those for whom our vows are none of their business and important people who require us to give them a satisfactory answer. To the former we need only reply that we take simple vows. Our answer to the others should be this: first of all our vows bind us to God, and secondly they bind the members to the company. Because of the vows there is no difficulty about sending a man to a seminary 50 leagues away, or to the Indies or to any other place. Thirdly, the vows make us more like Christ and more fit to carry out our ministries. Fourthly, they make for greater equality among us and are a bond of unity between individuals.'

He then went on to review the most frequently voiced objections to the vows.

First. The vows diminish the bishops' authority. Answer: A bishop's authority can be undermined in two ways, by refusing him the right to exercise some of his powers like administering confirmation or absolving from heresy and this is something the pope might do, or by removing people from his jurisdiction.

Jurisdiction is meant for subjects, not for prelates. If I remove myself from a bishop's jurisdiction by leaving his diocese I deny him the power he used to have over me but I do not do him any wrong. It is the same with the vows.

Second objection. The pope has not approved the vows. Answer: He would have done so if he had been informed about the matter at the start. A superior who destines somebody for a particular task must provide him with the necessary means to fulfil it. Besides, we do have papal approval though indirectly. The archbishop of Paris was commissioned by the pope and he studied the question for three years. He raised many difficulties but ended up saying he thought the vows were necessary. So I do not think we really need to go to Rome, but we will do.

Third objection. Missioners take vows that will have to be discontinued later on when the rules are modified. Answer: The Jesuits did this. But that is not the point. We do not vow to keep the rules, but in accordance with the rules, we promise to observe the vows.

Fourth objection: What sort of poverty do we practise? Answer: the canons of St Augustine take a vow of poverty and yet they can have parishes and hold the position of canon. The knights of Malta can have lands and revenues in spite of their poverty.

Fifth objection: We had no authority to establish this rule. Answer: We have the power to make rules about anything provided it is lawful, worthy and not contrary to canon law. The rule concerning our vows fulfils these conditions.

The conclusion was a practical one and took the form of an injunction; 'Gentlemen, we must all defend the vows.'

'They all agreed'

The matter was settled once and for all. The assembly minutes which made no mention of the vicissitudes of the debate, simply recorded the conclusion that was reached.

Everybody at the assembly agreed that the vows should be retained. To make these more authentic it was agreed that papal approval for them be sought without delay.[20]

---

[20] The official minutes of the Assembly are in *S.V.P.* XIII, pp. 326-332.

In compliance with the assembly's decision they immediately began negotiations with the Holy See, or, to be more accurate, they immediately resumed them. Meanwhile Vincent went a step further. They had to ask the archbishop of Paris to approve the rules and the assembly did this in the form of a document written in Latin and dated 11 August 1651,[21] the day that the assembly closed. Vincent used this occasion to obtain new approval, specifically for the vows, which was something the assembly had not requested. In the episcopal letters approving the rules and constitutions as a whole, there was a paragraph devoted *ex profeso* to the vows. No doubt Vincent thought that this new approval by the archbishop would put pressure on Rome. But there was an important difference between the approbation granted in 1641 and that of 1653, and this may have been the reason for Vincent's petition. In the first document, although the archbishop mentioned the authority delegated to him by the Holy See, he had approved the vows as a personal concession, *de nostra gratia*. In the new form of approbation the archbishop, who was doubtless aware of the arguments concerning the validity of the vows, had it stated that he gave them his approval in virtue of apostolic authority.

> And insofar as it may be necessary, we approve and confirm
> anew, with the same apostolic authority, the rule or ordinance
> contained in the said rules and constitutions promulgated by
> you ... twelve years ago and then approved and confirmed by
> us, concerning the simple vows taken in the congregation.[22]

This was on the 23 August 1653. Vincent had just won his second victory and with it ended the second stage in the development of the juridical statute concerning the vows.

'We had to have recourse to the oracle of God's will'

The third stage lasts from 1653 to 1660 and so goes beyond the limits of this section of the book. In order to avoid repetition, and so as not to lose the thread of the story, we will give its history now.

The first priest to take charge of negotiations with the Roman curia was Fr Thomas Berthe, who began the work early in 1653.[23] At this time Berthe was a young priest, thirty-one years old, very virtuous and highly

---

[21] *S.V.P.* XIII, pp. 357-359.

[22] Codex Sarzana, p. 116; COPPO, *La prima stesura* ..., p. 224.

[23] *S.V.P.* IV, p. 541.

intelligent.[24] Vincent thought so much of him that he suggested him, as well as Alméras, as his possible successor.[25] Berthe did the negotiating himself but long and detailed letters from Vincent instructed him on methods of procedure, the arguments to be put forward and the tactics to follow when dealing with distinguished personages in Rome. Progress was slow; partly because there was fierce opposition in Rome to the religious state of life so that Vincent had to keep on repeating that the missioners were not religious, but secular priests,[26] and partly because Vincent himself was slow to finalise the petition they were going to present. He was still working on it in October 1654.[27] It had to be completed by the end of the year. The petition contained a very long and erudite explanation that the vows in question would in no way make the congregation into a religious order and that the missioners were not asking for or claiming this; in fact they were deliberately avoiding this term.[28]

Berthe's negotiating skills meant that the affair was making good progress until an unpleasant episode, which we will recount later, put paid to all his efforts. In February 1655, the king of France (or rather Mazarin) was angry because the missioners had given shelter in Rome to Cardinal de Retz, and the French missioners were obliged to leave the Eternal City. Berthe had to leave in a hurry, having first taken the precaution of leaving all the papers connected with the congregation locked in a sealed chest in the house of the Benedictine Fr Placido which he decided would be the safest place for them.[29]

To add to these difficult circumstances there came another incident which was quite disturbing. The superior at Genoa, Fr Blatiron, who had put forward in the 1651 assembly the original suggestion that vows should only be taken by those appointed to positions of government, was imprudent enough to mention his ideas to the archbishop of Genoa, Cardinal Durazzo, who thought highly of him. Vincent was very alarmed at the influence the

---

[24] *S.V.P.* II, p. 532; III, p. 117. With regard to Thomas Berthe, *cf. Notices* II, p. 247ff.

[25] *S.V.P.* XIII, pp. 410-412.

[26] *S.V.P.* IV, pp. 578-589.

[27] *S.V.P.* V, pp. 204-205.

[28] *S.V.P.* XIII, pp. 365-370. This document published by Coste has the translated title 'A study of the Vows taken in the Congregation of the Mission and the privilege of exemption', and is probably the first part of the petition that Fr Berthe presented to the Sacred Congregation of Bishops and Regular Clergy. Coste put the date of this between 1653 and 1655 on the basis of his belief that the document from the archbishop of Paris granting approbation was dated 23 August 1653. Bearing in mind what has been said in a previous note, we can reduce the time margin because it must have been dated later than 9 October 1654.

[29] *S.V.P.* V, pp. 272 and 275.

cardinal might have now that Berthe was not on the scene. Blatiron was temporarily in charge of the negotiations. To repair the damage Vincent wrote a long letter to the superior at Genoa stating once more the arguments in favour of having vows and demolishing one by one the objections put forward by Blatiron.[30]

'Even if they were to tear my eyes out'

A further threat to the vows being approved came from outside the company, in the shape of opposition from certain important people, especially the Oratorian Fathers. The spiritual sons of de Bérulle were once again in conflict with Vincent. His reaction to this hostility was, if possible, even more heroic than in 1632. At least he expressed his feelings more strongly. This is not surprising considering that Vincent had not ceased to make progress from that time onwards in living out the evangelical counsels.

> 'As I see it', he wrote, 'we continue to meet with difficulties, but we cannot expect anything else since you have to deal with such a cardinal and such an important institution. This would not prevent me from honouring and loving them with the affection that children have for their parents, even if they were to tear my eyes out. I desire and beg of Our Lord that everyone in our congregation should share these dispositions. Do not stop urging our case, Father, and be confident that this is God's will for he sometimes allows contradictions to arise among the saints and even among the angels, not revealing the same things to each.'[31]

'It has pleased God and the pope to approve our vows'

Victory was in sight. The death of Innocent X and the election of his successor, Cardinal Chigi, as Alexander VII in April 1655 gave a favourable twist to the situation. It was not going to be all stalemate. Blatiron was replaced by a new negotiator, Fr Edmund Jolly, who knew the ins and outs of the Roman curia through having worked in the apostolic secretariat before entering the

---

[30] *S.V.P.* V, pp. 315-323.
[31] *S.V.P.* V, pp. 395-396.

congregation.[32] He continued Berthe's work.[33] His negotiations were very successful and he attributed this to God's special protection and that of the Blessed Virgin.[34] The new pope, whom Vincent had hastened to congratulate on his election,[35] published the brief, *Ex commissa nobis,* which accorded papal approval to the vows of the Congregation of the Mission under the same conditions, and even using the same terms, as Vincent had been describing them from 1641 onwards: simple and perpetual vows which could be dispensed by the sovereign pontiff and the superior general of the congregation, vows that did not designate the company a religious order but allowed its members to remain part of the secular clergy. As a bonus, the brief accorded the Congregation of the Mission exemption from the ordinary.[36]

The brief was a great consolation for Vincent. Exactly a month after its publication he gave the news to Fr Blatiron in these words:

> As regards the vows—it has finally pleased God and our Holy
> Father the Pope to approve the ones we take. We have offered
> this brief to Our Lord since it is the work of his hands.[37]

On that same day, during a ceremony held at St Lazare, and one that was to be repeated in all the other houses during the following months, the community formally accepted the brief[38] which was drawn up as a deed of notary.[39]

And on January 25, the missioners, with very few exceptions,[40] renewed their vows in accordance with the terms of the papal document.

There were still a few loose ends to be tied up. The main one concerned the scope of the vow of poverty. Vincent's thinking on this subject had changed considerably, partly through the complex nature of the question and partly because of the resistance he encountered. Vincent's original idea, which he set out clearly in the explanation he gave in 1641, was that

---

[32] *S.V.P.* IV, p. 231. Concerning Jolly *cf. Notices* ..., III, pp. 387-512.

[33] *S.V.P.* V, pp. 366-367, 384, 415.

[34] *S.V.P.* V, p. 474. As the negotiation were still entrusted to Fr Blatiron in July, Fr Jolly's efforts to have the vows approved lasted less than 3 months. The work must have been at an advanced stage when Fr Berthe handed it over.

[35] *S.V.P.* V, pp. 368-369.

[36] *S.V.P.* XIII, pp. 380-382.

[37] *S.V.P.* V, pp. 452-454.

[38] *S.V.P.* V, pp. 457-460, 501.

[39] *S.V.P.* V, p. 485; XIII, pp. 383-385.

[40] Men admitted into the congregation before 19 October 1641, were not obliged to take vows. We do not know the exact number of those who took advantage of this exemption. Coste based his list on the fact that some names were not included in the vow register. The absence of a name is not to be taken as conclusive evidence because some names do not appear in the register but we know from other sources that the individuals did take vows.

missioners, while retaining the right to inherit property, were obliged to give up the administration and income of these to the congregation and that if they left the company they would have no right to claim profits already received from them.[41]

Such a rule had an obvious ascetic and community value. Missioners who owned property were to act as though they were not owners by renouncing the administration, use and benefits of it. Private wealth was put at the disposal of all, thus establishing equality among all members of the community. It was right, thought Vincent, that those who had financial assets should help to support their brothers. This rule was still in force in 1651. During the assembly of that year Vincent repeated it in exactly the same words he had used when defining it ten years earlier.

There followed an exhaustive discussion which brought to light the many legal difficulties that might ensue. It was decided to consult a panel of experts.[42] These must have decided in favour of the text because the approbation given by the archbishop of Paris in August 1653 made no alterations whatsoever.

The first change came in 1656. The records of the collective taking of vows on 25 January of that year contain an explanatory note about poverty which shows a significant modification. The missioner must still renounce the administration and use of his personal wealth but he can now either give this right over to the community, as previously, or to his needy relatives. Vincent had given in to pressure. He was obliged to make even more concessions. So as to settle the obligations of the vow of poverty once and for all he went back to the Holy See, asking it to sanction the 'basic statute' of poverty for the missioners. The pope did this in a new brief, *Alias nos,* on 12 August 1659.[43]

The application of this newly approved statute differed considerably from the original one. From now on the missionaries would retain not only the ownership of their goods but also the administration of them, together with their accrued interest and benefits, but they were to use this income for works of charity and could not spend it on anything for themselves without permission from the superior.

Whether he liked it or not, the founder had bowed to the demands of many members of his community. He was flexible enough to give up his own point of view when essential values were not at stake.[44]

---

[41] Codex Sarzana, p. 41; COPPO. *La prima stesura* ..., p. 220 and pp. 242-245.

[42] *S.V.P.* XIII, pp. 350-352.

[43] *S.V.P.* XIII, pp. 406-409.

[44] New light has been shed on the way that the vow of poverty developed by the *Codex Sarzana* in Fr Angelo Coppo's *La prima stesura* ..., p. 242-245 and 'L'Évolution du voeu de pauvreté des prêtres de la Mission, jusqu'en 1659', *Vincentiana* 19 (1972), pp. 256-272.

Ideal and safeguard

The juridical structures of the Congregation of the Mission which had been tentatively mapped out in the 1625 contract, were definitively settled when final approval was granted to the rules and the vows. For thirty-five years Vincent had pursued his objective with great tenacity and we do not know which to admire most, the sureness of his intuition or the great patience with which he succeeded, in the teeth of all opposition, in seeing them take concrete shape in the juridical texts approved by the Church's supreme authority.

His efforts resulted in something that was entirely new: a congregation which belonged to the secular clergy and yet was exempt from the ordinary, and one that took vows. He had had his hesitations and his doubts but he never lost confidence that in the end his efforts would be rewarded. He had made concessions on minor points but had preserved the essentials. The final format was in keeping with the original plan; it had been developed and enriched with time but it had never been watered down or altered.

Perhaps the most original feature of Vincent's creation was the reconciling of two apparent opposites, the taking of vows and the secular nature of the institute.

Vincent's refusal to embrace the religious state never faltered. Was this a question of principle? We have no reason to think so from Vincent's writings. Was he afraid that religious structures might stifle the apostolic impetus of the company or weaken its charism? We have no documentary evidence to support such a claim.[45]

We will have to have recourse to other sources of information to decide this question. There is not the slightest doubt that Vincent held the religious life in high esteem. On more than one occasion he expressed regret at the suspicion and antagonism shown towards the religious state;[46] he often declared that he wished he had its spirit[47] and that he hoped to enjoy the reward promised to it.[48] St Chantal began to think it was Vincent's intention to combine the perfection of the ecclesiastical condition with that of the religious state of life, but he humbly protested that this was not so.[49] He was

---

[45] *Cf.* L. MEZZADRI, 'De la Misión a la Congregación de la Misión', *Anales* (1978), pp. 92-94.

[46] *S.V.P.* II, p. 28.

[47] *S.V.P.* II, pp.137-138.

[48] *S.V.P.* III p. 245.

[49] *S.V.P.* II, p. 100.

so determined to introduce vows into the company that at the most difficult point in the negotiations, in 1640, he was prepared to call it a religious congregation[50] and it appears he even went so far as to petition for religious vows.[51]

But these were extreme concessions which he made with great reluctance at a time when there seemed no other way out. In the event it proved to be a useless strategy because the difficulty they were encountering in having the vows approved came precisely from the fact that people thought taking vows would make the congregation into a religious order.

Apart from the temporary disparity we have just mentioned, the option to keep the Congregation of the Mission within the body of the secular clergy was a constant from the early years of the foundation[52] to the end of Vincent's life. There were both theoretical and practical reasons for this. The secular nature of the community was inherent from the very beginning, and the older missioners brandished this argument when they opposed the taking of vows: the vocation they had been called to was that of a secular priest.

There were other reasons at that particular time. Opposition to new religious orders was very strong in Rome, especially during the pontificate of Innocent X (1644-1655),[53] and opposition was even stronger in France where the bishops exerted a lot of pressure.[54] In 1645 they ordered the reprinting of the works of Petrus Aurelius (Saint-Cyran) who, in his polemics against the Jesuits and Benedictines, defended the eminent dignity of the priesthood as superior to the taking of vows which, according to him, were of human origin.[55] We should remember, too, that the first difficulties encountered in having the congregation approved by Rome, stemmed from the fact that it was considered to be a new religious order. And finally, we should remember the very unedifying spectacle presented by numerous religious orders at that particular moment in the history of the Church in France.

Vincent was unhappy about the hostility then being shown to the religious orders but he had to give way before it. However, he never gave up the idea of vows which had been part of the company's spiritual heritage

---

[50] *S.V.P.* II, p. 28.

[51] *S.V.P.* XIII, p. 338.

[52] *S.V.P.* V p. 458.

[53] *S.V.P.* III, p. 379; XIII, p. 339; IV, pp. 578-580.

[54] *S.V.P.* III, p. 246.

[55] J. ORCIBAL, *Saint-Cyran et le jansénisme*, p. 15-17; L.WILLAERT, *La restauración católica*, pp. 424-425.

right from the beginning.[56] The reason most frequently suggested for taking vows is that they help the individual to persevere in a difficult vocation which demands painful sacrifices.[57] But that is not the only reason. Vincentian spirituality with regard to the vows went beyond what was merely functional, and all through the years of controversy its development was perfectly coherent. Let us give a brief summary of this spirituality.

The initial inspiration to take vows sprang from a desire to be in the most perfect state possible and the wish to forge a bond with God and with the community.[58] The reasons given in the *ordinatio* of 1641 are that, besides the natural inconsistency of the human spirit, we can point to God's intervention in the Old Testament when he ordained circumcision and in the New Testament when he prescribed baptism; the example of the Church which only confers the priesthood on those who consecrate themselves to it for life, and the example of religious orders who always considered vows essential if members were to persevere in their vocation.[59] During the Assembly of 1651 Vincent argued that taking vows created bonds with God and with the community, that it was a way of imitating Christ; and that vows made all members of the company equal.[60] Four years later this same argument is presented in a letter to Fr Blatiron, and Vincent's reflections on the matter develop and give added weight to the reasoning. Vows are taken so that the company may be in the state which is most pleasing to God, namely that of perfection, and so that its members may strive more faithfully for personal sanctification and be drawn to give themselves completely to God in this way. On the other hand, opposition to the vows comes, not from the spirit, but from human nature which demands more and more freedom.[61]

It was Vincent's special genius that combined the secular nature of the company with the taking of vows. Or, as he would have said, the inspiration came from God.[62]

---

[56] *S.V.P.* V, pp. 319-320.

[57] *S.V.P.* III, pp. 379-380.

[58] *S.V.P.* V, p. 458. *Cf.* A. DODIN, 'Les voeux dans la spiritualité vincentienne', *M. et Ch.* 35-36 (1969), pp. 129-135.

[59] *Codex Sarzana*, pp. 39-41; COPPO, *La prima stesura ...*, pp. 219-220; *S.V.P.* XIII, pp. 283-286.

[60] *S.V.P.* XIII, p. 354.

[61] *S.V.P.* V, pp. 315-323.

[62] *S.V.P.* III, p. 246.

Chapter XXII
THE COMPANY IN ACTION: MISSIONS AND RETREATS

'Our main work is the instruction of poor country people'

Vincent and his collaborators were preoccupied with settling juridical structures but this in no way slowed down the day to day working of the congregation. These were complementary tasks. Legislation was defining ever more clearly the nature of the company and the spirit in which its works were to be undertaken; while structures were influenced by the demands of work and of life style.

From the outset, the main work of the congregation was to preach missions to poor peasants and this would always continue to have priority. There are very many statements in Vincent's writings to this effect. Let us be content with just one:

'Our main work is the instruction of poor country people.'[1]

It is true that this sentence is quoted from a letter written in 1650 to the bishop of Périgueux, who wanted Vincent to send just two missioners to take charge of his diocesan seminary so there would be no possibility of preaching missions. This was completely contrary to Vincent's practice of not sanctioning one work without the other.[2] An exception was made at Cahors only because of special circumstances.[3] The general tenor of Vincent's statement gives absolute and unconditional priority to this work. He was less categorical, however, with regard to the rule about not preaching in cities. For several years Vincent had interpreted this prohibition in the broad sense of taking it to refer simply to preaching, not to giving missions.

---

[1] *S.V.P.* IV, p. 42.
[2] *S.V.P.* II, p. 460; V, p. 252.
[3] *S.V.P.* IV, p. 43.

> When we decided, at the beginning of our foundation, that we
> would not work in towns that had a bishop, we meant that we
> would not preach or hear confessions because other orders
> were doing this in their religious houses or churches; we had
> no intention of abandoning our work of giving missions there.[4]

After 1651, when the rules were drawn up, this prohibition was
adhered to more strictly and only two exceptions were allowed: missioners
would preach if ordered to do so by the bishops,[5] or when poor peasants
came to take refuge in the towns because, in line with the laws on inheritance,
it is lawful to take possession of one's goods wherever they are found.[6] In
fact, Vincent preached several missions in Paris, including one in the church
of St Lazare itself, for the peasants who had fled to the capital during the
Fronde.[7]

'Would that everyone would prophesy!'

The Congregation of the Mission was not the only religious community
dedicated to the work of preaching missions. However original Vincent's
ideas may have been, and whatever the priority he gave to using missions as
a means of renewal for the ordinary people, his work must be judged within
the context of a general movement for reform or renewal; a movement that
had the backing of many famous names, St Peter Fourier (1565-1640) in
Lorraine, St John Eudes (1601-1680) in Normandy, the Jesuit, St John Francis
Regis (1597-1640), in the regions of Vivarois and Velay, Christophe Authier
de Sisgau (1608-1667) in Provence, Michel Le Nobletz (1577-1652) and
Julien Maunoir (1606-1683) in Brittany, Jean Jacques Olier (1608-1657) in
Paris. All these men were Vincent's contemporaries and shared his work of
animating religious communities dedicated wholly, or in part, to preaching
missions. Some of these communities, like those of Olier and St John Eudes,
also did similar work to that of the Congregation of the Mission in directing
seminaries. It would be impossible to establish a league table of merit from
among so many noble minds. But there is no doubt that Vincent was the first
to start this work. When he conceived the idea of founding the Mission in
1617, John Eudes was still studying humanities with the Jesuits at Caen;

---

[4]   *S.V.P.* II, p. 275. For information about missions that were preached in other places at this
time pp. 76, 367, 369. These texts date from the years 1640-1643.

[5]   *S.V.P.* IV, p. 373; V, p. 605; VI, pp. 329, 630; VII, pp. 86, 92. All these texts are later than
1651.

[6]   *S.V.P.* IV, p. 398.

[7]   *S.V.P.* IV, pp. 405-406.

Jean François Regis was a novice, and neither Olier nor Authier de Sisgau had reached the age of ten. As for Le Nobletz and Fourier, their work was confined to less developed regions and were not really part of the over-all movement within the Church in France.

It became fashionable to preach missions and Vincent was aware of this.[8] A whole host of new foundations seemed to be stirring up the Church in France: Blessed Sacrament Missionaries in Marseilles, Missionaries of St Joseph at Lyons, Missionaries of Forez, Missionaries to the Indies ... Several bishops started up their own missionary endeavours, in more or less open imitation of M. Vincent's work and style. Vincent reacted in a completely disinterested way. He even went against some of his own priests who were afraid of competition and he respected, and insisted that his congregation respect, the works of other communities and the action of the Holy Spirit even if this was not to his advantage.

> 'It would be better to have a hundred mission projects even if these proved prejudicial to our institute, than to hinder the working of even one of them on the pretext that we have to maintain our own works[9] ... 'We should want everyone to prophesy and the number of those who work to spread the gospel to multiply. No matter how many labourers there are in God's Church we will never be without work if we keep faithful to him.'[10]

The only area in which he defended the rights of the congregation was the matter of its title, which he insisted was exclusive, because experience had taught him that where communities had the same name there could be disagreeable misunderstandings.[11] Otherwise, his relationships with other apostolic workers were very cordial. In 1635 his missioners were working close to the region where St Francis Régis was operating. Neither congregation showed any sign of envy or jealousy.[12] On more than one

---

[8] *S.V.P.* VI, pp. 307, 399. For a comprehensive study of the seventeenth century missionary movement in France, 'Missionnaires catholiques à l'intérieur de la France pendant le XVII siècle', XVII *Siècle* 41 (1958), pp. 300-395. Cf. in particular R. CHALUMEAU, *Saint Vincent de Paul et les missions en France au XVII siècle,* pp. 317-327; *id.,* 'San Vicente de Paúl y las misiones' in *Vicente de Paúl, evangelizador de los pobres* (Salamanca, CEME, 1973). For the missions in the diocese of Paris, J. FERTE, *La vie religieuse dans les campagnes parisiennes (1622-1695)* (Paris, Vrin, 1962), pp. 196-223.

[9] *S.V.P.* IV, p. 348.

[10] *S.V.P.* IV, p. 363; see also IV, p. 399; VII, p. 468; VIII, pp. 189, 308.

[11] *S.V.P.* II, p. 423; III, p. 356; IV, pp. 56, 293-296, 338; VI, pp. 118, 349, 498-502.

[12] COLLET, *op. cit.*, Vol. 1, p. 248.

occasion Vincent spoke highly of St John Eudes[13] and in spite of some differences of opinion and differences in procedure, he did all in his power to help the holy founder from Normandy to have his communities approved (something that the Oratorians were opposing),and to establish them in Paris at the 'Hospital of the Three Hundred' where he had been offered the chaplaincy.[14] There were several attempts to amalgamate the community of Authier de Sisgau with that of the Congregation of the Mission but nothing came of them.[15]

'I would be offending God if I did not do everything possible for the peasants'

The rural areas of France were sufficiently vast to provide work for as many people as seriously wanted to transform them spiritually. The work done by Vincent and his missioners was on a colossal scale. The total number of missions preached in France by the Congregation of the Mission during the lifetime of its founder cannot be established, since the information we have available is incomplete. The house of Saint Lazare, alone, gave more than 700 missions between 1632 and 1660, and when this is added to the 140 given from the Bons Enfants between 1625 and 1632, it brings the total to 840.[16] Most of these were preached in the diocese of Paris and its immediate surroundings. Vincent took an active part in most of them, especially during the early years. Then, as he had to take on more responsibilities and as his physical health began to fail, he had to withdraw very unwillingly from mission work among the peasants. However, right to the end of his life, he ardently desired to have direct contact with, what for him, was his essential vocation, and he continued to work as long as he possibly could.[17] He worked in 1637 in the mission at Joigny. In 1647, when he was 66 years old, he preached a mission at Moüi, in the diocese of Beauvais,[18] and again in 1653 when he was 72, he took part in the missions given at Rueil and Sévran.[19] These are just random dates that tell us something about his activities. These must have been many, since the Duchess d'Aiguillon, who was always anxious about

---

[13] COLLET, *op. cit.*, Vol. 2, pp. 31-32; *S.V.P.* VIII, p. 308, 309.
[14] CH. BERTHELOT DU CHESNAY, 'Saint Vincent de Paul et Saint Jean Eudes', *M. et Ch.* 4 (October 1961), pp. 469-481.
[15] *S.V.P.* II, pp. 397, 415, 422.
[16] ABELLY, *op. cit.*, 1.2 c. 1, p. 21.
[17] *S.V.P.* I, p. 536.
[18] COLLET, *op. cit.*, Vol. 1, p. 424.
[19] COLLET, *op. cit.*, Vol. 2, p. 1; *S.V.P.* IV, pp. 584, 586-587, 589.

Vincent's health, took a hand in the affair. On 20 May 1653 she wrote a strong letter of protest to Fr Portail:

> I cannot help being astonished that Fr Portail and the other good priests of St Lazare should allow M. Vincent to go and work in country places in this heat, considering his age and the long hours he will have to spend out of doors in this great heat. I feel that his life is too precious and too valuable to the Church for him to squander it in this way.[20]

But Vincent regarded it as a serious obligation binding in conscience:

> I think that I would be offending God if I did not do everything possible for the peasants in this jubilee year.[21]

'The God of armies'

As it happened, the priests of St Lazare had to take part in another type of mission, something that had not been foreseen when any of the foundations were established.

For the third time in little more than a century, Paris was threatened, in 1636, by Spanish troops. Shortly after the French period of the Thirty Years War started, Cardinal Prince Ferdinand of Austria, the soldier brother of Philip IV, launched a fierce attack on northern France and routed the French army. He occupied Picardy and on August 5 took Corbie, about 60 kilometers from the capital. It was too late for troops to be rushed to the northern front from the other war zones of Savoy, Italy, Roussillon and the Basque country. The monarch, Louis XIII, and his minister, Richelieu, were jointly responsible for the defence and they mustered up a new army on the outskirts of the capital. Vincent witnessed these events:

> Paris is expecting to be besieged by the Spaniards who have entered Picardy and are laying waste to the region with a vast army whose vanguard has reached up to ten or twelve leagues from here. The people from the plains are fleeing to Paris and the people of Paris are so terrified that many of them are fleeing to other cities. The king, however, is trying to raise another

---

[20] *S.V.P.* IV, p. 586.
[21] *S.V.P., ibid.*

army to fight the Spaniards since his own troops are in action abroad or in the furthest corners of the realm. So it is here, in this very house, that soldiers are recruited and armed. Our cowshed, woodshed, all the halls and the cloister are full of weapons and the courtyards are packed with soldiers. Even today, the Feast of the Assumption, we have had no respite from this tumultuous din. The drum is beating again even though it is only seven o'clock in the morning and in just over a week 72 companies of soldiers have been organised. Well, in spite of all this, all the members of our congregation continue to make their retreat except for three or four who are going off to work in distant places, so that if the siege should happen, most of them will avoid the dangers such circumstances usually bring with them.[22]

Vincent's contribution to the war effort was not confined to lending his premises. A few days after writing this letter he had an order from Chancellor Séguier to send twenty priests to give a mission to the army. At that time there were only fifteen priests available at St Lazare (there were only twenty-nine altogether in the company) and these were immediately dispatched and allocated to different regiments. Vincent went in person to Senlis, where the king had set up his general headquarters, to offer the monarch the services of the congregation and to leave Fr du Coudray there as intermediary between the court and the missioners. On the spur of the moment, he drew up for the missioners a set of rules in which everything was provided for, the order of the day, community practices which were to keep as closely as possible to those of St Lazare, the ministry to soldiers and the spirit in which this was to be carried out. It is interesting to study the opening paragraphs of these rules which reflect the mixture of patriotism and religion which was prevalent at the time.

The priests of the Mission who are called to work with the army must remember that it is Our Lord who has called them to this holy work;

Firstly, to offer to God their prayers and sacrifices for the success of the king's good designs and the preservation of his army.

Secondly, To help those soldiers who are in a state of sin to be reconciled with God, and those who are in a state of grace

---

[22] *S.V.P.* I, p. 340.

to remain in this condition. And finally, to do everything possible to help the dying leave this world at peace with God.

With this in mind they shall have particular devotion to the name given to God in the Scriptures, 'God of armies' and to the sentiments of Our Lord who declared, 'I have not come to bring peace, but war' for the objective of war is to bring us peace'.[23]

The mission to the army lasted for six weeks and it was a huge success. By 20 September more than 4,000 soldiers had gone to confession and this was in addition to all the people from the places the army passed through, who also went to confession and communion. Once the mission was over, most of the priests returned to St Lazare; only a few of them were kept back a bit longer to serve as chaplains. One of these was Robert de Sergis who was appointed to the chancellor's personal retinue. For this reason, Vincent, remembering his days as chaplain to the de Gondis, sent him detailed instructions on how to fulfil his duties as chaplain to people of distinction. He warned de Sergis not to meddle in politics, or, as it was then called, 'affairs of State'.[24] In November the campaign ended with the French recapturing Corbie and all the missioners were allowed to return to St Lazare.

The other foundations emulated the house at St Lazare. Nearly a third of France was worked, inch by inch, by the Vincentian missioners. The Ile de France, Champagne, Lorraine, Artois, Picardy, Normandy, Brittany and Savoy were the regions that profited most. There were other missions in regions like Poitou, Saintonge, Provence and Gascony. This great wave of missionary endeavour had an even more widespread effect because, as we have seen, much of the missionary zeal in the seventeenth century was sparked off by Vincent.

'To help the poor find God'

They kept to the same mission techniques as those used in the early days: preaching in the morning, junior catechism just after midday, senior catechism or catechism for adults in the evening. All these emphasised the need to make a general confession and gave great importance to the explanation of

---

[23] ABELLY, *op. cit.*, 1.1, pp. 152-157. The regulation is found on pages 154-156 and it was repeated by Coste, *S.V.P.* XIII, pp. 279-281. See, too, *S.V.P.* I, p. 343-344, 347.

[24] *S.V.P.* I, pp. 351-356, 360-361.

basic doctrines, especially the mystery of the Trinity and of the Incarnation. In keeping with the theological ideas of his day, Vincent believed that nobody could be saved without explicit knowledge of these truths, or that, at the least, it would be highly dangerous to be ignorant of them, given the authority of the theologians who hold this.[25]

There were two types of missions preached in the seventeenth century: one was penitential in nature and the other was catechetical. Vincent's missions belonged to the second category and this was highlighted when he said:

> Everyone agrees that the success of a mission is due to the catechism classes.[26]

The ultimate aim was

> to help the poor to know God, to tell them about Jesus Christ, to say to them that the kingdom of God is at hand and that this kingdom is for the poor.[27]
> Knowledge of the great truths learnt during catechesis should lead people to frequent the sacraments, particularly confession and communion. They should be led to make a general confession which would put right any possible defects in previous confessions[28] and communions. Such were the most excellent means of honouring the central mysteries of the Trinity and the Incarnation.[29] The hope was that the mission would bring about the renewal of the whole parish and for that reason it went on until all had fulfilled their duties.[30] In other words, they were not to leave any village until all the people had been instructed in the things necessary for salvation and until each one had made a general confession.[31]

---

[25] *S.V.P.* I, p. 121; X, p. 336; XI, pp. 181, 382; XII, pp. 80-81.

[26] *S.V.P.* I, p. 429; cf. L. MEZZADRI, 'Le missioni popolari della Congregazione della Missione nello Stato della Chiesa' (1642-1700): *RSChI* (1979), p. 18ff.

[27] *S.V.P.* XII, p. 80.

[28] *S.V.P.* XIII, pp. 357-358.

[29] *'Common Rules'*, c. 10 art. 3.

[30] *S.V.P.* II, p. 151.

[31] *S.V.P.* I, p. 564.

'These fine discourses ... do not convert anybody'

The missions were directed to the poor, to poor country folk. Now most of the peasant population in the seventeenth century were illiterate. Even if they were not, they were not on the same cultural level as the middle class or the aristocracy.[32] They just did not have the necessary education to cope with the high-flown and subtle language used by the great preachers. At a time when the vogue was for a flowery, baroque style of oratory with its ponderous and affected phrases full of classical and literary allusions, Vincent advocated a simple and direct manner of speaking which the people would be able to understand. It was absolutely essential for Vincentian missioners to have a simple style of preaching. Vincent castigated the empty grandiloquence of famous orators with as much, or with more vigour, than Molière ridiculed the affected language of *Les Précieuses Ridicules*.

In this respect, too, Vincent belonged to a general movement in French culture which was to give rise to the classicism of the great century. We should not forget that the Académie Française was founded in Vincent's life-time and that among his contemporaries were Descartes (1596-1650), Corneille (1606-1684), Mansart (1598-1666), Poussin (1594-1665), Philippe de Champaigne (1602-1674), Le Nôtre (1613-1700), Le Vau (1612-1670) and Boileau (1636-1711).

So Vincent must be seen within the general context of a movement away from the Baroque. But in his own field, that of preaching, his style was original. His was a very individual style, so much so that this humble man almost considered himself as the author of the change in the French theatrical fashion of declaiming speeches, a phenomenon that came to the French stage following a new concept of drama and its presentation on stage:

> I have already said on other occasions, that Our Lord blesses those talks that are given in a simple down-to-earth style since he himself taught and preached in this way. Besides, since this is the most natural way of speaking, it is also easier to use than the other style which is more laboured. The people prefer it and take more profit from it. Would you believe me, Father, if I told you that even actors in the theatre have come to realise this and have changed their way of speaking; they do not declaim their lines in a high voice as they used to do. Now they moderate their voices as though they were speaking familiarly to their listeners.[33]

---

[32] R. MANDROU, *op. cit.*, pp. 74-106.
[33] *S.V.P.* VI, p. 378.

Vincent's disapproval of affectation in preaching was deeply rooted in his vocation to be an apostle to the peasants. These peasants had been abandoned and left in a state of ignorance, not only because there was a lack of good pastors, but also because they were not being offered the bread of the Word in a way that they could understand. All Vincent's work would have been jeopardised if his missioners had preached in the style that was then in fashion. In his eyes, this style was fundamentally flawed because it had no practical value whatsoever.

'It would be hard to find a single person who has been converted by many of these Advent and Lenten sermons. This is the case in Paris. What amendment of life has resulted from such eloquent preaching? Fathers, do you not see the great number of those who are converted? Oh, it would be very difficult to find even one![34] All these polished discourses normally appeal only to our lower nature. They may frighten people if they are preached in heaven knows what sort of voice, they might heat the blood or stir up desire but all this is in our lower nature; neither our reason nor our spirit is moved. And all responses of our lower nature are useless if our minds remain unconvinced; if there is no appeal to our reason then everything else will soon fade away and so that discourse will be useless.[35]

'The little method'

In contrast to this sterile eloquence Vincent introduced a form of preaching that was novel both in content and in style. He called it *la petite méthode*, which translated literally means 'the little method', though it really describes the humble but affectionate way Vincent speaks about all the things he has started. He dedicated several conferences and countless practical sessions to explaining the little method and giving his missioners practice in it.[36] While not wanting to suggest too many parallels, the conference of 20 August 1655 might be called 'the discourse on Vincent de Paul's method'

The little method was, more than anything else, a way of arranging the subject matter of a sermon so that it was reasoned, ordered and efficacious.

---

[34] *S.V.P.* XI, p. 270.
[35] *S.V.P.* XI, p. 286.
[36] *S.V.P.* I, p. 304; VIII, pp. 79, 80, 82; XI, pp. 256, 292; XII, pp. 289, 292, 295-297; XIII, p. 331.

If you follow this method you will first of all point out the reasons and motives that can lead a soul to detest sin and vice and to strive for virtue. But it is not enough for me to recognise how much I need to acquire a particular virtue if I do not know the nature of that virtue. I can certainly see that I have great need of it, and that this virtue is very important but, Father, I do not know what it is or how to acquire it. Wretch that I am, I just do not know. How can I practise this virtue unless you have the goodness to show me and to teach me what it basically consists of, how to practise it and what the results will be.

And so to the second point which will achieve all these results because, according to our method, as well as knowing the motives which would attract our hearts to virtue, we have to then understand what the practice of this virtue entails. Lift the veil and you will reveal this virtue in all its beauty and splendour and then, in a simple and natural way, you will show the meaning of this virtue and the practical actions that must follow, you must always go into detail.'

But 'quite frankly, do you think it is enough to tell somebody about the reasons for practising virtue and to show him what that virtue is, if you leave it at that and do not give him further help? I do not know, but to my mind more is needed. Also, if you leave things like that, and do not point out the means of putting into practice what you have taught, then I do not think you have achieved much ...' 'This would be a sham and you must not act in this way. On the contrary, you should point out to this person the way he can practise the virtue. This is the third stage of our method. Show him the way he can practise this virtue and he will be happy.'[37]

'To preach in the way that missioners do'

The little method was much more than just an outline which could vary according to the subject matter. It involved both style and language. It meant a return to the gospel way of preaching, to the style that Jesus himself used. The preacher used comparisons that his listeners would be familiar with, and he spoke in a normal tone of voice; he would address himself directly to his hearers and use language they could easily understand. Learned quotations

---

[37] *S.V.P.* XI, pp. 260-261.

from secular authors were anathema unless these were introduced to add weight to something in the gospel. The preacher was to be sparing in the use of allusions and he was to show respect for heretics who were never to be attacked, though the catholic truths they denied were to be explained. The first concern of such teaching was that it should be of practical value, that is to say, it should be directed to the conversion of souls and completely devoid of vainglory. According to Vincent the little method could be summed up in a single phrase, simplicity in preaching.

> O simplicity, how persuasive you are! Simplicity can convert everybody. Hurrah for simplicity and for the 'little method' which is, in fact, the most excellent method and one that brings more glory because it moves hearts more than all this speechifying which only irritates the listener.[38]

Vincent attached so much importance to using the little method that for three consecutive days he went down on his knees before a priest of the Mission whose style of preaching was very high-flown, begging him to preach humbly and simply in accordance with the little method. He could not persuade him to do this and Vincent was relieved when the conceited individual left the congregation.

> God's blessing was not with him; his preaching and his talks bore no fruit; all that mountain of words and sentences vanished like smoke.

Nicolas Sevin, the bishop of Sarlat, on the other hand, used to preach with admirable and moving simplicity, so much so that after one of his talks to the ordinands Vincent said to him:

> 'My Lord, you converted me today.'
> 'How is that, Father?'
> 'Well, everything you said was spoken so simply and plainly that I felt very moved and I could only praise God for it.'
>
> 'Father, I could, of course, speak in a more elegant style about loftier matters but if I did that I would feel I was offending God.'[39]

---

[38] *S.V.P.* XI, p. 286.
[39] *S.V.P.* XII, pp. 23-24; V, p. 572.

The new style of preaching gradually reached the pulpits, and the old style of fanciful rhetoric which was in such poor taste eventually disappeared. We know that there was a general movement in this direction and that preachers from different orders and congregations contributed to it, but Vincent was one of the pioneers. Within a few decades the style of preaching in France was transformed and Vincent himself recognised the part he had played in effecting this happy change.

'Nowadays, if a man wants to be known as a good preacher in all the churches in Paris and at court, this is the way he must preach, without any trace of affectation. And people will say of such a preacher, 'This man does wonders; he preaches just like a missioner, he preaches in the same way that a missioner does, like an apostle! Oh Saviour! And if the Lord had told me that everyone would end up preaching like this. I am certain that to preach in any other way is just play acting; it is preaching oneself, not preaching Christ. To preach in the way that missioners do! O Saviour, it was you who gave this small and lowly company the grace of being inspired to use a method that everyone now wants to follow.[40]

The success of the missions

At the close of every mission the priests would write a report which was read by Vincent and sometimes distributed to the members of the company, to everyone's edification. Most of these reports are now lost, but Abelly who was able to read them has kept a valuable anthology of the most edifying and noteworthy accounts of missions given.[41] But Abelly's account, which in common with many later versions that just repeated the story in different words, has the drawbacks common to many hagiographers: they lack a sense of history, give too much importance to what is edifying, and present facts out of context.

In spite of this, a careful study of the mission chronicles helps us to understand the religious and moral state of the people as well as the theological and pastoral thinking of the missioners.

With regard to the first point, the emphasis is on conversion of heretics and the correction of vices as a result of the mission. The main evils

---

[40] *S.V.P.* XI, p. 286.
[41] The accounts given by Abelly *op. cit.*, 1.2 c. 1, p. 29-45. I refer the reader to these pages as the over-all source of the information that follows.

of the time, though not necessarily in order of importance, were blasphemy, hatred and enmity, drunkenness, prostitution, concubinage and other sexual disorders, scandalous fashions and illicit pastimes. We may be somewhat surprised at the severity with which missioners condemned pastimes which, to our way of thinking, would appear quite innocent. On the other hand, there is rarely any mention of Sunday not being observed, or the breaking of other commandments of the Church. At this time society was officially Christian, so everyone practised his religion, though on more than one occasion this gave rise to serious abuses and to sacrilegious reception of the sacraments.

The missioners had two basic criteria for judging the success of a mission: the number of people who attended, and the number of general confessions heard. Other factors which were less easy to assess would be the people's devotion, as shown by the warm way they welcomed the missioners and bade them farewell, and in the spectacular demonstrations, that sometime occurred.

It would be a waste of time to search the reports for the root causes of these prevailing vices, for instance the question of marriage dowries which in many cases led to concubinage; the inadequate and irregular administration of justice which might explain the common occurrence of personal vengeance and the frequency of lawsuits; or the low level of culture which meant that drink was the only way of relieving long periods of boredom. In the missioners' eyes, everything boiled down to an attraction towards sin or the life of grace and, basically, to religious ignorance which was why the main emphasis of a mission was on catechising.

At any rate it is instructive and entertaining to read the accounts that Abelly has preserved. All of them repeat cases of heretics returning to the bosom of the Church, of hardened sinners renouncing their evil ways, of restitution of ill-gotten goods, of the appeasement of hatred and enmity, of public scandals being ended and places of sin closed down, of reconciliations between married couples and concubinage being abandoned.

The people of the villages would come in a body to the mission services, dragging with them the people who lived close by. In the diocese of Toul there was a huge attendance in spite of there being two feet of snow. In a small town in Brittany the number of general confessions was more than three thousand. In another place, more than 500 penitents waited 10 days for their turn to go to confession and the bishop had to administer confirmation in the cemetery because the church was full of people going to communion. In the diocese of Sens, M. de Saint-Cyr saw the transformation in his vassals after the mission and thought that God had sent a new colony to people his village. It sometimes happened, at Joigny, that preaching began at two o'clock in the morning and yet the church was full. In Usseau, in Saintonge, it was the custom to organise a public dance on Pentecost evening. More than once this ended up with girls being raped and there were even cases of murder. The missioners preached very strongly against these abuses but to no avail; the dance went ahead as usual. When he got to know this, the director of the mission went to the place with some of his priests. The dancers fled when they saw them. In the church, next day, the missioner went into the pulpit and thundered against the scandal given. To make his point more strongly he brandished the fiddle which the musician had been playing at the dance and had left behind at the scene of the crime. A few minutes later he smashed it to pieces against the rail of the pulpit. This gesture made such a deep impression on the men and women who had been at the dance that they confessed their fault in public and went on their knees to ask pardon of the missioner.

In Mauron, Brittany, all the taverns were closed as a result of the mission. The preachers had said that it was very difficult for innkeepers to be saved because, as was the custom in that region, they gave the parishioners too much to drink.

Farewells provided a moving spectacle everywhere; the faithful shed bitter tears and cried out to the missioners, begging them not to leave.

'They cannot bear the light'

Even during Vincent de Paul's lifetime, mission work was not all glory. Some censorious persons voiced criticism which had some basis of fact. Jean de Gaufretau, the author of a chronicle in Bordeaux, dismissed the mission preached in that diocese by Frs de la Salle and Brunet as 'just a fire made from straw that burns brightly but lasts no time.'[42]

The most fierce attack came from the Abbé de Saint-Cyran and the Jansenists in general. During his trial, Saint-Cyran admitted that he had objected to the excessive detail in which Vincent's missioners explained the sixth commandment, and their readiness to judge that ignorant peasants had made a good confession if they confessed their sins by answering the priest's questions, without enough attention being paid to their interior dispositions.[43] This clearly indicates the harshness of Jansenist teaching although the wording is somewhat toned down owing to the difficult circumstances Saint-Cyran found himself in. The main point of contention was whether absolution should be given before the penance was performed and also, though this was not

---

[42] The text is in A. DODIN, 'Critiques des missions au temps de M. Vincent', *M. et Ch.* (1967), pp. 281-283.
[43] *S.V.P.* XIII, pp. 116-117.

explicitly stated, whether it was sufficient to have attrition for the valid reception of the sacrament of penance.

Saint-Cyran's followers went even further. In 1660 the great Arnauld replied to a question put by an Oratorian, Fr Le Jeune, and stated categorically that the fruits of the mission were very short-lived. He dismissed them as 'passing emotion' and very imperfect and 'sketchy conversion', not well evaluated by imprudent confessors, so that confession degenerated into a situation where absolution was given without any change in the penitent's life-style and this was followed by unworthy communions. He attributed all this to certain impressionable people being affected by the extraordinary event of a mission even though this was nothing more than 'seeing new people who seemed to be very zealous.'[44] In brief, a summer shower that was all show.

These criticisms, or at least some of them, reached Vincent's ears. Contrary to his usual practice, he defended his way of acting and, in particular, the writing of mission reports. Those who were opposed to this were

> discontented spirits who are not usually inclined to do good;
> they make such little effort themselves that they dismiss as
> exaggerated the recognition of other people's hard work. This
> manner of thinking leads them to complain because they are
> embarrassed by the situation. Their eyes are so blinded that
> they cannot bear to look at the light.[45]

Also, the work of reforming the clergy was justified by the need to keep alive the good effects of the missions.[46] Missioners should act like conquerors who leave garrisons in the territories they have occupied so as to ensure the peace and security of these possessions.

Even in the worst cases, reflected Collet, such criticism could not be directed against the missioners but rather against some lax people who made bad use of the missions; and, in short, would it not have been worse to leave these souls in the state they were in then, than to awaken in them, albeit for just a short time, the desire and hope of goodness?[47]

If we leave aside mere anecdotes, and consider missionary endeavour in general during the seventeenth century, we find that these produced far more lasting effects than their critics would have us believe. A very considerable proportion of rural districts in France were profoundly changed.

---

[44] COLLET, *op. cit.*, Vol. 2, pp. 335-338; DODIN, reference article.

[45] *S.V.P.* IV, p. 614.

[46] *S.V.P.* IV, p. 43.

[47] COLLET, *op. cit.*, Vol. 2, pp. 337-338.

The missioners succeeded in changing local customs, removing abuses, planting the faith deeply in souls, imparting a truer understanding of religion and educating the people.[48]

According to a contemporary historian, 'Sociological studies carried out in our times have shown that the areas of France which remain Christian in the twentieth century were precisely those where missioners laboured most zealously 300 years ago, while those areas that the missioners did not go to are sadly and noticeably different, and are marked in red by Canon Boulard on his famous map showing the practice of religion in France today. No greater homage could be paid to the missioners of the seventeenth century and to the sound intuition of the men who directed them.[49]

One of these men, the most famous of them all, was Vincent de Paul.

'The word 'retreat'

Vincent de Paul had less spectacular but perhaps more deeply rooted results from the work that went hand in hand with giving missions, namely retreats. From early years in the history of the company, retreats had been given in St Lazare and the practice later spread to other houses of the congregation.

Even before 1635, they had begun to admit into the old priory, devout people who wanted to make a spiritual retreat. The first person to avail of this opportunity was an old friend of Vincent's from the far distant days of the first mission at Villepreux, Jean Coqueret, a man who belonged to the same circle as Duval and who was a theologian from the College of Navarre. We have already mentioned this man as one of those who advised Vincent on the question of the vows and later on he would work with him during the controversy with the Jansenists. After Coqueret had made the retreat he sent his students to do the same.[50] One retreatant drew another and the work, like so many of Vincent's undertakings, seemed to grow of its own accord. The founder took this to be a sign that the work came from God.

When Vincent de Paul started the retreats he was continuing something that was already a well-established tradition in the Church. St Ignatius of Loyola had produced the definitive formula for retreats a century earlier. Vincent was happy to drink from this spiritual source, particularly as

---

[48] R. MANDROU, *op. cit.*, pp. 94-96.
[49] DANIEL-ROPS, 'La Iglesia de los tiempos clásicos. El gran siglo de las almas', p. 107.
[50] *S.V.P.* XII, p. 437.

these retreats were approved by the highest authority in the Church. A brief note in Vincent's own handwriting gives us his definition of a retreat and Abelly has copied this out. It reads as follows:

> 'We understand the term 'spiritual retreat' or 'spiritual exercises' to mean the leaving aside of all worldly occupations and business with the object of seriously applying oneself to becoming deeply aware of one's spiritual state, examining one's conscience, meditating, contemplating and praying, and thus preparing the soul to purify itself of all its sins, evil inclinations and bad habits, and to be filled with the desire of acquiring virtues; of seeking and finding the divine will, and once this is known, of submitting to it, moulding oneself to it, and in this way to tend towards, to advance in, and finally, to achieve one's own perfection.'[51]

You only need to compare the work of the two men to realise just how much Vincent was indebted to St Ignatius for his *Spiritual Exercises*.[52] As did St Ignatius, Vincent considered the main objective of a retreat was to discover one's personal vocation and make a commitment to it.

> To be a perfect Christian and attain perfection in one's state in life; to be a perfect student if one is a student, a perfect soldier if one is a soldier, a perfect judge if one belongs to the judiciary, a perfect ecclesiastic like St Charles Borromeo if one is a priest.' In a word, 'to become perfect in one's vocation or to decide the way of life to which one is being called.[53]

'Noah's Ark'

Vincent's originality and his claim to distinction lay in the fact that he made

---

[51] This note is given by ABELLY (*op. cit.*, 1.2 c. 4, p. 270) and is reproduced in the text of *S.V.P.* XIII, p. 143-144.

[52] 'The expression *'spiritual exercises'* is understood to mean all the different ways of examining one's conscience and the different forms of mental and vocal prayer and other spiritual exercises as we will discuss later on. Because just as walking and running are physical exercises, in the same way, everything that prepares and disposes the soul to rid itself of all disorderly affections and then to seek and find God's will for one's state in life and the salvation of one's soul, is called spiritual exercises.' (IGNACIO DE LOYOLA, *Ejercicios espirituales* [Barcelona 1936], pp. 13-14)

[53] *S.V.P.* XII, pp. 441-442.

retreats a common practice and something that was accessible to all sorts of people. St Lazare, and in so far as they could, the other houses of the company, opened their doors to as many people who wished to withdraw there to make a retreat. 'Within a few months,' says Collet, 'the house at St Lazare received more visitors than it had previously done in a century'. Vincent himself compared it to Noah's Ark which welcomed all sorts of creatures, great and small.[54] In the former monastery's old refectory you could meet people of every type and condition: 'rich and poor, young and old, theologians, priests, clerics with benefices, prelates, noblemen, counts, marquises, procurators, lawyers, councillors, presidents, officials from the parlement or the justiciary, merchants, artisans, soldiers, pages and lackeys.'[55] It has been calculated that seven or eight hundred people a year passed through the former leprosarium, so that between 1635 and 1660 very nearly 20,000 retreatants went to St Lazare.[56]

'They are seeking salvation'

One of the reasons why the retreats proved so successful was that they were given absolutely free.Some people of quality might give a small alms before they left but this was a rare occurrence because there was a widespread belief that the expenses of the retreats were covered by the original foundation contracts. This was not so. The whole financial burden fell on Saint Lazare. This meant that periodically the house would fall into debt and this provoked more or less covert protests from some of the missioners.

In this matter Vincent showed a holy disinterestedness. When one brother in the congregation complained about the excessive number of retreatants and the exorbitant cost of looking after them, Vincent gave the laconic reply, 'Brother, they are seeking salvation.' And some days later he developed this thought during a community meeting called to discuss this question:

> If welcoming those who come here for retreats meant that we could only continue for 15 instead of for 30 years, we should not let that consideration prevent us from accepting these people. It is true that this makes for considerable expense but the money could not be spent in any better way, and if the

---

[54] COLLET, *op. cit.*, Vol. 1, p. 207.
[55] ABELLY, *op. cit.*, 1.2 c. 4, p. 273.
[56] ABELLY, *ibid.*

house gets into difficulties God will find means of helping us; we can expect this from his providence and infinite goodness.[57]

The objection was raised, too, that some of the retreatants came, not to profit spiritually from the experience, but to enjoy a few days' free board and lodging. Vincent's reply was both supernatural and resourceful:

> Well, it will always be almsgiving that pleases God. On the other hand, if you are reluctant to admit them, it could happen that you might be refusing somebody that Our Lord wishes to convert during this retreat and so your excessive zeal in questioning people's intentions could make some of them lose the desire they now have of devoting their lives to God.[58]

However, Vincent must have been somewhat influenced by his brothers' objections. So as to lessen the number of retreatants and the expenses of the house, he undertook to personally enquire into all those who asked to come. As a result numbers increased rather than diminished, and sometimes he had to say to those responsible for the domestic arrangements,

> If all the rooms are full, then give them mine.[59]

Spiritual disinterestedness was matched by a lack of concern regarding the cost of the work. In a conference wholly dedicated to the ways of looking after retreatants, he declared that the success of the work depended on this very question and he emphasised the point saying:

> Let us never say anything to them that might indicate that we would be pleased to have them in our congregation or even that we desire this, *'Non concupisces.'* You should know, Gentlemen, that if God has been pleased to grant any graces to this little company it is because of the complete lack of self-interest that we have always shown.[60]

---

[57] ABELLY, *op. cit.*, 1.2   c. 4, p. 275.
[58] ABELLY, *ibid.*, p. 276.
[59] ABELLY, *ibid.*, p. 275.
[60] *S.V.P.* XII, p. 441.

This thought is repeated in nearly all the talks he gave on the subject.[61] As we have seen, Vincent made it an inviolable rule never to put pressure on anyone to join his company.

'We have to mix three colours: modesty, joy and meekness'

These spiritual exercises differed from retreats for ordinands in that they were not given to groups. Each retreatant came when it suited him and made the retreat privately, with the help and guidance of a director who, in line with Vincent's regulations, (it was always a case of regulations!) was to take an interest twice a day in how the retreatant was getting on, show him the subjects for meditation, indicate the books he should read, and answer his questions. All the priests in the community, and sometimes the theology students, too, would be occupied in looking after one or more retreatants. Vincent was afraid that the missioners might get tired of such continuous effort and would render the congregation unworthy of receiving from God the grace of this saving ministry[62] which he regarded as a gift from heaven that had transformed the old leprosarium where nobody was healed, into a spiritual pest-house where all found wholeness.[63]

To guide them in their meditation Vincent suggested they read a recently published manual entitled. *Enchyridion piarum meditationum* or *Manual of pious meditations.* It was written by the Dutch Jesuit Jan Buys, and Vincent had the work translated so that lay people could use it more easily.[64] It was a serious work which appealed more to the mind than to the heart, and it left little scope for the imagination. It dealt with classic themes from the Ignatian exercises and was written in a dry, arid style but the author's

---

[61] St Vincent's conferences on spiritual retreats are in *S.V.P.* XI, pp. 14-20, 229-232 and XII, pp. 437-444. All these conferences except the last one are taken from ABELLY (*op. cit.*, 1.2 c. 4, pp. 277-281). The repetition of prayer on 10 August 1655, is also to be found in *'Recueil de diverses exhortations'* and Coste takes his material from this. There are very few differences between Coste's text and that of Abelly.

[62] *S.V.P.* XI, p. 15.

[63] *S.V.P.* XI, p. 16.

[64] The book written by Jan Buys whose name is given in Latin as Busaeus or Buseo, was published in 1624. The first reference to this book was made in 1633 (*S.V.P.* I, p. 197). At that time it was translated into French, probably by Fr Binet, SJ. The translation made under the auspices of St Vincent is dated 1644 and quite a number of new meditations are added to the original text. It was the work of Fr Portail or Fr Alméras. Coste changed his mind on this point between the publication of *S.V.P.* (p. 197 and III, p. 283) and that of *Monsieur Vincent* (Vol. 3, p. 13), where he is inclined to Alméras. The Vincentians adopted this book as the official manual for giving retreats and it was in use for a long time. The Spanish translation made in 1709 has gone through 13 editions. The last one was published in 1929.

solid arguments were irresistible. Vincent arranged for this to be studied after St Francis de Sales' method of making mental prayer but he always instructed the directors to recommend, also, the Ignatian practice of using the three faculties of the soul when reading the *Manual*.[65]

'Especially M. Vincent'

The dryness of the text was lightened by Vincent's own spirituality and when a distinguished retreatant, Louis Machon, canon of Toul, had finished his ten days retreat, he wrote:

> In your person, virtue is so attractive that it seems you have been chosen to be the one to reveal it to our bodily eyes; when we look at you we cannot help being attracted by what makes you such a loveable person and so praiseworthy.[66]

This testimony was repeated by other people. Vincent's demeanour, his very presence and his personality proved to be the most compelling aspect of those retreats. Just to have him there was enough to give the retreatants a happy sense of supernatural joy. His presence created an atmosphere of peace and trust. This is what a priest from Languedoc wrote, in 1640, to a colleague who had directed him to St Lazare:

> While I was in that house I was so well treated and shown such kindness by everyone I spoke to, that I was overcome. M. Vincent, especially, welcomed me with such affection that I am still overcome at the thought of it. I cannot find words to express what I feel in my heart. What I can say is, that while I was making that retreat I felt I was in heaven and now that I have come away from it, Paris seems like a prison.[67]

The results of the retreats were just as encouraging as those of the missions. Vincent was continually receiving grateful tributes from priests and laymen who had enjoyed his hospitality. Occasionally he would quote their words to the community so as to encourage the missioners to remain faithful to this retreat work.

---

[65] *S.V.P.* XII, p. 444.
[66] *S.V.P.* XIII, p. 134.
[67] ABELLY, *op. cit.*, 1.2 c. 4, p. 284.

'The last time I travelled to Brittany', he once related, 'I had only just arrived when a very distinguished person came to thank me for the favour which he said we had granted him by allowing him to make a retreat here. 'Father', he said, 'if it had not been for that retreat I would have perished; I owe everything to you; it was that retreat which brought me peace and made me embrace the way of life which, by the grace of God, I am still following and it makes me very happy. Father, I am so grateful to you, that I tell all my companions that I would have been damned if I had not, thanks to your goodness, made that retreat at St Lazare. How grateful I am to you, Father.' 'This,' said Vincent in conclusion, 'left me deeply moved.'[68]

Thanks to the missions and the retreats, the former being directed to the masses, and the latter to more selective minority groups, the Vincentian dream of transforming the fossilised Christianity of French country folk into a living, informed and dynamic practice of religion was gradually becoming a reality. As we know, Vincent was not the only worker in this field but his initiatives, which were imitated and continued by other people, and his impetus, which was not so easy to emulate but was so very contagious and stimulating, marked him out as the undisputed leader of the great reform movement.

---

[68] *S.V.P.* XI, pp. 230-231.

Chapter XXIII
THE COMPANY IN ACTION: ORDINANDS, SEMINARIES, CONFERENCES

'Our institute has just two main objectives'

Vincent's personal vocation, which he sensed from the very beginning of his spiritual quest, was not restricted to giving missions. No less important an element in this vocation was the reform of the clergy, so this was incorporated into the aims and activities of the Congregation of the Mission.

> 'Our institute', said Vincent, even before the definitive form of the rules was settled, 'has just two main objectives; instructing poor country people and working in seminaries.'[1]

Both these aims were explicitly stated in the foundation contracts for most houses and Vincent was most anxious that both should be seen as equally important, although at times, one of these works might seem unnecessary. The superior at Saintes who had very few vocations in his seminary, was reminded of this by Vincent who wrote:

> I hope this good work will not come to an end but that the situation will improve. You should not neglect this work in order to concentrate just on the missions; both are equally important and you have the same obligations with regard to both. I address these words to the whole family which was founded to undertake both works.[2]

When some missioner expressed disappointment at being sent just to train priests and not being able to give missions, Vincent, with some severity, pointed to the decision as a matter of principle.

---

[1] *S.V.P.* III, p. 273.
[2] *S.V.P.* V, p. 489.

Do you not know, Father, that we are just as much committed to the work of training good priests as we are to instructing the country people, and that a priest of the Mission who would wish to do one of these works and not the other, would be only half a missioner. I would go further and say that he stopped being a missioner the moment he refused to obey in one matter so as to devote himself to a work that was not judged necessary for him to do.[3]

'There is nothing better than being a priest'

As we have seen, the first concrete way of fulfilling this vocation to help the clergy, was to give retreats to ordinands. This was tried out in Beauvais in 1628, and had become a time-honoured institution in Paris by 1631. The episcopal letters that authorised the amalgamation of the priory and the Congregation of the Mission,[4] made the work a permanent and obligatory duty for the missioners at St Lazare after 1632.

This proved to be a serious financial burden on the house. Every year there were six ordination ceremonies in the diocese of Paris, although after 1643 this number was reduced to five when the mid-Lent ordinations were discontinued. This did not afford the missioners much relief, especially since after 1638 the Paris ordinands were joined for their retreat by clerics from other dioceses who wished to be ordained in the capital, and after 1646 candidates for minor orders added to the total. The number of participants in each group varied between 70 and 90. The retreats lasted for 11 days so that the end of year total worked out as 55 days of retreats and some 4,000 participants.[5]

Even though the house at St Lazare had considerable resources, it began to feel the pressure of such a heavy burden. Some ladies of Charity rushed to Vincent's aid. One of the first to do so was another of Vincent's good angels, Charlotte de Ligny, Madame Présidente de Herse. Her father and her husband both belonged to the aristocracy. Her husband, Michel Vialart, who had been a member of the Paris parlement and president of the Royal Tribunal of Petitions, died in 1634 and the widow devoted a large part of her fortune to works of charity.[6] She promised to subsidise the work for ordinands

---

[3] *S.V.P.* VII, p. 561.
[4] *S.V.P.* XIII, pp. 252, 274-275.
[5] ABELLY, *op. cit.*, 1.2 c. 2, pp. 116-117; *S.V.P.* VII, p. 298.
[6] *S.V.P.* I, p. 305.

for a period of five years and she kept her word. Between 1638 and 1643 she gave Vincent 1,000 *livres* for each ordination group. She also joined with some other ladies in paying out of their own purse the expenses incurred in furnishing the retreatants' rooms. When her contract came to an end it was taken over by the queen who was just beginning her regency but she only gave alms 'for two or three years.' 'Monarchs', commented Abelly with some irony, 'are not always able to do the good they would like to.'[7]

Most of the burden fell on St Lazare. In 1650, Marguerite de Gondi, Marquise de Maignelay and the saint of that family, bequeathed a legacy of 18,000 *livres* for the work and so completed the pious foundations started by her brothers.[8]

Even if economic assets were not very reliable Vincent worked hard to see that spiritual resources were as sound as possible. Vincent developed this message in his repetitions of prayer and in his conferences and letters to the community, with the object of making them all aware of the great dignity of the priesthood and the importance of working for priests.

Ever since his premature ordination at the age of twenty, Vincent had often reflected on the great dignity of the priesthood. His contact with the people of de Bérulle's circle had introduced him to a school of thought which regarded the priesthood as a call to perfection which was more demanding than a vocation to the religious life. Personal experience had shown him all too clearly that the dignity of the priesthood had to be reinstated; that priests themselves should be convinced of this dignity and that it should be equally appreciated by the faithful. This world of ideas which he had meditated on in depth, finds expression in short, impressive, sentences that would be carved on the hearts and memories of his listeners:

> 'Is there anything in the world greater than the priestly state? Kingdoms and principalities are nothing in comparison.[9] The character conferred by ordination is a participation in the priesthood of the Son of God.'[10] 'There is nothing greater than a priest to whom God has given all power over his natural and his mystical body.'[11] 'The office of priesthood is more exalted than any earthly dignity.'[12]

---

[7] COLLET, *op. cit.*, Vol. 1, p. 136.
[8] *Vincentiana* (1971), pp. 45-46.
[9] *S.V.P.* XI, p. 9.
[10] *S.V.P.* XI, p. 7.
[11] *S.V.P.* XII, p. 85.
[12] *S.V.P.* XII, p. 99.

'To make the Gospel fully effective'

Vincent's esteem for the clergy led him to cherish works connected with the training, development, and perfection of priests; and, in his eyes, such works were an essential part of a missioner's vocation. He worked hard to have every member of the community share this conviction. He was afraid that if they did not, God would take away the grace he had given them to work for the improvement of the clergy. He felt this all the more since he considered both himself and his community to be unworthy of the task, and it seemed to him that God had chosen them because of their insignificance, in accordance with the divine rule of choosing the most unworthy instruments for the most important enterprises. Not to respond to that grace would be a betrayal of the missioner's vocation. There would be something lacking in this vocation if it did not include the training of priests. The call to this work represented the coming of the fullness of time for the congregation. The evangelisation of the poor would only be completely effective when these were given good pastors. When some members of the community raised objections to the works of seminaries, ecclesiastical conferences and retreats for ordinands, Vincent made this reply:

> Let us now look at the difficulties we could come up against. First of all, the Son of God might have been asked, 'Why did you come on earth'? To evangelise the poor; that is what the Father commanded you to do. Then why do you have priests? Why do you give them the power to consecrate, to bind and to loose, etc.? It might be said that coming to evangelise the poor did not just mean teaching them the great truths necessary for salvation but doing everything that was foretold and prefigured by the prophets, to make the gospel effective. You know that in former times God rejected those unworthy priests that had profaned holy things; he held their sacrifices in abomination and declared that he would raise up others whose voices and words would resound from the rising of the sun to its setting. *'In omnem terram exivit sonus eorum.'* Through whom was he going to fulfil these promises? Through his Son, Our Lord, who raised up priests, instructed and trained them, and gave them the power to ordain others. *'Sicut misit me Pater et ego mitto vos.'* He would do this through the men he had made priests during his own lifetime to bring salvation to the nations by instructing them and administering the

sacraments.[13] Training priests was the way to make the gospel effective.

Vincent wanted every member of the community to join in the work of giving retreats to ordinands, not just those who directed the retreats. Everyone, including the lay brothers, could collaborate through humility, prayer, good example and careful celebration of the liturgy. Vincent would often say a word on this subject to the community at St Lazare just as a retreat was about to start. So he was gradually creating a collective consciousness of the importance and excellence of this work, and this was the best guarantee that it would survive.[14]

The retreat manual

As well as giving spiritual advice, Vincent would add practical recommendations on the way retreatants were to be welcomed to the house, how they should be directed and the way missioners were to relate to them. He immediately drew up, as he did for all his works, a relevant series of regulations. For those working with retreatants he devised something extra, a manual containing a summary of everything that an aspirant to the priesthood needed to know in order to attain and worthily perform his exalted ministry. The compilation of this manual was a collective effort. Working on it with Vincent were Nicolas Pavillon (1597-1677), François Perrochel (1602-1673) and Jean Jacques Olier (1608-1657).[15] These three belonged to the first group that attended the Tuesday conferences and they had been part of Vincent's circle for a long time, though each kept his own spiritual profile.

Pavillon soon became bishop of Alet and he accepted this position in 1637 on Vincent's advice. As a mark of esteem for his great friend, he was

---

[13] *S.V.P.* XII, pp. 84-85. The sentence *rendre effectif l'Évangile*, 'to make the Gospel effective', has been taken out of context and often interpreted as the Vincentian idea of evangelisation through word and work, namely, the essential combination of spiritual and corporal works of charity. Its original meaning, which is evident from the whole text, is that the evangelisation of the poor, if it is to be carried out in all its fullness, calls for the fulfilment of the prophetic promises to send a new kind of priest. It would be no use at all preaching missions if the people were not then confided to the care of zealous and well-trained pastors. For the gospel to be fully effective it was necessary to train good pastors.

[14] St Vincent's conferences on the work of retreats for ordinands, and more generally, on the excellence of the priesthood, have been preserved by Abelly (*op. cit.*, 1.2 c. 4, p. 222-232 and c. 5, pp. 298-299). These are the basis of the texts in *S.V.P.* XI, pp. 7-12, 308-312; XII, pp. 14-19.

[15] *S.V.P.* XIII, p. 291

consecrated bishop in the church of St Lazare.[16] He was noted for his firm discipline and the rigour of his doctrine which eventually led him to sympathise with the Jansenists. Six years after Pavillon,[17] Perrochel was consecrated bishop of Boulogne and this ceremony, also, took place at St Lazare. This man had such a reputation that Anne of Austria used to go to his talks for ordinands and she was so edified by them that she decided to give financial support to the work.[18] Olier was the youngest of them all and therefore the most submissive to Vincent who was his confessor. Vincent had helped him to overcome the hesitations he felt when the time came for him to be ordained. However, not long after this, he left Vincent's spiritual direction for that of Fr Condren, superior of the Oratory. It has been suggested, though there is no solid basis for this theory, that Olier made the change because Vincent was encouraging him to accept the bishopric of Langres whereas Condren advised the opposite. Events proved Vincent was wrong, because Olier would do much more important work as a simple priest and founder of Saint Sulpice than he would have done in any diocese. Whatever the reason may have been for their difference of opinion, it did not affect their friendship and the cordial relationship between master and disciple. Vincent regarded Olier as a man who would be blessed by God wherever he went, and Olier looked on Vincent as the father of his community.[19] We will find them working together on other occasions.

In 1634, or the following year, the four men were working together on the retreat manual. This came out as a small book entitled, *Entretiens des Ordinands*, which was never printed and the only copies preserved are handwritten.[20] When Vincent received a copy he had it studied by several theologians from the Sorbonne. These assured him that anyone who had mastered its contents would know everything necessary for the worthy exercise of the priestly ministry.[21]

Vincent made sure that the preaching to the ordinands was confined to subjects prescribed in the manual and that the style of preaching should reflect the little method's characteristic simplicity of thought and speech. Often preachers would come from outside the community and some of these were as famous as Bossuet.[22] However, as time went on, preference was

---

[16] *S.V.P.* I, p. 157.

[17] *S.V.P.* I, p. 296; *Annales* (1965), p. 495.

[18] ABELLY, *op. cit.*, 1.2 c. 2, p. 217.

[19] COLLET, *op. cit.*, Vol. 1, p. 204; *S.V.P.* I, p. 210.

[20] *S.V.P.* XII, p. 291. The list of topics to be dealt with during retreats is in ABELLY, *op. cit.*, 1.2 c. 2, p. 219ff. Extracts from *Entretiens,* in ROCHE, *op. cit.*, pp. 142-163.

[21] *S.V.P.* XII, p. 291, pp. 98-99.

[22] *S.V.P.* IV, p. 342; V, pp. 572, 575; VII, p. 17, 108.

given to the priests of the Mission,[23] especially to the younger ones who gave witness to the excellent training they had received and who were very proficient.[24]

A missioner known as 'The Director of Ordinands'[25] had over-all responsibility for the running of each retreat group but, as we have said, the whole community took part in the enterprise. When the ordinands arrived they were welcomed by the residents of St Lazare who took charge of their luggage, showed them to their rooms, explained the order of day and encouraged them to begin the retreat with an earnest desire to profit from it. After the talks and meditations, the retreatants were divided into small groups or 'academies' which were led by a priest, for dialogue and sharing of ideas about what had been discussed. Priests from the house were responsible for rehearsing the liturgy and also for reading in the refectory. This reading was usually taken from a classic spiritual work on the priesthood, *'Instructions for Priests'*[26] by the Spanish Carthusian, Antonio Molina. Throughout the day, the ordinands were immersed in an atmosphere of recollection and fervour that very few were able to resist.

But there were some exceptions. One of these was young de Gondi, the future Cardinal de Retz, who had been pressurised by his family into embracing the religious state. The meagre fruit of his retreat at St Lazare was a resolution to be as zealous for the salvation of others as he was careless about his own. He was prepared to do wrong deliberately, so as to avoid the absurd mixture of sin and devotion which he observed in other ecclesiastics.[27]

Antoine Arnauld's case was different. He, too, refused to be influenced by the environment but he had different reasons for his opposition. He had been trained by Saint-Cyran and had but scant regard for Vincent. He considered the spiritual nourishment offered at the Bons Enfants, where he made his retreat, to be very lacking compared with the solid teaching he had received from his master. The serious confrontation between Vincent and the famous Arnauld, undisputed leader of the Jansenists, was not far off.[28]

'Our company has contributed not a little'

These isolated cases have to be set against the great majority of successes. Among the great men of the Church in France who prepared for ordination

---

[23] *S.V.P.* II, p. 284.
[24] *S.V.P.* III, p. 258; IV, p. 114.
[25] *S.V.P.* IV, pp. 114, 342, 601; V, p. 588; XII, pp. 438, 442.
[26] ABELLY, *op. cit.*, 1.2 c. 2, pp. 219-222. *Cf.* M. A. ROCHE, *op. cit.*
[27] *Mémoirs* of Retz, 1.1, p. 216.
[28] The text of Arnauld's letter, in *M.V.* III, p. 163.

at St Lazare or at the Bons Enfants, were Olier himself, Armand de Rancé, the future reformer of the Trappists, Commander Brûlart de Sillery whom we mentioned earlier, Bossuet, Fleury and all the men who at diocesan level, or in abbeys, benefices or parishes in many different parts of France, would complete the work of ecclesiastical reform that was started by men of Vincent's generation. Vincent himself rejoiced in the good results that came from the retreats.

> At the present time, the secular clergy are receiving many blessings from God. It is said that our poor company has contributed not a little to this, by reason of its work for the ordinands and through the meetings of ecclesiastics that take place in Paris. These days, many distinguished people are embracing this state of life.[29]

Perhaps the greatest commendation of Vincent's work comes in the words of the founder, himself, 'Our poor company has contributed not a little ...' More important, maybe, than immediate results was the general retreat movement launched at St Lazare. Other communities, the Oratorians, Saint Nicolas du Chardonnet, the Company of Authier de Sisgau, were also committed to the work. Vincent could not meet all the requests that came from bishops wanting missioners to set up a house in their dioceses. Practically every foundation of the congregation, Crécy, Notre Dame de la Rose, Agen, Le Mans, Cahors, Saintes, Troyes, Luçon and Richelieu combined the work of retreats for ordinands with that of giving missions to the ordinary people. In dioceses where these was no house of the congregation, as at Rheims, Noyon, Angoulême or Chartres, the missioners were occasionally called upon to preach at some retreats for ordinands and so initiate the work.[30] Outside of France, the houses at Genoa and Rome were used, from the earliest days of their foundation, for the work of preaching retreats to ordinands. We shall see the successful results of their labours in later chapters.

'The Council's directives come from the Holy Spirit'

Retreats for ordinands led to another work which was to prove the perfect solution to the problem of training the clergy, *viz.*, the setting up of seminaries. In preceding chapters we have referred to the ordinances of the Council of

---

[29] *S.V.P.* II, p. 28.

[30] 30 ABELLY, *op. cit.*, 1.2 c. 2, p. 233-237. For the foundation of the houses mentioned, *cf. Notices ...*, I, pp. 510-535.

Trent regarding the establishment of diocesan centres for the training of future priests. The type of seminary envisaged by the council was meant for youngsters of twelve years of age and upwards who would receive religious education and be trained in the ecclesiastical disciplines, thus ensuring an on-going seedbed for God's ministers.[31] The council's decree was practically a dead letter in France though there were some unsuccessful attempts to implement it.

The first Vincentian attempt at founding a seminary was carried out along Tridentine lines. Unlike other Vincentian enterprises, we know nothing about who thought of the idea or what steps were taken to get the work started. Projects of this sort would doubtless have been bandied about in the reforming circles that Vincent frequented. Was there any particular incident or proposal that induced him to establish the first seminary? We do not know. The fact remains that in 1636 he decided to use the Collège des Bons Enfants as a junior seminary.[32] Eight years later, in 1644, there were 22 students and the numbers never exceeded 30 during this period.[33] It was a disappointing experience. In 1641 Vincent declared that not a single one of these seminaries had been of any use to the Church.[34] As time passed, these negative results were confirmed:

> 'We must respect the directives of the council as coming from the Holy Spirit', he wrote in 1644, 'but experience teaches us that fulfilling their requirements with regard to the age of seminarists has not been successful either in Italy or in France. Some leave the seminary early, others have no vocation to the priesthood, some go to religious communities and others move away from the region where they were born or where they are under some obligation, preferring to seek their fortune elsewhere. There are four seminaries in this country: at Bordeaux, Rheims and Rouen, and there used to be one at Agen. None of these dioceses has had much benefit from the seminaries and I am afraid that, with the exception of Rome and Milan, it is the same story in Italy ... We have 22 in our junior seminary at the Bons Enfants; of these only three or four are passable, and there is little hope that these will persevere. This is in spite of all the effort we might put into the work so I have my doubts, if not about the likely outcome,

---

[31] Dec. *Cum adulescentium aetas* sess.23.ª, can.18.
[32] ABELLY, *op. cit.*, 1.1 c. 31, p. 146 and 1.2 c. 5, p. 194.
[33] *S.V.P.* II, pp. 459, 489.
[34] *S.V.P.* II, p. 152.

at least about whether things will work out in the way proposed.'[35]

Vincent began to look for other solutions. However, and it is worth emphasising this point, he did not abandon the original project. As we shall see later on, in 1642 he started another type of seminary at the Bons Enfants but he had it functioning alongside the original work. In 1645, when the house became too small for both enterprises, he still refused to close down the junior seminary but had it transferred to a building at the extreme north-easterly end of the St Lazare precinct. It came to be known as 'little St Lazare' but Vincent soon changed its name to St Charles.[36] This seems to have functioned fairly well. There were quite a lot of students; in 1646 there were about 40[37] but the numbers dropped considerably during the Fronde[38] before gradually picking up again till the place was full.[39] However, it still did not measure up to Vincent's expectations because these young vocations lacked stability, and as he knew from experience, there was little guarantee that they would persevere.[40]

What, then, were his reasons for persisting in keeping it open? Perhaps it was because he did not want in any way to go against the orders of the Council of Trent, no matter how negative his experiences might prove to be. 'We have to respect the directives of the council as coming from the Holy Spirit.'[41] This is the explanation given by Abelly and he adds that Vincent did not want to leave unexplored any avenue that might produce good priests for the Church.[42]

'It's very different taking them between the ages of twenty and twenty-five.'

About the year 1642 (and let us not forget that this year is a watershed in the life of Vincent) a new idea seems to have taken shape in the minds of people working to reform the clergy in France; they planned to open seminaries for young clerics over the age of twenty.

---

[35] *S.V.P.* II, p. 459.
[36] *S.V.P.* IV, p. 291.
[37] *S.V.P.* III, p. 3.
[38] *S.V.P.* V, p. 69.
[39] *S.V.P.* VI, pp. 139, 238.
[40] *S.V.P.* V, p. 563.
[41] *S.V.P.* II, p. 459.
[42] ABELLY, *op. cit.*, 1.2 c. 5, p. 295.

'It is very different taking them between the ages of twenty and twenty five or at thirty', wrote Vincent in the letter quoted above.[43]

In 1642 Olier founded the seminary at Vaugirard which was later transferred to St Sulpice; the Oratorians set up their seminaries at St Magloire in Paris and at Rouen and Toulouse; St John Eudes began to develop the project which led him to leave the Oratorians in face of the intransigence shown by Condren's successor, Bourgoing. He founded a new congregation dedicated to the work of seminaries and missions, and the transformation of St Nicolas du Chardonnet began. About this time, too, some new projects were being tried out by the most zealous of the bishops: Juste Guérin in Annecy, Nicolas Pavillon at Alet, Alain de Solminihac at Cahors, Jacques Raoul at Saintes, etc.[44]

No one man can be given the credit for having the idea of establishing seminaries. The idea was in the air and each founder took it up and implemented it in his own way. It is significant that all the initiatives that were started around 1642, received financial backing from Cardinal Richelieu or his niece, the Duchess d'Aiguillon. Vincent received 1,000 *écus* (3,000 *livres*) to start up his project at the Bons Enfants[45] with twelve clerics. Olier, St John Eudes, Bourgoing, Authier de Sisgau and Bourdoise were to receive similar sums but in some cases the money did not materialise. We must not conclude from this, that the motives for giving this aid were purely political. It is just that reforming the clergy played an important and necessary part in Richelieu's vision of a new France. Political and religious change went hand in hand. Vincent was to make an original and important contribution to this change.[46]

The Vincentian idea of a major seminary, if we can use this term to describe the foundation in 1642, was merely a development and extension of the retreats for ordinands. So it might be more appropriate to refer to seminaries in the seventeenth century as 'seminaries for ordinands'. This was what generally happened; although the retreats had proved very successful it was soon realised that ten or eleven days was too short a time to give the candidates the training they needed. Some bishops who shared Vincent's views on this matter, began to extend the period of training for

---

[43] *Cf.* n. 35.
[44] *Cf.* L. COGNET, 'La vida de la Iglesia en Francia', in H. JEDIN, *Manual de historia de la Iglesia*, Vol. 6, pp. 62- 68; E. PRECLIN-E. JARRY, 'Luchas doctrinales', pp. 224-226.
[45] *S.V.P.* II, p. 225.
[46] *Cf.* the work of MAURICE ROCHE, *Saint Vincent de Paul and the formation of clerics* (Freiburg 1964), which deals with the subject in general.

ordinands to two, and to six months. Later on they doubled the training time by making it obligatory for clerics to be trained before the diaconate and again after ordination. They finally decided on a total period of two or three years' preparation. Training programmes developed along different lines but the general pattern is summed up by a contemporary witness, the Oratorian, Fr Cloyseault:

> In the beginning it was a great favour for us to obtain the bishop's consent to oblige all ecclesiastics to attend, for eight or ten days prior to ordination, a morning and an evening conference given in the churches or houses of the Oratorians. Later on, when the houses were suitably furnished, aspirants were obliged to stay there for 10 days; some prelates required them to stay for a month; others required two months, and finally, the more zealous among the prelates obliged them to stay for three months before each stage of ordination. In this way, almost imperceptibly, the first seminaries were established.[47]

'There are four seminaries in Paris'

Because of this training process, the Vincentian seminary was to differ quite considerably from seminaries that opened at a later date. At least in the early days at the Bons Enfants, they admitted not just clerical aspirants to holy orders, but also ordained priests who wanted to make up, *a posteriori,* the training they had missed. As the number of seminaries increased and as all clerics were required to pass through them, this latter type of seminarist naturally died out.[48]

Missioners who were in charge of seminaries had to do other work as well. In the intervals between one ordination ceremony and the next, they would close up the house and go off to preach missions in the country areas. They would often take the seminarists with them so that these could put into practice what they had learned. Vincent's reason for not accepting seminaries unless they were linked to the work of giving missions, is deeply rooted in his conviction that the chief aim of the company was to evangelise poor country people, but it also springs from his concern to have the missioners constantly occupied with one or other of these activities.[49]

---

[47] Referred to by S. POOLE, *op. cit.*, p. 86.
[48] *S.V.P.* II, p. 535; III, pp. 129, 249; VII, p. 483.
[49] *S.V.P.* IV, p. 43; V, p. 371; ABELLY, *op. cit.*, 1.2 c. 5, p. 301.

People did not regard the first seminaries as schools of theology, and even less as schools of philosophy. Their main concern was 'the spiritual formation of seminarists in the virtues proper to the priesthood; training them in liturgical functions (saying Mass and administering the sacraments); preparing them for their work as confessors and teaching them the moral theology, for the most part casuistic, that this work required. Training of a purely intellectual character continued to be the work of university faculties or colleges when these were near at hand. This explains why two or three priests were usually sufficient to direct a seminary. Vincent's ideal approximated more to what we might call today 'an ecclesiastical technical school' which did not aim at producing learned men (this was the province of the universities) but good parish priests, devout and spiritual men who were competent, zealous and well trained in pastoral work.[50]

In some cases the university centres were too far away and so chairs of theology and philosophy were set up in the seminaries. This became the general rule and all the seminaries gradually ended up as teaching centres in the strict sense of the word. Vincent bowed to these trends but not without some opposition.[51]

Ten days before he died, Vincent compared the four seminaries of Paris and came to this conclusion:

> In Paris there are four houses that specialise in this work: the Oratory, St Sulpice, St Nicolas du Chardonnet and the wretched little one at the Bons Enfants. The aim at St Sulpice is to subordinate everything to the spirit and then to purify this; to free the people from earthly desires and lead them on to higher inspirations and feelings. We notice that all who have been there show these characteristics; some more than others. I do not know whether they teach scholastic theology there.
>
> Those at St Nicolas are not quite so lofty-minded and tend to work in the Lord's vineyard by training men to labour at their priestly functions. With this intention they keep first of all to the practical application of their priestly training and, secondly, they take on lowly tasks like sweeping, washing up, scrubbing etc. They can do this because most of the students do not pay anything and the arrangement works well.
>
> We will leave the Oratorians out of it and not talk about them.

---

[50] ABELLY, *op. cit.*, 1.2 c. 5, pp. 294-295; *S.V.P.* III, p. 470; IV, pp. 596-597; VI, pp. 61, 385-388; VII, p. 593; VIII, p. 3.

[51] *S.V.P.* II, p. 188, 234.

There is no doubt at all, that out of these four houses the best results come from St Nicolas where the students are all like little suns. I have never known anybody complain about them; they are always very edifying.

So this is the most useful training programme. We should be aiming in the same direction or at least trying to imitate them. You are well aware that scholastic theology has never been taught there; only moral philosophy, and that they give practical conferences. It is for this reason that I am inclined to think that God wishes to give us the grace of following their example.

I understand that the scholastic theology taught at the Bons Enfants is of little or no use, and I have thought of discontinuing it, especially as the students go to the Collége de Navarre or the Sorbonne for scholastic lectures. They need to be instructed in moral theology and have plenty of practice in their priestly duties. I know that Fr Watebled will be upset to hear his but what can we do? Our aim must be to provide what is most useful.'[52]

'It is better to explain an author's works than to dictate notes'

Vincent died before he could order this type of teaching to be discontinued. What he had succeeded in doing was to impart a very different education from the purely speculative teaching given in the universities. It is moving to note his insistence that notes should not be dictated in class. Only the works of approved authors were to be taught; these writings were to be explained thoroughly, the seminarists were to learn them by heart and be able to repeat them, and the teachers should clear up any difficulties. On more than one occasion this decision by Vincent made for conflict between the founder and some of the professors who, from within the teaching situation, and sometimes acting not a little out of vanity, would question, 'What will they think of us if we just repeat what is in the text book?' They were turning the seminary classrooms into university lecture halls. The most obstinate among them, Bernard Codoing, received a long letter from Vincent who was supported in this matter by the council of the community which comprised seven of the most learned men in the company.

Vincent put forward all the reasons why he was against dictating notes. The main reason was that the seminary's principal objective was not

---

[52] *S.V.P.* XIII, pp. 185-186.

to produce learned men but men of piety who had practical training for their ministry. He also had recourse to the argument *ad hominem* and this reveals some less well known aspects of Vincent's character; he was well informed and he could be ironic, though this irony was not hurtful, and was only intended to curb the vanity of wayward subjects. Vincent says the method of explaining an author is better

> even for those who teach; it is more useful for them to explain an author's works than to make up notes on the subject, unless they take these notes from Bonacina or some other writer, like you did, and when the students discover who this author is they will ridicule their teacher.

Spanish people who have a devotion to St Vincent will be gratified to know that another of his arguments against dictating notes is based on the example of Spanish colleges and universities where, he said:

> They do not know what it is to dictate notes in class and they are quite happy simply to explain the texts, and yet everyone agrees that their theologians are more profound than any others.

This conviction, which was repeated several times by Vincent, must have come from his youthful experiences in the university lecture halls at Saragossa. It also explains Vincent's admiration for Spanish theology and Spanish universities though, unfortunately, it has to be said, that at the time Vincent was speaking, the teaching there had begun to degenerate into baroque verbosity.[53]

'We gave ourselves to God to serve him in seminaries'

In keeping with Vincentian traditions, the seminaries, too, were soon to have their particular regulations. The copies we now have were printed at the later date of 1722. This leads us to suppose that the early regulations were influenced by Jansenism and all the more so, since the rector of the Bons Enfants at this time was Fr Honoré Philopald de la Haye (1674-1762), who was a convinced Jansenist and was later expelled from the congregation for

---

[53] The paragraphs in quotation marks are taken from Codoing's letter, in *S. V.P.* II, pp. 231-240. Other texts that mention the ban on taking notes are in II, pp. 212, 219; IV, p. 322; VI, p. 55; VII, p. 291; VIII, pp. 107, 381. The work referred to in the text is that of the Italian theologian, Martino Bonacina, *Operum omnium de morali theologia compendium. Cf.* M. A. ROCHE, *op. cit.*, p. 92.

this reason.[54] Coste showed that the rules were drawn up before 1680[55] and in more recent times, Maurice Roche has given his support to the theory that Vincent wrote them in 1645.[56] To our eyes, these rules might appear, as they did to Daniel-Rops, 'somewhat draconian'.[57] Ecclesiastical customs have changed so much over three and a half centuries that what we would consider today to be harsh discipline, would have seemed a benevolent régime in 1645. At least there were no physical penances and the only fasting and abstinence was that imposed by the Church on all the faithful. Most of the religious practices and the order of day had their origin in the *Common Rules* for Missioners. Daily meditation, recitation of the Divine Office in common for those who had this obligation, two examinations of conscience—one general and one particular—Mass, reading of the New Testament, choir practice and rehearsing liturgical ceremonies, four hours study, domestic work, an hour's recreation after each meal; all this made up a long working day that started at four o'clock in the morning and finished at nine o'clock at night. Future priests were thus introduced to an austere and demanding life-style which was meant to inculcate the practice of piety and the habit of hard work which would save them from future temptations towards a relaxed way of life and from seeking their own ease.[58]

The Bons Enfants was not the first seminary to be set up by Vincent. Earlier he had founded one at Annecy in Savoy. The missioners had been in St Francis de Sales' city since January 1640.[59] The text quoted by Coste which would lead us to think that the enterprising superior, Fr Codoing, had gathered some seminarists together in the house, is suspect to say the least. This text would seem to refer rather to a renewal or second probation seminary that Codoing wanted to set up on his own initiative.[60]

In February 1641, the seminary at Annecy was still only at the planning stage and Vincent objected when they wanted to admit children.[61] The situation remained unchanged by 15 September of that year even though the bishop had officially inaugurated the seminary on the 8 September.[62] The first definite date we have is 31 January, 1642, when Vincent understood the

---

[54] [E. ROSSET], *Notices bibliographiques,* pp. 198-199.

[55] *M.V.* Vol. 2, p. 377.

[56] M. ROCHE, *op. cit.,* pp. 164-184.

[57] DANIEL-ROPS, *San Vicente de Paúl,* p. 45.

[58] 'Règlement du Seminaire de Saint-Firmin, de la Congrégation de la Mission établi au Collège des Bons Enfants' (Paris 1722) Text in ROCHE, *op. cit.,* pp. 188-196.

[59] *S.V.P.* II, p. 15.

[60] *S.V.P.* II, p. 102.

[61] *S.V.P.* II, p. 153.

[62] *S.V.P.* II, p. 188.

seminary to be functioning[63] and this is confirmed by a further letter of 9 February which clearly established Annecy as the earlier foundation.

> As the holy Council of Trent highly recommends this work of seminaries, we have given ourselves to God to serve him in this way wherever we can. You have already begun ... and we are going to start in this city; we will try it out with twelve students and for this purpose His Eminence (Cardinal Richelieu) is helping us with the sum of 1,000 *écus*.[64]

The seminaries at Annecy, the Bons Enfants and St Charles were followed by a dozen more in different dioceses as well as three or four (Alet, Marseilles, Périgueux and Montpellier) which did not last long. We can say that all the houses founded after 1642 fulfil the double rôle of mission station and diocesan seminary: Cahors in 1643, Saintes in 1644, Le Mans and St Méen in 1645; Tréguier and Agen in 1648, Montauban in 1652, Agde and Troyes in 1654, Meaux in 1658 and Narbonne in 1659.

They did not all prove to be equally successful and neither did they all function in the same way. Children were admitted to the seminaries of St Charles, St Méen, Le Mans and Agen.[65] At Saintes, which was a heretic stronghold, there were never more that just a few vocations.[66] We know the vicissitudes they suffered at St Méen. Of all the seminaries, the most prosperous one was that at Cahors, so much so that Vincent's great friend, bishop Alain de Solminihac, wrote to Vincent with justifiable pride:

> I imagine you would be very happy if you could see our seminary and meet the 35 seminarists who would be a source of great satisfaction to you. The priests of your company who have seen it say that it is the finest in the land and it is better ordered than any in Paris.[67]

All the seminaries would have had roughly the same number of seminarists. This is what Vincent would have us believe from a memorandum in 1647.[68] Thirty, forty or sixty seminarists may not seem very many to those who have known the great European seminaries of the nineteenth and early

---

[63] *S.V.P.* II, p. 219.
[64] *Annales* (1953), pp. 253-254.
[65] *S.V.P.* III, p. 379.
[66] *S.V.P.* V, p. 628; VI p. 424; XII, p. 66.
[67] *S.V.P.* III, p. 467.
[68] *S.V.P.* III, p. 167.

half of the twentieth century. This is quite a respectable number for the early stages of a work that was just starting up in the face of great opposition; it was only many years later that seminaries became the normal channel for the priesthood. Working alongside Vincent's missioners were the priests of St John Eudes' congregation, those of St Sulpice and the Oratory, and to a lesser extent, those of other communities, and their united efforts meant that eventually the whole ecclesiastical map of France was covered with seminaries. Whether or not it was historically true, Vincent regarded himself as the pioneer:

> We have the consolation of seeing that our small endeavours have seemed to others to be so good and useful that everyone has been inspired to emulate us and devote themselves to the works that we do, though with more graces; not only do they give missions but they also establish seminaries which are spreading all over France.[69]

The claim made by Daniel-Rops that over 400 priests were trained in the Vincentian seminaries every year, is an exaggeration[70] but it is certainly true that whatever their number may have been, they began to constitute a real priestly élite spread over the four compass points of the Church in France and that they were the effective leaven in its reform. Henry Kamen goes so far as to say that Vincent de Paul's main work, and his most effective contribution to the reform movement in France, was his work of training the clergy, 'changing the Christian people and starting by changing its pastors.'[71]

The Tuesday conferences spread

The Tuesday conferences put the finishing touches to what had been achieved by the seminaries and by the retreats for ordinands. Vincent put the same effort into the conferences as he did into the other two works and he believed that the priests of the Congregation of the Mission had a duty to promote them:

> because God has turned to them to promote in the world, through ecclesiastics, this way of discussing particular virtues. What would become of us, then, if we were the first to neglect

---

[69] *S.V.P.* VIII, p. 310.
[70] DANIEL-ROPS, *op. cit.*, p. 45.
[71] HENRY KAMEN, *El siglo de hierro*, p. 284.

it? What an account we would have to render to God if we
ever despised such useful and efficacious methods.'[72]

Soon the conferences began to expand, too. In Paris, conferences
were held at St Lazare and also at the Bons Enfants where most of those who
attended were ecclesiastics from the Sorbonne who came either as teachers
or as students. Tuesday was a free day at the university[73] and this was why
they chose this day for their meetings. Beyond Paris, the conferences started
up at Puy (1636), Noyon (1637), Pontoise (1642), Angoulême (1647), Angers,
Bordeaux and other places whose exact location is uncertain.[74] They were all
united by bonds of affectionate collaboration but even more by the veneration
they shared for the same founder. These lines taken from a report on the
conference at Pontoise in May 1642, are proof of this.

> After God, it is you, Father, that we have to thank for accepting
> us as members of your good and virtuous assembly in Paris. It
> was from you that we received our first instructions on how
> to set up this little company which for us has been a seed that
> produces all the good that comes to us each day and which
> God favours with his blessing and prosperity. We ask you one
> favour, that as we are mere infants in the practice of virtue and
> lack the strength to continue and direct our efforts, we beg
> you to send us from time to time, one of your company's
> ecclesiastics from Paris to pay us a visit.[75]

The works of the conferences

The conferences did other work besides helping their members towards
spiritual perfection. From the very beginning of its foundation, the members
committed themselves to apostolic work. Some of the tasks they undertook
were of a permanent nature and among these was the spiritual assistance
they offered at the Hôtel Dieu in Paris. In the early days the entire association
used to go there every day but later on small groups would take it in turn to
go and encourage the sick, prepare them to make a general confession, and
on Fridays they would preach and give instructions to those who were
convalescing. The General Hospital (a work we will discuss later on) was,

---

[72] *S.V.P.* XI, p.13-14
[73] ABELLY, *op. cit.*, 1.1 c. 27, p. 126.
[74] ABELLY, *op. cit.*, 1.2 c. 3, pp. 264-268.
[75] *S.V.P.* II, p. 252.

from the very outset, directed by a priest from the association. Many other priests went there on Sundays and holydays to preach and to hear confessions, and as there was a continuous turn-over of poor people in this centre, it was decided that missions would be given each year in every ward.[76]

The priests who attended the conferences also gave missions at the galley slaves' hospital and at the 'little houses' as they called the hospice which took in 400 people including married couples and those with contagious diseases. Vincent had given a mission there before he founded the company.[77] The mission preached by the priests of the Tuesday conferences was particularly successful. It was attended, not just by the inmates, but by people from the surrounding districts as well. So they drew up a leaflet entitled, *'The Christian Exercises,* and had it printed. It was written in clear, simple language and proved such a success that millions of copies were distributed throughout France.[78] This was not the only time that Vincent used printed material in his apostolate.

Missions were also preached at other places besides Paris. Between 1634 and 1637, for example, Olier gave missions on the estates of his abbey at Pébrac, and was helped by priests from the conferences and sometimes, too, by members of the Congregation of the Mission. The work was a great success. Olier speaks of it in glowing terms to his companions in the capital and ends with a long speech reminiscent of the style of St Francis Xavier.

> Paris, Paris. You hold back people who could convert several worlds. Alas, how many false conversions and how many pious discourses are wasted because the dispositions which God bestows on other places are not to be found there. Here, a single word is esteemed as much as a sermon and nothing is wasted. Here, they have not killed a single prophet. By that I mean that preaching has not been scorned as happens in the cities, and therefore, gentlemen, all these poor, unlettered folk are filled with graces and blessings from God.[79]

The master's spirit had been passed on to his disciple who would soon be ready to undertake his own works.

---

[76] ABELLY, *op. cit.*, 1.2 c. 3, pp. 257-258.

[77] ABELLY, *op. cit.*, 1.2 c. 1, p. 20.

[78] ABELLY, *op.cit.*, 1.2 c. 3, p. 257.

[79] ABELLY, *op. cit.*, *ibid.,* pp. 264-265; *S.V.P.* I, p. 333.

'The little method at court'

The two major works undertaken by the priests of the Tuesday conferences were the mission at St Germain en Laye, the court residence, and that given in the Paris suburb of St Germain des Prés.

The first was preached in January or February 1638, and on the king's orders, some priests of the Congregation of the Mission took part in it.[80] It was a mission that required delicate handling. The courtiers, the queen's ladies in waiting, and even the king and queen attended the mission services. Among the preachers was Nicolas Pavillon who was already the favourite candidate for the bishopric of Alet. A number of high-ranking gentlemen came to listen to him, just to see if they could catch him out in any wrong or imprudent statement so that they could denounce him to the king. Neither Pavillon nor any of his companions was put off by such difficulties. With evangelical directness they denounced the vices and frivolity of court life. They launched an offensive against immodest dress and in particular against the excessively low-necked dresses worn by the ladies. They were successful for a time but this did not last. It is easier to change behaviour than it is to change fashion. When the mission ended they set up a confraternity of Charity from among the court ladies, but this did not last long either.

> The mission at St Germain is over and God blessed it even though at the beginning we had to practise holy patience. There remain just a few people of the royal household who have not joined the townspeople in fulfilling their obligations; the rest did so and their devotion was very edifying. Our strong denunciation of low-necked dresses meant we had to practise patience, too. The king told M. Pavillon that he was very pleased with all the mission services; he added that this was the best approach, and that he would vouch for this everywhere. The ladies who caused most problems at the outset are now so fervent that they have joined the Charity. They go to serve the poor when it is their day to do so and they have gone through the town in four groups to collect money. These are the queen's ladies-in-waiting.[81]

We would be lacking a sense of history if we were to ask whether the missioners brought before the ruling class the injustice of a society based on the privileges of rank and fortune. Vincent felt, and how deeply did he not

---

[80] *S.V.P.* I, p. 450.
[81] *Ibid.*

feel the misery of the poor; their hunger and their pain? But he was no revolutionary. His work was directed towards changing people's consciences, not changing structures. His objective was charity, not social change. He was a child of his time and accepted the social framework he happened to be living in, while endeavouring to make this society more just and charitable.

The missioners remained faithful to the Vincentian style of preaching and to the simplicity of the little method. Vincent proudly recalled this in the last years of his life:

> The little method can be used at court—even at court. this little method has been used at court on two occasions and I make bold to say that it has been well received ...
>
> The little method was a great success; it brought marvellous results. The little method at court! And then you say it is something for common folk and for country parts! In Paris, in Paris; and at court, yes at court, and everywhere, you can't find a better or more successful method than this.'[82]

'The cesspit of France'

The most important work done by the priests of the Tuesday conferences in Paris, 1641, was the mission they preached in the slums of St Germain des Prés. This district, according to Abelly, was at that time 'the cesspit, not only of Paris, but of all France, and was a haven for all the libertines, atheists and other people who lived an impious and disordered life.'[83]

A pious lady of noble birth, the Duchess d'Aiguillon, suggested to Vincent that it would be a good idea to preach a mission in that dangerous quarter. The Congregation of the Mission could not take on the work because it would mean giving a mission in the city, so Vincent offered it to all the conference priests. Nobody would take it on. They were overcome by fear and a feeling of helplessness. Was it worth while starting a work which was so obviously doomed to failure because of the tremendous difficulties involved?

Vincent insisted so much that some of the priests became angry. He then went on his knees before the whole assembly and asked their pardon for being so tiresome in defending his point of view. His only excuse was that he felt a strong spiritual inspiration to promote this work as he believed that

---

[82] *S.V.P.* XII, p. 282.
[83] ABELLY, *op. cit.*, 1.2 c. 3, p. 261.

God was looking to their charity and zeal to have this service rendered. The victory was won. Those who had been most opposed to the work were the first to enrol. Straightaway they drew up a plan of campaign ...

How were they going to preach to these people who were so very different from simple peasants? Vincent had no hesitation in answering this question. This slum area was steeped in the spirit of the world and they had to combat this with the spirit of Christ. They were to use the same simple and humble style of preaching that they used in other places—the little method.

So the pious clergy, headed by Perrochel, went off to confront the host of actors, puppeteers, usurers, harlots, women of easy virtue, murderers, ex-convicts, vagrants, men with no belief in God and inveterate sinners acquainted with every type of vice ...

The miracle happened. That motley crowd came en masse to the confessionals, shedding bitter tears and loudly begging pardon for their sins. Then followed conversions, reconciliations, acts of restitution, atonement for scandal and remarkable changes of life-style. Those taking part in this wonderful event declared, 'The hand of God is in this.' The hand of God is with the humble, trusting works of M. Vincent.[84]

The work of giving retreats

Efforts to reform the clergy by means of retreats for ordinands, the seminaries, and the Tuesday conferences, were complemented by retreats for priests. For the most part, these retreats were integrated into the programme followed by individual retreatants who came every day to St Lazare. Realising this, Vincent had the idea of organising group retreats for priests. These would be a means of renewing, each year, the spirit they had assimilated at one or other of Vincent's foundations. But he met with an insuperable obstacle, financial problems. This meant he could not develop the project on too wide a scale and had to limit the facility to the more fervent members of the Tuesday conferences. Nevertheless, the retreats took place fairly frequently and with considerable success, both in Paris and in other places. Many bishops wrote to Vincent expressing their satisfaction with the retreats the missioners preached. [85]

In a letter dated 1641, Vincent summed up the works of the Congregation of the Mission when he wrote, one day, to Fr Lebreton, his delegate in Rome. The text is partly history and partly prophecy:

---

[84] ABELLY, *op. cit.*, 1.2 c. 3, pp. 261-264.
[85] ABELLY, *op. cit.*, 1.1 c. 4, pp. 284-292.

God will make use of this company to help the people by means of the missions that we give; to help those at the beginning of their priestly life through our work with ordinands; to help those who are already ordained because these will not be accepted for a benefice or a living unless they have made a retreat or been trained in a seminary, and to help people in general, by means of the spiritual exercises. May God, in his divine goodness, grant us his grace to perform these works.[86]

---

[86] *S.V.P.* II, p. 154.

Chapter XXIV
ITALY, IRELAND, POLAND:
THE MISSION IN EUROPE

'The principal houses are those of Paris and Rome'

Rome, the centre of Christianity, always had a great attraction for Vincent de Paul. As a young man, fate had led him there on two occasions. In later years he felt the urge to return and was always toying with the idea of going and maybe living there permanently. Illness, age and duties prevented this.[1]

Since he could not go himself, he would at least see his missioners settled there; first, on a temporary basis, as his delegates to the Holy See, and later in a more permanent capacity. François du Coudray resided in Rome between 1631 and 1635 when he was negotiating approval for the congregation. As we have seen, this work was crowned with success. Between 1639 and 1641 it was Louis Lebreton who was sent there to obtain approval for the vows. His early death on 17 October 1641, from a contagious illness contracted during the mission in Ostia, prevented him from completing the negotiations.[2] On the other hand, he did manage, before his death, to obtain from the vicar-general of the diocese of Rome, Monsignor Giovanni Battista de Altieri, a rescript dated 11 July 1641, authorising the Congregation of the Mission to establish a house where they would undertake the same ministries as those they had in France; retreats for ordinands and missions to the ordinary people. Before granting this concession, the vicar-general had been greatly influenced by the zeal shown by Lebreton during his missions to the shepherds in country districts near Rome.[3]

As soon as Vincent had word of this permission to establish a foundation, he decided to send two or three missioners to Rome.[4] These

---

[1] *S.V.P.* II, pp. 324, 409, 418, 427; IV, pp. 65-67, 98. For St Vincent's foundations in Italy, ABELLY, *op. cit.*, 1.2 c. 1, sec.3ª-6ª, pp. 55-91; S. STELLA, *La Congregazione della Missione in Italia*.

[2] *S.V.P.* II, p. 204; *Notices ...* II, p. 205 ff.

[3] *S.V.P.* II, p. 137; XIII, pp. 282-283.

[4] *S.V.P.* II, p. 188.

plans were not altered by the death of Lebreton, though a substitute had to be found for him. Vincent chose Bernard Codoing who had just completed the delicate task of securing the foundation at Annecy.[5]

It seems that the Rome house was the only foundation to be made on Vincent's own initiative, without anyone asking for, or offering to make the foundation. He was very keen on having a bridge-head in the Eternal City to give him direct communication with the Holy See and open up for the congregation areas of expansion outside of France. Vincent had very soon turned his gaze towards wider horizons than those of the de Gondi territories, the diocese of Paris and the frontiers of his native land. Rome could be the focal point for all these plans. In 1660 he wrote to the superior at Marseilles, describing that house as 'one of the principal houses of the company after those of Rome and Paris.'[6]

'It is no small humiliation to be poorly lodged in somebody else's house'

There was no financial capital to support the foundation at Rome and Vincent tried to remedy this without delay. Once more the generous patroness was the Duchess d'Aiguillon. In fulfilment of a promise made after her uncle was cured in 1642, she donated to the house an annual income of 2,500 *livres* from the royal postal service and, in 1643, a further income of 5,000 *livres* from the coach service to Rouen. Both these gifts were principally intended to finance retreats for ordinands.[7] The queen promised 3,000 *livres* for the same work but we do not know whether this was actually paid.[8] Some further donations improved the Rome foundation's financial situation but this would always be precarious. Income from the coaches and carriages fluctuated considerably on account of the wars, the unsafe highways and interference from the exchequer who frequently kept back part of the income.[9] So it was a long time before the missioners had their own house in Rome and they had to be content with hired lodgings which they changed frequently.[10] In the course of nineteen years they were offered various buildings; some of these they refused because the price was too high, and others because Vincent did not think they were in keeping with the aims and the works of the company.

---

[5] *S.V.P.* II, p. 205.
[6] *S.V.P.* VIII, p. 235.
[7] ABELLY, *op. cit.*, 1.1 c. 46, pp. 220-221; *S.V.P.* II, pp. 270, 390
[8] *S.V.P.* II, p. 452.
[9] *S.V.P.* II, pp. 322, 367, 413, 422, 426, 444, 466, 469, 474; III, p. 403; IV, p. 371, 371; VI, p. 161; VII, p. 522.
[10] S. STELLA, *op. cit.*, p. 7ff.

What they did acquire more readily was the church of St Yves; not Borromini's fine church of La Sapienza which was then being built, but the much more modest church of St Yves of the Bretons, one of the churches in Rome which belonged to 'the French nation'[11]. They also considered using the Pantheon but Vincent thought this project entailed too many problems.[12] What he really wanted was a modest house with a garden so that they could build extensions later on.[13] 'In the beginning we must be satisfied with a little', he said. Whether big or small it had to be called a house 'of the Mission' and the chapel was to be dedicated to the Blessed Trinity.[14] Vincent made a virtue out of necessity and was happy to think of the privations this would impose on the community:

> We would be very much at fault if we did not seem happy to be like Our Lord who said he had nowhere to lay his head. It is no small humiliation to be poorly lodged in someone else's house in a great city where people only seem to take note of well-established communities. But we should prefer to be unknown and looked down upon for as long a time as God wishes us to be in this situation. Perhaps God will use our love of poverty, if we have this sentiment, to provide us with a better place to live. If it pleases God to really fill us with this spirit then we can surely hope that our house will be a house of peace and of blessings.[15]

Right up to a year before Vincent's death the missioners did not have their own house. In 1659 they finally settled into a house bought from Cardinal Bagno, the man whose good offices while nuncio in Paris, had helped Vincent over the question of approval for the company. Two other cardinals, Brancaccio and Durazzo, also intervened on his behalf, and the latter gave a generous donation.[16] Vincent's wishes were more than fulfilled. The church was dedicated to the Trinity and not just the house, but the whole street it was in, was called 'The Mission'. This Roman street, high up in Montecitorio, still bears that name today.

---

[11] *S.V.P.* II, pp. 262, 271, 275, 325, 376-379, 392, 419, 424, 427. *Annales* (1936), pp. 408-409.
[12] *S.V.P.* II, pp. 26, 33, 34.
[13] *S.V.P.* II, p. 34.
[14] *S.V.P.* II, p. 49.
[15] *S.V.P.* VII, p. 312. the same ideas are duplicated in VII, pp. 328, 391, 543.
[16] *S.V.P.* XIII, p. 103, 119, 128.

Genoa and Turin

Cardinal Durazzo was archbishop of Genoa and it was he who promoted the second Italian foundation of the Congregation of the Mission, at Genoa. Impressed by the labours and the spirituality of Fr Codoing, whom he had got to know when the latter passed through Genoa on his way to Rome, he persuaded Vincent to send a team of missioners in 1645.[17] Their leader was Fr Blatiron, one of Vincent's most able men.

Helped by two distinguished priests from Genoa, Fr Baliano Raggio and Fr Cristoforo Monza, the archbishop had a new building constructed for the missioners.[18] He had such affection for the community that he used to join in their work, make his retreat with them and join them in giving missions.[19] In spite of all this, there was considerable delay in drawing up the foundation contract and the reasons for this were political. The contract was eventually authorised by the senate of the Republic and signed by Vincent in November, 1647.[20]

If Rome was responsible for the foundation at Genoa, then Genoa, in its turn, led to the foundation at Turin. Initial talks concerning the new foundation began in 1654 between Vincent de Paul and the Marquis of Pianezza, Filippo Emanuele di Sirmiano, prime minister of the duchy of Savoy-Piedmont. This was during the regency of Christine of France, the sister of Louis XIII, whose marriage to the heir of Savoy had been negotiated by St Francis de Sales in 1618.[21]

The marquis was edified by the works of the Vincentian missioners in Annecy and wanted to see them established in the capital of his duchy. Negotiations for this were protracted. The founder tried to persuade the congregation to take on works which in Vincent's eyes were hardly compatible with their commitment to working exclusively at giving missions and helping the clergy. Vincent told the superior at Genoa to explain this to him and he himself wrote letters in the same vein.[22] Everything was settled and although there were other differences of a political nature, the foundation was finally established in 1655.[23] Vincent chose as superior Fr Jean Martin who had had long experience in Italy since he had been part of the founding team at Rome and Genoa. He was a missioner of such tremendous zeal that Vincent feared

---

[17] ABELLY, *op. cit.*, 1.1 c. 46, p. 223; *S.V.P.* II, p. 544.

[18] *S.V.P.* IV, pp. 253, 437.

[19] *S.V.P.* III, pp. 59, 74, 187, 505.

[20] *S.V.P.* III, pp. 3, 140; *Notices ...* Vol. 2, pp. 158-159; S. STELLA, *op. cit.*, p. 15.

[21] ABELLY, *op. cit.*, 1.1 c. 46, p. 224; *S.V.P.* V, pp. 250-251.

[22] *S.V.P.* V, p. 371.

[23] *S.V.P.* V, p. 471.

for his health and personally saw to it that the priest was well nourished. On 18 July 1655, he wrote as follows to the cook at Turin:

> Please continue to look after good Fr Martin with your charitable services both on the missions and wherever he may need your help; and do not stop making him chicken broth to nourish and sustain him during his fainting fits, whenever the assistant judges this to be necessary and in spite of what others may say. I want you to know that the preservation of this servant of God is very important for the work of saving souls and something that is much appreciated by the company.[24]

Ineffable M. Vincent! 'A man with world-wide responsibilities as Vincent was at that time,' wrote one of his biographers, 'can think about soup and chicken broth for a missioner in Turin and this is the measure of his tenderness and great heartedness.'[25]

'Bandits are converted'

The three Italian houses were very similar. They all had the double ministry of preaching missions and giving retreats to ordinands; they all enjoyed the patronage of distinguished ecclesiastics, and in all three houses the missioners were called to practise heroism. At Vincent's express wish, all three houses began to recruit vocations from Italy and soon there was a novitiate, or internal seminary, in Genoa and in Rome.[26]

The most characteristic feature of the three Italian foundations was the spectacular success of their missions. In keeping with the Italian temperament which is less restrained than the French, everything seems a bit exaggerated. Throughout the Roman countryside, the Apennines, the dioceses of Viterbo and Palestrina, the country areas of Subbiaco, in the state of Genoa, in Lavagna, Sestri, Castiglione and throughout all Piedmont, it was the same story; people crowded into the churches which were overflowing, sinners openly confessed their crimes, bandits were rehabilitated into society; there was universal lamenting, terrifying shouts of 'pardon' and 'mercy', weapons were left on the altar and age-old hatreds forgotten. Abelly has left us an impressive collection of eye-witness reports either from the missioners

---

[24] *S.V.P.* VIII, p. 36.
[25] J. CALVET, *op. cit.*, p. 194.
[26] *S.V.P.* II, pp. 452-453, 456; VI, pp. 431, 508, 592; IV, 156; V, pp. 102, 375, 491.

themselves or from the bishops of the dioceses where the missions took place.[27]

A special feature of the Italian missions is that all the reports emphasised the peace that was brought to regions plagued by the endemic evil of 'vendettas'. The mission brought an end to long-standing hatred which was handed down from father to son with its ill-fated chain of murders, creating a climate of mistrust, suspicion and fear which could always be sensed, even at the most sacred moments such as the celebration of the holy sacrifice.

In no region was this evil as serious as in the island of Corsica. In 1652 Vincent was asked by the senate of Genoa to send some missioners to the island to preach in the most important places there. Vincent sent seven, and foremost among these were Frs Blatiron and Martin, the most fiery of his preachers. They gave four missions: at Campo Laura, Cotone, Corte and Niolo. They had to start by making peace among the priests themselves who were divided into two irreconcilable factions The missioners' persuasive words won over the townspeople. At Niolo the marvellous effects of the mission were outstanding and Blatiron gave Vincent a long account of it. No summary could do justice to the account itself.[28]

Vincent praised God for such great and abundant blessings. Although he refused to acknowledge it, it was Vincent who deserved the credit for that splendid harvest of souls. Instead, he attributed it to the graces God poured out on the little method.

> I would never stop talking if I were to tell you even a fraction of what God has accomplished through this method. We have so many examples of this that we would be here all night. Let us just recall one or two so that we can understand better the benefits of the little method. I remember one case where something happened that we had never experienced before, something unique, and I, with my grey hairs, can say that have never heard of any preacher who achieved such results. Oh Saviour, Oh Saviour! Bandits, as you know, are those robbers in Italy who have taken over the whole countryside; they steal

---

[27] ABELLY, 1.2 c. 1, p. 55-91. Here we have to repeat what has been said about the missions in France. L. Mezzadri has recently made a study of the Vincentian missions in central Italy in a work of historical criticism. In this the *Reports of the Missioners* are subjected to rigorous examination both as regards local customs and theology. Cf. L. MEZZADRI, 'Le missioni popolari della Congregazione della Missione nello Stato della Chiesa (1642-1700)', *RSChI* (1979), pp. 12-44.

[28] *S.V.P.* IV, pp. 411-416.

and they attack people everywhere. They are criminals and murderers. In that country there are a lot of murders because of feuds, which are carried out to the bitter end. These people destroy each other in their implacable fury; they are never ready to forgive. Once they have done away with their enemies they flee from justice and from men who are as evil as themselves; they take to the highways and live in the forests, robbing and looting the poor peasants' goods. They are called bandits and are so numerous that Italy is full of them. There is scarcely a village that does not have bandits. Well, after a mission in one of these villages, the bandits there gave up this evil way of life and were converted by the grace of God, who was pleased, in this instance, to make use of the little method! That is something unheard of up to now! It has never been known for bandits to give up crime for any reason. And this, Fathers, is what God has been pleased to achieve, through this poor, weak, community that used the little method in preaching.

To confirm what he had said, Vincent turned to someone who had taken part in these missions and began this spirited dialogue with Fr Martin.

'Is it not it true, Fr Martin, that bandits have been converted after our missions in Italy? You have been there, have you not? This is just an informal talk. Will you tell us, please, how all this came about?'
'Yes, Father. This is what happened. In the villages where we had given a mission, the bandits came to confession along with all the other people. This happens regularly.'
'Oh Saviour! What a marvellous thing! Bandits converted after sermons based on the little method! Oh, gentlemen. Even bandits were converted.'[29]

We can forgive Vincent this whiff of pride that his words reveal as he relates the anti-Italian black legend. These ideas were current at the time and the missioners' reports echo them. Shining through these words we have the clear picture of a man who is thrilled with the effects of grace working through the medium of his company.

---

[29] *S.V.P.* XI, p. 268.

The Irish Mission

A new foreign venture by the Congregation of the Mission was the direct outcome of the house founded in Rome. In 1645, the Sacred Congregation for the Propagation of the Faith asked Vincent to send some missioners to Ireland. The sacred congregation could see for themselves the work for ordinands that was beginning to take shape in the Rome house. This project was probably started by John Skyddie,[30] an Irish missioner based in Rome. Rome was interested in helping to bring about a Catholic revival in Ireland after the rebellion of 1641, under cover of the conflict between Charles I, the king of England, and his Parliament. A papal nuncio, Rinuccini, was sent there and several bishops appointed, among them the Bishop of Killala and the Bishop of Limerick who had both been consecrated in Paris, in the church of St Lazare.[31] The sacred congregation wanted to provide them with able personnel who would work with the clergy to restore the liturgy. At least this was what the cardinal prefect, Francisco Barberini, requested of Vincent.[32]

Vincent had been interested in Ireland for a long time. After the 1641 rebellion he asked Richelieu to help the Irish in their struggle. The cardinal said he regretted they could not help because at that time the king of France was having to shoulder some very heavy burdens, and so they could not possibly embark on any new ventures. When Vincent replied that the pope was ready to contribute 100,000 *écus*, Richelieu retorted:

> A hundred thousand crowns would go nowhere in providing
> an army. We would need soldiers, baggage, weapons and means
> of transport. An army is a weighty machine which is difficult
> to move.[33]

If it was not in Vincent's power to provide military aid, he certainly could help them spiritually. He was very happy to obey the order from Rome, but for reasons we do not know about, he was unable to comply with the order until the end of 1646. Vincent had about fifteen Irish missioners in the Congregation and the first of these was Skyddie, whom we have mentioned earlier, and who had joined them in 1638. Most of the others were exiles who

---

[30] *S.V.P.* II, p. 307. For the history of the C. M. in Ireland cf. ABELLY, *op. cit.*, 1.2 c. 1, pp. 145-155; PATRICK BOYLE, 'Les rélations de Saint Vincent de Paul avec l'Irlande', *Annales* (1907), p. 355 ff; *idem.*, *Saint Vincent de Paul and the Vincentians in Ireland, Scotland and England* (London, Washbourne, 1909); MARY PURCELL, *The story of the Vincentians* (Dublin, All Hallows College, 1973).

[31] *Annales* (1961), p. 495.

[32] *S.V.P.* II, p. 505.

[33] ABELLY, *op. cit.*, 1.1 c. 35, p. 170.

had discovered their priestly and missionary vocation while in France. He would naturally call on them to work in their own country but Fr Skyddie died in Rome while the business was still being negotiated. So six men were chosen. These were all lively young men: Gerard Bryan, Edmond Barry, Dermot Duggan, Francis White, Dermot O'Brien and Thaddeus Lee. Duggan, the eldest, had just turned thirty-three. The youngest, Lee, was twenty-three years old and neither he nor O'Brien was yet ordained. They were accompanied by a cleric, Philippe Le Vacher and a French priest, as well as two laybrothers, one of whom was French and the other English. At Skyddie's suggestion, the Superior was to be a Frenchman. Vincent first thought of Fr Bourdet, famous for his memorable flight from St Méen that summer. Bourdet, who had already shown that he was not cut out to be a hero, and who foresaw that life in Ireland was going to be even more hazardous than at the abbey in Brittany, declined the honour. Vincent named Fr du Chesne to replace him.[34]

'They have been delivered from the clutches of Satan'

The expedition arrived in Ireland early in 1647, after a hazardous journey. The missioners formed two teams and immediately set to work in the dioceses of Cashel and Limerick, respectively. They had the usual excellent results. The Irish Catholic population responded to the mission with the same enthusiastic fervour as the peasants in France and Italy.[35] The politico-military situation rapidly deteriorated and in the course of 1647 O'Brien's troops invaded the diocese of Cashel with fire and sword. 'Murrough of the fires' burned alive some 1,500 citizens who had taken refuge in the cathedral. The missioners found it impossible to continue their work, and their very lives were in danger. It was for this reason that the three Frenchmen and Fr White returned to France in 1648. The bishops of Cashel and Limerick both gave them letters for M. Vincent describing the work they had done.

They produced more fruit and converted more souls than all the rest of the ecclesiastics. Moreover, their good example

---

[34] *S.V.P.* III, pp. 79, 82. St Vincent used the French spelling of Anglo-Irish names. So Bryan is Brin; Duggan is Duiguin; White is Le Blanc; O'Brien is Aubriez; Lee is Lie, and so on. Coste (*M.V.* Vol. 2, p. 295) thinks that Lee did not take part in the first expedition. After comparing the different letters on this subject we are inclined to believe that he did. Coste is also unsure whether the said Fr White is Francis or George because another Irish priest had the same surname. All the documentation available suggests that his name was Francis.

[35] *S.V.P.* III, pp. 190, 274.

and upright conduct have converted a great number of the
nobility, both men and women, and these have become models
of virtue and piety. Such a thing was never seen here before
your missioners came to these parts.' 'And although these good
priests have suffered many trials since they arrived in this
country, that has not prevented them from devoting themselves
continuously to the works of the mission.[36]

In 1649 the storm broke over Limerick. Cromwell himself the
supreme commander in England after the execution of Charles I, landed in
Dublin with a formidable army and launched a systematic offensive against
the rebels. This was accompanied by a bloody persecution of Catholics. Br
Patriarch, who was English, was so disturbed by this régime of terror that his
mind was affected. Fr Duggan had to accompany him back to France.[37]

The number of missioners was now reduced to four, but they were
four heroes. Early in 1651, they gave a mission in Limerick where the people
had taken refuge after fleeing from the English troops. It was a memorable
occasion. This is how the bishop of the diocese described it to Vincent:

At the beginning of this year we began a mission in this town
and there were at least 20,000 communicants. It was so
successful and appreciated by everyone that I am sure, by God's
grace, that most of these people have been snatched from
Satan's clutches after so many evils were remedied; so many
bad confessions, so much drunkenness, swearing, adultery and
other disorders; all these have now been completely wiped
out.[38]

The most moving part of the mission was when the mayor, Thomas
Stritch, who had begun his term of office by making a retreat in the missioners'
house, went in procession on the closing day of the mission to the church of
Our Lady of Limerick, to put the keys of the city into her hands.

The spirit of martyrdom

If the mission had delivered the inhabitants of Limerick from the clutches of
the devil, these people could not escape from the clutches of the English.

---

[36] *S.V.P.* III, pp. 386-387.
[37] *S.V.P.* III, p. 486.
[38] *S.V.P.* III, pp. 420-421. This letter was dated by Coste as 1649 or 1650. M. Purcell (*op. cit.*, p.
17) dated it as 1651 basing this on the new research.

When Cromwell returned to England, his son-in-law, Ireton, took over and laid siege to Limerick in the spring of 1651. The siege lasted for six months and during this time more than 8,000 people died of the plague. When Ireton occupied the town he put to death the leading citizens, one of whom was the pious mayor. The worst savagery of the oppression was vented on priests. For them capture meant death. The bishop managed to escape, disguised as a soldier and so did the missioners but at first Vincent gave them all up for dead.[39]

In the letter he wrote to Fr Bryan at Mgr O'Dwyer's suggestion, Vincent had already faced the worst that might happen and tried to prepare them for martyrdom, or rather, he had praised their willingness to be martyred.

> We were very edified by your letter and we see in it two marvellous effects of God's grace. Firstly, we see how you have given yourself to God to persevere in that country amid all the dangers there, and your readiness to risk death rather than give up helping your neighbour. Secondly, we note the way you are thinking about your brothers' safety by sending them to France where they will be out of danger. In the first case you were motivated by the spirit of martyrdom and in the second case, by prudence; in both matters you have followed the example of Our Lord, who when he was about to suffer the torments of death for the salvation of mankind, was concerned for his disciples' safety and said, 'Let these alone and do not molest them.' As your companion priests share your dispositions, and this in spite of the real danger of war and of contagion, we think we should allow them to stay. How do we know what God has in store for them? the fact is that he would not have given them such a holy resolve to no purpose. Mon Dieu! How unsearchable are your judgements! You desire to harvest souls who are in good dispositions and to gather the good wheat into your everlasting granaries. We adore your designs, O Lord.[40]

As it happened, only one of the missioners was to shed his blood in the sacrifice which was anticipated and accepted by his father and founder with such submission to the divine will. In 1652 Frs Bryan and Barry managed to reach France after various setbacks. But Thaddeus Lee, the youngest of

---

[39] *S.V.P.* IV p. 290.
[40] *S.V.P.* IV, p. 15.

the group, who had earlier escaped from Limerick, was discovered by the English in his native town where he had taken refuge. It was here that he was brutally martyred in front of his mother. The executioners cut off his hands and his feet and then battered his head in. He is the protomartyr of the Congregation of the Mission.[41]

The mission to Ireland lasted barely six years. It was the Vincentian company's first adventure overseas and the first to be sealed in blood.

Scotland, the Hebrides and Orkney

Some of the missioners who came back from Ireland found it hard to settle down to the comparatively peaceful life of the French houses. Fr Bryan went back to Ireland with two fellow countrymen after Vincent's death.[42] Frs Duggan and White did not wait that long. They were soon ready to undertake a similar adventure in another part of the British Isles-Scotland and the Hebrides. On 7 October 1650, Vincent requested the necessary permission from the Sacred Congregation of Propaganda, confirming their suitability for the work; both men were native speakers of Gaelic, the language spoken in those islands.[43] A month later they were both at Antwerp disguised as merchants,[44] waiting for a Dutch ship to take them to Scotland.

It was in that densely populated city that they came into contact with a Scottish nobleman, Angus MacDonald, Laird of Glengarry. He had recently been reconciled to the Church, to use Fr Duggan's phrase and one that is repeated by Abelly, meaning that there was a moral conversion, not that he had changed his religion. The MacDonalds were one of the families that had remained proudly loyal to their religion and to their king.[45]

---

[41] *S.V.P.* IV, pp. 343, 481-484.

[42] M. PURCELL, *op. cit.*, pp. 22-27; *Recueil des principales circulaires ...*, Vol. 1, p. 4.

[43] *S.V.P.* IV pp. 91-94.

[44] This is mentioned in the *ex libris* of a book belonging to Fr Duggan which is preserved in the Scottish archives. In the *Commentaria in Sacram Scripturam,* of Tirino, we read: 'This book belongs to C. M., Paris. It was bought in Antwerp by the first missioners of that community that the pope sent to Scotland, viz Francis White and Diarmuid Duggan, 10 November 1650. They arrived here on the 1 March 1651 and on the isle of Uist 25 March 1651- D. Duggan C. M.' (M. PURCELL, *op. cit.*, pp. 43-44). This document resolves Coste's difficulty about Francis and George White (*M.V.* Vol. 2, pp. 201-202, in a footnote, and in *S.V.P.* Vol. 4 p. 305) It also makes clear that as Abelly specifically stated (*op. cit.*, 1.1 c. 11, p. 201) only two missioners were sent to Scotland. The third, Fr Lumsden, arrived the following year.

[45] M. PURCELL, *op. cit.*, pp. 44-46. A more complete version of Fr Duggan's letter than that preserved by Abelly and copied by Coste (*S.V.P.* IV, pp. 515-516) is in the Propaganda archives and this is the text used by Mary Purcell.

Protected by such an important gentleman, who was the real overlord of the regions they were going to evangelise, they made a successful crossing. Once they had arrived in Scotland they stayed at the imposing Glengarry castle perched on the craggy hill named Creag an Fhithich, 'The Rock of the Raven', where they 'converted' an elderly member of the family. Then the two companions separated. Duggan headed for the Hebrides and White remained in the Scottish Highlands. In 1653 he was joined there by a third companion, the Scotsman Thomas Lumsden. In 1652 Vincent had got permission from the Congregation of Propaganda for him to go. It was Vincent's intention to send two Irish missioners with him: Dermot Bryan, whom we have already mentioned, and John Ennery, but these could not reach their destination and had to remain in France.[46]

The work in Scotland offered a complete contrast to that carried out in Ireland. After the great missions which were attended by thousands of fervent people, came the hard life of a clandestine priest, the agonising wandering about through desperately poor regions, secret meetings with small groups of Catholics who had forgotten the basic elements of their faith and the constant fear that someone might denounce them. Such were the conditions that Fr Duggan had to face as he travelled to the isles of Uist, Barra, Eigg, Canna and Skye, and to the regions of Moidart, Morar, Knoydart, Glengarry and Arisaig, leaving everywhere the imprints of self-denial and heroism.[47]

The hard life of the missioner had its spiritual compensations: the good dispositions of the islanders when receiving religious instruction, the eagerness with which they repeated this teaching, their bravery in facing persecution, and the wonders, whether (or not) these might be called miracles, with which the Lord accompanied their preaching of missions in these primitive parts.[48]

Fr Duggan died on 17 May 1657, while he was preparing in South Uist another missionary expedition to the island of Pabbay, beyond Barra. The people still venerate his name. A chapel on Uist and a mountain pass in Barra are named after him. Compton Mackenzie attributed the islanders'

---

[46] *S.V.P.* IV, pp. 493-494.
[47] *S.V.P.* IV, pp. 315-316.
[48] *S.V.P.* V, pp. 116-117.
  According to information supplied by Fr Joseph Cunningham, C. M., the people of Barra call this mountain pass the Gap of Duggan (Gaelic Bealach a' Dhugain). There are two places in South Uist named as possible burial places for the body of Diarmuid Duggan. One is an ancient cemetery called Hogharor which has a ruin of a church or chapel to which his name is given though the chapel is said to predate him by three centuries. The more accepted place of his burial is called Kildonnan.

fidelity to the faith of their forefathers, to the labours of Fr Duggan and the affection the people had for this priest.[49]

News of Duggan's death did not reach Vincent until November. He hastened to inform the superior of every house and his words reveal both the pain of a father and the heroism of an apostle.

> We have received the very sad news that God has called to himself Fr Duggan who died on 17 May at his mission on the isles of Hebrides where it may be said he was working wonders. Those poor islanders mourned him as they would a father. They have not sent me details of the good that God worked through him, since nobody dares risk speaking about religion except in general terms, and only metaphorically, on account of the English who have organised a cruel persecution of Catholics, and more particularly of any priests they find. This, Father, is the way that God wishes to test the company everywhere, by taking away its good labourers. Since he is Lord he can dispose of things as he wills; it is up to us to beg him to raise up new workers after his own heart, to continue the work.[50]

While Fr Duggan was evangelising the Hebrides, Fr White was making his way through the Scottish Highlands. He went up the Great Glen and followed the Caledonian Rift, which divides Scotland, and went as far as Inverness. He worked for a time with Fr Lumsden who was a native of Aberdeen. There is a lovely story of something that happened at this time and the anecdote is definitely authentic. One day during the summer of 1654, they met two brothers who were tending their flocks. They told the missioners that their father was dying in a cottage nearby but no matter how much they begged him to make a will, he refused to do so, saying he was not going to die yet.

> He is very rich and we are just two of his many sons. We are prepared to accept whatever he decides to leave us but if he dies without making a will there will surely be many family quarrels, and up to now we have been a very united family.

One of the missioners, who had some knowledge of medicine, went into the cottage. He saw straightaway that the old man really was near the

---

[49] M. PURCELL, *op. cit.*, p. 49.

[50] *S.V.P.* VI, p. 602.

end and urged him to leave his affairs in order. But the man declared that he was a Catholic and for many years he had begged God not to let him die without the last sacraments. 'I am sure', he said, 'that God will not refuse what I ask. And since there are no priests round here that means I am not going to die yet.'

The missioner then told him that he was a priest, that he was on his way to Glengarry and that he had with him everything necessary to administer the sacraments. When he heard this, the old man told his sons to leave the cottage. He made his confession, received holy viaticum and extreme unction and then, after a few moments silence, he made his will. The missioners stayed with him until his death a few hours later.[51]

A short time after witnessing this modern version of the *Nunc Dimittis,* Frs Lumsden and White went their separate ways. The former spent several months travelling through the far northern parts of Scotland: Moray, Candie, and on the other side of the Great Glen, Ross, Sutherland and Caithness, from which point he reached Orkney. Lumsden wrote but seldom for fear his letters might fall into the hands of the authorities. Even so, he managed to tell Vincent of his success in converting Protestants and supporting Catholics in their faith, through preaching and the sacraments. At Easter 1654, he said Mass in a nobleman's house; fifty people went to communion and twenty of these were recent converts. He lived with the constant fear of being denounced. His zeal, and that of other missionaries from the Congregation of Propaganda, aroused the jealousy of Protestant ministers. When Cromwell was informed that many Scots, particularly in the western provinces, 'were going over to Papistry', he ordered new investigations, especially into the activities of priests who were to be imprisoned and punished, according to the law of the land.[52]

One of the first to fall victim to these laws was Fr White. In February 1655, he was arrested, together with a Jesuit and a secular priest, in Gordon Castle, the fortress of the Marquis of Huntley, and one of the most frequently used refuges for Catholic priests. He was taken first to Aberdeen prison and then to Edinburgh. Vincent feared for his life,[53] but he did not dare intervene from France. Any step he might have taken would have revealed the fact that the prisoner was a priest and this was just what his accusers wanted to prove.[54] He had to be content, therefore, with commending him to the prayers of the community. His words show the mixture of human tenderness, a supernatural

---

[51] M. PURCELL, *op. cit.*, pp. 49-50.
[52] *S.V.P.* V, pp. 124-125, 145; VI, pp. 530-531.
[53] COLLET, *op. cit.*, Vol. 2, p. 480; *S.V.P.* V, pp. 365, 367, 389.
[54] *S.V.P.* XI, p. 185.

outlook on life and the vision of faith that so characterised Vincent in his old age.

> Let us commend to God our good Fr White who was working in the Scottish highlands. The English heretics have imprisoned him, along with a Jesuit priest. They have both been taken to prison in Aberdeen, which is where Fr Lumsden comes from and he will continue to see and to help him. In that country there are many Catholics who visit and help priests in distress. Meanwhile, this good missioner is on the road to martyrdom. I do not know whether we should be glad or sorry about this, since on the one hand, God is glorified by his arrest since it is suffered out of love for him, and the company should reckon itself fortunate that God finds it worthy of being given a martyr who is happy to suffer in God's name and to offer himself, as this man is doing, for whatever God pleases to do with him and his life ...
>
> All this moves us, in God, to feelings of great joy and gratitude. But on the other hand, is not this our brother who is suffering? Should we not be suffering with him? As for me, I confess that humanly speaking I am very grieved and feel the pain deeply, but on a spiritual level, it seems to me that we should be blessing God as though he had granted us a very special grace.[55]

Fr White was set free since they could not prove that he had said Mass, something that English law regarded as a crime punishable by death. Vincent particularly admired the prisoner's courage in not denying his priesthood in order to gain his freedom. As soon as he was set free, White went back to the Scottish highlands to continue his work.[56]

The difficult conditions under which the mission to Scotland was carried out drew extraordinary signs (possibly miracles) that follow in the wake of those sent by the Lord.[57] This often happens in times of persecution. We cannot, *a priori,* attribute these events to the need for suffering, persecuted people to experience God's protection. But Vincent, who by nature distrusted extraordinary happenings, for he was a cautious and realistic man, was aware that divine interventions are a reality. He agreed that some of the events the

---

[55] *S.V.P.* XI, p. 173.
[56] *S.V.P.* XI, pp. 288, 304.
[57] ABELLY, *S.V.P.* XI, p. 173.

missioners described might be interpreted as extraordinary interventions on the part of God:

> But let us get back to our good Fr White and think about the way God treated him after he had done so much good in his mission. Here is something wonderful; some people would say it was a miracle. Some time ago the weather at sea was very bad so the men had only a very poor catch of fish and the people were in great want. They asked him to say some prayers and to sprinkle the sea with holy water because they thought this disturbance of the elements must be due to some evil spirit. He did as they asked and God was pleased to grant an immediate calm so they had a plentiful supply of fish once more. It was he himself who wrote and told me this.

No further reference was made to the alleged miracle. To be on safer ground, Vincent went on to talk about the real nature of Fr White's virtue and the true significance of his work.

> Other people, too, have spoken to me about his labours in the highlands, encouraging Catholics and converting heretics; the continual danger he was in and how he suffered want, having only oatcakes to eat.[58]

The mission to Scotland brings another dimension to the missionary labours of Vincent de Paul and his congregation. Lost in Scotland's remote and desolate highlands, these missioners added bravery and isolation to the usual features of the Vincentian vocation to evangelise the poor. They had to go about in disguise and were pursued from one place to another, hiding in noblemen's castles or in fishermen's huts, suffering unspeakable privations to keep the ancient Catholic faith alive in a country taken over by heretics. Vincent followed their work from afar, but he felt them as close to his heart as the groups of missioners who left the cloisters of St Lazare every autumn to evangelise the smiling countryside of France. Vincent, who was so closely attached to his native province, and so deeply marked by the culture of his own country, could make room in his company for that strange breed of priest-gentleman that so much reflected the British tradition. And these, in their turn, always felt the support of their founder's protective and understanding tenderness. Fr White returned to France in time to be there

---

[58] *S.V.P.* XI, p. 175.

when his father and friend died. Then he went back to Scotland where he lived and worked until his death in 1679. In 1663, three years after Vincent's death, Fr Lumsden made the final break from the scene of his labours. But the Vincentian mission in Scotland did not come to a complete end until 1704.[59]

The queen of Poland

It was a political coincidence that brought about the mission to Poland, the third European country to welcome Vincent's priests. In 1645, King Ladislaus IV of Poland (1595-1648), who was a widower, was looking for a French lady to be his wife. This position called for great sensitivity and Mazarin's choice fell on Princess Marie de Gonzague, the daughter of Charles de Gonzague, duke of Nevers and Mantua. It proved a very good choice. Marie de Gonzague was outstanding in high society for her piety, beauty and talent. Her piety meant that she was attracted to two of the most fervent groups of peoples, the Jansenists of Port Royal and Vincent de Paul's ladies of Charity, in whose work she shared. She wanted to have the same religious background in her adopted country as she had been used to in France. She brought as chaplain the French priest, François de Fleury, who had strong Jansenist sympathies and she asked Vincent to send missioners, Daughters of Charity and some Visitation nuns. Vincent agreed and he used this opportunity to extend to that far-off country the benefits of missions for the people and retreats for the clergy. The new queen wanted to confide both these works to the priests of the Mission.[60]

The first expedition arrived later than expected. The delay was partly due to the difficult circumstances in which the queen found herself. Three years after her arrival in Poland, her husband, Ladislaus IV, died. His brother, and successor to the throne, the former Jesuit and cardinal John Casimir II (1648-1668), took her as his wife. Once her position was secured she took up again the projects she had started earlier.

The first group of missioners arrived in Warsaw in November 1651. There were five of them: two priests, Fr Lambert aux Couteaux and Fr Guillaume Desdames; two clerics, Nicolas Guillot and Casimir Zelazewsky, together with a lay brother, Jacques Posny.[61] Fr Lambert was in charge. Years earlier when Vincent had recommended him to the Sacred Congregation

---

[59] M. PURCELL, *op. cit.*, pp. 52-64.
[60] *S.V.P.* IV, pp. 246-248: ABELLY, *op. cit.*, 1.2 c. 1, pp. 189-200; *Mémoires de la Congrégation de la Mission* Vol. 1, *La Congrégation de la Mission en Pologne*.
[61] *S.V.P.* XIII, pp. 359-361.

of Propaganda as bishop of Babylon, he said that letting him go was like tearing out an eye and cutting off an arm.[62]

In a letter to Vincent, the queen gave him news of the missioners' arrival and also shared with him a confidence that shows us the dangerous state of medical practice at that time. 'If God grants me the grace of not dying in childbirth ...'[63] she wrote. Every confinement was potentially fatal, even for a queen.

However, the illustrious lady's fears proved unfounded. Three months later, Vincent congratulated her on the birth of a 'fine prince'. The Lord had heard his prayer, just as he had done on a previous occasion when the queen gave birth to a daughter. This was a prayer that God would grant their Majesties, 'children of royal blood who would provide monarchs for Poland till the end of time.'[64] The prayer, however, was only partly answered. The infant prince died when he was only three months old. Vincent was deeply affected by the news although he recognised that God wanted, 'to deprive earth of this child, so that he could reign in heaven.'[65]

Vincent was allowed to share the lady's sorrows and her joys, both great and small. Years later, Marie de Gonzague begged him to send her a little dog. The Daughters of Charity promised to see to this royal request. They acquired a dog and kept it in their house until they had the opportunity of sending it to Poland. In the meantime Vincent became fond of the little animal. At the end of a long letter to the superior about very serious affairs concerning the mission in Poland, he added the following postscript:

> Mlle Le Gras brought to our parlour the little dog they are sending to the queen. It is so fond of one of the Sisters of Charity that it will not even look at the others; the minute she goes out of the room it starts to whine and to fret. I am filled with confusion seeing the particular affection this little creature has for the sister who feeds it while I show such little attachment to my sovereign benefactor and so little detachment from other things. You can assure Her Majesty that the sisters will take good care of it.'[66] Some months later he added this information. 'Tell Mlle de Villiers (the queen's French attendant) that the little creature is now deigning to look at me.[67]

---

[62] *S.V.P.* III, p. 158.
[63] *S.V.P.* IV, p. 272.
[64] *S.V.P.* IV, pp. 57, 318.
[65] *S.V.P.* IV, p. 349.
[66] *S.V.P.* V, pp. 360-361.
[67] *S.V.P.* V, p. 377.

Not everything about Vincent was serious and desperately important. His big, generous, heart found room for lesser joys, too. The poor queen would need all the consolations she could get during the serious trials that were to befall her.

'Send me another Fr Lambert'

Marie de Gonzague intended confiding to the missioners the seminary she proposed to establish in Vilna.[68] But the archbishop refused his consent. The Jesuits had persuaded him not to allow this because they thought the French priests who had a good relationship with Fr Fleury,[69] must therefore be influenced by Jansenism. In vain Vincent tried to get recommendations from the archbishop of Paris and the nuncio. The opposition lasted for years. It only ended when Vincent managed to persuade the French Jesuits to write to their brothers in Poland and ask them to desist.[70] This incident was deeply significant for the development of the Polish mission, which differed greatly from the mission in France, Italy or the British Isles.

The queen continued to look for work for the missioners. They were offered the parish of Sokolka near Grodno. Fr Desdames went there while Fr Lambert and the rest of his companions remained at court in Cracow. They found the city battling against a fierce epidemic of plague. The missioners devoted themselves fervently to the task of helping the sick.[71] Fr Lambert fell ill. He had only just recovered when news reached him that the epidemic had spread to Warsaw. Paying no heed to the queen's many recommendations to take care of himself, he rushed to the capital to organise aid for the poor. Marie de Gonzague ordered him to stay at the palace and to sleep in the king's own room.[72] The situation was desperate. Medical aid for the sick was conspicuous by its absence. Fr Lambert, helped by Br Guillot, had to improvise everything. Vincent recounts this with a father's justifiable pride:

> The work of our missioners in Poland is bearing much fruit ...
> there has been a serious outbreak of plague in Warsaw, where
> the king normally resides, so all the inhabitants who were able
> to flee have abandoned the city. Here, as in every other place

---

[68] *S.V.P.* IV, p. 272.

[69] *S.V.P.* IV, p. 349.

[70] *Mémoires* ...,Vol. 1, p. 12; POOLE, *op. cit.*, p. 194.

[71] *S.V.P.* IV. pp. 512, 521.

[72] *S.V.P.* IV. p. 487.

affected by the plague, there is hardly anything in the way of organisation; on the contrary, there is almost complete chaos because nobody buries the dead and these are left lying in the street and are eaten by dogs. As soon as somebody falls ill, he is thrown out into the street and will die because nobody will provide him with food. The poor workers, servants and serving maids, the poor widows and the orphans, are completely abandoned; they cannot find work and they cannot beg a bit of bread from anyone because all the rich people have fled. Fr Lambert was sent there, amidst all the desolation, to do something about all these needs. And, in fact, he has begun to restore order; he has had the dead buried, and abandoned sick people taken to suitable places where they can be cared for both spiritually and corporally, and this service was also provided for people whose illnesses were not contagious. And, finally, he ordered four separate houses to be prepared as hospices or hospitals; he had all the poor people who were not ill taken and lodged there, the men in one part and the women and children in another. He helped all these with alms and gifts sent by the queen.[73]

After the plague and famine came war. Poland suffered, as she was to suffer so many times in her history, from the covetousness of powerful neighbours. Russia and Sweden were preparing to attack the Catholic kingdom in what was to be the Thirteen Years War (1654-1667). King Charles Gustave X (1622-1666) and Tsar Alexis (1629-1676) put forward several pretexts as they hastened to prepare for war. The king and queen of Poland moved to the eastern frontier, which was the most dangerous area to be in, and Fr Lambert, who was part of their retinue, travelled with them. From Grodno, where he had another unsuccessful interview with the archbishop of Vilna about the seminary, he took a little trip to Sokolka, which was only five leagues away, to visit Fr Desdames. Death, which had failed to conquer him in Cracow or in Warsaw, was waiting for him there. It came in the shape of an illness which was so painful that, as he himself said, 'I could not suffer it for long and stay alive.' It only lasted three days. On 31 January 1653, Fr Lambert died at the age of 47. His death was universally mourned. The queen wrote a long letter to Vincent in her own handwriting, saying, 'If you do not send me another Fr Lambert I do not know what I will do.'[74]

---

[73] *S.V.P.* IV. pp. 533-534.
[74] *S.V.P.* IV, pp. 560-561.

'Famine, plague, war'

Finding another Fr Lambert was no easy matter. The man chosen to replace him was Charles Ozenne, who at that time was superior at Troyes. With him were sent the cleric Nicolas Duperroy and the first Visitation nuns, and they started their journey in August 1653. They set sail from Dieppe but had hardly left the port when the vessel was captured by an English pirate ship, which, after a dreadful crossing, took them to Dover. They had to remain in Dover for six weeks while the British Parliament and Admiralty debated whether the seizure of the boat was a legitimate act of war or not. Then the passengers were released and authorised to return to France. The nuns did so and landed in Calais on 5 October. Ozenne and Duperroy stayed in Dover until they were given their luggage back and the boat was authorised to continue its journey.[75]

They arrived in Poland about the middle of January 1654. They found many surprises there. The clerics Guillot and Zelazewski were now ordained and together with Fr Desdames they were negotiating the transfer of Holy Cross parish in Warsaw to the Congregation of the Mission.[76] There were still some traces of the plague and the missioners continued to attend to the sick. The church of Holy Cross was handed over to them during that same month but the formal agreement was not confirmed till the end of the year. The queen gave them a house with a kitchen garden near to the church.[77] Fr Desdames who was getting bored in his Sokolka retreat and who could now speak some Polish, hurried to join his companions in the capital, as instructed by Vincent. [78]

Things were beginning to go well. Shortly after this, Duperroy was ordained, but the mission received two setbacks, Fr Guillot returned to France and Fr Zelazewski left the company.[79] In spite of everything, the works flourished. In May they took over another parish at Skuly, near Warsaw. Fr Guillot had not long arrived back in France when he decided to return to Poland and he was accompanied by three students and a laybrother.[80] Zelazewski was feeling unsettled but he continued to work with the missioners. They gave their first mission in October. Frs Zelazewski, Desdames, Guillot

---

[75] Coste mistakenly supposed that Ozenne went back to Calais with the Visitation nuns. (*M.V.* Vol. 2, p. 211). We can see from St Vincent's letters that this was not so. *Cf. S.V.P.* V, pp. 24, 33, 42, 46.

[76] *S.V.P.* V, pp. 44, 74.

[77] *S.V.P.* V, p. 64.

[78] *S.V.P.* V, pp. 74, 77.

[79] *S.V.P.* V, pp. 86-87, 104-107, 108, 111.

[80] *S.V.P.* V, pp. 132, 137, 159, 177.

and Duperroy took part in it though Fr Zelazewski was the only one to preach because of the language problem.[81] The bishop of Posen had made up his mind to send his ordinands to Holy Cross. The ladies of Vilna asked for a confraternity of Charity to be established. Prince Wielopolski offered to found another house for the mission near Gdansk. The queen continued her plans to set up a seminary. The mission that was preached in Holy Cross parish was a great success.[82]

Such smiling hopes were dashed by the outbreak of war. Poland was attacked by Russia and Sweden simultaneously. The Russians occupied Lithuania, the Swedes went to Warsaw. The capital had to be evacuated. Fr Ozenne and the Daughters of Charity who had arrived in the meantime, moved with the court to Silesia. Fr Zelazewski and Br Posny both returned home and the youngest missioners were recalled to France. That left only Fr Desdames and Fr Duperroy in Warsaw. The capital was occupied by the Swedes on 30 August 1655, and regained by the Poles shortly afterwards. The following year it again fell to the Swedes who carried out a systematic sacking of the capital and Holy Cross church was not spared. Fr Duperroy protested and was so brutally beaten by the soldiers that he was left for dead. He was rescued thanks to the charity of some good ladies of the neighbourhood. Not long after recovering from this attack he was taken ill with a stomach complaint and asked to return to France. Thanks to the attentions showered on him by the Daughters of Charity at Oppeln, and to an operation he had, Fr Duperroy regained his health and stayed in Poland.[83]

In June 1657, the Swedes again occupied Warsaw. Fr Desdames who was on his own minding the house, had a presentiment that the city was about to fall and he left Warsaw on the very day that the Swedish troops entered it. The city was put to fire and sword and whole districts were reduced to ashes. Fire raged against the missioners' house and that of the Daughters of Charity with their orchards and poultry yards. When Fr Desdames returned he could not even find a chalice to say Mass. The situation at Skuly was equally catastrophic. The Swedes murdered the parish priest, burnt the church down and destroyed the missioners' cowsheds and wine cellar. Meanwhile, Fr Ozenne followed the court from one place to another, keeping pace with the enemy's advance. At Cracow, which was the last place of refuge for the worn-out monarchs, he and the Daughters of Charity devoted themselves to caring for the wounded.

As last the course of the war began to change. The Swedes were repulsed and Warsaw was reconquered in October 1657. Ozenne returned to

---

[81] *S.V.P.* V, p. 201.
[82] *Mémoires ...*, Vol. 1, pp. 18-20.
[83] *S.V.P.* VI, pp. 401, 541.

a desolate sight. Not a single building belonging to the company remained standing.

Faced with such an accumulation of disasters Vincent's reaction showed the same generous resignation as that aroused in him by the fate of the missioners in Scotland. Referring to Fr Desdames and Fr Duperroy, he said to the community:

> What things did they suffer in that country? Famine? That reigns everywhere. Plague? They both caught it and one of them had it twice. War? They were in the midst of armies and both fell into enemy hands. In short, God tried them in every possible way. My God, may you be for ever blessed and glorified for the graces you bestow on those who abandon themselves to you. Be, yourself, your own praise for having granted the Company two such wonderful men as these.[84]

'It would not have been right for you to have been spared'

He consoled Fr Ozenne, exhorting him to show solidarity with the sufferings of the people.

> You tell me that three of your houses in Warsaw and five in country parts have been destroyed in the war. That is a big loss but it would not be right for you to have been spared the sorrows that affect the people. God has allowed this and he will take care of repairing the damage in the measure that his Providence thinks fitting.[85]

Vincent, for his part, was not discouraged by adversity. He immediately began to prepare another expedition to replace the men lost. Yet another, and an equally sad loss, was to come. On 14 August 1658, Fr Ozenne died from a violent attack of fever. He was forty-six. In his typically spiritual way, Vincent broke the news:

> He had been preparing for this (to leave this life and be united with Our Lord) ever since he entered the company where he always avoided evil and did good in a most zealous and fruitful

---

[84] *S.V.P.* VI, p. 412.
[85] *S.V.P.* VII, p. 5.

way. He was very open, amiable and edifying. God is now his reward.[86]

The mission in Poland survived all these disasters. Circumstances had rendered the usual ministries of the company virtually impossible. On the other hand, they were able to take on works which were equally in keeping with its objectives: helping the sick, the soldiers and the injured. And it had ripened two men for heaven. Throughout the mission's eventful history it would be called on to practise the same virtues and to fashion the same sort of men. The spirit of the community was beginning to be lived out in different ways. France, Italy, Ireland, Scotland and Poland, all represented the start of different traditions within the Congregation of the Mission.

Sweden on the horizon

At that time, two further initiatives (those of Sweden and of Spain) were strangled at birth. Throughout the whole of 1654, attempts were made to send missioners to Sweden and in the beginning there was talk of sending men to Denmark, too, with a similar commitment to the work done on the Scottish missions to strengthen the faith of the few Catholics who had kept up the practice of their religion in that Protestant country.

On two occasions Propaganda Fide instructed Vincent to organise the work; the French ambassador, Baron d'Avaugour kept on asking for it and Fr Guillot wanted to do it. There was a time when everything seemed set. The superior in Poland was told to give Fr Guillot all the help he needed. But then came the difficulties. The queen of Poland refused to let Fr Guillot go, and so the ambassador looked elsewhere for workers. Vincent saw this as a manifestation of God's will and, not without some pain, abandoned the plan. He had lost the opportunity to extend the work of his missioners to a new field of endeavour but he had shown the measure of a zeal that was ready to go wherever God's glory and the salvation of souls was at stake.[87]

Spain, the unfinished project

There were three attempts at making a foundation in Spain and each one was for a different diocese: Barcelona in 1644, Toledo in 1657-1658 and Plasencia in 1660.

---

[86] *S.V.P.* VII, p. 266.
[87] The correspondence about Sweden continued all through 1654, from 30 January of that year till 26 February 1655. Cf. *S.V.P.* V, pp. 64, 163, 178, 212, 227, 247, 254, 325.

The house at Barcelona was meant to be a French, not a Spanish foundation. At that time the Catalans were in rebellion against the policies of Count-Duke Olivares and had proclaimed Louis XIII of France as Count of Barcelona. Between the years 1641 and 1654 there were ten French viceroys and several of these had some acquaintanceship with Vincent.[88] These were Brezé, Richelieu's brother-in-law (1641-1642), La Mothe-Fénélon (1643-1644 and then 1651-1652), who surrendered to the Spanish troops and so brought about the expulsion of the French from peninsular Catalonia, and the Duke of Mercoeur (1650).[89]

The real cornerstone of French politics in Catalonia was Pierre de Marca (1594-1642), former president of the parlement at Pau and nominee for the bishopric of Couserans. A fanatical supporter of Mazarin, he eventually became archbishop of Paris on the resignation of Cardinal de Retz. If the viceroys had military power, then civil and ecclesiastical authority was vested in Marca who, in his capacity as inspector and intendant general, took responsibility for civil and ecclesiastical government, assuming all these powers in the interregnum between each of the six viceroys who succeeded each other during the period that he was in office. (1643-1651).[90] The main feature of his ecclesiastical policy was the persecution of Catalan priests and religious who were opposed to the French government.[91] This policy proved to be counter-productive since he himself stated in 1645 that most of the clergy, monks, nobles, great ladies, people of rank and prominent business men ... were openly declaring themselves in favour of the Spanish party.'[92]

One aspect of this policy of frenchifying the Catalan Church was the project to bring French religious to Catalonia. On 4 December 1645, Louis XIV (or rather, Mazarin), wrote to the viceroy of Catalonia:

> Your reference to the advisability of sending French religious
> to Catalonia comes at an opportune moment and this would
> be very much to my advantage but I would need to know

---

[88] For information on the French domination of Catalonia it is not sufficient to consult books on general history, but it is essential to study the works of J. SENABRE, *La acción de Francia en Cataluña en la pugna por la hegemonía europea (1640-1652)* (Barcelona, Barcino, 1956); *Resistència del Rosselló a incorporarse a Francia* (Barcelona, Barcino, 1970); *El tractat dels Pirineus i la mutilació de Catalunya* (Barcelona, Barcino, 1978), 3ª ed.

[89] References to these three viceroys are to be found in *S. V.P.* II, p. 194; V, pp. 13, 618-619; VII, p. 236; VIII, p. 439.

[90] The references to Pierre de Marca are in St Vincent's correspondence *S. V.P.* III, p. 239; VIII, pp. 529-531; X, pp. 394, 453. For information on Pierre de Marca, *cf. Annales* (1953), p. 507.

[91] J. SANABRE, *La acción en Francia* ..., pp. 289-290.

[92] *Ibid.*, p. 320.

beforehand what needs to be done before I send them and I would have to be informed about who should be admitted. So M. Marca should send us a very detailed report about the status and the qualities we should look for in such religious, the manner in which they are to be introduced into the country, and as many details as possible about how the plan is to be put into operation.[93]

The plan to bring Vincentian missioners to Barcelona in 1644 was one more aspect of Mazarin and Marca's ecclesiastical policy. This is shown by the fact that the initiative came from Queen Anne of Austria who promised Vincent 3,000 *livres* for the foundation. Vincent showed little enthusiasm for the idea. Did he realise that he was only being used as a pawn in a game of political chess? Although he was ready, as always, to comply with a sovereign's wishes, he was very sceptical about the queen's intentions and about her reliability. After a while the matter was dropped.[94] We should not be sorry about this. If Vincentian missioners had gone to Catalonia as agents of French oppressors it might have ruined for ever any future hopes of establishing them in Spain.

The plans for Toledo and Plasencia during the final years of Vincent's life were quite different from the Catalonia project. The idea for both foundations was first thought of in Rome. A representative of the archbishop of Toledo in Rome was an Irish priest, James Dowley, (the latinised form 'Loeus' appears in Vincent's correspondence) and he interested his prelate, Mgr Moscoso y Sandoval (1646-1665), in the work of giving missions and retreats to ordinands, a work he had seen Fr Jolly's companions doing. Vincent was pleased to hear this and began to think of possible candidates for the Spanish mission. The most suitable choice seemed to be Fr Martin but he was needed in Turin. Fr Bryan, who had returned from Ireland, was equally suitable. However, the cardinal of Toledo did not make any firm offer, and Vincent, true to his principle of never starting a foundation on his own initiative, buried the project.[95]

The Oratorian priest, Luis Crespi y Borja (+ 1663), who was bishop of Plasencia and Spanish ambassador to the Holy See, showed a closer interest in the possibility of such a foundation. A priest in his diocese who had made a retreat in the house at Montecitorio told him about the aims and the methods of the Congregation of the Mission. The bishop had organised missions in

---

[93] *Ibid.*, p. 324.
[94] References to the question of a foundation in Catalonia are to be found in *S.V.P.* II, pp. 452, 456, 461, 472.
[95] *S.V.P.* VI, p. 342; VII, pp. 277, 311, 328, 377, 386, 392, 416.

Plasencia which were very similar to those given by Vincent's followers but retreats for ordinands were new to him. He asked Fr Jolly to send him a report on their method of working and he let it be seen that he wanted to bring the missioners to his diocese. Vincent had many reservations. He doubted whether he could find in the company subjects who were on the same cultural level as the Spanish clergy and he recommended Jolly to drag his feet in providing the report requested by the bishop of Plasencia. Again, he did not want to be the one to initiate a foundation.[96] Providence's clock had not yet struck the Spanish hour for the Congregation of the Mission.

Even excluding Spain, at the time of Vincent's death the congregation had taken solid root in European countries outside of France. Its international vocation was assured. The Vincentian way of interpreting Church reforms had shown that it could be adapted to societies which were very different from the one it was originally designed to serve.

---

[96] *S.V.P.* VIII, pp. 269, 279, 286.

Chapter XXV
TUNIS AND ALGERIA:
THE MISSION TO THE CAPTIVES

A clause in the foundation contract for the house at Marseilles, signed on 25 July 1643 by Vincent de Paul and Marie de Wignerod, Duchess d'Aiguillon, stipulated that:

> The priests of the Mission have the strict and lasting obligation to send priests of the said Congregation of the Mission to Barbary at such times as is judged fitting to console poor Christian captives and prisoners of that said place and instruct them in the faith and in the fear of God. They shall give these people the same sort of missions, catechesis, instructions and exhortations and they shall pray and say Mass in their customary manner.[1]

Was this just intuition on the part of the duchess or did the initiative come from a higher authority? According to Abelly, in 1642 the king felt inspired to help the poor captives and had 'cast his eyes on M. Vincent, judging him to be well able to undertake this charitable mission.' Some of Vincent's priests were sent to Barbary to give spiritual and material help to the poor captives, and to this end Vincent was given the sum of nine or ten thousand *livres*.[2]

Did Vincent himself play any part in initiating this new work? Judging from previous occasions we can well imagine that it was he who inspired the king and the duchess to show concern for the captives. And did Vincent's interest in their plight derive from the memory of his own captivity in Tunis?

---

[1] *S.V.P.* XIII, p. 300. For information about the history of the mission to Barbary *cf.* ABELLY, *op. cit.*, 1.1 c. 46, p. 223 and 1.2 c. 1, pp. 91-145; *Mémoires de la Congrégation de la Mission*, Vol. 2 and 3; R. GLEIZES, *Captivité et oeuvres de Saint Vincent de Paul en Barbarie* (Paris, Gabalda, 1930).

[2] ABELLY, *op. cit.*, 1.2 c. 1, p. 93.

The answers to these questions depend on whether Vincent really was a captive in his young days. For Abelly and all successive biographers till Coste, Vincent's basic motive for taking on the new work was his memories of being a captive.[3] Grandchamp, on the other hand, takes the view that if this captivity were authentic then the north African mission would not have happened because if Vincent knew what awaited his missioners then he would never have sent them there.[4] Turbet-Delof describes this argument as 'a masterpiece of *"a priori"* prejudice, contradictions and philistinism.'[5] The fact that Vincent sent his missioners to Barbary shows he was well aware of the captives' situation and their need for help and consolation.

Pirates again

Whatever his reasons may have been for sending missioners, Vincent remembered that an agreement made between the very Christian king and the consul of Constantinople gave French consuls in north Africa the right to have a chaplain. He suggested to the consul in Tunis, Martin de Lange, that he have a missioner as chaplain. The consul agreed on condition that the chaplain would be no financial burden. After this agreement Julien Guérin arrived in Tunis on 22 November 1645, accompanied by Br François Francillon. The following year, Fr Boniface Nouelly and Br Jean Barreau arrived in Algiers. The mission to Barbary had begun.[6]

In theory, the territories of Magreb, Morocco, Algeria, Tunisia and Libya were politically dependent on the Sovereign Turk in Constantinople. In practice, they were governed by semi-autonomous petty rulers: beys, deys, pashas and Turkish dignitaries, who acted on their own initiative. Their main activity was to harass European shipping in the Western Mediterranean as a sideline to the war which either openly, or covertly, was being waged between the Turkish empire and Christian nations, particularly Spain. Piracy provided a considerable source of revenue. Capturing Christian ships brought not only confiscated merchandise, but man power for the galleys and brigantines, labourers for agricultural projects, recruits for squadrons of soldiers of different nationalities, women for the harems and huge sums of money paid out in ransoms and in taxes on the sale of slaves.[7]

---

[3]   ABELLY, *ibid.*
[4]   R. GRANDCHAMP, 'La prétendue captivité ...', p. 18.
[5]   G. TURBET-DELOF, 'Saint Vincent de Paul, a-t-il été esclave à Tunis?', p. 338.
[6]   *Mémoires ...*, Vol. 2, pp. 17 and 138.
[7]   Information about Barbary is given by F.BRAUDEL, *El Mediterráneo y el mundo mediterráneo en la época de Felipe II* (México 1953), and particularly in the second volume:

Piracy continued for more than two centuries and proved a nightmare for Mediterranean countries. Spain in particular saw its communications with Italy put at risk. France was not affected so much and could afford to adopt a more temporising policy, even to the extent of making a treaty with the Sultan that would unite all forces hostile to Spanish supremacy. And yet France was not immune to pirate attacks. More than one French historian denounced, 'the humiliating picture of our relations (those of France) with the states of Barbary. Treaties made by Francis I and Henry IV with the Grand Sultan, treaties that Richelieu made with Barbary, tribute paid to the bey of Algeria, gifts, humiliations of every kind; none of this was very glorious. And the piracy continued and even prospered. We more or less condoned this by signing treaties and the terrible consequences were slavery and apostasy. This evil was the necessary outcome of temporising and people became used to these treaties. After doing all they could, our consuls shut their eyes to the situation.'[8]

Slavery and apostasy were, indeed, the other face of that policy. Along the North African coasts from the Straits of Gibraltar to the Gulf of Sidra, there teemed a captive population made up of all nationalities. They included Spanish, Italian, French, English and Greek slaves who at times numbered as many as 50,000. Abelly speaks of 20,000 in Algeria and 5,000 in Tunisia.[9] Other contemporary accounts put the figure much higher. Even more devastating than the numbers involved, were the sufferings that the captives were forced to endure. The vast amount of contemporary literature on this subject paints in stark terms their sufferings and humiliations.[10]

Even discounting propaganda reports, there is no doubt that a captive's life was pitiful and humiliating. Lodged in Moorish prisons that lacked even the most basic amenities, the captives were condemned to forced labour on the *canteras* or agricultural development areas where like beasts of burden they had to turn the mill wheels. Worse still, they might be put to

---

La piratería, forma complementaria de la gran guerra, pp. 97-124; G. FISHER, *Barbary, Legend, War, trade and piracy in North Africa, 1415-1830* (Oxford 1957) (the subject is treated most favourably, or at least with most understanding, in this work); P. HUBAC, *Les barbaresques et la course en Méditerranée* (Paris 1959); S. BONO, *I corsari barbareschi* (Turin 1964); P. EARLE, *Corsairs of Malta and Barbary* (London 1970).

[8] P. RENAUDIN, *op. cit.*, pp. 95-96.

[9] ABELLY, *op. cit.*, 1.2 c. 1, p. 95.

[10] See among others: J. GRACIAN, *Tratado de la redempción de captivos. En que se cuentan las grandes miserias que padecen los Christianos que están en poder de infieles y quán santa obra sea la de su rescate* (Brussels 1609); FR. DIEGODE HAEDO. *Topographia e historia de Argel ...*, (Valladolid 1612); G. GOMEZ DE LOSADA, *Escuela de trabajos en quatro libros dividida: primero, del cautiverio más cruel y tirano ...* (Madrid 1670); P. DAN, *Histoire de la Barbarie et de ses corsaires* (Paris 1649) second edition.

row in the galleys where their food ration was minimal and their diet reduced to ship's biscuits and a tiny portion of rice or badly cooked vegetables. Punishments were frequent and cruel. They included flogging, amputation of limbs, various forms of torture and even death.

The captives suffered mental as well as physical torment. They were far from their own country, separated from their loved ones, not sure whether they would be ransomed, and subjected to constant humiliation. Sometimes they suffered from lack of companionship or from treachery within their own ranks, from despair, and from attacks on their virtue especially if they were women or young men. The temptation to apostatise was often overwhelming because this was the only way of escaping such misfortunes.

'You have been sent to console the afflicted'

From a very early stage Vincent seems to have had information about living conditions for the slaves in Barbary. His aim in sending missioners to these lands was not to secure ransoms, for this work was already being done by the Mercedarians and Trinitarians. The latter were commonly known as 'Mathurins' in France and this is the word Vincent used when referring to them.[11] Even less was it his aim to convert Moslems or apostates. He knew that such activities were strictly forbidden by Islamic law. The price of any small victory in this field would be the incomparably worse consequences this would entail; the missioners would be expelled and their work for captives finished for ever.

> The souls of Turks and renegades are not your responsibility; your mission does not include them, it is directed to poor Christian captives.' 'You have been sent to Algiers just to bring consolation and encouragement to suffering souls and to help them persevere in our holy religion.[12]

According to Vincent, it was a question of keeping going a sort of permanent mission for captives, along the lines of those given to the peasants in France and Italy. But each work has its own dynamism which calls for action that was not envisaged in even the best laid plans. The mission to Barbary soon called on missioners to play a rôle that was very unusual for the company: they were to be French consuls. This idea came from the Duchess d'Aiguillon who claimed that this arrangement would put an end to

---

[11] *S.V.P.* II, p. 360.
[12] *S.V.P.* IV, pp. 120-123.

friction between consuls and chaplains, particularly when the consuls were engaged in commerce and at times might be troubled by the priests' spiritual ministrations. It was for this reason that she bought the consulate at Algiers and, when Martin de Lange died, that of Tunisia. She put both of these at Vincent's disposal.[13] But the Sacred Congregation of Propaganda did not look kindly on missioners working as consuls. Vincent got round this by arranging for the chaplain to be a priest and the consul to be a laybrother or unordained cleric.

The missioner-consuls had to put up with another sort of opposition. The consulate had often been used as cover for dubious activities, for smuggling arms and other goods prohibited by French and pontifical law. The missioners were inflexible in complying with these rules and they could not be bribed. An organisation in Marseilles masterminded these activities and Turbet-Delof refers to it as a 'gang'. In 1666 they managed to get Fr Le Vacher removed from office and one of their own men made consul in Algiers.[14]

In the face of such opposition, there came a time when Vincent was discouraged and had made up his mind to relinquish the consulates and withdraw his missioners, leaving captive priests to minister to their fellow captives. The Duchess d'Aiguillon was more up to date on the background of the affair and she opposed the plan. Even Vincent admitted that he could not put too much trust in the captive priests as their conduct was often most disordered and gave most scandal.[15]

The consuls did more than represent French subjects; they negotiated with the authorities the interests of all the other Christian nations except England, which had its own consul. They complained about the capture of French ships and protested against the abuse, ill-treatment and injustice that prisoners had to suffer; they negotiated ransoms and were arbiters in disputes among traders. The beys or pashas sometimes abused the consuls' position by holding them responsible for the debts or fines incurred by foreign citizens and very often the consuls were taken as hostages.[16]

As authorised by the Holy See, the missioners also acted as vicars general for the archbishop of Carthage and exercised ecclesiastical jurisdiction over the priests, religious, and faithful within their areas. This put into their hands 'the spiritual sword' that Vincent recommended them to use sparingly and only when other gentler and more persuasive methods had failed.[17]

---

[13] *S.V.P.* III, p. 404; V p. 84.
[14] G. TURBET-DELOF, article quoted, p. 338.
[15] *S.V.P.* V, p. 364; VI, pp. 300, 305, 315, 350; VII, pp. 230, 248.
[16] *S.V.P.* XIII, p. 313.
[17] *Ibid.* and IV, p. 120.

In spite of Vincent's reservations, the missioners ended up negotiating ransoms, too. This was the charitable service that the captives needed and appreciated most. The missioners intervened out of compassion, or because they were obliged to do so, but things did not always turn out well. The slave owners often made exaggerated demands. Some missioners paid the price of imprisonment or torture for agreements they had undertaken rashly and were not able to honour.[18]

Almost from the outset, the mission acted as storehouse or business office for dealings between captives and their families. Letters, gifts and ransom payments would be taken to St Lazare by the nearest parish priest or missioner. Vincent had them delivered to the house at Marseilles, and the superior there forwarded them to Barbary. Money was sent through letters of exchange between Messieurs Simmonet in Paris and the Napollon brothers in Marseilles who were Richelieu's bankers for business transactions with Barbary.[19]

The superior at Marseilles sent the money to Barbary with merchants or seamen who had links with both Mediterranean ports. Vincent's correspondence contains a whole string of names from every corner of France: Edmund Guillaume de Vaucouleurs from Champagne, Laurent Gramoissant and Jean Sanson from Le Havre, two Basque brothers surnamed La Roquette, Roque Hardy from Nancy, an old man from the Isle de Re ... a boring catalogue of names that makes Vincent's letters seem, at times, to be business correspondence. But no commercial enterprise could have been more lacking in self-interest; this was the commerce of charity. According to Abelly, the total number of captives rescued was more than 1,200 and, in monetary terms, this represented a sum of 1,200,000 *livres*.[20]

'But he is only a boy!': 'Monsignor, it is his vocation'

The enterprise could never succeeded if it had not been for the men trained by Vincent. The founder of the Mission raised up a team of priests and lay brothers who sacrificed not just their comfort but sometimes their liberty and even their lives to take to the prisons of Algiers and Tunis, to the desert quarries and the galley benches, that breath of Christian charity that he inspired.

Frs Julien Guérin and Jean Le Vacher were in Tunis with Br Francillon. They were joined there by a cleric, Benjamin Huguier, and a layman, the

---

[18] *S.V.P.* XIII, p. 386. There are innumerable references to the ransom of slaves in St Vincent's letters. Volumes, 5, 6, 7, 8, *passim*.

[19] The are frequent references to these bankers in St Vincent's letters. For a complete account *cf. S.V.P.* XIV, pp. 425-426, 572.

[20] ABELLY, *op. cit.*, 1.2 c. 1, p. 143.

lawyer Martin Husson, who acted as consul. The list of those working in Algiers is longer; Br Barreau and Frs Nouelly, Lesage, Dieppe and Philippe Le Vacher, brother of Jean, who, as already mentioned, first won his spurs in Ireland. There was also an attempt made to start up similar work in Salem, the Moroccan port near Rabat, but this failed. Vincent intended sending Fr Le Soulier here and had the requisite permission from the Congregation of Propaganda but the Augustinian Recollects were also interested in that mission and Vincent generously withdrew.[21]

When Guérin and Francillon arrived in Tunis in November 1645, they placed themselves at the disposal of the consul, Martin de Lange. They had to be more than cautious. They needed to make sure that no false step would shatter all their hopes. Guérin was the right man for this situation. He was extremely zealous but he knew how to act with moderation and avoid foolhardy risks. He began his work almost clandestinely. Little by little he won the Moslems' goodwill and then began to operate in public. He gave missions at the galley hulks in Bizerte, carefully prepared the prisoners at Tunis to fulfil their religious duties and set up several chapels in the prisons.[22] His zeal was not without a certain element of patriotism:

'You would be thrilled', he wrote to Vincent, 'to hear the *Exaudiat* and other prayers for the king of France being chanted in our churches and chapels on Sundays and feastdays. Even foreigners have great affection for the king and they respect him. You would also be delighted to see the devotion with which these poor captives pray for all their benefactors, most of whom are in France or come from France, and it is no small consolation to see people here from every nation, in chains and in fetters, praying to God for the people of France.'[23]

Fr Guérin's inexhaustible charity softened the bey's heart. One day Fr Guérin made so bold as to go to him and ask him to allow another companion to come from France and help him in his work.

'You can bring not just one, but two or three if you need them', replied the bey. 'I am sure that you are here to do good, not ill. Do not be afraid to come to me whenever you need my protection. I will never refuse it.'[24]

---

[21] *S.V.P.* II, p. 623; III, pp. 4, 27, 35, 69, 72, 81-82; IV, pp. 301-302, 330-331.
[22] On Guérin *cf. Notices* ... Vol. 3, pp. 57-82.
[23] *S.V.P.* III, p. 169.
[24] ABELLY, *op. cit.*, 1.2 c. 1, p. 94.

This authorisation led Vincent to send to Tunis Jean Le Vacher, a young priest who looked much younger than his 28 years of age. As they were saying goodbye at the gates of St Lazare, the papal nuncio chanced to arrive. Vincent took advantage of this opportunity to ask him to give his blessing to the missioner.

> 'Monsignor, you have just arrived in time. Will you bless this
> good priest who is going off to the missions in Tunis?'
> 'What!, exclaimed the nuncio, 'but he is only a boy!'
> 'It is his vocation, Monsignor,' replied Vincent.

This was how Vincent acted when he knew it was a question of God's will. He was absolutely sure about Le Vacher so no obstacle would make him alter his decision. When Le Vacher got to Marseilles he fell ill. The superior of the house broke the news to Vincent so that he could send him somewhere else, or at least postpone his departure. Vincent's reply was unexpectedly harsh:

> If he is too weak to travel to the boat then have him carried
> there and if, during the voyage, the sea proves too much for
> him, then throw him overboard.[25]

Coste thinks this remark is out of keeping with Vincent's customary gentleness and he doubts whether the words were ever said. But Vincent's charity was no sugary sentimentality. He knew Jean Le Vacher well and he was sure that God was calling him to Tunis. He treated heroes as heroes. Events would prove that Vincent was right.[26]

Guérin and Le Vacher were only together for a very short time. The latter had scarcely arrived in Tunis when plague broke out. The two missioners vied with each other in caring for the sick. Le Vacher caught the plague and was given up for dead. Fr Guérin and Br Francillon also fell ill. Against all expectations, Le Vacher recovered, thanks to the care he received from Br Francillon who got up from his sick bed to nurse him. 'The happiness that our brother and I feel', wrote Guérin, 'at our good Fr Le Vacher's recovery, has made us as strong as the lions in the mountains round here.'[27] This lion-strength was no defence against the plague. On 25 May 1648, Fr Guérin was struck down with it and a few weeks later it was the turn of Martin de Lange, the consul.[28] Le Vacher sent news of both deaths to Vincent.

---

[25] *Notices ...*, Vol. 3, pp. 611-612.
[26] *S.V.P.* III, p. 252.
[27] *S.V.P.* III, p. 300.
[28] *S.V.P.* III, pp. 352-355.

He also informed him that he had had to take over the duties of consul for the time being. Helped by the Duchess d'Aiguillon, Vincent bought the consulate of Tunis just as he had previously bought that of Algiers. In order to free Le Vacher from secular worries, Vincent named as consul Benjamin Huguier, a former court procurator, who had only recently joined the congregation. Le Vacher was delighted to welcome him but he was deeply disappointed when the bey informed him that he would recognise no other consul but Le Vacher himself. So they resorted to a legal fiction. Huguier was named 'chancellor' of the consulate which meant he could deal with most business matters and leave Le Vacher free to devote himself to his pastoral ministry.[29] This situation lasted until 1652 when the bey allowed another consul to be appointed. Huguier returned to France[30] and was replaced by a young lawyer, Martin Husson, for whom Vincent had a very high regard.

> I knew that he was one of the most virtuous men of his times but I was not aware that he was so intelligent and such a skilled negotiator in important matters.' 'Not only is he prudent, moderate, vigilant and pious, but he is also very competent all round, and he is always ready to work for his neighbour. He is going to serve God and the poor in Barbary, notwithstanding the distance and the perils of that place and of the seas.[31]

Vincent offered him the post with all the candour and respect for the man's freedom of choice that were so characteristic of his style of spiritual direction. On Easter Sunday 1653 he said to him:

> When I was celebrating Mass today, I offered to God your sorrows, your laments and your tears. As for myself, after the consecration I threw myself on my knees at the feet of Our Lord, begging him to enlighten me. After this I reflected on what I would have wished to say to you at the hour of my death. Well, it seems to me that if I were to die at this very moment I would have been greatly consoled to think that I had told you to go to Tunis and, on the other hand, I would have been filled with remorse if I had given you the opposite advice. I tell you this in all sincerity; this is what I think but nevertheless you are free to go there or not.[32]

---

[29] ABELLY, 1.2 c. 1, p. 97.
[30] *S.V.P.* IV, p. 379.
[31] *S.V.P.* IV, pp. 586, 625.
[32] ABELLY, *op. cit.*, 1.3 c. 24, p. 336.

Husson went off to Tunis. Vincent drew up for Le Vacher and him the rules for their respective offices and their relationship with each other. He did not forget to add the detail that the consul should be in lay dress.[33]

Husson was in Tunis for four years, from 1653 to 1657. He was then expelled for refusing to authorise the traders from Marseilles to deal in canvas for making ships' sails. This item was included in a list of goods that the Holy See and the French government had placed under embargo, as being what we would describe today as 'strategic supplies.' The Marseilles *gang* were probably not without a hand in the affair.[34] Once again Fr Le Vacher and Br Francillon were on their own and this state of affairs was not to be remedied during Vincent's lifetime.

'The ill treatment suffered by the French consul'

The mission in Algiers began in 1646 with the purchase of the consulate there. The seminarian Jean Barreau, who was nominated consul, had been a lawyer in the parlement of Paris. He withdrew from the bar to enter, first of all with the Cistercians, and then at St Lazare.[35] Frs Nouelly, Lesage and Dieppe worked in turn with him. After a very brief apostolate these three priests died, victims of their self-sacrificing labours for the plague-stricken.[36] Finally, Philippe Le Vacher, Jean's brother, arrived in 1651 and shared his labours for many years. They were both deeply pious and had the same capacity for suffering.

The observable history of the mission in Algiers can be summed up in two words: debts and imprisonment. Br Barreau was a very kindly man, so much so that he could never refuse to do a work of charity. To help his neighbours he would take on commitments that he could not honour, with no thought of the consequences. It was enough for any captive, merchant or religious, to be in difficulties, and this consul would stand guarantor for them. He did this so often that the beys would take him hostage whenever they wanted some payment exacted or compensation for some loss. In 1647 he went to prison against a debt of 40,000 *livres* owed by a Mercedarian priest; in 1650 he was imprisoned for not being able to settle the debts of a fugitive slave; in 1656 and the following year he was sent to prison again, for the debts of both groups of merchants in Marseilles and in 1658 he was

---

[33] *S.V.P.* XIII, pp. 363-365.
[34] *S.V.P.* V, pp. 335, 384, 405.
[35] *S.V.P.* II, p. 622.
[36] ABELLY, *op. cit.*, 1.2 c. 1, p. 96.

imprisoned in revenge for the flight of the governor of the French fortress who had fled to Leghorn taking with him 70 Arab prisoners and four horses ...

In vain did Vincent shower on him advice and instructions which alternated between severity and indulgence. The good Barreau promised to mend his ways but on the first occasion that presented itself his kind heart got the better of him. He was the one who had most to suffer. Algerian prisons were anything but holiday camps. He was not only imprisoned but practically every time he was badly treated. They beat him, hung him upside down, pushed bamboo canes under his nails ... Vincent, while never ceasing to reproach him for his rashness, and worse still, for his disobedience, did everything he could to extricate him from these troubles.[37]

The worst incident occurred in 1657. The bey demanded 40,000 *livres* to be paid in compensation for the bankruptcy of a merchant from Marseilles named Rapio. Vincent tried to have the merchant's properties in Leghorn impounded[38] and he authorised Philippe Le Vacher to go to France and organise a collection for the consul. The ladies of Charity made a collection in 1657 but it did not amount to much. In the wake of so many public calamities the purse strings of Paris remained tightly closed.[39] To rouse public sympathy, Vincent had printed and distributed a propaganda leaflet entitled *An account of the ill treatment suffered by the French consul in Algiers, Barbary, and the needs of poor captives*. He indicated in this leaflet, the places in Paris where people could leave their offerings.[40] This was the same procedure he had followed to alleviate the distress felt in different regions ravaged by war. The collection began in March.[41] It was just at that time (as we have mentioned previously) that Vincent learnt of the discovery of the letters he wrote, as a young man, about his slavery in Tunis. This was a serious blow. The picture painted in these letters was much rosier than that described in the propaganda leaflets and was closer in style to a recently published book by Emmanuel d'Aranda.[42] If the letters were to appear in such circumstances they could seriously compromise the success

---

[37] *S.V.P.* VI, p. 135. Similar places: V, pp. 329, 384; VI, pp. 55, 168, 178.

[38] *S.V.P.* VI, pp. 362, 393, 638-639.

[39] *S.V.P.* VI, p. 468.

[40] Copies of both these propaganda leaflets (1657-1658) have been preserved. They are published by F. COMBALUZIER in *Annales* (1938) pp. 825-828 and by G. TURBET-DELOF in *Revue de l'Occident musulman et de la Méditerranée* (1967), pp. 153-165, and *Saint Vincent de Paul et la Barbarie en 1657-1658;* this last-named work includes an interesting study of the subject.

[41] *S.V.P.* VIII, pp. 90, 98.

[42] *The relation de la captivité du sieur Emmanuel d'Aranda* had its first edition in Paris (G. Clousier, 1657); the second one in Brussels (1662), the third one in Paris (1665), and the fourth one in Leyden (1671).

of the collection. Vincent did everything in his power to make those 'wretched' letters disappear. He did not manage to do this but at least he stopped them being published. This may have been one of the reasons why Vincent kept silent about his captivity.[43]

'They work day and night'

More important than the vicissitudes suffered by the consuls was the pastoral work that the missioners did among the captives. To give an approximate idea of this work we would need to copy the passages from Abelly *in extenso*, as well as St Vincent's conferences or the descriptions given in the *Memoirs*. We have to be selective.

One of Fr Guérin's first concerns was to go to Bizerte where, on Easter Sunday 1647, a galley had arrived from Algiers with more than 300 Christian slaves aboard. The missioner asked leave of the captain to preach a mission to them. Every day the galley slaves were released from their fetters and went ashore to a private house where they had Mass. Fr Guérin, assisted by another priest, would preach and instruct them. Some had been away from the sacraments for twenty years. With the exception of a few Greek schismatics, they all went to Confession and Holy Communion. It was a real spiritual feast. For a few brief moments they rediscovered in their Christianity, their dignity as human beings. When the final day came Fr Guérin spent 53 crowns to provide a good meal for the celebration.[44]

What happened to Fr Le Vacher on a similar occasion is even more wonderful. Vincent related the incident to the community at St Lazare and there were tears in his eyes.

> I have had a letter from Fr Le Vacher who is in Tunis, telling me that a galley arrived in Bizerte from Algiers, ten or twelve miles away. He did not know whether to go or not because usually when he visits the galley slaves it is to see to their physical as well as their spiritual needs. Being short of money, he was very worried; he did not know what to do about going there because these people are as much in want materially as they are spiritually ...
>
> He collected all the money he could, took an interpreter and another servant to help him. When he arrived, as soon as he was in sight of the galley, the people recognised him by his

---

[43] *Cf. supra*, c. 5.
[44] ABELLY, *op. cit.*, 1.2 c. 1, p. 130.

habit and began to rejoice and shout out saying, 'Here comes our liberator, our pastor, our father.' When he climbed aboard the galley, all those poor slaves fell on him, weeping with joy and affection on seeing their spiritual and corporal deliverer. They knelt at his feet; some took hold of his soutane and others clutched at his cloak and both garments were torn in the people's anxiety to get near him. It took him more than an hour to cross the galley and pay his respects to the commander because they blocked his way and he could not move on for the applause and the rejoicing of these poor people. The commander ordered them all to return to their posts and welcomed the priest most courteously, telling him that he greatly admired the conduct and the charity of Christians who supported each other in their sufferings. Then Fr Le Vacher bought three of the fattest bulls he could find, had them killed, and the meat distributed. He also had a lot of bread baked and in this way he saw to the bodily needs of these poor slaves. At the same time he did all in his power to provide them with spiritual nourishment which is much more important for God's glory; catechising and instructing them in the mysteries of our holy faith and finally, comforting them with great charity. This went on for a week and it brought great blessings and extraordinary comfort to those poor galley slaves who called him their deliverer and their consolation since he had nourished them in soul and in body.[45]

In Algiers, Philippe was emulating his brother's zeal. He rescued slaves, reformed the clergy and captive religious, bore calumny and worked unceasingly. He was somewhat over-zealous and rigorous. Vincent had to take him in hand and give him a lot of advice about being sensible and observing moderation yet he never ceased to admire the man's consuming zeal and his exceptional capacity for work. He described him as 'a man who is all fire and so ready to put himself at risk, that knowing the dangers involved, he would have given up a hundred lives if he had them. He really is like fire ...'

He is a man who never stops working. I can tell you that last Easter, when he knew that he only had a week to help those poor people, and that he would not be able to do much unless he worked unbelievable hours, he shut himself up with them

---

[45] *S.V.P.* XI, pp. 447-449.

in their prisons. He spent that week working night and day, he had hardly any rest and so risked his life to help his neighbour.[46]

Just as they had done in Algiers, the missioners opened chapels in the main prisons at Tunis and Bizerte. In this way, as one of the missioners wrote, 'Our divine Saviour has made himself a captive among the captives, to console them in their trials as he promised.' In the two consulates there were proper churches. They were dedicated to St Louis and St Cyprian and served as parish churches for the traders. Reports sent to Vincent by his missioners indicate that religious services were conducted there with as much solemnity as in the churches of Paris. On Sundays and Feastdays they had solemn sung Mass and various pious associations and confraternities were started, among them the confraternity of the Holy Souls, the association to provide help for sick captives, the Rosary confraternity, the association in honour of the Carmelite scapular and other confraternities dedicated to various saints. The sanctuary lamp burned night and day. Holy Viaticum was taken to the dying in prison and was escorted with torches and lighted candles. In several chapels there was a procession for the feast of Corpus Christi and the Blessed Sacrament remained exposed for a whole week for adoration by the faithful.[47]

The missioners' efforts were not confined to prisoners in the cities but they also went inland to bring consolation and spiritual and material help to captives working in the quarries or in the *maceries* or country farms. The names of some of these places are quoted by Abelly—Alcantara (bridge), Grombalia (from Latin *columbaria*), Mamedia or Mahomedia etc ... and the missioners even penetrated the far-off mountain regions which were peopled more with lions than with men. On his first trip, Jean Le Vacher met some captives who had not seen a priest for 18 years. The good priest consoled them as best he could, heard their confessions, said Mass for them and then gave each man a quarter of a *piastre*.[48] In M. Vincent's school it was always taught that spiritual and material relief go hand in hand.

---

[46] *S.V.P.* XI, p. 307.
[47] ABELLY, *op. cit.*, 1.2 c. 1, pp. 120-121. A contemporary Spanish witness (FR GABRIEL G. DE LOSADA, *Escuela de trabajos* ...) corroborates these statements by the missioners. According to him there was never any lack of priests to administer the sacraments in the oratories of the Christian hospital and especially in the royal prison; the Blessed Sacrament was exposed on Holy Thursday, there were sung Masses with instrumental music and in 1665 there was a jubilee year that was celebrated as peacefully and freely as it would be in any convent in Madrid. The church attached to the hospital of the royal prison had three naves with silk hangings on the walls and the floor was covered with flowers. There was a baptismal font in the house of the French consul (this as we know, was Br Barreau) and it was here that they kept the holy oils used for extreme unction.
[48] ABELLY, 1.2 c. 1, p. 131.

The temple of the Holy Spirit

The chronicles of the Mission record incidents that rival those we read about in the annals of the early Church. In 1646 Guérin made reference to a little English boy of eleven 'one of the finest looking boys you ever saw,' who became a Catholic on Holy Thursday of that year. He had a great devotion to Our Lady and continually asked of her the grace to die rather than deny Christ. His master made every effort to entice him towards Islam and, on two occasions, even had him beaten to force him to comply. During the beating the child cried out. 'You can break my neck if you want to, but I am a Christian and will never be anything else'. And he told Fr Guérin that he was ready to be beaten to death rather than apostatise. 'I can assure you', concluded the missioner, 'that this was a little temple of the Holy Spirit.'[49]

There were many other similar cases, including that of two young boys, one English and the other French, who encouraged each other to suffer martyrdom and remain faithful to Christ.[50] But the story that most impressed Vincent was that of a young man aged twenty-one or twenty-two. His name was Pedro Borguny and he came from Majorca.

'A soul as pure as refined gold in the crucible'

According to Philippe Le Vacher, the boy had denied his faith and accepted the turban out of fear of being sent to the galleys. The missioner's preaching filled him with such deep remorse that he made up his mind to atone for his apostasy even if this cost him his life. With this in mind he began to speak in public against Islam and in favour of Christianity. He possessed that higher form of bravery which can admit to fear. 'Our Lord, too', he said, 'was afraid of dying but he willingly underwent sufferings far greater than those I will have to bear.' One day he presented himself before the pasha and told him that he had gone back to being a Christian. He took off his turban, threw it on the ground and began to stamp on it. The pasha condemned him to be burnt alive. The sentence was carried out on 30 August 1654. Fr Le Vacher witnessed the martyrdom and, hidden among the crowds, he secretly gave him absolution from a distance. 'Shortly afterwards', commented Vincent, 'he gave into the hands of God his soul which was as pure as refined gold in the crucible.'[51]

---

[49] ABELLY, *ibid.*, p. 133.
[50] ABELLY, 1.2 c. 1, pp. 135-138.
[51] *S.V.P.* XI, pp. 389-392.

On two occasions Vincent described to the community this heroic example of fidelity to the faith and he also wrote about it in his letters to missioners who were absent.[52] Le Vacher reverently collected the martyr's ashes and brought them to Paris in 1657 together with a picture representing the scene of the martyrdom. Both the relics and the picture are still to be found, today, in the House of the Mission in Palma, Majorca. In the eighteenth century they tried to introduce Pedro Borguny's cause for beatification in Rome.[53] Spain, which had not been able to welcome the sons of St Vincent de Paul, offered Vincent for his crown as apostle to the captives, this precious jewel of martyr's blood.

In the final years of his life, Vincent, who was weary of this labour of Sysiphus in rescuing slaves, attempted a sort of crusade which was meant to set free all the captive population of Barbary at one stroke. We will speak about this ingenious venture later on. It was unsuccessful. The mission to Barbary continued after Vincent's death. Jean Le Vacher and Br Francillon ended their lives with the crown of martyrdom. Both died in the same way; they were tied to the mouth of a cannon and when this was fired their bodies were cut in two and flung into the waters of the port of Algiers.[54]

---

[52] *S.V.P.* V, p. 341.

[53] The Vincentian Visitor of Spain, Fr Fernand Nualart, who was postulator of the cause, wrote the biography of the Majorcan martyr. *Vida y martirio del siervo de Dios Pedro Borguny, martirizado en Argel a los 30 de agosto de 1654* (Rome 1780). In the second edition of this work (Palma 1820) we have a repetition of the Latin account sent by Philippe Le Vacher to the Congregation of Propaganda Fide.

[54] *Notices* ..., Vol. 3, pp. 640-643.

Chapter XXVI
MADAGASCAR:
THE MISSION TO THE INFIDELS

'Vincent de Paul ... offers to send his missioners'

Although the work for captives in Barbary was carried out in heathen countries, it was still a Christian work and the missioners limited their efforts to helping only Christians. Vincent had a deep longing to work directly for the evangelisation of infidels.[1] He thought, and this idea was current at the time, that maybe God wanted to transplant the Church from European countries where heresy had taken root to some other continents. Even if this was a mistaken notion, any effort that contributed to the expansion of the Church would still be a great work.[2]

The Congregation of Propaganda, and its secretary, Mgr Ingoli, in particular, were looking for missionaries to go to distant countries. The Congregation of the Mission had earlier been approved as a simple 'mission' thanks to a favourable report from Ingoli and it met all the necessary requirements. The Congregation did not belong to either Portugal or Spain, the two nations that had sovereignty of these heathen lands, and it had all the dynamism of a young community. Several projects were bandied about. In the period 1643-1647 there was talk of confiding the work to the bishop of Babylon who had responsibility for the missions in Mesopotamia, Persia and parts of India. Fr Lambert was on the point of being named for this work. But the project came to nothing after a series of difficulties; the conditions imposed by Jean Duval, the retiring bishop, and the ambition or envy of other ecclesiastics such as Authier de Sisgau and Deslyons, the dean of Senlis.[3]

---

[1] St Vincent's plans for foreign mission are described by A. COPPO, 'San Vicenzo e i suoi rapporti con la S. Congregazione 'de Propagande Fide', *Vincentiana* (1972), p. 173-190; G. VAN WINSEN, 'Saint Vincent et les missions étrangères', *Vincentiana* (1978), pp. 150-182.

[2] *S.V.P.* III, pp. 35, 153, 182; V, p. 418; XI, pp. 309, 352-356.

[3] *S.V.P.* II, pp. 413-415, 422, 474; III, pp. 153-155, 158, 182-185, 380; IV, pp. 139, 142.

In 1643 Arabia was the centre of attention. This time Vincent petitioned for the work although we do not know whether the Holy See had previously offered it. There are lacunae in documents relating to this subject. The petition presented by Vincent eloquently expresses his desire to have his own corner of missionary territory.

> As the three regions of Arabia Felix, Arabia Petra and Arabia Deserta have not yet been confided to any congregation or to the secular clergy to be developed and evangelised according to the Christian tradition, Vincent de Paul, superior of the Congregation of the Mission, is offering to send his priests to those parts of Arabia whenever it pleases Your Eminences to confide to them that said mission *sub nomine proprio*.[4]

In 1656 there came an offer of Lebanon and Vincent was asked to nominate one of his priests for the work. After some hesitation he named Thomas Berthe, former superior at Rome. This project did not materialise either, though we do not know why.[5] At some point there seems to have been talk of sending missioners to Pernambuco in Brazil and to Canada,[6] the last a country where French policy at this time was to promote a big colonisation programme.[7] Vincent was always ready to evangelise and serve the poor wherever they were to be found.

'An island below Capricorn'

Only one of these plans came to fruition and that was Madagascar or the Ile Saint Laurent as it was officially called. In one of his letters Vincent described it as 'an island below Capricorn'.[8]

The French system of colonisation was closer to that of England or of Holland rather than the Spanish or Portuguese one. Trading companies were established and the state granted these the right to develop the colonial territories. Two rival societies wanted the island of Madagascar: the Indies Society or Society of the East, founded in 1642 by a group of traders from Paris which included President Lamoignon, and the company headed by one of Richelieu's cousins, Charles de la Porte, Duke and Marshal of La Meilleraye

---

[4] *S.V.P.* III, p. 335.

[5] *S.V.P.* VI, p. 19, 24.

[6] *S.V.P.* II, pp. 90; IV, pp. 292-296, 336, 377. According to Van Winsen (p. 165 in article mentioned) there was no plan to send Vincentian missioners to Canada, but to Guiana.

[7] V.L. TAPIÉ, *op. cit.*, pp. 241-242; S. DIAMOND, 'Le Canadá au XVII siècle: une société préfabriquée', *Annales* ESC. March-April 1961, pp. 317-354.

[8] *S.V.P.* III, p. 279.

who had been a staunch supporter of the missioners at the abbey of St Méen.[9] These companies were under obligation to provide their colonies with sufficient priests to serve the religious needs of French colonists and to evangelise the natives.

The French colony in Madagascar had settled in the southern-most part of the island and had built a fort—the fort of Delfin—and in time this became the city of Fort Dauphin.

Before the French came, Madagascar had been evangelised for a short time by Jesuits from Portugal but they had had little success. When the first French colonists arrived the place could well have been described as virgin soil.

In 1648 the Company of the Indies sent a petition to the nuncio in Paris asking for missionaries to be sent to Madagascar. The nuncio thought of the Congregation of the Mission and he went in person to suggest this to Vincent who consulted the most senior members of the company and then accepted the offer. The nuncio believed that he was acting with the authority of the Congregation for Propaganda but owing to a misunderstanding between Paris and Rome, the Sacred Congregation had already confided the mission to the Discalced Carmelites. As soon as Propaganda heard of the nuncio's concession they limited the faculties granted to the Vincentian missioners so that these were confined to parish foundations serving French colonists.[10] The difficulty was resolved when the Carmelites withdrew. After this the missioners of St Lazare assumed full responsibility for the island's evangelisation.[11]

Humanly speaking, the mission to Madagascar was an impossible one. Distances, and communications systems in particular, gave rise to many discouraging problems. Of the first three expeditions that Vincent sent out there, the second one (1654) was the least behind schedule, arriving at its destination five months late. The first one, in 1648, was six months late and the third (1655-1656), arrived nine months late. The three final expeditions never arrived at all. One was shipwrecked in the Loire before it even reached

---

[9] *Cf. supra*, c. 19. For information about French colonisation in general see H. BLET, *Historie de la colonisation française,* vol. 1: *Naissance et déclin d'un Empire (Des origines à 1789)* (Paris 1946); R. MOUSNIER, *Les XVIe et XVIIe siècles* (vol. 6 of *Histoire générale des civilisations* by M. Crouzet), pp. 490-493. For information on Madagascar: see H. DESCHAMPS, *Histoire de Madagascar. L'éveil missionaire de la France d'Henri IV à la fondation des missions étrangères* (Lyon 1942).

[10] *S.V.P.* XIII, pp. 317-318.

[11] *S.V.P., ibid.,* and IV, pp. 85, 337. Information about the Vincentian mission in Madagascar is given in ABELLY, *op. cit.,* 1.2 c. 1, pp. 155-189; *Mémoires de la Congrégation de la Mission,* Vol. 9: Madagascar; H. FROIDEVAUX, *Les Lazaristes à Madagascar au XVII siècle* (Paris 1903).

the high seas (1656); another had to take shelter in Lisbon and when it left the port was captured by a Spanish vessel that conducted it to Galicia (1658); and the final expedition was shipwrecked in the Bay of Biscay, returned to France to begin the trip again, and was becalmed at the Cape of Good Hope so that the missioners were obliged to return to Paris via Amsterdam in a Dutch ship (1659-1661). As if this was not bad enough, there were disagreements between the company of the Indies and the Duke of La Meilleraye and this complicated embarking procedures. The duke was very jealous when the missioners travelled in the other company's ships. Vincent had to go to great lengths of diplomacy to keep on the right side of both of them.[12]

Those missioners who managed to set foot on the island found the French population more of a hindrance than a help to their apostolate. Most of the colonists were dissolute characters who had joined this overseas adventure after being enticed by the lure of easy riches. When they had to face the harsh reality of a poor country whose inhabitants were not disposed to be submissive they reacted by falling into every kind of abuse and outrage. To crown it all, there were a good number of Huguenots among them and the native people were very perplexed by dissensions between these and the Catholics. Moreover, the first governor of the colony, M. de Pronis, was a Huguenot, although his conduct in no way reflected the strictness of Calvinism. The second governor, Etienne de Flacourt, was the typical colonial official concerned only with his company's commercial interests; authoritarian towards those who served under him but extremely easy-going as regards morals. There was constant friction between these governors and the missioners.[13]

A third difficulty stemmed from the climate and sanitary conditions of that exotic location. The missioners were to pay the price of being new boys; they suffered frequent illness and premature death. Toussaint Bourdaise had the longest apostolate which lasted two years and ten months. All the others died, we might say, almost as soon as they began their apostolic labours.[14]

The natives were docile, approachable and affectionate but they were timid and mistrustful of strangers, particularly if these tricked them, as frequently happened with the military from the fortress. They practised a primitive form of religion with additional elements introduced by Arab traders who taught them Islamic practices and beliefs. Faith in a supreme God was overshadowed by a much stronger belief in the evil spirit mingled with an

---

[12] *Cf. Mémoires* ..., Vol. 9, pp. 49, 177, 257, 353, 363, 399, 387-391.

[13] *S.V.P.* III, pp. 580-582, 590, 603.

[14] *Notices* ..., III, pp. 14-23, 43-57, 93-110, 129-146, 157-163, 180-214.

idolatrous polytheism directed towards the *olis*, a sort of lesser gods, whose carved images were carried about by the people who attributed magic powers to them. A complicated ritual known only to the *ombiases* or sorcerers ensured protection by the good *olis*.[15]

'Have courage and let down the nets'

For this difficult and perilous mission Vincent chose a succession of priests who were outstanding for their human and spiritual qualities. It is amazing how in less than 25 years the little company, whose members were described by Vincent as lowly in virtue, knowledge and social status, should have had sufficient men available for such varied and demanding tasks. The mission in Italy demanded talent, finesse and eloquence; Ireland and Scotland called for bravery in the face of persecution and martyrdom, while Poland would test a missioner's self-sacrifice and disregard for his own life. In Algeria and Tunis missioners would have to display compassion, business acumen, and astuteness in dealing with the Moslem petty rulers. In Madagascar everything had to be started from scratch and they had to be able to improvise, to have a bent for languages as well as a sympathetic understanding of strange customs, and more than anything else, they had to be of great integrity and show tact in their dealings with the Huguenots ... In spite of all these difficulties, Vincent never had any problems in finding personnel. Vincent sent as many as twenty or so missioners in successive groups to Madagascar but out of these only eight arrived at the mission. None of the priests named showed any repugnance in going to that distant island and many of them volunteered to go.

The first two missioners that Vincent chose were Charles Nacquart and Nicolas Gondrée. The letter of appointment that he wrote to them is the model of a courteous, affectionate and pressing invitation to join this enterprise for the glory of God.

> 'The company', he told Nacquart on 22 March 1648, 'has cast its eyes on you as its best victim to give homage to our sovereign Creator by serving him in this way.' 'My very dear Father, what is your heart saying at such news? Do you feel suitably humbled and confused at receiving such a great grace from heaven? It is as great and wonderful a vocation as that of the greatest apostles and saints in God's Church! God's eternal designs are being accomplished in our times through you! It is

---

[15] *S.V.P.* III, pp. 553-559.

only humility that will help you bear this grace, together with complete abandonment of all that you are and all that you could become, with joyful confidence in your sovereign Creator. You need to have the deep faith of Abraham and the charity of St Paul as well as zeal, patience, deference, poverty, solicitude, discretion, integrity and a great desire to give yourself completely to God; all these will be as necessary for you as they were for the great Saint Francis Xavier.' 'When you reach that island you will have to start by arranging things as best you can—you may have to separate so that you can work in different areas but in that case it would be advisable for you to meet as often as possible to console and encourage one another.

The main thing is that after trying to live in the odour of sweetness with the people you have to deal with, and after setting them good example, you must help these poor people born in darkness and in ignorance of their Creator, to understand the truths of our religion. You must not do this by subtle theological arguments but should take as your starting point examples drawn from nature and you should help them to understand that you are only developing the traces of God's presence which he himself left with them but which corrupt human nature has been obliterating by many years of clinging to evil ways.

I would like you to show them the weakness of our human nature by pointing out that they, too, condemn bad conduct since they, too, have laws, kings and sanctions.

If his divine Majesty is pleased to grant you the grace of cultivating the seed of those Christians already settled there, and living in charity with these good people, then I am absolutely sure that Our Lord will make use of you to prepare an abundant harvest for the company there. Go, then, Father, and since it is God's will that sends you there through his representatives on earth, have courage and let down the nets ...'

In the postscript to this letter Vincent reveals his own feelings, 'What more can I say to you ... that there is nothing on earth I would like more than to go with you and be your companion, if only I could, instead of Fr Gondrée.'[16]

---

[16] *S.V.P.* III, pp. 278-285.

Deep down Vincent saw himself a missionary in the person of his sons.

As well as giving them spiritual counsel, the prudent organiser had advice about essential things for the journey. The missioners were to take 100 gold crowns for emergencies, a Mass kit, two rituals, two bibles which should be small and not too bulky, two copies of the teachings of the Council of Trent, two manuals of Binsfeld's *Morality,* two books of meditations by Busaeus, some copies of *The Devout Life* and lives of the saints, the life and letters of St Francis Xavier, irons for making hosts, safety pins, three or four pocket-size containers with the holy oils ...

Gondrée died the very year they arrived in Madagascar. He caught sunstroke while accompanying the governor on a visit to the town of Fanshere, the home of Adrian Ramaka, a black petty king who had been baptised in his youth by the Jesuits.[17] Nacquart held out for another year, completely on his own. He died on 29 May 1650, worn out by his apostolic journeys in the Fort Dauphin area.[18] During the two years of his apostolate he suffered a lot because he could do nothing to change the disorderly conduct of the soldiers and the French colonists. His efforts in this direction provoked many clashes with governor Flacourt who reneged on the company's agreement and reduced the amount of material aid it had promised to give the priest. He was very consoled, however, by his apostolic work for the natives. He soon learnt enough Malagasy to be able to give catechism lessons with the help of some pictures he had brought from France. He won the confidence of Adrian Ramaka and other chiefs. He visited Fanshere on several occasions and also went to many other places though his freedom of movement was restricted after Gondrée's death since he had to be in Fort Dauphin every Sunday to say Mass for the colonists. On all sides he met a submissive people who were ready to accept the seed of the gospel. He baptised only seldom because he wanted to be sure that the catechumens were properly instructed and that they were not acting from purely natural motives:

> 'You sent me to let down the nets', he told Vincent, 'up to now I have only caught 57 fish and except for 3 big fish all the rest were tiny ones but there are so many to be caught that I am sure you will send enough people to the sea to bring in nets at breaking point with so many fish.'[19]

---

[17] *S.V.P.* III, pp. 438-439.
[18] *S.V.P.* V, p. 285, *Notices ...,* III, pp. 106-108.
[19] *S.V.P.* III, p. 606.

He had made a lot of plans. He thought of building a church inside the fortress and to have it served by the secular clergy; he planned to establish a community of six priests and a seminary in Fanshere; to found another mission post in Matatane with twelve priests; and he even wanted to bring four lay brothers who would work as tailor, teacher, surgeon and administrator. He dreamt of bringing a group of Daughters of Charity to look after the young Malagasy girls ... he was preparing a catechism in the native language ...

Such fine projects were cut short by the premature death of this apostle endowed with such breadth of vision. In the space of a very short time he had understood the need for a comprehensive plan for the territory confided to his care. Carried away by the thought of the possibilities that island held for his zeal, he echoed the lament of all discoverers:

> Where are all those theologians, as St Francis Xavier said years
> ago, who are wasting their time in academies while so many
> poor infidels are begging for bread and there is nobody to give
> it to them? May the Lord of the harvest send labourers.[20]

'I am the only one left to break the news to him'

More than four years passed between Nacquart's death and the arrival of the second group of missioners. At last, on 16 August 1654, Frs Bourdaise and Mousnier, together with Br Forest, landed on the island.[21]

Nacquart's work had been wiped out. They had to begin all over again. Bourdaise was ready to tackle the work. He was not reckoned to be very intelligent and when he was a student they thought of asking him to leave the community, so limited was his ability. Vincent had sensed his spiritual potential and refused to let him go. In Madagascar he was to demonstrate a common sense and great-heartedness which more than made up for intellectual gifts. He followed Nacquart's example and began an itinerant apostolate to the native towns. This revived the enthusiasm of earlier years. The great and the lowly, petty kings and subjects, sorcerers and ordinary pagans, men and women: all rushed out to hear his teaching. The detailed reports he sent to Vincent are full of anecdotes that describe better than any learned treatise the conditions and the difficulties of the missioners' work. His companion, Fr Mousnier, who was the learned member of the group, died after nine

---

[20] *S.V.P.* III, p. 576. Nacquart's letters to St Vincent constitute four long reports. They are published in *S.V.P.* III, pp. 438-448, 545-577, 580-593, 603-609.
[21] *S.V.P.* V, p. 285.

months following a difficult expedition he had undertaken to serve a colonists' camp.[22] Bourdaise, like Nacquart before him, was left on his own to do all the work. This he did wholeheartedly, very ably and with sureness of touch. In less than 3 years he baptised about 600 pagans. In 1656 he was overjoyed to have reinforcements in the shape of Frs Dufour and Prévost. A third companion, Fr Belleville, died during the voyage. Sadly Dufour and Prévost died, two and three months respectively after their arrival. They were victims of their imprudent zeal that ignored the precautions Europeans had to take against the climate of Madagascar. So once again Fr Bourdaise was left on his own. When he sent the sad news to Vincent his words seem like an echo of the biblical lamentations:

> Fr Belleville, whom I only know by name, and by his reputation
> for virtue, has died on the journey. Fr Prévost died a short
> while after recovering from the fatigue of his journey and Fr
> Dufour, whom I met only so that I might know the value of
> what I was to lose, has also died. So there is only myself, your
> humble servant, to give you this news ...[23]

Fr Bourdaise, himself, did not survive his companions for long. On 25 June 1657, he, too, succumbed to an attack of dysentery.[24] It took so long for this news to reach Paris that Vincent thought Bourdaise was still alive and he continued to write to him. Vincent obtained from the Holy See his appointment as apostolic superior of the mission and brandished this document in front of Marshal de la Meilléraye, to try and get him to send ships more quickly. One day, on 11 November 1658, he sent the absent solitary missioner this greeting which in the circumstances we find poignant.

> Fr Bourdaise, are you still alive or not? If you are alive, may
> God preserve you. If you are already in heaven then pray for
> us.[25]

Tragic destiny of the Madagascar mission which was to prove a constant blood-letting for Vincent. But it was a glorious destiny, too, and it shows us in a way that none of his other enterprises could do, this man's unconquerable zeal and his readiness always to begin again, even at the cost

---

[22] The 24 May, 1655 (*S.V.P.* V, pp. 505-508).
[23] *S.V.P.* VI, p. 195. The reports given by Mousnier, Dufour and Bourdaise are in *S.V.P.* V, pp. 276-313, 501-524; VI, pp. 9-16, 192-235.
[24] *S.V.P.* VIII, p. 156; *Notices ...*, III, p. 212.
[25] *S.V.P.* XII, p. 69.

of his finest sons. No obstacle, no loss, could alter his determination to serve those poor people in unknown and distant lands through the Church's mission *ad gentes*.

'This retiring, humble and gentle youth'

Three other groups of missioners were sent out between 1656 and 1660, and all these enterprises were doomed to failure. As mentioned earlier, the expedition of 1656 was shipwrecked and more than half the passengers perished. Thirty out of the 64 died. The three missioners were among the survivors and this was partly due to circumstances and partly to the bravery and resoluteness of one of them. They were two priests and a brother. On All Souls Day the ship was anchored at the mouth of the Loire, opposite Saint Nazaire. The two priests had gone ashore so that they could say Mass more easily and the captain of the boat went with them. When they returned they could not get back on board because the waves were so powerful and nobody dared to cross the bay. That night the storm became so violent that—but let Vincent tell the story :

> At about eleven o'clock it began to hurl the boat towards a sandbank where it was dashed to pieces. But God immediately inspired some of them to make a sort of raft from pieces of wood roped together. How did they manage this? I do not know yet but I do know for certain that sixteen or seventeen people climbed on to it and they were at the mercy of the waves and the mercy of God. Among these sixteen or seventeen people was our poor brother, Christophe Delaunay, who with his crucifix in his hand encouraged his companions.
>
> 'Have courage', he said to them, 'let us have great faith and trust in God; let us hope in Our Lord and he will save us from danger'. And he began to spread out his cloak so that they could use it as a sail. I do not know whether the others did not have a cloak, but anyway, he spread out his, getting one person to hold out one side and somebody else to hold out the other, and in this way they all managed to reach land alive except for one person who died of cold and the fright he had in that danger.'
>
> Do you not admire the strong spirit of God that filled that young man, our good brother Christophe, who is a retiring, humble and gentle lad. Yes, he is the most humble and gentle young man that I know. And here he is, with his crucifix in his

hand, shouting encouragement to his companions ... And I will say in passing, brothers, that this shows us we should never be without our crucifix. It was not he who did this, my brothers, it was God alone, working through him, who did it. But after all, even if they had died leading all those people who were in the boat, we can well believe that they would have been happy to die, serving God and leading their sheep.[26]

'God be praised for life and for death'

The final expedition was the most hazardous one of all and for Vincent it was an opportunity to show his total submission to God's will and to show how much he was in control of his feelings.

Nantes was the point of embarkation but when the travellers, three priests and a brother, arrived there they were told they had to make for La Rochelle. The superior, Nicolas Etienne, went by sea and took the brother with him while the others went overland. Not long after they left Nantes a fierce north-east wind broke the masts of the ship and shattered the main sail, dragging the ship on to a sandbank. The pilot begged Fr Etienne to give absolution to the passengers and crew. The priest had just made the sign of the cross when the wind suddenly changed direction and blew the ship away from the dangerous reef. Two young passengers had not waited this long and had helped themselves to a skiff which they launched into the sea. They thought they saw the ship sink beneath the waves so when they got to La Rochelle they wasted no time in telling the news and writing to Paris. A Requiem Mass was celebrated in La Rochelle for the people who had drowned. In Paris, Vincent named somebody else to be superior for the expedition and told the priest to keep quiet about the appointment for the time being.

Meanwhile, Fr Etienne's ship was now without mast or sail and was at the mercy of the waves for a whole fortnight. It was dragged towards the coast of Spain, pushed back towards the French coast and eventually ran aground near St Jean de Luz. Etienne wrote to Vincent from Bayonne and Bordeaux, bringing him up to date with the situation. The letters arrived in Paris just as the new superior for Madagascar was having a meal before setting out that evening for La Rochelle. Vincent was in his room dictating a note to one of his secretaries telling the surviving missioners about the change of superior. At that moment the assistant of the house brought him the post. Vincent thought he recognised Etienne's handwriting on two of the letters.

---

[26] *S.V.P.* XI, pp. 373-378.

He opened them straightaway and there, right enough, was the missioner's signature and the news that he was setting off once more by sea. Vincent's heart somersaulted from desolation to joy but not a muscle of his face nor anything in his voice betrayed the transformation. He had learnt to master his feelings and all he did was to praise and bless God 'for life and for death'.[27]

'Are we going to abandon God's work for five or six setbacks?'

For Vincent, Madagascar was the crowning of the company's missionary labours. For this reason he held on to it at all cost in spite of a long and sad list of men sacrificed. But other people began to complain about an enterprise which up to that moment had brought nothing but disaster. Vincent countered their objections in a talk which was partly a harangue and partly prophecy.

> Can we be so cowardly of heart and so lacking in manliness that we would abandon the Lord's vineyard that his divine Majesty has called us to, just because four, five, or even six men have died there? Tell me, would it be a good army that abandoned everything because it had lost two, three, or five thousand men (as they tell me happened during the last attack on Normandy)? A fine thing that would be, to see such a cut and run army that thought only of its own comfort. Well, we would have to say the same thing about the Mission! It would be a fine company, this Mission, if it abandoned the works of God after five or six losses. A cowardly company, too attached to earthly things. No, I do not believe that there is a single man in the company who is so lacking in spirit that he is not prepared to go and take the place of those who have died.[28]

In no other enterprise did Vincent display so much tenacity and put so much labour and effort into the work. When Bourdaise died there were no missioners in Madagascar until three years after Vincent's death when the last of the missioners sent out by the founder arrived. Vincent's successor, Fr Alméras, continued the work until France withdrew the last of the colonists. Vincentian missioners returned there in the nineteenth century and today they are still in Fort Dauphin, continuing the work started by Nacquart and Gondrée in such very different circumstances.[29]

---

[27] ABELLY, *op. cit.*, 1.3 c. 21, pp. 312-313.
[28] *S.V.P.* XI, p. 422.
[29] *Mémoires ...*, Vol. 9, pp. 452-593.

Chapter XXVII
CHARITY'S ARMOURY—
CONFRATERNITIES AND LADIES OF
CHARITY

'To evangelise by word and by action'

If Vincent de Paul's biography were to end at the preceding chapter, the reader who had no access to any other source of information would really think that this was end of the story, for his missionary activity was more than enough for one life's work. But if we stopped at this point we would have to omit the most brilliant and admirable aspect of his life, his works of charity. We should not use that phrase because charity characterised everything that Vincent did, whether it was the Mission, seminary work, or giving retreats. All these activities were to include works of charity which were not seen as a marginal extra to the work of evagelisation, but rather as an additional way of spreading the gospel. Vincent de Paul's torrent of charitable works flows simultaneously from the double source of mission and charity. The systematic approach we adopted towards our subject has necessarily led us to deal separately with works and foundations which were, in fact, mutually dependent and supportive. If a distinction has to be made between the two, it is the distinction of results. There is no difference in the spiritual sap from which both draw nourishment, evangelical charity with all the demands that this makes.

The pivot of all these works was the Congregation of the Mission. When Vincent was explaining to the missioners the real essence of their vocation he made this point very strongly:

> If there are any among us who think that they are in the Mission in order to evangelise the poor and not to look after them, to see to their spiritual but not to their temporal needs, then I have to tell them that we must assist the poor and see that they are helped in every possible way, either by ourselves or by other people, if we hope to hear those beautiful words spoken by the sovereign Judge of the living and the dead, 'Come, you

blessed of my Father, and enter into the kingdom that is prepared for you because I was hungry and you gave me to eat, I was naked and you clothed me, I was sick and you cared for me.' When we do this we are evangelising by word and by action; it is the most perfect way of acting and this is what Our Lord did. Those who represent him on earth by reason of their calling and their mission, as priests do, are called to act in the same way.[1]

These words were spoken in 1658 but they only summarise and justify what had been written 25 years earlier in the bull *Salvatori nostri*:

They [the members of this congregation] will endeavour to establish confraternities called charities in every place where they preach or give instructions, so that poor sick people will be helped.[2]

We have already noted the establishment and the spread of these confraternities throughout the de Gondi territories and in certain towns that Vincent himself passed through: Paris, Mâcon, Beauvais ... After 1633 the increased number of missions and the founding of new houses of the Congregation of the Mission meant that the confraternities of charity also multiplied. These proved successful because they responded to a real need and they offered a solution that was not difficult to organise. Soon charities sprang up, not only in those dioceses where there were missioners or where they preached, but also in other areas of France where they were not directly involved. Vincent's formula was copied by bishops, parish priests and religious associations. The Company of the Blessed Sacrament sent its associates *a memo about the practices of the company of the ladies of charity ... so that they could set up similar associations in other parts of the country*.[3] Nicolas Pavillon, the bishop of Alet, approved the rules for a charity in his diocese and these rules repeated word for word those drawn up by Vincent.[4]

In documents that are still extant we find references to about sixty parish charities.[5] There were many more than that. A veritable network of charity covered almost the whole of France or, to use Abelly's words,

---

[1] *S.V.P.* XII, pp. 87-88.
[2] *S.V.P.* XIII, pp. 260-261.
[3] COSTE, *M.V.* Vol. 1, p. 335.
[4] M. BORIES, 'Une charité dans le diocèse d'Alet aux XVII et XVIII siècles', in *Mélanges d'histoire religieuse offerts à Mgr. Elie Griffe* (Toulouse 1972), pp. 251-259.
[5] *S.V.P.* XIV, p. 105.

'confraternities were established in so many places that we just do not know how many there were.'[6]

Most of these charities were for ladies. The men's charities or those confraternities that admitted both men and women members seem to have been abandoned after the first few were tried out. A failure? It would be nearer the mark to speak of the triumphant development of the ladies' charities which marked the first serious attempt to promote the position of women in the Church after centuries of being relegated to a merely passive rôle. It was thanks to the charities that the Church could be a mother to the destitute. At a time when women were regarded as nothing more than men's servants or, worse still, as instruments of the devil, Vincent de Paul gave them pride of place in the noblest work of the Church, the proclamation of charity.

The aim of parish charities was to help the poor sick people in their area. Many began to work for all poor people, not just those who were sick. The pressures of the times led to a broader concept of poverty. People complained that the term 'poor' was restricted to those had no possessions. It was often said that people who could not sell their lands because of mortgages were in a worse state as they got no profit from their lands and no help from the charities.[7]

The charities provided an on-going remedy for problems arising from inadequate social planning. They were charities for times of peace. In a relatively stable society the administrative authorities should have been able to eliminate the problem of poverty completely by making the comfortably-off in every area help those who were destitute. Vincent could not be accused of excessive optimism: in his time he had sounded the terrifying depths of poverty. He knew, though, that it was possible to at least reduce poverty to tolerable levels, to make the rich aware of their obligations and to move gradually closer to the ideal of a Christian society.

But society is not something static. It was not static in the seventeenth century either. A long period of economic depression marked the progressive impoverishment of most country areas and this led to the unending series of revolts recorded in Porchnev's studies[8] and to the emergence of colossal hordes of beggars. In addition, there were the catastrophic consequences of the wars. For a period of 25 years (1635-1659), France was continually at war with other countries and the situation was made worse by frequent wars at home, revolts by the nobility, uprisings among the common people and the long, drawn-out, blood-letting of the Fronde. As

---

[6] ABELLY, *op. cit.*, 1.2 c. 8, p. 340.
[7] LOUISE DE MARILLAC, *Pensées,* e.a., p. 127ff.
[8] B. PORCHNEV, *Les soulèvements populaires en France de 1623 à 1648* (Paris 1963).

well as the calamities of war there were occasional outbreaks of plague, that terrible scourge which periodically devastated the cities and rural areas of Europe.

Conventional charitable associations proved inadequate for dealing with these new forms of poverty and so the ladies of the Charity of the Hôtel Dieu took on an increasingly important rôle in tackling the problem. They gradually began to take on all Vincent's enterprises: galley slaves, foundlings, captives, foreign missions, disaster areas.[9]

'Our hearts are burning within us when M. Vincent speaks'

As happened with the Tuesday conferences, Vincent was the guiding spirit of the association and also its director for life.

The ladies used to meet every week and either Vincent or one of his delegates would preside. Some items on the agenda dealt with administrative problems but he also gave spiritual encouragement. We still have some manuscripts containing the notes he made to prepare for these meetings. They are too brief for us to recapture the passion of his spoken words but at least they show us the subjects dealt with as well as the tone of these meetings. Vincent would talk about the particular work under consideration and the spirit in which it was to be undertaken. As in all assemblies convoked by Vincent, the tone was informal, so that everyone present felt part of the proceedings and called to action.[10]

A few anecdotes help to recreate the atmosphere. As a rule, Vincent accepted majority decisions. One particular lady thought he was too ready to accept other people's opinions and was not slow to reprove him for this. This was Vincent's disarming reply to the lady:

> Madame, God does not want my poor ideas to override those of other people. You do not know how delighted I am that God should perform these works without any help from a wretched sinner like me.[11]

On another occasion during the effusive farewells after the meeting was over, three ladies spoke to each other about M. Vincent's address.

---

[9]   *S.V.P.* XIII, p. 818.
[10] *S.V.P.* XIII, pp. 761-802.
[11] ABELLY, p. c. , 1.3 c. 13, p. 205.

'Do you not think, Madame,' said Mme de Lamoignon to Louise Marie de Gonzague, 'that when M. Vincent was speaking we could say, like the disciples at Emmaus, that our hearts were on fire with the love of God? I must confess that although I am very indifferent to spiritual things, my heart was burning within me after what the holy man said to us.'

'That is not surprising', replied the future queen of Poland, 'M. Vincent is an angel of the Lord and his lips are touched with the glowing coals of that divine love which burns in his heart.'

'Yes, yes, that is true', added the third speaker, 'and all we have to do is to share that fire.'[12]

It was not until 1660 that the rules for the ladies were ultimately settled.[13] In fact, the association continued to function without written rules, or perhaps we should say with rules that were operational even though they had not been formally approved. These rules were as much concerned with the spirit in which the ladies should visit the Hôtel-Dieu as they were with defining the association's structures. One particular thing that was specifically laid down was the way in which they were to exhort the sick to make a general confession, for this was the original aim of the association together with the distribution of food. After 1636, only fourteen ladies undertook to give spiritual assistance to poor sick people and they took turns in doing this, the rota being changed every three months.[14] Two of them would go through the wards each day, to instruct and catechise the sick. The ladies financed a group of chaplains who were to work exclusively at instructing sick men and hearing confessions. At first there were two chaplains and then the number increased to six. Each one received 40 crowns a year as well as a stipend for the Mass they said each day in the cathedral. This payment was in addition to their board and lodging in the hospital. They were required to make a retreat at St Lazare before taking on the work and to do the same annually.[15] The ladies' efforts were very successful. In the first year alone, 760 non-Catholics were converted. These included Lutherans, Calvinists and Turks. Years later Vincent speaks of 200 heretics being converted.[16] Another group of ladies

---

[12] ABELLY, *op. cit.*, 1.3 c. 4, p. 30; COLLET, *op. cit.*, Vol. 2, p. 112.
[13] *S.V.P.* VI, p. 52.
[14] ABELLY, *op. cit.*, 1.1 c. 29, p. 138.
[15] ABELLY, *ibid.*, p. 139.
[16] ABELLY, *ibid.*, p. 140.

would serve the meals and very soon these ladies were helped by the Daughters of Charity.[17]

The society's organisation was confided to its director and a few committee members who were the 'superior' and two assistants who were originally named treasurer and assistant. The first superior was Mme Présidente Goussault, who founded the association. She held this office from 1634-1639. During Vincent's lifetime she was succeeded by Mme de Souscarrière (1639-43), Mme de Lamoignon (1643-51) and the Duchess d'Aiguillon (1651-75).[18]

'The party of God and the party of charity'

The number of ladies fluctuated quite a bit. We know this from remarks that Vincent made though perhaps we should not take his words too literally. Shortly after the association was founded there were 120 ladies[19] and this number soon increased to more than 200.[20] By 1656 there were only 50 and in 1657 they numbered 150.[21]

Each lady had to make sure she would be replaced and she named her successor from among her relations and friends. Vincent refuted, in advance, the shallow jibes made by the more frivolous sector of society at that time, by demanding that his aspirants be people completely dedicated—he repeated and emphasised the word 'completely'—to the service of God and to charity, and they must have renounced vain or dangerous pastimes such as gambling or the theatre. Above all, they were 'not to be motivated by vanity or the desire to gain a reputation for being pious'.[22] Vincent was far from naive. Even before Molière, he had unmasked the false piety of all Tartuffes.

Some of these ladies are already known to us. Others must always remain anonymous since the list of names we have is incomplete and nobody has made a systematic study of the social class, income, and the family or political links of what we might call the higher estate of charity. And so, many of the references are generalisations. Taking into account some of the very distinguished names that appear, it has even been said that the whole of France's aristocracy joined in performing the works of charity which were

---

[17] *S.V.P.* I, pp. 230, 371: IX, p. 8.

[18] COSTE, *M.V.* Vol. 1, p. 324.

[19] *S.V.P.* I, p. 253.

[20] *S.V.P.* XIII, p. 807.

[21] *S.V.P.* VI, p. 52; XIII, p. 807.

[22] *S.V.P.* XIII, p. 813.

the fruit of Vincent de Paul's genius. This observation is not altogether true. Vincent was not as influential among the highest ranks of that society and with the ladies at court as he would have wished. Around the year 1641, perhaps as a result of the second mission in St Germain en Laye, he drew up the rough draft of a set of rules for an association of charity for ladies at court. It was his intention to bring all the other charities under the patronage of these influential ladies and the members of this charity were to be 'the sacred person of the queen' and the noble ladies she saw fit to nominate.[23] This association never saw the light of day. Vincent could count on the queen's help on many occasions but this help was to come through other channels as we shall see in due time.[24]

The ladies of Charity had among their members some of the most distinguished ladies of noble birth. These included, among others, Charlotte Marguerite de Montmorency, Princess de Condé, Marie d'Orléans, Duchess de Nemours and Louise Marie de Gonzague who was later to become queen of Poland. These three were destined to play a very significant part in the historical events of that period. As a young woman Charlotte de Montmerency had married the elderly Condé to please Henry IV, who considered him to be a suitable husband for her, and she nearly provoked a war between France and Spain when King Henry made ready to take the beautiful princess by force away from the Low Countries where she had been taken by her husband. Ravaillac's dagger put a stop to that crazy adventure.[25] In later years she was involved in a web of political and military intrigues hatched by her husband and three sons. The great Condé, the Prince de Conti, and the Duchess de Longueville all paid for their share in the intrigues with different prison sentences. Though she was caught up in these turbulent events, she was prepared to devote much of her time and her fortune to works of charity.

Life was more peaceful for the Duchess de Nemours but her great wealth and extensive lands aroused the envy of powerful enemies like the kings of France and Prussia as well as the Duke of Savoy.

As we have mentioned earlier, Louise Marie de Gonzague was outstanding among the ladies of France for her intelligence, piety and beauty and so came to occupy the throne of Poland.

These three ladies would all be present, at least from time to time,

[23] *S.V.P.* XIII, p. 813.
[24] R. DARRICAU, 'L'action charitable d'une reine de France: Anne d'Autriche', *XVIIe Siècle* 90-91 (1971), pp. 111-125.
[25] P. CHEVALLIER, *op. cit.*, p. 60.

at the meetings of the ladies of Charity[26] but their main support was in the form of financial aid.[27]

As well as these ladies of royal blood there were equally distinguished people such as the Duchess d'Aiguillon and the Duchess de Ventadour who, at various times, held the office of president of the association,[28] and several other countesses and marchionesses.

Most of the ladies belonged to the upper middle class of the parlement, known as the *noblesse de robe*, a class of people whose social and economic progress played such a decisive part in changing the *Ancien Régime*.[29] Nearly all the important names connected with parlement, the palace secretariats, the royal household and tribunals are featured in the register of these ladies. Mme Goussault was the daughter of one president of the exchequer and the wife of another, Mlle Pollalion was a widow whose husband had been a gentleman of the royal household, Marie Lhuiller, Châtelaine de Villeneuve, belonged to the provincial aristocracy and had brothers-in-law in the government and in parlement, Mme de Miramion was related by birth and by marriage to noblemen with extensive estates, the name Lamoignon is inseparably linked, through mother and daughter, with the celebrated first president of the parlement; Mmes Fouquet, Herse and Traversay were all married to councillors of the parlement, while the husbands of Isabel de Aligre and Magdalen Fabri both held the office of chancellor.[30]

All these ladies were more famous for their devotion to works of charity and for their generosity than they were for their high rank and fortune. In Vincent's school, which was so different from Molière's famous *école des femmes*, they learnt to put their lives and their wealth at the service of the poor. Some of them founded or endowed religious congregations which were dedicated to answering the most pressing needs of the Church. The Daughters of Providence, dedicated to the education of poor girls and young people at risk, owe their origin to Mlle Pollalion. Their work was later amalgamated with that of the Nouveaux Catholiques and the sisters eventually became known as the Religious of St Chaumont. Mme de Villeneuve came to the rescue of the Daughters of the Cross who were about to die out because of the war and because they were falsely accused of illuminism, a charge that Vincent played an important part in refuting. Mme de Miramion founded the

---

[26] *S.V.P.* II, p. 6; ABELLY, *op. cit.*, c. 10, p. 358; COLLET, *op. cit.*, Vol. 1, p. 235 and Vol. 2, p. 112.

[27] *S.V.P.* III, pp. 510, 512.

[28] *S.V.P. ibid.*

[29] *Cf.* R. MANDROU, *op. cit.*, pp. 33-38; R. MOUSNIER, *La vénalité des offices au temps de Henry IV et de Richelieu* (Ruan 1945).

[30] COSTE, *M.V.* Vol. 1, 337ff.

Daughters of the Holy Family who were later amalgamated with the Daughters of St Genevieve and devoted themselves to the difficult work of helping fallen women.

Vincent helped all these foundations; sometimes by drawing up their statutes, sometimes by negotiating their approbation, sometimes by getting money for them and, in every case, by giving spiritual guidance to the foundresses. The association of ladies regarded this as one of their works and often sent gifts of money to these communities. Sometimes they sent one of their members to lead these congregations when the foundress died.[31]

We could go on for ever about the virtues of these pious ladies. Vincent liked to talk about them to the missioners and the Daughters of Charity.

One day when he was speaking about how we should put up with our disabilities and have sympathy for those of other people, he told the story of Mlle du Fay, one of the oldest members of the association:

> 'We all knew good Mlle du Fay, the sister of M. de Vincy,' he said. 'This lady had one leg two or three times heavier than the other but she was so close to God—I do not think I have ever known anyone so united to God as she was. She used to refer to her leg as "her blessed leg" since it was this which kept her out of company and even stopped her from getting married, in which state she might have lost her soul.'[32]

To the Daughters of Charity who sometimes complained about the heavy work involved in carrying heavy soup pots to dwellings that had many steps, he quoted the example of the Princess de Condé.

> The story is told that when the princess went one day to visit the sick she had to climb up eighty steps. When she came back, her servants were amazed to see her clothes all splashed with mud. What do you think led her to do this? It was because she realised her need to practise penance.[33]

Speaking about Mme de Fouquet, the mother of two bishops and of five Visitation nuns he said, 'If by mischance the Gospel were to disappear we would find its spirit and its maxims in the actions of Mme de Fouquet.'

---

[31] COSTE, *M.V.* Vol. 1, p. 334ff.

[32] *S.V.P.* XI, p. 131.

[33] *S.V.P.* X, p. 398.

And he went on to say, 'She makes piety seem so attractive that others are drawn to practise it.'[34]

'Join this holy company'

It was largely due to Vincent's efforts that this great upsurge of goodness came from the best elements of French society. The captivating influence of a priest of such lowly origins on the privileged classes of such a structured society is truly remarkable. The reason for his success may be simply that Vincent represented the voice of the people, and he made this voice heard even by those who had it in their power to inflict the most misery. It is no rhetorical expression to describe him as the voice of the voiceless. His words translated the lament of the masses into a language that the ruling classes prided themselves on being able to understand, the language of the gospel. The most sincere among them could not help but comply with its precepts. Vincent never led any of the peasant rebellions which other more or less enlightened priests often directed, but he achieved much more than any of these. While Chancellor Séguier was crushing with an iron hand 'the barefooted of Normandy'[35] his wife, who had something of a reputation for being tight-fisted, was generously contributing to Vincent's charities that cared for orphans, widows and those wounded in the war. Vincent was calling them to a non-violent struggle and for this reason people listened to his call and responded to it.

> 'Join this holy company' he exclaimed during the general assembly of 1657, 'Join us, you ladies who have not yet enrolled. This company's sole aim is to have a heart only for God alone, a will only to love him and time only to serve him.'[36]

The works performed by the association of ladies of Charity are incorporated into those of Vincent de Paul himself. We will illustrate this as we describe their works.

---

[34] *S.V.P.* III, p. 175.
[35] B. PORCHNEV, *op. cit.*, pp. 492-502.
[36] *S.V.P.* XIII, pp. 814-815.

Chapter XXVIII
CONSOLIDATION OF
THE DAUGHTERS OF CHARITY

'It was God who started this work'

We must now go back and follow the development of Vincent de Paul's most important creation, the Daughters of Charity. The parable of the mustard seed has been so over-used that one hesitates to quote it even in the most appropriate context. The four young women who met together on 29 November 1633 in a small house belonging to Louise de Marillac in the rue de Versailles which no longer exists and facing at that time L'Epée Royale,[1] were destined to increase over three centuries and to come to number tens of thousands.

Vincent would repeat ad nauseam that neither he, nor Louise de Marillac, nor M. Portail, nor Marguerite Naseau had ever thought of founding the community:

> Mlle did not think of it, Fr Portail and myself had no notion of doing it and neither had that poor girl. St Augustine used to say that when there was a doubt about who started a particular work then it was God himself who began it. It was God who started this work so it is God's work. Always remember that what was not done by men was done by God.[2]

It is the same old song from Vincent. Perhaps in this case there was more justification for it. The Daughters of Charity started off in a modest

---

[1] *S.V.P.* I, p. 215. Information about the Daughters of Charity in general is given in the works quoted in *Les Filles de la Charité de Saint Vincent de Paul* (Paris 1923), 6ª edition; P. NIETO, *Historia de las Hijas de la Caridad desde sus orígenes hasta el siglo XX* (Madrid 1932); P. COSTE, *M.V.* Vol. 1, pp. 385-535; R. MEYER and L. HUERGA, *Una institución singular: el superior general de la Congregación de la Misión y de las Hijas de la Caridad* (Salamanca, CEME, 1974).
[2] *S.V.P.* IX, p. 602.

way as helpers for the confraternities of Charity. It was hard to imagine the wonderful way the concept would develop but the original idea was so rich in potential that it very soon outgrew the narrow limitations that marked its beginnings. And the idea was really Vincent's idea.

It was a way of rounding off and perfecting what Vincent had in mind for the confraternities of charity: for every parish to have a small group of women who would be wholly dedicated to the service of the poor, and for all these groups to be united with each other, animated by the same spirit and following the same rules.

'Servants of the poor'

Vincent always had the objectives of this new association clearly in mind.

> 'The principal end to which God has called and assembled the Daughters of Charity is to honour and venerate Our Lord Jesus Christ as the source and model of all charity; serving him corporally and spiritually in the person of the poor, whether these be sick, children, prisoners or any others who are too embarrassed to make their needs known.'[3]

> 'And so', commented Vincent, 'you should aim at honouring Our Lord Jesus Christ, servant of the poor, in the person of children and so honour his infancy; in poor, needy people like those you will meet at the *Nom de Jesus* , and in the poor people you help when they come to take refuge in Paris because of the wars. You must, then, be ready to serve the poor wherever you may be sent—to soldiers, as you have done when sent to the battlefields, to poor criminals and to any other place where you can help the poor; this is to be your aim.'[4]

This was the guiding spirit of the new company, a spirit that was reflected in its official title, confraternity or society of charity, 'servants of the poor'.[5] Translation has tended to upgrade the original word 'servant' which comes from the Latin word *serva*. In Vincent de Paul's emphatic phrase, which reflects his understanding of the demands made by the gospel, they were literally to be servants, the serving maids, of those difficult masters, the

---

[3] *Common Rules of the Daughters of Charity*, c. 1 art. 1 (ed. of Madrid 1831).

[4] *S.V.P.* X, p. 126.

[5] *S.V.P.* XIII, pp. 558 and 571.

poor. Wealthy people had plenty of servants but the poor had only the humble, self-sacrificing 'Daughters of Charity',[6] their other name which was given them by the people and by which they would come to be known throughout the whole world. Vincent was to give a beautiful interpretation of this title.[7]

They were not meant to give just material relief to the poor but they had also to be concerned for their spiritual welfare. This is the counterpart of what Vincent asked of his missioners. When speaking to the Daughters of Charity he emphasised this different aspect and in this way he achieved, through both communities, a balance between man's material and his spiritual needs.

> It is very important to help the poor in a material way but in fact it was never Our Lord's plan in establishing this company that you should only look after their bodily needs. There will never be any shortage of people for that. Our Lord's intention in setting up the company was that you should give spiritual help to poor sick people. A Turk or an infidel can give material help. You must be resolved to add spiritual help to the material relief you give.[8]

Missioners and Daughters of Charity were to be the two arms of Vincent's vocation and so he regarded them as dependent on each other. In spite of all objections he confided the direction of the Daughters of Charity to the priests of the Mission. The words 'to have the poor helped either by ourselves or by other people'[9] were most fully lived out by the Daughters of Charity. This is how he explained the matter in depth to Jacques de la Fosse who was always worried and ready to criticise.

> Our little company has given itself to God to serve the poor corporally and spiritually. This has been so from the very beginning, and while we were labouring for souls during the missions we were trying at the same time to find ways of helping the sick through the charity confraternities.
>
> ... The ladies of the Charity of Paris, too, are so many witnesses to the grace of our vocation which helps us to contribute, with them, to so many good works both in the city and outside it. With this in mind and remembering, too, that

---

6   *S.V.P.* IX, p. 509.
7   *S.V.P.* III, p. 174; IX, pp. 14, 27, 52-53, 435, 568; X, pp. 125, 128, 473, 651.
8   *S.V.P.* X, pp. 333-334.
9   *S.V.P.* XII p. 87.

the Daughters of Charity are part of God's providential design since they are to take on works that we cannot do and provide material help for the sick poor, giving them little instructions for their salvation or some words of comfort, we, therefore, are obliged to help them advance in virtue so that they can dedicate themselves to their works of charity.[10]

The great danger, the biggest danger of all, was that the servants of the poor might be taken for a religious order. It was not that Vincent shared the aversion that some people felt at that time for the religious state as such. On the contrary, he had an unusually high regard and veneration for it. The danger was juridical and it could have had immediate and practical repercussions. In canonical terms at that time 'religious' meant cloistered and the cloister would have spelt death for the works of the community.

You are not religious in name but you must be so in spirit and you are more obliged to strive after perfection than professed religious are. But if any agitators or wrong-minded individuals among you should say, 'It would be much better if you were religious' then, my dear sisters, the community would be ready for extreme unction. That is what you must fear, my sisters, and as long as you have any breath left in you, prevent that happening. You should weep, lament and speak of it to your superior. Because whoever says *religious* means *cloistered* and Daughters of Charity have to be able to go anywhere.[11]

Vincent wanted to avoid terms used by religious orders so in spite of opposition from some sisters[12] he wished the community to be known as a confraternity. But common practice and possibly pressure from those who were unhappy with the term confraternity led to their finally being called a 'company'. When this title was applied to a community of women it meant that these were not nuns.

They did not wear a religious habit for the same reason. The first sisters continued to wear the costume of their native villages, the long grey gown and white coiffe which was the normal dress of country girls living on the outskirts of Paris. Girls coming from other regions adopted the same form of dress so as to preserve uniformity. This costume soon became

---

[10] *S.V.P.* VIII, pp. 238-239.
[11] *S.V.P.* X, p. 638.
[12] *S.V.P.* VII, p. 440.

distinctive and in quite a number of contemporary documents we find references to 'the grey sisters'. Neither Vincent not Louise made any concession to changes in fashion or to individual caprice. The question of whether to allow sisters, even in such distant places as Poland, to use a more serviceable headdress that would cover the neck and ears and give some protection from the cold, was a serious matter that had to be discussed in council.[13]

Female vanity invented little stratagems for being a bit different; they tried to have their hair showing, to show their chemise sleeves and to have these made from a finer or a whiter linen than others.[14] Vincent unmasked these abuses with a severity that might have been more apparent than real.

> I received a letter only today, telling me about one of your sisters who had bought herself a hooded cloak without permission and had gone out in it. Now do you think it's a nice thing to see one sister wearing her usual coiffe and another wearing a hood? If we do not come down on this with a firm hand there will be some sisters dressed in one style and some in another, some will wear clothes of finer material, some will want to take more pains with their hair and others will want to have their hair showing. Indeed, if we do not do something about this, uniformity will be lost and that will be the end of the company. [15]

Poor M. Vincent! If only he could have known how the years would change his daughters' simple costume into an imposing monument of material and starch. And how right it is for our sisters today, that in line with the thinking of Vatican II, they have gone back to a simpler style of dress which is more in keeping with the garb of those first sisters.

This was a confraternity, then, of ordinary laywomen. They were not religious; they had no cloister to protect them from the dangers of the world and no distinctive religious habit to set them apart but they were meant to be different so that everyone would recognise them as servants of the poor. Did Vincent have no qualms about the tremendous innovation his company was bringing to the style of women religious? He had no fears because he had discovered the secret of inspiring his daughters with a community spirit that would protect them from danger and make them

---

[13] *S.V.P.* II, p. 620; XIII, pp. 746, 750.
[14] *S.V.P.* X, pp. 18, 187-188, 285, 295-299, 350.
[15] *S.V.P.* X, p. 314.

conscious of the greatness of their vocation which was something new and different. His final summary of what the ideal Daughter of Charity should be is in the classical text that appears in every collection of his writings. All the elements of religious life are there, but reinterpreted in secular terms:

> They will have for monastery the houses of the sick, for cell a hired room, for oratory the parish church, for cloister the streets of the city or the wards of hospitals, for cloister obedience, for grille the fear of God and for veil holy modesty. They shall therefore lead as holy a life as they would if they were professed nuns in a convent.[16]

'Providence has brought the twelve of you here'

As happened with the Congregation of the Mission, the Daughters of Charity got off to a slow start but as people got to know and appreciate them their numbers increased more rapidly. Eight months after they were founded on 31 July 1634, they numbered twelve.[17] It has been calculated that between 1645 and 1646 that figure had risen to more than a hundred.[18] In 1660, the year that Vincent died, there must have been more than 200. The number of houses they had would indicate this. A further pointer to the growth of this community is a document relating to the election of sisters to office, dated 8 August 1655. This list contained 142 names but we have to remember that not every sister was present and this total does not include sisters who had died or left the community.[19]

Most vocations came from among uneducated peasant girls living in the outlying districts of Paris. These were recruited by Vincent during his missions or by Louise de Marillac and other ladies during their visitations of the charities. A fair number of these girls could neither read nor write.[20] There were some who came from a higher social class but Vincent doubted whether girls who had been brought up in refined and comfortable surroundings would be able to cope with the laborious work of the company.[21] The company admitted both young, single women and widows who had no small children to look after.[22]

---

[16] *Common Rules of the Daughters of Charity*, c. 1 art.2 (ed. de Barbastro 1815).
[17] *S.V.P.* IX, pp. 1-13.
[18] *S.V.P.* II, pp. 549-551 (July, 1645); III, pp. 54-55 (September, 1646).
[19] *S.V.P.* XIII, pp. 575-577.
[20] *S.V.P.* IX, pp. 7, 31, 42, 43, 217, 219, 427; X, pp. 509, 545, 568, 574, 577, 717.
[21] *S.V.P.* XIII, pp. 716-717.
[22] *S.V.P.* I, p. 278; XIII, pp. 551, 557, 559, 566, 570.

'Solid virtues'

After a probationary period working for the poor in a parish confraternity, the aspirants had a brief training session in the house of Louise de Marillac. This developed later into a formal programme like that of a novitiate and was called a seminary.[23] Vincent was working out the guidelines for such training as he went along and he personally took part in the talks. One thing preoccupied him more than anything else: they were to acquire 'solid virtues' and the true spirit of the company. He was very suspicious of virtue that went no further than acts of piety. The real test of a true vocation is every day living.

> 'You would do well to tell them', he wrote to Louise de Marillac, 'what is meant by solid virtue and teach them especially to perform interior acts of mortification of their judgement, will and memory; to practise recollection of the eyes and ears and to exercise control over their other senses as well as their attachment to things that are evil or frivolous, as well as those things which are good in themselves but which they should mortify out of love for Our Lord who acted in this way. You should help them to grow stronger in this practice, particularly with regard to the virtues of obedience and holy indifference. It would be a good thing if you told them that they will need help in acquiring this virtue of mortification and they must be given the opportunity to practise it. I will tell them the same thing so that they will be more ready to act like this.'[24]

Vincent pointed to the conduct of young village girls as a model for these solid virtues and this was something that would have been familiar to them. On Sunday 25 January 1643, shortly after the feast of St Genevieve, he devoted the entire weekly conference to this theme. Memories of his country childhood, of his mother and sisters, things he had seen during the hundreds of missions he had preached in French villages, all his priestly experience and his intuitive knowledge of the feminine psyche, are all summed up in this talk. The simple girls listening to him would have recognised in this the story of their own lives touched by divine grace. Holiness was within their grasp; all they had to do was to perfect the good qualities they already

---

[23] *S.V.P.* I, pp. 238, 278, 315.
[24] *S.V.P.* I, p. 278.

had. It was not a question of becoming different but of living out in a holy and perfect way what they already were. Even today, after three centuries, Vincent's words are the greatest praise that can be offered to those French peasants whose solid goodness had been nurtured by centuries of Christianity.

The spirit of genuinely good village girls—Vincent was quick to emphasise the word 'genuine' because he was by no means naive and he knew that his listeners could have had very different experiences from the idyllic picture he was painting—is that they would be simple, humble, free from ambition, sober, pure, modest, poor, hard-working and obedient; and he illustrated all this with true examples from country life. He ended by saying:

> Know this, my daughters, that if I have ever told you anything
> that is true and important it is what you have just heard. You
> must strive to practise and to keep the spirit of genuinely good
> village girls.[25]

Do these words suggest contempt for life at court and the greatest praise for rural life? Was it an early and intuitive notion of the good savage? There may be something of that in these words but more importantly, they reflect the early Christian concept of rural life even though this description could be more what Vincent wished it to be rather than the real picture. The Daughters of Charity were not the slightest bit interested in the literary origins of the model he was putting before them. The important thing for them was that their lives should correspond to the ideal that their father and founder was presenting to them.

'Our dear mother'

Vincent's key collaborator in the work of training the sisters was Louise de Marillac. Many different circumstances have helped to obscure the rôle that this extraordinary woman played in the development and consolidation of the company founded by Vincent de Paul. She wrote little, compared with Vincent, not a lot is known about her progress in the spiritual life, and she was always happy to remain in the shadow of her director and spiritual father. Three centuries passed before she was canonised so she did not enjoy the same recognition as other saints in the Church who are more well known. A contemporary study of St Louise is throwing increasing light on the hidden figure of Mlle le Gras who was one of Vincent de Paul's most brilliant

---

[25] The conference on the virtues of good village girls is in *S. V.P.* IX, pp. 79-94.

masterpieces. Vincent himself moulded the spirit of his closest collaborator but only after a long period of instruction and training.

By the time Louise took over the work of directing the sisters in 1633, she had overcome her main spiritual difficulties. She was forty-two and a mature woman in the best sense of that word. She was beginning to blossom spiritually and the joy she felt in knowing that she was following God's call was more intense than the spiritual trials that still tormented her. Her son's behaviour and worries about his future still caused her much concern. The poor young boy still had no idea what he wanted to do. Sometimes he seemed happy enough and was ready to be ordained[26] but at other times the thought of this filled him with horror and he said that he would only be ordained to please his mother; sometimes he even wished himself and his mother dead.[27] In the end he had to give up the idea of being a priest. Michel returned to ordinary life and was involved in some not very honourable incidents.[28] Vincent appointed him bailiff at Saint Lazare[29] and in 1650 he married a young woman of considerable social standing. The girl's uncle procured for him the post of counsellor in the finances tribunal and Vincent gave his blessing to the marriage.[30] But this was not to be the end of his troubles. He became profoundly deaf and had to give up his post as magistrate.[31]

While grieving over so many misfortunes, Louise tried to supernaturalise her maternal feelings. She wanted to reach the stage of regarding her son as just a child of God. She did not quite achieve this but she did succeed in not letting her personal problems interfere with her duties as superior of the company.

After 1635 or 1636 her letters begin to take on a different tone. From being the person directed, she has to become directress. The advice that she kept seeking from Vincent was passed on to her daughters with increasing confidence and sureness of touch. Although she was subordinate to the director and founder, her responsibility for training the sisters and her administration and government of the company were not simply delegated tasks. She took decisions, kept records, and guided and directed the sisters. She did all these things with increasing skill and confidence. On some occasions she was bold enough to put forward opinions that were very different from those held by Vincent, and her arguments prevailed. We will see an example

---

[26] *S.V.P.* I, pp. 519-520.

[27] *S.V.P.* I, pp. 441, 516.

[28] *S.V.P.* II, pp. 542, 576; III, p. 31.

[29] *S.V.P.* III, p. 437.

[30] *S.V.P.* III, p. 544.

[31] *S.V.P.* V, p. 445.

of this later on. In 1647 she personally took charge of the seminary[32] and this was only a part of the training programme. Through her correspondence she was able to extend her influence to the sisters in the provinces, while the sisters in Paris were able to benefit from her talks and admonitions; she participated in Vincent's conferences and, finally, she gave them the example of her daily life which was like a living rule for the company. Vincent even confided to her direction the ladies who used to go to the sisters' house to make a retreat. So it is not surprising that the Daughters of Charity spontaneously began to refer to her as 'our dear mother.'[33]

She never had good health but this did not prevent her from visiting the charities.[34] In 1639 she travelled to Angers and in 1646 made the journey to Nantes to supervise, like St Teresa had done for her order, the establishment of the two most important foundations of the Daughters of Charity,[35] and in 1644 she made a pilgrimage to Chartres.[36] Meanwhile, Louise was making progress in the spiritual life, and a careful reading of her writings reveals the different stages of her spiritual development. Sometime around the year 1644 she went through a period of spiritual renunciation which might even be called spiritual annihilation and this led her to practise still greater self-sacrifice. From the year 1651 until her death in 1660 she reached a state of union with the sovereign Lord of souls which bears all the marks of total mystical fulfilment.[37]

'With the help of God you will have your rules one day'

The process of compiling rules for the Daughters of Charity was similar to that used for drawing up the rules for missioners. In both cases Vincent wanted a long testing period to check that the prescriptions were both useful and practicable before he promulgated the definitive version.

In 1634 we already have some general regulations written out by St Louise, and Vincent used to explain these to the sisters.[38] These regulations continued to be modified and added to throughout the forties. There was one copy, or two at most, and these were reserved for the superiors. By 1643 it contained 32 points which were divided into two sections. The first section dealt with regulations concerning the order of day and exercises of

---

[32] *S.V.P.* XIII, p. 658.

[33] *S.V.P.* X, p. 719; GOBILLON, *op. cit.*, pp. 78-80.

[34] *S.V.P.* I, pp. 239, 242-247, 325-327, 503, 504.

[35] *S.V.P.* I, pp. 603-606, 609-613; III, pp. 5-7, 11-14, 17-19.

[36] *S.V.P.* II, p. 478.

[37] J. CALVET, *Louise de Marillac*, pp. 131-152.

[38] *S.V.P.* IX, pp. 1-13, 18-26, 113-127.

piety, the second contained the basic norms dealing with the spirit in which the various works were to be performed, the virtues special to the community, and relationships the sisters should have with each other and with those who did not belong to the company.[39] The rule was short and simple. The sisters only knew it from hearing it read aloud and from the explanations given during the weekly conference. It was not long before the sisters began to ask for written copies.[40]

Vincent promised to see to it—'With God's help you will have your rules one day'[41]—but he was a long time producing them. He foresaw several difficulties, one of which was the need to draw up different regulations for 'the variety of poor people' they served, that is, for the different foundations and works.[42] The most serious problem was that the community had still not been formally granted ecclesiastical approval. When this approbation was finally granted by the archbishop of Paris in 1655 it included, as we shall see, the basic statutes of the congregation. Vincent then drew up a set of rules which comprised the basic or common rules for every sister and every house, and particular rules for sisters working in parishes, hospitals, schools, etc. On 29 September 1655, Vincent began the systematic reading and explanation of the common rules and this went on until 11 August 1659.[43] During the following months he explained the particular rules for sisters in the parishes.

Even at this point Vincent decided not to have the rules printed. He thought it might be better to have them written out by hand and a copy sent to each house. He was still hesitating about this when death overtook him. So there was no formal ceremony for distributing the rules as happened with the missioners. Vincent's first successor did not have them printed either; he just signed a copy of the text, thus guaranteeing its authenticity and preventing any variations being introduced at a later date. It was then that he rearranged Vincent's text, dividing it into chapters and adding footnotes. This meant that we now have 75 points of rule instead of the original 70. There is no substantial difference between the text that Vincent explained in his conferences and the version we have now. All the same we will always regret not having the text that came directly from the pen of Vincent.[44]

---

[39] *S.V.P.* IX, pp. 115, 118.

[40] *S.V.P.* IX, pp. 18, 113, 213.

[41] *S.V.P.* IX, p. 18.

[42] *S.V.P.* IX, p. 115.

[43] *S.V.P.* X, pp. 105, 653.

[44] The authentic copy was signed by René Alméras and Sister Mathurine Guérin on 5 August 1672. It was also signed by the superior of every house in Paris and by a few representatives. They arranged that any future copies that were sent to the houses had to be signed by the superioress general and one of her assistants and it had to be sealed with her seal. The copy that we have consulted, dated 1790, bears, in fact, the signatures of the then superioress general, Mother Renée Dubois, and her assistants.

'Although you have not vows just now'

It was quite soon after their foundation that Vincent began to think of the possibility that the Daughters of Charity, in line with the missioners, might make some sort of vows. This was no easy matter. A community of women who made vows was automatically classed as a religious community. Vincent's fears for the future of the company might well have been justified. No doubt this was why he were more hesitant and cautious in dealing with this question than he had been in soliciting vows for the missioners.

The first reference to the vows of the Daughters of Charity is found in a conference given on 5 July 1640. In a way that is almost subliminal, the text hints at Vincent's intentions.

'The Daughters of Charity although they do not have vows just now, are none the less in that state of perfection if they are living as true Daughters of Charity.'[45]

The phrase 'just now' is a clear indication that the founder was thinking that they would make vows. A fortnight later he made the same suggestion and it is obvious that he was looking for a positive response from the sisters.

My dear sisters I was very consoled one day. I must tell you about it. I heard the vow formula used by nursing religious in Italy and it went like this, 'I promise and vow to God to spend my whole life in poverty, chastity and obedience and to serve our lords, the poor.' My daughters, see how pleasing it is to our good God for his members, the beloved poor, to be honoured in this way.

M. Vincent read this vow formula with such fervour that some sisters were moved to share what they felt about it. They spoke of the happiness those good religious must have felt in being able to consecrate their whole lives to God and they asked whether sisters in our community could not be allowed to do something similar.

After this successful start, Vincent went a step further, and taking it for granted that the sisters would be able to make vows, he told them what this would involve.

---

[45] *S.V.P.* IX, p. 14.

Yes, of course, my daughters, but with this difference; those good religious took solemn vows which cannot be dispensed even by the pope, whereas the bishop could give a dispensation from the vows that you would take. However, if you thought you could get a dispensation whenever you like, it would be better not to take vows at all.

The following question shows that the matter was now considered a *fait accompli* since it referred to the manner of making vows and who was to give authorisation for them.

To the question: Would it not be a good thing for the sisters to make them [vows] in private when they felt moved by grace to do so?' his charity replied that they should be very wary of this. If any sister wanted to do this she should discuss it with her superiors and then be at peace whether the permission was granted or not.

This answer to the query clearly indicates that there was a definite formality about making vows. Although these vows were private and only binding in conscience, they could only be made with the superiors' approval. Vincent had done what he set out to do and he finished with a prayer that was almost an early version of the vow formula:

Fr Vincent raised his heart to God and with great fervour spoke as follows:
'Oh my God, we consecrate ourselves entirely to thee; grant us the grace to live and to die in true poverty. I ask this for all our sisters, those here present and those who are far away. Do you not wish this, too, my daughters? Grant us also the grace of living and dying in chastity. I ask this grace for all sisters of charity and for myself, as well as the grace to live in perfect obedience. My God, we give ourselves to you to honour and serve our lords the poor all our life long, and we ask this grace through your holy love. Isn't this what you wish, too, my dear sisters?
All our sisters immediately gave their assent with great fervour and they all knelt down.'[46]

---

[46] *S.V.P.* IX, pp. 25-26.

The arrow had found its target and the Socratic dialogue had led the sisters to find for themselves the answers to their questions.

Almost at the same time as Vincent was skilfully handling the rudder and steering the Daughters of Charity towards introducing into their company the practice of making vows, Fr Lebreton was in Rome during July 1640 to negotiate approval for the missioners' vows. Nothing like this was done for the Daughters of Charity. In October of the following year the archbishop of Paris gave his approval to the decree which recognised the vows taken by the priests of the Congregation of the Mission. Nothing could have been done because ecclesiastical authorities had not yet given formal approval to the company. However, the actual practice of taking vows developed, strikingly enough, at the same pace for both communities.

On 24 February 1642, the missioners took their vows together as a community for the first time. A month later, on 25 March of that same year, the first five Daughters of Charity, including Louise de Marillac, pronounced their vows. We can only be certain that Barbe Angiboust, 'Big Barbara', was one of these sisters but the others were most probably Isabelle Turgis, Marie Denise and Jeanne Gesseaume. They made perpetual vows. Vincent must have wanted both congregations to have similar vows and that year marked a decisive stage in the incorporation of these into their respective constitutions.[47]

The sisters' vows followed a longer and more tortuous path than those of the missioners. From all the documentation that is still preserved we can deduce that some sisters made perpetual vows and this practice persisted right until the time of Vincent's death. In 1650 there were quite a number of sisters who had made perpetual vows.[48] Barbara Bailly made perpetual vows in 1656[49] and by 1659 'all the older members of the company' had done likewise.[50] It was the custom for sisters to make annual vows after being in the company for five years. They did this for a further five, six or seven years and then made perpetual vows which they renewed periodically out of devotion.[51]

Did Vincent intend to make this practice a general rule? Current research can give no answer to this question. But the fact remains that at the time of the founder's death, some sisters made perpetual vows while others made vows annually. In either case these were strictly private vows since the

---

[47] *S.V.P.* V, p. 353; X p. 638; XIII, p. 660.

[48] *S.V.P.* IX, p. 534.

[49] *S.V.P.* VII, p. 393; VIII, p. 188.

[50] *S.V.P.* VIII, p. 207.

[51] *S.V.P.* III, pp. 298, 301; V, pp. 438, 460; VI, pp. 61, 118, 358, 397; VII, pp. 71-72, 283, 393, 448, 455, 472; VIII, pp. 91, 163, 391.

company was still not formally approved by the Church. However, sisters still had to have permission from the superior to make or to renew their vows. After Vincent's death it became the custom to make temporary vows only and these were renewed each year on 25 March. This was the definitive formula that was approved by the Holy See and it is still adhered to by the Daughters of Charity today. Vincent's intuition had led him to create the most original form of taking vows to be found anywhere in the Church; he founded a community whose members would be perfectly free each year to renew these vows. The fact that the company has lasted all these years proves just how right their founder was.[52]

'You now have your own special identity'

Vincent de Paul was not in the same hurry to seek ecclesiastical approval for the Daughters of Charity as he had been for the Congregation of the Mission. Even as late as 1645 he had not made any move to have them accepted even at diocesan level. He did draw up, that year, a preliminary petition which must have gone unheeded,[53] because the following year he wrote another one.[54]

The archbishop was not against it. It was in his name that Jean François Paul de Gondi, his nephew and coadjutor, signed a decree on 20 November 1646, giving canonical recognition within the diocese of Paris to the 'confraternity of Charity, servants of the poor.'[55]

Some months later, Vincent gave the news to the Sisters during a conference that he was giving to explain the rules and the statutes which were approved at the same time as the institute was formally recognised. This marks the definitive beginning of the company.

> Up to now you have not been a separate organisation from that of the confraternity of ladies of charity and now, my daughters, God wants you to have your own special identity and even though you will still be working with the ladies you will now have your own exercises of piety and your own special functions.[56]

---

[52] *Circulaires des supérieurs généraux ... aux Filles de la Charité*, Vol. 2, p. 3, 7, 19.

[53] *S.V.P.* II, pp. 548-553.

[54] *S.V.P.* III, pp. 53-56.

[55] *S.V.P.* XIII, pp. 557-565.

[56] *S.V.P.* IX, p. 323.

The decree of approval granted by the archbishop confided the direction of this new association to Vincent de Paul but placed it 'under the authority of and dependent on' the archbishop of Paris. Moreover it was not accorded the title 'Daughters of Charity'. Louise de Marillac was worried.[57] She was particularly concerned that at some later date the sisters might have other directors than the Vincentian superiors. Through her friends, she got the queen, Anne of Austria, to petition the pope to appoint 'the superior general of the Mission and his successors as directors of the confraternity of charity of the servants of the poor in perpetuity.'[58] We do not know for certain who it was that suggested this petition to the queen but all the indications are that it was Louise.[59] Neither do we know anything about how this petition was received in Rome, if, in fact, it was ever discussed.

The company needed to be recognised by the civil authorities and for this to happen as soon as possible. They had no difficulty at all in obtaining letters patent from the king but something unforeseen happened when the parlement was to have ratified these. All through April 1650 they were expecting the approbation to be granted any day. At least this is what Louise de Marillac was given to understand by Blaise Méliand, the procurator general.[60] But shortly after this date the distinguished official died and so did his secretary. The new procurator general was a gentleman from whom they could expect a very favourable judgement, because Nicolas Fouquet was the son of one of the ladies of Charity we mentioned earlier. Negotiations were resumed but when the new procurator asked to see the documents these had disappeared. They could not be found either among the dead man's papers or in the archives of St Lazare or anywhere in the sisters' house.[61]

It has been commonly thought that Louise de Marillac was responsible for this loss though she believed them to be in the hands of Vincent's secretary.[62] She had ample opportunity and sufficient motive for engineering the loss. For one thing, she was anxious to suppress the clause that would put the company under the authority of the bishop. And then her friendship with Mme Fouquet meant that she had easy access to the documents. Perhaps this is stretching things a bit far. The situation could simply have arisen because of the death of Méliand and his secretary. This, at any rate, is the official version of what happened.

So they had to start again from scratch. A second petition was addressed to the archbishop who was formerly the coadjutor; and this was

[57] *S.V.P.* III, p. 121.

[58] *S.V.P.* XIII, p. 567.

[59] MEYER-HUERGA, *op. cit.*, pp. 97-100.

[60] *S.V.P.* IV, pp. 4-5.

[61] *S.V.P.* XIII, pp. 570-571, 581.

[62] *S.V.P.* IV, p. 275.

granted on 18 January 1655. Strangely enough there is only one significant difference between the two letters of approval. In the second one, and in compliance with Louise's wishes, the government and direction of the confraternity was confided, in perpetuity, 'to Vincent de Paul and his successors as superior general of the Congregation of the Mission', and all references in previous clauses to the archbishop's delegate were replaced by the word superior.[63] The king granted the new letters patent in November 1657,[64] and these were ratified by the parlement in 1658.[65] The confraternity of Daughters of Charity was at last recognised as a juridical entity.'[66]

The archbishop's decree of approval included some briefly worded statutes concerning the election of the superioress general and her assistants, as well as a summary of the rules governing the aims and spirit of the company, its order of day and the principal works. Vincent had these rules implemented straight away although, as this was the first time for it to happen, he dispensed with the rules about electing sisters to office. He named these himself and then had the appointments ratified by the sisters.[67] As regards the office of superioress general, he had already explained in 1646 that the rule stating she should be replaced every three years was not to come into force until after the death of Mlle le Gras. Louise knelt down and begged that there would be no exceptions but Vincent was adamant.

> Your sisters and I, mademoiselle, must beg God to grant you many more years of life. It is often the case that God preserves, in an extraordinary way, those who are indispensable for the accomplishment of his works. And when you think about it, Mademoiselle, it is a wonder you've been alive at all for the past ten years.[68]

We know for certain that during the last years of his life Vincent sounded out the possibility of having the Daughters of Charity recognised by the Holy See. We know this from a letter he wrote in September 1659, to his representative in Rome, Fr Jolly.[69] But if any serious attempts were made to

---

[63] *S.V.P.* XIII, pp. 569-572. *Cf.* For a comparison between both approvals, see MEYER-HUERGA, *op. cit.*, p. 102.

[64] *S.V.P.* XIII, pp. 578-585.

[65] *S.V.P.* XIII, pp. 585-587.

[66] For canonical difficulties arising from this approval *cf.* MEYER-HUERGA, *op. cit.*, pp. 104-105.

[67] *S.V.P.* X, pp. 97-104; XIII, pp. 572-577.

[68] *S.V.P.* IX, p. 324.

[69] 'I will send you the rules of the Daughters of Charity and their approval by Cardinal de Retz in Rome, together by a copy of the letters patent and their registration parlement, so that we can see how to make them be approved' (*Annales* [1945-1946], p. 199).

negotiate this, then they were not successful during the founder's lifetime. It was only in 1668 that the Daughters of Charity were formally approved by the pope, in a decree issued by Cardinal Louis de Vendôme who was the legate *a latere* of Clement IX.[70] We cannot help but be surprised at Vincent's slowness in this matter which is so different from the vigorous efforts he made to negotiate formal approval for the missioners. Perhaps he was afraid that the nature of the institute would provoke too much opposition in Rome and that he would rather have it approved at diocesan level than risk its rejection by Rome.

---

[70] The Latin text of Cardinal Vendôme's letter is in MAYER-HUERGA, *op. cit.*, pp. 209-212.

Chapter XXIX
EXPANSION OF THE COMPANY OF DAUGHTERS OF CHARITY

In the beginning, the field of action for the Daughters of Charity was limited to Paris. It was here that they were being asked for by the charities. Very soon they were established in every parish where there was a confraternity. The aspirants, or seminary sisters, continued to live in Louise de Marillac's house which was the mother-house of the community.[1] But this soon became too small for their needs and they had to look for another house. Finding one was not easy because money was scarce. In 1636 they rented a small house in the village of La Chapelle to the north of Paris and not far from the capital.[2] Some years later, in 1641, they had to move again. The house they chose, and again it was a rented one, was opposite St Lazare in the parish of St Laurent. Soon after they moved in Vincent bought the property for 12,000 *livres* because at that time the company was not officially recognised. In 1653 it was sold by public auction to Mlle Le Gras who had at her disposal the 9,000 *livres* bequeathed her by Mme Présidente Goussault. The property was now valued at 17,650 *livres* and the difference in the price was met by donations from other ladies. The Daughters of Charity now had their own mother-house at last. Improvements and extensions were begun during the lifetime of both founders and were continued in later years. It remained the mother-house until the French Revolution, a century and a half later.[3]

'May the company be rooted in humility'

The mother-house was not just an administrative centre. Guided and inspired by Louise de Marillac, the sisters there did the same works as those taken on

---

[1] GOBILLON, *op. cit.*, p. 51.
[2] GOBILLON, *op. cit.*, p. 74.
[3] GOBILLON, *op. cit.*, pp. 97-98; COSTE. *M.V.* Vol. 1, p. 450.

by all the other houses: they visited the sick, instructed young girls and gave medicines to those who came to their door ...[4]

Life was hard and they had to live within a tight budget. Vincent and Louise wanted it to serve as a model for the other foundations. The house had neither a pump nor a well so the sisters went to the public fountain where they saw many unedifying things, heard scandalous talk and were insulted and badly treated. One day, the sister who was responsible for fetching the water could not stand it any longer. She picked up her pails and straightaway headed for St Lazare. Just at that moment Vincent came out. He listened to the sister's complaints and then took the buckets, filled them from the well in that house, and then carried them back himself.[5] Not long afterwards, Mlle Le Gras obtained permission from the municipal authorities to use water from the public supply system outside her house for domestic purposes.[6]

Extensions were made to the house when funds allowed. Louise and Vincent both agreed that the new buildings should avoid any suggestion of luxury. Louise even wanted them to use old stone that had been discoloured by the weather, if they could. And Vincent admitted that in a spirit of poverty he had decided not to renovate one of the buildings.

> Whenever M. le Lieutenant comes here he never stops remonstrating with me ... When he complains I just laugh and I do not tell him why I will not have the repairs done but the real reason is that I want the company to be rooted in humility and to imitate, as far as possible, the Son of God's manner of acting.[7]

Louise in her turn, tackled the architect:

> 'May I remind you' she wrote, 'that it is absolutely essential for this building to reflect the simple style of a village house and it must be as unpretentious as possible. I know that you are accustomed to doing things on a grand scale and that you will find it hard to go to the other extreme, but when you reflect on what I told you, that it is absolutely necessary for the survival of our company that it be poor and lowly in all

---

[4] GOBILLON, *ibid.*; *S.V.P.* II, p. 550; III, p. 55.

[5] Evidence given by Sr Marie de la Ruelle in the *Beatification Process of St. Vincent de Paul*, pp. 469v-472v.

[6] *S.V.P.* VIII, p. 84.

[7] *S.V.P.* XIII, p. 716.

things, then you will realise that this is Our Lord's work and
you will even be happy to contribute to it.'[8]

'You are being asked for on all sides'

The sisters in Paris worked in the parish charities and also served in another
five establishments set up for particular works, as we shall be seeing later on.
In 1638 the works began to extend beyond the boundaries of the capital
when a foundation was made at St Germain en Laye at the request of Mme de
Chaumont, superior of the ladies of Charity in that district.[9]

After that the process of making foundations never stopped. 'You
are being asked for on all sides', says Vincent on several occasions.[10] And
this was true. Most of the requests were made by the ladies of Charity who
asked for sisters to work in their respective confraternities.'[11] Some houses,
like those of Fontainebleau, Châtillon, and Sedan were royal foundations,
while others were set up by bishops or municipalities. The sisters were a
good bargain: their food and clothing only cost about 100 *livres* a year and
some managed on only 75 *livres*.[12] The lessons of frugality and poverty that
the founder gave to his daughters were not just empty words.

Within a few years the number of houses of the Daughters of Charity
increased to fifty, and as well as those founded in the capital there were
houses in many parts of France. Between 1638 and 1648 there were twenty
new foundations: St Germain en Laye, Richelieu, Angers, Nanteuil-le-
Haudouin, Sedan, Issy, Fontenay aux Roses, Liancourt, Crespières,
Fontainebleau, Le Mans, Nantes, Maule, St Denis, Serqueux, Chantilly,
Chartres, Montrueil-sur-Mer, Fréneville and Valpuiseaux. Another fifteen
were established between the years 1648 and 1660: at Hennebont, Montmirail,
Brienne, Varize, Bernay, Chateaudun, La Roche-Guyon, St Marie du Mont,
La Fère, Arras, Cahors, Ussel, Metz, Narbonne, Vaux-le-Vicomte, Belle Isle-
sur-Mer. And beyond France itself, there was the foundation at Warsaw
(1652). The sisters were summoned here, as were the missioners, by the
queen of Poland.[13]

It would be exaggerated to suggest, as some people have done,
that these foundations covered the whole of France. Most of the houses of

---

[8] LOUISE DE MARILLAC, *Ecrits* ..., p. 509; R. CASTAÑARES, *op. cit.*, II, p. 292.
[9] *S.V.P.* I, pp. 421, 433.
[10] *S.V.P.* III, p. 210; X, p. 222.
[11] *S.V.P.* II, p. 549; III, p. 54.
[12] *S.V.P.* II, p. 549; III, p. 54.
[13] For the date of these foundations and the circumstances in which they were made, *cf. S.V.P.*
XIV, pp. 109-111.

the Daughters of Charity were concentrated in the northern half of the country though the foundations made at Ussel, Cahors and Narbonne point to a movement southwards and this would continue relentlessly after the death of the founders.

These were small communities. Most of them had two or three sisters living either in rented accommodation, in the house of the lady of charity who had asked for them, or in lodgings provided by the confraternity, parish or municipality. Very few foundations needed to have more sisters; at most there would be half a dozen. Nevertheless, these small teams scattered over French soil were hardy plants that took root, thus ensuring the extraordinary expansion of the community. The sisters had certainly taken the 'solid virtues' to heart.

Parishes, schools, hospitals

There was little variation between the works of one foundation and another.

The main work was serving the poor in their homes and this was done by sisters in practically every house. It was the original work of the community. The sister would go through the streets of the parish carrying the soup pot that the ladies had prepared. She did not just bring food and medicine to the house but consolation, too, and pious exhortations which the poor needed as much, if not more, than the material help she gave. Sisters were servants, nurses and catechists all rolled into one. They made beds, applied poultices, gave purges, did blood-letting, stayed up at night with the sick, and cleaned and scrubbed the rooms of the most abandoned people. Each visit, and especially those made in the evening, gave them the opportunity to teach the truths of religion to these sick people and also to their families, and encourage them to go to confession. They also instructed them in the duties of a Christian. All this they were to do with humility, respect, joy and cordiality and they were to take particular care not to treat the sick in a brusque or disdainful manner even when these refused to take the medicines or behaved roughly.[14]

In each parish one sister would attend to the sick while the other instructed little girls. This, too, was one of the earliest works of the company. Marguerite Naseau, the dairymaid from Suresnes, began her works of charity, as we have already mentioned, by teaching girls to read, once she had learnt this skill herself. Vincent never forgot that first vocation. He wanted all the sisters to learn to read and write so that they could teach others.[15] We find it

---

[14] *Règles particulières de soeurs des paroisses.*
[15] *S.V.P.* IX, p.7.

strange, today, to think that people who had just become literate should be teachers. This situation was due to the backward state of primary education in France during the seventeenth century. The state provided no system of public education at all. The only small contribution it made in this field was to encourage parish priests and curates to procure 'prudent, wise, virtuous and diligent teachers.' In each village they could impose a tax of 100 or 150 *livres* a year for this work but such ordinances were a dead letter.[16] In these circumstances any help, however small, that could be given was most valuable. Help given by the sisters was particularly welcome in villages, so half the foundations were made in such places. All they were asked to do was to teach reading and writing, and Vincent trained them in this. Later on he was concerned that they 'should learn how to teach' and in spite of some reservations, he allowed them to go to the Ursulines. He did not want his daughters to get too involved with nuns and was happier to have them trained by a young lady who had spent six years with the Ursulines.[17] This network of small urban and rural outposts carried out a real teaching apostolate and it is now recognised that they played a very important part in the literacy programme for the female population.[18]

A third work, and one that was to have a decisive influence on the development of the company, was that of nursing the sick in hospitals. Even before the company was formally established, the first sisters had begun to work at the Hôtel-Dieu in Paris, as assistants to the ladies. In 1639 they took charge of the hospital at Angers which was the first one to be completely confided to their care, and in so doing they fulfilled the wish that Mme Goussault had expressed before her death.[19] The work required first nine, and later twelve, sisters. Even though she was not well at the time, Louise de Marillac accompanied the first group in person there. The journey by coach and barge took a fortnight.[20] They signed a contract with the municipality and Vincent drew up a special rule for them.[21]

Working in hospitals was different from working in the parishes or in schools and so required a different life-style but the same spirit prevailed. Sisters were faithful to community exercises, obedient to superiors and to the doctors, directors and administrators of the hospital and they combined the spiritual and corporal service of the poor as they carried out even the most menial tasks, seeing Jesus Christ in the person of the sick.[22] The hospital

---

[16] M. MARION, D*ictionnaire ... Enseignement primaire*, pp. 205-208.

[17] *S.V.P.* I, p. 437.

[18] J. DELUMEAU, *Le christianisme va-t-il mourir?*, pp. 106-107.

[19] *S.V.P.* I, pp. 479, 606.

[20] GOBILLON, *op. cit.*, p. 89.

[21] *S.V.P.* XIII, pp. 539-547.

[22] *Règles particulières pour les soeurs qui sont dans les hôtels-Dieu et hôpitaux.*

at Angers was a success and its history a peaceful one. Vincent was overjoyed.[23]

This success led other municipalities to ask for sisters to work in their hospitals. The authorities did not always make a clear distinction between working in hospitals and working in old people's homes or orphanages. However, the foundations at St Denis, Nantes, Hennebont, Chateaudun, La Fère, St Fargeau, Ussell and Cahors were all hospitals in the strict sense of the word.[24] This is not a complete list because it does not as yet include the hospitals in Paris or take into account the occasions when the sisters gave their services in military and civil hospitals in times of war or other public disaster.

Even though Vincent appreciated all the work that was being done in hospitals he did not want the community to concentrate too much on this work. He was worried that nursing the sick in hospital might eventually take over from the basic work of the company which was to care for poor people in their own homes.[25] At that time it was the policy to have poor and infirm people shut away in institutions where they were isolated from society. This trend was to lead to the founding of the General Hospital in 1657 but Vincent's aim was to have the poor served in their own homes where they would be with their family. For Vincent they were people, and they were like the sacrament of Christ's presence among men.

Difficulties, problems, tribulations

There was no lack of difficulties, problems or tribulations for the new foundations. Life there could be very hard at times and it tested the mettle of the young girls that Vincent was training. In some cases their lodgings lacked even the most basic amenities, in others they had so little money that the sisters had to go out and beg; in other places they had to contend with local customs which were very much against the rules and spirit of their company, and in several places the administrators or the local clergy showed a want of understanding.

Perhaps the hardest trial of all was endured by the community at Liancourt. As they knelt outside the confessional on the Feast of St Joseph 1652, they were met with a torrent of abuse. The confessor, who belonged to the community of Fr Bourdoise, said to them through the grille, 'Go away.

---

[23] *S.V.P.* III, p. 428.

[24] ABELLY, *op. cit.*, p. 349.

[25] *S.V.P.* I, pp. 244-245; *cf.* X, p. 144.

You are a bunch of hypocrites. You come here to confess trifling little faults and keep quiet about the horrendous sins you commit. Go and find another confessor. I'm not going to give you absolution.'

The sisters were bewildered. Whatever could these words mean? They were not long finding out. Two young men from the town had been spreading the most terrible calumnies about them. It was said that they admitted strange men into their house at night and during Mass times on Sundays. They described the sisters as loose women and went into scurrilous details. It was a terrible scandal in that small village. The priests were the first to believe the story and they refused the sisters the sacraments and would not even let them receive communion at Easter. This went on for four months.

One day, Sr Mathurine Guérin, the boldest member of the group, wrote to Vincent, telling him of their tribulations. Vincent immediately informed Louise de Marillac and the foundress of the hospital, the Duchess de Liancourt. The duchess hurried to the village and began an investigation. The sisters protested their innocence and Sr Mathurine said she had complete confidence that God would vindicate her because this was a matter concerning God, even more than the sisters. The director and the parish priest, however, were still convinced that the sisters were guilty.

Like a second Daniel, the duchess summoned the two young men to the inquiry. While she was questioning them, the confessor was hiding in the next room, listening to it all. The two young men immediately embarked on a whole lot of contradictory statements. Pressed by the duchess, they eventually confessed that the whole story was a lie. A public announcement was made that the sisters were innocent, and important people, starting with the gullible parish priest, offered their deepest apologies. Sr Mathurine wanted no revenge and begged that the guilty parties should go unpunished. She was a great-hearted soul. In later years she would be in charge of the community as St Louise's second successor.[26]

The difficulties at Nantes went on for a longer time and there were all sorts of trials. These included disagreements between sisters, tension between the confessor and the superior, opposition from the bishop who regarded them as nuns, arguments between the sick and the administrators over the question of food, and calumnies and gossip. The strangest thing that happened was in 1653, when a very capable sister was moved to the hospital at Hennebont. The administrators at Nantes did not want to lose her so they accused her, in front of all her colleagues, of having stolen things from the hospital and said she must therefore return to Nantes with them. The councillors at Hennebont informed the superior about these charges. This

---

[26] *Circulaires des supérieurs généraux ...*, Vol. 2, pp. 561-562.

sister was very quick on the uptake, saw through their game, and said to the administrators:

> 'Look, gentlemen, Sr Martha (the sister in question was Martha Dauteil) is a good servant of God and of the poor. She did not even bring back the rest of her clothes from Nantes. All she had was some medicines and she left these behind for the sick. If you are as much concerned for your hospital as these gentlemen from Nantes are concerned for theirs, then you will take as much trouble to keep her as they are taking to have her removed.

That opened the Hennebont councillors' eyes.

> 'Do not worry, Sister,' they said, 'these gentlemen will get the answer they deserve.'[27]

The problems at Fontainebleau and Chantilly were more financial than anything else. These houses were royal foundations and the income due to them was always paid late. The sisters at Chantilly did not even have enough money to pay their rent so the owners of the house obtained a court order, seized their furniture, and sold it at a public auction.[28]

At Chartres, the sisters had spiritual problems. The parish priest there was a convinced Jansenist. He kept the sisters away from communion and only allowed them to go to confession on rare occasions. This meant the poor sisters could not keep their rules and they had to put up with unpleasant interference in their community life. There was nothing to be done except close the foundation:

> 'As long as those priests are here,' reasoned Vincent, 'we cannot expect anything else. Besides, I would be very much afraid they might persuade some of the sisters to their way of thinking. The only thing we can do is leave the place.'[29]

The foundation at Poland went through a long period of uncertainty because of the twists and turns of the wars, and also, in a way, because of the queen's whims. The first three sisters arrived in Warsaw in September

---

[27] *Ibid.*, p. 231.
[28] LOUISE DE MARILLAC, *Pensées,* e.a., p. 194; *Écrits ...*, pp. 542, 617, 747.
[29] *S.V.P.* XIII, p. 736.

1652. Vincent had solemnly bidden them farewell. This was the first time that the company was to cross a frontier. The founder saw this as the start of a movement which was to see his daughters spread throughout the whole world. The queen welcomed them very affectionately.[30] It was not long, however, before there were problems. The lady ordered two of the sisters to go to Cracow to serve the poor there and the third, Sr Marguerite Moreau, to stay at the palace and be her servant.

'Madame, what are you saying?' exclaimed the sister in question. 'The three of us are here to serve the poor. You have many other people in your country who are better able to serve your Majesty. Allow us, Madame, to do here what God wants of us, the same work that we do in other places.'

'So sister, you do not want to work for me?'

'Forgive me, Madame, but God has called us to serve the poor.'[31]

The sisters' duties were not clearly laid down. They were put in charge of a sort of Noah's ark which housed a number of old people, some orphan children, a few sick people, and even a mother and a daughter who were detained there by royal decree. The queen, too, was dissatisfied. She asked for better qualified sisters than the first group to be sent from France and for a superior who would be on good terms with Mme Villiers, her lady in waiting, whom she described as a very charitable and humble lady who never gave any cause for complaint. This lady may also have been rather bossy and interfering because as soon as she died the problems disappeared as if by magic. The queen became fond of the sisters and she would spend a lot of time in their house, talking to them and helping them to spin. Once the troubles of the war were over, she bought them a fine property in Warsaw that had a park, orchard, farm and other buildings. It was here that the sisters established St Casimir's home for orphan girls.'[32]

---

[30] *S.V.P.* IV, p. 487.
[31] *S.V.P.* IX, p. 588.
[32] P. NIETO, *Historia de las Hijas de la Caridad*, Vol. 1, pp. 103-107; *S.V.P* V, pp. 163, 167; XIII, p. 93.

'Chosen souls spread their perfume everywhere'

Vincent kept in close touch with the problems that beset all the foundations, instructing, encouraging, and reprimanding, as circumstances demanded. He gave the sisters in Paris all the news from the other houses, the good news as well as the bad. Naturally he was happier to relate edifying things and there were plenty of these. The works that sprang from Vincent's creative intuition could not possibly have succeeded and developed if it had not been for the virtue and the calibre of a whole host of anonymous sisters who had caught something of his ardent, contagious charity. As we have already seen, he possessed the rare quality of being able to appeal to people's good will and get them to join him in projects. We will give just a few examples.

People had nothing but praise for Sr Jeanne Dalmagne and the virtues she practised. Whenever a sister died it was Vincent's practice to give a conference on the virtues of the deceased. After Sr Jeanne's death the sisters vied with each other in describing her edifying qualities. They spoke of her spirit of faith, her constant joy, her indifference to what she was sent to do, her love for the poor and her extraordinary humility. She used to say, 'I do not know how they can use me. I am no good at anything and never have been.'

A former companion of hers said,

> During the eighteen months I lived with her I never observed the slightest imperfection. Another said, 'The way she cured some wounded people was miraculous. One day she went to the superior to ask for some food for a poor man. The superior said, "There is some stale bread there, give him that." But she answered, 'That is not the way we should act, sister. I will eat that. We should only give good things to God.'

Vincent said:

> I tell you, sisters, that whenever I met her I always felt recollected, not because of any virtue on my part, poor wretch that I am, but God allows certain souls to be like musk which fills every place with its sweet perfume. I have read the lives of many saints and I can tell you that few of them had more love for God and their neighbour than our sister did.

She died a saintly death and Vincent thought they would do well to pray to her in private. She was only thirty-three when she died.[33]

---

[33] *S.V.P.* IX, pp. 179-203.

Sr Barbe Angiboust, 'Big Barbara', to use Vincent's phrase, was of a different mould from Sr Jeanne but she was no less saintly. The Duchess d'Aiguillon asked Vincent if she could have a Daughter of Charity to serve in her household. Vincent could not very well refuse the request considering the lady's rank and the outstanding favours they had received from the duchess. With the consent of Louise de Marillac, he chose Sr Barbara but things did not turn out the way they expected. Let Vincent tell the story:

One day I told her to go to the place (the duchess's palace) where I happened to be at the time. The lady was informed that the Daughter of Charity she asked for had arrived. She sent two of her lady companions to fetch her and when these found out what she had come for they said, 'You are very welcome, Sister. Madame wishes to see you.' I told her to go and she followed them, holding back her tears as best she could.

When they went out into the courtyard of that lady's palace she noticed a great number of carriages, almost as many as you would see at the Louvre. She was very astonished at this and said to the ladies, 'May I go back? I forgot to tell M. Vincent something.' They said 'Yes, Sister, and we will wait here for you.' She came back and said, 'Oh Father, where are you sending me? This place is just like the court.' 'Come, sister,' I answered, 'you're going to meet someone who has a great love for the poor.' The poor sister went back and she was taken to the lady who embraced her very affectionately and then waited for her attendants to withdraw before she told the sister what she wanted her to do. And although that sister knew that she could do a lot of good for the poor by living in that palace she was still very sad. She kept sighing and could hardly eat. When the lady we have been talking about noticed this she asked her, 'Do not you like being with me, my daughter?' And the sister, without trying in any way to hide the reason for her sadness replied, 'Madame, I left my parents' house in order to serve the poor. You are a great lady, you are rich and powerful. If you were poor, Madame, I would be very happy to serve you.' And she would say the same thing to everybody, 'If the lady were poor I would serve her with all my heart, but she is rich.' In the end the lady saw that she continued to be sad and upset so after a few days she sent her back.[34]

---

[34] *S.V.P.* X, pp. 643-644; *cf.* I, pp. 329-331.

Love for the poor was the virtue that Vincent emphasised most to his daughters. One day he told them another moving story. A certain Sr Andrée, about whom we know nothing except for her name, was dying. Vincent went to the bedside of the dying woman as was his custom.

> 'When I put a question to her' he said, 'Sr Andrée replied that she felt no regret or remorse for anything except that she had taken too much delight in serving the poor. And I asked her, "So there is nothing in your past life that worries you, sister?" And she answered, "No, Father, unless it is that I felt too much satisfaction in going to the villages to see those good people. I was so happy to serve them that I felt my feet had wings when I went there ..." Have you ever known anything like that? Would you not have to have led a very innocent life to be in such dispositions? Would you not need to have lived a holy life not to have anything troubling your conscience at a moment when even saints themselves have felt threatened by the enemy?'[35]

'All this is a miracle'

Some of the stories that Vincent told were embellished to the point that people began to describe the events as miraculous. He preferred to think of them rather as signs of God's predilection for the company but sometimes he had to see in them an extraordinary intervention of providence.

One day he was going to preside at an important meeting in the sisters' mother house. Before the meeting began, Mlle Le Gras went into the room to make sure that everything was in order. It was just at this point that

> ... a sister heard a creaking noise and told her the room was not safe. She took no notice. Then another sister, who was older, said the same thing and out of respect for the older sister she came out and went into the next room (just think, sisters, that was only three steps away) and just then a beam snapped and went crashing to the ground. Would it have worked out like this without God's special intervention? I had to be here that evening as we had to have a meeting to discuss important business. With all the noise that goes on at a meeting

---

[35] *S.V.P.* IX, p. 684.

nobody would have noticed a creaking beam. That sister would not have been around because sisters do not attend these meetings and we would all have been crushed to death. But God allowed other business to crop up and this detained me and kept all the ladies from going there. All this did not happen by chance, my daughters; beware of thinking that it did.[36]

This event was to prove highly significant for both Louise de Marillac's spiritual development and for the history of the company. She always looked on it as a sign from providence and a reminder of God's care for her and for her work. With Vincent's help she tried to understand what Our Lord was trying to tell her through this event; maybe it was that he wanted the destiny of both companies to be more closely linked to each other.[37]

Something else happened that strengthened Vincent's conviction that God was exercising a special providence over the Daughters of Charity. This time, and at Vincent's insistence, the sister involved will tell the story. He said to her:

'What happened, my Daughter? I heard that a house had fallen down. Which district was this in? Were you in the house or not? What day did this happen?'

The sister replied that it happened on the last Saturday of carnival week[38] when she was taking soup to a poor person. As she climbed the stairs, a poor water seller who was a little ahead of her called out, 'We are done for.' She was going up from the first floor to the second and the poor man had just shouted these words when the house began to collapse. Our poor sister was terrified and she crouched down in the corner of one of the landings. The neighbours were very frightened and went to fetch somebody to give the last sacraments to anyone able to receive them. Unfortunately 35 or 40 people were buried under the rubble and only one boy of about eleven was rescued. When the onlookers saw that our sister seemed to be in danger of death, they urged her to jump down and

---

[36] *S.V.P.* IX, p. 248; *cf.* II, p. 258.
[37] LOUISE DE MARILLAC, *Écrits* ..., pp. 80, 120, 913-915. According to Coste this accident happened in 1642. The dating of the letters is questionable so we cannot be sure that it did.
[38] 10 February 1646.

about a dozen of them got ready to catch her. She handed them down the soup pot and they hung this from a hook on the end of a rod. Then, trusting to God's providence, she threw herself into the cloaks that they had spread out. She did not know how it happened but by God's special providence she found that she was safe; and trembling all over, she went off to serve the rest of the sick people.[39]

'Do you think, my daughters, that God allowed that new house to fall down without his having some special purpose in mind? Do you think that it was just by chance that she escaped completely unhurt? Not at all, my daughters. All this is a miracle. God had ordained it all to show the company the care he is taking of it.'[40]

The company was God's work. God had founded it and God was seeing that it would continue.

---

[39] *S.V.P.* IX, pp. 240-241.
[40] *S.V.P. ibid.*, p. 247.

Chapter XXX
CHARITY IN ACTION:
CHILDREN, GALLEY SLAVES, BEGGARS

'Paris has as many foundlings as there are days in the year'

Pictures of Vincent de Paul, and this is specially true of nineteenth century representations of the saint, often show him holding a baby in his arms and with two little ones pulling at his cassock. There is no historical basis for such pictures and yet they contain an element of truth. One of the most striking aspects of Vincent's works of charity was the way that this man could stoop down to abandoned little ones and show them, through the ladies, the Daughters of Charity and also the missioners, how tenderly he cared for them. It was children, more than anybody else, who gave him the title 'Father of the Poor'.

There were hundreds of abandoned babies. In a hypocritical society that was scandalised by conduct they judged to be immoral, the only answer to the single mother situation was for babies to be left abandoned on the public highway. Quite often mothers had to abandon their new born babies because they simply could not feed them. Other and less pardonable reasons for abandoning children were selfishness, vice and perversion.[1]

At any rate, hundreds of abandoned babies appeared on the streets of Paris and particularly in the doorway of churches, where people left them as if appealing to the Church's maternal instincts. Vincent reckoned that there were 'as many foundlings as there are days in the year.'[2]

This was no new evil. Throughout the sixteenth century, royal and municipal directives aimed at improving the lot of these poor, defenceless

---

[1] On the subject of foundlings, *cf.* J. DE HAUSSE, *L'assistance publique à l'enfance. Les enfants abandonnés* (Paris 1951); L. LALLEMAND, *Un chapitre de l'histoire des enfants trouvés. La maison de la Couche à Paris* (Paris 1885); J. F. TERME and J. B. MONFALCON, *Histoire des enfants trouvés* (Paris 1837); G. RENOUX, *L'assistance aux enfants du premier âge à Paris aux XVI et XVII siècles* (Paris 1924).

[2] *S.V.P.* XIII, p. 807; ABELLY, *op. cit.*, 1.1 c. 30, p. 142.

children,[3] were issued at intervals but they did not come to much. Those children who did not die of hunger or cold during the hours or even days that they were left lying abandoned, were taken to an official institution, the Couche (or foundling hospital), which was run by a widow and two servants. The cathedral chapter was responsible for this place. Funds were scarce at the Couche, but worse still, the staff were very inhuman.[4] Vincent gave this stark description of conditions there.

> A wet nurse would be attending to four or five babies at once. Babies were given a few drops of alcohol or some laudanum pills to make them sleep. Some babies were sold at 8 *sous* each, to beggars who used to break the babies' arms or legs so that people would feel sorry for them. Others were procured by immoral women for similar or even worse purposes and some were used to stimulate a mother's mammary glands. And to add to all these evils, the children were not baptised, and this filled Vincent's Christian soul with horror. To all appearances, it is almost sure that none of the foundlings admitted to the Couche in the first 50 years of its history survived.[5]

This is a frightening picture and if it did not come from the pen of such a perfectly reliable witness we might be tempted to think it was exaggerated. A contemporary historian states that child cruelty, whether directed at foundlings or other infants, produced more victims during that century than wars did.[6]

We do not really know how Vincent first came into contact with this particular form of misery. In the last century the story went round that Vincent was returning, one day, from a mission and when he came to the gates of Paris he met one of these beggars who used to break the babies' limbs. 'You monster', shouted Vincent as he went for the wretch, 'I was wrong. From the distance I thought you were a man.' Then he took the babe in his arms and carried it to the Couche where he witnessed the scene that he was to describe, years later, to the ladies.[7]

---

[3] COSTE, *M.V.* Vol. 2, pp. 453-455; M. MARION, *Dictionnaire ...*, art. *Enfants trouvés,* pp. 202-204.

[4] ABELLY, *ibid.*

[5] *S.V.P.* XIII, p.798.

[6] J. MAUDUIT, *op. cit.*, p. 133.

[7] U. MAYNARD, *op. cit.*, Vol. 3, p. 400. A romantic biographer, Capefigue, claimed that he had discovered the diary of a Daughter of Charity in which she relates Vincent's nightly strolls in search of abandoned children whom he would collect and take

It did not take such horrifying scenes as these for Vincent's heart to be moved. Everyone knew about foundlings and the terrible consequences of this but nobody was willing to tackle the dreadful problem. They would have to start by overcoming prejudice. Foundlings were regarded as 'children of sin' and illegitimacy was a degrading social stigma. At least this is what the high-minded bourgeoisie thought, though kings and nobles could boast about their bastard sons and even procure bishoprics for them. Even a Daughter of Charity, when the queen of Poland once suggested that Vincent might recruit vocations from girls at the Couche, was very offended and said, 'Oh no, Madame. Our company does not take that sort of person. We only accept virgins.'[8] The good sister was unconsciously echoing the social prejudice which laid what they presumed to be the sin of the parents at the doors of the children.

'We will give it a try'

It took courage to go against the whole climate of opinion for the sake of the gospel. Vincent had this courage. The first thing he did was to invite the ladies of Charity to visit the Couche. His reason for doing this was not so much to let them see the evil as to encourage them to suggest a remedy.[9] The ladies discussed the matter, prayed about it, and decided to give it a trial.[10] This was towards the end of 1637.

On the 1 January 1638, Vincent spoke to St Louise about the outcome.

> At the last meeting it was agreed that we should ask you to try and see if there was any way we could get cow's milk for the children and whether it would be possible to buy two or three cows for this purpose. I was very consoled to see how providence was turning to you to deal with the matter. I do realise that this question needs to be discussed fully and so we will talk about it later.[11]

---

personally to the foundlings' home. While it is quite possible that St Vincent could have come across an abandoned child at some time we have to say that the diary in question is completely spurious. *Cf.* J. B. CAPEFIGUE, *Vie de Saint Vincent de Paul* (Paris 1827), pp. 40-41.

[8] *S.V.P.* IX, p. 590.
[9] ABELLY, *op. cit.*, 1.1 c. 30, p. 142.
[10] *S.V.P.* XIII, p. 798.
[11] *S.V.P.* I, p. 417.

It was a very modest first attempt. They began by taking in twelve infants who were chosen by lot so that there would be no favouritism and also in order 'to honour divine providence.'[12] At first the babies were taken to Mlle Le Gras's house and later on to a rented building in the rue des Boulangers. Several Daughters of Charity took on this work. They bought a goat but this did not solve the problem and they had to go back to employing wet nurses.[13] There were many difficulties to be overcome. To save money allocated for this work, one of the ladies suggested that the babies should stay at the Couche and that the ladies should visit them there.[14] The first Daughter of Charity to take over this work was a widow of some standing, called Mme Pelletier. She wanted the direction of this establishment to be taken out of the hands of the superiors and when this proposal was rejected she left the company.[15] And yet, in spite of everything, this first attempt was a success. The number of infants being looked after increased and they continued to be chosen by lot. The increase in numbers was only a modest one because resources were limited to 1,200 *livres* a year.

'We will take in all the foundlings'

After two years Vincent decided to take over the whole enterprise and with this in mind he called an extraordinary meeting of the ladies. This took place on 17 January 1640. High society was well represented , including the Duchess d'Aiguillon and the Princess de Montmorency.[16] Vincent prepared his talk very carefully. He knew he would have to move their hearts, forestall objections and indicate ways of solving the problem. He did not hesitate to attack their pseudo-religious prejudices head on, and did not mince his words. 'It will be said that God has condemned many of these little ones because of the circumstances of their birth and that could be why the problem cannot be solved.' This was a horrible way of reasoning but it reflected what people and many of the ladies thought. 'My answer to that is that man was cursed by God because of Adam's sin. But it was precisely for this reason that Our Lord became man and died. Taking care of these little ones, even if they are cursed by God, is to do the work of Jesus Christ.'

The main problem was money. How could they be responsible for two or three hundred infants if it cost 150 *livres* a year to maintain six or

---

[12] ABELLY, *op. cit.*, c. 30, p. 143.
[13] *S.V.P.* I pp. 421, 433.
[14] *S.V.P.* I, p. 433.
[15] *S.V.P.* I, pp. 436-437.
[16] *S.V.P.* II, p. 6.

seven? Vincent, who was realistic as well as an optimist, replied, 'The answer is we must do what we can.'

It was suggested, too, that they might set up another association of ladies who would be known as 'the Foundling Ladies' as distinct from the Ladies of the Hôtel-Dieu. After considering the pros and cons Vincent decided against this.

He ended by saying, 'If we do what we can we shall be honouring the Eternal Father who handed over his Son to the mercy of the world and subjected him to Herod's persecution.' The cause was won. 'The decision was taken that they would look after all the foundlings.'[17] Two months later on 30 March 1640 the work began.

A special feature of Vincent's works of charity is particularly striking in the case of the foundlings. Vincent's three great institutions all collaborated, in their own way, in this work. The ladies were patrons of the work and they provided the funds, the Daughters of Charity were directly involved in the work, while the priests of the Mission supervised and directed it. Charity is all one and it is to be served by all available helpers.

Moving house

The first problem was that of finding accommodation. The little house in the rue des Boulangers was too small so some of the children were moved to the sisters' mother house which was then in La Chapelle. From there, they moved with the sisters to the new house in the Faubourg St Laurent, but still there was not enough room. In 1645 Vincent took a decision which went some way towards solving the problem. Using the foundation capital from the missioners' house in Sedan, he had 13 small houses for children built alongside the sisters' house. For these, the ladies paid an annual rent of 1,300 *livres*.[18] The latest group of foundlings to be rescued now had somewhere to stay. Some remained there and were looked after by the sisters and by wet nurses. Others were put in the care of foster mothers who came from Paris or the surrounding districts. Louise de Marillac kept a register of the different placements for these children. Vincent checked this register and (a touching detail) signed it with his own hand. At intervals a brother from the mission would come to inspect the places where the children were.[19]

Every week the ladies would visit both refuges, the one in the rue des Boulangers and the other that comprised the thirteen small houses. But

---

[17] *S.V.P.* XIII, pp. 774-778; II, p. 6.
[18] *S.V.P.* I, p. 543; II, p. 260; III, pp. 172, 198, 511; IV, pp. 170, 382; V, p. 135; X, pp. 607, 611; XIII, pp. 305, 780.
[19] ABELLY, *op. cit.*, 1.3 c. 11, p. 127.

the great number of babies and older children was still a problem. There just was not room for them in the house so another place had to be found. The ladies decided to ask the queen to let them have the Château of Bicêtre, a royal property near Gentilly, south of Paris, which had been empty for years.

Louise was against the plan because she foresaw that they would have difficulty in adapting the place to meet the needs of the children and the sisters. For example, how could the sisters go to Mass in the parish of Gentilly and leave the children on their own? In spite of these objections the move went ahead. Louise's fears were justified. There were all sorts of problems. The administrator appointed by the chapter claimed that he was the only one who had the right to instruct the children. The ladies objected and threatened to withdraw from the work.[20] Quite a number of the infants died.[21] In 1649 all their lives were in danger because of the Fronde. Condé's troops were camped outside Paris and the sisters lived in a permanent state of anxiety and in fear of the outrages committed by the soldiery.[22]

Of course Paris was not a safe place either. On 13 May 1652, there was an incident in the St Denis conflict between Condé and Touraine which took place right outside the doors of the sisters' house and they feared the worst:

> The fierce fighting that went on close by and the men that they saw lying dead outside their door terrified the wet nurses so much that everyone of them left with the other sisters. They each carried an unweaned babe in their arms and left the rest of the children asleep in bed.[23]

In 1649, the children were moved from Bicêtre to Paris. They were provisionally lodged in the sisters' mother house. Later on it was requested that they occupy part of the prison hospital but negotiations for this came to nothing. The ladies then rented a house near St Lazare.[24]

'These good ladies are not doing all they could'

Finance posed a much more serious problem. The initial income of 1,200 *livres* was soon found to be inadequate. By 1644 expenditure had risen to

[20] *S.V.P.* III, pp. 226-227.
[21] *S.V.P.* III, pp. 230, 265.
[22] *S.V.P.* III, p. 422.
[23] *S.V.P.* IV, p. 383.
[24] *S.V.P.* II, pp. 401, 545-546; III, pp. 210, 226, 230, 253, 262, 265, 298, 406, 423, 428, 436, 508, 511, 522-524; IV, pp. 3-4, 21, 188, 385.

40,000 *livres*.[25] Vincent knocked on all doors. First Louis XIII, and then his widow, assigned him an income of 12,000 *livres* from various royal properties.[26] The gap between income and expenditure was still enormous and the only way of narrowing it was to have generous donations from the ladies. In 1649, these felt they had reached their limit. The war (this was the first year of the Fronde) and the economic crisis affected everybody, even the wealthy ladies of Charity. Everything was in short supply, clothing, food and money. Louise, who was responsible for dealing with the day to day administrative problems, was on the point of giving up and abandoning the work. Her letters to Vincent at this time are constant appeals for help.

> I am very sorry to keep troubling you but we are finding it just impossible to take in any more children. At present we have seven children who are not ready to be bottle-fed and we have only two wet nurses. We have not any more money to hire more nurses, we have no supplies of linen or clothing, and no hope of getting a loan. Please tell us whether in conscience we can expose these children to the risk of dying since the ladies are not bothered about our situation and I am sure they think that we are supporting ourselves at their expense. This is just not true because we have only kept 100 *livres* out of the money they agreed to pay for the nurses' board. I can only think of one way to help all those who are suffering in this work and that is to ask the first president of the parlement, on behalf of the company, to first of all relieve us of the obligation of admitting any more children. He can transfer that responsibility to anybody he likes. But we would need to have the ladies' approval for such a step so that nobody would be surprised by our decision. If we do not do this I feel we will be in a perpetual state of mortal sin.

> They brought us another four children yesterday. As well as the seven babies who are being breast fed, we have three others that have just been weaned and these were only brought in recently; one of them is sick and we really should put these back with foster mothers if at all possible. I wish we could bear these trials without telling you about the situation but we are so helpless to deal with it that we have to let you know. These good ladies are not doing all that they could, they have

---

[25] ABELLY, *op. cit.*, 1.1 c. 30, p. 143.
[26] *Ibid.*

not sent us a thing and even the ladies of the company, most
of whom have paid their subscription for the year, have not
sent us anything either ...[27]

'Now is the time for you to pass sentence'

Louise's anxious plea touched Vincent's heart and he decided to call an
extraordinary meeting of the ladies of Charity. Mme de Herse very nearly
prevented this meeting from taking place. She spread the rumour that the
ladies would need to take plenty of money with them to this meeting so some
ladies began to send their excuses for not attending.[28] The danger was averted
just in time and the meeting was held at the end of December 1649. Once
again Vincent prepared a talk that was to move these ladies' hearts.

He realised that these were hard times and that everyone was feeling
the pinch but he really was not asking all that much. If every one of the
hundred ladies present each contributed a hundred *livres* then the problem
would be solved; if only half donated a hundred *livres* and the rest gave as
much as they could, then the situation would not be so desperate. What
would this involve? Well, what about all the trinkets they wore and the knick-
knacks they had decorating their houses? One lady, recently, had given all
her jewels ... And thus he finished his now famous exhortation which in itself
is ample proof of his great eloquence.

> Ladies, pity and charity led you to adopt these little ones as
> your children. You have been their mothers according to grace
> ever since their natural mothers abandoned them. Now we
> have to see if you, too, are going to abandon them. Stop being
> their mothers for a minute, and see yourselves as their judges.
> The life or death of these little ones is in your hands. I am
> going to take a vote. The time has come to pass sentence. Let
> us see if you are going to be merciful to them. If you continue
> to collect alms for them then they will live, if you abandon
> them they will die. Make no mistake about it, they will die, as
> we know from experience.[29]

---

[27] *S.V.P.* III, pp. 508-509. *Cf. ibid.*, pp. 510-512, 522-523.

[28] *S.V.P.* III p. 523.

[29] *S.V.P.* XIII, pp. 797-801. Coste is inclined to give 1647 as the date of this talk. His
reasons for this are not wholly convincing. The letters of St Louise quoted in the two
preceding notes were written in 1649. These led to the convocation of an extraordinary
meeting and the talk that was given there.

The ladies responded generously to this moving appeal and the work for foundlings was saved. After 1653 there does not seem to have been any further financial problems. In 1656 they had nearly reached a balance between income and expenditure: 16,248 *livres* as against 17,221.[30]

The ladies were not the only people to grumble. Discontent was expressed by some missioners, too. These claimed that the foundlings were ruining the company, not just because mission funds were being used for this work, but because benefactors of the mission had stopped helping them because they thought that the foundlings needed the money more. When Vincent heard these complaints he was saddened.

> May God forgive you for this failing which is so opposed to the spirit of the gospel. What a lack of faith! To think that Our Lord will be any less good to us if we do good to these poor abandoned children; he who has promised to reward a hundredfold whatever is given for love of him! If our gracious Saviour could say to his disciples, 'Let the children come to me', how can we reject and abandon them when they come to us, for to do this would mean rejecting Him? We would not be faithful to his grace if, after being chosen by his providence to preserve and give spiritual help to these poor foundlings, we were to grow weary of this task and abandon them because they caused us some problems.[31]

'You will be both mothers and virgins'

Only the sisters remained steadfast in this work though the heaviest burdens fell on them. Vincent had taught them to value the spiritual dimension of the work they were doing. These little ones were the children of God and the sisters who acted as mothers to them were mothers, then, of God's children.

> In this you are something like the Blessed Virgin because you are both mothers and virgins.

They were also the guardian angels of these children and theirs would be the merit for the Lord's praises that came from these little ones'

---

[30] *S.V.P.* XIII, p. 807.
[31] ABELLY, *op. cit.*, 1.3 c. 11, pp. 127-128.

lips. Theirs would be a far greater reward than the children's natural mothers or the paid nurses could ever hope for.

> What reward will you have for serving these poor little ones that the world has cast aside? You will enjoy God's presence for all eternity. My daughters, is there anything to equal that?[32]

The instructions that Vincent gave in the conferences were summarised and formally written down in their particular rules. Some of these may seem too strict to modern eyes but others reveal a remarkable understanding of child and of feminine psychology. They also anticipated, in a very striking way, our present day teaching methods. Punishment was to be used sparingly and introduced by degrees, while rewards were presented as desirable. Boys and girls were to be taught how to read and the former also learned how to write. Naturally, religious instruction was given first priority. But all the children were taught a trade. When the boys reached the age of twelve they became apprentices. The girls were found a situation, usually in domestic service, when they were fifteen.[33]

Concern for the welfare of young children would seem to be one of the greatest advances of our times. The change in people's attitudes which has made this possible has its roots in the charitable works of Vincent de Paul in the second half of the seventeenth century and continued for three centuries more by Daughters of Charity in all the countries of Europe.

'Nothing is more meritorious in God's eyes than charitable work for prisoners'

If the foundlings were a blot on society then the galley slaves were a reproach both to society and to the state. The latter was responsible for the appalling situation whereby thousands of men were condemned to waste away their lives on the benches of the galley ships. This spectre was to haunt every navy in the world until the development, first of sailing boats, and later of steamships, meant that vessels could be powered by other means than men's arms. In the second third of the seventeenth century this solution was still a long way off and the fact that the country was at war only added to the evil. Richelieu's policy of naval expansion in his bid for European supremacy meant

---

[32] *S.V.P.* IX, pp. 128-142.
[33] *Cf.* the Spanish translation of the particular rules for sisters working with foundlings in J. M. IBAÑEZ, *op. cit.*, Appendix, pp. 347-373.

that the number of galley slaves was increased and that the prisoners had to serve longer sentences.[34]

If the evil could not be eradicated then it should at least be mitigated. Vincent de Paul had been principal chaplain to the galley slaves since 1619. Such authority as he had was limited to those prisoners who were already serving sentences in the galleys. He was not responsible for the prisoners who were locked up in the galley slaves' institution in Paris, waiting to be transferred to Marseilles, since all prisons in the capital were under the procurator general and not the naval authorities.[35] Nevertheless, he was concerned with improving their conditions and he did manage to have them moved to somewhat better accommodation. In 1632 he succeeded in having them moved again and this time the prison assigned to them was a tower set into the old walls of the city and situated on the left bank, between the Seine and St Bernard's gate in the rue de la Tournelle.[36]

Many people were involved in this work for galley slaves and there were several associations devoted to the same end, particularly the Company of the Blessed Sacrament. Its members tried hard to have the worst abuses stopped and they fought against the unjust practice of extending the sentence passed on galley slaves. They tried to procure better treatment for the prisoners by paying the wages of extra guards so that the prisoners could take exercise in the courtyard; they paid for soup and medicine as the authorities only provided bread and water, and they maintained a chaplain to look after the prisoners' spiritual needs.[37] This last provision upset the parish priests in the capital because they considered themselves responsible for any prisons in their parishes. The prison for galley slaves was in the parish of St Nicolas du Chardonnet and an episcopal decree in 1634 had specifically appointed its priests as chaplains for prisoners.[38] So the Company of the Blessed Sacrament had to give up the work.[39]

The details just given will help us to understand the relatively small effort made by Vincent and his congregation to help the galley slaves of Paris between the years 1625 and 1632. This does not signify any want of concern. Even though he was not directly involved, Vincent was mindful of the difficulties that people experienced in providing spiritual and material help for prisoners. We know this from the part he played in having them moved to La Tournelle and also from a brief letter he wrote about this time to Louise de

---

[34] *Cf. supra*, c. 10; *cf.* R. LA BRUYERE, *La marine de Richelieu* (Paris 1960).

[35] COSTE, *M.V.* Vol. 2, p. 523.

[36] ABELLY, 1.1 c. 28, p. 127; R. CHALUMEAU, *Guide* ..., p. 37, pl. 7.

[37] R. DE VOYER D'ARGENSON, *Les Annales de la Compagnie du Saint Sacrament* (Paris 1900); referred to by COSTE, *M.V.* Vol. 2, pp. 521-525.

[38] COSTE, *M.V.* Vol. 2, p. 523.

[39] *Ibid.*

Marillac in which he sounds out the possibility of the charity confraternity at St Nicolas du Chardonnet taking on the care of those galley slaves who had just been moved within the limits of the parish.

> Nothing is more meritorious in God's eyes than charitable works for poor prisoners. You did well to assist these poor men and it will be very good if you can continue to help them in every way possible until I can come and see you, probably in two or three days' time. Give some thought as to whether the charity at St Nicolas du Chardonnet might take charge of this work, even if it is only for a short time; you can help them with any money you have left over. But what else can we do? I know it is difficult and that is why I venture to put this thought into your mind.[40]

The results of this experiment could not have been very encouraging. Not much was done during the years that followed; the community at the Bons Enfants gave a little help, some missions were preached to the galley slaves before the 'chain gang' left for Marseilles, and some charitable people visited them occasionally.[41] This was the time when the parish priests of Paris were so suspicious of the Congregation of the Mission and complained about them. Vincent had to proceed with great caution and now, more than ever, he was careful 'not to poach on other people's preserves.'

In 1639 the situation changed. It was in that year that one of those small events that Vincent regarded as signs from providence took place. M. Cornuel, the former financial administrator and president of the Ministry of Finances, bequeathed the sum of 6,000 *livres* to be used for helping galley slaves.[42] Collet observes philosophically: 'These legacies that the deceased often bequeath in order to salve their consciences are frequently opposed by other members of the family. What they get is not as important in their eyes as what they were hoping to get'.[43]

---

[40] *S.V.P.* I, p. 166. Coste puts the date of this excerpt taken from Abelly (*op. cit.*, 1.1 c. 28, p. 128) as 1632. I think it should rather be 1634 which is the year when the parish of St Nicolas was formally given responsibility for the galley slaves' prison. St Vincent tried to act in conformity with the requirements of the law as much as possible and since the parish was responsible for looking after the galley slaves, he used a parish organisation, the Confraternity of Charity, to reach out to the prisoners.

[41] ABELLY, *op. cit.*, p. 127.

[42] *S.V.P.* II, p. 20.

[43] COLLET, *op. cit.*, Vol. 1, p. 177.

M. Cornuel's daughter was to have seen to the legacy but her husband was reluctant to comply with his father-in-law's wishes. Vincent had to be very patient during the negotiations. He made many applications for the money, had several interviews with the other legatees, and discussed the matter with the procurator general. At last they came to an agreement. M. Cornuel's family handed over to the procurator the sum of money stipulated in the will and they appointed him executor of the trust for life. The money was allocated to a community of the Daughters of Charity whose sole work was to look after prisoners. Vincent also succeeded in introducing a clause into the agreement which would give the parish clergy an annual income of 300 *livres* for the additional work involved in their spiritual ministrations to the galley slaves. There was some opposition to this. Why should they be given anything since this work was part of their normal duties? Vincent gently insisted and this gesture took away the bitterness felt by clergy who had previously opposed him and who now became his allies ...[44]

'One of the most dangerous and difficult works'

In 1640 the Daughters of Charity went into action. There were only two or three of them[45] to take on this very onerous work which was described in the regulations drawn up by Louise de Marillac and Vincent as 'one of the most difficult and dangerous works'.[46] The sisters were required to purchase the food, prepare the daily meals for the galley slaves and carry the food to the prisons, to wash the prisoners' clothes, look after the sick, kit the prisoners out when they left for Marseilles, scrub the cells, and wash and mend the mattresses. They really were the servants of these fearsome and demanding masters who used to jeer at them, make improper suggestions, were insolent and insulting and even, at times, made false accusations about the sisters 'while these were doing everything they could to help them.' We are amazed at the audacity shown by Vincent and Louise in sending their daughters to these dens of iniquity that housed the scum of society. It would be no exaggeration to compare their situation with that of the three young men in the fiery furnace of Babylon.[47]

The sisters needed to be very virtuous to be able to put up with all the trials mentioned in their rule. The work would have tried the patience of

---

[44] ABELLY, *op. cit.*, pp. 127-128; COLLET, *op. cit.*, Vol. 1, p. 178.
[45] *S.V.P.* II, pp. 259, 550.
[46] *S.V.P.* II, p. 114; LOUISE DE MARILLAC, *Écrits* ..., p. 991.
[47] *Règles pour les Filles de la Charité qui ont soin des Galériens.*

a saint. Vincent wondered if it might not be too much even for Barbara Angiboust who, in spite of being tall, was not very strong.[48] Once again Barbara showed her mettle. During the conference on her virtues that was held after her death, a sister who had worked with her said:

> I worked with her, looking after the galley slaves. She showed great patience in dealing with difficulties caused by those persons' ill humour. And even though they were sometimes so angry with her that they threw the soup and meat on the floor, she bore it all in silence and gently picked up the food as pleasantly as though they had not said anything. Not only that, but five or six times she stopped the guards from beating them.

Vincent meant his daughters to learn from these conferences so he drew a lesson from what had just been said.

> My daughters, you could all be called on to serve these poor people so learn from your sister how you should conduct yourselves, not just in the galleys but in every other place too, learn from our sister how to bear patiently with the poor.[49]

Sometimes it was so difficult to bear patiently with the poor ... But Vincent's whole life had been spent bearing with them and teaching others to do the same. And not just bearing with them, but serving them lovingly and joyfully. Once more he conjured up the spirit that was to animate their work.

> They shall try to win them over by their gentleness and their compassion, always keeping in mind the pitiable state of soul and body these people are usually in, but remembering that this does not stop them from being members of the one who became a slave to rescue us all from the dominion of the devil ... They should be like rays of sunlight that continually pass through filth and yet remain untouched by it.[50]

> What happiness to serve these poor prisoners who are abandoned into the hands of merciless men. I have seen these poor people treated like animals and it is this situation that has brought them God's compassion. He had pity on them and in

---

[48] *S.V.P.* II, pp. 174, 259.

[49] *S.V.P.* X, p. 645.

[50] *Règles* ..., art. 8 and 18.

his goodness did two things for these people. First of all he had a house bought for them, and then he arranged for them to be looked after by his own daughters, for the name Daughter of Charity means daughter of God.[51]

Mission to the galleys

Once they were on board the galleys the prisoners became the responsibility of Vincent who was chaplain royal. Moreover, the foundation contract of the Congregation of the Mission stated that its members should, whenever possible, spend part of their time looking after the spiritual needs of galley slaves.[52]

From the earliest days of the congregation, Vincent had delegated his functions to ordinary chaplains and limited himself to co-ordinating and supervising the work. But he felt the need to be more directly involved. This feeling was shared by other people who knew at first hand the terrible reality of the galleys. Others who joined in the work at Marseilles included the bishop of that diocese, the Oratorian priest Jean Baptiste de Gault (1593-1643), and Gaspar Sirmiane de la Coste (1607-1649), a pious layman who had received spiritual direction from Vincent and from him had learnt to have a great love for the poor.[53] In Paris the cause was taken up by the Richelieu family; by the cardinal who had over-all responsibility for these poor men who were cannon fodder for his policies, by the Duchess d'Aiguillon who was her uncle's conscience, and by the Duke of Richelieu because he had been appointed General of the Galleys by his great uncle who had wrested this office from the hands of the de Gondis to keep it in his own family.

After the cardinal died, early in 1643, all these forces banded together to organise a general mission for galley slaves. Vincent sent five missioners, four of whom were priests, and a laybrother who was a surgeon by profession. The leader of this group was the ever efficient Fr François du Coudray and they left Paris on 22 February.[54] The bishop had intended postponing the mission but he changed his mind. The work was too much for Vincent's five missioners so he had to ask other communities to help and he appealed to Authier de Sisgau's community, the Oratorians, the Jesuits and some Italian

---

[51] *S.V.P.* X, p. 125.

[52] *S.V.P.* XIII, p. 201.

[53] *S.V.P.* II. On Mgr. Gault and M. de la Coste: F. MARCHETTY, *La vie de Messire Jean Baptiste Gault évêque de Marseille* (Paris 1650); M. DE RUFFI, *La vie de M. le Chevalier de la Coste* (Aix 1659).

[54] *S.V.P.* II, p. 368.

priests. The bishop took part in the work, too, and did this with so little regard for self that he died from a disease that he caught while giving the mission.[55] As usual, the mission was a success, and a special feature of it was the conversion of many heretics and Turks, who were baptised with great solemnity.[56]

'Compassion takes on different forms'

This mission was only the first stage in a much more ambitious project. After an initiative made by Philippe de Gondi and by Vincent in 1618,[57] it was proposed that a hospital for galley slaves should be established. This time they were serious about the project. The Duchess d'Aiguillon contributed 9,000 *livres* and, prompted by Vincent, the queen allocated to the work 12,000 *livres* which were to come from taxes at Marseilles.[58] The death of Mgr Gault would have been a serious setback if it had not been for the enthusiastic perseverance of M. de la Coste who was the guiding spirit behind the enterprise.[59] Thanks to his efforts the hospital was completed within two years. When the sick were transferred there from the galleys they thought they were moving from hell into paradise.[60]

At the insistence of M. de la Coste, a house of the mission was founded at the same time and this was endowed by the Duchess d'Aiguillon.[61] The principal objective of this house was to provide spiritual help for sick prisoners at the hospital and to give a mission to the galley slaves every five years. They also had the right to appoint and to dismiss chaplains to the navy.[62] With this in mind, Vincent obtained authorisation to delegate his office of chaplain royal to the superior of the house. This chaplaincy was invested in the person of the superior general of the Mission in perpetuity.[63]

The first superior at the house of Marseilles was François Dufestel. In 1648 Fr Firmin Get, a man of extraordinary talent, arrived, and in 1654 was appointed superior.[64] Thanks to his many activities, his talent for organising, his greatheartedness, and his administrative ability, the Marseilles

55 ABELLY, *op. cit.*, 1.2 c. 1, pp. 36-37.
56 *S.V.P.* II, pp. 395, 398.
57 *Cf. supra*, c. 10.
58 ABELLY, *op. cit.*, 1.1 c. 28, pp. 129-130.
59 *S.V.P.* III, p. 474.
60 *S.V.P.* II, p. 526.
61 *Cf. supra*, c. 19.
62 *S.V.P.* XIII, pp. 298-301.
63 *Ibid.*, pp. 302-303.
64 *S.V.P.* III, p. 258.

house became the third most important foundation in the company. Firmin Get cannot take all the credit for this for he was constantly backed up by Vincent de Paul. We know this from Vincent's letters to him and these numbered more than a hundred and fifty. The letters contain all sorts of things: advice, instructions, prohibitions, words of encouragement, reprimands, praise, consolation ... Perhaps it would be a slight exaggeration to say that Vincent himself was directing the house from a distance. It was Vincent who made the important decisions but it was Fr Get who had to see that these were implemented. He often had to take on very serious responsibilities, appointing chaplains, supervising their way of acting, and paying them; this latter was not always an easy thing to do because funds came in from the exchequer at very irregular intervals. Occasionally he had to use community money to pay the chaplains.[65] He organised missions for the galley slaves, found confessors for the different language groups, and attended the sick. In addition, and with Vincent's approval, he also set up a sorting office and depot like the one that was used for the captives in Barbary. He had to compile a list of the galley slaves who, through the ministrations of Vincent and his delegate in Marseilles, received messages and tiny sums of money, maybe thirty *sous* or fifty pennies, from their relations. The galley ships bore such fine names as *La Douce, La Ducal, La Capitaine, La Reine, La Duchesse, La Princesse de Morgue*, and these names appear more than once in Vincent's letters. Mothers, sisters, sweethearts and wives of the galley slaves would confide to Vincent's care the little present they had made such sacrifices to send, or their loving messages and words of encouragement which would often have been written down by some other priest of the mission.[66] Vincent's pen allows us to see what this terrible institution was like and it puts a name and a suffering face to its inmates. Perhaps it was one of these who threw the plate of hot soup at Sr Barbara Angiboust.

For Vincent the galley slaves were yet another group among the countless poor people crying out for help. None of these groups was to be excluded from the benefits of Christian charity because, as Vincent explained to the missioners:

> 'Compassion takes on different forms so the company is called on to serve the poor in a variety of ways; to serve the galley slaves, the captives in Barbary ...[67]

---

[65] *S.V.P.* VI, p. 104.
[66] For the letters to Firmin Get, *cf. S.V.P.* XIV, p. 238.
[67] *S.V.P.* VIII, p. 238.

Martyrs of charity

The missioners were steeped in the spirit of self-sacrifice imparted to them by Vincent so it was not long before charity had its martyrs. Just two years after the Marseilles house was founded, Fr Louis Robiche died from a disease he caught while serving the galley slaves. He was thirty-five. He had so won the admiration of the people of Marseilles that his funeral was marked by scenes of hysteria. One man took a bite out of the cushion that was stained with the martyr's blood so that he could keep it as a relic. Somebody else scratched a few splinters off the chair he used to sit in, and someone else took the wax from the funeral candles. Vincent gave details of this display of veneration by the people and ended by saying:

> The voice of the people (which is the voice of God) proclaimed him a saint and we could almost say he died the death of a martyr since, for love of Our Lord, he risked his life working for the corporal and spiritual welfare of these poor sick people and died from a disease which is nearly always fatal and which he knew to be contagious.[68]

Robiche was not the only martyr. Six years later Fr Brunet, 'such a good worker for the Lord, such a friend of the poor and such a shining light for the whole company,' died in similar circumstances. At this time, M. Sirmiane de la Coste, described by Vincent as, 'founder and benefactor of the hospital at Marseilles,'[69] also fell victim to the plague and died.

The work for galley slaves exacted payment in blood. Vincent made this payment with a sorrowful heart, knowing that this was the price they had to pay for practising charity.

Vagrancy, another scourge

French society was plagued by a third scourge which took the form of vagrancy. Beggars were to be found all over France, both in the country areas and in the cities, but they were most in evidence in Paris which was the nation's sponge and its sewer. These beggars formed a floating population that hung around the public square or the streets of a town, crowded outside convents, surrounded the coaches bringing travellers to the towns and pestered

---

[68] *S.V.P.* II, pp. 517-521.
[69] *S.V.P.* III, pp. 471, 474.

better-off people in the streets. Roguery flourished alongside begging. There were countless ways of playing on people's pity: people pretended to be blind or crippled, others feigned madness, some swallowed soap so that they would be taken for epileptics foaming at the mouth, women padded their stomachs with rags to pretend that they were pregnant or had a whole troupe of little ones with them ... These represented every shade of petty criminal that walked the streets of Paris by day and, when night fell, melted into Monopodio's courtyard or the 'Court of Miracles.'

The state regarded vagrancy as a political problem and dealt, or rather tried to deal with it, by political, or maybe we should say, police methods. Countless decrees against vagrancy were promulgated during the sixteenth and seventeenth centuries. The very fact that these had to be repeated so often is clear proof that they did not work. As long as the causes of the misery remained, there was no hope of curing its effects.[70]

Beggars were a public enemy for society in general. They were regarded as enemies and feared as such. These fears were well-founded because bands of armed beggars would often demand money, not beg for it. Furetière's dictionary gives the laconic comment, 'people are murdered by the poor.'

As a general rule the Church remained faithful to the traditional practice of almsgiving. Abbeys, monasteries and convents gave a tremendous lot of help to beggars, usually in the form of food. But this easy access to sustenance was, itself, an open invitation to lead a life of idleness.[71]

'I am concerned for the company, but I'm even more concerned for the poor'

Vincent, too, gave alms. Until such times as a more radical solution to the problem could be found, no charitable soul could refuse to meet the urgent needs of those in distress. All sources of contemporary evidence are in emphatic agreement about Vincent's exorbitant almsgiving. He gave everything he had. He turned St Lazare into the greatest welfare centre in

---

[70] Very many books have been written about pauperism and mendicity in seventeenth century. Among the most interesting ones for our purpose are: J. P. GUTTON, *La société et les pauvres. L'exemple de la généralité de Lyon. 1534-1789* (Paris 1971); *id.*, *La société et les pauvres en Europe (XVI-XVII siècles)* (Paris 1977); H. KAMEN, *El siglo de hierro* (Madrid 1977), pp. 455-486; R. MOUSNIER, *Les institutions de la France sous la Monarchie absolu.* (Paris 1974), Vol. 1, pp. 217-220.

[71] E. CHILL, 'Religion and mendicity in seventeenth century France', *International Review of Social History* (1962), pp. 400-425.

Paris. Every year the house contributed 200 *livres* to the charity confraternity in the parish of St Laurent and every day they distributed bread, soup and meat to poor families in the neighbourhood. And every day, two poor men were invited to eat in the community refectory where they were given the places of honour, on either side of the superior. Poor beggars who rang at the door were given a portion of bread and a few *sous*. Three times a week soup would be distributed to every beggar that came and there would usually be about six hundred. When times were worse, as during the siege of Paris by the Fronde, this distribution was made every day. Three great cauldrons of soup were needed to provide for nearly two thousand people. The brother who was in charge of making bread reckoned that in the space of three months they had gone through 1,200 kilos of wheat.[72] Vincent's generosity was a serious threat to the community's finances. The bursar complained that they had no money left. Some of the missioners protested and they complained that M. Vincent was taking it on himself to dispose of the community's goods. But Vincent could give good reasons to justify his actions.

> Of course I am concerned about the company, but I am even
> more concerned about the poor. When we are in difficulties
> we can always ask our other houses for bread if they have any,
> or we could find work in the parishes as curates. But what can
> the poor do or where can they go to find something to eat?
> The poor are my burden and my sorrow.[73]

When the house finally ran out of money, he borrowed the sum of 16,000 *livres*. In addition to the regular distribution of alms, help was given on other occasions. Vincent could not see anyone in need without helping them. If the faceless poor man behind the statistics called into play his organising skills, then the poor person in the flesh melted his heart. Anecdotes abound about Vincent's spontaneous giving and we should put some of these on record.

One day, when Vincent was passing by in his carriage, he saw a boy crying in the street. He stopped the carriage, got out, and went up to the boy to ask him why he was crying. When he saw the boy's injured hand he took him to a surgeon who attended to the wound, then he paid the doctor and

---

[72] The price of a *muid* of wheat in 1649 fluctuated around 150 *livres* so the bread that was distributed would have cost about 1,500 *livres*. For a table of dry measure weights in seventeenth century, *cf.* M. MARION, *Dictionnaire*, pp. 373-376.

[73] ABELLY, *op. cit.*, 1.3 c. 11, p. 120.

gave the lad a few coins. On another occasion he gave 100 *livres* to a carter who had lost his horses. It's impossible to count the number of times he used his carriage to take sick people that he found in the streets to the Hôtel-Dieu. A soldier, nicknamed 'the Sieve' because he had so many scars, came to St Lazare and with all the effrontery of the *miles gloriosus* asked Vincent for lodgings. Vincent took him in. Next day the veteran beggar fell sick. Vincent had him moved to a room with a fireplace, and he lived there for two months as their guest, with a brother to wait on him hand and foot. At other times Vincent would waive the rent due from tenants, he took in orphans at St Lazare, sent a hundred needles to a tailor, and he personally gave some women the money they asked for. As we said, the list is endless.[74]

'Here you have the poor people of the Nom de Jésus Hospital'

Vincent was not content just to give alms when these were urgently needed but he tried to view the problem of vagrancy from a new perspective. Ever since his Châtillon days he had been good at organising and putting things in order. For many years he had been toying with the idea of setting up some sort of institution for vagrants but as yet providence had given him no sign. Then one day a gentleman gave him a considerable sum of money, 100,000 *livres*, to be used for any charitable work he liked and under one condition only, that the donor remain anonymous. After consulting Louise, Vincent suggested to the donor that they use the money to set up a refuge for old people. He immediately started to make plans and get the work under way. He bought a house quite near to St Lazare and on the front of the building was the name *Nom de Jésus*.[75] This house would give him many a headache. Noël Bonhomme, the man who was selling it, took as long as he could to hand over the premises and Vincent was obliged to file a suit with the parlement.[76] Once this problem was solved he set to work. His plan was to provide a comfortable and pleasant dwelling for old people and for those who were unable to work. If they made the best use of the money they had available, he reckoned they could take in forty people, twenty men and twenty women. These would be looked after by a community of Daughters of Charity. The men and women were to live in separate units with a church and a dining room between the two wings so that they could all hear Mass and listen to the same spiritual reading during meals though they would not be able to see

---

[74] ABELLY, *ibid.*, pp. 128-137.
[75] R. CHALUMEAU, *Guide ...*, p. 16, p1. 3.
[76] *S.V.P.* II, pp. 628, 633; III, pp. 633, 637.

each other. In this matter, as in many others, Vincent was acting in accordance with the customs and the outlook of his times.

Neither Vincent nor Louise wanted the people they took in to live a life of idleness. In the first few years after the institution opened, they had people who could teach their skills to the elderly so there were weavers, cobblers, silk weavers, buttonmakers, wool carders, lacemakers, glovemakers, seamstresses, pinmakers ... At the benefactor's special request, religious instruction and taking devotional services was entrusted to the priests of the Mission and these activities took up a good part of the day. As always, Vincent regarded corporal and spiritual charity as inseparable, and he committed his two congregations to working at both.[77]

It was Vincent, himself, who gave the first talk, in his customary simple and familiar way which involved the old people in a dialogue with him. He tried in his talk to teach them the basic truths of religion and also to instil in them the spirit of work.

> Tell me, is it not right that you should work out of gratitude to God for giving you the grace of providing you with all that you need for soul and body? What more could you wish for? You have your meals; they may not be quite as good as the meals the presidents eat, but they meet your needs. How many poor people in Paris and elsewhere have not got what you have! How many impoverished noblemen would be glad to have the food you have! How many farm labourers have to toil from morning till night but are not as well fed as you are! All this should encourage you to do manual work for as long as you can, and according to your strength, instead of thinking to yourself 'I do not need to bother doing anything because I'll always have what I need.' Oh my brethren be on your guard against that. Instead, you should be telling yourselves that you ought to work for the love of God, since He himself has given us the example of always working on our behalf.'[78]

This novel type of institution, which became operational in 1653, proved very successful. The residents could enjoy a peaceful and leisurely old age and they were happy with the way they were being looked after. The only drawback was that the institution could only take in a limited number of residents. Places only became vacant when residents died, and there was

---

[77] ABELLY, *op. cit.*, 1.1 c. 45, pp. 211-214.
[78] *S.V.P.* XIII, pp. 156-163.

always a long waiting list as people applied years in advance.[79] The institution may have been just an experiment for Vincent, a first step in a new direction, but politicians took up the idea and decided to implement it on a big scale. Later on we will see the consequences of this.

Some of the missioners had misgivings. The objection was made that this hospital was distracting the company's attention away from its main work, which was to preach missions. Vincent took these objections on board and strongly refuted them.

> Someone will say to me, why should we be running this hospital? The poor people at the Nom de Jésus are wearing us out. We have to go and say Mass for them, give them instructions, administer the sacraments and be generally responsible for them ... Gentlemen, would we not be lacking in piety if we criticised this good work? If priests dedicate themselves to caring for the poor, was not this just what Our Lord did, and many of the great saints did likewise. They did not just exhort us to look after the poor but they themselves consoled and encouraged them. Are not the poor the suffering members of Our Lord? Are they not our brothers? And if priests abandon them, who will be there to help them?[80]

Every kind of misery

Foundlings, galley slaves and beggars were not the only needy people. Poverty had a thousand other faces. It is typical of Vincent that his charity could be aware of all these and reject none of them. Whether on his own initiative or acting through his missioners, the ladies of Charity, his daughters, the priests from the Tuesday conferences or other congregations that he inspired and helped, he ministered to 'every kind of misery' as the liturgy would later say about him. We can only give a brief mention of these works here.

From time immemorial Paris had had the Hôpital des Petites Maisons ('Hospital of the Little Houses') or the hospital for married couples, for the mentally ill, for people with contagious diseases, and other sick people. Vincent had given a mission here before he founded the congregation, and so, too, had the priests from the Tuesday conferences.[81] In 1655 the municipal welfare department asked Vincent to send Daughters of Charity to work in the hospital

---

[79] ABELLY, 1.1 c. 45, p. 213.
[80] *S.V.P.* XII, p. 87.
[81] ABELLY, *op. cit.*, 1.2, pp. 20 and 257.

and Vincent agreed.[82]

The bishop of Cahors, Alain de Solminihac, also put in a request for sisters to work in a home for orphan girls. Vincent agreed[83] but only after some hesitation, since he was afraid that this work for orphans might prove detrimental to the service of the poor in their own homes.

Irish immigrants, bishops, priests, soldiers, widows and orphans were all in desperate need. The help they all received from Vincent was both generous and discreet.[84]

Many other groups, including the young girls in moral danger who were taken in by Mme de Pollalion's Daughters of Providence, the orphans who were cared for by Mlle L'Estang, the fallen women of St Magdalen, the little school girls of the Daughters of the Cross and many others were indebted to Vincent de Paul for assistance, spiritual direction, legal advice and his negotiations with the civil and ecclesiastical authorities.[85]

And we still have to consider one of the most spectacular aspects of Vincent's all-embracing charity, his wonderful work for those who suffered in the war.

---

[82] *S.V.P.* V, p. 419; X, p. 114.

[83] *S.V.P.* V, p. 631; X, pp. 117, 578-579; XIII, p. 711.

[84] ABELLY, 1.2 c. 11, pp. 134, 154, 172; *S.V.P.* V, p. 414; VI, pp. 133, 252.

[85] COLLET, *op. cit.*, Vol. 1, pp. 426-430.

Chapter XXXI
CHARITY IN ACTION:
WAR BRINGS DISASTER

Lorraine, a country caught between two firing lines

France's entry into the Thirty Years' War in May 1635, after the Swedish débacle of Nordlingen, only served to endorse the 'covert' or cold war that had been going on for many years. However, the transition from 'covert' to 'open' warfare brought protests from a wide section of public opinion in France because many people were in favour of making a treaty with Catholic Spain.[1]

During the first year of hostilities, Spain clearly held the upper hand. The troops of the Cardinal-Infante, the hero of Nordlingen, reached Corbie, in August 1636 on the outskirts of Paris. As we have already mentioned, this was the first time that Vincent sent missioners to the army. That same year witnessed the triumph of a French drama that had a Spanish hero, Corneille's play *Le Cid*. As yet, wars between nations had not become as fierce as they would be later on with the growth of nationalism. There were still some traces of medieval chivalry left and in 1641 the French opened their border for the funeral cortège of their great enemy, the Cardinal-Infante, who was allowed to make his posthumous journey back to Spain.[2]

One of the main theatres of war between the years 1636 and 1643 was the duchy of Lorraine. This tiny, autonomous state, that had France to the west, the Empire to the east, the Spanish possessions in Flanders to the north, and Franche-Comté to the south, was destined to be the victim of any and every confrontation between its powerful neighbours. To add to its misfortunes, the triple wedge of the episcopal cities of Metz, Toul and Verdun, had been annexed by France since 1552. So, ethnically and linguistically,

---

[1] J. M. JOVER ZAMORA, *Historia de una polémica y semblanza de una generación* (Madrid 1949).
[2] A.VAN DER ESSEN, *Le Cardinal-Infant et la politique européenne de l'Espagne* (Brussels 1944).

Lorraine was partly French and partly German. Its geographical and strategic position made it equally desirable for both contenders. In such circumstances, it would have been nothing short of a miracle if this country could have stayed neutral during the great European conflagration.[3]

Duke Charles IV and his brother and successor, François Nicolas, pursued the political policies they judged most advantageous to their country's interests. They were suspicious of Richelieu's plans to annexe it to France, and so they sided with Spain and the Empire. The flexible, semi-feudal structure of the Empire would have made it easier for Lorraine to preserve its national identity and independence. But Lorraine just did not have adequate military forces to follow this option and so had to gamble on political ruses and shrewd alliances. St Vincent de Paul's eighteenth century biographer, Pierre Collet, who in fact chose Lorraine as the place where his book should be published, roundly condemns the policies followed by Duke Charles IV, policies which, he says, were 'vigorous enough to alarm his neighbours, but too feeble to resist them; he was always ready to sign an agreement and even more ready to break it.'[4] What else could a minor prince do, when he was surrounded by such formidable enemies?

The full violence of the Thirty Years War erupted over the duchy. France had occupied this territory in 1633, even before her formal entry into the war. This was in reprisal for the asylum Lorraine granted to Gaston d'Orléans, the brother of the French king, and for his secret marriage to Margaret of Lorraine. Louis XIII accused Duke Charles IV of abducting his brother. Charles had to take refuge in Germany and he abdicated in favour of François Nicolas, the unconsecrated bishop of Verdun. The Duke continued to work for his country's independence, from his place of exile. France operated a policy of repression and of cultural assimilation. The city of St Mihiel from whose walls a lucky cannon shot destroyed Louis XIII's carriage in 1635, was made to pay a fine of nearly half a million *livres*, its leading citizens were shut up in the Bastille, 36 officers were imprisoned, and 'two or three thousand' soldiers were sentenced to the galleys.

The governor appointed to carry out this programme of repression, Count de La Ferté-Senectère, proved to be an implacable governor and was known as the 'butcher of Lorraine'. Castles were razed to the ground, people were sent into exile and property was confiscated. He forced all the inhabitants to swear an oath of allegiance to the king of France. The people, following

---

[3] On Lorraine *cf.* J. A. LESOURD, *La Lorraine* (Nancy 1962); G. CABOURDIN, *La Lorraine entre France et l'Empire germanique de 1480 à 1648*; see, in addition these old but still valid works; A. DIGOT, *Histoire de Lorraine* (Nancy 1856); D'HAUSSONVILLE, *Histoire de la rèunion de la Lorraine à la France* (Paris 1856).

[4] COLLET, *op. cit.*, Vol. 1, p. 286.

the lead of the clergy, adopted an attitude of passive resistance. St Peter Fournier, the saint of Lorraine, refused to take the oath and had to take refuge in Spanish Franche Comté where he died in exile in 1640.[5] The Oratorians in Nancy, who were French, were the only ones to obey the order to recite the *Exaudiat* prayer for the king of France in the liturgical office. But when it came to the petition 'God save the king', more and more of the choir changed the response to 'God save the duke' so the practice had to be abandoned.[6]

It is impossible, in the space of a few lines, to give a coherent outline of the tangled events of this war. Between 1635 and 1643 the war is nothing more than a series of moves and counter-moves by both armies. As many as seven armies with a total of 150,000 men were camped, at the one time, within the narrow confines of the dukedom. Most notable among these soldiers were the Swedes, captained by the bloodthirsty Prince Bernard of Sax-Weimar whom Richelieu had attracted to his cause. He had three French armies fighting on his side. Opposing them were two contingents of imperial troops led by John de Werth, who in 1635 seized Toul and was one of the leaders of the Spanish march on Corbie the following year. The army of Charles IV of Lorraine completed the picture. None of these forces corresponded to our modern notion of a national army. They all had in their ranks mercenaries from very different countries. As well as Germans, Spaniards and Frenchmen, there were Swedes, Scots, Poles, Croatians, Hungarians, Swiss, and even Turks and barbarians. Neither was there any clearly demarcated combat line. Troops from different armies had no over-all commander so military engagements were just haphazard events, the object of which was pillage and revictualling the troops. Mercenaries were badly and irregularly paid so they lived off the land. The atrocities they committed in search of sustenance added to the war's savagery.[7]

'Sola Lotharingia Ierosolyman calamitate vincit'

All the scourges of the Apocalypse were unleashed over the unfortunate duchy. *'Mother Courage's* waggon travelled through the countryside of

[5] H. DERRÉAL, *Un missionnaire de la Contre-Réforme, Saint Pierre Fourier* (Paris 1950); id., *Saint Pierre Fourier et ses rapports avec la cour de Lorraine*, in *L'Université de Pont à Mousson et les problèmes de son temps* (Nancy 1974), pp. 217-233.

[6] J. GIRARD, 'Saint Vincent de Paul. Son oeuvre et son influence en Lorraine', *Annales* (1951), p. 330. This extensive study published in *Annales* [1951], pp. 321-368, [1952] pp. 96-145 and 376-408 remodels and brings up-to-date all previous studies on St Vincent's work in Lorraine.

[7] J. GUIRARD, ref. art. (1951), pp. 326-328.

Lorraine for years.* One of Bernard de Weimar's bands of troops had, on its standard, the picture of a woman split in two from head to foot and flanked by two soldiers carrying a flaming torch and a sword. On the banner was blazoned the single word 'Lorraine'. Nothing could have summed up better the state of that region.[8]

The Swedes, who were rabid Lutherans, vented their savagery with special fury on places and objects connected with Catholic worship. More than 600 churches were desecrated; chalices, albs and chasubles were stolen, relics were burned, altars pulled down, and the sacred species trodden under foot. For their part, the duke's Croatian and imperial troops hunted down the 'traitors' of Lorraine, requisitioned the harvests and burned down villages. All the armies vied with each other in cruelty. After the troops had passed through a village, the roads would be littered with corpses and dead animals. They used some very sophisticated forms of torture. Men would be slowly burned over the fire in their own hearth to force them to confess where they had hidden their money or provisions; others had their arms and legs cut off and others still were beaten to death. Women and children were not spared.

Plague and famine added to the destruction. Food was so scarce that people ate grass and roots; acorns and wild fruits were sold as sweetmeats in the market and people were glad to eat dead animals, particularly the army's dead horses. People spoke of mothers eating their children and of a man who killed his brother for a bit of bread ... The Jesuit Caussin, who was confessor to Louis XIII, made the rhetorical comment: *Sola Lotharingia Ierosolyman calamitate vincit,* 'Only Lorraine suffered more calamities than Jerusalem', an allusion to Vespasian's troops whose atrocities were not nearly as horrendous.'[9]

'My Lord, give peace to France'

The first news that Vincent had about the devastation in Lorraine came from the missioners in Toul, a house that had been founded in 1635. These priests did not wait for instructions but put themselves at the service of the injured. They converted part of their house into a hospital and lodged between forty

---

* Mother Courage, the main character in Bertolt Brecht's *Mutter Courage und ihre Kinder* was a camp-follower who drove a canteen waggon during the Thirty Years War.
[8] COLLET, *op. cit.*, Vol. 1, p. 287.
[9] *Ibid.*, p. 288. Descriptions of atrocities committed in Lorraine are a commonplace in works on this subject where the authors have based their findings on contemporary reports. There might have been an element of propaganda in these, but as we shall see, the reports that St Vincent received confirmed the gravity of the situation.

and sixty sick people there. They looked after a further hundred or a hundred and fifty in another place on the outskirts of the town.[10]

Vincent immediately took the measure of such a horrific catastrophe. The scale of the relief operation had to match the need.. This period of Vincent's life coincides with what we might call his first involvement in politics. One day he paid a visit to Cardinal Richelieu. He explained to him the misery that war brought in its train, the suffering that people had to endure and the sins that were committed in times of war. At the end of his speech he went down on his knees and exclaimed, 'My Lord, give us peace. Have pity on us. Give France peace'! The Minister's reply was what we might have expected from a man of his political astuteness. 'Peace? But that's something I never stop working for, M. Vincent. It does not just depend on me. A lot of people, both here and abroad, are involved.'[11]

Was this just a polite excuse offered to a well- intentioned visitor? It could be that the reply might have a different interpretation. This anecdote, related by Abelly, is surprisingly backed up by the cardinal's letters. In a letter to Chancellor Séguier in 1638, he is recommending a priest friend of 'M. Vincent' and he adds a postscript which perhaps reflects the impression made on him by his interview with the founder of the Mission, 'I beg you to redouble your prayers for peace. This is something that I desire so sincerely, and so earnestly, that I do not hesitate to ask God to punish those who are thwarting it.'[12] Is not this the same answer that he gave Vincent, though couched in conventional terms.

Vincent realised he would have to take the initiative himself. He started by making the community do penance. Remembering the words of Joel, he ordered his priests to pray for the people who were suffering such calamities and he imposed various privations on the community as a way of lessening the evil. At the outbreak of war with Spain he ordered one course of the meal to be cancelled. When he first heard about the devastation in Lorraine he gave orders that only black bread should be served at meals. This order remained in force for three or four years.[13]

But if any aid was to prove effective it would need to have far greater resources than any the missioners could provide from the economies they made. Letters arrived from Toul describing the terrible plight of the people in Lorraine. Vincent read these letters to the ladies and to other influential people. It was obvious that a massive aid programme was called for, and Vincent's long experience of organising relief at Châtillon, Mâcon,

[10] COLLET, *op. cit.*, Vol. 1, p. 291; *S.V.P.* I, p. 538.
[11] ABELLY, 1.1 c. 35, pp. 169-170.
[12] Referred to by CHEVALLIER, *op. cit.*, p. 564.
[13] ABELLY, 1.3 c. 19, p. 298.

Beauvais and in the charities of the towns and villages, was now to be used to the best advantage. Four things were lacking in the beginning: the collection of funds, distribution centres, information about what was needed, and liaison services.

Fund-raising

Right from the outset it was the ladies who took charge of fund-raising. The ladies gave out of their own pockets and urged others to do the same.[14] They appealed to the most high-ranking people. The king contributed 45,000 *livres* which was to be allocated, particularly, to religious orders whose members were among the most needy.[15] The Duchess d'Aiguillon proved generous on many occasions and to help people in distress she donated the funeral hangings and the linen used at the funeral of her uncle, the cardinal. The queen did the same after the funeral of her husband,[16] the king, and she also gave many donations in cash, including the sum of 2,000 *livres* which was to be used specifically for impoverished nobles.[17] Collet deemed this action all the more meritorious as the sovereign 'had no reason to love the country she was being asked to help.'[18] The last thing charity needs is discrimination between friends and political enemies! But all the donations that came in were trifling compared with increasing needs. At the beginning of the campaign, in May 1639, Vincent estimated that they would need 2,000 *livres* a month.[19] In February 1640, this figure rose to 2,500. Vincent was afraid they would not be able to keep up that level of fund-raising.[20] His tenacity, coupled with the enthusiastic support of the ladies and many other anonymous benefactors, saw the project through to the end in spite of the fact that, when the French troops lost control of the province, Richelieu thought that the king had no reason to continue helping those who suffered because of the war.

Relief aid

The work of distributing alms was confided to the missioners. Vincent sent twelve of his best priests and clerics to help the missioners at Toul and he also sent brothers who had some knowledge of surgery or medicine.[21] As

---

[14] COLLET, *op. cit.*, Vol. 1, p. 288.
[15] *S.V.P.* II, p. 80.
[16] ABELLY, 1.2 c. 11, p. 388.
[17] *S.V.P.* II, p. 483.
[18] COLLET, *op. cit.*, Vol. 1, p. 288.
[19] *S.V.P.* I, p. 551.
[20] *S.V.P.* II, p. 32.
[21] COLLET, *op. cit.*, Vol. 1, pp. 289-290.

always when a new work was being undertaken, Vincent drew up for them a set of rules which established strict standards of conduct and administrative practice.[22]

The missioners worked in pairs from seven strategic points: Toul, Metz, Verdun, Nancy, Pont à Mousson, St Mihiel and Bar-le-Duc and from these centres they looked after the needs of people in the surrounding areas.[23] On a less regular basis, but with no less commitment, they helped out at many other places including Lunéville.[24] Each centre was allocated a monthly sum of 500 *livres* and Vincent appointed Fr Dehorgny as regional visitor to supervise the work from June to July 1640.[25]

Basic aid consisted of food, particularly bread and soup, medicine and clothing. The same method of distribution was followed in every place. Each week the missioners would go round their districts and with the help of the parish priest they would draw up a list of poor people. Then they would give the priest, or some charitable lady, the flour needed for the week's baking, and after the first distribution of bread they would gather the poor people together for a pious exhortation, catechise the children, and help those who were most seriously ill to prepare well for death.[26]

At the regular centres every type of need was addressed. Letters from missioners, reports by the visitor and the testimony of people from the towns that received aid, all give us some idea of the colossal relief work carried out by the missioners, even though this evidence is incomplete.

The missioners' first priority was the distribution of food to starving people in the townships. In Verdun they distributed bread and soup to some five or six hundred people each day, they did the same for a further four or five hundred at Nancy and for a similar number of people at Pont à Mousson, where some of the poor were so famished that they died after swallowing the first mouthful. At Bar-le-Duc there were sometimes more than 800 needy people and, to add to the difficulty, missioners from other districts would send people to this city as it was the gateway to Lorraine and these people thought they would find the answer to their problems by going into exile. At St Mihiel the people used to eat snakes and dead horses. During March 1640 food was distributed to 1,132 poor people. Sometimes the number of needy people who begged the missioners for bread rose to between four and five thousand.

---

[22] COLLET, Vol. 1, p. 290.

[23] ABELLY, *op. cit.*, 1.1 c. 35, p. 165 and 1.2 c. 11, pp. 375-384; *S.V.P.* I, pp. 552, 590.

[24] ABELLY, *op. cit.*, 1.2 c. 11, p. 385.

[25] ABELLY, 1.2 c. 11 pp. 380-381; *S.V.P.* II pp. 55, 58-60, 67-68.

[26] These facts and the information which follows are to be found in ABELLY, *op. cit.*, 1.2 c. 11, pp. 375-381. As I am following a different type of outline I would have to keep on repeating references so I have put all the references together in the pages indicated.

Famine led to an increase in the number of sick people. Many of these were lodged in the missioners' houses at Toul and Nancy. In other places like Bar-le-Duc, and even in Nancy itself, the sick were sent to hospital and the missioners sent clothing, food and medicine there. The sick who remained at home were not neglected either. About fifty of these were visited in the town of Nancy. Sick people were provided with a more substantial diet than the ordinary poor people had; they were given bread, soup and meat as well as clothing and medicine. One of the most common infections was ringworm. The brothers had discovered a 'sovereign remedy' for this, which made the infection disappear within a few days. More than twenty-five people at Bar-le-Duc were cured by this remedy.

The 'bashful poor', to use a popular expression of the time, were even more deserving of pity because being people of rank, and even of the nobility, they felt they could not make their situation known. This class of people was to be found in many places. At Nancy, the missioners reckoned there were about fifty middle-class people in need and they delivered bread to these people's homes. They found thirty of the nobility in reduced circumstances and these were given money. At Pont à Mousson there were fifty or sixty people of this social class who were dying of hunger; at Verdun there were thirty, and at Toul and St Mihiel they were 'numerous'.

There was also a serious shortage of clothing. At Nancy, clothing was distributed and the old clothes of the poor were washed and mended. In this way they were able to recycle 6 or 7 dozen shirts which were given to people in even greater need. The same thing happened at Bar-le-Duc. Here, clothing was distributed to 260 poor people and any clothes that were too old to use, were carefully washed and made into bandages for the injured. Shoes and tools were also distributed.

The relief workers were very concerned about the plight of many young women who were reduced to great poverty and so were open to the temptation of selling their virtue, or, as reports described it, their 'honour' for a piece of bread or a little money. This was happening throughout the whole province. The missioners congratulated themselves on rescuing countless young women, including some ladies from distinguished families, from this peril.

Amidst all these forms of misery there was perhaps no situation more distressing than that of nuns in enclosed orders. Shut up in their convents, unable to collect the income from their dowries, and deprived of the usual alms because of the poverty that prevailed all round, some would ring the convent bells for hours on end in a vain appeal for help. A good number of nuns were forced to leave their convents, either to look for assistance outside, or because they were turned out by the troops. One of the best documented aspects of Vincent's work is the charity he showed towards nuns. Between

1642 and 1649, in the city of Verdun alone, 2,740 *livres* were given to the Carmelites, 1,338 *livres* to the Poor Clares, and 1,630 *livres* to the Benedictines of St Maur.[27] Reports for the year 1647 tell us that from 28 January to 8 April, 8,495 *livres* were distributed to fifty-two convents and monasteries of different orders: Sisters of the Annunciation, Poor Clares, Dominicans, Daughters of St Francis, Benedictines, Visitation nuns, Carmelites, Magdalens and the Congregation of Our Lady.[28] As well as money, they were given a lot of help in kind: blankets, furniture, habits, clothing and medicines[29] Others discovered, in the upheaval of war, an opportunity to found new convents. The Benedictine nuns at Rambervilliers, who had taken refuge in St Mihiel, moved to Paris on Vincent's advice. At the head of this community was Mother Catherine de Bar who transferred from the Annunciation Order to the Benedictines and changed her name to Mechtilde of the Blessed Sacrament. In the Paris district of St Germain they founded the Benedictine Nuns of the Blessed Sacrament. The queen and high-ranking ladies vied with each other in being the nuns' patrons so as to obtain for the city the blessings that come from perpetual adoration.[30]

In Lorraine, too, spiritual help went hand in hand with material aid. The missioners spent long hours preaching, instructing, and administering the sacraments. At Pont à Mousson they preached a short mission to the refugees. A missioner in Verdun reckoned that he had helped more than a thousand people to prepare well for death. 'How many souls will enter paradise thanks to poverty!' he exclaimed. More than 2,000 people attended the catechism classes at St Mihiel. It was such a heavy task that one of the missioners became ill. At Bar-le-Duc, the missioners heard over 800 general confessions in just over a month and a half. Religious instruction was given every day at Nancy, and the priests successfully exhorted the people to go to confession and communion every month. The Lorraine campaign was one of the best examples we have of the priests of the Mission working hand in hand with the charities.

'It is enough that God knows our works': publicity

Reports about help given to the needy and on the distribution of relief aid arrived punctually at St Lazare. Vincent had instructed the missioners to

---

[27] *Annales* (1939), pp. 691-692.
[28] J. GIRARD, article quoted (1951), pp. 348-349.
[29] COLLET, *op. cit.*, Vol. 1, pp. 306-307.
[30] ABELLY, *op. cit.*, 1.2 c. 11, p. 388; COLLET, Vol. 1, pp. 310-322; J. GIRARD, article quoted (1951), pp. 354-355.

obtain a receipt for the alms they distributed[31] but on the other hand, he did not want these receipts to be seen as so many certificates of merit. 'It is enough', he said, 'that God knows our works and that the poor are being helped.'[32] But he could not prevent the inevitable. The vicar general and the Dominican nuns from Toul, the councillors and the 'thirteen' from Metz, the mayor and the magistrates of Pont à Mousson, the deputy, the provost and the governor of St Mihiel, the officials and councillors of Lunéville, as well as countless private citizens, priests, and religious, all wrote to Vincent, praising to the skies the missioners' charity and spirit of self-sacrifice. They hailed Vincent as father of the poor and saviour of their country. Some witnesses remarked: 'M. Vincent must be a native of Lorraine since he does so much for that region.'[33]

Although at the outset he was very much opposed to the idea, Vincent decided to capitalise on that enormous stack of reports and mount a publicity campaign to attract further support. Every month he would read out to the ladies in Paris the amount of aid distributed, and in this way he encouraged them to persevere in their efforts; 'they were very encouraged'.[34] He started something else—a technique he was to perfect later on—to send the most heart-rending of the letters he received to various places, 'to move the rich to compassion by describing such suffering, and also to give encouragement to benefactors by letting them see the happy results of their almsgiving.' These letters were passed round from hand to hand so the effect was multiplied. Unfortunately for us, it is precisely for this reason that an incomparable source of first-hand documentation has been lost for ever.[35]

'They think they are not made of flesh and blood'

The fervour that Vincent had inculcated in his missioners was the dynamism that made such a great outpouring of charity possible. In Lorraine, as had happened in Ireland, Tunis and Marseilles, there were numerous examples of heroism. The most outstanding case was that of Fr Germain Montevit, who died at Bar-le-Duc on 19 January 1640, at the age of twenty-eight, after contracting an illness while serving the poor. He lived at the Jesuits' house and the superior of that community gave this wonderful eulogy.

---

[31] *S.V.P.* II, p. 60.
[32] The statements referred to here can be found in ABELLY, *op. cit.*, 1.2 c. 11, pp. 375-385.
[33] J. GIRARD, article quoted (1951), p. 357.
[34] *S.V.P.* II, p. 60.
[35] ABELLY, *op. cit.*, 1.2 c. 11, p. 378.

He suffered a lot during his illness which was a very long one and I can say, in all honesty, that I have never seen patience and resignation like his. We never heard him utter a word of complaint or show the slightest impatience. All his words revealed an extraordinary piety. The doctor often told us that he had never treated such an obedient and simple patient. He received communion frequently during his illness, as well as on the two occasions that he had holy viaticum. Even when he was delirious for a week, he was fully conscious when he received extreme unction, though he lost consciousness immediately afterwards. In a word, I would like to die in same dispositions as he had, and I beg God to grant me this grace.

The two canonical chapters at Bar attended his funeral, as did the Augustinian priests, but the greatest honour paid him during his obsequies was that six or seven hundred poor men accompanied his remains. They each carried a lighted candle and they wept as though it were their own father's funeral. This was the poor people's way of showing their gratitude for the fact that he had caught this illness while he was curing their ills and alleviating their poverty. He was always with them, breathing in their foul odours. He was so diligent in hearing their confessions during the mornings and after the mid-day meal that I could never get him to take any rest or come out for a stroll with me. We had him buried next to the confessional where he had taken ill and where he stored up the merits he is now enjoying in heaven.

Two days after this priest's death, his companion fell ill with continuous fever and for a whole week he was at death's door. He recovered. His illness was due to overwork and long periods of time spent serving the poor. On Christmas Eve he went 24 hours without food or sleep and only left the confessional to say Mass. Your fathers are very docile and reasonable except when they are advised to take a little rest. Either they think they are not made of flesh and blood or else they think they have only one year left to live.[36]

---

[36] ABELLY, *op. cit.*, 1.2 c. 11, pp. 384-385.

'Our brother Mathieu does marvels': the link-service

Heroic deeds and willingness to work were not enough. It would have been impossible to bring aid to Lorraine if there had been no communication link-service between that region and Paris. Given the dangerous conditions of those times, one could come upon bands of soldiers lying in ambush at any bend in the road, waiting to set upon any unwary traveller. To deal with such dangers you would need to be very astute and cool-headed. Br Mathieu Regnard had both these qualities. Vincent appointed him his emissary and he soon became famous. The story of his adventures spread from mouth to mouth and Anne of Austria summoned him to her palace to hear the accounts at first hand. Some incidents could have cost him his life. Br Mathieu wrote an account of his exploits which is now lost but Abelly made a very good summary of it. People called him *The Fox,* a pun on his surname, because of his proverbial astuteness.[37]

There were 18 incidents that Mathieu described as extremely dangerous but the total number of journeys he made was 54 and each time he carried with him twenty or thirty thousand *livres*. One can imagine the temptation his satchels must have been for bands of marauders but he always managed to escape them.

On one occasion he fell into the hands of some footpads who searched every fold of his clothing but did not find anything of value. When they got tired of searching him they made him an offer: 'Fifty *pistoles* or your life.'[38] 'Fifty *pistoles*!' exclaimed the brother in astonishment. 'Even if I had 50 lives I could not give you even a Lorraine *sou* for them.' The miscreants were almost ready to give him an alms! As soon as they disappeared, Mathieu picked up his satchels which he had hidden at a bend in the road.

On another occasion, a horseman who was armed to the teeth, stopped him, threatened him with his pistol and then led him to the edge of a precipice where he could take his time in searching him. The brother's satchels contained no less than 34,000 *livres*. As they walked along Mathieu would turn to the rider every so often and make a little bow. He noticed, out of the corner of his eye, that his pursuer had turned his head away for a few moments. Quick as a flash, Mathieu threw away the satchels. A hundred paces further on, he turned round again and bowed deeply several times, making sure that his footprints were clearly marked in the recently ploughed soil. The only thing found on him after the rigorous search that followed was a knife. The robber immediately took possession of this and then he let this strange traveller,

---

[37] The summary is given by Collet in *op. cit.*, Vol. 1, pp. 320-322. Our account of the episodes that follow is taken from this. *Cf.* ABELLY, *op. cit.*, 1.2 c. 11, pp. 390-391.

[38] The *pistole* was a valuable coin which was worth 10 *livres*.

whom he took to be a bit crazy, go free. When the danger was over and the coast clear, the brother retraced his steps and, guided by the footprints he had left, was able to recover his treasure.

Most of Charles IV's 'Croatians' were really men from Lorraine and they were among the worst for looting. On one occasion Mathieu came across a band of them in the open countryside. He sensed danger and acted quickly. He hid his satchel in some thick bushes, and four or five paces further on, he dropped his stick. Then he deliberately walked towards the soldiers, looking the picture of innocence. The Croatians searched him and then let him go on his way. Mathieu waited till it got dark. Then he went back and started to look for his bags but he could not find them all night. At daybreak, and after much prayer, he found the stick. A few yards further on lay the bag, hidden in the undergrowth where he had left it the previous day.

The 'Fox's' adventures became legendary and this proved no help at all in his difficult work. Not far from St Mihiel he was recognised by a captain who pointed him out to his men and said, admiringly, 'This is the famous Br Fox.' The soldiers were about to rush at him when the captain, pistol in hand, stopped them and said, 'Anyone who dares to harm a man who does so much good will have his brains blown out.' The brother arrived at his destination with no further mishap.

On another occasion some Croatians discovered that Mathieu was lodging at the castle of Nomény, and they posted sentries on every road so that he could not escape. Before it was daylight the brother left his hiding place by a false door, took to a footpath that nobody knew about, and presented himself in Pont à Mousson before his besiegers knew he had even left. When the people in the castle said that the brother had left Nomény, the Croatians could not believe their ears and in their rage they cursed and blasphemed saying: 'Either God or the devil must have carried him over the woods.'

Travelling with Mathieu was like having a guarantee against all accidents. The Countess of Montgomery was travelling on a journey and she had a passport from the king of France, the king of Spain and the Duke of Lorraine. In spite of having all these safe-conducts she had been attacked on various occasions. She was just about to set out again from Metz to Verdun when she learned that the brother was travelling along the same road. She immediately begged him to get into her carriage saying, 'Your company will be more use to me than all the passports in the world.' And in fact, they did both arrive at Verdun without encountering either soldiers or bandits.

As he finished telling the story of his adventures, the brother assured them that if he had been able to come safely through so many dangers, then this was due to the special protection that God granted him because of the faith and the prayers of M. Vincent. This is no doubt true, but Vincent's more matter-of-fact comment was, 'Our Br Mathieu does wonders and this is due to a very special grace given him by God.'[39]

Exiles

It was not just the people living in the duchy of Lorraine who received help. The war was responsible for the exodus of thousands of people of all ages and every social class. Half the country was left uninhabited. The principal centre that these poor, harassed and destitute people made for was Paris. Vincent poured out his tenderness on these poor exiles, too, and he started with the most vulnerable groups: young girls and children.

Br Mathieu was also given the job of leading this flood of humanity to Paris. If he could not save all of them, he gave priority to helping the weakest and those most at risk. In September 1639, he brought 46 girls and 54 boys to the capital.[40] He guided many more there in the course of later expeditions.

Young girls were chosen from among the 'best developed', to use Abelly's phrase, because these were more in danger of being raped by soldiers. They were temporarily lodged at the Foundlings' Home and later were found situations as maids or servants in better-off households. The boys were housed at St Lazare until such times as work could be found for them.[41]

Adults who were in exile received spiritual as well as material help. Vincent was for all those people from the provinces the refuge of the afflicted. They were sent to him by their relatives and their parish priests and brought with them eloquent letters of recommendation, but even without these the compassionate superior of St Lazare was ready to open his arms and his house to them.[42]

He set up a refuge camp at La Chapelle, at the gates of Paris and not far from St Lazare. Vincent had his priests and those of the Tuesday conferences (so here we have the fourth Vincentian work taking part in the action) preach three missions to these people in 1639, 1641 and 1642. During the first mission these people were given food as well as spiritual nourishment. Vincent's great friend, François Perrochel, preached at the final mission. We have already mentioned this man who, by this time, was appointed bishop of Boulogne.[43]

---

[39] *S.V.P.* I, p. 591.
[40] *Ibid.*
[41] ABELLY, *op. cit.*, Vol. 2, c. 11, p. 386; 1.3 c. 20, p. 307.
[42] *Id.*, Vol. 2, c. 11, pp. 386-387.
[43] *S.V.P.* X, p. 552; ABELLY, 1.1 c. 30, p. 166; COLLET, Vol. 1, p. 309.

A good number of the exiles were noblemen who had been ruined by the war and whose rank and dignity prevented them from publicly asking for help. Vincent showed great ingenuity in finding ways of helping them without hurting their feelings. He gathered together a group of his friends who were also noblemen, brought them to St Lazare and put the problem to them. The group included the Duke of Liancourt, the Count of Brienne and the Marquis of Fontenay, but the most notable person there was Baron Gaston de Renty (1611-1648).[44] These men set up an association whose first priority was to find out the number of refugees and what their needs were. Gaston de Renty himself took on this task and his outstanding piety soon gained him the reputation of being a saint.[45] Once the census had been taken, they calculated how much money would be required to meet all the needs and then every member of the association, including Vincent, pledged himself to contribute. There was a meeting on the first Sunday of every month to review the situation, to update the list of those needing help, and to collect contributions.

At one of these meetings they found they were 200 *livres* short of their target. Vincent sent for his bursar and asked him how much money they had in the safe.

'Just enough to feed the community tomorrow', answered the bursar.
'And how much is that?'
'Fifty *écus*'

It was almost the amount they needed. So Vincent insisted:

'Have we not got any more?'
'No, father. There are only fifty *écus*.
'Well, bring them to me, please.'

The bursar, somewhat displeased, obeyed, and Vincent used his community's money to make up the amount of money needed to help the people of Lorraine. The next day, one of the gentlemen who had overheard the superior's conversation with the bursar, sent 1,000 *livres* to St Lazare.

---

[44] *S.V.P.* II, p. 42.

[45] The life of de Renty was written by another great friend of his and of Vincent de Paul, the Jesuit J. B. de Saint Jure: *La vie de Monsieur de Renty* (Paris 1651). Fr Blanchet has published a perceptive study on Saint Jure's book, 'Notes sur le livre de Saint Jure: "La vie de Monsieur de Renty"', *Études* (1970), pp. 74-85. For a modern biography of Renty, see Triboulet, Raymond: *Gaston de Renty. 1611-1649. Un homme de ce monde. Un homme de Dieu*, Préface d'Henri Gouhier (Paris: Beauchesne, 1991), p. 435.

Vincent's trust in divine providence was never disappointed.

The members of the association were very discreet in giving alms and they used the occasion to show friendship and solidarity with their comrades from Lorraine, so that these would not feel offended at being given alms. The association was in operation for seven or eight years until the troubles in Lorraine began to subside. Even then, Vincent made sure that the refugees' return journey would be paid for and he gave them something towards initial expenses when they got back. Years later, Vincent gave similar help to English and Scottish nobles who were fleeing from Cromwell's persecution. [46]

The final total

Systematic help continued to be given to Lorraine until 1643, the year which saw an end to distributions of bread and soup. But aid continued, on a less regular basis, for a further five or six years. According to Br Regnard's calculations the total amount of money distributed in Lorraine came to 1,500,000 *livres*. This is the figure given by Abelly. Other sources suggest a sum of two million *livres*.[47] There is no contradiction between these two estimates if we remember that the brother was only referring to the amount of money in cash that he took there himself. We should add to this the cost of help given in kind (14,000 yards of cloth were supplied) as well as the cost of looking after the refugees, the expenses incurred in their travels, and other help they received.

Besides, it would be childish to measure Vincent's charity only by the amount of money distributed. There was a much deeper significance to the aid given to Lorraine. Vincent proved himself a genius at organising and a real statesman. His name broke out of purely ecclesiastical circles to reach coteries that decided the nation's fate. Everyone realised that Vincent had at hand the organisational procedures to tackle successfully even the direst catastrophes. It would not be long before these mechanisms would be called into action again.[48]

---

[46] ABELLY, *op. cit.*, 1.1 c. 35, pp. 167-169; 1.2 c. 11, p. 387; COLLET, *op. cit.*, Vol. 1, pp. 312-314.

[47] ABELLY, *op. cit.*, 1.2 c. 11, p. 389; COLLET, *op. cit.*, Vol. 1, pp. 318-319.

[48] U. MAYNARD (*op. cit.*, Vol. 4, p. 140-141) drew attention to the silence of chroniclers and historians in the seventeenth and eighteenth century regarding the relief given by St Vincent to their country. The explanation is simple. The people of Lorraine still felt strongly about their nationality and had vivid memories of the outrages committed by French troops so they were not interested in presenting the other side of the story. Even today, after two centuries, the people of Lorraine are still inclined to be reticent about this; the work done by St Vincent is regarded as a feeble attempt by the French to make amends for the harm they themselves did to Lorraine.

Chapter XXXII
MONSIEUR VINCENT AT COURT

All eyes were fixed on Vincent after his relief work in Lorraine. This obscure priest who reformed the clergy, promoted missions and inspired associations of charitable works, was also someone who could touch people's hearts and could successfully tackle problems that had defeated the authorities. Vincent passed through the door of Lorraine on to the great stage of history but his appearance there was no sudden leap to fame but rather the end of a long journey.

Quite a long time prior to 1643, the date we can take as marking the end of the basic relief aid to Lorraine, Vincent had come into contact with three great personages who were the most powerful people in France: Richelieu, Louis XIII and Anne of Austria. Vincent had left his mark on each of these three but he influenced each in a different way, according to the circumstances in which he met them and the works they watched him develop.

'A few days ago, I said to His Eminence'

Richelieu was probably the first of the three to meet Vincent personally. We know that he was very quick to find out about the motives and objectives of the Tuesday conferences. That first interview with Vincent led to the drawing up of a list of possible candidates for bishoprics.[1] Later on, and probably through the influence of his niece, the Duchess d'Aiguillon, he founded the house for Vincent's missioners at Richelieu.[2] Although we have no record of other meetings between Vincent and the cardinal, we can safely say that the two men must have met on many occasions during the years 1635-42. In November 1640, for example, Vincent remarked, 'A few days ago I said to His Eminence ...'[3] 'We gather from the tone of these words that these meetings

---

[1] Cf. supra, c. 17.
[2] Cf. supra, c. 19.
[3] S.V.P. II, p. 143.

happened regularly. They must have generated a certain level of confidence between the two men or Vincent would never have had the audacity to tackle the cardinal over two important matters of state, the question of peace at home at the beginning of the war against Spain,[4] 'and the proposal to send military aid to Ireland in 1641.'[5] These two requests might seem contradictory but Vincent had the same reason for making both. It was a question here of adopting a coherent religious policy: peaceful relations with Catholic countries and firm opposition to the spread of Protestantism. This suggestion was very much in line with the policies of the former 'Devout Party' and very different from the cardinal-minister's stratagems. Collet makes the comment that Vincent's interventions 'let Richelieu see that he thought the cardinal could be doing more than he was doing.'[6] Vincent, who was never a man to sin by rashness, must have been very sure that his words would not be misinterpreted when he made bold to put forward these suggestions.

Richelieu, too, had increasing confidence in Vincent. We are told that he appreciated Vincent's works and supported them. As well as making the foundation at Richelieu in 1640, he gave 700 *livres* for Masses,[7] 'and in 1642 he donated a further 12,000 *livres* to the Bons Enfants Seminary.'[8] The cardinal had recourse to Vincent on two occasions when important state negotiations needed the support of leading ecclesiastics. Around 1634-35, Vincent was one of the people consulted about the validity of Gaston d'Orléans' marriage to Margaret of Lorraine. Unlike Saint-Cyran, Vincent was of the opinion that the marriage should be declared null, a verdict that was in accordance with Richelieu's interests.[9] 'In 1639, as we shall see later on, Richelieu summoned Vincent to appear as a witness for the prosecution at Saint-Cyran's trial and on two occasions questioned Vincent himself. This time, however, his hopes of being supported by Vincent were disappointed.'[10]

No doubt there were times of tension in the relationship. On one occasion Vincent was accused, we do not know in what way, of acting against the cardinal's interests. Vincent immediately went to see the cardinal. 'My Lord', he said, 'here is the miscreant that people are accusing of acting against Your Eminence's interests. I have come here in person so that you may dispose of me and all the congregation in whatever way you please.'

He must have been very sure of his innocence, to take such a bold step, and he must also have had a good measure of confidence in the integrity

---

4 *Cf. supra*, c. 31.
5 *Cf. supra*, c. 24.
6 COLLET, *op. cit.*, Vol. 1, pp. 316-317.
7 COLLET, *op. cit.*, p. 307.
8 *Cf. supra*, c. 23.
9 A. DODIN, *Saint Vincent de Paul et la Charité*, p. 46.
10 *Cf. infra*, c. 36.

of his interlocutor. Vincent's openness disarmed his accusers and won over the cardinal. Neither Vincent nor his congregation were ever troubled again.[11]

It was after one such encounter that Richelieu confessed to his niece, the Duchess d'Aiguillon, 'I thought highly of M. Vincent before, but after my last interview with him I consider him to be different from other men.'[12] Vincent was, indeed, very different from the servile courtiers or the implacable enemies the cardinal met up with every day. His was the the incorruptible voice of a man whose only motivation was the glory of God and the salvation of the poor.

Richelieu's death on 4 December 1642 is not referred to in detail in Vincent's correspondence but we have to remember that we now have only one letter written by Vincent in that month: the letter to Bernard Codoing, dated 25 December. We know from this letter that Vincent ordered the Office of the Dead to be solemnly recited morning and evening and for several Masses to be celebrated for the repose of the soul of this great man who did not have time to put the business affairs of the Richelieu foundation in order before he died, and neither did he see fulfilled his wish to have the missioners established in the church of St Yves of the Bretons in Rome.[13] 'For Louis XIII, who esteemed but had no liking for the man, and for many people in France, Richelieu's death came as a relief.'[14] Fate has not allowed us to learn Vincent's personal feelings on the subject.

In the king's service

Vincent had less contact with Louis XIII but their encounters were certainly more cordial. Apart from meetings to discuss official business such as petitions regarding the congregation, which could well have been dealt with through bureaucratic channels, the first known interview between Vincent and the king took place in 1636 when the chancellor asked Vincent to send missioners to the army. According to Abelly, Vincent made the journey to the army's general headquarters in Senlis to offer the king his services and those of his congregation.[15]

Two years later, in 1638, Vincent sent the conference priests to the court residence at St Germain en Laye where they preached the famous *décolletées* mission.[16] It was the first time that Louis XIII had come into

[11] M. BARCOS, *op. cit.*, p. 40.
[12] COLLET, *op. cit.*, Vol. 1, p. 190.
[13] *S.V.P.* II, pp. 320-326.
[14] P. CHEVALLIER, *op. cit.*, pp. 628-632; V.-L. TAPIÉ, *op. cit.*, pp. 399-400.
[15] ABELLY, *op. cit.*, 1.1 c. 33, p. 154.
[16] *Cf. supra*, c. 23.

direct contact with the work done by Vincent's followers. The king paid no heed to the gossip and the protests of the courtiers and when the mission ended, the monarch could not have given it any higher praise than his comment, 'This is how it should be done and I will tell that to everybody.'[17]

Vincent gradually became on more intimate terms with the king. Louis XIII was a sincere and deeply religious man but his was a somewhat troubled piety that reflected his general outlook on life. Historians have noted in him the opposite traits of timidity and boldness, indecision and firmness, an almost feminine tenderness coupled with implacable authoritarianism, and abnormal sexual complexes. He earnestly desired the spiritual good of his subjects. For religious as well as political reasons he wanted to promote the Catholic faith in areas tainted by Protestantism. He was very concerned that good men should be appointed bishops. The work of Vincent de Paul could not fail to attract his attention and, together with the queen, he followed with interest Vincent's works of charity, the missions and training of the clergy.[18]

In 1638, the year that the mission was preached in St Germain, the king and queen had their first child after 22 years of marriage. The future King Louis XIV was born at St Germain on 5 September. Nine months earlier, on 5 December 1637, the king had paid a visit to Louise Angélique Lafayette with whom he had once had a platonic affair and who was now a novice in the Visitation convent in Paris. A violent storm blew up while he was there and the king was unable to return to Versailles. The nuns suggested that he stay the night at the Louvre where his wife was in residence. According to court rumours, the fruit of his encounter was the dauphin.

Be that as it may, on 14 January 1638, the royal physician informed Louis XIII that his wife was definitely pregnant. The news soon reached Vincent and this suggests he was in close communication with the palace. Indeed, in a letter dated 30 January, he urged Fr Lucas: 'Pray, and get others to pray for the queen's safe delivery.'[19] The mission to St Germain was in progress at the time so it is not surprising that Vincent should have had the news at first hand.

'The Sacred Person of the queen'

Anne of Austria was very different from her husband. Rumours passed down through the ages, and historical novels, have all ranted against this

---

[17] COLLET, Vol. 1, p. 281.
[18] *Cf.* V.-L. TAPIÉ, *op. cit.*, pp. 90-93.
[19] *S.V.P.* I, p. 432. *Cf.* P. CHEVALLIER, *op. cit.*, pp. 549-560; V.-L. TAPIÉ, *op. cit.*, pp. 352-353.

beautiful Spanish princess who at the age of fourteen was married to the king of France, himself an adolescent at the time and no way mature enough to take on the duties of a husband.[20] Disdained by her husband and mistrusted by Richelieu, whose suspicions were in some measure justified because of the young queen's political mistakes, she was left abandoned and isolated for twenty-five years. Her passionate temperament naturally sought compensation in petty flirtations—and despite what is written in novels, her relationship with the debonair Buckingham was no more than that—and in her fondness for the theatre. Present day historians are now presenting the true picture of Philip III's daughter as she appeared to her closest contemporaries: a Christian queen brought up in the baroque style of piety that was usual for princesses in Madrid and Vienna, she was pious but not fanatically so, and she knew how to combine joie de vivre with great and noble virtues.[21]

Anne was quick to hear about M. Vincent. We know that she attended the retreats for ordinands preached by Perrochel and that she had pledged to support this work by donating funds.[22] She was even more involved in works of charity and the most pious among the ladies in her retinue belonged to Vincent's association. As we know, there was even a proposal to set up a 'court charity' and its leading member would have been 'the sacred person of the queen.'[23] The birth of the dauphin brought the royal couple closer together. In thanksgiving to God for such a signal blessing, Anne of Austria donated to St Lazare a set of cloth of silver vestments which were so costly that Vincent had scruples about being the first person to use them, even for midnight Mass. He put them aside and donned an everyday woollen chasuble. The deacon and subdeacon had already vested in the precious dalmatics but they had to follow Vincent's example so that their vestments would match.[24]

In 1641 the queen had further contact with the missioners who were preaching the second mission at St Germain which was primarily for the benefit of people working at the palace. Every evening she attended the talk that Fr Louistre gave, at her request, to the ladies of the court. She also arranged for a young priest of the Congregation of the Mission to give catechism lessons to the dauphin who was then three years old.[25] Could it be

---

[20] P. CHEVALLIER, *op. cit.*, pp. 101-102.
[21] R. DARRICAU, 'L'action charitable d'une reine de France, Anne d'Autriche', *XVIIe Siècle* 90-91 (1971), pp. 115-125.
[22] *Cf. supra*, c. 23.
[23] *Cf. supra*, c. 27.
[24] ABELLY, *op. cit.*, 1.3 c. 13, p. 123.
[25] COLLET, *op. cit.*, Vol. 1, pp. 281-282; *S.V.P.* XI, p. 282.

that this gave rise to the delightful story he told the Daughters of Charity in 1647?

> I remember, six or seven years ago, that the previous king, Louis XIII, was out of countenance for about a week because when he came back one day from a journey, he sent for the dauphin, but the prince (who was only a child) did not want to see his father and turned his back on him. The king was angry and blamed those who attended the dauphin saying, 'If you had instructed my son properly and if you had taught him the proper way to welcome me, then he would have come into my presence like a dutiful son and shown pleasure at my return.[26]

Once again Vincent lifts the veil on his familiarity with everyday life at the palace. The queen came to have great confidence in him. Above all, she trusted his integrity and his disinterested charity; so much so that at one time she gave him a diamond valued at 7,000 *livres*, and on another occasion some earrings which the ladies sold for 18,000 *livres*.[27] Painters and novelists have exaggerated these gestures and have portrayed the queen putting all her jewels, including the crown, into Vincent's cloak. The legend should not take over from history but neither should it let us forget what she did.

Vincent's integrity, the growing importance of his apostolic enterprises and his increasing influence on the religious life of the kingdom, all brought him to the notice of the king and queen. His aid to the people of Lorraine opened to him the doors of those who wielded power. When Br Matthieu recounted to Anne of Austria his exploits on the dangerous highways of Lorraine, the queen agreed with the brother's observation: 'If I have been able to overcome so many obstacles it has been thanks to the prayers and the faith of M. Vincent.'[28]

'His Majesty wished me to attend him on his death bed'

Shortly after this interview the king died, following a long illness. The first symptoms of this illness were seen in February but from April onwards it was clear that the king was not going to get better. As he came closer to death, the king reviewed current ecclesiastical affairs with his Jesuit confessor,

---

[26] *S.V.P.* IX, p. 338.
[27] ABELLY, *op. cit.*, 1.3 c. 11, p. 126.
[28] ABELLY, *op. cit.*, 1.2 c. 11, p. 391; COLLET, *op. cit.*, Vol. 1, p. 322.

Fr Dinet. The most urgent matter still to be dealt with was the great number of vacant bishoprics and the monarch wanted to see to this before he died. He confided this work to his confessor who was to consult with other distinguished and devout people, and especially M. Vincent, and then present him with a list of names. The king was probably influenced by a similar step taken by Richelieu about eight years previously. Vincent thought so and on 17 April 1643, he wrote to Fr Codoing:

> If this matter of the *vescovandi* turns out well, then it will prove to be very important. Priests who have been trained here are outstanding among all the rest, and everyone, including the king, recognises that they have had a different formation. It is for this reason that His Majesty has asked me, through his confessor, to send him a list of those I think most worthy of this office.[29]

A week later there was a serious deterioration in the king's condition and on 23 April he received Extreme Unction. Then Vincent was summoned to the palace. Apparently it was the queen who suggested this to her husband. The king asked his confessor if he minded. Fr Dinet readily approved the idea. This is Fr Dinet's version of what happened. Vincent's account of it is practically the same though he does not mention the negotiations and says simply, 'His Majesty asked me to attend him on his death bed.'[30]

It is worth noting that both royal partners were anxious that the dying man should have this famous priest beside him at his last hour. There was no lack of spiritual assistance available to the king because he had with him, not just his confessor, but the bishops of Meaux and Lisieux as well as Canon Ventadour. So we must conclude that Vincent was asked to be present because people considered him a saint. Perhaps the king was remembering how his distant ancestor, Louis XI, had brought St Francis of Paula from Calabria to comfort him in his last moments.

When Vincent entered the royal bedchamber he greeted the sick man with the words from Scripture, 'Blessed be the man who fears the Lord, it will go well with him at his last hour.' The king replied with the versicle, 'And he will be blessed on the day of his death.'

There then followed a conversation between the sick man and his visitor, though only a few isolated phrases have been handed down to us. At one point in the conversation the king said: 'M. Vincent, if I recover my health I will see that all the bishops spend three years in your house.'

---

[29] *S.V.P.* II, p. 387.
[30] *S.V.P.* II, p. 393.

They must have been discussing the list of candidates for bishoprics. In the king's eyes Vincent's most important work was the reform of the clergy, and from a political point of view there can be no question that it was.[31]

Another matter that caused the king concern was the question of how to consolidate the Catholic religion in areas where Protestantism was gaining ground. In his will he left Vincent 24,000 *livres* to fund two missions annually in Sedan for ten years. But they must have discussed this question during the first interview because in his letter of 7 May, which was some time before the monarch died, Vincent informed Fr Codoing that the king had ordered him to 'prepare for the mission in Sedan.'[32]

After receiving Extreme Unction the king rallied, and there was hope that he might recover. Vincent was authorised to return to Paris and he left the palace, consoled in the knowledge that he had seen his king face death in a truly religious manner. He told the Daughters of Charity this in a conference given on the following Sunday 26 April.

> 'I beg you all to pray for his (the king's) intentions that God many restore him to health, or if in his goodness God judges it to be for his greater glory; that he keep him in those dispositions that he had on Thursday (23 April when he received Extreme Unction) when he thought he was dying and prepared for death in a generous and Christian way.'[33]

M. Vincent, who had just a few minutes earlier been speaking in such a simple, natural way about his visit to the king, remembered that he was only the son of a peasant and that he had been a poor swineherd, and he said: 'If you speak to common folk and preserve your integrity; if you walk alongside kings and offer them your inspiration ...' Vincent had reached that high degree of serenity that left him indifferent to human greatness.

'I have never seen anybody die a more Christian death'

The improvement in the king's health was only a passing one. On Thursday 7 May, his condition worsened again and this time it was final. The illness

---

[31] ABELLY, *op. cit.*, 1.1 c. 36, pp. 171-172.

[32] *M. et Ch.* 19-20 (1970), p. 45.

[33] *S.V.P.* IX, p. 112.

was probably phthisis of the bowel and left no grounds for hope. On 12 May Vincent was again summoned to the palace. He did not leave until after the king had died. Through various letters and conferences Vincent helps us to picture his last conversation with the monarch.

The doctors kept urging the king to eat, in spite of his serious condition and the aversion he felt for food. The king asked Vincent what he should do.

> 'M. Vincent', he said, 'the doctor insists that I eat something and I have refused because I am dying. What do you advise me to do?' I said to him, 'Your Majesty, the doctors have recommended you to take some food because they think they should always urge sick people to eat. They think that as long as a sick man has breath in his body there is a chance that the patient might recover. So, if it please your Majesty, I think it would be better if you take what the doctors order.' That good king then called M. Bouvard, the physician, and ordered soup to be brought.[34]

The next question showed that the king was even more ready to accept death.

> M. Vincent, what are the best dispositions to be in when you are dying?

Vincent did not need to think twice about the answer. It came from the depths of his religious experience and the principle that had guided his whole life.

> Your Majesty—complete and utter submission to the divine will. This was what Our Lord Jesus Christ practised during his agony when he cried out, 'Not my will but thine be done.'

The king immediately took up this holy counsel and exclaimed:

> 'O Jesus, I, too, desire this with all my heart. Yes, my God, I declare and I wish to say till my last breath: Thy will be done. *Fiat voluntas tua.*'[35]

---

[34] *S.V.P.* X, p. 342-343.
[35] ABELLY, *op. cit.*, 1.3 c. 8, pp. 87-88.

A few moments later, the king entered into his last agony. While the memory of the event was still fresh in his mind, Vincent gave his impressions of what happened:

> Yesterday God was pleased to call to himself our good king, on the very same day that he became monarch thirty three years ago ... Never in my life have I seen a more Christian death. About a fortnight ago he asked me to go and see him. And as he was somewhat better the next day, I came home. Three days ago he summoned me again and Our Lord granted me the grace of being with him at that time. I have never seen anyone in that situation reach out so much to God and to show such peace, such horror of the smallest thing that might be sinful, such goodness, and such a sense of responsibility. The day before yesterday the doctors found him in a stupor with the whites of his eyes showing and, fearing that he would not recover, they alerted his confessor who immediately roused him and told him that the doctors thought it was time for him to recommend his soul to God. Then that great soul, imbued with the spirit of God, gave a long and affectionate embrace to the good priest, thanked him for the good news and immediately afterwards raised his eyes and his arms to heaven and said the *Te Deum Laudamus*. He finished it with such devotion that I am touched by the memory of it even as I write.[36]‘

The king died on 14 May 1643, at half-past-two in the afternoon. Thirty-three years earlier, to the very day, his father, Henry IV, had been assassinated. Vincent had good reasons to remember it well. That was also the date when he had signed the contract which transferred to Vincent the Abbey of St Leonard de Chaumes.[37] ‘What a long way that ordinary young priest had come in the thirty-three years that Louis reigned. From being just a curious passer-by, he became one of the leading protagonists in important events.

‘There was still the formidable Spanish infantry’

Five days after the king’s death, the French forces achieved their most outstanding victory of the Thirty Years War, Rocroi. The old Spanish infantry

---

[36] *S.V.P.* II, pp. 393-394.
[37] *Cf. supra*, c. 7.

regiments suffered their first defeat in open battle and were demolished by the great Conde's powerful artillery. Young Condé was then only twenty-two years old. The French were victors and the Spaniards were vanquished in spite of the great wave of heroism that resulted in the death of 6,000 veterans together with their general, the Count de Fuentes. 'Count the dead ...' Bossuet would say, at the funeral oration for the great Condé, as he recalled the impression that the bravery of the Spanish soldiers had made on their enemy:

> But we still had to reckon with the formidable Spanish infan-
> try. Its powerful and dangerous squares of soldiers were like
> so many towers—towers that could, of themselves, repair any
> breeches made in them, and with defeat all round them, could
> remain invincible, spouting fire in all directions.[38]

The battle of Rocroi and, within the space of just a few months, the disappearance from the political scene of its leading figures: Richelieu, the Count-Duke of Olivares (dead in January 1643), Louis XIII, and Urban VIII (in 1644), signalled a decisive turning point in the history of France and of Europe. There began a new period in Vincent's life, too. His influence had increased steadily over a period of ten years and had now reached its peak.

---

[38] BOSSUET, 'Oraison funèbre de Louis de Bourbon, prince de Condé ...', in *Orateurs Chrétiens* (Ed. Migne, 1875), Vol. 25, col. 1312.

Chapter XXXIII
M. VINCENT IN THE GOVERNMENT

The Italian cardinal

On the day after Louis XIII died, the parlement of Paris abrogated part of his last will and testament by conceding to the queen mother: 'the care of the education and upbringing of the king; and the full, absolute and entire administration of the kingdom's affairs' until the new monarch's coming of age. The king was then four years and eight months old.[1] This meant that Anne of Austria would be regent for ten years and have absolute power. Richelieu had kept her in isolation so she was ill-prepared to take on such a mission but she had the sense to gather round her a competent team of advisers.

Richelieu had named his successor and this choice was ratified by the king before he died. The inflexible and resolute bishop of Luçon was replaced by another churchman who gave the impression of being more pliable and easily led, but who was basically just as ruthless. This man was the Italian, Giulio Mazzarino (1602-1661).

Mazarin's political career began when he was a member of the pontifical delegation at the Peace of Cherasco (1631) where he very obviously supported the French. Richelieu recognised the young diplomat's ability and took him under his wing. At the cardinal's request, Mazarin, who was later to become vice-legate at Avignon, was appointed nuncio to France (1634-1636). In 1639, and again on the cardinal's advice, Mazarin withdrew from the pontifical service and adopted French nationality. In the years that followed, he proved a faithful servant to Richelieu who secured for him the cardinal's hat and recommended him to Louis XIII as his successor. Court gossip has it that he also praised him highly to the queen, in a phrase that was not without a touch of malice: 'You will like him, my Lady. He looks like Buckingham.' After Richelieu's death, Louis XIII followed this minister's

---

[1] M. MARION, *Dictionnaire ...*, art. *Régence* p. 476; R. MOUSNIER, *Les institutions ...*, Vol. 2, 101-103.

advice and soon confided matters of state to Mazarin. By May 1643, when the king died, Mazarin was in effect, prime minister. The queen did no more than formally confirm his appointment. So there is little foundation for Collet's suggestion that the queen had made up her mind to exclude all Richelieu's henchmen from state affairs, and that she had intended to dismiss Mazarin but only left him in office at the insistence of Vincent who preached to her about pardoning one's enemies.[2] Mazarin had full control over the government of France throughout the whole regency period and during the first years of Louis XIV's rule.

The Council of Conscience

At the time that Anne of Austria was placing the administration of the kingdom into the hands of Mazarin, she confided the direction of her soul to Vincent de Paul and brought the two men together to direct ecclesiastical affairs in the Council of Conscience.[3] This organisation was already functioning in the last years of Louis XIII's reign. Anne of Austria made it into a more formal institution though it never had any official place among the agencies of government of the kingdom. It consisted, really, of a small group of people whose function was to advise the queen about state affairs which would be her duty in conscience to direct and, in particular, to offer advice about the allocation of benefices, especially bishoprics where the right of appointment had been granted to the French monarchy by the concordat. Vincent's appointment to the council meant that Anne of Austria was assured of the collaboration of the men she valued most: Vincent de Paul and Giulio Mazarin.

A very old tradition in Vincentian history often portrays these men as two incompatible and irreconcilable geniuses. Collet, who may have been the first to suggest this, says that Vincent and Mazarin, 'had such a different moral outlook that one would be tempted to think that they had studied different gospels.'[4] He is just one step away from presenting Mazarin as the queen's bad angel and Vincent as her good angel. The reality was not as simple as that.

Mazarin is, perhaps, the politician who has had the worst press in French history. During the Fronde, the anti-Mazarin propaganda campaign was scandalous and it spared neither his public actions nor his private life.[5]

---

[2] COLLET, *op. cit.*, Vol. 1, p. 364. For information on Mazarin, *cf.* P. GUTH, *Mazarin ...*, *Biographie* (Paris 1972).

[3] M. MARION, *Dictionnaire ...* art. *Conseil de Conscience,* p. 137; R. MOUSNIER, *op. cit.*, t. 2 p. 134, 157, 163, 169.

[4] COLLET, *op. cit.*, t. 1, p. 366.

[5] M. N. GRAND-MESNIL, *Mazarin, la Fronde et la presse* (Paris 1967).

This is something we need to keep in mind when judging the Italian Minister's actions. Whatever his moral failings might be—and these were many, ambition for power, cupidity, vanity, baseness and the desire to win at any cost, he still possessed some great qualities. Everyone recognised his affability, his personal charm, his devious cunning, his passion for politics and his efforts to make France a great country and to establish the authority of the crown. With sureness of touch, he continued Richelieu's work and, together with him, was the artificer of his adopted country's greatness. Without Mazarin we would not have had the splendour of Louis XIV's reign. As a politician he subordinated everything, including Church interests, to the good of France. And if he managed at the same time to procure the advancement of his family and to accumulate a colossal personal fortune, then this was a fairly common failing among politicians of that era, and not only in France.

In the early days at least, Vincent de Paul had no reason to oppose Mazarin. In fact he never did oppose him, however much they disagreed. Unlike the cardinal, Vincent was not a politician but a man of God. The clash would come when there was conflict between religion and politics or when Mazarin's natural wariness tended to see Vincent as an enemy. This is how we should interpret Mazarin's notes, for in his files Vincent is considered the agent of what might have been an anti-Mazarin group which included, among others, Fr de Gondi, Potier, De Noyers, Lambert, Maignelay ... ' M. Vincent who is in the ranks of La Menelay, Dans, Lambert and others, is the channel through which everything reaches her Majesty's ears.'[6]

Too much importance has been attached to these notes and it has even been suggested that Mazarin felt a morbid resentment against Vincent. It was said that Vincent's name 'appeared on every page and nearly every line' of Mazarin's private diary.[7] This is not true. There are fewer than a dozen references to Vincent and they all date back to the first year that Mazarin was in office (1643-1644). These were the months when Mazarin needed to establish his position and to determine that of other personages on the political scene. M. Vincent falls under suspicion because of his links with important people in the opposing faction, especially the de Gondis and some of the ladies of Charity. Mazarin does not accuse him so much of acting against him as of being used, perhaps, by other people to discredit him in the eyes of the queen. 'They have gone to see M. Vincent and under the pretext of showing affection for the queen, they tell him ...' 'De Noyers ... claims to have the support of the Jesuits, the monasteries, devout people and especially M. Vincent ...' The only note which accuses Vincent directly is written in Spanish, a language that Mazarin had learnt during his studies at Alcalá and Salamanca.

---

[6] Passages from Mazarin's notes that refer to Vincent can be found in *S. V.P.* XIII, pp. 136-138.
[7] J. MAUDUIT, *op. cit.*, p. 198.

It reads: 'Fr de Gondi criticised me and so did Fr Lambert and M. Vincent.'

It was just at this time that rumours went around that Vincent had fallen out of favour and had been removed from office. But as Vincent himself said, although

> 'they possibly did not want me to hold office any longer; it has, for my sins, turned out differently and God has not been pleased to accept the sacrifices I made for this intention. *In nomine Domini.* I hope they will grow tired of me some time.'[8]

Vincent's irreproachable conduct dispelled this initial mistrust and both men collaborated on many matters. We have ample proof of this. If relations between the two men were never particularly cordial, at least they worked together for the good of France. The bitter feelings engendered by the Fronde would eventually put paid to the 'entente' which in general had been very successful.

'That is as false as the devil'

Something else that made for confrontation between the priest and the minister was the rumoured love affair between Mazarin and Anne of Austria. So much has been written on this subject and the source material is so biased, that it is hard to separate fact from fancy. But the reported marriage of the queen to her prime minister is most definitely false, as is the allegation that Vincent conducted the ceremony. Br Robineau, one of Vincent's secretaries, speaks of the time that he asked his superior if there was any truth in this rumour. 'That is as false as the devil' exclaimed Vincent angrily and the brother adds, 'What they were saying about him was untrue; as was the whole question of the marriage. In spite of what people said, there never was such a marriage between these two important people. It was quite untrue.'[9] Recent research is proving that good Br Robineau was right.[10]

---

[8] *S.V.P.* II, p. 500; *cf.* ABELLY, *op. cit.*, 1.1 c. 37, p. 173.

[9] Manuscript of ROBINEAU, p. 10.

[10] M. LAURAIN-PORTEMER, *Le statut de Mazarin dans l'Église. Aperçus sur le haut clergé de la Contre-Réforme* (Paris 1970) Off-print from *Bibliothèque de l'École de Chartres* (1969), pp. 355-419 and (1970), pp. 5-80. According to the authoress, Mazarin never renounced the purple and he never married Anne of Austria or anybody else. At the end of his life he was granted an indult allowing him to be ordained a priest, something that would have been impossible if he were married. It is strange that such a serious work as *La civilización de la Europa clásica* should accept as authentic the marriage between Anne and Mazarin. *Cf.* P. CHAUNU, *op. cit.*, p. 659.

Leaving aside the marriage question, historians will continue to wonder how intimate was the relationship between queen and minister. According to the anti-Mazarin pamphleteers, the two were lovers. The fact that a man of such integrity as Vincent continued to be the queen's spiritual director obliges us to reject such a theory. He would never have consented to be their accomplice in such a flagrant violation of Christian morality. And we have to say, too, that such conduct would not be in keeping with the queen's character or her sincere piety. At the risk of appearing ingenuous, we can only conclude that this was a spiritually based friendship, a more or less platonic relationship; and according to some witnesses, Anne herself recognised this. What we read in novels may sometimes be true.

'Look how M. Vincent is dressed'

Vincent often went to court to hear his royal penitent's confession or to take part in the meetings of the council but he was never a courtier. In the beginning he tried his best to avoid both appointments and he never ceased to pray that he would be relieved of them.[11] He begged the queen not to oblige him to live at court and to give her consent to his appearing there only when summoned.[12]

The presence of this humble priest soon made itself felt in the palace. His threadbare cassock was very different from the fine habits worn by the abbots and monsignori who went there. Vincent was content with 'a modest and humble appearance' and this provoked some ill-concealed smiles. One day Cardinal Mazarin brought him in front of some elegant courtiers. He took hold of the worn sash that Vincent was wearing and said with a smile, 'Look how M. Vincent is dressed to come to court; just look at the beautiful sash he is wearing.' The onlookers naturally guffawed at the joke. Underlings always find their master's jokes funny.[13]

Other great lords took the liberty of making jokes that were in even worse taste. The Prince de Condé was returning from Paris with some companions when he spied Vincent ahead, mounted on his white horse and riding in the same direction. The gentlemen of leisure decided to make sport of him. They galloped after him, firing their pistols in the air. Poor Vincent dug his spurs into his horse and joined the race that left him dizzy. 'As soon as he comes to a church you will see him go in and give thanks to God for having escaped from bandits,' said the prince. And indeed, shortly after this,

---

[11] ABELLY, *op. cit.*, 1.1 c. 27, p. 173.

[12] *Ibid.*, 1.2 c. 13, p. 443.

[13] ABELLY, *op. cit.*, 1.3 c. 18, pp. 273-274.

Vincent felt that the danger had passed and he knelt down at the door of the first church he came to on the way. [14]

Such jests were really an admiring tribute to Vincent's kindly simplicity. On another occasion this same Condé, who had done him such a bad turn, showed just how able Vincent was. During one of the early sessions of the Council of Conscience, Condé was in conversation with some gentlemen when Vincent arrived and the prince invited him to sit down with them. Vincent, with his usual humility, declined.

'My Lord, it is an honour for me even to allowed in your company. I am only the son of a poor swineherd.'

'Moribus et vita nobilitatur homo' (it is his conduct and way of living that ennoble a man), replied the prince and immediately asked him a number of question that made Vincent reveal his solid grasp of theology and canon law.

'M. Vincent, you tell everybody that you are just an ignoramus and yet in a few words you have answered the trickiest questions that the Huguenots put to us', was the prince's comment.

There was, perhaps, some motive of self-interest behind Condé's flattery. Politicians try to make friends with anyone who seems to have a bit of influence. The queen's increasing esteem for Vincent was a topic of conversation at court. It was common knowledge that, in obedience to him, she practised mental prayer every day and used the little method that Vincent recommended to the Daughters of Charity,[15] that she made the jubilee stations with unusual fervour,[16] strictly observed the fast days of Lent, and was almost ready to forbid plays to be performed.[17] Vincent could not persuade her to go to this extreme as her Majesty's very Spanish fondness for the theatre prevailed, but he did manage to have indecent and scandalous scenes banned.[18] There was even a rumour that the queen had petitioned Rome for Vincent to be made a cardinal.[19] Did she want to revive the Richelieu-de Bérulle combination of political cardinal and devout cardinal? Neither Mazarin nor

---

[14] COSTE, *M.V.* Vol. 3, p. 108. For the following anecdote *cf.* ABELLY, *op. cit.*, 1.3 c. 13, p. 210.

[15] *S.V.P.* IX, p. 427.

[16] *S.V.P.* IX, p. 621.

[17] COSTE, *M.V.* Vol. 3, pp. 98, 101-104.

[18] ABELLY, *op. cit.*, 1.2 c. 13, p. 467.

[19] ID., *op. cit.*, 1.1. c. 37, p. 175; COLLET, *op. cit.*, Vol. I, p. 400.

Vincent would agree to the proposal, Mazarin for reasons of state and Vincent from humility. The plan, if in fact there ever was one, was just one of many corridor rumours. Vincent's influence would be exercised in other ways and in weightier matters for the good of the Church.

'M. Vincent has more influence with the queen than I have'

M. Vincent was not, as is often thought, president of the Council of Conscience.[20] That position was held by Mazarin[21] but Vincent was the most influential member of the council. His decision was final, even when he disagreed with the prime minister. We know this from two letters: one from Le Tellier, minister of war, and the other from Mazarin.

During the French occupation of Catalonia there were several proposals to appoint French bishops to vacant dioceses there. In 1645, the French viceroy, Count d'Harcourt, sent to Paris a list of three names for the bishopric of Solsona. The minister, Le Tellier, wrote to inform him that where benefices in Catalonia were concerned, the queen would only listen to the opinion of the French visitor, Pierre de Marca, whom we mentioned earlier,[22] and that in the case of French benefices she relies entirely on M. Vincent's recommendations.

> As for M. Vincent, she feels so obliged to follow his advice that if the cardinal nominated as bishop somebody that M. Vincent thought was unsuitable, then she would accept the latter's decision and neither the recommendation of His Eminence nor of anybody else would prevail over M. Vincent's decision.[23]

The cardinal corroborated his representative's statements.

> 'M. Le Tellier has told you the absolute truth when he assured you that in these matters M. Vincent has more influence with the queen than I have ...' Even I, who know more about her Majesty's intentions than anyone, dare not intervene until M. Vincent has studied the matter as much as he wishes.'[24]

---

[20] COLLET, *op. cit.*, Vol. 1, p. 365.

[21] ABELLY, *op. cit.*, 1.2 c. 13, p. 445.

[22] *Cf. supra*, c. 24.

[23] *Annales* (1953), p. 508.

[24] *Annales* (1954), p. 184. These documents which were not included in Coste's researches were published by the Spanish historian Josep Sanabre in the work we have already mentioned. F. Combaluzier published them in *Annales,* using the original text.

The testimony of Le Tellier and Mazarin confirms what we already know from other sources. Even though he was not president of the council, Vincent was its cornerstone.[25] In today's language we would call him the final referee, even though the Council included ecclesiastics of higher rank and some very distinguished laymen. At various times it had among its members the bishops of Beauvais, Lisieux and Limoges, the penitentiary of Notre Dame, Chancellor Séguier, the secretary of state, Hugo de Lionne, Fr Dinet and others. But Anne of Austria wanted to hear the voice of her conscience and nobody but Vincent de Paul could echo that. This was why he had been appointed.[26]

As we have already indicated, the council was concerned with all questions which one way or another were matters of conscience for the monarch, especially the business of ecclesiastical appointments. But it also dealt with matters of general religious concern, the suppression of blasphemy and of duelling, vigilance against heresy, and the censorship of books and theological writings. Anne of Austria regarded the council as a sort of Ministry of Spiritual Affairs. It may be an exaggeration, though, to describe Mazarin as minister for temporal affairs and Vincent as minister for the spiritual.[27] During the *Ancien Régime*, the temporal and the spiritual were so interwoven that it would be difficult to trace the dividing line between them.

Criteria and attitudes

Vincent's first concern was to define very precisely the criteria for nomination to office. Almost as soon as he was appointed, he proposed for the council's approval, a set of rules to be followed for this. By today's standards these rules may not seem to be very rigorous but, in his time, even to establish fixed criteria for the process represented a considerable advance. Among these rules were directives that nobody should be appointed bishop unless he had been a priest for at least a year, and that coadjutor abbesses had to be at least twenty-three years old and a professed religious for at least five years. In a country that had seen children of four years of age appointed bishop, such progress was remarkable. The fact that men appointed as abbots only needed to be 18 years old, priors 16 years old, and canons 14 years old, was an unavoidable evil within the general framework of the customs of those times, and at least it set some limit to the anarchy of former days.[28]

---

[25] ABELLY, *op. cit.*, 1.1 c. 37, p. 174; 1.2 c. 13, p. 445.
[26] *Ibid.*, 1.1 c. 37, p. 137; *S.V.P.* III, pp. 248, 521, 529; IV, p. 589.
[27] J. CALVET, *op. cit.*, p. 126.
[28] ABELLY, *op. cit.*, 1.2 c. 13, p. 444.

More important than the rules were the candidates. Methodical man that he was, Vincent drew up a list of aspirants in order of merit, ability and needs. As a matter of fact, there was nothing revolutionary about this either; Vincent was a man of his time and he could not shake off the mentality that linked high ecclesiastical office with noble birth. In any case it would have been useless to try and act otherwise. But at least he saw to it that appointments were given to worthy candidates.[29]

One thing is certain, beyond any shadow of doubt, Vincent continued to act with complete lack of self-interest. He never used his position to obtain worldly favours for himself or for his congregation. He did not even seek compensation for losses suffered during the Fronde.[30]

'Blessed be God for the embarrassment I have just been caused'

In a society where the sale of public offices was normal practice, the usual way of obtaining favours was to offer a bribe. Vincent, of course, had some very attractive offers but he never accepted any of them. On one occasion a group of influential people used the services of a mutual friend to offer him the tempting sum of 100,000 *livres* for his support in a matter which, while it was not immoral, could have been prejudicial to the interests of the clergy. Vincent's response was emphatic: 'God preserve me. I would rather die than say anything on the subject.'[31] At other times there were promises of support for a house of the congregation,[32] of influence in an important lawsuit,[33] the gift of a library.[34] As opposed to bribery, there were also threats, calumny and abuse. All these were used against Vincent by people whose hopes had been disappointed.[35] The best-known anecdote on this subject concerns a lady of high rank. She had requested that her daughter, who was a novice at the time, be made abbess. Vincent opposed the appointment and the good lady's indignation knew no bounds. She went round all the court with her protests and levelled all manner of insults against Vincent. He decided to pay her a visit and gently explain why he had refused her request and so make her see reason. In fact, he went to her palace and spoke to her about the dangers attached to being in high office, something that was particularly

---

[29] *Ibid.*, pp. 445-447.
[30] *Ibid.*, pp. 473-475.
[31] *Ibid.*, p. 474.
[32] *Ibid.*, 1.3 c. 17, p. 262.
[33] *Ibid.*, 1.3 c. 18, p. 278.
[34] *Ibid.*, 1.3 c. 13, p. 211.
[35] *Ibid.*, 1.3 c. 22, p. 317.

true for young people; he reminded her of the terrible judgement that people in authority can expect, and he tried to make her see that the highest positions should only be given to those who had shown that they could worthily discharge the duties of lesser offices. It was all in vain. The lady would not listen to reason. She answered Vincent's words with screams and insults and, at the height of her wrath, she grabbed the nearest stool and hurled it, in fury, at his head. Vincent dodged the blow, and without losing his composure, he made her a deep bow and left the room. As they went downstairs he said to his companion, 'Blessed be God for the embarrassment I have just been caused. It was only for his glory that I exposed myself to it'[36]

There were no fixed times for the Council of Conscience to meet. Mazarin sometimes made use of the intervals between sessions to make appointments without Vincent's knowledge. These were little tricks that the astute politician used to further his own interests and to place his own men in key positions. This did not always work out the way he wanted.[37] Sometimes, even though the candidate was appointed, the queen demanded a report from M. Vincent or at least required the new bishop to be sent to him to be instructed in the duties of his office. This was the case with Edouard Molé, son of the first president of the parlement, who was nominated bishop of Bayeux because of his father's position. Mazarin broke the news to Vincent very circumspectly, giving him to understand how much the queen was under obligation to the illustrious member of the parlement. Vincent did not consider the son worthy of this high office but, as the nomination had been made, the only thing left was to try peaceful persuasion. He went to see the first president and tried to make him understand that his son would not make a good bishop. He ended by saying: 'Do not risk bringing the anger of God down on him and on your family. Mathieu Molé was a conscientious man and Vincent's words made a deep impression on him. But he was also a father, and a father who was

---

[36] Coste does not accept that this incident is authentic because Abelly and Collet have nothing to say on this subject (*M.V.* Vol. 2, p. 426-427). Coste is mistaken with regard to Collet as we can prove from Collet's work (*op. cit.*, Vol. 2, p. 274) where he gives as the reason for Abelly's silence the fact that when the latter's book was published the lady in question was still alive and was well-known. This is not the only mistake that Coste made about this subject. In 1929 he stated that the first person to relate this incident was Maynard in 1860. 'Nobody had ever read it in any previous work' (*Annales* [1929], p. 273). He corrected this in *M.V.*, accepting that it had appeared in the Lisbon edition of the *Common Rules* (1743, p. XXVII), but he did not realise that Collet had also referred to this incident using the *Summary of the Beatification Process*, p. 308. Maynard did change quite a few details and instead of a young woman wanting to be an abbess, he speaks of a bishopric for a young man. Vincent's original comment is changed into the more dramatic phrase: 'How marvellous is a mother's love!' *Cf.* MAYNARD, *op. cit.*, Vol. 3, pp. 496-499.

[37] *S.V.P.* III, p. 248.

concerned for his children's future. After thinking the matter over for some time, he believed he had the answer and he told Vincent the solution.

What terrible nights you have caused me, M. Vincent. Although there is something in what you say, I think that if my son has a good team of wise and prudent ecclesiastics round him, he will be able to tackle his duties.

It was a *fait accompli* and Vincent could do no more. He left the matter in the hands of providence. Edouard Molé was not a good bishop.[38]

'The Church in your hands'

Apart from the anecdotes that have been handed down to us, there is no denying the fact that Vincent, through the Council of Conscience, had a very considerable influence on the reform of the Church in France. A new generation of bishops, abbots, canons, priors, holders of benefices, parish priests and curates held the key posts in the ecclesiastical machinery and they carried the spirit of reform to all parts. The change was quickly noticed and the most discerning observers realised what was happening. In 1648 the Cistercian, Jean Baptiste de la Place (1612-1678), abbot of Val Richer, dedicated his book, *L'Union Mystique,* to Vincent de Paul in the following words whose flowery, baroque style cannot hide the admiration which Vincent's reform of the bishops had aroused.

Before the most just of monarchs placed the nation's Church in your hands, men were born to the mitre and the ring. You administer the goods of illustrious young men with blind impartiality. Your choice inclines more to rustic knowledge than to noble ignorance, and the virtue that might deplore its cradle of poverty is indebted to you for the throne it has risen to, in preference to others more favoured.[39]

Vincent's influence on the episcopate lasted long after the candidates' appointment. Many bishops came to consult him, to tell him their problems and ask his advice and recommendations. There is hardly a bishop of that time who did not have contact with Vincent, either personally or by letter. Vincent always replied with tact and circumspection. We should not be misled

---

[38] ABELLY, *op. cit.*, 1.2 c. 13, pp. 451-452.
[39] *Annales* (1947-1948), p. 323.

by the flowery courtesies of the language he used, courtesies that were exaggerated by the saint's humility. Behind these polite conventions there often was great firmness and a very clear understanding of problems.[40]

Equally important to the reform of the episcopate was the reform of religious orders which Richelieu had started with great determination and which met with fierce opposition. There was a general trend towards a return to a more austere way of life and towards the abolition of abuses. Vincent used his important position in the council to do everything he could to encourage this. He gave particular help and protection to the Benedictines of St Maur, the Canons Regular of St Augustine, the religious of Grandmont, the Dominicans and the Cistercians. As well as the help given to the major religious orders we have to remember what he did for other convents and monasteries, especially the convents of nuns where Vincent laboured day in and day out for the election of worthy prioresses and abbesses, for the suppression of scandals, the elimination of abuses and the reintroduction of their primitive observance.[41]

'My heaviest cross: the Daughters of St Mary'

In addition to his work for the Council of Conscience, Vincent was directly responsible for another religious order, the Daughters of the Visitation of St Mary, whose direction in Paris had been confided to him by the two holy founders, Francis de Sales and Jane Frances de Chantal.

Between 1622 and 1660, that is to say for a period of 38 years, Vincent was the ecclesiastical superior of the first Visitation monastery in Paris and of the three later foundations, that of St Jacques in 1626, that of St Denis in 1639 and that of Montorgueil in 1660. He very nearly had to take charge, too, of the monastery at Chaillot which was founded in 1651. The first monastery also had an annexe in the convent of St Madeleine. Although this was an independent foundation for repentant women or 'Magdalens', from 1639 onwards it was directed by four Visitation nuns acting as superior and councillors.[42]

The superior's duties were many. He had to preside at the monthly chapter, make the canonical visitation, give talks and spiritual conferences,

---

[40] *S.V.P.* II, pp. 434-435; III, pp. 150, 168, 384 ,503, 630, 631; IV, pp. 31, 47, 105, 148, 165, 171, 198, 314, 334, 517.

[41] ABELLY, *op. cit.*, 1.2 c. 13, pp. 456-466.

[42] *S.V.P.* I, pp. 136, 186; II, p. 84, 420; V p. 344; VIII, pp. 39-42; XIII, pp. 84, 632.

be present at the elections, at profession and clothing ceremonies, celebrate the major feasts of the order, designate confessors, accept new foundations and appoint the nuns who would be placed there.[43]

Vincent's close relationship with Francis de Sales and Jane de Chantal helped him to keep alive the spirit of the founders in their daughters. The nuns were extremely grateful for the benefits that came from Vincent's direction. They appreciated his spiritual discernment, his zeal for the observance of rule, his kindly firmness in giving correction. A number of chosen souls, Mother Hélène Angélique Lhuiller (1592-1655), Mother Anne de Beaumont (+ 1656), Mother Anne Marie Bollain (1599-1683), and many others that it would be tedious to mention, found in Vincent, consolation in their spiritual trials, the prudent and realistic advice they needed, and spiritual direction.[44]

Some extraordinary events happened and Vincent's intervention was looked upon as miraculous. There was one nun who was tempted to despair and was driven to utter terrible blasphemies against God and sacred things. She even went so far as to say that her only God was the devil. A tiny piece of St Francis de Sales' surplice and St Vincent's prayers quickly restored her to health even though the efforts of various prelates, religious and doctors had all failed.[45] On another occasion a lay sister became seriously ill. Vincent went to see her and, when the good nun told him that she was ready to die, Vincent, who had great regard for her virtue, replied gently: 'Oh no sister, not yet', and bending over her he traced the sign of the cross on her forehead. The sister felt that she was instantly cured and she had no more pain or fever.[46]

Did Vincent have anything to do with the vocation of the famous Mlle de Lafayette, Louis XIII's favourite? It was Richelieu who urged her to become a nun so that he could dispose of a rival for the monarch's favour, and this was the indirect cause of the downfall of the Jesuit, Caussin, who was the king's confessor. Vincent's involvement in the affair was strictly in accordance with his official duties as superior of the monastery.

Neither was it Vincent's responsibility to supervise the education of the Visitation nuns' pupils, who included young ladies of the highest rank. Any suggestions to the contrary are completely without foundation.[47] On some occasions he made recommendations about disciplinary matters concerning the students where these affected the religious life of the

---

[43] *Cf. S.V.P.* XIV, pp. 637-640.
[44] ABELLY, *op. cit.*, 1.2 c. 7, pp. 318-322.
[45] *Ibid.*, pp. 331-333; *S.V.P.* XIII, pp. 64-66.
[46] *Ibid.*, p. 319.
[47] *Cf.* A. MENABREA, *Saint Vincent de Paul, le maître des hommes d'État*, p. 85ff.

community but that was all. One such occasion was when Louis XIV came to Paris with his beautiful young wife, Maria Theresa of Austria, the daughter of Philip IV of Spain. This solemn entry took place on 26 August 1660. Bowing to pressure from the most important people at court, Vincent gave permission for all the students to go out with their families and watch the magnificent procession.[48]

The social rank of many of the Visitation nuns meant that Vincent had to mix with high society. In one or other of the monasteries would be found the sisters, cousins or nieces of presidents of parlement, royal councillors, counts, marquises, dukes and royal princes. This world was not unfamiliar to Vincent as the ladies of Charity came from the same background. There were family ties between both, and the illustrious family names of the ladies, Maupéon, Fouquet, Lamoignon, Lhuiller ... are found again in the registers of the Visitation nuns.

In all circumstances Vincent acted with the same impartiality. One of the defects of the old religious orders, and something, which contributed greatly to their laxity, was the easy way that ladies of high rank used family influence to become prioress or abbess in convents or monasteries. Vincent made sure that such abuses did not creep into the houses of the Visitation order. With this in mind, he had them draw up a list of people who, according to the deeds of foundation, could be admitted to the convents, and he made no concessions for others. He even refused to allow one of Queen Anne of Austria's ladies-in-waiting to be accepted into the first monastery.[49]

However, Vincent felt ill at ease with this huge task, not so much because it involved mixing with high society but because the rules forbade missioners to undertake the spiritual direction of nuns. Vincent feared he was giving bad example to the company but defended himself by saying he was acting in obedience to Church authorities.

> 'It is true that I am acting out of step in directing the Daughters of St Mary but I want you to understand that this duty was confided to me before ever the Mission existed; this duty was imposed on me, for my sins, by the blessed bishop of Geneva. On rather, I should say, by providence because I find it a cross, the hardest cross I have to bear, but one that I am obliged to carry though I have made many efforts to be free of it.'[50]

---

[48] *S.V.P.* VIII, pp. 387, 392.

[49] *S.V.P.* 1.2 c. 7, pp. 322-323.

[50] *S.V.P.* VII, p. 200.

We know, in fact, some of the steps he took. After making his retreat in 1646, he took the resolution to resign and he even went on a sort of strike, not putting a foot in the monasteries for 18 months. But the coadjutor archbishop of Paris, under pressure from his aunt, the Marquise de Maignelay, who was an important patron of the Visitation nuns, obliged him to resume office.[51] Shortly before his death he again tendered his resignation. Again the same archbishop, now in charge of the diocese, refused to accept it.[52] By this time Vincent had become an institution and nobody could imagine anyone else leading the works he had founded or directed.

Morality and orthodoxy

The Council of Conscience was also concerned with many other aspects of the moral and religious life of the nation. One of these was the suppression of blasphemy. Vincent had the decrees prohibiting blasphemy renewed as a matter of urgency and he collaborated with the efforts made in this direction by the other great apostle of his time, the famous Fr Claude Bernard, who was known as 'the poor priest.' Another scourge of this period was duelling, and this was vigorously attacked by the Company of the Blessed Sacrament which had the support of Vincent's implacable opposition to the practice, and his many efforts to eradicate it. He was no less active in the struggle to prevent harmful books from being published. There was a striking increase in the number of these that appeared during the turbulent years of the Fronde. Vincent alerted the Council of Conscience and secured the confiscation of published copies and a ban on the printing of others.[53]

Vincent also opposed the Huguenots who often went beyond the concessions allowed them by the Edict of Nantes and the Peace of Alais. Although he was more inclined towards charitable persuasion than violent repression when dealing with heretics, he was adamant that established laws had to be obeyed. The movement of the Illuminati which originated in Spain, had disturbing repercussions in France. By 1630 Vincent had already taken part in the investigation into the *guérinets* sect and the outcome judged in favour of the accused. In the Council of Conscience he had to deal with periodic outbreaks of 'illuminism' in convents. He suggested that learned and prudent visitors be sent there and these discovered quite a number of misguided souls.[54]

---

[51] *S.V.P.* III, pp. 63, 75, 194, 276; IV, p. 287; V p. 603; XI, p. 167; ABELLY, 1.3 c. 14, p. 231
[52] COLLET, *op. cit.*, Vol. 2, p. 276; *S.V.P.* VIII, p. 272.
[53] ABELLY, *op. cit.*, 1.2 c. 13, p. 468.
[54] *Ibid.*, p. 467; A. DODIN, 'Saint Vincent de Paul et les illuminés', *RAM* (1949), pp. 445-456.

Another sect, which was known by the rather conventional name of Jansenism, was the most unorthodox of all the movements at that time and it found in Vincent a determined and invincible opponent. But his dealings with the Jansenists need to be treated in a separate chapter and we will return to this subject later.

Some biographers have presented Vincent de Paul's activities in the Council of Conscience as something of a deviation from the main direction his life was taking, an unexpected addition which is difficult to fit into an otherwise unified and coherent career. This is an optical illusion. Vincent's membership of the Council of Conscience is the logical culmination of his vocation as reformer. The Congregation of the Mission and the charities, the two channels of that same call to transform the Church in France from within, had, of necessity, to lead to changes in structures and in the people who had positions of responsibility. There could be no reform of the clergy without a reform of their leaders, the bishops. This was the view held by Vincent's contemporaries and especially by Anne of Austria, so they put into his hands the means of effecting this work. As royal adviser for ecclesiastical affairs, he had it in his power to effect not a political, but a religious and charitable transformation. In 1644 he declared that he would limit his activities in the Council of Conscience to matters of religion and questions concerning the poor.[55] Taken in this light, rather than the emphasis being put on anecdotes about his position on the fringes of political power, Vincent's years with the Council of Conscience represent the high point of his career.

---

[55] *S.V.P.* II, p. 448.

Chapter XXXIV
M. VINCENT IN POLITICS:
THE FRONDE

An unprecedented revolution

In 1648, people in France might have thought that their country was emerging from the nightmare of war and its train of misery. The victory at Lens (19 August), which consolidated that of Rocroi, was yet another triumph for Condé and coupled with the Peace of Westphalia between France and the Empire (24 October), presaged a speedy and successful outcome to the war against Spain. It was just at this moment that an unexpected domestic problem arose, in the shape of civil war, or rather the series of civil wars, known as the Fronde.

Collet, the eighteenth century biographer of Vincent de Paul, thought that Mazarin was chiefly responsible for the Fronde. He wrote: 'An Italian who had come to the fore in affairs of state and had astutely made himself indispensable to the queen, who was not aware of her own talents in this direction, was partly the reason, and partly the pretext, for an unprecedented revolution in our history.'[1]

Collet's simplistic assessment has long been shared by a good number of French historians but in actual fact the situation was much more complicated.

The timing and the features of the Fronde wars bring them into the framework of a general climate of rebellion throughout Europe which affected, almost simultaneously, the England of Charles I, the Spain of the Count-Duke of Olivares (uprisings in Portugal, Catalonia and Naples), the Holland of William II, the Sweden of Queen Christina and the Ukraine of the Cossack, Jmelnitski.[2] It would be wrong to label all these movements alike. Each one

---

[1] COLLET, *op. cit.*, Vol. 1, p. 466. From among the many books written about the Fronde we would single out, with other works mentioned later on, the book by E. H. KOSSMANN, *La Fronde* (Leiden 1954).

[2] *Cf.* H. KAMEN, *op. cit.*, pp. 363-390.

had its own individual characteristics and the outcome of each was different. But each one had determining features or 'preconditions' which could have turned them all into full-scale revolutions.

'The Fronde', wrote Mousnier, 'was the outward expression of a society and a state in deep crisis.'[3] One of the chief causes of the Fronde was the war that was being waged abroad. It laid an increasingly heavy burden on all sections of society through the range and increased level of taxation which threatened to change the traditional monarchy into a dictatorship. To this must be added economic recession, adverse weather conditions and periodic epidemics which wore down the impoverished people. This led to a permanent state of unrest and a growing number of peasant revolts. One might say that between 1623 and 1648 not a single year went by without some uprising by the peasants.[4] Mazarin continued Richelieu's political policy and everything was subordinated to the prestige of the state, even though achieving this meant ignoring or violating traditional laws and privileges. It was the relentless march towards absolute monarchy.

Both the bourgeoisie of the parlements, and the nobles, regarded this policy as a permanent violation of the laws by which monarchs had governed from time immemorial, and also as an attack on their interests and their influence on society. Both sides set themselves up as defenders of the old order and as opponents of political change. The parlement of Paris, and to a lesser degree the provincial parlements, claimed that they were trying to restore customs that had been in force earlier but this was really only an excuse for rebellion. The parlements argued that since they had the right to ratify royal decisions, it followed that they should have access to all matters of state, and that they had the right to deliberate and pronounce on these, to convoke meetings of the country's representatives and even to accept or reject laws that were already in force after a *lit de justice*.[5] The rebellion of the princes and barons was rooted in the idea that the monarch's powers were shared by all the royal family, particularly during the minority of a young monarch. It was also coloured by their understanding of a subject's duties, a concept which was closer to the feudal ideal of voluntary subjection (whereby each man was free to choose his own liege lord) than the modern idea of the citizen being subject to the state. When the two kinds of rebellion happened simultaneously, the state was ready to disintegrate, especially since the nobles

---

[3] R. MOUSNIER, 'La Fronda', in J. H. ELLIOT, *Revoluciones y rebeliones en la Europa moderna*, p. 145.

[4] *Cf.* B. PORCHNEV, *Les soulèvements populaires en France de 1623 à 1648* (Paris 1963).

[5] The term *lit de justice* refers to the king appearing in person before parlement. In such circumstances parlement could not refuse to ratify the king's decisions. *Cf.* R. MOUSNIER, *Les institutions* ..., Vol. 2, pp. 378-379.

and the members of the parlements had the support of the people, or perhaps we should say the rabble, of Paris, Bordeaux and other big cities.

Rebellion did not split French society horizontally but vertically. There were Frondist and anti-Frondist nobles; there were members of the parlements who were pro-Mazarin and others who were against him; and there were townsfolk who fought for either side. The Fronde was not a class struggle and most of the country remained loyal to the king and to the state. Neither was the Fronde a revolution against the monarchy. Its war cry was not: 'Down with the king', but as in Catalonia, Naples, Sweden and Holland (in England it was a very different story), 'Long live the king and down with bad government', or 'Long live the king but down with taxes.'[6]

Chronicle of events

It is customary to divide the chaotic events of the Fronde into two main stages: the Fronde of the parlement (1648-49) and the Fronde of the princes (1651-1653). In fact, it was one continuous succession of incidents, in spite of the intrigues and criss-crossing of interests that made more than one protagonist change his allegiance.

The disturbances of the Fronde began on 26 August 1648, a week after Lens, and they were sparked off by the arrest, on Mazarin's orders, of two very popular councillors, Broussel and Blancmesnil. Mazarin held them responsible for a document approved in the preceding July, which asked, among other things, for the repeal of extended jurisdiction powers and that taxes should be approved by the parlement. After the arrest of the two councillors, the people of Paris took to the streets and their leader was the coadjutor archbishop, Jean François Paul de Gondi. The streets were bristling with barricades for three days. The royal family retreated to St Germain and after some difficult negotiations and the release of the two members of parlement, they eventually signed the pact of St Germain, on 24 October, the same day as the Peace of Münster. But the people's unrest continued; there was growing discontent with Mazarin, and the royal family found itself in an impossible situation. On the night of 6 January 1649, the court fled once again to St Germain and Mazarin entrusted to Condé the siege of the city. Organised resistance to this was led by the first president of the parlement, Molé, and by de Gondi. They laid in a stack of provisions and prepared to

---

[6] For the causes of the Fronde and the ideology behind it we have used R. MOUSNIER, *'La Fronda'*, in H. H. ELLIOT, *op. cit.*, pp. 144-173; *cf. ibid.*, 'Quelques raisons de la Fronde. Les causes des journées révolutionnaires parisiennes de 1648', *XVII Siècle* (1949), pp. 33-78; H. KAMEN, *op. cit.*, pp. 369-375; R. MANDROU, *op. cit.*, p. 55.

defend the city walls. But time was on Mazarin's side. After two months the citizens of Paris asked for negotiations to begin, and on March 11 1649, the Concorde of Reuil was signed with concessions made on both sides. This marked the end of the parlement Fronde.

The years 1649 and 1650 saw an uneasy truce with the web of alliances being woven and unwoven hundreds of times. Mazarin and Condé became sworn enemies. De Gondi supported first one and then the other as he became involved in the web of intrigue, ambition, envy and greed where the ordinary people were just pawns or puppets in the game. The three protagonists, Mazarin, Condé and Gondi, hated each other because all three wanted power. The aristocracy which followed Condé, and the ordinary people who were led by de Gondi and the parlement, eventually joined forces against Mazarin. When the minister ordered the arrest of Condé, Conti and Longueville (21 January 1650), the second Fronde erupted.

Plots against Mazarin continued to be hatched all through the year 1650. In February of the following year, the parlement persuaded the queen to set the princes free and Mazarin was sent into exile. This was a strategic retreat. From his distant exile in Cologne, Mazarin continued to rule the heart and the government of Anne of Austria. There was no reconciliation of minds and hearts even when the king was proclaimed of age on 7 September 1651. Civil war raged throughout the whole kingdom and the situation was made worse by the wars that France was fighting abroad. Condé thought to strengthen his position by making an alliance with the Spanish but this caused dissension in his own party.

Mazarin saw that popular discontent with Condé was on the increase and judged that the time was ripe to return to France with an army of 7,000 mercenaries. This was a mistake because all his enemies joined forces against him. Condé was summoned to Paris and de Gondi, who had been appointed Cardinal de Retz since 19 February 1652, once again inflamed the people against the hated minister. In the outlying districts of Paris there were battles that lacked glory and brought desolation and famine to an already impoverished people. The situation in the capital itself was even worse. Food was scarce and this led to famine and to looting. On 4 July, a mob that went wild after rumours that the parlement was considering unconditional surrender, attacked the town hall to vent their savagery on people that they took to be followers of Mazarin. The situation deteriorated rapidly. The forces of the Parlement could not stomach either the atrocities committed by Condé's soldiers or the anarchy of the masses. They entered into negotiations with the court. The king agreed to dismiss Mazarin in August though his intention was to restore him to power once calm was restored. But the minister's removal was put off indefinitely. In September a delegation of the clergy of Paris, headed, most ironically, by de Retz himself, begged the king to return to Paris. Louis XIV promised an amnesty on condition that the leaders of the Fronde left Paris. Condé, who could expect no mercy from Mazarin's implacable hatred, went over to the Spanish side and took with him his weaponry and provisions. The king's demands having been met, the royal family made their triumphal entry into Paris on 21 October, amid the acclamations of the people who up to then had been in revolt. The Fronde was over. All that remained was for outstanding accounts to be settled. In December 1652, de Retz was accused of inciting the king's uncle, Gaston d'Orléans, to rebellion, and was imprisoned in the château de Vincennes. Three months later, in February 1653, Mazarin came back and was acclaimed, in his turn, by the fickle masses.[7]

The Fronde took its name from the catapults that the urchins of Paris used in their street fights or to show defiance of the city constables. Its rebellion was no more successful than that of the urchin gangs. Its failure accelerated rather than delayed the triumph of the very policies it fought against. From now on nothing could halt the advent of absolute monarchy.

'We must continue distributing alms'

Vincent, and his two houses of St Lazare and the Bons Enfants, suffered the privations and inconveniences caused by these events, as did all the other people living in Paris. In January 1649 Vincent went on a journey, which we will discuss in detail later on. In his absence, and notwithstanding the good will of the magistrates who appointed an armed guard of four men 'to protect M. Vincent's grain'[8] at St Lazare, the house was commandeered on the instructions of a councillor who claimed he was acting with the authority of the parlement . Under the pretext of inspecting the premises and making an inventory of its provisions, six hundred soldiers billeted themselves at St Lazare for three days, and requisitioned the wheat and flour to sell them at the market. Not content with this, they got their hands on the keys of the house and searched it from top to bottom, looking for the treasures they imagined it contained. They caused untold damage. To crown it all, they set fire to the wood shed and reduced it to ashes. Fr Lambert, who was temporarily deputising for Vincent, was devastated, and had recourse to parlement. The officials there were indignant that such outrages had been committed in their name. They arranged for the immediate withdrawal of the soldiers but none of the damage was repaired.[9]

---

[7] The events of the Fronde have been narrated an infinite number of times. Most of our account is based on R. MOUSNIER, *Les institutions* ..., Vol. 2, pp. 587-606.
[8] COLLET, *op. cit.*, Vol. 1, p. 503.
[9] ABELLY, *op. cit.*, 1.1 c. 39, pp. 182-183.

Vincent followed each day's events from afar, and sent detailed instructions to Fr Lambert. St Lazare and the Bons Enfants were almost completely evacuated and at the seminary of St Charles numbers were reduced to the minimum[10] so as to be able 'to continue distributing alms.'[11] No setback could make Vincent give up his active and effective works of charity.

The farm at Orsigny had been pillaged, too, so Vincent instructed them to take out a loan of 16,000 *livres* so that they could help people in distress. The amount of aid distributed broke all records. More than 2,000 people received a daily ration of bread and soup at the gates of St Lazare. The parlement had decreed that anyone with surplus food should sell wheat at the fixed price of 10 *livres* a bushel; Vincent ordered his wheat to be sold for 6 *livres*. St Lazare was in such bad financial straits that Vincent thought one of his priests might go as chaplain to the galleys and so bring in a much-needed salary.[12]

When the concordat of Rueil brought temporary peace during the spring of that year, the food reserves at St Lazare were just about exhausted. In three months they had distributed ten *muids* of wheat, each of which would be the equivalent of about 57 gallons in liquid measurement. The summer was a hard one. The community at St Lazare was reduced to eating rye bread and when this ran out they ate bread made from oats.[13]

'We were more frightened than anything else'

The second Fronde meant just as many headaches for Vincent. He himself was in danger one day when he was coming back from St Denis; most probably he had been discussing business matters with the queen. The sentries did not recognise him at first and they forced him to get out of his carriage and face shouting, threats and violence.[14] The attacks that took place in the outlying areas of Paris grazed the walls of St Lazare on a couple of occasions. The first time this happened was on 13 March 1652, the same day as the battle of St Denis, when some of the skirmishes took place near the priory and at the very doors of the foundlings' home. Nothing worse happened than that they all got a fright. Vincent was not easily rattled. 'Yesterday there was a bit of a disturbance round here', was his only comment.[15] On the night of 1 July the danger was greater. Condé's army was trying to find some point of

---

[10] *S.V.P.* III, p. 417.

[11] *S.V.P.* III, p. 413.

[12] *Ibid.* and ABELLY, *op. cit.*, 1.3 c. 11, pp. 133-134; COLLET, *op. cit.*, Vol. 1, p. 467.

[13] COLLET, *op. cit.*, Vol. 1, p. 479.

[14] COLLET, *op. cit.*, Vol. 1, p. 605.

[15] *S.V.P.* IV, p. 382.

entrance into the capital and surrounded Paris during that night's sortie. As they were passing St Lazare, eight soldiers took it on themselves to pillage the seminary of St Charles. They did not think twice about it but entered the building, and not content with the money and the provisions Fr Alméras offered them, they searched the entire house, going into all the rooms, forcing open chests and cupboards, and taking away anything that caught their fancy. All of a sudden two men from the king's army appeared; one was a Swiss and the other was one of the Duke de Bouillon's coachdrivers. They set upon the intruders, forced them to abandon their booty, and drove them away. Then they stayed all night to guard the house. Vincent believed that the two men must have been sent by God since he had no idea who they were, but from then on he took precautions. On his instructions, a small detachment of armed men remained in the house, and he himself kept guard at night with another six or seven members of the community. There were no further incidents. In fact, Vincent commented: 'We got more of a fright than anything else.'[16]

Fr le Gros got rather more than a fright on the famous day of 4 July. Vincent had commissioned him to represent St Lazare at a meeting, so he made his way to the municipal offices. When fighting broke out and Mazarin's supporters started to kill people, he found somewhere to hide and stayed there all night, 'in grave danger of being killed or injured.' During the final days of the revolt Vincent began to think that these frenzied mobs would destroy the capital completely.[17]

St Lazare suffered serious financial losses. No coaches could travel, so this meant the tax on this service could not be collected, and Vincent calculated their lost income as 23,000 *livres*.[18] Added to that would be the loss of their entire harvest which would have come to something between 26 and 30 *muids* of wheat.[19] Vincent thought of sending the students at St Lazare to Le Mans as the cost of living was lower there than in the capital.[20]

But one way or another the missioners were able to overcome their difficulties. Many people were worse off and had less chance of improving their situation; there were the poor, 'the poor people who do not know where to go or what to do, they are suffering and their numbers increase every day—these are my burden and my sorrow.'[21]

---

[16] *S.V.P.* IV, pp. 418-420.
[17] *Ibid.*
[18] *S.V.P.* IV, p. 327.
[19] *S.V.P.* IV, p. 463.
[20] *S.V.P.* IV, p. 307.
[21] COLLET, *op. cit.*, Vol. 1, p. 479.

'Cast yourself into the sea and the tempest will be calmed'

It was not enough to suffer with others, or even to suffer more than others. Vincent's acute awareness of the sufferings of the poor, who are the principal victims of every war, goaded him into action. He could not remain unmoved while people were dying in every part of France. First he had to rush to their assistance and later on we will see what a torrent of self-sacrifice and tenderness he would set in motion to alleviate the effects of both Frondes and of the war abroad. But he had to try, also, to cut out the roots of so many miseries. This is the sole motive for what has been called Vincent de Paul's political action, an unfortunate term if people take it to mean that Vincent was motivated by party interests, personal preferences, ambition for power, or a particular ideology. You will not find any of these in any of Vincent's words or actions. His only concern was to alleviate the sufferings of the poor.

The disturbances had hardly begun when Vincent took a step, which was so daring and courageous that we can only explain it as his anxiety to shield the poor people of France from further horrors and misery. As already mentioned, the court had fled from Paris on 6 January 1649, to set up residence at St Germain. Just over a week later, on 13 January, Vincent set off in the same direction. The duties which kept him in contact with the important people in both factions had convinced him that peace could only be achieved if Mazarin were dismissed. He decided to act in a way that had always been very successful in his direction of his congregation: he would give a charitable admonition and a measure of fraternal correction. With just one brother for company, Vincent left St Lazare in the early hours of the morning and set off for St Germain. So that no wrong interpretation would be put on this action, he left a written note for his old friend, Mathieu Molé, president of the parlement, and the man he had given sleepless nights to after his son had been nominated bishop. In the note he explained that his only reason for taking such a step was that he wanted to do all in his power to achieve peace. If he had not gone to see Molé before setting off, it was because he wished to assure the queen that he had not spoken to anyone in the opposite party about his intentions. At the same time he made it perfectly clear that he was not going over to the enemy or switching his allegiance. The only party he supported was the party of peace.

The journey proved to be full of incident. As they passed through Clichy it was still dark, and the sentries, some armed with picks and others with guns, forced the two riders to halt. Vincent's former parishioners were suspicious of everything. Only the day before, a band of German soldiers had sacked the town, and the good peasants did not want to be taken by surprise a second time. Br Ducournau, who was Vincent's companion, had little experience of such dangerous situations and began to tremble with fear. But one of the peasants recognised his former parish priest and suspicion gave way to respect. The people of Clichy gave Vincent all manner of advice about which paths to follow in order to avoid the enemy soldiers. Vincent continued his journey.

At Neuilly there was another scare: the river was so swollen that the waters covered the bridge. It was very dangerous to cross and the people advised Vincent not to attempt it. But Vincent was a good horseman and had many hours of riding experience. Nothing daunted, he dug in his spurs and crossed the angry torrent. Once he was safely on the other side he sent his horse back, so that a good man who had no other way of dealing with the obstacle, could get across. He arrived at St Germain about ten o'clock in the morning and immediately begged an audience with the queen.

Perhaps it was then that the delicate nature of his mission dawned on Vincent. There were rumours at court that the queen would not have a word said against her first minister. One night, one of her attendants was helping her to undress, and the lady remarked that she had been told by the Duke of Elbeuf that Paris was ready to lay down arms as soon as the cardinal was dismissed from office. The queen dismissed her instantly with the words: 'So you are in contact with the enemy! Get out of here! I never want to see you again.'

In spite of his influence with the queen, Vincent could expect to have a similar reception. More important people than Vincent had been sent into exile for less. When the doors of the royal chamber were opened he went in, prepared for anything. Six years earlier, in that same palace, he had soothed this same lady's grief as she looked on her dead husband. Now his words were forceful and insistent. The sufferings of the poor called for sacrifices to be made. The only way to have peace was for the cardinal to go. The queen listened to him in silence, and perhaps in sorrow, because she believed that she needed Mazarin to direct state affairs and perhaps, too, because of the attraction that the Italian minister had for her. To avoid responsibility for such a decision she sent Vincent to Mazarin himself. The situation was getting more and more difficult for the ambassador of charity.

His interview with the cardinal was a long one. Vincent drew on all his powers of persuasion but he was nonetheless forthright. Echoing the prophets, he ended by saying: 'My Lord, bow to misfortune. Cast yourself into the sea and the tempest will be calmed.'

Mazarin, too, tried to shrug off responsibility. Good diplomat that he was, he answered Vincent courteously but did not commit himself in any way. He did not want to make an enemy of the man whose goodwill was so obvious. But neither was he prepared to commit political suicide. Triumphantly he produced the solution.

'Well, Father, I will resign if M. Le Tellier thinks the same way as you do.'

The cause was lost and Vincent knew it. Le Tellier, the minister for war, was Mazarin's creature and it was a delusion to imagine that such a man would turn against his master. That day they held a council meeting to discuss what they were pleased to call M. Vincent's proposal. Le Tellier opposed it for reasons of state and it was agreed that the cardinal should not give up power nor leave the country. The decision came as no surprise to Vincent. All he was worried about was the reason for his failure and he was quick to realise his mistake. Two days later he explained to Br Ducournau: 'I have never found harsh words to do any good. If you want to change people's hearts you have to be very careful not to hurt their feelings.' He was referring to the way he had spoken during his interview with the queen.

A week later he wrote to Antoine Portail: 'I went to St Germain to perform some small service for God but my sins rendered me unworthy of it.'[22]

He almost considered himself personally responsible for the Fronde. Such is the humility of the saints.

'I left with a flock of 240 sheep'

After the failure of his mission at court Vincent made other plans. For the time being, circumstances prevented him from returning to Paris. People in the capital would think that he went to court because he was a follower of Mazarin; people at court would interpret his return to Paris as showing solidarity with the rebels. This is often the fate of an intermediary. Vincent decided to use the time to go round the main houses of the congregation. This was the last of Vincent's journeys that we know about in detail and the account is full of anecdotes. We can only describe it briefly.

From St Germain he sent out to visit Fr de Gondi in Villepreux. From there he went on to Fréneville where the house of St Lazare had a farm. That winter was exceptionally severe and he was obliged to stay there for nearly a month. At the end of February he left for Le Mans. But he did not leave alone. One of the armies, (friends or enemies it does not matter which) had pillaged the farm at Orsigny which was the granary of St Lazare. They had made off with the wheat and the provisions but had left the cattle scattered about in the fields. At the age of sixty-seven, Vincent recalled with nostalgia

---

[22] *S.V.P.* III, p. 402.

his young days as a shepherd boy. He went around gathering as many of the strayed animals as he could, until he had rounded up a flock of 240 sheep. Even after sixty years he had not forgotten how to do this and he knew that the sheep had to be counted one by one. He went on horseback, guiding them through snowy passes, just as in earlier days he had been a shepherd on stilts, and he stayed with the sheep until he was able to leave them in the safety of a farm that belonged to a lady who was a friend of his, at Étampes.[23]

Then, still on horseback, he went on to Le Mans, Angers, Rennes, St Méen, Nantes and Luçon. The whole journey was spiced with adventure. In the little village of Durtal, between Le Mans and Angers, he fell into the river and was nearly drowned. Fortunately, he was rescued, thanks to the speedy intervention of a missioner who jumped into the water. Not far from Rennes, he nearly fell into the waters round a mill. When he reached the city, an angry Frondist made a threatening gesture as if to shoot him and said: 'I would not be a bit surprised if somebody blew your brains out.' And saying this, he left the inn where they had been and went off to sleep in the hedgerow. The local magistrates made Vincent change his travel plans.

'My ignominy'

Vincent had intended to go from Luçon to Saintes. But in the meantime the concorde of Rueil had been signed and the queen ordered him to return to Paris. So he started the return journey via Richelieu, but when he arrived there he fell ill. Everyone was worried. From St Lazare they sent an infirmarian, Alexandre Veronne, who was the best person to look after Vincent. Louise de Marillac was very concerned and wrote to him. The Duchess d'Aiguillon sent a pair of horses and the carriage which the ladies of Charity had given him some years earlier and which he was reluctant to use. He returned to Paris in it towards the middle of July. As soon as he got back to St Lazare he returned the two horses to the duchess. He would rather stay shut up in St Lazare than go about in a carriage. But the duchess was adamant. She spoke to the queen and to the archbishop, and both the civil and the ecclesiastical authorities formally ordered him to use it. After this, Vincent travelled about like a gentleman, in his own carriage. He always referred to it as 'his ignominy.'[24]

---

[23] *S.V.P.* III, p. 412.

[24] An account of this journey, which is now lost, was written by Vincent's companion, Br Ducournau. We have used the summary of this made by Abelly (*op. cit.*, 1.1 c. 39, pp. 181-186) and Collet (*op. cit.*, Vol. 1, pp. 468-478).

'Yesterday I spoke to the queen'

During the second Fronde, the Fronde of the princes, Vincent intensified still further his efforts to secure peace. His friendship with people on both sides and his unique position as a man of God who had neither interest in, nor ambition for political power, marked him out as the ideal mediator between them. He exercised this rôle with discretion and impartiality and was very successful. The gaps in documentation for this period do not allow us to reconstruct every step in the negotiations but the texts that do still exist give us at least a glimpse of the main outlines.

In a letter dated July 1652, and preserved by Abelly,[25] Vincent informed Mazarin of the dialogue he had had with both sides. On the previous day Vincent had had an interview at St Denis with Anne of Austria, to tell her of the proposals made by the Duke of Orleans and the Prince of Condé after he had spoken to each of these separately. In Paris he had another interview with the Duke of Orléans and told him what the queen thought. Orléans met up with Condé to compose a joint reply and one of Condé's secretaries, D'Ornano, was to communicate this reply to Vincent who would see that it was delivered to the queen and the cardinal.

The gist of the king's demands was that he required the total submission of Paris and recognition by the princes that the cardinal's policy had been the right one. Given these conditions, he was prepared to make concessions, such as Mazarin's dismissal. Agreement was to be reached through men that both parties could trust, rather than through official delegates.[26]

These initiatives were overtaken by events. The gulf that already existed between the parties was widened on 4 July. On 20 July, the duke of Orleans accepted the title of Lieutenant General of the Realm, setting himself up in open rebellion against his nephew, the king. Vincent continued to maintain contact with both factions. He obtained from the Duke of Orleans a safe conduct which would protect him from unpleasant incidents like the one at St Denis.[27] That same month he would risk his life to help Mazarin's friend, Chancellor Séguier, who was trapped in Paris, to leave the capital by way of the St Lazare's enclosure, so that he could join the court at Pontoise[28] and beg the queen and her generals, Rameville and Touraine, for protection against the troops who were setting fire to crops and preventing wheat from being brought into Paris.[29]

---

[25] ABELLY, *op. cit.*, 1.1 c. 43, p. 206.
[26] *S.V.P.* IV, p. 423.
[27] COLLET, *op. cit.*, Vol. 1, p. 605.
[28] ABELLY, *op. cit.*, 1.3 c. 11, p. 110.
[29] *S.V.P.* III, pp. 429-432.

Negotiations got bogged down and then Vincent thought of another initiative. He would ask the pope to mediate in the conflict. On 16 August he sent a strongly worded petition to the pope in which he gave a graphic account of the country's catastrophes and begged him to intervene and remedy the evils.

'There is no greater remedy for our ills', he concluded, 'than the help that can come to us from your fatherly concern, your affection for us and from the authority exercised by Your Holiness.'[30]

'It does not matter whether you come back before or after'

The Fronde, however, was drawing to a close. Two days after Vincent's letter to the pope, Louis XIV invited Mazarin to leave the country. This was yet another manoeuvre by the crafty Italian. The letter made it clear that his dismissal was only temporary, but for the moment it represented a major concession. An increasing number of men defected from the Frondist ranks at a time when there was growing dissatisfaction with Condé's intransigence.

Mazarin continued to remain at court, and as the cardinal's presence there was the last remaining obstacle to the ending of hostilities, Vincent went a step further. He wrote to Mazarin in what has been described as 'one of the great political moves of the century.'[31] Vincent was asking for the monarchs to be allowed to enter Paris without the cardinal being there to accompany them. Basically this was just the repetition of a suggestion he had made three years earlier at St Germain. To make it more palatable he described the mood in the capital:

I now see Paris recovering from the sad situation it was in before, begging the king and queen to return and loudly acclaiming them. Everywhere I go, and everyone I meet, tells the same story. Even the ladies of Charity, who come from the most important families in Paris, tell me that if Their Majesties return, there will be a regiment of ladies ready to give them a triumphant reception.

Vincent did well to mention the ladies. Mazarin knew that a good number of them came from families that were his bitterest enemies though

---

[30] *S.V.P.* IV, pp. 455-459.
[31] J. MAUDUIT, *op. cit.*, p. 205.

there were also some ardent Mazarinists among them, such as the chancellor's wife and Mlle Lamoignon. One of Vincent's miraculous achievements was to have kept such an assembly of different political persuasions, united in the cause of charity.

Then Vincent studied every single objection to the cardinal's removal and refuted them all. So as to make it abundantly clear that he was not acting from any personal consideration, he ended up by presenting the resignation as a long-term victory. When it came to cajolery, the Gascon, Vincent de Paul, needed no lessons from the Italian Mazarin.

> 'It does not really matter whether Your Eminence comes back before or after the king's arrival, provided you do come. And once the king is established in Paris he can bring Your Eminence back whenever he thinks fit.' In this way 'he will win the support of the people, and in a very short while they will acclaim him again, I am sure.'[32]

Quite a few biographers think that Mazarin's initial reaction on reading this letter was one of anger.[33] There is no reason to suppose that this was the case. Vincent's letter fitted in with Mazarin's own plan. Events took their course in accordance with Vincent's advice and forethought. Mazarin withdrew for a while. The monarchs returned to Paris without him. Vincent, himself, witnessed their majesties' triumphal entry into the capital.

> You cannot imagine how much rejoicing there is on all sides at their return. There is no trace of past troubles and this gives us good reason to hope that the country's internal disorders will soon come to a complete end.[34]

In some sense Vincent had contrived to bring about this happy ending because he had helped to persuade Mazarin to go.

Shortly before the return of the royal family to Paris, Vincent had stopped being a member of the Council of Conscience.[35] This has commonly been interpreted as Mazarin's revenge for Vincent's attitude during the

---

[32] *S.V.P.* IV, pp. 473-478.

[33] *Cf.* COSTE, *M.V.* Vol. 2, pp. 700-701; J. CALVET, *op. cit.*, p. 167; J. MAUDUIT, *op. cit.*, p. 206.

[34] *S.V.P.* IV, pp. 513-514.

[35] We do not know the exact date that Vincent left the council or when the document concerning his retirement was issued, if such a document ever existed. From a letter written by Alain de

Fronde, and in particular, for his letter of 11 September.[36] Such an explanation is in line with the biased view of those who represent Vincent as Mazarin's constant enemy but this is not a true picture of the situation. Other factors have to be taken into consideration.

Vincent had been appointed to the Council of Conscience because of his position as confessor to the queen. Once the king was declared of age this office became the responsibility of the king's confessor. In fact, the Jesuits, Dinet and Annat, who succeeded each other as confessor to Louis XIV, took over Vincent's post in the Council of Conscience. Furthermore, Vincent was now seventy-one years old and although he remained clear-thinking and energetic, he was nevertheless an old man in the eyes of the younger generation. And Mazarin, whose power was consolidated after the defeat of the Frondists, had no further need of support from those sectors represented by Vincent, whose goodwill had been so important to him in the early years of his government.

Looking back over all Vincent's actions in the slippery field of politics, we must conclude that none of these actions was motivated by party politics. The only party he belonged to, and would always belong to, was 'the party of God and the party of charity.'[37] So he was never a politician in the strict sense of the word.

Solminihac to St Vincent, and dated 2 October 1652, we can deduce that this retirement took effect before October 1652. The bishop of Cahors congratulates Vincent on the relief he must feel at leaving office, but he regrets the loss this will mean for the Church. *Cf. S.V.P.* IV, p. 491.

[36] COSTE, *M.V.* Vol. 2, p. 701; J. CALVET, *op. cit.*, p. 167; J. MAUDUIT, *op. cit.*, p. 207.

[37] *S.V.P.* XIII, p. 813.

Chapter XXXV
WAR AGAIN:
PICARDY, CHAMPAGNE, ILE DE FRANCE

Did Vincent really imagine that his influence over the protagonists in France's great drama would put an end to these calamities? Probably not, but it was his duty to try and achieve this, and he had acted accordingly. However, there continued to be wars both at home and abroad. The peace of Münster had eliminated only one adversary, but from a military and political point of view this was nonetheless quite a considerable achievement. But war with Spain was to continue for another eleven years. This, coupled with the Fronde, brought devastation to the frontier zones of Picardy and Champagne and even to the very heart of France, changing the pleasant countryside of Paris into battlefields.

We are not going to describe particular events in the war. Attacks and counter-attacks followed each other as they did during the Lorraine campaign and with equally tragic results. They brought appalling misery for the populace who were victims of brutal harassment by the armies. It did not matter whether the army was friend or foe; both sides were equally guilty of bringing ruin to the people. Generals, whose names have been written on the pages of this sad time in history, are more famous for the havoc they wrought than for any great feat of arms. There was no second Corbie, no second Rocroi, no second Lens. Only the Battle of the Dunes is notable for the valour of those taking part and for its important consequences. On the French side: Erlach, the sinister Rosen, Du Plessis-Praslin, and La Ferté, and on the Spanish side Fuensaldaña, Charles of Lorraine, the Archduke Leopold and Condé; all closed their eyes to the abuses of the soldiery, if they did not actually encourage or sanction them. 'I was given all the territory between the Aisne and the Marne to pillage,' said Rosen when four generals complained to Mazarin about the unbelievable violence of this man's troops.[1]

---

[1] The classic work on the aid given by St Vincent to devastated regions is that of A. FEILLET, *La misère au temps de la Fronde et Saint Vincent de Paul* (Paris 1868), 4th edition, which is the one we used. Notwithstanding the passage of time, this continues to be the indispensable

What happened at Lorraine was being repeated here but on a larger scale. Vincent's works of charity were also repeated but this time the relief measures were even more organised and methodically carried out because Lorraine had been a preparation for this.

'War on all sides; misery on all sides'

For a start, war had the effect of quickening Vincent's religious awareness. He saw the conflict as an evil that God permitted as a punishment for man's sins. The poor were suffering as a consequence of their ignorance and their sins, while the missioners were also guilty because of their neglect and failure to act.[2] For this reason the priests and the brothers were exhorted to offer continuous prayer and to perform acts of penance to turn away God's wrath.

> 'I repeat the recommendation I made to you and which I cannot stress often enough; that you should pray that God will unite the hearts of Christian princes. There is war in every Catholic country; in France, Spain, Italy, Germany, Sweden, and in Poland, which is being attacked on three sides, and also in even the poorest mountain parts and most deserted regions of Ireland. Scotland is not much better and you know the sorry situation England is in. War on all sides, misery on all sides. In France there are countless numbers of suffering people. Oh Saviour, Oh Saviour! If in the four months that we have had war hanging over us, there has been so much misery in France where there is plenty of food every where; what must it be like for those people living near the borders who have suffered this misery for 20 years? Yes, they have known continuous war for 20 years. If they sow crops they have no guarantee that they will be able to harvest them; the armies come along and loot and pillage on all sides, and what the soldiers do not steal is carried off by the constables ...'[3]

As always, Vincent preached by example. Every morning when the community recited the Litany of the Holy Name he would repeat solemnly, the invocation 'Jesus, God of Peace.' In June 1652, he implemented the

---

reference book on account of its accumulation of information and documents used. The sentence we have quoted is on pp. 293-294.

[2]   *S.V.P.* XI, p. 202.

[3]   *S.V.P.* XI, p. 200.

archbishop's instructions that special prayers be said and acts of penance performed on the occasion of the solemn translation of the relics of St Genevieve, by ordering two priests or clerics and two lay brothers to fast each day. A priest would say Mass assisted by the clerics and brothers and they all offered their communion for peace. He did the same himself when his turn came. This practice was continued for nine months, until the signing of the peace of the Pyrenees.[4] Vincent's exhortations to prayer and penance were not confined to the community. He recommended these practices to the ladies, the Daughters of Charity and to all the pious people he knew.[5]

Mobilisation on a large scale

Prayer was just the first thing, and it had to lead on to action. The first news of the alarming situation in these regions reached Vincent in 1650 during the Spanish blockade of Guise and the relief expedition sent by the king of France. The retreating French army had left behind countless numbers of sick or wounded soldiers who had to make the long journey back and left the waysides littered with dying men and corpses. Vincent did as Mlle de Herse wanted, and rushed to the aid of these needy people. He sent two missioners to the area with 500 *livres* in cash and a horse laden with provisions. The resources of this expedition fell very much short of the need. It was not just in the countryside that sick and dying people needed help. The towns were just as badly off if not worse. The armies had reaped the harvest and looted the villages, leaving the peasants without a shirt to their backs. The people had fled to the towns for refuge but nobody could help them because the people here had also been reduced to poverty and had neither bread nor money. Hunger and misery were everywhere. The missioners wrote to Vincent telling him about the situation and begging for help. Vincent immediately called into action his relief-aid procedures. His first step was to convoke a meeting of the ladies of Charity.[6] The first delivery of relief supplies left Paris on 15 July 1650.[7]

      Other people and other religious bodies in Paris also got to hear of the scourge that was devastating the frontier regions. There were initiatives on all sides to combat the tragedy. The Jansenists of Port Royal and the

---

[4] ABELLY, 1.1 c. 43, pp. 199-201; *S.V.P.* XII, p. 458. There is a slight difference between Abelly's information and that given in the conference records. According to Abelly there were three people practising penance: a priest, a cleric and a brother. The records state that there were four people involved, two would be priests or clerics and two would be laybrothers.

[5] ABELLY, *ibid.*, p. 202.

[6] ABELLY, *op. cit.*, 1.2 c. 11, pp. 391-392.

[7] *S.V.P.* XIII, p. 804.

Company of the Blessed Sacrament involved their members and supporters in the movement. Vincent would not be working alone. His greatness lay in being able to consolidate and organise that great outpouring of charity without worrying about where the aid came from or the motives or ideology of the people who helped.[8]

Publicity once more

The first thing they had to do was to organise a publicity campaign. His experience in Lorraine had shown him that this was absolutely essential. On that occasion the missioners' letters had proved a very effective lever for moving people's hearts and gathering in funds. Vincent decided to use the same method again and he would perfect his techniques and extend the range of his influence. Instead of using hand-written copies, he decided to have pamphlets printed and these were distributed all over Paris. These pamphlets indicated the places where alms should be deposited. All this must seem self-evident today when worldwide campaigns for all sorts of needs are a commonplace. In seventeenth century France it was a novelty. The credit for inventing the system should be given to Vincent de Paul.

The printing of these pamphlets was confided to Charles Maignart de Bernières (1616-1662), a former official in the parlement who had resigned his post to dedicate himself to the service of the needy. His close links with the Jansenists of Port Royal did not stop him collaborating with Vincent.

Bernières took the most interesting paragraphs from a selection of letters sent by the missioners and put them together in a short article entitled *Report*. This gave rise to the *Reports on what has been done to help the poor people of Paris and surrounding areas as well as in the provinces of Picardy and Champagne*. Each *Report* was usually eight pages long and had a circulation of 4,000 copies. Its publication fluctuated quite considerably. Between September 1650, and February 1651, it appeared monthly, but after that it came out less regularly. Other ecclesiastical writers such as the Jansenist, A. Lemaistre, and Vincent's great friend Godeau, the elegant bishop of Grasse, published religious works that exhorted the people of Paris to be generous in giving help to the needy.[9]

---

[8] A. FEILLET, *op. cit.*, pp. 225-229; R.TAVENAUX, 'Port Royal, les pauvres et la pauvreté', *Actes du colloque sur le jansénisme* (Leuven 1977), pp. 65-88.

[9] A. FEILLET, *op. cit.*, pp. 226-232; A. LEMAISTRE, *L'aumosne chrétienne ou la tradition de l'Église touchant la charité envers les pauvres* (Paris 1651); A. GODEAU, *Exhortations aux parisiens pour le secours des pauvres de Picardie et Champagne ...* (Paris 1652). The *'Reports'* were put together in one volume which appeared in 1655. *Recueil des relations contenant ce que s'est fait pour l'assistance des pauvres, entre autres, ceux de Paris et des*

The *Reports* were a great success. Alms poured in from generous people and this in spite of the difficulties that were being experienced in Paris itself. Donations, either in kind or in money, were collected in every parish in the capital as well as in the houses of the leading ladies of Charity such as Mesdames Lamoignon, Herse, Traversay, Viole, etc. We know this from the concluding lines of each *Report*. Various other sums of money were collected by the ladies, by generous noblemen or by Vincent himself. Between 1650 and 1652 the average monthly collection was 16,000 *livres*. The administrative part of this work was taken on by the ladies who were also responsible for distributing the alms. They held weekly meetings for this purpose and on these occasions reports from the front line of operations would be read out and there would then follow a discussion about which needs were most urgent, and how they should spend the money that had been collected.[10]

'Br Jean Parre is in charge of distributing alms'

The missioners took on the direct service of the poor and the distribution of alms just as they had done in Lorraine. Other missioners went out to join those who had been sent in the beginning, so that by March 1651, the priests and brothers numbered eighteen,[11] These were organised into small groups and they settled in strategic places in the dioceses of Noyon, Laon, Rheims, Soissons and Châlons. In the *Reports* we find mentioned over and over again the names of small towns and villages in the two provinces: Guise, Chauny, La Fère, Riblemont, Ham, Marles, Vervins, Rosay, Plomyon, Orson, Auberton, Montcornet, Arras, Amiens, Peronne, St Quentin, Catelet, Basoches, Brenne, Fismes, Rheims, Rethel, Château-Porcien, Neufchâtel, Lude, Boul, St Étienne, Vandy, St Souplet, Rocroi, Mesières, Charleville, Donchéry, Sedan, Vaucouleurs ... These same names figure in the great successes of the war but they show the other side of the story, too. Every glorious victory brought terrible misery with it and this was recorded in detail by the missioners in their letters. These same details went into the *Reports* that were circulated to appeal to the compassion of the people in Paris. For centuries, history has just repeated the communiqués issued by general headquarters and has ignored

---

environs eet des provinces de Picardie et de Champagne pendant les années 1650, 1651, 1652, 1653 et 1654* (Paris 1655) Another collection of the *'Reports'* can be found in what is known as the Thoissy source references and these were used by Feille and Maynard (*op. cit.*, Vol. 4, p. 170ff). As well as reports about Picardy, Champagne and Ile de France, there is also information about aid given to Berry, Poitou, Beauce, etc.

[10] ABELLY, *op. cit.*, 1.2 c. 11, p. 397.

[11] *S.V.P* IV, p. 156.

the humble reports of the missioners. But it was these who had their finger on the real pulse of history. According to Abelly, Vincent's envoys visited and worked in more than 200 localities.[12] A visitor was appointed to be in charge and to co-ordinate and supervise the work. Fr Berthe[13] was appointed to this office in 1651-52.

The missioners stayed in Picardy and Champagne from July 1650 to August 1652 without a break. Then there was a breathing space in the conflict so the missioners were able to withdraw and it was thought that the nightmare was coming to an end.[14] The truce was providential because in the months that followed Paris suffered from the Fronde. The missioners who returned from the provinces were sent by Vincent to help to relieve distress in the capital. But the 'rest' was only a brief one. In January 1653 the situation again deteriorated.

Once more the missioners hurried back to Picardy-Champagne but this time they were fewer in number. Fr Alméras was in charge as Fr Berthe had been posted to the house in Rome to negotiate with the Holy See about papal approval for the vows. Alméras was in Picardy-Champagne until May 1654.[15]

When Alméras left, the mission team was reduced to three men: Br Proust, Br Mathieu Regnard (the ingenious courier of the Lorraine campaign) and Br Jean Parre who was the trusted envoy for Picardy-Champagne.

> 'At the meetings of the ladies of Charity which are held to assist the poor people of Picardy and of Champagne,' Vincent told his community, 'they read the letters sent to us by Br Jean Parre who is responsible for distributing the alms sent by these good ladies.'[16]

Parre was, perhaps, less resourceful than his companion, Mattieu, but he was better at administrative work and leadership. He acted like a real quartermaster general. Following Vincent's instructions, he found out what the poor people, and especially the clergy, needed. He sent out reports, received and distributed relief supplies, and he even set up confraternities of Charity. When she heard about his activities, the widow of Omar Talon, the attorney general, exclaimed enthusiastically:

---

[12] ABELLY, *op. cit.*, 1.2 c. 11, pp. 396-397.
[13] *S.V.P.* IV, pp. 183, 463, 465, 498.
[14] *S.V.P.* IV, 433.
[15] *S.V.P.* V, pp. 72, 132, 144.
[16] *S.V.P.* XI, p. 339.

If the brothers of the Mission have been given the grace to perform all the good works we have just heard about, how much more will the priests accomplish!

Vincent could not help feeling a bit complacent when he heard these words of praise but he accused himself of this fault in front of the whole community.[17]

Aid to Picardy and Champagne continued, though to a lesser extent, until 1659. The missioners' works were ably backed up by the Daughters of Charity.[18]

'General review'

As we said earlier, the scene facing the missioners when they arrived was heart-breaking. Some thought it was worse than the situation in Lorraine ten years earlier.[19]

The general picture might be summed up as follows: the military campaigns which had inevitably entailed violence, arson, destruction of crops, sacrilege and every form of cruelty and abuse, had brought poverty to the country by depriving it of its natural resources. The country people had fled en masse to take refuge in the towns but these were unprepared for this avalanche of misery and lacked the resources to deal with it. The most immediate and obvious consequence of this was famine, which was universal, and affected even the wealthiest townsfolk. Added to this, the exceptional cold of some unusually severe winters raged against the hordes of refugees, very many of whom had abandoned their homes and had nothing but what they stood up in. In these circumstances it was impossible to prevent the spread of disease. People's weakened constitutions had no defence against scabies, ringworm, dysentery and all kind of fevers. The situation was made worse by lack of sanitation. The over-all result of this was that many people died all over the country. Sometimes the mortality rate was so high that there were not enough people to bury the dead, so infection spread rapidly.

Suffice it to quote the *Report* of December 1650, which gives an over-all view of the desolation and the particular conditions operating in the region of Guise.

'We have reviewed the number of sick people in our department. The figure stays more or less the same because if

---

[17] *Ibid.*
[18] *Report* of December, 1650, in IBAÑEZ, *op. cit.*, p. 382.
[19] *Report* of October, 1650, *ibid.*, p. 376.

some people recover, others fall ill. There are nearly 900 sick people and that does not include people from villages further away. We have no means of finding out about these. In the last four months 4,000 people have died through want of aid. If it had not been for the help that God sent the survivors, then all the sick would have perished. It would make you sad to see them; some are covered with scabies or purpura, others are full of tumours or abcesses, many suffer from swellings in the head, stomach or feet and there are some whose whole body is swollen up. When the swellings burst they discharge so much pus and give off such a terrible smell that the people are a horrible and pitiful sight to behold. The basic cause of all these ills is the awful food they eat. For a whole year now, they have eaten nothing but roots, grass, rotten fruit and some scraps of bread that even the dogs would not eat. Another reason is that they have been living underground; all the caves round Guise are full of refugees. They sleep on the ground and have neither straw nor blankets. The weather is so damp that they might be better off sleeping in the fields than spending the night in those places that are soaking wet.

As we go from one place to another we hear nothing but lamenting. Some people complain that they have been abandoned in their sickness while others mourn for their parents who died of hunger. One poor woman threw herself at our feet, shouting that her husband and children died because she had not a morsel of bread to give them. Another said that if we had arrived earlier she would not have seen her father and mother die in want. They run after us, howling like famished creatures. Some ask us for bread and others ask for wine. People from further off ask us for a little meat. They are so desperate that even the sick will drag themselves the two leagues journey to Guise and they will brave the rain and the bad state of the roads to get some soup from us. This means we have to make more frequent trips to the villages to take them food, and more importantly, to give them spiritual help. All the frontier towns have been left without priests so a lot of people have died without the sacraments and even without burial. This is so true, that only a few days ago, as we were going to visit the sick in the village of Lasquielle, near Guise, on the Landrecy side, we found a house where somebody had died for want of assistance; the head was torn to pieces and the whole body gnawed by animals which had wandered into the house. Is it not heart-rending to see Christians abandoned both in life and in death? We fear there will be more such cases this winter because the people have neither firewood, blankets or clothing and so the cold and the rain will kill just as many people as hunger does.[20]

Soup, clothing, medicines, implements, graves

Organised relief followed a similar pattern to that given in Lorraine. The basic form of aid was soup and this was distributed daily in places that the people had been notified about in advance. Soup was given out by the missioners, by pious volunteers, by the Daughters of Charity or by people who were paid for this work. And soup was taken to the homes of those who were not able to walk.[21] There were different recipes for this soup, which usually contained bread, meat and vegetables. From the end of October onwards, there was more money available and this meant a better diet could be provided. The missioners gratefully acknowledged this.

> We have seen God's very special providence in the increased amount of alms sent from Paris. This is the only place that we can hope to have assistance from. In this region, even the most comfortably off families have only harvested enough to feed themselves, so that those who used to give to others have now got to receive. We have improved the soup by putting in more meat and have increased the number of helpings. Up to now it was one bowl of soup between two or three people; now they have a bowl each. This is putting new life into the people and giving them back the will to work.[22]

Medical supplies were an important part of the aid given by the missioners. They used powders, which seemed to work miracles against dysentery.[23] Whenever they could, the Daughters of Charity used bloodletting, which was the commonest remedy in those times.[24]

---

[20] *Report* of December, 1650; *ibid.*, p. 381-382.
[21] *Ibid.*, p. 382.
[22] *Report* of October, 1650; *ibid.*, p. 375.
[23] *Ibid.*, p. 376.
[24] *Report* of December, 1650; *ibid.*, p. 382.

Bed linen and clothing were distributed to protect people from the cold. The *Reports* give graphic descriptions of the ingenuity displayed by the helpers.

'The sick people have neither clothing nor shifts so we are appealing to you for material. These people sleep on the bare ground or on rotten straw so they are perished with cold. Some old blankets would give them some protection. If you could replace the old ones in your house with new ones then our sick people would benefit and so would your servants. The sick people here who are beginning to recover soon fall ill again because they have no shoes for their feet—an old pair of shoes or clogs costing about 12 *sous* would save them.[25]

Another need that was attended to was the lack of vestments and sacred vessels. Many churches had been desecrated, either from the hatred of religion felt by Protestant soldiers on both sides, or from covetousness of the sacred vessels.

Churches have been desecrated, the Blessed Sacrament has been trodden underfoot, chalices and ciboria have been stolen, baptismal fonts have been destroyed and vestments torn to shreds so that in this tiny area alone, there are more than 25 churches where Mass cannot be said,' stated the reports of November 1650.[26] In the following January they were able to report, 'We have now distributed the vestments to the churches.[27]

Yet another type of aid given went beyond providing bare necessities. In areas that were relatively peaceful, they distributed tools for various trades, farming implements and grain for sowing.[28] Vincent insisted on this form of aid because the gifts had the added value of helping the needy to do something for themselves so that aid could be targeted to the most desperately poor. Help of this kind was given priority as the general situation began to improve. In 1659, when the war was drawing to a close, Vincent wrote to Br Parre:

---

[25] *'Report'* of November, 1650, *ibid.,* p. 380.
[26] *Ibid.*, p. 378.
[27] *'Report'* of January, 1651, *ibid.*, pp. 385-386.
[28] *'Report'* of January, 1651, *ibid.*, p. 385; *Report'* of March-April, 1652, *ibid.*, p. 388.

We have set aside a small amount of aid for these poor peasants who are able to sow a tiny bit of land; I am referring to the very poorest people who would not be able to do anything if they did not get help. We have not anything organised just yet but we will try to collect at least 100 *pistoles* for the work before the sowing season starts ... We would also like to help those who have no land at all to earn their living, and provide work for both men and women by giving the men some tools to work with and giving the women a distaff, tow and wool for spinning. Again, we would only be helping the very poorest people. Now that peace seems to be near, everyone can find something to do and as the soldiers will not be robbing them of all that they have, they can now get something together and gradually get back on their feet.[29]

It was just as necessary to bury the dead as it was to care for the living. This task was all the more urgent because as well as being a work of mercy, it helped to eliminate sources of infection; no distinction was made between civilians and soldiers, or between friends and enemies. In 1650, Touraine's army which then supported the Spanish cause, left more than 500 dead unburied on the outskirts of St Etienne. Vincent instructed Fr Deschamps, the priest in charge of that region, to attend to that need. The missioner was quick to comply with this directive and the work was done effectively and at not too much cost. Thanks to him and his helpers, 'These bodies that will one day rise again' could now be laid to rest, 'in the bosom of mother earth.'[30]

Countless were the young women rescued from the danger of losing their virtue,[31] the orphans that were rescued,[32] the nuns who were helped to survive,[33] and the priests who were saved from starvation by periodic gifts of money and so were able to continue their ministry ...

'You go to war to repair the damage'

As well as helping the missioners, the Daughters of Charity started a new work which had been unheard of up till then, but which was to have a glorious future: they were to help as nurses in military hospitals.

---

[29] *S.V.P.* VIII, p. 72.
[30] *S.V.P.* IV, p. 143.
[31] *'Report'* of November 1650, *ibid.,* p. 378; of January 1651, *ibid.,* p. 385.
[32] *'Report'* of December 1650, *ibid.,* p. 383.
[33] *'Report'* of October 1650, *ibid.,* p. 376.

At the queen's request, they took charge of the hospitals at Châlons, St Menehould, Sedan, La Fère, Stenay; and after the Battle of the Dunes, Calais.[34]

Vincent encouraged them by his conferences and his letters and he drew up for them the spiritual guidelines that were appropriate for those circumstances. With unusual depths of discernment he gives us a picture of the deeply spiritual and warmly human character of these rural nurses.

> The queen is asking for you to be sent to Calais to look after poor wounded soldiers. How humble this should make you feel; to think that God wants to make use of you in such a marvellous way! Oh Saviour, men go to war to kill each other, and you go to war to repair the damage that is done there! What a blessing from God! Men kill the body, and very often they kill the soul if people die in a state of mortal sin; you go to bring them back to life, or at least to preserve life by the care you give to those who survive, and your efforts to show them, by your good example and your exhortations, that they should be resigned to God's will.[35]

Vincent's charity reached out to others as well as his fellow countrymen. A good number of Irish exiles had enrolled in the French army because they could not find any other work or means of support. They played a very active part in the taking of Bordeaux and were then transferred to the northern front where they joined the siege of Arras. When their services were no longer needed there, they were billeted at Troyes in Champagne. The troops were accompanied by a pitiful retinue of the widows and orphan children of soldiers who had died in the campaign. Soldiers and civilians were without any kind of help. Naked and hungry, they fought with dogs in the street over scraps of refuse.

The priests in the house at Troyes informed Vincent about this situation. Once more Vincent called a meeting of the ladies and put before them this new calamity. Then the Irish missioner, Fr Ennery, was sent there with 600 *livres* and a good supply of clothing. The women and girls were housed in the hospital and were taught how to sew and spin. The orphans were placed in charitable institutions or in appropriate employment. After seeing to his countrymen's bodily needs, Fr Ennery prepared them for their Easter duties by preaching a mission in their own language. When the

---

[34] *S.V.P.* V, p. 59; VI, pp. 137, 382; X, p. 507.
[35] *S.V.P.* X, p. 510.

townspeople saw the missioners' works of charity, they, too, were moved to help the Irish people and other needy persons in that area.[36]

'Father of this nation'

The poor people who received help were extremely grateful to their benefactors in Paris and especially to Vincent de Paul. This is frequently mentioned in the *Reports*.

> 'We cannot tell you how grateful our poor people are to their benefactors; they raise their hands to heaven to pray for their prosperity and beg God to grant eternal life to the people who have helped to preserve their mortal life.' 'We cannot describe the response that your charity has aroused throughout all the frontier region; people talk about nothing else; the poor people who have been restored to health by the aid that you sent, are storming heaven for their benefactors.'[37]

Vincent de Paul, in particular, received the most moving messages from governing bodies and from private individuals. Still preserved are seven letters from the councillors at Rethel and messages were sent by the deputy governor of St Quentin and of Rethel, the knight commanders and the chapter of Rheims and the parish priests of many towns who all expressed their gratitude.[38] The most eloquent testimony came from the deputy governor of St Quentin.

> The alms which, thanks be to God and to your kindness, have been sent to this province and which have been distributed so impartially by your delegates, have given life to millions of people who were reduced to direst poverty, by the calamities of war. For this reason I feel myself obliged to send this testimony of the humble gratitude that all these people feel for your goodness. Last week when the troops passed through, we had as many as 1,400 poor refugees in this town and the poor were fed each day thanks to the alms you sent. Besides the peasants there are another thousand people in the town

---

[36] ABELLY, *op. cit.*, 1.2 c. 11, p. 403; *Report* of April-June 1655; *op. cit.*, pp. 414-415.

[37] *Report* of December 1650 and January 1651; *op. cit.*, pp. 382 and 385.

[38] *Cf. S.V.P.*, v.4 and 5 *passim*. Abelly had at hand many more letters which have since been lost (*op. cit.*, 1.2 c. 1, p. 407).

and their only sustenance comes from your charitable help. There is so much misery. The people in the villages have only a little straw to lie on and even the leading citizens of these parts have not anything to eat. There are even some people who can count on an income of 20,000 *écus* but who, in actual fact, have only a scrap of bread and have not eaten for two days. For this reason, and in virtue of the office I hold, I feel obliged to entreat you to continue to show yourself a father to this country and to save the lives of countless poor people who are sick and dying and whom your priests look after in such an impartial and conscientious manner.[39]

An incomplete balance sheet

The best summary of Vincent de Paul's charitable works and the help given to Picardy and Champagne, was the one that he himself presented to the general assembly of the ladies of Charity when he gave them the statement of expenses accounts on 11 July 1657.

'From 15 July 1650, until the previous general assembly, 348,000 *livres* have been sent out and distributed to the poor, and from the last general assembly until today, 19,500 *livres*, which is not much compared with previous years. These sums of money have been used to feed poor, sick people, to gather together and maintain about 800 orphans from the devastated villages and place these in employment after they had been given clothes and training; to support many priests in their parishes that have been badly damaged and which they would have had to abandon as they could not have stayed alive without the help you sent; and finally, to repair some churches which were in such a dreadful state that I cannot describe this without shocking you.

The money was distributed in the towns and neighbouring districts of Rheims, Rathel, Laon, St Quentin, Ham, Marle, Sedan and Arras. This is in addition to money spent or clothing, material, blankets, shirts, albs, chasubles, missals, ciboria, etc. which would come to a lot more.

---

[39] *S.V.P.* V, pp. 377-378.

Indeed, Ladies, we are lost in admiration at the thought of such great quantities of clothing provided for men, women, children and priests, not to mention the vestments sent to churches that had been pillaged and ruined. We might even say that if these vestments had not been donated the sacred mysteries would not have been celebrated and these holy places would have been used for profane purposes. If you had visited the ladies who were in charge of sending these goods you would have found their houses looking like shops and stores belonging to some big business enterprise.

Blessed be God who has given you the grace to clothe Our Lord in the person of these his poor members, most of whom were covered in rags, and many of the children went about as naked as the day they were born. Young people and women had so little clothing that anyone with any modesty at all would not dare to look at them, and all these people were nearly dead with the cold that terrible winter. How grateful you should be to God for giving you the inspiration, and the means, of helping to relieve such great need. How many sick people have had their lives spared! They had been abandoned by everybody, they slept on the ground, exposed to the elements, and were reduced to absolute destitution by the troops and by lack of grain. A few years ago they were even worse off, and at that time 16,000 *livres* were sent every month. People were enthusiastic about giving because they knew that these people were in danger of perishing unless they received help immediately, and they encouraged each other to contribute to charitable relief; but in the last year or so, the situation has improved a bit and there has been a big drop in almsgiving. And yet there are still about 80 churches in ruins and the poor have to travel long distances to hear Mass. This is the situation at present. Thanks to God's providence for the company, we have begun to do something about it.'[40]

This information provided by Vincent shows that Abelly did not exaggerate when he calculated that the total amount of aid given to the provinces of Champagne and Picardy came to more than half a million *livres*.[41] Maynard increased that estimate to two million. Perhaps the romantic historian

---

[40] *S.V.P.* XIII, pp. 804-805.
[41] ABELLY, *op. cit.*, 1.2 c. 11, p. 407.

got carried away and exaggerated a bit, but the information he provides to back up his calculation leads us to think that Abelly's estimate is much too conservative.[42]

The miseries of the Fronde

We have already referred to the temporary halt in the charity campaign for Champagne and Picardy during the summer and the winter of 1652. This was partly due to the relative improvement in the situation prevailing in the frontier zones but more importantly, it was because the Fronde had brought ruin and disaster to the outlying districts of Paris, and this meant that resources from the capital were diverted there.

The general picture of misery here is a repetition of the scenes witnessed in Lorraine, Picardy and Champagne. It is not necessary, then, to repeat the details because the only difference would be in the names of places, the dates of the pillaging and the amount of damage done. A special feature of the desolation in the Paris region is that it was caused by Frenchmen only, and this gives special poignancy to the tragedy.

The reaction of Paris

The proximity of these sad events and the suffering inflicted on Paris itself, led to the relief movement becoming more widespread. Not just Vincent de Paul but all the religious orders as well, the civil and ecclesiastical bodies, the religious associations, the merchant and craftsmen's guilds, as well as private individuals, all collaborated in the work of relieving the catastrophe. The Company of the Blessed Sacrament and the Jansenists played an important part in this work, as they had done in the frontier towns, and this was particularly true of the abbey of Port Royal. The archbishop took over-all command of the movement, but Vincent, because of his experience and his many resources, played a very important part in it, together with his priests, the ladies and the Daughters of Charity.[43] There was bound to be friction and jealousy among such a wide variety of workers, some of whom were deeply divided on religious grounds. There was a misunderstanding between the

---

[42] U. MAYNARD, *op. cit.*, Vol. 4, pp. 242-243.

[43] In addition to Feillet's work that we have already mentioned, for this section *cf.* J. JACQUART, 'La Fronde des princes dans la région parisienne et ses conséquences matérielles', *RHMC* (1960), p. 257-290; L. MEZZADRI, 'Caridad y política: San Vicente de Paúl y la Fronda', *Anales* (1978), pp. 395-412.

ladies of Charity and the religious of Port Royal over a donation sent by the queen of Poland. Vincent was quick to clear up the matter.[44] What interested him was that the poor should be helped, not who did the work. His praise for the work of the Company of the Blessed Sacrament could not have been warmer or more completely free from self-interest.[45]

The charity warehouse, 'this holy storehouse'

The organisation for sending relief supplies had its central headquarters in an institution called 'the charity warehouse' which was thought up by Christophe du Plessis, Baron de Montbard (+1672).[46] Two general store depots were set up: one at the house of Mme de Bretonvilliers, on the Ile St Louis because it was close to the wharves of the Seine, and the second at the palais de Mandosse. Each of these provided for a different part of the diocese, depending on whether the goods were to be transported by water or by land, but both services were co-ordinated. Benefactors could leave their gifts at either of the central depots or at parish collection points.[47]

The stores would accept anything: church books and vestments, medicines, sheets, mattresses, shoes, shirts, food, tools, shrouds, furniture, crockery, kitchen utensils. The list of things asked for and the list of things donated are like some second-hand dealer's catalogue which throws more light on daily life in the seventeenth century than many learned works do.[48] Vincent was full of admiration for this organisation, or to use his own phrase, 'this holy storehouse' which he himself had helped to create.[49]

Religious were given the responsibility for distributing aid and personally caring for the sick. The diocese was divided into ten areas and each was directed by a different religious community: Corbeil was served by the Capuchins, Villeneuve-St-Georges was served first by the priests of St Nicolas du Chardonnet and later by the Jesuits, Brie was directed by the Picpus Fathers, Tournan by the Discalced Carmelites, Gonesse and Lazarches by the Reformed Dominicans, Mont Valérien by Fr Charpentier's priests, and St Denis by the Recollect Fathers. Vincent's missioners were in charge at Lagny and Juvisy. Later on they would leave Juvisy to the Jesuits so that they could care for a new district, Étampes. This was outside the diocese but

---

[44] *S.V.P.* IV, pp. 445-446.
[45] *S.V.P.* IV, p. 540.
[46] ABELLY, *op. cit.*, 1.1 c. 42, pp. 194-195; *S.V.P.* IV, p. 624.
[47] *Mémoire des besoins de la campagne aux environs de Paris*, p. 403.
[48] *Ibid.*, p. 404-406 and 429-431
[49] *S.V.P.* IV, p. 540.

it received help because the people there were in such desperate need.[50]

Full use was made of the publicity measures which had been so successful in the relief of Picardy and Champagne. The *Reports* provided information on the state of affairs in the Paris region and new publications appeared: two documents recording the most pressing needs and the *Magasin Charitable* which was very much in the spirit of today's social welfare information, and gave the public a detailed balance sheet of goods received as well as details of what was sent to each centre and how the funds were used.[51]

Paris itself, had a great number of poor people. When the city was under siege from the royal army, the landed gentry were prevented from collecting their dues and casual day-labourers were unable to go out and work in the fields. All this had social repercussions; there was no demand for articles other than basic necessities so craftsmen, too, were reduced to poverty. Refugees from the country districts added to the army of those in need and this led to hardship all round and a great increase in the number of mendicants. This had happened before, in 1649. The effects of the Second Fronde in 1652 proved more disastrous and lasted longer.

'This is the way that God wishes us to take part in such holy enterprises'

Let us first of all examine the help that Vincent gave to the poor people in the capital. During the most difficult months of the war, May-July 1652, every work of charity was intensified. In a letter dated 21 June 1652, Vincent himself gave a summary of 'the good works that are being performed in Paris' and listed these as:

1. To distribute soup daily to about 15,000 people; some of these are the bashful poor and others are refugees.

2. To accommodate young refugee girls in private houses where they are looked after and receive training. Just think of the awful things that might have happened if they had been left to wander the streets. We have about 100 of them lodged in a house in the St Denis area.

3. To help, also, the nuns that the troops expelled from their convents in the

---

[50] 'Magasin charitable', in J. M. IBAÑEZ, *op. cit.*, p. 417-429.
[51] *Report* of March, 1652ff; 'Etat sommaire des misères de la campagne et besoins des pauvres aux environs de Paris. Mémoire des besoins de la campagne aux environs de Paris', 'Magasin charitable'.

country areas and made them flee to Paris. Some of these were thrown out on to the street; others were lodged in very dubious places, and some had to return to their families. They were all dispersed and at risk so we thought it would be very pleasing to God if they could be brought together in a convent of the Daughters of St Mary. Finally, we have been sent all the poor parish priests, curates and other clergy who had to leave their parishes and flee to this city. They come here every day and we give them food as well as instructing them in the things they should know and the duties they should perform.

This, then, is the way that God wishes us to participate in so many and such holy works. But the poor Daughters of Charity are still doing even more than we are to look after the material needs of the poor. At the house of Mlle Le Gras, in the Faubourg St Denis, they prepare food every day and distribute it to 1,300 bashful poor and to 800 refugees in the St Denis area; four or five sisters give out food to 5,000 poor people in St Paul's parish alone, as well as to the 60 or 80 sick people that they have to look after. And other sisters are doing the same elsewhere.'[52]

In this account Vincent makes no mention of the work done at St Lazare. Here, too, soup was distributed twice a day to some 800 people and after the food was given out, a short mission service would be preached. After the sermon, the men and boys went into the enclosure where they were divided into nine or ten groups or 'academies' and received more specialised catechism instruction from a priest. The women were similarly catered for in other parts of the building. Vincent himself took an active part in this work.[53] A similar mission was organised at St Nicolas du Chardonnet.

'There are too many poor people in Étampes'

In the country areas confided to the missioners the work was even more exhausting. Étampes was one of the worst hit war zones. In January, 1653 it was said that:

> There are too many poor and sick people for us to list them all. By and large we could say that all the inhabitants are either sick or living in extreme poverty. These good missionaries have put the hospital back into working order and, together with

---

[52] *S.V.P.* IV, pp. 406-407.
[53] ABELLY, *op. cit.*, 1.1 c. 42, p. 197.

the Daughters of Charity, they look after the sick. In Étampes there is also a soup kitchen for about 200 poor people. Kitchens have been set up in four other places; at Etréchy, Villeconin, St Arnoult and Guillerval. The kitchen at Etréchy which serves 34 poor widows and orphans uses 12 loaves at 8 *sous* each, so they spend more than 60 *sous* a week and the other kitchens spend proportionally the same amount. They also help the poor people of Boissy-le-Sec, Saclas, Fontaine, Boissy, Guillerval, Dormoy, Marigny, Champigny, St Marc Mineur and Brières at a cost of more than 100 *écus* a week.[54]

The worst thing about Étampes was the tremendous number of deaths caused by repeated sieges and epidemics. The streets were full of corpses and dead animals all piled up together in a most pitiful way. Vincent kept on recommending them to clean up the city and give Christian burial to the dead. The missioners set about this work diligently and afterwards they disinfected the houses and streets to make them habitable again.[55]

Soon the missioners, too, fell victim to the epidemic. Fr David died in July 1652, and Vincent said of him:

'In a short time *explevit tempora multa*. He had only been helping the poor of Étampes for 10 days or a fortnight ...' Fr Deschamps, who was with him, told me that he did all that any man on earth could have done: he heard confessions, gave catechism instructions, gave material help to the poor and the sick, and buried the decomposing bodies of the dead. He had 12 corpses buried at Etrechy because they were infecting the whole village, and after that he fell ill and died.' He was 25 and had been a priest for only one year.[56]

Fr David was the first victim but not the last. Fr de la Fosse (the classicist) who replaced him, was brought back to St Lazare on a stretcher after working at Étampes for a month. Fortunately, he recovered.[57] In September, all the missioners at Étampes fell ill[58] and two of them, Frs Watebled

---

[54] 'Magasin charitable', in *op. cit.*, p. 424. This is our translation.
[55] ABELLY, 1.1 c. 42, pp. 192-193.
[56] *S.V.P.* IV, p. 438.
[57] *S.V.P.* IV, p. 463.
[58] *S.V.P.* IV, p. 488.

and Deschamps, succumbed.[59] A Daughter of Charity also died, the victim of her selflessness.[60]

'Our loss is greater than words can say, that is, if we can call it a loss when God calls people to himself,'[61] was Vincent's terse but supernatural epitaph.

'A waggon pulled by three horses'

A similar incident occurred at Palaiseau, a place which Vincent helped as well as the other districts confided to his care. The first five missioners fell ill and had to be sent back to St Lazare. The same thing happened to the priests who came to replace them. The town had no provisions whatsoever because the army had destroyed the crops. Vincent provided for the townspeople's needs at his own expense. Every morning a waggon loaded with food set out from St Lazare and returned empty each evening. This daily ritual aroused the curiosity of the sentries at the gates of Paris. One day they stopped the driver and asked him what was going on. They suspected him of ferrying contraband or of being in league with the enemy. The good man's explanation failed to satisfy them and they demanded a certificate from M. Vincent. Vincent sent them one and it is thanks to it that we know that every day they sent to Palaiseau, 'sixteen large white loaves, fifteen pints of wine, eggs, and yesterday (4 June 1652) some meat; and as they told me they need flour and a *muid* of wine for the poor sick people of that place, I have sent them today a waggon drawn by three horses and loaded with four sacks of flour and two *muids* of wine ... St Lazare, 5 June 1652.[62]

By 24 July, Vincent had spent 663 *livres* on Palaiseau and this is not counting donations in kind. When he had no money left he appealed to the ladies of Charity for help and asked the Duchess d'Aiguillon to convoke a meeting of the ladies at her house for this purpose.[63]

'We must spare nothing to help the poor'

It would be useless to try and calculate the exact, or even the approximate, amount of money and provisions provided by Vincent de Paul over more

---

[59] *S.V.P.* IV, p. 514-515.
[60] *S.V.P.* X, p. 510.
[61] *S.V.P.* IV, pp. 514-515.
[62] *S.V.P.* XIII, p. 362; ABELLY, *op. cit.*, 1.3 c. 11, p. 124; COLLET, *op. cit.*, Vol. 1, p. 496.
[63] *S.V.P.* IV, p. 424.

than 20 years of continual aid to the devastated regions. Other things are more important. Vincent, who had been so assiduous in consolidating the finances of the houses he founded, now squandered their assets in the service of his neighbour. His conduct and his teaching showed he believed it to be literally true that the money of the company was the money of the poor. 'Spare nothing to save the lives of these poor sick people' was the motto he passed on to Br Nicolas Sené who was so outstanding a worker at Lagny.[64]

They spared neither resources nor effort. During the most critical periods of the Fronde, St Lazare was almost completely deserted. Some of the empty places would never be filled again as the occupants had died, 'arms in hand' to use Vincent's phrase, and 'martyrs of charity.'[65]

The mighty wave of active and compassionate charity towards the poor which Vincent unleashed, rescued France from the charge of inhumanity. This France was notorious for its ambitious cardinals, its scheming bishops, its merciless generals and a soldiery that was crazed with cruelty and envy. Thanks to Vincent and his magnificent band of helpers, another, underground France, started to flourish beneath mountains of self-interest and hypocrisy, the France which, ever since the days of St Ireneus, had taken to itself the gospel message of compassionate charity.

---

[64] *S.V.P.* IV, p. 530.
[65] COLLET, *op. cit.*, Vol. 1, p. 495: *S.V.P.* X, p. 510.

Chapter XXXVI
VINCENT DE PAUL CONFRONTS JANSSEN

Divided generations

The Church reform in France that Vincent championed showed a decided option for the poor but at the same time it was directed towards a vigorous programme of clerical renewal. It was a reform that was undertaken in charity and for charity. Other reformist movements that operated alongside the Vincentian projects, emphasised different values from among the common Christian heritage. There was no lack of confrontation between the different schools of thought.

The first generation of reformers in that century (the generation of de Bérulle, St Francis de Sales, Michel de Marillac, André Duval, Mme d' Acarie) had branched off in two different directions and, although these two lines of thought were not always clearly defined, it was obvious that they clashed with each other. Towards 1618 this led to a violent confrontation between de Bérulle and Duval who were the leading figures in the movement now that the saintly bishop of Geneva was no longer on the scene.

Even more dramatic were the clashes between members of the second generation of reformers who included, among others: Vincent de Paul, the abbot de Saint-Cyran, the two de Gondi brothers Philippe Emmanuel and Jean François, Nicolas Cornet, Garasse, Adrian Bourdoise, Richelieu, Janssen, Bourgoing, Condren, Abra de Raconis, Mère Angélique, Louise de Marillac and Alain de Solminihac.

It could be said that the two generations which followed each other seemed to be divided into irreconcilable factions from the very first moment they appeared on the historical scene.[1]

---

[1] For the classic way of dealing with this subject see ABELLY, *op. cit.*, 1.2 c. 12, pp. 409-440 and COLLET, *op. cit.*, Vol. 1, p. 518-581. The opposite point of view is given in M. DE MARCOS, *Défense de feu Mr. Vincent de Paul, instituteur et premier supérieur général de la Congrégation de la Mission contre les faux discours du livre de sa vie ...* (1668). From among more recent works, apart from the documented synthesis in Coste's *M.V.* (Vol. 3, c.

Jean Duvergier de Hauranne, abbot of Saint-Cyran

The men of Vincent's generation had started off with the same zeal for reform, and at some time or another during their respective careers they were united by the bonds of friendship. It was only gradually that they began to distance themselves from each other until this reached the point where the original close-knit group split up into two opposing factions. A typical example of this was the case of Vincent de Paul and Jean Duvergier de Hauranne, abbot of Saint-Cyran.[2] They had met each other and become good friends in 1624 when their public career was just beginning.[3] The two men had both undergone a conversion experience at about the same time and for a while, at least, they had the same spiritual director.[4] But the human, intellectual and religious path of Duvergier was very different from the one that Vincent de Paul travelled.

Jean Duvergier came from a family that owed its wealth to commerce and its members had come to occupy the highest positions in the municipality of Bayonne, his native city.[5] His father's fortune allowed him to pursue his studies in the most prestigious centres of learning: the Jesuit college at Agen, the Sorbonne where he graduated with an arts degree in 1600, the University of Louvain where he studied theology from 1600-1604, and the Sorbonne again where he came back to study from 1604-1606 though he failed to gain his doctorate.[6]

During this second period in Paris he became friendly with another student whose name will always be linked with that of Duvergier; this was the Flemish student, Cornelius Janssen, future bishop of Yprès and more

---

49-51, pp. 135-208), we have to give special mention to the masterly study by L. MEZZADRI, *Fra giansenisti e antigiansenisti. Vincent de Paul e la Congregazione della Missione (1624-1737)* (Florence 1977), which gives an in-depth treatment of the subject using source material and the most recent writings on Jansenism.

[2] For information on Saint-Cyran it is now essential to read J. ORCIBAL, *Les origines du jansénisme* (Leuven-Paris 1947-1962), 5 vols. Particularly important are Vol. 2. *Jean Duvergier de Hauranne, abbé de Saint Cyran et son temps* (1581-1638); Vol. 3. *Saint Cyran et son temps. Appendices, bibliographie et tables;* Vol. 5. *La spiritualité de Saint Cyran avec ses écrits de piété inédits.* A brief but solid summary is given in J. ORCIBAL, *Saint-Cyran et le jansénisme* (Paris 1961).

[3] *Cf. supra,* c. 12.

[4] J. ORCIBAL *(Les origines* II, pp. 211-248) dated the 'first conversion' of Saint-Cyran between 1617 and 1622.

[5] J. ORCIBAL, *op. cit.,* II, pp. 94-100.

[6] J. ORCIBAL, *op. cit.,* II, pp. 113-137.

commonly known as Jansenius which was the Latin version of his surname.[7] The two friends decided to set up house together so as to share more easily their mutual passion for study. They did this first of all in Paris and later at Camp-de-Prats, the family estate of Duvergier's mother, on the outskirts of Bayonne. The bishop of this city, Bertrand d'Eschaux, appointed Duvergier as canon of the cathedral chapter and Jansenius was made principal of one of the colleges. The seven years that the two men lived together at Camp-des-Prats (1609-1616) have usually been regarded by historians as the period during which the future bishop of Ypres worked out his doctrine on grace. Recent investigations, however, have gone into this question more carefully. The two friends certainly devoted themselves to feverish study and to such an extent that Duvergier's mother complained that her son was killing Jansenius with study.[8] They were anxious to improve on the scholastic methods of research used in the universities; so, they put all their efforts into gaining direct knowledge of the Scriptures and on systematic study of the Fathers of the Church, particularly St Augustine.[9] Jansenius was ordained priest in 1614 and returned to his own country two years later. Shortly after this, Duvergier settled in Poitiers and was appointed theological adviser there by the bishop, Mgr de la Rocheposay.

In spite of his assiduous study, Duvergier was a man who had wide dealings with society. Thanks to these he had access to the highest social and political circles. While at Poitiers he decided to be ordained a priest to defend himself against the criticism of his fellow canons in the chapter. The preparations he made for the taking of holy orders and the acquaintances he made at this time—Sébastien Bouthillier, the Capuchin Joseph de Tremblay, Fr Condren and, especially after 1620, Pierre de Bérulle—all resulted in Duvergier's 'conversion'. The bishop made him abbot of Saint-Cyran and from that time onwards the theologian from Bayonne was known by this title.[10]

Both by temperament and by training, Saint-Cyran was a polemicist. He had taken an active part in intellectual controversies from his early youth. His first two publications, *Question Royale* (1609) and *Apologie en faveur de l'évêque de Poitiers* (1615) were polemic writings. His close friendship with de Bérulle drew him into further dialectical battles. He made devastating attacks on the Jesuit, Fr Garasse; upheld the rights of the secular clergy

---

[7] J. ORCIBAL, *ibid.*, p. 138. So Saint-Cyran did not get to know Jansenius in Leuven, contrary to what was thought by ABELLY (*op. cit.*, 1.2 c. 12, p. 410) and rightly contradicted by Barcos (*op. cit.*, p. 52).

[8] J. ORCIBAL, *ibid.*, p. 139.

[9] J. ORCIBAL, *ibid.*, pp. 139-153.

[10] J. ORCIBAL, *ibid.*, pp. 211-248.

against the religious during the conflict these had with the vicar apostolic in England, R. Smith, who was a follower of de Bérulle; and with the Jesuits E. Knott and J. Floyd. In a book published under the pseudonym *'Petrus Aurelius'*, he defended de Bérulle's principal work, *Les Grandeurs de Jésus* against the charges of illuminism; he supported the founder of the Oratory in his lawsuit against the Carmelites; opposed the introduction of vows into de Bérulle's congregation when their founder died, and wrote a defence of *Le Chapelet Secret,* a work of very dubious orthodoxy published by Mère Angélique, the abbess of Port Royal.[11]

His polemical activities made Saint-Cyran a partisan. Around him were emerging two distinct camps. On the one hand, the numerous friends he had made during the most brilliant period of his career called him 'the oracle of the cloister of Notre Dame', and he was consulted by all the most devout people in Paris, while his influence over the nuns of Port Royal was the decisive lever which gave him an opening into the most important religious circles.[12] On the other hand his adversaries were also increasing in number as controversies multiplied. Lining up against him were the Jesuits, Carmelites, Cistercians, Capuchins and the politicians like Fr Joseph and Chancellor Séguier amongst others.[13]

After 1620, he found himself in opposition to his former friend, Richelieu, and the confrontation became more violent from 1629 onwards. The final break happened for religious, political and personal reasons. When de Bérulle died in 1629, Saint-Cyran became the leader of the defeated devout party. In 1635 he was seriously compromised by the publication of *Mars gallicus,* a Jansenist pamphlet that fiercely attacked Richelieu's foreign policy. Animosity increased when Saint-Cyran pronounced in favour of the validity of Gaston d'Orléans' marriage. The abbot's teaching that attrition does not suffice for sacramental absolution clashed, or at least seemed to clash, with the cardinal's writings on the subject.[14]

Fierce controversy and heated argument often brought to Saint-Cyran's pen, or to his lips, phrases that smacked of unorthodoxy. His zeal for reforming the Church led him to exaggerate her defects. He defended the excellence of the priesthood in a manner very reminiscent of de Bérulle, and this led him to attack, not just the conduct of individual religious, but the religious state itself, and the vows as a means to sanctity. His very demanding notion of the integrity we should have before entering the divine Majesty's presence (another idea he inherited from de Bérulle) inclined him towards a

---

[11] J. ORCIBAL, *ibid.*, pp. 249-375.
[12] J. ORCIBAL, *ibid.*, pp. 377-404.
[13] J. ORCIBAL, *ibid.*, pp. 435-476.
[14] J. ORCIBAL, *ibid.*, pp. 477-517.

very rigorous morality which at times went to excess. His deep study of the works of St Augustine led him imperceptibly towards a pessimistic view of human nature and the corresponding high value he put on the power of grace, something which undervalued the creature's co-operation in his own sanctification.

It was not difficult to exaggerate some of the many ideas in Saint-Cyran's work to the point of interpreting them as heresy, and his numerous enemies were quick to do just that. When the Jansenist scandal broke out, following the publication of *Augustinus,* an accusing finger was pointed at the friendship that had existed between Jansenius and Saint-Cyran. Suspicions were confirmed when the abbé's followers gave their unequivocal support to the doctrines contained in the book.

Issues, and stages in the action

In St Vincent's dealings with Jansenism we have to distinguish the following issues and the stages in the action and these sometimes overlap:

1. His relationship with Saint-Cyran from the early days of their friendship till it came to an end, and to the abbé's death (1624-1643);

2. The controversy over frequent communion (1643-1646);

3. The struggle to have Jansenism condemned (1643-1653);

4. The controversies that arose following the bull *Cum occasione* (1653-1660).

Vincent and Saint-Cyran: from friendship to conflict[15]

We have already mentioned the early stages in the friendship between Vincent de Paul and the abbot of Saint-Cyran.[16] It has to be pointed out that a good deal of the information we have about the closeness of their relationship comes from Jansenist sources and we must be cautious about this. There is

---

[15] P. COSTE, *Rapports de Saint Vincent de Paul avec l'abbé de Saint Cyran* (Toulouse 1914). Coste put together the essential points of his conclusions in *M.V.* (Vol. 3, pp. 135-165). Recently, an interesting interpretation of the subject has been given by J. S. SYMES, *The contrary estimation of Saint Vincent de Paul on the Abbé de Saint Cyran* (New York 1972).

[16] *Cf. supra,* c. 12.

no doubt at all that such a friendship really did exist and this should come as no surprise. In the beginning they both belonged to de Bérulle's circle and they both had a great desire to cleanse and improve the Church. Saint-Cyran gave valuable assistance to Vincent in various matters such as the pontifical approval of the Congregation of the Mission and the acquisition of St Lazare.[17]

Round about 1634 the friendship began to cool off. Vincent refused to allow Saint-Cyran to stay at the Bons Enfants when the abbot had to leave the cloister of Notre Dame.[18] Vincent and Saint-Cyran stopped seeing each other. At the inquiry during his trial, Saint-Cyran attributed this to the distance they lived from each other. Living as he did in St Lazare, Vincent was some distance from Paris and this made it more difficult for them to meet frequently. But he admitted that 'for three or four years there had hardly been any communication or closeness between them.'[19] It is difficult to explain such a breakdown in the relationship on the grounds of physical distance alone. The causes were, in fact, much more profound.

Vincent was uneasy about his former friend's spirituality which was too much in the realms of theory. Vincent's down-to-earth attitude; the active life he led and the practical training and guidance he had from St Francis de Sales and André Duval had led him to join that movement in the Church of France that reacted against mysticism. We have to keep this reaction in mind, and remember that it was not simply a clash of interests that led to the crisis which, over the thirties decade, saw Saint-Cyran rejected by many of his former friends: Fr Joseph, Condren, Zamet, Duval, Vincent de Paul ...[20] Saint-Cyran's theories were completely at odds with the essential values that governed Vincent's line of thought and action. The former's strictness with regard to the sacrament of penance; his insistence on contrition, and on the penance being performed before absolution could be given, were not in keeping with missionary work and the practice of making general confessions. He undermined the value of religious vows and this went against Vincent's intuition that these were necessary to ensure the missioners' perseverance and to keep before them the ideals of the life to which they had been called. His pessimistic view of human nature was in sharp contrast with Vincent's vision of the poor person as an image of Christ. In fact Saint-Cyran had reproached Vincent for this way of thinking. Vincent, in turn, had taken Saint-Cyran to task for having such different views. So, gradually, there was a rift

---

[17] *Cf. supra,* c. 15 and 16.

[18] *S.V.P.* XIII, p. 109.

[19] *S.V.P.* XIII, p. 94.

[20] J. ORCIBAL, *op. cit.,* II, pp. 435-476. The author tends to exaggerate when he gives a clash of interests as the reason for the anti-Saint-Cyranists' reaction against former friends.

between the two men. But Vincent continued to be on the best of terms with many of the abbot's enemies: Fr Condren, the abbot of Prières, Abra de Raconis, the Jesuits Dinet and Annat, young Olier ... He had heard these men condemn Saint-Cyran's unorthodox views and he probably joined in with them. Vincent tried to bring about a reconciliation before the gulf widened into a chasm.

'I went to see M. de Saint-Cyran'

With this in mind, Vincent had a personal interview with his former friend in October 1637.

> I went to see the said M. de Saint-Cyran at his house in Paris which is opposite the Carthusians, to tell him about the rumours that were being spread against him and to find out where he stood in regard to certain ideas and practices which are contrary to the Church's teaching, and which he is said to support.[21]

There were no witnesses to the interview. Statements made by both men during the trial, together with occasional reports given by confidants of each party, make it possible for us to reconstruct, if not a verbatim account of their conversation, then at least its general outlines and the tone of the discussion.[22]

Vincent tried to make Saint-Cyran see the bad impression he was making and to gently persuade him to be more prudent. Basically he reproached him about four matters, the first of which was Saint-Cyran's practice of deferring sacramental absolution for months.[23] The other three points were probably Saint-Cyran's idea that God had decided to destroy the Church and that people who tried to preserve it were acting wrongly; that the Council of Trent had altered the Church's doctrine, and that the just man need follow no law except the interior promptings of grace. At least this is what all the documentation suggests and we can be fairly safe in accepting this as both Saint-Cyran and Vincent stated that they could not remember the precise subjects they spoke about.[24]

During all these discussions Vincent spoke in prudent and measured terms, trying to make his interrogator reflect on the intellectual dangers of

---

[21] *S.V.P.* XIII, p. 87; *cf.* p. 94.
[22] J. ORCIBAL, *op. cit.*, II, pp. 578-579.
[23] *S.V.P.* XIII, p. 87.
[24] COSTE, *M.V.* Vol. 3, pp. 138-146.

the stance he was taking, and of the practical problems that could ensue. At the same time he did not hesitate to say bluntly that he thought the accusations were well-founded.[25] Saint-Cyran could not appreciate the real motive for the visit. He considered it an insult that Vincent should reproach him in this way, and in his own house, and he would give no definite answer about the controversial points raised. He accused Vincent of abandoning him and of letting himself be ensnared by people who were Saint-Cyran's enemies.[26] Then, in a personal attack on Vincent, he made it abundantly clear that he did not think much of the founder of the Mission's intellectual ability. At one point he asked Vincent what he understood by the term 'Church'. Vincent replied that 'it was the union of the faithful under the authority of our Holy Father the pope', to which the abbé replied scornfully, 'You know as little about this question as you do about High German.'[27] He went on to say: 'You are an ignoramus, you are so totally ignorant that I am amazed your congregation can put up with you as its superior.'[28] Perhaps Catholic historians have sometimes exaggerated Saint-Cyran's arrogance but not even his most sympathetic exponents could disguise the complete confidence he had in his own intelligence and the scant regard he had for those who did not share his point of view. This comes across very clearly in all his abundant polemic writings. An equally well-substantiated fact of history is Vincent's long struggle to acquire the virtue of humility. This is exemplified in the answer he gave to the abbot's harsh outburst, 'I am even more amazed than you are, Monsieur, because I am more ignorant than you could ever imagine.'[29]

But Vincent did not want the break to be final. His training in the school of Francis de Sales, and his experience in apostolic work, had taught him that gentleness is the best way of winning over an opponent. So he ended the interview by offering the abbot who was about to leave for his abbey, a horse for the journey. Saint-Cyran accepted the offer and promised to return the horse.[30]

True humility

The incident worried Saint-Cyran very much. A man who was so prone to introspection as he was, needed to explain to himself, and to other people, the reasons for Vincent's opposition. The disapproval of his other adversaries

---

[25] J. ORCIBAL, *op. cit.*, II, p. 579 nt.2.

[26] *Ibid.*, nt. 6; *S.V.P.* XIII, pp. 88-89, 109; I, p. 403.

[27] C. LANCELOT, 'Mémoires touchant la vie de M. de Saint Cyran ...' Vol. 2, p. 301.

[28] ABELLY, *op. cit.*, 1.3 c. 13, p. 203.

[29] *Ibid.*

[30] *S.V.P.* XIII, p. 100.

could be shrugged off as a clash of interests but the case of the superior of St Lazare was something very different. Vincent had a reputation for impartiality and this was borne out by his works of charity and by his virtue, especially his humility. This latter virtue had come across strongly during the interview and Saint-Cyran spent a long time pondering on this during the weeks that followed. His reflections led him to write two long documents.

The first was a letter addressed to Vincent and dated 20 November. Once again he steered away from the essential point of the questions raised and attributed Vincent's attitude to two things: the influence of certain of Saint-Cyran's enemies who claimed to be authorities in matters of doctrine, and Vincent's inability to grasp the subtle problems raised by the controversies.[31]

The second manuscript was a short treatise on humility which Saint-Cyran gave to his friends Le Maître and Lancelot.[32] Why should it have been written specifically about humility? Because if Vincent were really humble, as his conduct and reputation seemed to suggest, then he, Saint-Cyran, had against him the force he feared most, the power of God. He needed to prove to himself that Vincent was not really humble. Without putting this in so many words, this was the whole burden of his treatise.

He gives a penetrating analysis of the characteristics of true humility and the demands that this virtue makes on people, and every line of this analysis is full of Augustinian overtones about corrupt human nature. He then embarks on a description of true humility and it is here that he resolves, to his own satisfaction, the enigma of Vincent de Paul. In the abbot's opinion, Vincent's apparent humility is really secret pride, because one of the conditions for spiritual humility is that, and here we give Saint-Cyran's own words:

> Whatever position a person may hold as superior or administrator in a particular community or in the Church, it does not entitle him to pronounce on matters of conscience or ecclesiastical questions when he knows before God that he does not understand these matters. However, this is precisely what is happening with certain people who undeservedly enjoy a reputation for holiness and prudence. Indeed it sometimes happens that a person can be responsible for a house, and be respected by priests, even though he lacks the knowledge and other necessary qualities for being in charge. God allows this for reasons known only to himself, and often it is to test the person who has this reputation and who should therefore be

[31] The text of the letter is in *S.V.P.* I, pp. 401-406.
[32] C. LANCELOT, *op. cit.*, Vol. 2, p. 302.

watchful over himself, and fear the judgement of God who has allowed him to have this reputation, and consequently, the spiritual direction of other souls. So unless he is very careful, he cannot fail to become conceited and to fall into secret pride, though in his lack of understanding, he will not be aware of this. On the contrary, he will believe that he is following the will of God who draws so many people to this man's house without any effort on his part, and he will answer the questions put to him so as not to disappoint the people God confides to his care. In my judgement, this would be most unfortunate because such a man cannot help but realise that he has absolutely no knowledge of the real nature of the Church and without this he cannot possibly provide an answer to problems that arise in the Church or even discern which people are qualified to do so.[33]

In spite of such subtle reasoning, Saint-Cyran still had some doubts because he could not deny that the Lord was bestowing great graces through Vincent de Paul. In a second, and more extensive study, he tried to resolve these doubts.

God has given some people the grace of helping their neighbour and he has not given this gift to others who have different talents. These should humble themselves at the thought that talented people may not be good at everything.'[34] 'Nothing encourages a person to be humble more than the realisation that God achieves through the apparent knowledge, ability or virtue of some people, what he does not effect through the genuine knowledge, ability and solid virtue of others.[35]

So to Saint-Cyran's way of thinking, the Vincent de Paul question was settled and put in its pigeon hole. His followers would just repeat the opinions of their master, though with less subtlety and more effrontery.[36] In

---

[33] J. ORCIBAL, *Les origines ...,* V, pp. 402-403.

[34] *Ibid.,* p. 394.

[35] *Ibid.,* p. 396.

[36] Saint-Cyran's scornful opinion of St Vincent's learning came to be a cliché among Jansenist authors. So G. Gerberon will say in his *Histoire générale du jansénisme ...,* p. 418, that 'M. Vincent had more zeal than enlightenment' and will call him 'the pious ignoramus', Mère Angélique said that he had 'ignorant zeal' and the RECUEIL D'UTRECHT, states that 'his simplicity prevented him seeing the consequences of the difficult matters he was taking up' (p. 171). *Cf.* these statements are in L. MEZZADRI, *op. cit.,* p. 66.

actual fact the subject had not even begun to be studied. A close analysis o fthe paragraphs we have just quoted, leads us to the conclusion that Saint-Cyran had a complex about Vincent de Paul whom he envied. The rejection he had just suffered amounted to failure and he tried to compensate for this by denigrating his opponent without at all justifying his motives for this.

Vincent's attitude, on the other hand, was one of transparent integrity. He did not reply to Saint-Cyran's letter but interpreted it as a friendly act and an attempt at reconciliation. When Saint-Cyran returned to Paris he visited him again and they dined together though their conversation was on non-controversial subjects only.[37] Most probably it was during this second interview that he showed Saint-Cyran a further mark of affection. It was already common knowledge that Richelieu was beginning to suspect Saint-Cyran and was collecting evidence against him. Vincent suggested to the abbot that he should approach the cardinal directly to vindicate himself and clarify the position he was taking. Vincent himself had done just that when he was in similar difficulties and had been very successful.[38] Saint-Cyran did not think that it was the right moment to approach the cardinal. The threatening clouds that were hanging over his head were too dense to be dispelled by a simple declaration of good intentions. Besides, he did not feel as innocent as Vincent had been. In fact, Richelieu was about to start proceedings against Saint-Cyran. The opportunity to do this came when Paris was disturbed by the withdrawal of the first solitaries to Port Royal, and even more so by the publication of Saint Augustine's treatise on virginity. This included an unfortunate prologue by the Oratorian, Claude Séguenot, (1589-1676) which disseminated many of Saint-Cyran's ideas without the caveats and nuances proposed by the master.[39]

In May 1638, Richelieu gave orders for the arrest of Saint-Cyran and his imprisonment in the château de Vincennes. Shortly after this his trial began.

'I reckon M. de Saint-Cyran to be a good man, one of the best'

One of the witnesses called to give evidence at the trial was Vincent de Paul. This was because among the papers that were confiscated when Saint-Cyran was arrested, was a copy of the letter he had written to Vincent de Paul on 20

---

[37] *S.V.P.* XIII, p. 89.
[38] M. BARCOS, *op. cit.*, p. 40-41.
[39] L. MEZZADRI, *op. cit.*, p. 54-56.

November of the preceding year. Saint-Cyran had written in such ambiguous terms that if they had not been present at the interview, nobody could have said for certain what the meeting was about. And yet it was obvious from it that there were important doctrinal differences in the two men's way of thinking. Richelieu decided to explore this avenue further. The testimony of such an upright man as Vincent de Paul would be crucial. He ordered the latter to appear as a witness.

But Vincent was not prepared to be a docile witness. First of all he refused to make a statement to Laubardemont, the judge in charge of the case, claiming, and very rightly so, that an ecclesiastic could not be summoned to appear before a lay court. His real reason for refusing was probably the sinister reputation that Laubardemont had acquired from previous trials. The expression 'to be a Laubardemont' came to mean being an unjust judge.[40] So Richelieu summoned Vincent on two occasions in order to question him personally. But the cardinal-minister also failed to get Vincent to make a condemnatory statement. The only thing he managed to clarify was that the letter was authentic. The cardinal was enraged and perplexed and he sent Vincent away. Not long after this, he at last appointed an ecclesiastical judge, Jacques Lescot (1593-1656), who summoned Vincent to appear on 31 March and on the 1 and the 2 April 1639. These three interrogation sessions resulted in a document signed by Vincent's hand, which contained the main points of his statements.[41]

In all Vincent's writings it would be difficult to find a text more full of evasions. On the subject of his personal relationship with Saint-Cyran, Vincent acknowledged that he had known him for fifteen years and considered him, 'a good man, one of the best I have ever met', but beyond that his response was that he was not informed or he did not remember what Olier and the others had said about Saint-Cyran; he did not recall advising Caulet not to visit him or forbidding the missioners to have any dealings with the abbot. He did not know what persecution or cabal the abbot was referring to in his letter, or what was the service Saint-Cyran had wanted to perform for the Congregation of the Mission and that he, Vincent, had declined ...

With regard to the main points of the indictment, Vincent did not deny these outright but he sought to present them in an orthodox light. If Saint-Cyran had said somewhere that God had destroyed, or that he wanted to destroy his Church, this should be interpreted in the light of a statement ascribed to Pope Clement VIII, that it might be God's will to transfer the Church to other continents and allow it to disappear from Europe. If people

---

[40] COLLET, *op. cit.*, Vol. 1, p. 266 (nt. f) and 576 (nt. f).
[41] *S.V.P.* XIII, p. 89; M. BARCOS, *op. cit.*, p. 20.

attributed to Saint-Cyran the idea that the pope and the bishops did not constitute the true Church, what he really meant to say was that many bishops were 'children of the court' and had no real vocation to the priestly state. If he was accused of denying the lawful authority of the Council of Trent, what he really meant was that this council was riddled with intrigue. Neither was it correct to accuse him of saying that it was an abuse to give absolution immediately after confession; what Saint-Cyran had said was that the opposite practice was to be commended, that is to say, that absolution should be deferred until the penance had been performed. As for interior promptings of grace, Vincent had heard him speak highly of these but he had not heard him state that these should be the only guiding principles for the godly man.[42]

By and large, Vincent's statement amounted to a defence of the accused. Neither the judge nor Richelieu could find sufficient evidence to condemn the man. However, two statements made by Vincent are highly significant: firstly, that he had kept Saint-Cyran's letter so that he could prove, if necessary, that he did not agree with the writer, and secondly, that he had never regarded the said abbot as his master. Vincent may not have considered Saint-Cyran a heretic but he was not prepared to have any misunderstanding about their differences.

It is not easy to reconcile Vincent's attitude in 1639 with the accusations of heresy that he later made against Saint-Cyran. We will try to find a satisfactory explanation for this later in the chapter.

Saint-Cyran was imprisoned for nearly five years and during all that time Vincent showered on him every possible mark of friendship. When he was released after the death of Richelieu, Vincent was quick to visit him and offer his congratulations. When Saint-Cyran died in October 1643, Vincent went to pray over the abbot's remains though he did not attend the funeral.[43]

---

[42] The complete text of Vincent's declaration is in *S.V.P.* XIII, pp. 86-93. This document, which was lost during the seventeenth century, was published in the following century by the pro-Jansenist, Mgr Colbert, bishop of Montpellier, from the original declaration preserved in his archives. Collet denied its authenticity. Among his reasons for doing so was the fact that the Jansenists refused to put the original in some public place where it could be studied by friends and enemies alike. (*op. cit.*, Vol. 1, pp. 266-267 and 574-580). The Jansenist, Lancelot, however, accepted it as authentic and included it in his book (*op. cit.*, Vol. 2, pp. 493-501). Vincent's biographers continued to believe it was apocryphal until Coste admitted that it was basically true. His reason for accepting the document as genuine is that it gives Vincent's age as 'about fifty-nine' and this would be in accordance with the theory that Vincent was born in 1581, something that would never have occurred to anyone falsifying the document. For the document's history *Cf.* COSTE, *M.V.* Vol. 3, pp. 151-161.

[43] M. BARCOS, *op. cit.*, p. 28.

The controversy over frequent communion

The Jansenist scandal, properly so-called, broke out in 1640 with the posthumous publication of the first edition of Jansenius' *Augustinus*. Jansenius had died in 1638 after expressly declaring his submission to the judgement and the authority of the Church. So the personal orthodoxy of the bishop of Ypres cannot be called into question. On the other hand he does not appear quite so orthodox in his book which claimed to be an account of authentic Catholic doctrine on grace, as taught by St Augustine to refute the Pelagians.

The Leuven edition was quickly followed by two others in France: one was published in Paris (1641) and the other in Rouen (1643). They caused immediate controversy and Belgian and French theologians split into two factions.

There were those who made the accusation that the book showed leanings towards Baianism and Calvinism. On the other hand, Saint-Cyran's friends were quick to defend its orthodoxy. Earlier prohibitions of public debate on the question of grace were renewed by the Holy Office on 1 August 1641, and by Pope Urban VIII in a brief dated 11 November 1642, and again in the bull *In eminenti* of 6 March 1642 and published in July 1643; but all of these went unheeded. Isaac Habert (1598-1668), the future bishop of Vabres, strongly denounced Janssen's teachings in three sermons that he preached in Paris during Advent 1642, and at Septuagesima of the following year. On the other hand, Saint-Cyran's closest follower, Antoine Arnauld, 'the great Arnauld' (1612-1694), published various works in defence of the bishop of Yprès. From his not too uncomfortable prison, the master encouraged him with the words, 'The time has now come to speak. It would be criminal to remain silent.'[44] So it came about that in the eyes of the public, Saint-Cyran's cause was linked with that of his life-long friend, Cornelius Janssen. It did not matter too much that the personal concerns and doctrinal positions of both men were not always identical.

Vincent de Paul did not take part directly in this first Jansenist controversy until 1643 when Arnauld published his book about communion entitled, *De la fréquente communion,* a work that was inspired by Saint-Cyran and written with his help. A trivial incident led to the writing of this

---

[44] L. MEZZADRI, *op. cit.*, p. 65. The documentation concerning the origins of Jansenism is in L. CEYSSENS, *Sources relatives aux débuts du jansénisme et de l'antijansénisme, 1640-1643* (Leuven 1957); *idem.*, *La première bulle contre Jansénius. Sources relatives à son histoire (1644-1653)* (Rome-Brussels, 1961-1962) 2 vols; *id.*, *La fin de la première période du jansénisme. Sources des années 1654-1660* (Brussels 1962-1963) 2 vols. There is a good synthesis of the vicissitudes and the significance of the controversy in L. COGNET, 'Origen y desarrollo del jansenismo hasta 1653', in H. JEDIN, *Manual de historia de la Iglesia* Vol. 6, pp. 68-91; *cf. DTC* VIII, col. 318-529.

book. One of Saint-Cyran's penitents, Anne de Rohan, Princess de Guémené, had received a letter from her confessor advising her to space out the times that she received communion in order to increase her awareness of her unworthiness and stir her to greater repentance. The princess spoke about this to her friend, Madeleine de Souvré, the Marquise de Sablé, whose spiritual director was the Jesuit, Pierre de Sesmaisons (1588-1646). This priest wrote a short treatise for the use of the lady he was directing and this contained ideas that were diametrically opposed to the advice written to her friend. Naturally, it found its way into Saint-Cyran's hands and he confided to his friend, Arnauld, the task of replying to the Jesuit.[45]

De la fréquente communion was a learned work in which Arnauld, while admitting that the ideal would be to have as frequent recourse to holy communion as possible, and even to receive the sacrament daily, restated the right of the faithful to stop receiving holy communion for a while in order to intensify their feelings of unworthiness and repentance. He based his arguments on the practices of the early Church. Whatever Arnauld's intentions might have been, (even today, the interpretation put on the work is very much an open question), the book was, in fact, inviting the ordinary faithful to stop receiving the sacraments. Many theologians regarded it also as an embryonic synthesis of numerous heretical doctrines. This was the opinion of the Jesuit Jacques Nouet (1605-1680), Charles François, Abra de Raconis, bishop of Lavaur, and Denis Petau (1583-1652), to mention just a few. What laid the book even more open to suspicion was the prologue which was written by Saint-Cyran's nephew, Martin de Barcos. He had slipped into this prologue some ambiguous phrases which might be interpreted as a denial of Peter's primacy in favour of hierarchical equality between St Peter and St Paul, a notion which led people to talk about the doctrine of 'the two heads of the Church.'[46]

In the beginning, the controversy was just a speculative exercise. There were bitter arguments at the Sorbonne; anti- and pro-Jansenist stratagems in the cloister of the faculty of theology and the entrenched warfare of the pamphleteers, something we do not need to go into in detail. The book in general, and its prologue in particular, was denounced to the Holy See. The Jansenists sent a delegation to Rome to present their defence of the work and these representatives were Doctor Jean Bourgeois (1604-

---

[45] Arnauld's work was entitled: *De la fréquente communion, où les sentiments des Pères, des Papes et des Conciles touchant l'usage des sacrements de Pénitence et d'Eucharistie sont fidèlement exposés* (Paris 1643).

[46] *S.V.P.* III, p. 66. For the dispute about 'not two heads of the church but only one', *cf.* L. WILLAERT, *La restauración católica* (Vol. 20 of *Historia de la Iglesia*, FLICHE-MARTIN) p. 429-430.

1687) and Doctor Jérôme Duchesne. The latter was a former friend of Vincent and one of his companions during the first missions and the early retreats to ordinands.[47] This was another friendship under threat and yet another proof of the way the reforming generation was being torn in two by the violent storms of the Jansenist controversy.

In a society where civil and ecclesiastical matters were inextricably intertwined, the affair had immediate political repercussions. The principal figures in the government: Anne of Austria, Mazarin, Séguier, and Condé the elder, spoke out against the new ideas. The Council of Conscience had to take a stand vis à vis a problem which so deeply affected the country's religious peace. Vincent, who had been so cautious during Saint-Cyran's trial, was now outstanding for his determined opposition to the followers of his former friend, and in retrospect, to Saint-Cyran himself. His important position in the Council of Conscience made him the key figure in the anti-Jansenist offensive. His contribution was more in the line of organising and co-ordinating activities rather than doctrinal lucubrations, though he did not neglect personal study of the subjects under discussion.[48]

Both within, and outside of, the Council of Conscience, Vincent came to an understanding with Mazarin, Condé, Abra de Raconis and others, by which they worked out the lines of action to be followed. Within the council he kept to Mazarin's unyielding stance even though this meant distancing himself from another old friend, Potier, bishop of Beauvais, who was more in favour of seeking a compromise, but Mazarin interpreted this as connivance with the innovators.[49]

At the insistence of Jacques Charton, the penitentiary of Paris, who had been his adviser on the matter of the vows, Vincent negotiated with Mazarin so that the vacant chair of theology in the faculty was awarded to an ardent anti-Jansenist, Nicolas le Maître.[50]

He used his influence with Cardinal Grimaldi, one of his patrons in the Roman Curia, to deal with the question of two heads of the Church. Vincent recommended to the cardinal books that were written against this doctrine and he urged him to condemn the teaching. This was done almost immediately.[51] But he was still very worried about Arnauld's teaching on frequent communion. What added to his concern was the fact that one of the Jansenist apologists, Bourgeois, was a student friend of Fr Dehorgny, superior

---

[47] *Cf. supra,* c. 10 and 14.

[48] *S.V.P.* XIII, pp. 147-156.

[49] *S.V.P.* II, pp. 498-499; L. MEZZADRI, *op. cit.*, pp. 70-71.

[50] *S.V.P.* pp. 40, 45; ES, p. 41, 45.

[51] *S.V.P.* III, pp. 65-67.

of the house in Rome, and that he had persuaded the latter to take up the new doctrines very enthusiastically.[52] Vincent felt that the orthodoxy of his own congregation was being threatened. To defend this he wrote two extremely long letters to Dehorgny.[53]

'M. de Saint-Cyran ... did not even believe in the councils'

The tone of both letters is one of alarm and this was fully justified in the circumstances. We can leave aside, for the moment, the attacks he makes in the letters on Jansenism in general, because we are more interested just now in noting his judgement of Saint-Cyran as a person, as well as the abbot's teaching and Vincent's evaluation, of the doctrine of frequent communion.

Nine years after stating during Saint-Cyran's trial that he regarded him as 'a good man; one of the best I have ever known',[54] he now affirmed that he was well aware of the plans made by that 'author of new ideas' and that these were just

> to destroy the Church in its present form and have it in his power. One day', he added, 'he told me that God wanted to bring about the downfall of the Church in its present state and that those who were trying to support the Church were, in fact, acting against the designs of God. When I told him that this pretext has often been used by such heretics as Calvin he replied that Calvin had not been altogether wrong but he had not been able to justify his teachings adequately.[55]

In the second letter Vincent revealed the abbot de Saint-Cyran's thinking on the subject of sacramental absolution:

> You would have to be blind not to see ... that M. Arnauld thinks it necessary to withhold absolution from all mortal sins until the penance has been performed. Indeed, I myself have known the abbot de Saint-Cyran to do this, and those who have gone over completely to his ideas continue the practice. But this is outright heresy.[56]

---

[52] The testimony of Bourgeois is in L. MEZZADRI, *op. cit.*, p. 79.
[53] *S.V.P.* III, pp. 318-332 and 362-374.
[54] *S.V.P.* XIII, p. 87.
[55] *S.V.P.* III, pp. 318-319; ABELLY, *op. cit.*, 1.2 c. 12, p. 410.
[56] *S.V.P.* III, p. 365.

The final point concerning Saint-Cyran that we would like to emphasise is that Vincent accused the abbot of duplicity in the tactics he used to conceal his real views. Vincent's testimony lends weight to the idea of 'two Saint-Cyrans' which has recently been the subject of much debate by historians.

> All innovators act like this. They scatter contradictory statements about in their writings so that if somebody takes them up on some point they can always defend themselves by saying they took up the opposite position in another part of the book. I have heard it said that the now deceased abbot de Saint-Cyran would discuss certain truths with people who could understand them in one room, and then go to another room and say the opposite to people who were less able to understand them. He declared that Our Lord acted in this way and recommended others to do the same.[57]

Vincent was even more categorical with regard to Saint-Cyran's heresy when in 1651, he wrote to the bishop of Luçon. On the subject of the proposed Jansenists' submission to the judgement of the Holy See, he thought that most obstacles to this might come from the abbot's followers because

> not only was he unwilling to submit to the pope's decisions but he did not even believe in the councils. I know this very well, Your Lordship, because I had many dealings with him.[58]

In view of this evidence which flatly contradicts Vincent's defending statements on these same subjects during the trial, it is not surprising that for centuries the trial documents have been regarded as dubious, since there is no denying the authenticity of his letters to Dehorgny. Let us see whether an analysis of the circumstances in which the two sets of documents were written cannot validate both of them.

In 1639 Saint-Cyran was accused of heresy and until the man was proved guilty he had to be presumed innocent. So Vincent tried very hard to find an acceptable explanation of words and phrases that could be interpreted in different ways. By 1648, the doctrinal and disciplinary consequences of Saint-Cyran's teaching which were taken up by his adherents, no longer allowed any such favourable interpretation.

---

[57] *S.V.P.* III, pp. 365-366.
[58] *S.V.P.* IV, p. 178.

In 1639, Saint-Cyran was alive and he was being harassed. At worst he was a man with mistaken ideas who had to be given every opportunity to return to the right path. By 1648 Saint-Cyran was dead so his religious stance could not be altered. The man could not retract his opinions so these had to stand.

In 1639 Saint-Cyran was subject to a civil procedure which only secondarily was also a religious one. In 1648 the problem was regarded as a question of faith and of conscience and this was dealt with by the highest ecclesiastical court, the Holy See. The charges, then, should be presented just as they really were, without fear of the political capital that could be made out of them.

Finally, in 1639 Saint-Cyran's followers were only a small handful of ecclesiastics and lay people and they posed only a very remote threat to the faith of Christian people. By 1648 their teachings had become a public danger and their influence is shown by the fact that there were supporters of Saint-Cyran even in Vincent's own community. It was absolutely essential to unmask those who were spreading such pernicious doctrines because these would end up ruining all the work of reform that had been so patiently developed over half a century.

As for the teaching on frequent communion, Vincent set aside all subtle talk about the number of times it was advisable to go to communion and whether it should be a weekly or a monthly practice (a long established tradition tended not to make this too frequent);[59] and he attacked, instead, the ideas of Arnauld whom he judged to be a mere figurehead of Jansenism.[60]

> I think it is heresy to say that it is an act of great virtue to put off going to communion until you are dying, because the Church commands us to go to communion every year. It is also heresy to value this supposed humility more than any kind of good works; martyrdom, for example, is much more excellent. And it is also heresy to state categorically that God is not honoured by our communions and that these serve only to outrage and dishonour him.[61]

Moreover, Vincent attributed the noticeable falling off in numbers of communicants in various churches in Paris, to the ideas circulated by Arnauld.[62] Recent studies have not been able to prove he was mistaken. Other

---

[59] L. MEZZADRI, *op. cit.*, pp. 71-78.
[60] *S.V.P.* III, pp. 321-323.
[61] *S.V.P.* III, p. 371.
[62] *S.V.P.* III, pp. 322, 369-371.

reasons might be given for this decline, but the uncompromising observations made by Vincent are still valid.[63]

The struggle against Jansenism: 'I am ready to lay down my life'

The controversy about frequent communion and the long letters Vincent wrote to Dehorgny, were just a very small part of a much wider conflict, the struggle against Jansenism properly so-called. We have already hinted that his part in the struggle was not primarily an intellectual one. Such was neither his charism nor his mission within the Church. However, Vincent did not neglect to study these questions in so far as they concerned him. This is shown by his documented and lucid study on grace to which we have already referred. We do not know whether he compiled this for his own personal use or whether he meant to distribute it to other people involved in the controversy.[64]

Vincent was mainly concerned with practical matters. He was the undisputed leader and the tireless promoter of the appeal that was made to Rome to have Jansenism condemned. The truths he fought for were so dear to Vincent's heart that he could say that for these 'I am ready to lay down my life.'[65]

This is not a book on theology and so it is not our brief to enter into a detailed analysis of Jansenist teachings. It is an incontrovertible fact of history that the work *Augustinus* exploded like a bomb in theological circles and that many men of good will and sound theological training discovered formal heresies in it. The enthusiastic following of such doctrines by Saint-Cyran's adherents and the defence of these teachings by his most important followers, who in the early days were encouraged by their master; the setting up of a party which did not reject the name 'Jansenist' though they preferred to call themselves 'the disciples of St Augustine'; all gave the movement the recognised characteristics of a religious sect. The idea that Jansenism gained ground, especially among the middle-class, as being the religious protest of the *noblesse de robe* against the blue-blooded aristocracy, would seen to be a fairly accurate assessment, provided the idea is not taken to extremes.[66] To

---

[63] *Cf.* L. MEZZADRI, *op. cit.*, p. 81.

[64] *S.V.P.* XIII, pp. 147-156.

[65] *S.V.P.* III, p. 373.

[66] L. GOLDMANN in 'Remarques sur le jansénisme: la vision tragique du monde et la noblesse de robe', *XVII Siècle* 19 (1953), pp. 177-195, where he anticipates the conclusions he comes to in his work *Le Dieu Caché* (Paris 1955). Another interesting work is that of R. TAVENEAUX, 'Jansénisme et vie sociale en France au XVII siècle', *RHEF* (1968), pp. 27-46.

regard it as a sort of spiritual Fronde, running parallel, and even coinciding in time with the political Fronde, is an interpretation of events that places the rigorous asceticism of the 'party' within a general framework of puritanical rebellion.[67] On the other hand, we should not reduce the phenomenon to purely political terms. Neither Arnauld's allegations and Pascal's diatribes on the one hand, nor Mazarin's opposition on the other, should be interpreted in a purely political sense.[68] This is even more applicable to the attitude adopted by Vincent. In his eyes it was religious values that were being threatened. He saw in Jansenism the embodiment of something he had been afraid of all his life.

> All my life I have dreaded being present at the start of anything heretical. I have seen the terrible disaster caused by the teaching of Luther and Calvin, and how so many people of every class and condition have sucked in their dangerous poison through wanting to taste the sweetness of what was called a reformation. I have always been afraid of falling into the errors of some new doctrine without realising it. Yes, I have been afraid of this all my life.[69]

And this fear was justified. Moving, as he did, in the advance party for reforms in the Church, the danger of a 'pseudo reform' was by no means a remote one. Jansenism gave name and fame to just such a pseudo-reform. At first sight, nothing could have been more pious or well-meaning. Jansenist teaching summed up a whole new spiritual movement, and the most sincere supporters of these doctrines had been among those who started the reform movement but who had gone to extremes, as is always the case with false reforms.[70] Ideas that had originally been acceptable were taken out of context. De Bérulle's concept of humility was transformed into the notion that it is impossible to keep the commandments and to resist grace. The idea of God's sovereign autonomy was reinterpreted as a denial of his will that all men should be saved.

---

[67] R. TAVENEAUX, article quoted p. 34.
[68] P. JANSEN, *Le Cardinal Mazarin et le mouvement janséniste français (1653-1659) d'après les documents inédits conservés dans le Ministère des Affairs étrangères* (Paris 1967); R. TAVENEAUX, *Jansénisme et politique* (Paris 1965).
[69] *S.V.P.* XI, p. 37; ABELLY, *op. cit.*, 1.2 c. 12, p. 409.
[70] Y. CONGAR, *Vraie et fausse réforme dans l'Église* (Paris 1969), pp. 238-239.

'What should we not do to rescue the bride of Christ'

Vincent deplored the spread of these new doctrines. On 2 May 1647, he wrote to Dehorgny:

> The new ideas are causing such havoc that half the world seems to have taken them up. It is to be feared that if some of this party came to power in this country, they would defend this teaching. What would we not have to fear in that case, Father, and what should we not do to rescue the bride of Christ from this shipwreck![71]

An active person like Vincent could not be content with just bemoaning the situation. The important thing for him was action; 'What must we not do!' We have a great deal of documentation about Vincent's activities but all this is just the tip of a much larger iceberg.

His first concern was to combat these new ideas that had spread among the clergy of Paris. With this in mind he set aside two or three sessions of the 1648 series of Tuesday conferences to put them on their guard against these doctrines. As a result of this he got the parish priest of St Nicolas, Hippolyte Féret, and others to retract their allegiance. Féret had been won over to the new teachings during his stay in Alet with the Jansenist devotee, Nicolas Pavillon. With Féret and the parish priest of St Josse, Louis Abelly (who was to become his biographer), Vincent created a sort of secret society to defend orthodox teaching.[72]

Defining positions

In the spring of 1648, and under the aegis of Vincent, a meeting took place at St Lazare between the penitentiary Charton, the syndic Nicolas Cornet, and Doctors Pereyret and Coqueret.[73] Together they worked out the five propositions which summarised the basic ideas contained in Janssen's book. Cornet had these same propositions condemned by the Sorbonne at its first

---

[71] *S.V.P.* III, p. 183.

[72] *S.V.P.* III, pp. 331-332.

[73] L. CEYSENNS has made a study of the leading anti-Jansenist figures in a long series of articles which were later put together in *Jansenistica minora* (Malines, 1951ff.). Outstanding for their information on St. Vincent in particular are Nicolas Cornet (1592-1663), 'Promoteur des cinq propositions antijansénistes', *Antonianum* (1977), pp. 395-495; 'L'antijanséniste Isaac Habert (1598-1668)', *Bulletin of the Belgian Institute in Rome* (1972), pp. 237-305.

meeting on 1 July 1649,[74] and the general assembly of clergy would ask the Holy See to condemn them in a petition drawn up by the bishop of Vabres, Isaac Habert, and presented in May, 1650.[75] Without attributing these propositions directly to Janssen, himself, he made it very clear that these had been taken from Janssen's book. The final text that was presented to the Holy See reads like this:

1. Given their limitations and the fact that they lack the grace necessary to accomplish this, it is impossible for the faithful to keep certain of God's commandments, no matter how much they would wish to do so or try to observe them.

2. Given the state of fallen human nature, promptings of divine grace are never resisted.

3. Given man's fallen state, for him to gain or to lose merit it is not necessary for him to have inner freedom; it is enough that he be free from external constraint.

4. The semi-pelagians admitted the need for interior, prevenient grace, for all actions, even for the first stirrings of faith. Their heresy consisted in claiming that the nature of this grace was such that the human will could either co-operate with it or resist it.

5. To say that Jesus Christ died, or shed his blood for all men together, is semi-pelagianism.[76]

Collecting signatures

After setting the anti-Jansenist campaign in motion, Vincent gave it his unconditional support. In this phase of the operation, his work consisted in using the influence he exerted over many prelates to make sure they continued to support the petition sent to Rome to have the movement condemned. We still have some copies of the circular he wrote with this in mind, and which were addressed to the bishops of Cahors, Sarlat, Périgueux, Pamiers, Alet, La Rochelle, Luçon, Boulogne, Dax, Bayonne and other places.[77] Other people

---

[74] L. Ceyssens ('Nicolas Cornet ...', pp. 442-461) gives a detailed account of this stormy session.
[75] The text of this petition is in *M.V.* Vol. 3, pp. 176-178.
[76] I have translated the Latin text of the 5 propositions as given in the minutes of the meetings of 1 July, 1649 in L. CEYSSENS, 'Nicolas Cornet ...', pp. 445-446.
[77] *S.V.P.* IV, pp. 148, 152-153, 172, 175, 198.

must have received the circular, too, because in April 1651, he wrote to Fr Dinet, the king's confessor, asking him for more copies of the petition because his earlier supplies had run out.[78] At the same time he conspired with his great friend, the bishop of Cahors, to collect more signatures and he worked out a strategy for winning over some reluctant bishops.[79] He sent a second letter to Nivelle of Luçon, using all manner of arguments to convince him that he should sign.[80] He wrote extensively to Pavillon of Alet and Caulet of Pamiers, the two men most opposed to having recourse to Rome, and discussed with them the pros and cons of such a move. Vincent's ultramontanism, something he learned from Duval, is shown at its best in the balanced and moderate contents of these letters.[81]

He had his failures, too.[82] Eleven bishops presented a counter-petition to the Holy See asking for any judgement on the incriminating doctrines to be postponed.[83] Others, including Pavillon of Alet who had been a close friend of Vincent for many years, preferred to abstain. This was a great disappointment for Vincent, particularly as from that date, this old comrade in so many battles for reform, (remember the mission at St Germain and the charities at Alet) was to refuse bread and salt to good M. Vincent.[84]

Co-ordinating forces

But Vincent was not discouraged. The next phase of the operation took place in Rome and the two sides sent their representatives there. The Jansenist delegates were Louis Gorin de Saint Amour, who has left us the most precise if not the most accurate account of these negotiations,[85] and La Lanne, Angran and Brousse who were later reinforced or replaced by Fr Desmares and Dr Manessier. The anti-Jansenist delegation comprised François Hallier, Jérôme Lagault and François Joysel.

In spite of some gaps in Vincent's correspondence for those years, it can be proved that both before their departure as well as during their stay in Rome, Vincent planned the tactics they were all to follow; advised them,

---

[78] *S.V.P.* IV, p. 171.

[79] *S.V.P.* IV, pp. 152-153.

[80] *S.V.P.* IV, pp. 175-181.

[81] COLLET, *op. cit.*, Vol. 1, pp. 538-539; *S.V.P.* IV, pp. 204-210.

[82] *S.V.P.* IV, p. 206.

[83] *S.V.P.* IV, p. 172.

[84] *S.V.P.* IV, p. 210; XIII, p. 195.

[85] L. GORIN DE SAINT AMOUR, *Journal de ce qui s'est fait à Rome dans l'affaire des cinq propositions* (s.1 1662).

provided them with the money they needed, made arrangements for their lodging, and encouraged them at every turn. For their part, the delegates gave Vincent an account of how the discussions were going, told him about difficulties that cropped up and asked his help and advice.[86]

Vincent was the first person they notified about the condemnation of the five propositions and this was even before the bull was published on 9 June 1653.[87] Vincent was delighted at the good news and passed it on to his community[88] and to his friends, particularly his good comrade in labour, Alain de Solminihac.[89] However, he did not look on the Holy See's decision as some personal triumph, but rather as a victory for faith and for truth. From then onwards he worked as hard as he could to prevent the successful party going to extremes and the losers from being humiliated. He multiplied his efforts to persuade the recalcitrants to submit to Rome, and with this in mind he visited the most distinguished among them, starting with the monastery of Port Royal. He did all in his power to win over those who were wavering, especially the dean of Senlis, Jean des Lions, with whom Vincent maintained a lasting if not always easy relationship, and who ended up joining the rebel side.[90]

On the sidelines of the controversies

For Vincent, the bull settled once and for all the question under discussion. All that remained was to accept the judgement wholeheartedly. But not everyone thought in that way. Almost from the very moment that the bull was published, the Jansenists had recourse to the subtle distinction between the question of *de facto* and *de iure*, a controversy that was to continue well into the eighteenth century. Conflicts broke out again and were made worse by the inflammatory language and literary talents of some of the leaders. This was the era of Pascal's *Provinciales* and the fiery responses it provoked from the Jesuits.[91] But that was not Vincent's battle. For him, Rome's word had put an end to it all. As well as this, his departure from the Council of Conscience a few months before the bull was published, relieved him of his

---

[86] *S.V.P.* IV, pp. 400-403, 422, 534.

[87] *S.V.P.* IV, pp. 607-613.

[88] *S.V.P.* XI, p. 156.

[89] *S.V.P.* IV pp. 620-622.

[90] ABELLY, *op. cit.*, l.2 c. 12, pp. 433-438; *S.V.P.* VI, pp. 38, 266-270.

[91] The only possible allusion that St Vincent made to *Les Provinciales* is found in a letter dated 12 December 1657, in which he acknowledges receipt of two copies of a work *Réponses aux Lettres provinciales,* published that same year (*S.V.P.* VII, p. 15).

heaviest reponsibilities concerning ecclesiastical affairs. He therefore confined himself to carefully shielding from contagion the congregations confided to his care: the missioners, Daughters of Charity and the Visitation nuns; and keeping the din of controversy far away from them.[92]

Champion of orthodoxy

In the story of Vincent's life, his struggle against Jansenism is not just an isolated incident which has no connection with his other activities; it is the necessary consequence of the whole direction of his life.

The advent of Jansenism meant that reform of the Church in France was in danger of dying in some cul de sac, or, what was worse, of being a tardy imitation of the Protestant reformation. If Jansenism had triumphed, the real significance of all Vincent's labours would have been lost.

The charities would have been deprived of the theological basis that sustained them, *viz.*, the universal, redeeming love of God revealed in Christ who died to save all. The missions would have lost their *raison d'être*: the forgiveness of sins through general confessions followed by absolution, something which gave new birth to the spiritual lives of the poor. How many of these would have done penance for months or for years while waiting for sacramental absolution? The seminaries could not have continued to instruct good apostolic workers who were well trained in administering the sacraments of penance and the holy eucharist. The Congregation of the Mission would have lost the powerfully binding force of aspiring to evangelical perfection and being supported in this by the vows. Vincent's vision of the Church, something that gave coherence to all his activities, would have been truncated if he had not firmly insisted on unconditional loyalty to the sovereign pontiff.

Although the anti-Jansenist campaign is far from being Vincent's main work, as there was a tendency to claim at one period,[93] there is absolutely

---

[92] *S.V.P.* VI, pp. 88, 533; VII, p. 424; XIII, pp. 678, 734.

[93] The beatification and canonisation of St Vincent coincided with the re-emergence of Jansenist Jansenist manoeuvre in the canonisation process of our saint. A statistical study of the bull contradicts some slight suggestions that this was so. *Cf.* M. EMERIT. 'Une manoeuvre antijanséniste: la canonisation de Vincent de Paul', in *Actes du 99 Congrès des Sociétés savantes,* Vol. 1, pp. 139-150.disputes in France and Italy. This fact was not without its repercussions on the processes. The newly-beatified was used as propaganda by supporters of both sides. The Jansenists tried to block the publication in France of the bulls, by means of the royal veto. Collet had to avail of hospitality in Lorraine, which was not at this time annexed to the French crown, so that he could publish his biography of St Vincent. But it would be wrong to see this as just an anti-Jansenist manoeuvre in the

no doubt that it represents an essential and ineradicable feature of his true historical physiognomy.

Neither is it true to say that Vincent himself embodied the anti-Jansenist movement; we have seen how his actions have to be considered as part of other very powerful forces in the movement as a whole. But without Vincent de Paul, the anti-Jansenist movement ran the risk of degenerating into a squalid clash of interests and sterile disputes between different schools of thought. Vincent de Paul's most valuable contribution was to tip the balance on the scales of the controversy against Jansenius and Saint-Cyran, with the weight of the most sincere man among all the reformers. By doing this he came to the rescue of the movement's orthodoxy and he showed that it was a fundamental error to believe that the Church could be reformed except from within.

The Jansenists had no doubts at all about the important and decisive rôle played by Vincent de Paul in bringing about the defeat of their movement. One of them, Gerberon, wrote this revealing sentence: M. Vincent was 'one of the most dangerous enemies of the disciples of St Augustine.'[94] In all later Jansenist publications there is a continual attempt to discredit Vincent de Paul. The most subtle and comprehensive example of this is the libel written by Saint-Cyran's nephew, Martin de Barcos.

---

canonisation process of our saint. A statistical study of the bull contradicts some slight suggestions that this was so. *Cf.* M. EMERIT. 'Une manoeuvre antijanséniste: la canonisation de Vincent de Paul', in *Actes du 99 Congrès des Sociétés savantes,* Vol. 1, pp. 139-150.

[94] G. GERBERON, *op. cit.*, p. 422.

Part Five

HIS LUCID OLD AGE

(1653-1660)

Chapter XXXVII
FINAL ACHIEVEMENTS, LAST TRIALS

In 1653, when Vincent was 72 years old, he had seen his main works successfully established. He had retired from the Council of Conscience (September 1652), domestic peace was restored to France once the Fronde wars were over (February 1653), Jansenism had been condemned (June), the rules and the vows of the Congregation of the Mission were approved by the archbishop of Paris (August), and Vincent now moved into old age, his final years being physically painful but he remained lucid and hard-working. There was no retirement or seclusion for him. He used the last seven years of his life to tie up loose ends, to prepare to hand over office to his successor, to ensure the continuance of the congregations he had founded, and to fight his last battles.

Loose ends

The most important matters still in hand concerned the definitive establishment of the two communities. The Congregation of the Mission had approval for its vows from the archbishop of Paris but not from the Holy See. Its rules were not yet printed. The Daughters of Charity had not been granted full recognition by the Church and were not officially recognised by the civil authorities.

We know all the effort and labour that Vincent put into achieving these objectives between the years 1653 and 1660, and in every case he was successful as we have shown earlier.[1] On 22 September 1655, the brief *Ex commissa nobis* was issued and this gave approval to the vows of the Congregation of the Mission.[2] On 12 August 1659, another loose end was tied up when a further papal brief, *Alias nos,* gave a ruling on the vow of

---

[1] *Cf. supra*, cs. 20, 21 and 28.
[2] *S.V.P.* XIII, pp. 380-382.

poverty.[3] Previous to this, on 17 May 1658, Vincent had at last been able to distribute to the missioners their *Common Rules* which had just been printed.

The Daughters of Charity were granted full episcopal approbation on 18 January 1655.[4] In November 1657 they received letters patent from the king[5] and on 16 December 1658 these were ratified by the parlement.[6] In 1660, when he had one foot in the grave, Vincent drew up the final version of the rules for the ladies of Charity.[7]

All the institutions set up by Vincent could now calmly face the loss of their founder as well as the passage of time. They were going to live on.

'We read the brief about the vows in Latin and in French'

Vincent wanted to celebrate with some solemnity the ceremonies during which he told them the news about the brief concerning the vows and the *Common Rules*. With regard to the first of these, nothing has come down to us except the official record of proceedings and a brief note by Vincent himself. We know from this that the meeting opened with a conference given by the founder in which he summarised the history of the vows. Then he went on to say:

> We had the brief read out in Latin and in French and I asked everyone if they were willing to accept and abide by it. They all answered out loud that they did accept it and they wanted to thank God and the Holy Father for it. Afterwards they all signed a statement saying more or less what I have just told you and attached to it was a copy of the brief. All this was validated by two notaries.[8]

This was on 22 October 1655.[9] The other houses did likewise during the months that followed[10] and there was great rejoicing. On 25 January 1656, the anniversary of the founding of the company, the priests, clerics and brothers of St Lazare renewed their vows together to comply with the conditions laid down in the brief.[11]

---

[3] *S.V.P.* XIII, pp. 406-409.
[4] *S.V.P.* XIII, pp. 569-572.
[5] *S.V.P.* XIII, pp. 578-585.
[6] *S.V.P.* XIII, pp. 585-587.
[7] *S.V.P.* XIII, pp. 823-828.
[8] *S.V.P.* V, pp. 459 485 496.
[9] *S.V.P.* XIII, pp. 383-385.
[10] *S.V.P.* V, pp. 496 501.
[11] *S.V.P.* V, p. 496.

'Am I dreaming? Can I be the one to distribute rules!'

A much more vivid and picturesque account of the distribution of the rules is given by Br Ducournau who was commissioned by the superior general's assistants to transcribe Vincent's conferences.[12]

Those present were deeply affected by the solemnity of the occasion. There was a feeling that they were witnessing a ceremony that was both a leave-taking and the handing over of an inheritance. The chronicler did not hesitate to compare it to Our Lord's discourse during the Last Supper, 'when he, too, handed the apostles their rules when he gave them the commandment of love and charity.'[13] The atmosphere was heightened by Vincent's words which were spoken in a low voice and with humility, gentleness and fervour.'[14] The subject of the conference was the reasons for observing the rules and the manner in which this was to be done. When Vincent came in, the meeting had already started and a brother was speaking. He said that if they did not keep the rules well at this time, they would not be kept at all after a hundred or two hundred years. M. Vincent made him repeat these words.[15] which summed up the deep feelings of those present at that assembly and their desire to launch the company into the future. Then Vincent took over and gave a short talk on the subject of the conference.[16] Practically every time he made a point, his clear and lucid explanation would give way to an outburst of emotion. Vincent could not hold back the feelings that choked him:

> Oh Saviour! Oh Fathers! Can I be asleep? Am I dreaming? To think that I am the one to be distributing rules! I do not know what we have done to come to this, I cannot understand what has happened; I keep thinking we are just at the beginning, and the more I think about it the further this all seems from human thinking and I realise more and more that only God could have inspired the company to do this. Yes, Fathers, the company.

If this scene reminded the chronicler of the Last Supper, then Vincent evoked for him the figure of Moses giving the law to the people. In imitation of Israel's aged leader, he repeated his blessings on all who faithfully kept the rules:

---

[12] *S.V.P.* XII, pp. 445-450.
[13] *S.V.P.* XII, p. 13.
[14] *Ibid.*
[15] *S.V.P.* XII, p. 2.
[16] The text of the conference is in *S.V.P.* XII, pp. 1-14. The texts quoted and the information that follows are taken from these pages.

A blessing on them, a blessing on their plans and on all their works, a blessing on their coming and on their going, in short, a blessing on them in every way.

But we also ... have reason to fear, and greatly fear, that those who do not observe the rules that God has inspired this company to make, will be cursed by Him, cursed in body and cursed in soul, cursed in all their plans and enterprises; in short, cursed in every way.

'Come, Fr Portail'

All that remained now was to distribute the copies of the rules. Before doing this Vincent made another dramatic gesture. Taking the book of rules in his hands, he invoked God's blessing on them:

Oh Saviour, you who have given such blessings to many books like, for example, the one we are now reading at table,[17] so that people can profit greatly from these, rid themselves of their faults and make progress in virtue. Grant, Lord, your blessing to this book, and pour out on it the unction of your spirit to act on all those who read it, and lead them to shun all that is sinful, renounce all worldly vanities, and to find union with you.

The emotional atmosphere intensified as the distribution began. Vincent called each missioner by name. He began with the most senior member who had been his companion since his days at Clichy and in the de Gondi household and in the heroic days of the Bons Enfants. 'Come, Fr Portail. You who have always put up with my shortcomings. God bless you.' After this it was the turn of Frs Alméras, Becu and Gicquel who were nearest him and sitting on either side of the president's table. One by one they knelt in front of the founder, received the book and kissed it, they also kissed the founder's hand and then kissed the floor. All the priests did likewise and many of them could not hold back their tears. As time was running short Vincent postponed the distribution of copies to the students until the following day, and he said he would give them to the lay brothers as soon as the French edition was available.

Once the rules had been distributed, Fr Alméras, the first assistant,

---

[17] The copyist points out that the book referred to here is *Ejercicio de perfección y virtudes cristianas,* by Fr. Alonso Rodríguez, S.I.

knelt down and, expressing the feelings of all the community, begged Vincent to bless them. The founder prostrated himself on the ground and then pronounced the words that brought this historic ceremony to a close:

> Oh Lord, you are eternal law, unchanging reason, and you rule the whole universe with infinite wisdom. All living things are ruled by you, and all laws governing right conduct have their true source in you. Bless those to whom you yourself have given these rules, and may they receive them as coming from your hand. Grant them, Lord, the grace to observe them perfectly, and right to the end of their lives. Confident that they will do this, and in your name, I, a wretched sinner, give the blessing: *Benedictio Dei omnipotentis descendat super vos et maneat semper, in nomine Patris, et Filii, et Spiritus Sancti. Amen.*

This took place on 17 May 1658, and it brought to an end a long chapter in the history of the Congregation of the Mission and in the life of Vincent de Paul. Vincent would use the conferences he gave during the last years of his life to explain and comment on the text of the rules, both for the Priests of the Mission and the Daughters of Charity. These talks were a final summary of his thinking on these matters and they are truly his legacy.

'We have gained much from this loss'

Vincent was concerned about putting the finishing touches to the company but not just in the spiritual domain. He multiplied his efforts to get outstanding economic questions settled. He obtained from Rome the bull that annexed St Lazare to the Congregation of the Mission[18] and this was ratified by the king in March 1660,[19] while another bull conceded the contested abbey of St Méen to the seminary of the same name.[20] So two longstanding problems were settled satisfactorily. This was also the time when the missioners in Rome at long last got their own house on a farm in Montecitorio, which they bought from Cardinal Bagno.[21]

Not everything turned out to his satisfaction. In 1658 Vincent suffered the biggest financial loss that the Congregation had known since it

---

[18] *S.V.P.* XIII, pp. 372-380.
[19] *S.V.P.* XIII, pp. 412-415.
[20] *S.V.P.* XIII, pp. 387-395.
[21] *S.V.P.* VII, pp. 103 119 128.

was founded. In 1644, under pressure from Prior Le Bon, he had rather unwillingly accepted from the Norais family a large country estate in Orsigny, not far from Paris. In exchange for the property he promised to pay the benefactors a substantial pension for life. The estate was valued at some 50,000 *livres*.[22] Vincent did extensive repairs and had the farm developed. It was a good farm and its produce was a great help to St Lazare. Together with Rougemont, it was the granary of the mother house.[23] A team of lay brothers did the farm work and Vincent paid frequent visits to the place.[24] Sometimes there were losses. Its sacking by troops from the Fronde in 1649 was a catastrophe. That was the time when Vincent personally rescued 240 sheep and 2 horses from the débris left by the attackers.[25]

The worst was to happen in 1658 when the two benefactors died. Two brothers, surnamed Marsollier, inherited the estate from their sister, Mme Norais, and after their death it was to pass to a son of M. Norais by his first marriage.[26] They filed a suit against Vincent, claiming that the property ceased to belong to the Congregation of the Mission once the donors died. Vincent was convinced they were wrong. Eight lawyers and a procurator had given him every assurance that he had nothing to fear and that there was no question that the property legally belonged to him.[27] On the basis of this advice he went to litigation. Vincent was prompted to do this by a sense of duty:

> I could not in conscience relinquish a property which was so legitimately acquired and the possessions of a community whose administration was in my hands without doing everything possible to retain these.[28]

The lawyers were proved wrong. In September 1658, parlement gave judgement against Vincent.[29] A more decisive factor than purely juridical considerations in the verdict, was parlement's tendency to make it difficult for the Church to acquire private property. The decision might also have

---

[22] *S.V.P.* II, p. 486; ABELLY, *op. cit.*, 1.3 c. 18, p. 380; COLLET, *op. cit.*, Vol. 2, p. 55; M. Denigot has taken up again the subject of the Orsigny estate and has contributed many documents. *cf. Au plateau de Saclay, Ile-de-France Monsieur Vincent et sa Congrégation à la ferme d'Orsigny* (Paris 1978) Mimeographed.

[23] *S.V.P.* IV, p. 327.

[24] *S.V.P.* III pp. 3 58 412 416 417; IV pp. 529 530; V, p. 362; VI, p. 38.

[25] *Cf. supra*, c. 34.

[26] M. DENIGOT, *op. cit.*, p. 10.

[27] *S.V.P.* VII, p. 405; ABELLY, *op. cit.*, 1.3 c. 2, p. 311.

[28] *S.V.P.* VII, p. 407.

[29] *S.V.P.* VII, p. 251.

been influenced by the calumny spread abroad by the other party, to the effect that the pension paid by Vincent to the donors was merely a bait to attract other gifts. Several of the magistrates had leanings towards Jansenism and this helped to swing the balance of opinion against Vincent. So he lost the case by just three votes.[30]

This event gives us one of the finest proofs of Vincent's spiritual stature and his detachment from material things. He was away from St Lazare when the news came. Br Robineau, his second secretary, told him the verdict when the evening meal was over. Vincent's only reaction was to exclaim several times, 'Blessed be God', and then he went off to the church to adore the Blessed Sacrament.[31] He wanted everyone to share these sentiments and so gave a beautiful conference to the community that September. In it he gives his thoughts on accepting contradictions and his reflection on the gospel maxim of not going to law are summed up perfectly for us:

> We have gained much from this loss because God has taken way from us, not just the property, but the satisfaction we took in owning it and the pleasure we would have had in going there from time to time. This pleasure of the senses would have been like sweet poison that kills, or like fire that burns and destroys. And now, through God's mercy, we are freed from this danger. And since there is now a greater possibility that we could lack material goods, His divine goodness wishes to draw us to have greater confidence in his providence, and abandon to his care all our anxieties about the necessities of life as well as the graces we need for salvation.

One lesson that the company should learn from this incident was

> Never to go to court, no matter how much we may be in the right; or if we have to go to litigation then this will only be after we have tried every way imaginable to come to an agreement; unless the justice of our cause is absolutely unquestionable since we are often mistaken in trusting to men's judgement. Let us practise the maxim of Our Lord who said, 'If they take your cloak, give them your tunic also.[32]

---

[30] *S.V.P.* VII, p. 405.
[31] ABELLY, *op. cit.*, 1.3 c. 21, p. 310.
[32] *S.V.P.* XII, p. 56-57.

There was the possibility of contesting the parlement's verdict. Several of Vincent's friends, including one of the judges, told him this and urged him to put in a civil claim. A famous lawyer who took part in the tribunal was of the same opinion. He undertook to defend the case at his own expense and also to indemnify St Lazare if they lost the case. Another good friend, M. des Bordes, who was a judge in the Financial Tribunal, also urged him to appeal.[33]

Vincent resisted all these pressures. He had made up his mind to accept the verdict as if it were the judgement of God. He had two reasons for doing this: firstly, he was afraid of giving scandal to those who might interpret the appeal as showing too great an attachment to worldly goods, a very common failing among ecclesiastics; and secondly, he thought that by participating in the first lawsuit he had amply fulfilled his duty to defend the rights of the congregation:

> Now that God has relieved me of this duty, since it was his sovereign decree that my efforts should be in vain, I believe we should let the matter rest there, especially since if we were persuaded to plead a second time, we might get a bad reputation which could be prejudicial to the service and the edification we should give people ...
>
> Since one of our practices during missions is to settle differences between people, it is to be feared that if the company persisted in presenting another civil claim against this decree, as those who are most fond of going to law would do, then God might deprive us of the grace of working to reconcile people.[34]

Vincent had reached that high degree of spiritual indifference that makes a person regard material losses as a divine favour. Shortly after this, his spirit of resignation was rewarded by the Lord with a new legacy that equalled in value the amount he had lost at Orsigny.[35]

More painful trials than just financial ones were waiting for Vincent in the last years of his life. Strangely enough (this is not a systematic account), each of these trials came from a different apostolic work. It was as if God were testing the mettle of each of these and at the same time purifying the man who created these works from any imperfections they may have caused him to have.

---

[33] ABELLY, *op. cit.*, 1.3 c. 18, p. 283.

[34] *S.V.P.* VII, p. 405.

[35] *S.V.P.* XII, p. 53.

'My relatives are begging for alms'

It was Vincent's deepest feelings, his detachment and his gratitude, that God particularly wished to put to the test.

Round about 1653, Vincent's family had suffered serious financial loss because of the civil war. Various friends, such as Canon St Martin, the parish priest of Pouy, and the bishop of Dax, told Vincent about his family's circumstances and begged him to help them. The bishop was the most outspoken of these and on 15 March 1656, when he happened to be visiting St Lazare, said:

> M. Vincent, your poor relations are in a very bad way; they will find it hard to survive unless you do something to help them. Some of them died during the war and others are going around begging.

Vincent felt again the temptation he had in his young days, to use his priesthood to improve his family's finances. He rejected the temptation. He would not allow himself to use community money to help his relatives, even though, theoretically, he might have been justified in doing this. Had not he used this money to help thousands of poor people? During a conference he spoke to the whole community about his feelings:

> So, Fathers and brothers, that is the sad situation my poor relations are in; they are begging, begging! And if God had not given me the grace of being here, I would be begging with them.[36]

What was he to do, then? He could not use community money and he could not ask the community to help them. This would have given scandal and would have created a dangerous precedent. Then he remembered that some years earlier he had received a gift from another great friend of his, M. du Fresne. This former secretary to the de Gondis had given him 1,000 *livres* for his family. These did not need the money at the time so Vincent had kept it aside to pay for preaching a mission in the place where they lived. This plan failed so the small amount of money remained intact. Vincent saw this as a sign from providence. But he consulted the most senior missioners before taking any decision and it was only when they had given their consent, that he decided to send the money to Canon St Martin to help his relatives. It was

---

[36] *S.V.P.* XI, p. 329.

not a lot of money but it would help one relation to buy a pair of oxen; it would help another to repair his house and it would buy a small plot of land, clothing and farming implements for the rest.[37] Once again Vincent had found the right balance between the feelings of his heart and the demands of virtue, the balance between charity and justice.

'God did not wish to leave this diocese without its pastor'

The problem of seeing to his family's needs was followed by a difficulty with regard to the de Gondis. Vincent owed his early career and a good number of his works to this wealthy and noble family of politicians, bishops and generals. If some of them (the general and his wife) had founded the Congregation of the Mission, others (the archbishops and cardinal), had established him in St Lazare and had approved his communities and associations, while others (the Marquise de Maignelay and the duke) had given him important financial support. Would he ever be able to do anything to help such important benefactors? An incident in the latter years of his life provided the answer to this question. In 1647 he had paid part of his debt of gratitude by receiving into the community the widower of Madeleine de Silly, M. de Fargis, who had become disillusioned with the turbulent, treacherous world of politics.[38] He was soon to be given the opportunity of doing something much more important.

Cardinal de Retz had been arrested on 19 December 1652, on the orders of Mazarin who could never forgive him for his part in the Fronde and his strong opposition both to Mazarin himself and to his policies. Perhaps the turbulent coadjutor deserved this punishment. Perhaps if Mazarin had been less exacting and more generous in spirit, he might have been able to use the undeniable talents of one of the most vigorous and active men of his times, for the benefit of France and her king. At all events, the prime minister's rancour was just as much responsible for the harsh measures taken against the younger de Gondi, as were the foolish actions of this leader of the Fronde. De Retz was imprisoned at Vincennes, in the same château that the abbot de Saint-Cyran had languished in for nearly five years. Fr de Gondi, the former general of the galleys, was invited to retire to his estates at Villepreux, which was tantamount to exile. Vincent was quick to sympathise with both father and son. He went to Villepreux to console his grieving old friend[39] and kept up a regular correspondence with him, keeping him informed about the prisoner's condition even down to such small details as the toothache he

---

[37] ABELLY, *op. cit.*, 1.3 c. 19, pp. 292-293.
[38] *S.V.P.* VII, p. 290.
[39] COLLET, *op. cit.*, Vol. 2, p. 475; *S.V.P.* IV, p. 535.

was suffering or the permission granted him to say Mass on Easter Sunday 1653, as well as rumours about his possible release, which was something Vincent earnestly desired.[40]

Vincent's sympathies clearly lay with the de Gondis. One has only to read the letter in which he tells how the prisoner from Vincennes took possession of the archdiocese of Paris, to realise this. The archbishop, Jean François de Gondi, died at four o'clock in the morning of 21 March 1654. A few days before his imprisonment at Vincennes, his nephew, who was also his coadjutor with right to succession, had taken the precaution of authorising his delegate to take possession of the archdiocese in his name should that situation arise. Indeed, at five o'clock in the morning, barely an hour after the death of the archbishop in office, the delegate, M. Labour, presented his papers to the cathedral chapter and had the archbishop's successor formally appointed. The minister, Le Tellier, had been sent in all haste by Mazarin to prevent such a ceremony from taking place but by the time he arrived at Notre Dame it was too late. There was nothing he could do about an archbishop who had been formally and rightfully appointed. A scheme was devised to inform de Retz, who was still in prison, about developments in the question of succession. The chaplain who was saying Mass, raised his voice at the *Te Igitur* and in a louder voice than usual he pronounced the name of the new archbishop, *antistite nostro Ioanne Francisco Paulo* ...[41]

Vincent regarded the whole event as an act of providence:

'Last Saturday', he wrote on 27 March, 'God took to himself the archbishop of Paris and on that same day Cardinal de Retz took possession of this see through a proxy acting in his name, and he was accepted by the chapter even though he is still in the forest of Vincennes. Providence inspired him to name a proxy for this purpose and to appoint two vicars general, just a few days before he was imprisoned, because at that time he was thinking of going to Rome and wanted to make these appointments in case God took his uncle while he was making this journey. So these two vicars general, who are canons of Notre Dame, are already exercising their office and it is on their instructions that we are receiving ordinands. Everyone is in admiration of this foresight and of its very happy results, or perhaps we should say that it was not in God's plan to leave this diocese without a pastor for even a single day when they were wanting to appoint somebody who was not his choice.'[42]

---

[40] *S.V.P.* IV, pp. 573-575.
[41] *S.V.P.* V, p. 110.
[42] *S.V.P.* V, pp. 109-110.

The last sentence is significant. Vincent, who was well aware of Mazarin's plans to impose Pierre de Marca as archbishop, regarded young de Gondi as the only legitimate pastor. All the prescriptions of canon law were in his favour but so, too, would have been Vincent's affection for the young son of his benefactors.

'We have performed a big act of gratitude towards our founder'

The matter was not completely settled. On 8 August 1654, de Retz escaped by being let down from the walls of Nantes castle where he had been transferred. In spite of a dislocated shoulder he rode half way across France, and reached Spain. He travelled through Spain, set sail again from a Mediterranean port, and finally arrived in Rome towards the end of that year. He was warmly received by Innocent X. The pope convoked an extraordinary meeting of the consistory to confer on him the cardinal's hat which he had not received up till then, and he arranged for him to stay at the house belonging to the Congregation of the Mission. This was the start of problems for Vincent and his company.

The Holy Father gave express orders for the missioners to welcome the persecuted cardinal into their house but the French ambassador was no less adamant in forbidding this. Fr Berthe, the superior, was caught between two fires and did not know what to do. He went in turn to the papal palace and to the French embassy and got contradictory orders in each place. 'The pope means to be obeyed', he was told at the palace. 'Beware of harbouring an enemy of the king', was the embassy's response. In fact the problem solved itself because when he went back to the house to reflect on the situation again and urgently consult M. Vincent, he found the cardinal's servants already unloading the baggage. A few days after this, another of Mazarin's envoys, Hugo de Lionne arrived in Rome with uncompromising instructions. He summoned Fr Berthe to appear before him and ordered him to leave the city immediately with all members of the community who were French citizens, and this under pain of incurring the king's displeasure.[43]

Berthe safely stored away all the congregation's papers, wrote in duplicate to Vincent to tell him what had happened, and left Rome en route for Florence and France while his companions took refuge in Loreto and Genoa. Only four Italian missioners were left in Rome.[44] In political circles in Paris there was strong indignation against the priests of the Mission for having

---

[43] R. CHANTELAUZE, *op. cit.*, pp. 355-362.
[44] *S.V.P.* V, pp. 269-275, 336, 341.

sheltered an enemy of the king. The court's anger was directed at Vincent, too, since he was in charge and was responsible for the conduct of his subjects.[45] Vincent accepted what was happening with his usual spirit of faith.

> We have reason to thank God for what has just been happening with regard to Cardinal de Retz who was welcomed into the house of the Mission in Rome: firstly because in this way we have shown great gratitude to our founder and prelate; secondly, because we obeyed the pope in this since it was he who ordered the superior of the Mission in Rome to welcome that said cardinal to that house, and thirdly and lastly, by doing another good act of obedience in obeying the orders of the king who ... commanded the superior of the Mission in Rome and all French priests of the Mission there to leave Rome and return to France ... See how all these virtues are linked together; one virtue leads to another and this leads to yet another.[46]

Mazarin's anger was short-lived. The queen's continued affection for Vincent and the fact that it was in the minister's interests to keep a French presence in Rome, made him quickly agree to the appointment of someone to replace Fr Berthe. This, as we know, was Fr Jolly.[47]

'Where will we find another Blatiron?'

Even greater trials were in store for the Italian foundations, one of them being in Rome, where the missioners had taken on the spiritual direction of the College of Propaganda Fide where it was proposed to confide a seminary to them.[48] In October 1656, there was an outbreak of plague and a student from the college died of the disease. The college was put into isolation. An Italian missioner, Fr di Martinis, shut himself up there in order to help the seminarists. Vincent praised his courage as well as that of Fr Jolly who was equally ready to risk his life to help the plague-stricken.[49]

[45] R. CHANTELAUZE, *op. cit.*, p. 360.
[46] *S.V.P.* XI, p.172.
[47] *S.V.P.* V, p. 366; VI, p. 20.
[8] *S.V.P.* VI, pp. 526, 538-539, 607-608; VII, pp. 270, 346, 418: VIII, p. 368. *Cf.* A. COPPO, 'San Vincenzo e i suoi rapporti con la S. Congregazione de Propaganda Fide', *Vincentiana* (1972), pp. 187- 189.
[49] *S.V.P.* VI, pp. 116, 138; XI, p. 365.

Catastrophe struck in Genoa. During the summer of 1656 plague broke out there with devastating fury. The sick people were piled up in hospital wards that were inadequate, or else died in the streets with nobody to attend to them. Food supplies left on the beach remained untouched because there was nobody to go out and collect them. Four or five thousand people died every week. Soon the whole city became one vast silent pesthouse. The superior of the missioners was Fr Blatiron. Vincent urged to him the need for caution, but to no avail. Blatiron converted the house into a hospital and volunteered to attend the sick. The first one to have his offer accepted was the Italian, Luca Arimondo. He was also the first to succumb. Twelve days after entering the pesthouse of La Consolazione he fell ill and three days later gave up his beautiful soul to God. Fr Blatiron caught the infection while administering viaticum to three people who had the plague. He died a holy death after a brief illness. Other missioners died during the summer of 1647. Of the nine priests in that community only two survived. Three of the four lay brothers and the four seminarists also managed to survive.[50]

Vincent's desolation was very great. 'Where will we find another Blatiron? Where will we find another Duport, Ennery and Tratebas?' he exclaimed.[51] But he was able to rise above this terrible loss. The trial served only to strengthen his resignation and his confidence in God:

> After shedding some tears over what we feel at this separation, we are resigned to it; we raise our hearts to God and we praise and bless him for all those we have lost, since what has happened is in accordance with his most holy will.[52]

The year 1657 was a bad one for Vincent. It was the year of the disastrous mission to Poland where the house in Warsaw was destroyed by Swedish troops,[53] the year of the Madagascar failure when not a single missioner was left alive there,[54] the year when Fr Duggan died in the Hebrides,[55] and the year when so many of the community at Genoa perished. It might be said that the Lord was heaping disasters on Vincent to test his mettle and his virtue. The vigorous old man courageously overcame all these adversities. And he still had enough spirit left to take on new enterprises.

---

[50] *S.V.P.* VI, pp. 58, 151, 354 ,375, 411, 450. *Notices* ..., III, pp. 82-87.
[51] *S.V.P.* XI, p. 432.
[52] *S.V.P.* XI, p. 430.
[53] *Cf. supra,* c. 24.
[54] *Cf. supra,* c. 26.
[55] *Cf. supra,* c. 24.

Chapter XXXVIII
FINAL VENTURES

The General Hospital

Works of charity had come into fashion. The movement started by Vincent de Paul gained new supporters every day as more people imitated his relief services. But as the movement became more widespread it became less pure. The original charism turned into institutionalised service and the religious dimension was lost. What had started out as an effort to help the poor was turned into a weapon against mendicants.

In the years that followed the Fronde, social bodies of very different complexions, the ladies of Charity, the Company of the Blessed Sacrament, the parlement, the government, all took up the question of mendicants with the idea of solving the problem once and for all. One of Vincent's works, the Nom de Jésus hospital, was a case in point. Why could they not do on a larger scale what he had begun in a small way?[1]

The ladies of Charity were the first to float the idea. It was immediately taken up by the gentlemen of the Blessed Sacrament and then by politicians. They copied the idea but not the spirit behind it. Vincent had approached the problem from the angle of a poor person needing help. Those in public office had a political end in view: society had to be protected from the rabble of beggars. So, basically, there were two completely different ways of seeing the poor: the Christian view which regarded the poor as an image of the suffering Christ, and the secular view which considered them a threat to established social order. Vincent wanted to help the poor, the politicians wanted to eliminate them. The juxtaposition of these two ideas in Furetière's dictionary speaks volumes: 'before (the General Hospital was founded) people were being killed by the poor who were begging for alms. Beggars, poor

---

[1] ABELLY, 1.1 c. 45, pp. 211-218. New information and documents concerning the General Hospital in F. COMBALUZIER, 'L'Hôpital Général de Paris et Saint Vincent de Paul', *Annales* (1949), pp. 238-246.

people, are called the members of Christ.'[2] It is not surprising that it was impossible to reconcile both these attitudes.

The ladies took up a position somewhere between these two extremes. Coming, as they did, from the upper classes of society, it was natural that they should share the prejudices and concerns of their husbands and sons who might be members of the parlements, judges, or have some high position in the government. But, trained in the school of St Vincent, the ladies had an earnest desire to serve the poor. One day, in 1653, they told Vincent what they had in mind. They would try and set up a large institution which would take in all the poor people of Paris and provide them with board and lodgings as well as giving work to the able-bodied. They had it all very well worked out. They had even calculated how much money would be needed: the Duchess d'Aiguillon had promised 50,000 *livres* and another lady had offered an income of 3,000. On the face of it, it was an excellent plan which would be the crowning point of Vincent's life-long works of charity. So they were exceedingly surprised when M. Vincent showed no enthusiasm at all and asked for time to think about it.[3] The first thing he did was to consult Louise de Marillac. On the whole she was inclined to favour the idea but she had some reservations. 'If this is a political venture,' she commented, 'then the work should be taken on by men; if it is a charitable work, then the ladies should do it ...'[4] And as the gentlemen of the Blessed Sacrament were planning a similar project, Louise was against any collaboration with that famous organisation.

The ladies brought the matter up again at their next assembly. Everything was ready. Funding would not be a problem since some very distinguished people had undertaken to make a generous contribution. What they really needed was a building with plenty of space. They suggested the Salpêtrière, a former gunpowder depot, which was lying empty at the time, in the Faubourg St Victor. Vincent asked the queen for it and she readily granted his request. There was some difficulty when a man claimed he had certain rights over the building but the problem was solved when one of the ladies agreed to pay him a pension of 800 *livres*.[5]

'If we used force we could be going against God's will'

Vincent was not at all convinced. He gave a second conference to the ladies and told them his many reservations. It would be better to go slowly because

---

[2] A. FURETIERE, *Dictionnaire universal,* ed. 1690, art. *Pauvre.*
[3] ABELLY, *op. cit.,* 1.1 c. 45, p. 214.
[4] LOUISE DE MARILLAC, *Pensées, op. cit.,* p. 286.
[5] ABELLY, *ibid.,* p. 215.

this was the way all God's works are done. Is not this what happened with Noah when he took a hundred years to build the ark and were not the people of Israel wandering in the desert for forty years? They would have to try out the work and begin gradually, perhaps with just a hundred or two hundred poor people. The most important thing would be to change the attitude of those involved in the work. The poor had to enter the institution voluntarily and nobody was to force them: 'If we used force we could be acting against God's will.' This was his biggest objection to the plan.[6] But the ladies would brook no delay. The most enthusiastic members grew impatient at M. Vincent's slowness. Work began immediately on adapting the Salpêtrière.

This was how matters stood when the parlement intervened in the affair. It decided to take over the project and the grand master ordered the work to be stopped.[7] Vincent accepted this decision and persuaded the ladies to do likewise, in spite of the considerable sums of money they had invested in the project and their determination to continue with the work and to have it directed by Vincent.[8] They could not do anything about it. A royal edict of 1656 ordered the setting up of 'The Grand General Hospital for the Poor' and provided for an administrative council whose members would be the first president of the parlement, the procurator general, the president of the relief tribunal, the president of the accounts department, the general commander of police and the leading representative of the merchants. The hospital was allocated ten buildings in Paris and the surrounding areas and included the Salpêtrière and the castle of Bicêtre, the former home for foundlings.[9] So the project passed into the hands of administrators.

Vincent must have heaved a sigh of relief. This was not his way of dealing with the poor. He had given many hours thought to the problem. One day when he was going to Villepreux to see Fr Gondi, he stopped at St Cloud to have something to eat. While people continued to talk after the meal Vincent sent for his secretary, Br Robineau, and began to dictate the reasons for and against shutting the poor away. For the moment he could not come to a definite decision either way. We must presume from his later actions that he eventually decided against it. One of the things that saddened him most about the project was that they planned to exclude from this hospital peasants from the country areas, and refugees, so these would be forced to return to their native parts. If Paris was the sponge of France that sucked up the best part of the country's wealth, what right had they to prevent poor people from other areas enjoying the benefit of these resources?[10]

6   ABELLY, *op. cit.*, 1.1 c. 45, p. 215.
7   *S.V.P.* V, p. 47.
8   *S.V.P.* VI, p. 110.
9   F. COMBALUZIER, ref. art., p. 239.
10 [L. ROBINEAU], *Remarques*, pp. 151-153.

'We still do not know whether it is God's will'

Vincent's delight in seeing himself rid of this dubious enterprise was short-lived. He was amazed to find out that the priests of the Mission had been named chaplains to the institution.[11] This was set out in the edict and in a triumphant propaganda leaflet which praised the advantages that such an establishment would bring for the poor, for pious people, and for the public in general.[12] He had to think it through carefully once again.

The plan had been put into action with complete disregard for the comments he had made and, what was worse, against his strong conviction that the poor should not be coerced. They had taken this decision purely to stop people begging.[13] In such circumstances was he right in collaborating? He did agree to the priests of the Tuesday conferences and some from his own congregation giving a mission to the beggars in the capital,[14] but as for taking permanent charge of religious services at the Hospital he 'still did not know whether this was God's will'.[15] He consulted the community about whether they should take it on. They advised him against it, saying that priests were needed for other community commitments. Vincent reported their findings to the Duchess d'Aiguillon,[16] the superintendant of finances,[17] and some other people. He also told the news informally to the hospital administrators.[18] These demanded an official reply so Vincent brought the community together again on 9 April 1657. They were unanimous in rejecting the proposal. This is recorded in the minutes which also stated their reasons for the decision and put into writing the formal renunciation of any benefits which might have accrued from the appointment.

> 'We have unanimously decided that our company cannot undertake it [the work] because of its many commitments which prevent it taking on any new works. We are hereby notifying the administrators about this decision so that they can find other ecclesiastics to do the work and we consequently renounce the benefits that would have accrued to the company from this appointment.'[19]

---

[11] *S.V.P.* VI, p. 239. Edict concerning the establishment of the General Hospital, arts 23-26.

[12] *L'Hôpital Général charitable* . Trad. *ibid.*, pp. 437-451.

[13] ABELLY, *op. cit.*, 1.1 c. 45, p. 217.

[14] *L'Hôpital Général charitable*, 1.c., p. 444.

[15] *S.V.P.* VI, pp. 239, 245.

[16] *S.V.P.* VI, pp. 250-251, 257.

[17] *S.V.P.* VI, p. 256.

[18] F. COMBALUZIER, article quoted, p. 240.

[19] The document which was not known to Coste, was published by F. COMBALUZIER, article quoted, p. 241.

To avoid any difficulties Vincent gave the hospital administrators the names of some priests from the Tuesday conferences who would be reliable in fulfilling these duties. Their choice fell upon Louis Abelly, who would later write the saint's biography, but for health reasons he was only in office for five months.[20] The ladies of Charity continued to give their valuable assistance to the hospital[21] and so did the Daughters of Charity for a brief period but this was only when the work was just beginning.[22]

'They are blaming you'

Although he disapproved of the project Vincent was very careful not to criticise the hospital. On the contrary, he praised the intentions of those who had promoted the enterprise and he suffered in silence the fact that public opinion, and more especially the poor people, attributed this idea to himself. In accordance with the terms of the edict which strictly forbade begging, he discontinued the customary practice of distributing alms at the gates of St Lazare. One day, as he was going into the house, some beggars came up to him and complained about not being given the usual alms.

'Father, did not God tell people to give alms to the poor?' Vincent tried to avoid entering into the argument and just replied, 'Yes, my friends, but he also tells us to obey the magistrates.[23] One of the more daring spirits among those who were complaining went on to say:

'Do you know what they are saying round here?'
'Tell me, my friend.'
'Well, they are blaming you for having the poor shut away in the General Hospital.'

So that was it! The father of the poor stood accused of being their gaoler. Nothing would have been easier than for Vincent to protest his innocence at this point but in keeping with his respect for the authorities, and his practice of never defending

---

[20] F. COMBALUZIER, article quoted, p. 245. Not two years as Coste thought. (*cf. M.V.* Vol. 2, p.506).

[21] *S.V.P.* VI, pp. 376-377.

[22] LOUISE DE MARILLAC, *Ecrits,* p. 659.

[23] ABELLY, *op. cit.,* 1.3 c. 11, p. 133.

himself against false accusations, he replied meekly, 'Well, my friend, I will go and pray for them.'[24]

The official and adulatory propaganda praised the General Hospital to the skies, speaking of it as the greatest charitable enterprise of the century. Vincent had voluntarily renounced the credit for this project, which far from being the crown of all his works of charity, was a distortion of their true meaning. It had never been his intention to eliminate begging by some artificial means but rather to get to the roots of the problem of poverty and dig these out with love.

The mission in Metz

Vincent had just got himself out of the tangled situation at the General Hospital when he was offered the mission in Metz, a work which was more in keeping with the aims of the company but which also had a serious drawback because Metz was a cathedral city and the priests of the Mission never preached in such places. Queen Anne of Austria had visited this city in Lorraine during the summer of 1657 and had witnessed grave abuses there.[25] She was particularly concerned about the strong Protestant influence in this frontier, and still semi-Germanic, town. Catholicism had to be bolstered there. The queen had in mind a mission after the style of M. Vincent, her former adviser on the Council of Conscience, with whom she remained on good terms and to whom she would occasionally grant audience. She summoned him to the palace to explain what she wanted done. Vincent was not able to accept the work but he did find a satisfactory solution.

> My lady, Your Majesty is not aware that the poor priests of the Mission are called to serve only poor country people. If we are established in Paris and other episcopal cities it is only so that we can work in seminaries, with the ordinands, and to those who come for retreats, and to go out and give missions in country places; not to preach, instruct or hear confessions for people in these cities. But we have another company of priests who meet every Tuesday at St Lazare, and if Your Majesty agrees, they could fulfil your wishes much more worthily than we could.[26]

---

[24] ABELLY, *op. cit.*, 1.3 c. 11, p. 176.
[25] ABELLY, *op. cit.*, 1.3 c. 46, p. 225.
[26] *S.V.P.* XII, p. 4.

The queen accepted this counter-proposal and Vincent was given charge of organising the mission. He chose about 20 of the most fervent priests for this work[27] and named as its director, Louis de Rochechouart de Chandenier (1660), abbot of Tournus, and nephew of Cardinal de la Rochefoucauld. Vincent considered him 'one of the best abbots in the country.'[28] Both he and his brother Claude, abbot of Moutiers-St-Jean, had been members of the conference right from the beginning. Both were benefactors to Vincent and his company and they had given an abbey to the congregation. Louis had refused several bishoprics out of humility, and Vincent, most unusually, allowed him to live at St Lazare as if he were a missioner.[29]

In Metz itself, the man in charge of preparations was another great friend of Vincent, Jacques Bénin Bossuet, who was at that time archdeacon of the cathedral in that city and a member of the Tuesday conferences. Just five years earlier, on 16 March 1652 he had been ordained in the church of St Lazare.[30] Vincent arranged for Fr Demonchy,[31] a priest from the house at Toul, to move to Metz and help organise the mission.

At first there were a lot of problems. To start with, it cost a fortune to employ a cook. Once more Vincent helped out and he appointed a lay brother to do this work.[32] The mission was to have been preached during Lent of 1658 but the cathedral had already engaged a famous Lenten preacher, the Dominican Antoine Guespier. The problem was that the usual Lenten sermons would not be preached if a mission was in progress. How could they dispense with the services of this eloquent preacher in such a way that neither his prestige nor his payment would be affected? Vincent put the situation to the queen and the conflict was discreetly resolved by a gift of 100 gold coins in addition to the normal stipend, as well as the firm promise to call on the Dominican's services the following year.[33]

The missioners set out towards the end of February. Then another difficulty cropped up. In northern France there was such torrential rain that the whole region seemed to be one great lake. According to Vincent, there

---

[27] We cannot be sure about the exact number of missioners. Abelly (l.c., p. 225) says there were more than 20. On one occasion St Vincent mentions 15 or 16 (*S.V.P.* VII, p. 92.) and at another time he speaks of 18 or 20. (*ibid.*, p. 76).

[28] *S.V.P.* IV, p. 79.

[29] *S.V.P.* V, p. 365; VI, pp. 33, 381; VII, pp. 298-300.

[30] *Annales* (1958), pp. 620-622.

[31] *S.V.P.* VII, pp. 69, 87, 92.

[32] *S.V.P.* VIII, p. 92.

[33] *S.V.P.* VII, pp. 63, 96.

were more boats in Paris than there were carriages.[34] Speaking from Metz, Bossuet talked of a 'veritable flood' and begged God to open a pathway through the waters for the mission priests. Br Mathieu, the 'fox' of Lorraine, found a way of arriving safely in Metz and he prepared this route for the mission team.[35]

'I have never seen anything more apostolic'

The mission finally started on the date that had been fixed and it lasted for two and a half months. Vincent followed its progress with keen interest through the letters sent by Chandenier and other mission priests. He read these letters to the community and to the members of the conferences. He was not the only person to read them. The queen, also, asked for detailed accounts of the mission, and for reports to be sent to her.[36]

As usual there were some spectacular conversions, especially among some Protestants. More priests had to be sent for so that they now numbered more than forty. Bossuet himself put his eloquent, ardent preaching at the service of the mission. Vincent thought that the missioners' conduct was just as effective as their preaching and he spoke to the community at St Lazare on this subject:

> You might not speak a single word but if you are filled with God's spirit you will touch people's hearts just by your presence. The abbés de Chandenier and other priests who have just given a very successful mission at Metz in Lorraine used to walk in pairs from their residence to the church, and from the church back to their residence, wearing their surplices and walking in complete silence; they were so recollected that everybody who saw them was greatly impressed by their modesty, never having seen anything like it before. So their modesty was a silent sermon but one so efficacious that it has been said it contributed greatly, and perhaps more than anything else, to the success of the mission.[37]

For his part, Bossuet gave fulsome praise to Vincent for the marvellous work that the missioners did:

---

[34] *S.V.P.* VII, pp. 92, 94.
[35] *S.V.P.* VII, p. 96.
[36] *S.V.P.* VII, pp. 120-121.
[37] *S.V.P.* XII, p. 17. For the increase in number of missioners *cf.* COLLET, *op. cit.*, Vol. 2, p. 40.

'Everything has gone so well, Father, that you have every reason in the world to rejoice in Our Lord ...' 'There has never been anything so well-ordered, so apostolic and so exemplary as this mission. How many things I could tell you, especially about the director and all the others who preached the gospel to us in such a holy and Christian way ...' 'They raised the hearts of everybody here. And now they come back to you, worn out in body but rich in spirit from the spoils they have snatched from hell and from the fruits of penance that God has worked through their ministry. So, Father, welcome them back with a blessing and with thanksgiving.'[38]

These words show how much Vincent's missionary work was appreciated by someone who was to prove the greatest preacher of that century. Humanly speaking, he could not have asked for a greater reward. Metz was the ultimate confirmation of missions as Vincent de Paul's most important work in life.

Retreats for ordinands in Rome

Retreats for ordinands were appreciated by an even higher authority and this was shown in the last years of life of the man who started them.

From the year 1642 onwards, and thanks to the generosity of the Duchess d'Aiguillon, the house in Rome had taken in priests who had asked, of their own accord, to make a retreat there.[39] Gradually people began to recognise the importance of this work. The solid virtue of priests who had prepared for ordination at the missioners' house could not fail to be noticed. A decisive factor in the work was the election of Alexander VII who played an important part in other Vincentian enterprises. The new pope was aware of the excellent results that Vincent's followers had, and he wanted their work to be extended throughout the whole diocese of Rome. In 1659 he published a decree obliging all candidates for ordination to make a retreat, beforehand, at the missioners' house.[40] Vincent received the news with a mixture of delight and caution. He did not tell the community straightaway as he wanted first of all to think about what this would entail. But he recognised

---

[38] *S.V.P.* VII, p. 155.
[39] *S.V.P.* II, pp. 270, 284, 293, 368, 406, 490.
[40] *S.V.P.* VIII, p. 183.

in the pope's instruction, a further sign of God's providence and, with a grateful heart, he prayed:

'I thank God for having brought the question of retreats for ordinands to this point and I am deeply grateful to Him for it. It seems that divine providence wishes to give us the opportunity to be of some little service in such an important matter.[41]

The first session took place during Advent of that year. By chance, the de Chandenier brothers happened to be present, because they were visiting Rome and were lodging at the mission house. They both made a personal contribution to the splendid liturgical ceremonies. Louis celebrated High Mass every day and his younger brother, Claude, was acolyte and thurifer. The order of the day and the subjects dealt with, followed the same pattern as those at St Lazare.[42] The Italian missioners were responsible for preaching. The fervour and devotion aroused by this retreat were so noticeable that the pope publicly expressed his gratitude for it during a consistory. Two further retreats were given during Lent in 1660, and another group of retreatants came at Pentecost. Fr Jolly, the superior at Rome, gave Vincent a careful account of the results each time.[43]

We know from these reports that the retreats were becoming more and more successful and that they aroused the curiosity of other ecclesiastics, not just in Rome but in other Italian dioceses as well. We know that the retreats were welcomed on all sides and that the priests of the Mission were encouraged by the gratitude of those who made them. We also learn the social standing of some of the ordinands; these included canons of the Lateran and St Peter's, pontifical princes and nephews of cardinals. Some came back for retreats and one celebrated his first Mass in the missioners' church after he had prepared for this event by making another retreat.[44]

Present at one of those retreat sessions was the secretary to the bishop of Plasencia, who, as we mentioned earlier,[45] was planning a mission foundation in that Spanish city. The saintly bishop of Bergamo, Gregorio Barbarigo, came to one retreat and was so enthusiastic about it that he could not rest until he had taken the missioners to his own diocese to be in charge

---

[41] *S.V.P.* VIII, p. 182.

[42] *S.V.P.* VIII, p. 222, 244.

[43] *Ibid.*, Jolly's letters have come down to us through Abelly who copied them or made extracts but he did not date them. When Coste reproduced them in *S.V.P.* he gave approximate dates.

[44] *S.V.P.* VIII, pp. 269, 275, 285, 294, 302.

[45] *Cf. supra*,c. 24.

of training ordinands. One saint can recognise another even though they are separated by distance.[46]

'We will show our support for that company'

Not everything was congratulations and blessings; they met opposition, too. Jolly told Vincent that the success of their retreat work had roused the envy of certain long-established and prestigious communities in Rome. This was particularly true of the Jesuits, and one of their reasons for mistrusting the congregation was the fact that the missioners were French. This prompted Vincent to intensify his recruitment of vocations from Italy.[47] His opponents used the prevailing situation and the fact that the humble Congregation of the Mission was still not very well known as a pretext for having recourse to the cardinal-vicar, and then to the Holy Father, himself, asking that people of high rank should not be obliged to make the retreat. They also pleaded for the priests of the Mission to be withdrawn and the work confided to another congregation.[48] The cardinal and the pope remained firm and they refused to make any exceptions.[49]

This was an opportunity for Vincent, now in the last months of his life, to put into practice what he had always taught about how to act in the face of calumny and persecution. It was calumny, and being accused of theft, that had sparked off Vincent's conversion fifty years earlier. His only comment then had been, 'God knows the truth.'[50] Now, as he neared the end of his long journey towards the God of his youth, he methodically analysed the different ways he might react to the situation which still stirred in him feelings of rebellion. What was he to do? What avenues were open to him? Vincent weighed in the balance the conflicting options prompted by nature and by grace.

Human nature and common prudence suggested he ought to:

1. Complain about this congregation, about all its members or about some particular individuals;
2. Complain to their friends so that these might speak to them;
3. Complain to our own friends so that these could use their authority and influence;

---

[46] S. COPPO, 'De S. Gregorii Barbadici in vincentianos sodales benevolentia', *Vincentiana* (1961), p. 346-347.

[47] *S.V.P.* VIII, p. 246.

[48] *S.V.P.* VIII, p. 290.

[49] *S.V.P.* VIII, p. 294.

[50] *Cf. supra*, c. 6.

4. Join forces with those who opposed this congregation and seek to humiliate them. This is how human nature and a worldly spirit would proceed.

Following the inspirations of grace, and this was something he had to do at all costs, his duty would be:

1. Not to say a single word to this community;
2. Much less to their friends;
3. Not a word to our friends either;
4. Not to take sides; and not only to refrain from acting against the interests of this company but to go much further, and following the counsels of Our Lord, we should actively take their part and try to get people to praise them etc. It is not enough for us to remain indifferent towards them and to say, 'Oh well, this will not stop us serving God' and leave it at that. That is human nature speaking. We have to do more than that. We must really serve them and seek out occasions for doing so.'[51]

This is the admirable, serene, attitude of a man who had succeeded in completely mastering his natural feelings and who had made the gospel teaching an integral part of himself. Not for a single moment would he allow something that happened at the eleventh hour to cast a shadow over his long friendship with the Society of Jesus and his appreciation of it.

God rewarded his integrity. The little company of the Mission continued to direct the retreats for ordinands for many years to come. After Vincent's death, Alexander VII published a new brief in favour of the company, and his instructions about the retreats were now made to apply in the outlying districts, too. So the supreme authority of the Church ratified the humble work that started many years earlier, and had first been conceived during that journey to Beauvais in a creaking carriage.[52]

'Union of minds, peace for the Church'

It was not easy for Vincent to avoid taking sides against the Jesuits during those years. Not only was there the clash that he had with them in Rome, but many people were urging him to oppose them. At that time the battle against casuistry or laxism was at its height, and the controversy was fiercely exacerbated by the caustic pen of Louis de Montalto, Pascal's pseudonym in *Les Provinciales.*

---

[51] *S.V.P.* XIII, pp. 175-177.
[52] *Cf. supra*, c. 14.

Vincent's tireless companion in the struggle against Jansenism, Alain de Solminihac, wrote to his friend asking him to take part in a new campaign, this time against the Jesuits:

> 'I feel I have to write to you (this was on 3 May 1659) to tell you that you must take up arms again, just as you did before to combat Jansenism; not to fight them, this time, but to oppose the most pernicious doctrine that has perhaps ever been seen in the Church and which is trying to gain ground under the pretext of combating Jansenism. I am referring to that monster of abomination, the *Apologie des casuistes*.[53]

Vincent must have given the prelate the help he asked for, because a month later Alain de Solminihac wrote again, thanking him for his help and asking more favours.[54] Vincent did not like extremes of any kind and this was why he was against laxism.

'Strictness in religious matters which is so much recommended in the sacred precepts of the Church, and which was restored by St Charles Borromeo, produces incomparably more fruit that excessive indulgence',[55] he had written in 1655, quite some time before laxism was condemned.

We know from Abelly and Collet that he welcomed the condemnation of laxist principles as eagerly as he had welcomed the condemnation of Jansenism.[56] But he took very little part in this controversy. He did not have the same opportunity to intervene and he never confused the Society of Jesus as a whole with the opinions of some of its members. As we have just seen, he did not oppose the Society even to refute their attacks in Rome. His rôle, especially after the publication of the bull *Cum occasione*, had been a silent one. It was with these sentiments that he wrote to Fr Pesnelle, the new superior at Genoa, about the anti-casuistry controversy:

> We have given ourselves to God to take no part whatsoever in all these discussions that so many and such holy people are having, and which are being debated by such influential congregations within the Church. We give our word that we will not think about or read all these books that have been

---

[53] For the anti-Laxist controversy *cf.* E. PRECLIN and E. JARRY, *Luchas doctrinales* (Vol. 22 from the *Historia de la Iglesia*, FLICHE-MARTIN, pp. 47-49); H. TÜCHLE, *Reform y Contrarreforma*, p. 270.

[54] *S.V.P.* VII, p. 614.

[55] *S.V.P.* VII, p. 324.

[56] ABELLY, *op. cit.*, 1.2 c. 12, p. 440: COLLET, *op. cit.*, Vol. 2, pp. 148-149.

printed on this subject, and which are being circulated in Paris
and even in the provinces. We are content to beg God to unite
minds and hearts and to establish peace in his Church.[57]

'If the captives are not freed by force of arms ...'

And yet, at the very end of his life, this man who was such a pacifist, thought
up a plan that involved armed combat. This is how it came about.

In 1658, the consul in Algiers, Br Barreau, was a prisoner for the
umpteenth time in the hands of the Turks. The younger of the Le Vacher
brothers, Philippe, had returned to France to organise a collection to pay for
Barreau's release. Vincent had some leaflets printed (he always believed it
was good to advertise), appealing to the charity of the people of Paris. These
leaflets were not only about Barreau, for there were thousands of French
captives in the Algerian prisons. It would be impossible to ransom them all.
Vincent was deeply afflicted by the plight of these hapless people.

At that time there was an adventurer going round the wharves at
Toulon and Marseilles. He went by the name of 'M. Paul' and he offered to
lead an armed expedition to Algiers to liberate the captives. Rumour had it
that this man had been born in the Château d'If of a washerwoman and an
unknown father. He had served with the Knights of Malta and the French
navy, distinguishing himself by his reckless bravery, and had reached the rank
of captain and lieutenant general.[58]

Vincent thought that this gentleman's plan was the only way to end
the North African nightmare once and for all. No price would be too high if
it meant that all the captives could be rescued at a single stroke. He spoke
about this to the superior at Marseilles, Fr Get, and told him to contact M.
Paul; to remind him that they had once met at Mazarin's house and to tell him
that Vincent was proud to share the same name. In the months that followed,
the gentleman's name frequently crops up in Vincent's correspondence so
we can follow the progress of the negotiations, step by step. Vincent
interested the Duchess d'Aiguillon, and her brother, who was consul at
Marseilles,[59] in the project, and procured letters from Mazarin and from the
king authorising the expedition.[60] He consulted M. de Verthanon and M.
Lamoignon, 'two of the cleverest men in Paris', about the viability of the

---

[57] *S.V.P.* VIII p. 86.
[58] *S.V.P.* VII, pp. 78-79.
[59] *S.V.P.* VII, pp. 130, 139.
[60] *S.V.P.* VII, p. 160.

project[61] and tried, though unsuccessfully, to have the enterprise financed by the king. The monarch could not give him financial aid because all the resources he had were being put into the siege of Dunkirk. He did arrange for the city of Marseilles to be responsible for maintaining the fleet during the two months that the ships would have to remain at that port.[62]

Finally, on 7 June 1658, Vincent informed Fr Get that the king had given M. Paul secret orders to go ahead with the expedition and he gave him the letters he had received from the king and from Mazarin.[63] Then they talked about money. Vincent undertook to give the man 20,000 *livres* from the money Fr Get had for ransoming the captives, but the money would only be handed over after the mission had been successfully accomplished. They had to come to this arrangement because if the plan failed they would have to use the money to ransom captives through the ordinary channels:

> If all this cannot be achieved by force of arms, then this money
> will have to be used to bring about these results in the usual
> way, which would mean paying this brother's debts and giving
> the poor Christians the sums allocated to them so that they
> can use these to pay their ransom.[64]

Before Vincent could spend the money, he needed to have the consent of the ladies of Charity who had provided most of the funds. They agreed wholeheartedly. This was yet another occasion when all the institutions founded by Vincent collaborated in his projects.[65]

The fleet was held up for months on end and a series of unforeseen events prevented it from sailing. Vincent did not give up hope but he felt his own life was slipping away and he grew more and more anxious about his brothers in Algiers. His last letter on this subject is dated 17 September 1660, just ten days before his death. In this letter he could not hide the pain and anxiety that gripped him.

> I feel very deeply, as you do, about what is happening to our
> brothers in Algiers. What an anxiety it is! How much
> uncertainty there is in the present circumstances! God protect
> them!

---

[61] *S.V.P.* VII, pp. 165-166.
[62] *S.V.P.* VII, p. 171.
[63] *S.V.P.* VII, p. 174.
[64] *S.V.P.* VII, pp. 197, 211.
[65] *S.V.P.* VIII, p. 25.

My concern is causing me indescribable anguish. The rumour is going round here that Commander Paul has laid siege to Algiers but we do not know how that has turned out; you tell me that ships are beginning to set sail for Algiers but you make no mention of our poor brothers; in God's name tell me what is happening.[66]

He never did find out. Perhaps this was just as well because the expedition ended in failure. M. Paul, after transferring troops to the Ionian islands, turned up at Algiers to rescue the captives. He could not get near the coast for about five days because of adverse winds. Wearied by this delay, he veered round and left the area. They only rescued about forty slaves who jumped into the sea and swam to the ships.[67] But Vincent was dead by now. He had left unfinished the final task of his life, an enterprise which his young heart had embarked on at the age of eighty. What impulse had urged the gentle and charitable Vincent to sponsor that armed adventure? Doubtless it was his conviction that this was the only way of liberating the captives since the Turks were not open to persuasion or to payment. But perhaps it was also some secret desire to close that circle which had been opened in his early years by the three Turkish brigantines that had carried him off by force, to Barbary. It was not God's will that fate should come full circle. It would have been too happy an ending if Vincent could have left this life retracing his steps to where he had set out. Such things only happen in novels.

---

[66] *S.V.P.* VIII, pp. 448-449.
[67] *S.V.P.* VIII, p. 449.

Chapter XXXIX
FAREWELLS

Because he lived to such an old age, Vincent de Paul had seen most of his friends and collaborators off to heaven. One after another there disappeared the men of his generation with whom he had shared the joys and sorrows of their work to reform the Church: Condren in 1641, Abra de Raconis in 1646, Jean François de Gondi in 1654 and Bourdoise in 1655, as well as other younger men whom he had trained and directed. So Vincent's old age was darkened by the added sorrow of loneliness. He was particularly moved by some of these deaths, either because he had lost his closest collaborators or because in the years and months prior to his death, they seemed to give him a premonition of his own passing.

Jean Jacques Olier, an untimely death

In 1657 it was the turn of M. Olier. He had been more than a companion to Vincent and was more like a son, this very gifted son, whose progress Vincent followed with great affection even, or perhaps especially, when Olier left this fatherly care to make his own way in life. Indeed, the founder of St Sulpice would often say to his followers, 'M. Vincent is our father and we should honour him as such.'[1] He had every reason to speak like this. Vincent had helped him make up his mind to become a priest when the young cleric had doubts about taking holy orders. He had introduced him to the work of the missions, to the retreats for ordinands and to the Tuesday conferences. After the tumultuous mission in the Faubourg St Germain, Vincent was also indirectly responsible for Olier being given the parish of St Sulpice where he founded his community and started his seminary.[2]

---

[1] COLLET, *op. cit.*, Vol. 1, p. 414.
[2] *Cf. supra*, c. 23.

In fact, an unpleasant incident over who should be in charge of this parish showed just how much Vincent identified himself with the interests of the man he had been directing. A short time after Olier had been appointed to St Sulpice, the former incumbent, who had moved to a more prestigious parish, thought better of the bargain and spread the rumour that he had been misled and had accepted a benefice that was much less important than he had been led to believe. His followers reacted so violently to this that they came to attack St Sulpice by force of arms. They occupied the presbytery, and Olier himself was pursued by a fanatic who drove him out at sword point. The parlement issued a decree in favour of Olier and the parish was returned to him but his adversaries did not give up. They again laid siege to his residence and tried to break down the doors and scale the walls. The queen sent a detachment of guards to repel the troublemakers and they only just managed to prevent the building from being set on fire. At court, the friends of the former incumbent thought that Olier's community was an off-shoot of Vincent's. They blamed Vincent for what had happened and on one of his visits to the queen there were ministers, and even royal princes, who reproached him bitterly. Nothing would have been easier than for Vincent to have cleared up the matter by simply saying that the two communities were completely separate. He did not do this and, in fact, he strongly defended his friend. When the storm was over, and feelings had calmed down, everyone recognised the loyalty of M. Vincent who had chosen to be thought guilty rather than abandon a friend in his time of need.[3]

When Olier was dying, the news was quickly relayed to Vincent who came straightaway and stayed with the dying man till he breathed his last. This was on Easter Sunday[4] 1 April 1657. Restraining his feelings of deep sadness, Vincent spoke these beautiful words to the dead man's companions:

> 'Earth has his body and heaven has his soul,' he told them,
> 'but his spirit remains with you. If God has judged him worthy
> of a place among the angels in paradise, you should deem him
> worthy of a place in your hearts.'[5]

In the three years of life left to him, Vincent always referred to this friend who had died an untimely death (Olier was only 48 when he died) as a saint, and had no hesitation in praying to him.[6]

---

[3] COLLET, *op. cit.*, Vol. 1, pp. 413-414.
[4] COLLET, *op. cit.*, Vol. 2, p. 144; *S.V.P.* VI, p. 275.
[5] *S.V.P.* XIII, p. 166.
[6] COLLET, *op. cit.*, Vol. 2, p. 144.

It was at the insistence of the priests of St Sulpice, and at the request of the abbot of St Germain who was responsible for the parish, that Vincent presided at the assembly where M. de Bretonvilliers (1612-1676)[7] was elected Olier's successor. Their grief at Olier's absence was tempered by their certainty that they had a father in heaven. Sadly, Olier's beatification cause has not been successful. In the catalogue of the Sacred Congregation which deals with canonisation, his cause is entered under the heading *quae silent*, that is to say 'frozen'.[8]

Alain de Solminihac, a reforming prelate

No less painful for Vincent was the loss of another great friend and a companion in numerous campaigns, Alain de Solminihac, bishop of Cahors. This happened on 31 December 1659. Certainly this was the bishop who was closest to Vincent, who looked on him as a saint.[9] He had given ample proof of holiness by his austerity of life,[10] his zeal for monastic reform, starting with his own abbey of Chancelade,[11] and his devotion to looking after the plague-stricken, so zealous a devotion that Vincent often had to advise him to be prudent.[12] He had collaborated with Vincent in the foundation and organisation of the seminary at Cahors and of a house of the Daughters of Charity.[13] Together they had fought Jansenism and laxism[14] and they had struggled to reform the episcopate by their efforts to have worthy men appointed as bishops.[15]

By the time he died, his diocese was completely reformed thanks to the missions, to the seminary (which was one of the best in the country) to the confraternities of charity and to the orphanage.[16] Solminihac was twelve years younger than Vincent and a very different type of person. He was noted for his strictness[17] and his fondness for lawsuits, qualities which gained him not a few enemies.[18] This did not prevent the two men from being very close friends.[19]

---

[7] *S.V.P.* ES VI, p. 262-253.
[8] SACRA CONGREGATIO PRO CAUSIS SANCTORUM, *Index ac status causarum beatificationis servorum Dei canonisationis Sanctorum* (Rome 1975), p. 229.
[9] *S.V.P.* X, p. 578.
[10] *S.V.P.* X, pp. 247, 687; XII, p. 420.
[11] *S.V.P.* II, p. 442; IV, pp. 135, 220.
[12] *S.V.P.* IV, pp. 497, 520.
[13] *Cf. supra*, c. 19, 23.
[14] *Cf. supra*, c. 36, 37.
[15] *S.V.P.* II, pp. 389, 564, 624-626.
[16] *S.V.P.* I, p. 207.
[17] *S.V.P.* X, p. 580.
[18] *S.V.P.* III, p. 229; IV, p. 62.
[19] *S.V.P.* III, p. 88; XIII, p. 194.

Vincent felt the prelate's death very deeply. Despite his firm belief that the saints are happier in heaven than on earth, he could not help but regret the loss of these living models of sanctity whose witness was so urgently needed by the Church.[20]

The beatification cause of Alain de Solminihac, which was put forward by the clergy of France, also failed to make any progress with the Sacred Congregation over long years of time. Only recently the final obstacles have been overcome, Alain de Solminihac was finally beatified on 4 October 1981 by Pope John Paul II and now it is possible for these two men to be honoured together at the altars of the Church, just as they were so closely united while they were on earth.[21]

'God has been pleased to take good Fr Portail from us'

The last year of Vincent's life started the day after Alain de Solminihac died. The Lord was about to demand even more painful farewells of Vincent. Three deaths in less than four months deprived him of the three helpers who had been with him at the foundation of each of his major works, the Congregation of the Mission, the Daughters of Charity and the Tuesday conferences.

The first to go was good Fr Portail, the first of Vincent's spiritual sons and his friend through thick and thin during all the vicissitudes of the history of the Mission. He was Vincent's eyes and ears during visitations of the houses, he was director of the Daughters of Charity, he was Vincent's confidant, sharing his every concern and counselling him in his doubts. So this death brought to an end fifty years of companionship and friendship. Vincent wrote a circular letter to the superior of each house giving them the news:

> God has seen fit to take good Fr Portail from us. He died on Saturday, the fourteenth of this month, (February) and on the ninth day of his illness. It started off as a kind of lethargy which then turned to continuous fever and convulsions. Then he regained consciousness and could speak clearly. He had always been afraid of dying but when he realised that death was near he accepted it with peace and resignation, and on several occasions when I visited him, he told me that his earlier fears had completely vanished. He ended his life as he had lived it,

---

[20] COLLET, *op. cit.*, Vol. 2, p. 68.
[21] SACRA CONGREGATIO PRO CAUSIS SANCTORUM, *op. cit.*, p. 175.

making good use of his suffering, practising virtue and desiring to honour God and end his days, as Our Lord did, fulfilling the divine will ... His death would have been a great loss to us if God did not arrange things for our greatest good and help us to recognise blessings in what might appear to be contradictions. We have reason to hope that this, his servant, will do even more for us in heaven than he would have done on earth.[22]

It was with this sober and supernatural comment that Vincent bade farewell to his lifelong friend. Vincent was now coming to the highest point of detachment from human friendship and this was very evident when he had to part from Louise de Marillac.

'Be of good heart my daughters, you have a mother in heaven'

Mlle Le Gras had been delicate all her life. As far back as 1647 Vincent could say of her: 'Humanly speaking, I would have said she was dead ten years ago. She was so physically weak and so extremely pale that if you saw her you would have thought she had risen from the grave, but God knows her strength of spirit ... if it were not for her frequent illnesses and her strong spirit of obedience, she would still be going about from one place to another, visiting her sisters and working with them, though the only life left in her is the life of grace.'[23]

Her anxiety to look after the sisters, and to help them by her advice, her decisions and her example, had kept her going despite labours and worries that were far beyond her physical strength. She continued to make progress in the spiritual life which deepened over the years, and led her, finally, to the very heights of mystical union.[24]

She became seriously ill on 4 February 1660, the same day that Fr Portail's illness started. It was feared that Louise would die first but she rallied for a time. 'Thanks be to God,' wrote Vincent, 'that he has spared us a double sorrow.'[25]

She was critically ill and an inflammation of the left arm required three incisions. Her condition improved for a short while after she had an operation and when the sisters piously applied to the arm a stole belonging

---

[22] *S.V.P.* VIII, pp. 248 254; *Notices ...*, Vol. 1, pp. 1-14.

[23] *S.V.P.* III, 'p. 256.

[24] J. CALVET, *Luisa de Marillac. Retrato*, pp. 146-150.

[25] *S.V.P.* VIII, pp. 248 258.

to St Charles Borromeo and a tiny piece of the heart of St Francis de Sales, and then she received the last sacraments and said goodbye to her son, the great sorrow of her life, who was there with his wife and little daughter.

> I beg the Father, Son and Holy Spirit, through the power that God has given to parents to bless their children, that he will give you his blessing, detach you from things of earth and draw you to himself. Live as good Christians[26]

Both she and Vincent accepted what was happening with complete resignation to God's will.

> 'Everything possible is being done to keep her alive,' wrote Vincent, 'but this is God's work and as he has preserved her life, against all human expectations, for twenty years, he will continue to do so for as long as this is to his glory.' 'The great secret of the spiritual life is to place all that we love into his hands and to abandon ourselves to whatever he wills.'[27]

On March 9 she again fell seriously ill and had all the symptoms of senile gangrene. For a second time Louise asked for holy viaticum and had the consolation of receiving the sacrament. On the other hand, she was denied another spiritual consolation she most fervently desired, a visit from her spiritual father and director. Vincent, too, was ill at this time and unable to move from his room. The sick woman begged him to at least send her a little note of comfort as he had done before when she was ill. But Vincent did no more than send a verbal message through one of the missioners, 'You are going on ahead of me; I hope to see you soon in heaven.' Not another word. The terseness of this farewell message to a kindred spirit he had directed for 38 years in its stormy spiritual journey, is quite astonishing. It is hard to understand Vincent's lack of feeling at such a critical moment. We can never completely fathom the mind of a saint. Maybe Vincent thought it necessary to impose such a painful sacrifice both on himself, and on the dying woman, as a final purification. At least this was how St Louise understood and accepted it.

Her final days were a mixture of spiritual consolation and bouts of fear of divine justice. Simply and eloquently she gave her blessing to her daughters and received the ladies of Charity with whom she had worked so

---

[26] GOBILLON, *op. cit.*, p. 173.
[27] *S.V.P.* VIII, p. 255.

hard for the poor. The Duchess de Ventadour spent the night of 14-15 March at her bedside. At about half-past eleven on the morning of 15 March, her death agony began. Before that she had followed the prayers for the dying with attention and devotion and had received the apostolic blessing *in articulo mortis*, something she had petitioned Innocent X for some years previously. In the end she died peacefully. Her last word was 'yes', her heroic response to the call of her divine Lord. The parish priest of St Laurent was present and when she breathed her last he exclaimed: 'What a beautiful soul. She is leaving for heaven with the grace of baptism.'[28]

In spite of his apparent indifference, Louise's death was a terrible blow for Vincent. We are so used to thinking of his words of resignation as just the expression of his natural feelings, that we find it hard to understand that these words covered a raging sea of human grief. He devoted two conferences to the virtues of Louise de Marillac. He spoke little, himself, so as to leave the sisters more time to give testimony to the edifying qualities they had noted in her. So the few words he did speak, are even more precious, and they all reveal his hidden pain, as well as the deep admiration he had for that chosen soul.

> Sometimes I began to reflect before God and I said to myself, 'Lord, you wish us to talk about your servant and the work of your hands' and I asked myself 'What have you noticed in the 38 years you have known her? What did you notice in her?' I thought of some tiny imperfections but mortal sin, never! The slightest irregular movement of the flesh filled her with horror. Hers was a pure soul in every way; she was pure in her youth, pure during her marriage and pure as a widow. She was very careful about examining her conscience so that she could confess her sins and all the attendant circumstances that troubled her. She confessed her sins in a very direct manner. I have never known anyone so pure. And she used to weep so much that it was difficult to comfort her. Be of good heart. You have a very powerful mother in heaven.[29]

Vincent's certainty about Louise de Marillac's heavenly glory was solemnly ratified by the Church, when Mlle Le Gras, as he always called her, was canonised on 11 March 1934 by Pope Pius XI.

---

[28] Information about the death of St Louise is in ABELLY, *op. cit.*, 1.1 c. 49, pp. 238-239 and GOBILLON, *op. cit.*, pp. 172-187.

[29] *S.V.P.* X, pp. 716-717.

The abbé de Chandenier 'lived like a saint and died a missioner'

Vincent still had not recovered from the upheaval caused by these deaths when providence dealt him a further blow which was no less painful than the others. The abbot of Tournus, Louis de Chandenier, made a pilgrimage to Rome in 1659, together with his brother and two priests of the Mission. Pope Alexander VII showed him every mark of esteem on his arrival in the Eternal City. Everyone at the house of the Mission where he lodged was edified by his piety and the fervour with which he joined in the retreat for ordinands.[30] On several occasions Louis de Chandenier had begged to be allowed to join the Congregation of the Mission but Vincent had always put this off on account of the abbé's high rank and his many ecclesiastical and social commitments. But he consoled him by promising to receive him into the congregation before he died.

In March 1660, while Chandenier was staying in Rome, he fell ill and he thought the time had come for this promise to be fulfilled. Fr Jolly, the superior of the house, did not think that the sick man was so near death and, in fact, de Chandenier was able to start the journey back to Paris in April. The rigours of this journey and the slow rate of travel affected his health once more, and when he arrived at Chambéry in Savoy, he fell ill again. His brother, Claude, was with him and so were Fr Berthe and another missioner. Fearing that this illness would prove fatal, Chandenier begged Fr Berthe to receive him into the company. Fr Berthe sadly granted his request, and the good abbé died on 3 May clothed in the missioner's soutane.[31] Vincent wept when he heard the news. It is the only time that we hear of him doing this. The accumulation of so many and such sad losses had finally worn down his resistance.

On Vincent's instructions, de Chandenier's remains were buried at the Mission house at Annecy. Later on they would be transferred to Paris for interment in the church of St Lazare. As was the custom with other missioners, the community held a conference on the virtues of the dead man. He had so many virtues that one conference was not enough and they had to hold four. In addition, Vincent outlined the deceased's panegyric in a letter addressed to the superiors of the congregation. What impressed him most was the dead man's extraordinary affection for the little company.

> 'The abbé de Chandenier', he said, 'lived like a saint and died a missioner. Before he died he repeatedly asked one of our priests who was with him to receive him into the company and

---

[30] *Cf. supra*, c. 38.
[31] *S.V.P.* VIII, p. 288.

this he did. On several occasions he had asked me to do this but, as he was far superior to us both by birth and in virtue, I was reluctant to do so. We were not worthy of such an honour. And indeed it is only our house in heaven that has merited the grace of owning him as a missionary; our earthly houses have merited only to inherit his holy life's example so that we can admire and imitate this. I do not know what he could see in our wretched company that could have given him this devotion to it, and the desire to appear before God clothed in our rags and with the name and the habit of a priest of the congregation of the Mission.'[32]

'I will pray for you in this world and in the next'

Vincent did not really need providence to send him any warnings like this procession of his closest collaborators making their journey towards heaven. He could already feel his own death was fast approaching. Before all these friends died, he had a relapse into his usual illness and in January 1659 he felt that his departure from this life was not far off. He did not want to be taken unawares and so began to make his preparations. One of the first things he did was to take leave of his two most important benefactors, Fr de Gondi and Cardinal de Retz, his son. He did not want to leave this life until he had fulfilled this important duty. The letters of farewell that he wrote reveal Vincent's great human and supernatural qualities.

'The poor state of health I am in, and the little fever I am suffering from,' he wrote to the former General of the Galleys, 'and in view of what might happen, make me prostrate myself in spirit at your feet, to ask your pardon for any unpleasantness my rustic upbringing may have caused you and very humbly to thank you, as I do, for the great charity you have shown to me, and for the countless benefits that our congregation, and myself in particular, have received from your kindness. Be assured, monsieur, that if God continues to give me the strength to pray, I will use that strength in this world and the next to pray for you and for all those you hold dear.'[33]

---

[32] *S.V.P.* VIII, pp. 302-303. *Cf.*, also, VIII, pp. 294, 299, 300, 305. The rest of the information on Louis de Chandenier is in ABELLY, *op. cit.*, 1.1 c. 49, p. 239-242, and COLLET, *op. cit.*, Vol. 2, pp. 77-79.

[33] *S.V.P.* VII, pp. 435-436.

Vincent's fears, or more accurately, his hopes, were not realised for a further twenty months, but he felt more at peace once his debts of gratitude had been settled. Some months later, in October 1659, he took further measures. In accordance with the constitutions, he nominated a vicar general of the congregation and two candidates for the position of superior general. These documents were dated 7 and 9 October, respectively. Fr Alméras was named vicar and the two candidates for the office of superior general were Fr Alméras again, and Fr Berthe.[34] With these matters attended to he could peacefully await his time to depart.

---

[34] *S.V.P.* XIII, pp. 409-412.

Chapter XL
THE PARTING

'When I was young I suffered from the same complaint'

Vincent would often go to see missioners who were ill. When he came across any who were feeling depressed or fearful he would encourage them by quoting his own experience and would say about the different illnesses:

> Do not be afraid, brother, when I was young I had this same complaint and I got better. I used to suffer from asthma but I do not have it now. I had hernias but God cured me. I, too, used to have the vapours but I never have them now. I used to have chest pains and stomach ailments but I got over them. Just be patient for a while. There's every reason to hope that yours is just a passing sickness. God has more work for you to do. Let him act and give yourself to him in peace and tranquillity.[1]

Was Vincent exaggerating past illnesses in order to raise the spirits of these sick men who were feeling afraid? The opposite would seem to be the case. That extraordinarily active man had suffered serious and frequent illnesses, three of which were chronic, and he regularly suffered from these all year round.[2]

A serious illness he had contracted in 1615 when living with the de Gondis had left him with periodic swelling of the legs, which gave him a lot of pain and meant that he could hardly walk.[3] Between 1620 and 1625 he

---

[1] ABELLY, *op. cit.*, 1.1 c. 50, p. 246.

[2] Together with the additional references that are given in the following notes, the information about Vincent's illnesses and his death comes from Abelly (*op. cit.*, 1.1 c. 50-52, pp. 243-259) and Collet (*op. cit.*, Vol. 2, pp. 70-86). We will not tire the reader by repeating these.

[3] Collet and Abelly and Br Robineau's manuscript (p. 104) agree that this inflammation of the legs might also have been caused by Vincent's sufferings while he was a captive in Barbary.

began to have recurrent attacks of fever, (the 'little fever' as he used to call it), and these attacks would come on at irregular intervals, sometimes lasting three or four days, and at other times more than three weeks. In an effort to cure these Vincent went fairly regularly to the medicinal spas near Paris[4] but the chief remedy he used was sweating. Even in the height of summer he would sleep with three blankets on the bed, and on either side of this he would have a big tin bowl filled with boiling water. He would spend the night bathed in perspiration which soaked the bed clothes so that he was not able to sleep. He also suffered from another type of fever, the quartan, which would last for three or four days and this happened two or three times a year.

None of these regular illnesses interfered with his work or business. No matter what state of health he was in, he would rise at four o'clock in the morning to be with the community for meditation, and would then follow the customary order of day. Sometimes, lack of sleep the previous night would cause him to accidentally nod off during a meeting. When he realised this he would humbly apologise and attribute it to 'his wretchedness' without making any reference at all to his long, sleepless night.

Each of these illnesses reached a critical stage so that Vincent's life was in danger on more than one occasion. In 1644, the quartan fever was so bad that Vincent was delirious for many hours, and the community feared the worst. It happened that a young priest of thirty-one years of age, Antoine Dufour, was ill at the same time. When he learned about Vincent's serious condition, he offered his life to God in exchange for that of the founder. From that time onwards, Vincent began to get better and the missioner began to get worse. A few nights later when Vincent was dozing and two brothers were staying with him, there were three loud knocks on the door of his room. The brothers in attendance opened the door but there was nobody there. They did not say anything to Vincent but he woke up and told them to say the Office for the Dead. They found out next morning that good Fr Dufour had died at exactly that time.

In 1649, when he was on his way from north-west France after his meeting with Mazarin, the 'little fever' came on him unexpectedly at Richelieu. For several weeks he hung between life and death and the illness left him so weak that he could never ride a horse again as the pain in his legs and joints was just unbearable when he tried to mount or dismount. It was then that the Duchess d'Aiguillon sent him her carriage and the archbishop ordered him to use it from then onwards. Otherwise he would never have been able to leave St Lazare again.[5]

---

[4]   *S.V.P.* I, pp. 63, 581; II, p. 148.
[5]   *Cf. supra*, c. 34.

We might say that his final illness began in 1656. He had a very high temperature and his legs were swollen right up to the knee. He recovered sufficiently to take up work again but he was never completely well. He had more frequent bouts of fever and he lost his appetite, especially during one Lent when he hardly swallowed a mouthful, and his legs became permanently swollen. To crown these misfortunes, he had an accident early in 1658. One day when he was coming back from Paris, one of the carriage springs broke and the vehicle overturned. Vincent suffered a heavy blow to the head. A few months after this, a new complication set in: he had problems with one eye. Various remedies were tried without success and then the doctor ordered them to bathe the eye with the blood of a freshly killed young pigeon. The infirmarian brought the little creature up to the room. He was just about to kill it when Vincent objected violently. The innocent little bird reminded him of our Saviour who shed his blood to redeem us. There was no way that Vincent could be persuaded to use this remedy.

'I never go to bed without putting myself in the right dispositions to die that night'

Towards the end of 1658, and right through the following year, these illnesses all recurred at the same time. The Lord seemed to be purifying him for the last time in a crucible of pain. Running ulcers, which were probably varicose, opened up on his legs so that he could not walk. First of all he used a stick and then he had to have crutches. By this time he could not leave St Lazare, even by carriage, but throughout the year he continued to come down to the chapel for Mass and for community exercises. He found it very difficult to manage the sacristy steps so he used to put his vestments on at the altar and this made him joke: 'Now I am quite a somebody, I vest at the altar just like a bishop.' He was never without fever and could never sleep at night.

The missioners realised that his end was near and tried to postpone it as long as possible. The Duchess d'Aiguillon gave advice as to how he should be cared for, and she was very upset that they would not allow her to take him to her house where she could have him looked after properly. Louise de Marillac, who was ill herself at this time, sent him lots of home recipes and these eased his pain a bit. The infirmarian at St Lazare, Br Alexandre Veronne, selflessly gave his time to the difficult work of applying remedies and, especially, of treating the running ulcers. Nobody was under any illusion. A missioner wrote to an absent companion telling him that Vincent had not much longer to live. As usual, he put the missive through the superior's letter box for posting. Vincent read the letter and thought he detected a veiled admonition in the message and possibly some cause for scandal since the missioner had not seen him make any special preparation for death. He sent for the writer, thanked him for the admonition, and begged him to mention any other defect he had noticed. The embarrassed priest did not know what to do to make up for his indiscretion. He protested as best he could that he had never had any intention of correcting his superior and eventually Vincent was convinced. Even so, to dispel any possible cause for scandal, Vincent explained to him:

> As for the admonition I thought you wanted to give me, I will tell you, in all simplicity, that God has granted me the grace of not acting in the way you mentioned. I tell you this so that you will not be scandalised at not seeing me make any special preparation. For the past eigthteen years I have never gone to bed without first putting myself in the right dispositions to die that night.

Neither pain nor increasing immobility prevented him from attending to everyday business. His correspondence between 1659 and 1660 deals with all matters concerning his different works—help for the latest areas of deprivation in Champagne and Picardy, advice to the superiors of the different houses, negotiations with the Holy See, organisation of the Tuesday conferences, problems concerning the ladies and the Daughters of Charity, messages of encouragement to missioners in difficult circumstances, the sending of personnel to Madagascar, the rescue plan at Algiers, reprimands, admonitions, recommendations. He also continued to receive visitors, to preside at councils and to give conferences. His last conference to the sisters and to the priests of the Mission were given on 14 and 19 December, respectively.[6]

The Lord granted him the consolation of seeing one of his most cherished dreams come true: peace was restored to Europe. On 7 November 1659 the Treaty of the Pyrenees was signed and this put an end to the Franco-Spanish war. The Treaty of Oliva, signed on 13 May 1660, restored peace to Poland. Vincent received the news of both events with a sigh of relief.[7] A month before his death Vincent followed with interest another public event which represented—or at least this is what was thought at the time—the final seal on the friendship between France and Spain: the triumphal entry into Paris of another Spanish queen, Maria Theresa of Austria, the beautiful

---

[6] *Cf. S.V.P.* VIII, *passim*; X, pp. 698-708; XII, pp. 424-433.
[7] *S.V.P.* VIII, p. 258.

young wife of Louis XIV.[8] How things had changed from the dark days of the campaigns in Lorraine and Picardy! A cycle in the history of France and of Europe was drawing to a close. All the leading figures were disappearing from the scene almost at the same time as Vincent was departing. The last to do so would be Mazarin in 1661, and Anne of Austria in 1666. For the last time the crucial phases of France's history would run parallel with the events of Vincent's life. After long years of preparation would come the epoch of glory and supremacy. Vincent had contributed to this.

'The brother is going on ahead to say the sister is coming'

In the early months of 1660 Vincent's health deteriorated still further. By now he found it impossible to leave the second floor of St Lazare, even to go to Mass. He painfully dragged himself on his crutches to the infirmary chapel and said Mass there. The conferences on the virtues of Louise de Marillac given on 3 and 24 July as well as the election of her successor had to take place at St Lazare.[9]

People from all walks of life were concerned about his health. Pope Alexander VII sent him a brief dispensing him from reciting the divine office.[10] Cardinals Ludovisi, Bagno and Durazzo wrote to him, begging him to let himself be cared for by those whose office it was to do this. 'Avoid any worry that might shorten your life,' was Durazzo's affectionate recommendation.[11]

Vincent did not find it easy to follow this advice. Anything that brought relief, but which presupposed a dispensation from community customs, clashed with his idea of humility and his sense of duty. The doctor ordered him a light diet based on soups and chicken. After being served this a couple of times, Vincent said it was bad for his heart so the diet had to be discontinued. So that he would not have the painful trip to the chapel to hear Mass (by this time he was not able to celebrate Mass himself), the confrères suggested setting up a small oratory in the room next to Vincent's. He would not allow it. He said that domestic oratories could only be authorised for very serious reasons and these did not apply in his case. It was only at the very end, on 15 August, that he allowed himself to be carried to the chapel in a kind of *sedia gestatoria* since he could not manage the crutches any

---

[8] *S.V.P.* VIII, pp. 387, 392.
[9] *S.V.P.* X, pp. 709-743.
[10] *S.V.P.* VIII, p. 455.
[11] *S.V.P.* VIII, pp. 427, 455, 456.

longer. Further complications set in and these aggravated his suffering. Urine retention caused him intense pain. He had to grip a rope hanging from the ceiling in order to be able to move in the bed. Even then, this brought on a painful jerking of his badly ulcerated legs. He was in continual agony from the hardening of pus on his knees and ankles. His sleepless nights alternated with intermittent naps during the day when he would doze off for long periods. 'It is the brother going on ahead to say the sister is coming,' he would say with a smile. Indeed, death's coming was imminent.

'Oh God, come to my aid'

The detailed diary that Fr Gicquel kept helps us to follow Vincent's last days step by step. We do not intend to copy or to summarise this. Nothing can equal the actual text which is eloquent in its raw pathos.[12]

On the night of Sunday 26 September Vincent was asked if he would like to receive the last sacraments. He replied with a simple 'yes' and Fr Dehorgny administered them. His spiritual sons took it in turn to sit up with him all through the night and every so often they would suggest ejaculatory prayers or phrases from the gospel. He seemed to like repeating these even when he was falling asleep. He prayed, or mumbled antiphons, and those present noticed that he seemed to have a particular liking for the opening invocation of the divine office, 'Oh God come to my aid.' At the urgent request of Fr Dehorgny, he gave his blessing, in turn, to each of the associations he had founded: the priests of the Mission, Daughters of Charity, Tuesday conferences, the Foundlings, the old people of the Nom de Jésus, and to friends and benefactors.

His last word before entering the death throes was 'Jesus'. At a quarter to five on the morning of Monday September 27 1660, without any convulsions or struggle, he breathed his last and went to meet the God of the poor whom he had loved and laboured for so ardently.

He was fully dressed when he died and was sitting in a chair by the fireplace. The chronicler tells us that he looked 'finer and more majestic and venerable than ever.'

He had lived his life to the full and there was nothing left for him to do. All his works could face the future with confidence.

---

[12] *S.V.P.* XIII, pp. 175-193.

EPILOGUE

St Vincent de Paul's story continued after his death and was no less eventful and stirring than the record of his earthly life. Everyone agreed that he had died a saint. Bishops and cardinals, the aristocracy and common folk, kings and beggars, all vied with each other in testifying to his extraordinary virtues. Among the many distinguished people who attended his funeral on 28 September were the Prince de Conti, the Nuncio Piccolomini, and the Duchess d'Aiguillon. There was another memorial service, two months later, at St Germain l'Auxerrois which was organised by the priests of the Tuesday conferences. On that occasion the preacher was the bishop of Puy de Dôme, Mgr Maupas du Tour. The orator preached for more than two hours and declared that he had not said half of what he intended to say because there was so much in M. Vincent's life to talk about that he could have given a whole series of Lenten sermons on it.[1]

Two hundred and ninety witnesses gave evidence at the beatification process which went on for 69 years after Vincent's death. On 21 August 1729 Benedict XIII inscribed him in the catalogue of the blessed. He was canonised on 16 June 1737.[2]

Meanwhile, the works started by Vincent were beginning to develop in an extraordinary way. The Missioners or 'Lazarists' in France, 'Paúles' in Spain, 'Vincentians' or 'Vins' in other countries, were spreading all over the world. They came to Spain in 1704. Today they are working all over Europe, in America, from Canada as far as Argentina, in Asia, and in Oceania.[3]

Even more spectacular has been the expansion of the Daughters of Charity which is the biggest religious community in the Church. Today they number 35,000 and one-third of these are Spanish.

---

[1] COLLET, op. cit., Vol. 2 pp. 86 93; H. DE MAUPAS DU TOUR, *Oraison funèbre* ... *prononcée le 23 novembre 1660* , Paris 1661.
[2] SACRA CONGREGATIO PRO CAUSIS SANCTORUM, *op. cit.*, p. 327.
[3] J. HERRERA, *Historia de la Congregación de la Misión*, Madrid 1949.

At the present day, the confraternities of charity are a splendid, world-wide body of volunteers who work for the benefit and the social advancement of 'poor country people' as Vincent liked to call them. They work in collaboration with the Society of St Vincent de Paul which was founded in 1833 by Frederic Ozanam. These were inspired by St Vincent de Paul and have him for their patron.

Altogether there are nearly a million people in the Church who are working and striving to keep alive and active the spirit of Vincent de Paul which is perhaps more necessary today than ever before. This is the spirit of God, himself, who sent Jesus to evangelise the poor by word and by deed.

TABLE OF EVENTS

	LIFE OF ST VINCENT	POLITICAL AND SOCIAL HISTORY	CHURCH HISTORY	CULTURAL EVENTS
1581	Birth of St Vincent in Pouy		Birth of Saint- Cyran	
1582			Death of St Teresa of Jesus	Gregorian reform of the calendar
1585			Death of Gregory XIII Election of Sixtus V	
1589		Assassination of Henry III of France		
1590			Death of Sixtus V Election and death of Urban VII Election of Gregory XIV	
1591	Birth of Louise de Marillac		Death of St John of the Cross Death of Gregory XIV Election and death of Innocent IX Election of Clement VIII	
1593		Abjuration of Henry IV	Death of Montaigne	

	LIFE OF ST VINCENT	POLITICAL AND SOCIAL HISTORY	CHURCH HISTORY	CULTURAL EVENTS
1594		Coronation of Henry IV and his entry into Paris	Expulsion of Jesuits from France	
1595	St Vincent begins his first studies at Dax Tutor in the Comet household.	Papal absolution for Henry IV		Re-issue of Montaigne's 'Essays'
1596	St Vincent receives the tonsure and minor orders at Bidache			Birth of Descartes
1597	He begins his theological studies at Saragossa and Toulouse (till 1604). Tutor at Buzet.	Henry IV recaptures Amiens	Birth of St John Francis Régis (+ 1640)	
1598	Death of St Vincent's father, John de Paul. Vincent receives subdiaconate and diaconate at Tarbes.	Edict of Nantes. Peace of Vervins. Death of Philip II of Spain.	Death of Fr Luis de Granada. Birth of Charles de Condren and J. B. Saint Jure.	
1599		Annulment of the marriage between Henry IV and Marguerite de Valois	Birth of Blessed Mary of the Incarnation	Publication of *Guzmán de Alfarache* by Mateo Alemán
1600	St Vincent is ordained to the priesthood at Château l'Évêque, first Mass at Buzet. Appointed parish priest of Tilh.	Marriage of Henry IV and Marie de Medici		Birth of Velázquez. *El Guzmán* is translated into French.

LIFE OF ST VINCENT	POLITICAL AND SOCIAL HISTORY	CHURCH HISTORY	CULTURAL EVENTS
1601 St Vincent's first journey to Rome. He is moved to tears.		Birth of St John Eudes	
1603	Death of Elizabeth I of England	Return of the Jesuits to France	
1604 St Vincent obtains his Batchelor of Theology degree at Toulouse	Institution of La Paulette		
1605 St Vincent travels to Bordeaux, Castres, Toulouse and Marseilles. He is captured by Barbary pirates and taken to Tunis.		Death of Clement VIII Election of Leo XI and Paul V	Publication of first part of *Don Quijote*
1606 St Vincent a slave in Tunis		Birth of Julien Maunoir	Birth of Corneille
1607 Freed from slavery. Stays at Avignon. 2nd journey to Rome. First letter about his captivity.			Publication of *L'Astrée* by Honoré d'Urfé

	LIFE OF ST VINCENT	POLITICAL AND SOCIAL HISTORY	CHURCH HISTORY	CULTURAL EVENTS
1608	Second letter from captivity. St Vincent moves from Rome to Paris.	Birth of C. Authier de Sisgau and J.J. Olier.	Publication La Vie Dévote.	
1609	The judge from Sore accuses Vincent of theft. St Vincent makes the acquaintance of de Bérulle.		Benet of Canfield publishes *The Rule of Perfection*.	
1610	Letter to his mother. He is appointed chaplain to Marguerite de Valois and abbot of St Leonard de Chaumes. His journey to La Rochelle.	Assassination of Henry IV. Marie de Medici appointed regent.	St Francis de Sales founds the Visitation order.	
1611	St Vincent stays at the house of de Bérulle. He visits the He makes the acquaintance of a theologian tempted against the faith.	Concini, Councillor of Marie de Medici.	Death of B. de Canfield. De Bérulle founds the Oratorians. Charity Hospital.	
1612	He is appointed parish priest of Clichy. Probable date of temptation against the faith (it lasted 3 or 4 years).		Condemnation of Richer. Paul V approves the Ursulines.	Birth of Arnauld.
1613	He enters the de Gondi household as tutor to the children			Birth of J. F. Paul de Gondi

	LIFE OF ST VINCENT	POLITICAL AND SOCIAL HISTORY	CHURCH HISTORY	CULTURAL EVENTS
1614	Appointed canon and treasurer of Écouis. He contracts an illness that affects his legs.	Louis XIII comes of age. The Estates General.	*Ejercicio de Perfección* by Fr Alonso Rodríguez	
1615	Resigns the post of abbot of St Leonard de Chaumes. Asks permission to absolve reserved sins. Sermon about the catechism and communion.	Marriage of Louis XIII and Anne of Austria. Philip IV marries Isabelle de Bourbon.	The Assembly of the Clergy promulgates in France the decrees of Trent.	
1616		Richelieu enters the government for the first time.	*Traité de l'amour de Dieu* by St Francis de Sales	Death of Cervantes
1617	Confession of the peasant at Gannes and the sermon at Folleville. He leaves the de Gondis. Parish priest of Châtillon. Foundation and rules of first Charity Confraternity. He returns to the de Gondi household.	Assassination of Concini. Louis XIII begins to reign in his own right. Luynes is his favourite.	Approbation granted to the Clerks Regular of Christian Schools of St Joseph of Calasanctius.	
1618	Preaches mission at Villepreux, Joigny and Montmirail. Becomes friendly with St Francis de Sales in Paris.	Start of the Thirty Years War.	St Francis de Sales travels to Paris. Death of Mme Acarie.	

LIFE OF ST VINCENT		POLITICAL AND SOCIAL HISTORY	CHURCH HISTORY	CULTURAL EVENTS
1619	Appointed Chaplain to the Galleys	Ferdinand II, Emperor		
1620	Mission and Charity Confraternities throughout the de Gondi estates. Conversion of two heretics at Montmirail. Another heretic voices his objections.			
1621	Mission at Marchais. Conversion of the third heretic at Montmirail. St Vincent affiliated to the Minims. The Charity at Mâcon. He makes his retreat at Soissons.		Death of Paul V Election of Gregory XV	*Ejercicio de Perfección* is translated into French
1622	St Vincent named superior of the Visitation nuns in Paris. He travels to Marseilles.			Birth of Molière
1623	Mission to galley slaves in Bordeaux. Journey to Pouy. He is tempted to help his family. Obtains his degree in canon law.	War of La Valtelina between France and Spain. Edict against the illuminists of Seville.	Death of Gregory XV. Election of Urban VIII.	De Bérulle publishes *Discours de l'état et de la grandeur de Jésus*

LIFE OF ST VINCENT	POLITICAL AND SOCIAL HISTORY	CHURCH HISTORY	CULTURAL EVENTS
1624 He makes a retreat at Valprofonde and Soissons. He is named prior of Grossesauve and principal of the Bons Enfants. Pastoral visitation of Clichy by Mgr de Gondi. He makes the acquaintance of Saint-Cyran and of Louise de Marillac.	Richelieu is Prime Minister. Franco-Dutch alliance.		
1625 Foundation of the Congregation of the Mission. Death of Mme de Gondi. St Vincent travels to Provence to tell her husband. Death of Antoine Le Gras, husband of Louise.	Cardinal Barberini legate during the conflict of La Valtelina	Mère Angélique tranfers her abbey to Paris.	
1626 The archbishop of Paris grants approval to C.M. The Bons Enfants joined to it. The Missioners sign the deed of aggregation. St Vincent bequeaths his possessions.	Peace of La Rochelle with Spain. Peace of Monzón	Jansenius has the Oratorians founded in the Low Countries.	Death of Malherbe and Francis Bacon

LIFE OF ST VINCENT	POLITICAL AND SOCIAL HISTORY	CHURCH HISTORY	CULTURAL EVENTS
1627 The Sacred Congregation of Propaganda approves Vincent de Paul's Mission. The first lay brother enters the community.	Conflict between France and England. Franco-Spanish alliance.	De Bérulle, cardinal. Foundation of the Company of the Blessed Sacrament.	Philippe de Champagne paints Jansenius' portrait. Birth of Bossuet.
1628 St Vincent gives testimony during the beatification process of Francis de Sales and gives the first retreat to ordinands at Beauvais. Propaganda refuses to approve C.M. Opposition from de Bérulle.	Fall of La Rochelle. Succession of Mantua. Spain opposed to French candidate, Charles de Gonzague.		
1629 Vows are introduced into the C.M. Foundation of the Charity at Beauvais. Louise de Marillac visits the charities.	Louis XIII gives aid to Charles de Gonzague. Hostility of Richelieu and de Bérulle. Peace of Alais.	Death of Cardinal de Bérulle. He is succeeded by Fr Condren.	
1630 St Vincent makes a will to bequeath his goods. He is visited in Paris by his nephew. Louise de Marillac visits the charities of Beauvais. Opposition to the C. M. from the clergy of Paris.	France captures Pignerol. Day of the Dupes. Downfall of the Devout Party.		

LIFE OF ST VINCENT	POLITICAL AND SOCIAL HISTORY	CHURCH HISTORY	CULTURAL EVENTS
1631 The archbishop of Paris confides the work of retreats for ordinands to St Vincent. Fr du Coudray arrives in Rome to negotiate the approbation of the C.M.	Marie de Medici flees to the Low Countries		Start of publication of *La Gazette de France*
1632 St Vincent takes possession of St Lazare. Lawsuit with the canons of St Victor. Death of Marguerite Naseau.	Death of Michel de Marillac and execution of Louis. Battle of Lützen. Secret marriage of Gaston d'Orleans.		Galileo: *Dialogo sopra i due massimi sistemi.*
1633 Bull *Salvatoris Nostri* giving approval to the C.M. Foundation of the Tuesday conferences and of the Daughters of Charity.	Invasion of Lorraine by Louis XIII	Priestly ordination of J.J. Olier. Saint-Cyran in Port Royal.	Holy Office condemns Galileo.
1634 Foundation of the ladies of Charity of the Hôtel-Dieu. Louise de Marillac renews her vows of widowhood and service of the poor.	Battle of Nordlingen. Victory for the Cardinal-Infante.	Saint Jure publishes *De la connaissance et l'amour de Dieu.*	

	LIFE OF ST VINCENT	POLITICAL AND SOCIAL HISTORY	CHURCH HISTORY	CULTURAL EVENTS
1635	Foundation of the house at Toul	Pierre Séguier, Chancellor. France declares war on Spain.		Foundation of the Académie Française
1636	St Lazare military recruitment centre. Chaplains are sent to the army. St Vincent visits the king at Senlis. Bons Enfants, Tridentine seminary.	Taking of Corbie. Spanish threat to Paris. Rising of the 'croquants'.		First performance of *Le Cid* by Corneille
1637	Establishment of the internal seminary of C.M. Foundation of the house Notre Dame de la Rose. St Vincent reproaches Saint-Cyran.	Mlle La Fayette joins the Visitation order. Downfall of P. Caussin.		Descartes: *Discours de la Méthode.*
1638	The Tuesday conference priests give a mission in St Germain-en-Laye and to the Court. Beginning of the work for foundlings Foundation of the houses at Richelieu, Troyes and Luçon.	Death of Fr Joseph de Tremblay. Birth of Louis XIV. Saint Cyran imprisoned. Death of Jansenius.	Death of M. Duval, spiritual director of St Vincent. The first recluses at Port Royal.	Poussin: *The Arcadian Shepherds.*

	LIFE OF ST VINCENT	POLITICAL AND SOCIAL HISTORY	CHURCH HISTORY	CULTURAL EVENTS
1639	Beginning of aid for Lorraine. Mission to the refugees. St Vincent gives evidence at the trial of Saint-Cyran. Foundation of the house at Alet and the hospital of Angers. Aid to the galley slaves. P. Lebreton in Rome.	Uprising of the 'Va-nu-pieds' in Normandy	Publication of *L'Esprit de Saint François de Sales* by Camus	
1640	St Vincent pleads with Richelieu for peace. Aid for Lorraine continued. St Vincent unsure about the vows.	Rebellion of Catalonia and Portugal	Jansenius' *Augustinus*	Publication of Pascal: *Les Sections Coniques*.
1641	Foundation of the house at Annecy. St Vincent has a vision of the three globes. Foundation of the house at Crécy. 'Ordinance of the *Vows*' in C.M. approved by the archbishop. Authorisation to found houses in Rome.	The French in Catalonia. Cromwell in power. Mazarin, Cardinal. Death of Cardinal-Infante.	First condemnation of *Augustinus* Death of J.F. de Chantal and Fr Condren.	Descartes: *Méditations*.

LIFE OF ST VINCENT	POLITICAL AND SOCIAL HISTORY	CHURCH HISTORY	CULTURAL EVENTS
1642 Establishment of seminaries at Annecy and the Bons Enfants. First collective taking of vows and first General Assembly of C.M. St Vincent's resignation not accepted by the Assembly.	Plotting and execution of Cinq-Mars. Death of Richélieu. Mitigation of Saint-Cyran's imprisonment.	Olier founds the seminary and community of St Sulpice. Habert preaches against Jansenius.	Corneille: *Le Menteur*. Death of Galileo.
1643 St Vincent helps Louis XIII to die well. Appointed member of the Council of Conscience. Mission in the galleys at Marseilles. Foundation of houses at Cahors, Marseilles and Sedan.	Death of Louis XIII. Anne of Austria, regent. Mazarin Chief Minister. Saint-Cyran is released.	Death of Saint-Cyran. Arnauld: *De la Fréquente Communion*. St John Eudes founds the Congregation of Jesus and Mary (Eudists).	
1644 A. Dufour offers his life for that of St Vincent who is gravely ill. Foundation of the houses at Saintes and Montmirail. Project for a foundation in Barcelona.		Death of Urban VIII. Election of Innocent X.	
1645 Foundation of houses at St-Méen, Le Mans and Genoa. Missionaries arrive in Tunis.			

LIFE OF ST VINCENT	POLITICAL AND SOCIAL HISTORY	CHURCH HISTORY	CULTURAL EVENTS
1646 Arrival of Missioners in Algeria and Ireland. The coadjutor of Paris gives approval to the Daughters of Charity.			
1647 Project for a mission in Persia. John Le Vacher arrives in Tunis.		Condemnation of the Doctrine of 'the two heads'	
1648 Foundation of the houses at Tréguier and Agen. Missioners arrive in Madagascar. Letters of St Vincent about frequent communion and Jansenism. Meeting at St Lazare to prepare the propositions.	Arrest of Broussel. The Parlement Fronde breaks out. Battle of Lens. Peace of Westphalia.	Innocent X condemns the Treaties of Westphalia	Philippe de Champaigne paints Mère Angélique's portrait.
1649 St Vincent goes to St Germain to ask for Mazarin's dismissal. He visits the houses of west France. Falls ill at Richelieu. Begins to use the carriage. Discourse to the ladies about the foundlings. Aid given to Paris and surrounding districts.	Paris rebels against Mazarin. The Court at St Germain. Concorde de Rueil. Execution of Charles I of England.		Cornet submits the Jansenist propositions to the Sorbonne.

LIFE OF ST VINCENT	POLITICAL AND SOCIAL HISTORY	CHURCH HISTORY	CULTURAL EVENTS
1650 Foundation of the house at Périgueux. Marriage of Michel Le Gras. Start of relief given to Picardy and Champagne. Les Relation appear.	The Spaniards lay siege to Guise. Arrest of Condé.		Death of Descartes
1651 Increased aid for Picardy and Champagne. Missions to Limerick. Death of Thaddeus Lee, protomartyr of C.M. Second general assembly of C.M. Missioners arrive in Poland and Scotland. St Vincent collects signatures against Jansenism.	Condé is released. The Fronde of the Princes breaks out. Louis XIV comes of age.	Foundation of the Foreign Mission of Paris	
1652 Period of most intensive aid to Paris and surrounding districts. St Vincent mediates in the Fronde. Interviews with the queen and the princes. Letters to the pope and to Mazarin. Leaves the Council of Conscience. Foundation of house at Montauban.	Campaigns of the Fronde. Paris surrenders and the monarch's return. Cardinal de Retz a prisoner at Vincennes.	Bossuet is ordained a priest at the church of St Lazare.	

LIFE OF ST VINCENT	POLITICAL AND SOCIAL HISTORY	CHURCH HISTORY	CULTURAL EVENTS
1653 St Vincent gives support to the anti-Jansenist delegation in Rome. The archbishop of Paris approves the rules and constitutions of C.M.	Return of Mazarin. End of the Fronde.	The five Jansenist propositions are condemned in the bull *Cum occasione*	
1654 Foundation of the houses at Agde and Turin and establishment of Nom de Jésus hospital. Martyrdom of Pedro Borguny in Algiers. Aid to Picardy continued.	Flight of Cardinal de Retz	Death of J. F. de Gondi, archbishop of Paris	
1655 Approval for the vows of C.M. in the brief *Ex commissa nobis*. Cardinal de Retz approves the Daughters of Charity. Election of its officers. French Missioners expelled from Rome for giving hospitality to de Retz.	Cardinal de Retz in Rome	Death of Innocent X. Election of Alexander VII. Dispersion of the recluses of Port Royal. Death of A. Bourdoise.	
1656 The Missioners renew their vows in conformity with the brief *Ex commissa nobis*. Plague in Rome.		Further condemnation of Jansenism	The first *Provinciales* by Pascal

	LIFE OF ST VINCENT	POLITICAL AND SOCIAL HISTORY	CHURCH HISTORY	CULTURAL EVENTS
1657	St Vincent at the death of Olier and the election of his successor. Plague in Genoa. Death of the Missioners. Royal approval for the Daughters of Charity. Project for a foundation in Toledo. St Vincent refuses the work of directing the General Hospital.	Foundation of the General Hospital in Paris	Death of J. J. Olier	
1658	Mission at Metz. St Vincent distributes the rules to the Missioners and begins his explanation of them. Foundation of the house at Meaux. Loss of the farm at Orsigny. Daughters of Charity in the hospital of Calais. Brother Barreau is in prison in Algeria.	Battle of the Dunes. Death of Cromwell.		
1659	St Vincent is ill and unable to leave Saint Lazare. He takes his leave of de Gondi. Proposes Alméras as his successor. Foundation of the houses of Montpellier and Narbonne. Brief *Alias Nos* on the vow of poverty in the C.M.	Peace of the Pyrenees between Spain and France	Condemnation of *L'Apologie des casuistes.* Death of Alain de Solminihac.	

LIFE OF ST VINCENT	POLITICAL AND SOCIAL HISTORY	CHURCH HISTORY	CULTURAL EVENTS
1660 St Vincent confined to his room. Death of Fr Portail, Louise de Marillac and the abbé de Chandenier. Project for a foundation in Plasencia (Spain). Death of M. Vincent (27 September).	Marriage of Louis XIV to Maria Teresa of Austria. They both enter Paris. Peace of Oliva, between Sweden and Poland.		

BIBLIOGRAPHY

Note. This translation aims to reproduce the Spanish edition of 1981 as closely as possible. In the bibliography a small number of works in English have been added. References to the Spanish edition of the writings of St Vincent have been omitted as well as translations into Spanish of works more easily available to the English reader in the original.

ABELLY, L., *La vie du vénérable serviteur de Dieu Vincent de Paul...* (Paris 1664). English translation: *The life of the Venerable Servant of God Vincent de Paul, founder and First Superior General of the Congregation of the Mission.* 3 v. (New York, 1993);
La vraie défense des sentiments du vénérable serviteur de Dieu Vincent de Paul.. contre les discours injurieux d'un libelle anonyme... (Paris 1668).

ACAMI, D., *Vita del ven. servo di Dio Vincenzo de Paoli ...* (Rome 1677).

ANSART, S. I., *L'esprit de saint Vincent de Paul* (Paris 1780).

ARANDA, E., *Relation de la captivité du sieur Emmanuel d'Aranda* (Paris 1657).

ARNAULD, A., *De la fréquente communion, où les sentiments des Pères, des Papes et des Conciles touchant l'usage des sacrements sont fidèlement exposés* (Paris 1643).

ARMANDI, A., 'Une étrange coïncidence: Saint Vincent de Paul à Rome et les conférences dites de Saint Vincent', *M. et Ch.* 10 (1963), pp. 224-226.

D'AVENEL, L. M., *Lettres, instructions diplomatiques et papiers d'Etat du cardinal Richelieu* (Paris 1853-1857) 8 vols.

BARCOS, M., *Défense de feu Mr. Vincent de Paul contre les faux discours du livre de sa vie publié par Mgr. Abelly, ancien évêque de Rodez* (s.1. 1668), *Réplique à l'écrit que M. Abelly a publié pour défendre son livre de la vie de M. Vincent* (s.1. 1669).

BATIFFOL, L., *La journée des dupes* (Paris 1925). *Richelieu et le roi Louis XIII. Les véritables rapports du souverain et de son ministre* (Paris 1934).

BAUNARD, L., *La Vénérable Louise de Marillac, Mademoiselle Le Gras, fondatrice des Filles de la Charité de Saint Vincent de Paul* (Paris 1898).

BELLESORT, A., *Le mystère de Monsieur Vincent: Journal des Débats,* 22 August 1928.

BERCÉ, Y.-M., *Histoire des croquants* (Paris 1974), 2 vols.

BERTHELOT DU CHESNAY, Ch., 'Les missions de saint Jean Eudes Contribution à l'histoire des missions en France au XVII siècle (Paris 1967). Saint Vincent de Paul et Saint Jean Eudes', *M. et Ch.* 4 (1961), pp. 469-481.

BÉRULLE, P., *Oeuvres complètes* (Paris, Migne, 1856).

BICAIS, J., 'Notice du général des galères Philippe-Emmanuel de Gondi', *Annales* (1940), pp. 272-287.

BLANCHET, A., 'Note sur le livre de Saint Jure, *La vie de Monsieur de Renty'*, *Études* (1970), pp. 74-85.

BLET, P., 'L'Église de Paris et les Gondi, in *Recueil des travaux sur l'histoire de la cathédrale et de l'Église de Paris (*Paris 1967), pp. 345-357. 'L'Ordre du clergé au XVII siècle', *RHEF* 54 (1968), pp. 5-26.

BONO, S., *I corsari barbereschi* (Turin 1964).

BORIES, M., 'Une "charité" dans le diocèse d'Alet aux XVIIe et XVIIIe siècles', *Mélanges d'histoire religieuse offerts à Mgr. Elie Griffe...* (Toulouse 1972), pp. 251-259.

BOSSUET, J. B., *Sermons choisis* (Paris 1894).

BOUDIGNON, J. B., *Saint Vincent de Paul, modèle des hommes d'action et d'oeuvres* (Paris 1886). English translation: *Saint Vincent de Paul, model of men of action* (St Louis, 1925)

BOUGAUD, L., *Histoire de Saint Vincent de Paul* (Paris 1889) 2 vols. *Histoire de Sainte Chantal et des origines de la Visitation* (Paris 1874) 2 vols.

BRÉMOND, H., *Histoire littéraire du sentiment religieux en France depuis la fin des guerres de religion jusqu'à nos jours* (Paris 1925-1936) 13 vols. (Edition of Paris 1967).

BROUTIN, P., *La réforme pastorale en France au XVII siècle. Recherche sur la tradition pastorale après le concile de Trente* (Tournai 1956) 2 vols.

BURCHARDT, C. J., *Richelieu* (Paris 1970-1975) 3 vols.

[BUYS, J.], *Enchiridion piarum meditationum...* (Paris 1645). French translation: J. BUZEE, *Manuel de méditations dévotes* ... Paris 1649.

CABOURDIN, G., *La Lorraine entre France et l'Empire germanique de 1480 à 1648* (Strasburg 1975).

CALVET, J., *Histoire de la littérature française* Vol. 5: *La littérature religieuse de François de Sales à Fénelon* (Paris 1938);
'Saint Vincent de Paul et la Compagnie du Saint Sacrement (1636-1660)', *Petites Annales de Saint Vincent de Paul* (1903) pp. 46-43;
Saint Vincent de Paul (Paris 1948). English translation: *Vincent de Paul and his world* (London, 1978);
Louise de Marillac par elle même (Paris 1958).

CAMPO, F., '1580-1980. IV centenario del nacimiento de San Vicente de Paúl', *Anales* (1977), pp. 551-555.

CANFIELD, B., *Règle de perfection, contenant un bref et lucide abrégé de toute la vie spirituelle réduite à ces seul point de la volonté de Dieu* (Paris 1609) (Latin edition: *Regula perfectionis continens breve et lucidum compendium totius spiritualis vitae redactae ad unicum punctum voluntatis divinae* ... Paris 1610). There is a modern French-English edition: *La Règle de perfection. The rule of perfection.* Edition critique publiée et annotée par Jean Orcibal (Paris: P.U.F., 1982).

CAPEFIGUE, J. B., *Vie de Saint Vincent de Paul* (Paris 1827).

CARVEN, J., 'The poor. An attempt to fathom the mind of St Vincent', *Vincentiana* 23 (1979), pp. 42-56.

CARRE,THOMAS, *Pietas Parisiensis or a short description of the charities commonly exercised in Paris* (Paris: Moutier, 1666).

CASTAÑARES, R., *Cartas y escritos de Santa Luisa de Marillac* (Madrid 1945) 3 vols.

CATALOGUE *du personnel de la Congrégation de la Mission depuis l'origine (1625) jusqu'à la fin du XVIIIe siècle* (Paris 1911)

CERTEAU, M., 'La réforme dans le catholicisme', *Histoire spirituelle de la France* (Paris 1964), pp. 194-216;
'Crise sociale et réformisme spirituel au début du XVIIe siècle', RAM 41 (1965), pp. 339-386.

CEYSSENS, L., *Sources relatives aux débuts du jansénisme et de l'antijansénisme. 1640-1643.* (Leuven1957);
La première bulle contre Jansénius. Sources relatives à son histoire (1644-1653) (Rome-Brussels, 1961-1962) 2 vols;
La fin de la première période du jansénisme. Sources des années 1654-1660 (Brussels 1962-1963) 2 vols;
Jansenistica minora (Malinas 1951ss) 11 vols;

'François Hallier', *Bulletin de l'Institut belge de Rome* 40 (1969), pp. 157-264;

'L'antijanséniste Isaac Habert (1598-1668)', *ibid.*, 42 (1972), pp. 237-305;

'Nicolas Cornet (1592-1663), promoteur des cinq propositions jansénistes', *Antonianum* 52 (1977), pp.395-495.

CHALUMEAU, R., 'Saint Vincent de Paul et les missions en France au XVII siècle', *XVIIe Siècle 41* (1958), pp. 317-327;

La vie et l'âme de M. Vincent (Paris 1959);

Guide de Saint Vincet de Paul à travers Paris (Paris 1960);

'Saint Vincent de Paul missionnaire', *M. et Ch.* 11 (1963), pp. 248-261 (pen name Jules Melot);

'Les pensionnaires de Saint Lazare au XVII et XVIII siècles', *M. et Ch.* 13-14 (1964), pp.49-55;

'Saint Vincent de Paul, pèlerin de Rome', *M. et Ch.* 28 (1967) pp. 322-325.

CHANTELAUZE, R., de, *Saint Vincent de Paul et les Gondi* (Paris 1882).

CHAUNU, P., *La civilización de la Europa clásica* (Barcelona 1976).

CHEVALLIER, P., *Louis XIII* (Paris 1979).

CHILL, E., 'Religion and mendicity in seventeenth-century France', *International Review of Social History* 7 (1962), pp. 400-425.

CIRCULAIRES *des supérieurs-généraux et des soeurs supérieures aux Filles de la Charité et remarques ou notices sur les soeurs défuntes* Vol. 2 (Paris 1845).

COCHOIS, P., 'Bérulle, hiérarque Dionysien', *RAM* 147 (1961), pp. 314-353.

Bérulle et l'École française (Paris 1963).

COGNET, L., *Les origines de la spiritualité française au XVII siècle* (Paris 1949);

'Bérulle et la théologie de l'Incarnation', *XVIII Siècle* 29 (1955) pp. 330-352;

De la dévotion moderne à la spiritualité française (Paris 1958);

Histoire de la spiritualité chrétienne Vol.3: *La spiritualité moderne. I. "L'essor (1500-1650)"* (Paris 1966);

'La vida de la Iglesia en Francia', in H. JEDIN, *Manual de historia de la Iglesia* Vol.6: *La Iglesia en tiempo del absolutismo y de la Ilustración* (Barcelona, Herder, 1978), pp. 39-181.

[COLLET, P.], *La vie de Saint Vincent de Paul ...* (Nancy 1748) 2 vols.

[COLLOT, P.], *L'esprit de saint François de Sales recueilli de divers écrits de Jean Pierre Camus...* (Paris 1727).

COLLUCCIA, G. L., *Spiritualità vincenziana, spiritualità dell'azione* (Rome 1978).

COMBALUZIER, F., 'L'Abbaye de Saint Léonard de Chaumes et Saint Vincent de Paul (14 mai 1610-20 octobre 1616)', *Annales* (1941-1942), pp. 249-265;

'M. Vincent, prieur de Grosse Sauve', *ibid.*, pp.265-269;

'L'Hôpital Général de Paris et Saint Vincent de Paul', *Annales* (1949), pp. 238-246.

CONGAR, Y., *Vraie et fausse réforme dans l'Église* (Paris 1969) 2nd edition.

CONTASSOT, F., 'Saint Vincent de Paul et le Périgord', *Annales* (1949), pp. 161-203;

Saint Vincent de Paul, guide des supérieurs (Paris 1964)

COPPO, A., 'La prima stesura delle Regole e Constituzioni della Congregazione della Missione in un inedito ms. del 1655', *Annali* (1961), pp. 206-254;

'*De antiqua Domus S. Lazari forma nuperrime inventa*', *Vincentiana 4* (1960), p. 266;

'De antiqua S. Lazari forma iuxta casalense ms. nuper repertum', *Vincentiana 5* (1961), pp. 361-366;

'*Antiquissimus codex Regularum ac Constitutionum Congregationis anno 1655. Manuscriptus archivo generali dono datus*', *Vincentiana* 16 (1972), pp. 115-124;

'San Vincenzo e i suoi rapporti con la S. Congregazione "de Propaganda Fide"', *Vincentiana* 16 (1972), pp. 173-190;

'De S. Gregorii Barbadici in vincentianos sodales benevolentia', *Vincentiana* 5 (1961) pp. 346-347;

'La prima approvazione pontificia della Missione nel 1627', *Annali* (1972), pp. 222-246;

'Le due suppliche del 1628 per l'erezione dell'Istituto in Congegazione di diritto pontificio non accolte della Sacra Congregazione', *Annali* (1973), pp. 37-65;

'L'évolution du voeu de pauvreté des prêtes de la Mission jusqu'en 1659', *Vincentiana* 16 (1972), pp. 265-272.

CORBINELLI, J., *Histoire généalogique de la maison de Gondi* (Paris 1705).

CORERA, J., 'La revolución perdida. El lugar de San Vicente de Paúl en la historia de la espiritualidad', *Anales* (1977), pp. 1031-1081;

'Las Hijas de la Caridad no son religiosas', *Anales* (1979), pp. 75-86;

'La noche oscura del Señor Vicente', *Anales* (1980), pp. 413-428.

COSTE, P., 'Histoire de la maison de Ranquine avant le XIXe siècle', *Bulletin de la Société de Borda* (1906);

Rapports de St. Vincent de Paul avec l'abbé de Saint Cyran (Toulouse 1914);

'La vraie date de la naissance de Saint Vincent de Paul',
Summary from *Bulletin de la Société de Borda* (Dax 1922);
Le grand saint du grand siècle. Monsieur Vincent (Paris 1932) 3
vols. (English transl., *The life and works of Saint Vincent de Paul*,
Burns Oates, 1934; reprinted in New York : New City Press, 1987);
'L'abjuration du 29 juin 1607 à Saint Pierre d'Avignon. Un document nouveau', *Annales* (1936), pp. 182-188.

CUZACQ, R., *Géographie historique des Landes, les Pays landais* (Paris 1962).

DAGENS, J., *Bérulle et les origines de la restauration catholique* (1576-1611) (Paris 1952).

DAN, P., *Histoire de la Barbarie et de ses corsaires* (Paris 1649).

D'AGNEL, A., *Saint Vincent de Paul, directeur de conscience* (Paris 1925);
Saint Vincent de Paul, guide du prête (Paris 1928);
Saint Vincet de Paul, maître d'oraison (Paris 1929).

DANIEL-ROPS: *San Vicente de Paúl* (Barcelona 1960).

DARCHE, J. F., *Le saint abbé Bourdoise* (Paris 1883-1884) 2 vols.

DARRICAU, R., 'L'action charitable d'une reine de France: Anne d'Autriche', *XVII Siècle* 90-91 (1971), pp. 111-125;
'Saint Vincent de Paul et le cardinal Durazzo archévêque de Gênes', *M. et Ch.* 11 (1963), pp. 262-270.

DEBONGNIE, P., 'La conversion de Saint Vincent de Paul', *RHE* 31 (1936), pp. 313-339;
'Vincent de Paul a-t-il menti?', *RHE* 33 (1938), pp. 320-331;
'Pour mieux connaître Saint Vincent de Paul', *RHE* 34 (1939), pp. 774-778;
'Saint Vincent de Paul et Abelly', *RHE* 45 (1950), p. 688-706;
'Saint Vincent de Paul étail-il à Tunis en 1606-1607 et à Rome en '1607-1608?', *RHE* 58 (1963), pp. 862-865.

DEFOS DU RAU. J., 'La date de la naissance de Saint Vincent de Paul', summary from *Bulletin de la Société de Borda* (Auch 958);
Il a été esclave...! (Mont de Marsán 1963).

DEFRENNÉS, P., 'La vocation de Saint Vincent de Paul. Étude de Psychologie surnaturelle', *RAM* 13 (1932), pp. 60-86, 164-183 294-321, 389-411.

DEGERT, A., *Histoire des séminaires françaises jusqu'à la Révolution* (Paris 1903) 2 vols.

DE GRAAF, H., *De votis quae emittuntur in Congregatione Missionis* (Rome 1955).

DELUMEAU, J., *Le christianisme va-t-il mourir?* (Paris, Hachette, 1977).

DELAURE, J., *L'idéal missionnaire du prêtre d'après Saint Vincent de Paul* (Paris 1946);

Sainteté de M. Vincent (Paris 1959).

DENIGOT, M., *Au plateau de Saclay, Ile-de-France. Monsieur Vincent: sa Congrégation à la ferme d'Orsigny* (Paris 1978).

DEPLANQUE, L., *Saint Vincent de Paul sous l'emprise chrétienne* (Paris 1936).

DERRÉAL, H., *Un missionnaire de la Contre-Réforme, saint Pierre Fourier* (Paris 1965);
'S. Pierre Fourier et ses rapports avec la cour de Lorraine', in *L'Université de Pont-à-Mousson et les problèmes de son temps* (1974) pp. 217-233.

DESCOURVEAUX, Ph., *La vie de Monsieur Bourdoise...* (Paris 1714).

DE VEGHEL, O., *Benoît de Canfield (1562-1610). Sa vie, sa doctrine et son influence* (Rome 1949).

DIEBOLD, D., 'La première messe de Saint Vincent (1600)', *Annales* (1957), pp. 490-492;
'Saint Vincent de Paul. Sa nomination à la cure de Tilh (diocèse de Dax) in 1600', *Annales* (1959), pp. 389-397;
'Antoine Godeau et Saint Vincent de Paul', *Annales* (1952), pp. 232-239.

DODIN, A., 'Lectures de Saint Vincent ...', *Annales* (1941) pp. 239-248; *ibid.* (1945), pp. 447-464; *ibid.* (1947), pp. 479-497;
'Saint Vincent de Paul et l'évangile', *La Vie Spirituelle* (1948), pp. 50-59;
'Saint Vincent de Paul et les illuminés', *RAM* (1949), pp. 445-456;
En prière avec M. Vincent (Paris 1950);
Saint Vincent de Paul et la charité (Paris 1960) (English translation: *Saint Vicent de Paul and Charity. A contemporary portrait of his life and apostolic Spirit,* New York 1993);
'Monsieur Vincent et les prisonniers', *M. et Ch.* 13-14 (1964), pp. 56-63;
'Critiques des missions au temps de M. Vincent', *M. et Ch.* (1967), pp. 281-283;
'La promotion de la femme à l'apostolat missionnaire', *M. et Ch.* 28 (1967), pp. 307-321;
'Saint Vincent de Paul, mystique de l'action religieuse', *M. et Ch.* 29-30 (1968), pp. 26-47;
'Esprit de Saint Vincent, esprit de Mission', *M. et Ch.* 31-32 (1968), pp. 135-143;
'La espiritualidad francesa en el siglo XVII', in *Historia de la espiritualidad* Vol.2 (Barcelona 1969), pp. 438-444;
'Les voeux dans la spiritualité vincentienne', *M. et Ch* 35-36 (1969), pp. 129-135;

'El culto a Maria y la experiencia religiosa de San Vicente de Paúl', *Anales* (1975), pp. 388-404;

'Théologie de la charité selon Saint Vincent de Paul', *Vincentiana* 20 (1976), pp. 263-284;

Lecciones sobre vicencianismo (Salamanca 1979).

DUDON, P., 'Le VII centénaire de l'Université de Toulouse', *Études 199* (1929), pp. 724-738.

ELLIOT, J. H., *Revoluciones y rebeliones de la Europa moderna* (Madrid 1978).

EMERIT, M., 'Une manoeuvre antijanséniste: la canonisation de Vincent de Paul', in *Actes du 99 Congrès des Sociétés savantes* Vol.1, pp. 139-150.

ERLANGER, Ph., *Richelieu* (Paris 1972).

EARLE, P., *Corsairs of Malta and Barbary* (London 1970).

ÉTAT SOMMAIRE *des misères de la campagne et besoins des pauvres aux environs de Paris.* 22, 23, 24 and 25 October 1652.

EUSEBIO DEL SANTISIMO SACRAMENTO, *Compendio chronológico de la vida admirable y virtudes heroicas de el Beato Vicente de Paul* (Rome 1730).

FEILLET, A., *La misère au temps de la Fronde et saint Vincent de Paul* (Paris 1868) 4th edition.

FELIU Y PEREZ, B., 'De la patria y estudios de San Vicente de Paúl'. Spanish edition appendix of A. LOTH. *San Vicente de Paúl y su misión social.* (Barcelona 1887) pp. 459-480.

FERTÉ, J., *La vie religieuse dans les campagnes parisiennes* (1622-1695). (Paris 1962).

FILLES (LES) *de la Charité de Saint Vincent de Paul* (Paris 1923). 6th edition.

FISHER, G., *Barbary Legend. War, trade and piracy in North Africa, 1415-1830* (Oxford 1957).

FOISIL, M., *La révolte des Nu-Pieds et les révoltes normandes de 1639* (Paris 1970).

FOSEYEUX, M., *L'Hôtel-Dieu de Paris au XVII siècle et au XVIII siècle.* (Paris 1912).

FRANÇOIS DE SALES, S., *Oeuvres* (Annecy 1892-1932).

FURETIERE, A., *Dictionnaire universel* (La Haya-Rotterdam 1960) 3 vols.

GERBERON, G., *Histoire générale du Jansénisme ...* (Amsterdam 1700) 3 vols.

GIELEN, C., *La charité demeure* (Paris 1960).

GIRARD, J., 'Saint Vincent de Paul. Son oeuvre et son influence en Lorraine', *Annales* (1951), pp. 321-368; *ibid.* (1952), pp. 96-145, 367-408.

GIRAUD, Y., 'Antoine Godeau (1605-1672). De la galanterie à la sainteté', *Actes des journées commemoratives; Grasse, 21-24 April 1972* (Paris).

GLEIZES, R., *Captivité et oeuvres de Saint Vincent de Paul en Barbarie* (Paris 1930).

GODEAU, A., *Exhortation aux parisiens pour le secours des pauvres des provinces de Picardie et Champagne ...* (Paris 1652).

GOMEZ DE LOSADA, G., *Escuela de trabajos* (Madrid 1670).

GOBILLON, A., *La vie de Mademoiselle Le Gras, fondatrice et première supérieure de la Compagnie des Filles de la Charité, servantes des pauvres malades* (Paris 1676).

GOLDMANN, L., 'Remarques sur le jansénisme: la vision tragique du monde et la noblesse de robe', *XVII Siècle* 19 (1953) pp. 177-195;
Le Dieu caché. Étude sur la vision tragique dans les "Pensées" de Pascal et dans le théâtre de Racine (Paris 1955).

GONDI, J. F. P., *Mémoires,* ed. M. ALLEN (Paris 1956).

GRACIAN, G., *Tratado de la redempción de captivos ...* (Brussels 1609).

GRANDCHAMP, P., 'La prétendue captivité de Saint Vincent de Paul à Tunis (1605-1607)'. Summary of *La France en Tunisie au XVII siècle (1651-1660),* Vol.6 (Tunis 1928);
Ibid. 'Observations nouvelles'. Summary of *ibid.*, Vol. 7 (Tunis 1929);
'Un document nouveau sur Saint Vincent de Paul et l'abjuration du 29 juin 1607 à Saint Pierre d'Avignon', *Revue Tunisienne* (1936, 2nd term), pp. 80-84;
(The three last articles were reproduced in *Les cahiers de Tunisie 49-52* [1965], pp. 51-84);
'De nouveau sur la captivité de Saint Vincent de Paul à Tunis', *Revue Tunisienne* (1931), pp. 155-157;
'A propos de la prétendue captivité de Saint Vincent de Paul à Tunis', *ibid.*, pp. 294-300.

GRAND-MESNIL, M. N., *Mazarin, la Fronde et la presse* (Paris 1967).

GUICHARD, J., 'Saint Vincent de Paul esclave à Tunis', *Étude historique et critique* (Paris 1937);
'Saint Vincent de Paul et les monastères de Verdun', *Annales* (1939), pp. 689-692;
'Saint Vincent de Paul, catéchiste', *Cahiers Catéchistiques* (1938-1939).

GULLICK, E., 'The life of Father Benet of Canfield', *Collectanea Franciscana* 42 (1972) pp. 39-67.

GUTH, P., *Mazarin* (Biographie) (Paris 1972).

GUTTON, J. P., *La société et les pauvres. L'example de la généralité de Lyon* (1534-1789) (Paris 1971);
La société et les pauvres en Europe (XVI-XVII siècles) (Paris 1974).

HAMSCHER, A. N., 'The Parlement of Paris and the social interpretation of early French Jansenism', *The Catholic historical Review 63* (1977) pp. 392-410.

HAEDO, D., *Topographia e historia general de Argel.*(Valladolid 1612).

HERNANDEZ Y FAJARNES, A., *San Vicente de Paúl. Su patria: sus estudios en la Universidad de Zaragoza* (Zaragoza 1888).

HERRERA, J., and PARDO, V., *San Vicente de Paúl. Biografía y selección de escritos* (Madrid 1950);
Historia de la Congregación de la Misión (Madrid 1949);
El santo Patrón de San Vicente: Anales (1961) pp. 220-223;
Teología de la acción y mística de la caridad (Madrid 1960).

HOUSSAYE, M., *Le Père de Bérulle et l'Oratoire* (Paris 1872-1875) 3 vols.
Le cardinal Bérulle et le cardinal Richelieu. 1625-1629. (Paris 1875).

HUBAC, P., *Les barbaresques et la course en Méditerranée* (Paris 1959).

HUIJBEN, J., 'Aux sources de la spiritualité française au XVII siècle', *La Vie Spirituelle,* Suppl. 25 (1930), pp. 113-139; 26 (1931), pp. 17-46, 75-111; 27 (1931), pp. 20-42, 94-122.

IBAÑEZ, J. M., *Vicente de Paúl y los pobres de su tiempo* (Salamanca 1977).

IGNACIO DE LOYOLA. San, *Obras completas* (Madrid, BAC, 1977)

JACQUART, J., 'La Fronde des princes dans la région parisienne et ses conséquences matérielles', *RHMC* 7 (1960), pp. 257-290.

JANSEN, P., *Le cardinal Mazarin et le mouvement janséniste français (1653-1659) d'après les documents inédits conservés dans le Ministère des Affaires Étrangères* (Paris 1967).

JIMÉNEZ DUQUE, B., *Historia de la espiritualidad* vol. 2 (Barcelona 1969).

JOVER, J. M., *Historia de una polémica y semblanza de una generación* (Madrid 1949).

JUAN DEL SANTISIMO SACRAMENTO, Fr., *Vida del Venerable Siervo de Dios Vicente de Paúl...* (Naples 1701).

JUVA, S., *Monsieur Vincent. Évolution d'un Saint* (Bourges 1939).

KAMEN, H., *El siglo de hierro* (Madrid 1977).

KOSSMAN, E. H., *La Fronde* (Leiden 1954).

LA BRUYERE, R., *La marine de Richelieu* (Paris 1960).

LAJEUNIE, E. M., *St. François de Sales et l'esprit salésien* (Paris 1962);
St. François de Sales, maître spirituel (Paris 1967).

LANCELOT, C., *Mémoires touchant la vie de Monsieur de Saint-Cyran ...*

(Cologne 1738).

LAURAIN-PORTEMER, M., *Le statut de Mazarin dans l'Église.Aperçus sur le haut clergé de la Contre-Réforme* (Paris 1970).

LAURENTIN, R., and ROCHE, P., *Catherine Labouré et la Médaille miraculeuse* (Paris 1976-1979) 2 vols.

LAVEDAN, H., *Monsieur Vincent, aumônier des Galères* (Paris 1928).

LAVISSE, E., *Histoire de France* Vol.6: *Henri IV et Louis XIII;* Vol.7: *Louis XIV* (Paris 1911).

LE BRUN, J., 'Le Grand Siècle de la spiritualité française et ses lendemains', in *Histoire spirituelle de la France* (Paris 1964) pp. 227-285.

LEMAISTRE, A., *L'aumône chrétienne ou la tradition de l'Église touchant la charité envers les pauvres* (Paris 1651).

LEURET-DUPANLOUP, *Le coeur de saint Vincent de Paul* (Paris 1971).

LOPEZ, A., 'La obra catequética de Santa Luisa', *Anales* (1980), pp. 220-230.

LIVET, G., *La guerre de Trente Ans* (Paris 1963).

LOTH, A., *San Vicente de Paúl y su misión social* (Barcelona 1887).

LOUISE DE MARILLAC, *Lettres,* autobiographical edition (Paris);
    Pensées, ed. autóg. (Paris);
    Sa vie, ses vertus, son esprit (Bruges 1886) 4 vols;
    Ses écrits. Correspondance. Méditations. Pensées. Avis (Paris 1961);
    Cartas y escritos de Santa Luisa de Marillac (see CASTAÑARES);
    Spiritual writings of Louise de Marillac. Correspondence and Thoughts. Edited and translated from the French by sister Louise Sullivan, D.C. (New York, New City Press, 1991).

MANDROU, R., *Francia en los siglos XVII y XVIII* (Barcelona 1973).

MARCHETTY, F., *La vie de Messire Jean Baptiste Gault, évêque de Marseille* (Paris 1650).

MARION, M., *Dictionnaire des institutions de la France aux XVII et XVIII siècles* (Paris 1969).

MARTINEZ, B., 'Rasgos más sobresalientes de la fisonomía humana y espiritual de Santa Luisa', *Anales* (1977), pp. 134-141;
    'El nacimiento de Santa Luisa', *Anales* (1978), pp. 95-101;
    'Sobre la fundación del hospital de Nantes', *Anales* (1979), pp. 466-483;
    'Santa Luisa y las obras en Courteau Villain', *Anales* (1974), pp. 8-12.

MASSAUT, J. P., 'Thomisme et augustinisme dans l'apologétique du XVII siècle', *Revue des sciences philosophiques et théologiques 44* (1960), pp. 617-638;

'L'humanisme au début du siècle (XVI siècle)', in *Histoire spirituelle de la France* (Paris 1964), pp. 185-193.

MAUDUIT, J., *Saint Vincent de Paul* (Paris 1960).

MAUPAS DU TOUR, H. de, *La vie du vénérable serviteur de Dieu ,François de Sales* (Paris 1657);

La vie de la Vénérable Mère Jeanne Françoise Frémiot (Paris).

Oraison funèbre à la mémoire de feu Messire Vincent de Paul ... prononcée le 23 novembre 1660 dans l'église de S. Germain l'Auxerrois (Paris 1661).

MAYNARD, U., *Saint Vincent de Paul. Sa vie, son temps, ses oeuvres, son influence* (Paris 1886) 3rd edition;

Vertus et doctrine spirituelle de Saint Vincent de Paul (Paris 1864) (English translation, *Virtues and spiritual doctrine of Saint Vincent de Paul*. Niagara, 1877)

MAZZINI, G., 'Per l'approvazione della Congregazione della Missione. Un documento dell'anno 1632', *Annali* (1925), pp. 174-186.

MÉMOIRES *de la Congrégation de la Mission* (Paris 1863-1866) 9 vols.

MÉMOIRES DES BESOINS *de la campagne aux environs de Paris* (1652)

MENABREA, A., *Saint Vincent de Paul, le maître des hommes d'État* (Paris 1944);

La révolution inaperçue. Saint Vincent de Paul le savant (Paris 1948).

MEUVRET, J., 'La situation matérielle des membres du clergé séculier dans la France du XVII siècle', *RAM* 54 (1968), pp. 47-68.

MEYER, R., and HUERGA, L., *Una institución singular: el superior general de la Congregación de la Misión y de las Hijas de la Caridad* (Salamanca 1974).

MEZZADRI, L., *Fra giansenisti e antigiansenisti. Vincent de Paul e la Congregazione della Missione (1624-1737)* (Florence 1977);

'De la Misión a la Congregación de la Misión', *Anales* (1978), pp. 88-94;

'La conversión de San Vicente de Paúl', *Anales* (1978), pp.9-15.

'Caridad y política: San Vicente de Paúl y la Fronda', *Anales* (1978), pp. 395-412;

Le missioni popolari della Congregazione della Missione nello Stato della Chiesa (1642-1700): RSChI (1979) pp. 12-44.

MOMMAERS, P., 'Benoît de Canfeld. Sa terminologie "essentielle"', *RAM* 47 (1971), pp.421-454; 48 (1972), pp.37-68.

'Benoît de Canfeld et ses sources flamandes', *Revue d'histoire de la spiritualité 48* (1972), pp. 401-434; 49 (1973), pp. 37-66.

MONGRÉDIEN, G., *10 novembre 1630. La journée des dupes* (Paris 1961).

MOTT, E., *Saint Vincent de Paul et le sacerdoce* (Paris 1900).

MOUSNIER, R., *La vénalité des offices sous Henri IV et Louis XIII* (Ruán 1945);

'Quelques raisons de la Fronde. Les causes des journées révolutionnaires parisiennes de 1648', *XVII Siècle* (1940), pp. 33-78;

L'assassinat d'Henri IV (Paris 1964);

Faureurs paysannes: les paysans dans les révoltes du XVII siècle (Paris 1967);

Los siglos XVI y XVII (vol. 6 from *Historia general de las civilizaciones)* (Barcelona 1967);

*Les institutions de la France sous la Monarchie absolue (*Paris 1974-1980) 2 vols.

NIETO, P., *Historia de las Hijas de la Caridad desde sus orígenes hasta el siglo XX* (Madrid 1932) 2 vols.

NOTICES *sur les prêtres, clercs et frères défunts de la Congrégations de la Mission* (Paris 1891-1893) 3 vols.

NUALART, F., *Vida y martirio del siervo de Dios Pedro Borguny, martirizado en Argel a los 30 de agosto de 1654* (Rome 1780).

O'BOYLE, P., 'Les relations de Saint Vincent de Paul avec l'Irlande', *Annales* (1907), p. 355 ff.

ORCAJO, A., 'La promoción de vocaciones a la C.M. según San Vicente', *Anales* (1978), pp. 17-32.

ORCIBAL, J., *La recontre du Carmel thérésien avec la mystique du Nord* (Paris 1959);

Les origines du jansénisme (Paris 1947-1962) 5 vols;

Saint Cyran et le jansénisme (Paris 1961);

Le cardinal Bérulle: évolution d'une spiritualité (Paris 1965);

'Vers l'épanouissement du XVII siècle (1580-1600)' in *Histoire spirituelle de la France* (Paris 1964) pp. 217-226;

Port Royal entre le miracle et l'obéissance (Paris 1957).

PAGES, G., 'Autour du "Grand Orage". Richelieu et Marillac:deux politiques', *Revue Historique* Vol.179 (1937), pp. 63-97.

PARDO, V., *Renovación de la mística de la acción y de la caridad según San Vicente* (Madrid 1960);

Espiritualidad vicenciana y renovación conciliar (Madrid 1967).

PARRANG, J., 'Un mécène de saint Vincent de Paul: Pierre François Montoro (dit Montorio), vice-légat en Avignon (1604-1607)', *Annales* (1937), pp. 245-259; *ibid.* (1938), pp. 615-623; *ibid.* (1943-1944), pp. 224-228.

POHAR, A., *Octogenarius ille: Vincentiana* 22 (1959) pp. 153-155.

POINSENET, M. D., *De la angustia a la santidad. Luisa de Marillac, fundadora de las Hijas de la Caridad* (Madrid, Studium, 1963).

POOLE, S., *The Tunisian captivity of Saint Vincent de Paul. A survey of the controversy* (1978).
A History of the Congregation of the Mission. 1625-1843 (1973).

PORSCHNEV, B., *Les soulèvements populaires en France de 1623 à 1648 (Paris 1963)*).

POURRAT, P., *La spiritualité chrétienne* vol. 3 (Paris 1918).

PRAVIEL, A., *Monsieur Vincent chez les turcs* (Paris 1935).

PRECLIN, E. and JARRY, E., 'Luchas doctrinales' (vol. 22 of *Historia de la Iglesia* by FLICHE-MARTIN, Valencia, Edicep, 1976) *Luchas políticas* (vol. 21 of *ibid.*, Valencia, Edicep, 1977).

PURCELL, MARY, *The world of Monsieur Vincent* (Dublin, Veritas Publications, 1989).

PURCELL, MARY, *The story of the Vincentians* (Dublin 1973).

RECUEIL *des principales circulaires des supérieurs généraux de la Congrégation de la Mission* (Paris 1877-1880) 3 vols.

RECUEIL *des relations contenant ce qui s'est passé pour l'assistance des pauvres, entre autres de ceux de Paris et des environs et des Provinces de Picardie et Champagne ...* (1655).

REDIER, A., *La vraie vie de Saint Vincent de Paul* (Paris 1947) 26th edition;
'Péchés de jeunesse de Monsieur Vincent', *Revue Hebdomadaire* (1939), pp. 186-215;
Règles communes des Filles de la Charité servantes des pauvres malades. Ed. ms. 1840;
Regulae communes, Constitutiones et regulae particulares C.M. Ms. de Sarzana, in the archives de la Curia Generalicia C.M;
Regulae seu Constitutiones communes Congregationis Missionis (Paris 1658).

REMIREZ, J., *La espiritualidad de San Vicente de Paúl* (Madrid 1956).

RENAUDIN, P., *Saint Vincent de Paul* (Marsella 1927). English translation: *St. Vincent de Paul*, (London and Edinburgh, 1930).

RIQUET, M., *La charité du Christ en action des origines à Saint Vincent de Paul* (Paris 1963).

RISTRETTO *cronologico della vita, vetù e miracoli del B. Vincenzo de Paoli* (Rome 1729).

[ROBINEAU, L.], *Remarques sur les actions et paroles de feu Monsieur Vincent. Ms.* in the Archives of Saint Lazare (Paris). Now edited by André Dodin (Paris 1991).

ROCHE, M., *Saint Vincent de Paul and the formation of clerics* (Friburg 1964).

RODRIGUEZ, A., *Ejercicio de perfección y virtudes cristianas* (Barcelona Edition 1857).

ROMAN, J. M., 'San Vicente de Paúl y la Compañía de Jesús', *Razón y Fe*
162 (1960), pp. 303-318; 163 (1961), pp. 399-416.
'Nuevos datos para el tema de la cautividad tunecina de Vicente
de Paúl:I. Corsarios berberiscos y cautivos cristianos', *Anales*
(1979), pp. 445-465; II. 'Las cartas de la cautividad, ¿novela
picaresca?', *Anales* (1980), pp. 137-147.
'El nacimiento de San Vicente de Paúl. Preguntas en torno a una
fecha', *Semana Vicenciana de Salamanca* (10ª) *Vicente de Paúl,
la inspiración permanente*, Salamanca, CEME, 1981, pp. 147-172.

[ROSSET, E.], *Notices bibliographiques sur les écrivains de la Congrégation
de la Mission* (Paris 1878).

ROSSI, G.F., 'La schiavitù di San Vincenzo de Paoli é un fatto storico',
Divus Thomas 63 (1960), pp. 468-522;
'La storicità della schiavitù tunisina di San Vincenzo de Paoli
(1605-1607)', *Divus Thomas 48* (1964), pp. 449-458.

ROUANET, J.B., *Saint Vincent de Paul, prêtre, instrument de Jésus-Christ*
(Bourges 1960).

SACRA CONGREGATIO PRO CAUSIS SANCTORUM, *Index ac status
causarum Beatificationis Servorum Dei et canonisationis
Sanctorum* (Rome 1975).

SAINT AMOUR, L.G. de, *Journal de ce qui s'est fait à Rome dans l'affaire
des cinq propositions ...* (s.l. 1962).

SAINT-JURE, J. B., *La vie de Monsieur Renty ...* (Paris 1651).

SAINT VINCENT DE PAUL, *Corespondance. Entretiens. Documents* (Paris
1920-1925), ed. P. COSTE. 14 vols + vol.15: M. et Ch. 19-20
(1970) (English translation, New York 1985-... Vols. 1-7 only) .
The Conferences of St Vincent de Paul to the Sisters of Charity,
translated by J. LEONARD, vols. 1-4 (London 1938).

SANABRE, J., *La acción de Francia en Cataluña (1640-1659) en la pugna
por la hegemonía europea* (Barcelona 1956).

S. R. C. PARISIENSIS, *Restrictus probationum circa zelum Servi
Dei contra mores Sancyranii et Jansenii* (Rome 1727).

SÉROUET, P., *Jean de Brétigny (1556-1634). Aux origines du Carmel de
France, de Belgique et du Congo* (Leuven1974).

SERPETTE, S., *Le berceau de Saint Vincent de Paul* (Dax s.a.).

SOULET, J.F., *La vie quotidienne dans les Pyrénées sous l'Ancien Régime
(du XVI au XVII siècles)* (Paris 1974).

STELLA, S., *La Congregazione della Missione in Italia* (Paris 1884-1889).

SYMES, J. S., *The contrary estimation of Saint Vincent de Paul on the
Abbé de Saint Cyran* (New York 1972).

TALLON, ALAIN, *La Compagnie du Saint Sacrement(1629-1667)
Spiritualité et société* (Paris, 1990).

TAPIÉ, V.-L., *La France de Louis XIII et de Richelieu* (Paris 1967).

TAVENEAUX, R., 'Jansénisme et vie sociale en France au XVII siècle', *RHEF* 54 (1968), pp. 27-46.

Jansénisme et politique (Paris 1965).

'Port Royal, les pauvres et la pauvreté', *Actes du colloque sur le jansénisme,* (Lovaina 1977), pp. 65-68.

TRIBOULET, RAYMOND, *Gaston de Renty. 1611-1649. Un home de ce monde. Un homme de Dieu.* (Paris 1991).

TERESA DE JESUS, Santa, *Obras completas* (Madrid, BAC, 1976).

TÜCHLE, H., *Reforma y Contrarreforma* (Vol. 3 of the *Nueva historia de la Iglesia)* (Madrid 1966).

TURBET-DELOF, G., 'Saint Vincent de Paul et la Barbarie en 1657-1658', *Revue de l'Occident musulman et de la Méditerranée* 3 (1967), pp. 153-165;

'Saint Vincent de Paul, a-t-il été esclave à Tunis?', *RHEF* 58 (1972), pp. 331-340;

L'Afrique barbaresque dans la littérature française aux XVI et XVII siècles (Geneva 1973).

VAN DER ESSEN, A., *Le Cardinal-Infant et la politique internationale espagnole* (Brussels 1944).

VAN WINSEN, G., 'Saint Vincent et les missions étrangères', *Vincentiana* 22 (1978), pp. 150-182.

VICENTE DE PAUL, *Pervivencia de un fundador* (Salamanca 1972);

evangelizador de los pobres (Salamanca 1973);

inspirador de la vida comunitaria (Salamanca 1975);

y la acción caritativo-social (Salamanca 1976);

y la evangelización rural (Salamanca 1977);

y los enfermos (Salamanca 1978);

y la catequesis (Salamanca 1979);

VIVES, J. L., *De subventione pauperum* (Bruges 1526).

WILLAERT, L., *La restauración católica* (vol. 20 of *Historia de la Iglesia* by FLICHE-MARTIN) Valencia 1976.

INDEX OF NAMES OF
PERSONS AND PLACES

G